Metuchen, N.J., London, 1982 Studies in Jazz No. 1

Volume II

The Scarecrow Press and the Institute

Benny Carter

A Life in American Music

MORROE BERGER

EDWARD BERGER

JAMES PATRICK

of Jazz Studies, Rutgers University

VOLUME II

1

CHRONOLOGY

This Chronology supplies details of Benny Carter's professional life: his formation and dissolution of regular big bands from 1928 to 1946, his formation of bands for specific engagements since 1946, the dates and places of all his engagements on which information has been found. Most of these details are not given in the text, but the general index includes the names of persons and venues. This Chronology gives the personnel for all the regular and pickup bands, led by Carter, for which such information has been found; to save space Carter's name is omitted from these lists. Also included are the dates of those issues of Billboard and Down Beat in which their band routes (showing where the bands were or would be playing) listed Carter's bands. The band routes are not always reliable because schedules often changed, but they do provide useful leads.

This Chronology omits Carter's recording dates and the films he wrote for. This information is given in the Discography and the Filmography. Together, these three compendia embrace the facts of Carter's musical activity.

The sources of the Chronology are: (1) published statements in periodicals and books, which are cited if full details are available and if the source is not too obscure, (2) Carter's careful recollections, backed by his files including photographs, programs, newspaper clippings, etc., and stimulated by the authors' myriad questions to him since 1973, (3) the authors' interviews with many people associated with Carter's career, and (4) the authors' own observations and notes since 1970 when they became associated with Carter. These last three types of primary sources are not cited in this Chronology and are to be taken as the sources of those entries not documented and as supplementing those that are documented.

ABBREVIATIONS

Periodicals

AA	Afro-American (Baltimore)
AN	N.Y. Amsterdam News
BB	Billboard
CD	Chicago Defender
DB	Down Beat
IM	International Musician
IST	Inter-State Tattler
LAT	Los Angeles Times
Met	Metronome
MM	Melody Maker
NYA	N.Y. Age
NYT	N.Y. Times
OW	Orchestra World
PC	Pittsburgh Courier
PT	Philadelphia Tribune
Var	Variety

Instruments

as	alto saxophone
b	bass
bj	banjo
cl	clarinet
d	drums
g	guitar
p	piano
t	trumpet
tb	trombone
ts	tenor saxophone
v	vocalist
vn	violin

Venues

Th	Theater
Bm	Ballroom

Others

JATP	Jazz at the Philharmonic
NARAS	National Academy of Recording Arts and Sciences
NEA	National Endowment for the Arts

CHRONOLOGY

1907   Aug. 8. Born, N.Y.

1917   First music lessons, piano, from mother.

1921   Buys first instrument, cornet, which he exchanges soon for C melody saxophone. Takes saxophone lessons from neighborhood teachers.

1922   Sits in with professional musicians in Harlem.

1923   Family moves from San Juan Hill (N.Y.) to Harlem. Probably first professional job, Connor's Inn, Harlem. Summer. Plays at Asbury Park, N.J., with Rex Stewart, Bobby Stark.

1924   Plays in trio or quartet, Harlem, with Willie the Lion Smith. Switches from C melody to alto saxophone. Possibly first recording, not verified, with Charles Matson group. Plays with June Clark band, N.Y. Plays briefly with Sidney Bechet and James P. Johnson, Kentucky Club, N.Y.

1925   Summer. With June Clark band, Saratoga Springs, N.Y.

        Summer. With Billy Paige's Broadway Syncopators, Capitol Palace, Harlem, and in Pittsburgh.

        Summer. With Earl Hines band, Pittsburgh.

        Fall. Joins Wilberforce Collegians based at Wilberforce U., O., dates in Harlem, New England, Baltimore.

1926   Jan. Leaves Wilberforce Collegians, joins Charlie Johnson band, Small's Paradise, Harlem.

        April. Leaves Charlie Johnson, joins Billy Fowler band at Strand Roof Cascades; also Cameo Club, N.Y.

        April. Joins Duke Ellington band for about two weeks as temporary replacement, Ciro's club, N.Y.

        Sept. With Fowler band in Baltimore and Newark, en route to N.Y. --AA Sept. 11, p. 5.

Oct.   Joins Fletcher Henderson band briefly as replacement for Don
Redman, at Roseland Bm, N.Y., then returns to Fowler band.

Late.   Leaves Fowler, rejoins Charlie Johnson band at Small's
Paradise (remaining until Feb. 1928).   Starts arranging.

1927   Composes first published song, collaborating with Fats Waller on
"Nobody Knows."

With Charlie Johnson band all year.

April 28.   Perhaps first arrangement recorded, "P.D.Q. Blues,"
by F. Henderson.

1928   Jan. 28.   First confirmed recording as sideman and of a BC arrangement, with Charlie Johnson's Paradise Ten, N.Y.

Feb.   Leaves Johnson, rejoins Collegians at Savoy Bm, Harlem.

Spring.   Tours with Collegians, to Graystone Garden, Detroit.

Summer.   Elected leader of Collegians--first time leading a band.

Aug. 13.   Leads Collegians to victory, in battle of bands, over
McKinney's Cotton Pickers led by Don Redman, Graystone Garden,
Detroit.

Fall.   Leads Collegians as Savoy Play Boys, Savoy Bm, Harlem,
intermittently to March 1929.   Personnel.   Shelton Hemphill,
Wardell Jones (t), Henry Hicks, Danny Logan (tb), Ted McCord,
Bobby Sands (reeds), Gabby Rogers (p), Lavert Hutchison (b,
tuba), Talcott Reeves (bj), Bill Beason (d).   In late 1928:   Clarence Powell (t) added, Elmer Williams (reeds) replaces Sands,
Joe Turner (p) replaces Rogers.

Nov. 26-Dec. 2.   Leads band, Lafayette Th, Harlem. --AN Nov.
28, p. 8.

1929   Starts playing trumpet regularly.

March, early.   Band leaves Savoy after intermittent residency since
fall 1928. --IST March 22, p. 10.

March 20.   Leads band, one-nighter, Shadowland Bm, Philadelphia.
-- PT March 14, p. 6.

July 4.   Leads band, one-nighter, Pythian Temple, Pittsburgh.
-- PC local edn., June 29, p. 7.

Aug. 4.   Leads band, boat-ride, Pittsburgh. --PC local edn.,
Aug. 3, p. 7.

Aug. 5.   Leads band, Pythian Temple, Pittsburgh. --Ibid.

Sept. 13.   Leads band, with four others, for reopening of Alhambra
BM, Harlem. --AN Sept. 4, p. 8.

Oct.-late Dec. Leads band, Arcadia Bm, N.Y., then disbands.
--OW Oct., pp. 4, 15, 17, and Nov., pp. 15, 16, 21.
Personnel. In Oct. Edward Anderson, Wardell Jones, Shelton
Hemphill (t), Henry Hicks, Charlie Green (tb), Bob Carroll,
Howard Johnson, Ted McCord (reeds), Joe Turner (p), Lavert
Hutchison (b, tuba), Talcott Reeves (bj), Bill Beason (d). --OW
Oct., p. 7. In Nov. Russell Procope (as) replaces Johnson,
John Truehart (bj) replaces Reeves, omit Anderson. --OW Nov.,
p. 21.

1930   Jan. Joins F. Henderson band, remains to March 1931. W. C.
Allen, pp. 254-255.

1931   March. Leaves F. Henderson to join Chick Webb band.

Aug. Leaves Webb band to join McKinney's Cotton Pickers, De-
troit, as musical director (not leader), remaining to April 1932.
Personnel. Doc Cheatham, Joe Smith, Rex Stewart (t), Charlie
Green, Quentin Jackson (tb), Elmer Williams, Jimmy Dudley
(reeds), Todd Rhodes (p), Billy Taylor (b), Dave Wilborn (g, bj),
Cuba Austin (d). Changes: see Discography, Sept. 8.

1932   First BC tune played in a feature film: "Hot Toddy" played on
screen by Cab Calloway band in The Big Broadcast of 1932.

April. Leaves McKinney's Cotton Pickers.

Summer. Forms new big band: Benny Carter and His Orchestra.

July 10-23. Leads new band in show, "Connie's Inn Ace in the
Hole Revue," Central Th, N.Y. --AN July 13, 20, p. 8.

Aug.-Sept. Leads band, four weeks, in revue "Cocktails of 1932"
in a Boston Th (name not given). -NYA Oct. 8, p. 6. Personnel.
Leonard Davis, Louis Bacon (t), Dicky Wells (tb), Chu Berry,
Hilton Jefferson, Wayman Carver (reeds), Rod Rodriguez (p),
Ralph Escudero (b), Bernard Addison (g), Sidney Catlett (d).
Also: Alfred C. Thomas, James M. Herbert, instruments not
given. --IM Oct., p. 3.

Oct. 7. Leads band in benefit for "Scottsboro Boys," Rockland
Palace, Harlem. --NYA Oct. 15, p. 7; PC Oct. 15, p. 6.

Oct. 8-14. Leads band, Lafayette Th, Harlem. --NYA Oct. 15,
p. 6.

Oct., late. Leads band, a week, Howard Th, Wash., D.C.
Personnel. Leonard Davis, Howard Scott, Shad Collins (t),
George Washington, Dicky Wells (tb), Howard Johnson, Wayman
Carver (reeds), Rod Rodriguez (p), Ernest Hill (b), Bernard
Addison (g), Sidney Catlett (d). --IM Dec., p. 7.

1933   Feb. 9-ca. 23. Leads band to open Empire Bm., N.Y. --N.Y.
Daily News, Feb. 9, p. 33; --MM March, p. 185, and May 27,
p. 3.

Feb. 11-17.   Leads band, Lafayette Th, Harlem. --AN Feb. 8, 15,
    p. 8.

March 8.   Leads band in benefit for "Scottsboro Boys," Savoy Bm,
    Harlem. --AN March 1, p. 8, "Observations."

April 1-7.   Leads band, Lafayette Th, Harlem. --AN April 5, p. 8.

May, late.   Leads band, Savoy Bm, Harlem, about two weeks.
    --MM June 24, p. 5.

June, early.   Leads band, Empire Bm, N. Y. , to early Aug. --W.
    C. Allen, P. 285.

June, late.   Leads band, Howard Th, Wash. , D. C. --AA July 1,
    p. 9. Personnel.   Clifton "Pike" Davis, Otis Johnson, John
    Brown (t), Wilbur de Paris, Fayette Williams (tb), Johnny Rus-
    sell, Alberto Socarras (Estacio) (reeds), Rod Rodriguez (p),
    Ernest Hill (b), Lawrence Lucie (g), Walter Conyers (d). --IM
    July, p. 5.   Other sidemen in late 1933: Shad Collins, Bill
    Coleman, Lincoln Mills (t), Dicky Wells, Charlie Green (tb), Chu
    Berry, Hilton Jefferson (reeds), Cozy Cole (d). --Lucie in Dance,
    World of Swing, p. 349; Cole, ibid. , p. 186. See Discography,
    Oct. 16.

July 22-25, July 29-Aug. 1.   Leads band, Harlem Opera House,
    Harlem. --AN July 19, 26, p. 7.

Oct. 6 ca.   Leads band at new Harlem Club, Harlem, remaining to
    late Feb. 1934. --CD Oct. 7, p. 8; AN Oct. 11, p. 7; Ottley,
    AN Feb. 21, 1934, p. 9; advt. , ibid. , Feb. 28, 1934, p. 9.

Oct. 23-29.   Leads band, Lafayette Th, Harlem. --AN Oct. 25, p.
    7.

Dec. 20-26.   Leads band, Harlem Opera House, Harlem. --NYA
    Dec. 23, p. 6; AN advt. , Dec. 20, p. 7 and review, Dec. 27,
    p. 7; Albertson, p. 191.   Bessie Smith was advertised for Dec.
    23-26 but did not appear.

1934   Jan. 15 ca.   Leads band, several days, Louis Sherry's, club, N. Y.
    --Var Jan. 23, p. 1.

Jan. 26-Feb. 2.   Leads band at reopening, with "new" band-show
    format, Apollo Th, Harlem. --AN Jan. 24, p. 14, and Jan. 31,
    p. 8. Personnel.   Bill Coleman, Bill Dillard, Lincoln Mills (t),
    Charlie Green, Keg Johnson (tb), Johnny Russell (reeds), Teddy
    Wilson (p), Lawrence Lucie (g), Cozy Cole (d). --Cole in Dance,
    World of Swing, p. 186.

Feb. , late.   Leaves Harlem Club.

Feb. 16.   Leads band in benefit for "Scottsboro Boys," Savoy Bm,
    Harlem. --NYA Feb. 10, p. 6.

Feb. -April.   Leads band, Empire Bm, N. Y. --Rosenkrantz, pp. 7,
    32-36; NYA May 12, p. 5, Outram.

Spring. Arranges for new Benny Goodman band. --Goodman, pp.
133-134, 139.

May, early, to mid-June. Leads band, Empire Bm, N. Y. --BB
band routes, May 5-June 16.

June 1. Breaks arm in auto accident en route from N. Y. to Tren-
ton, N. J. This injury exempted him from military service in
World War II.

Nov. 16-22. Leads band, Apollo Th, Harlem. --NYA Nov. 24, p. 4.

Nov. 29. Leads band in Thanksgiving Day dance after Wilberforce-
W. Va. St. Coll. football game, Arcadia Bm, Detroit. --PC Dec.
1, sec. 2, p. 1.

Dec. 31. Leads band, New Year's Eve dance, Webster Hall, N. Y.
--Labor Defender (International Labor Defense), Jan. 1935, advt.
p. 23.

Band routes. BB May 5-June 16.

1935 Jan. Gives up regular band formed in 1932.

Feb. Joins Willie Bryant band as trumpeter and arranger, remaining until May. --NYA March 23, p. 4.

May 24. Sails for France to join Willie Lewis band at Chez Florence, club, Paris, returns to U. S. May 2, 1938. --AN June 8,
p. 1.

July. Starts playing with Willie Lewis band, Chez Florence, remaining until ca. March 17, 1936.

1936 Jan. 29, 31. Plays concerts with Quintette of the Hot Club of France
in Barcelona. --Tendes; Delaunay, Django Reinhardt, p. 83.

March 18. Arrives London to arrange for BBC dance orchestra.
--MM March 21, p. 11.

March 27. BBC dance band broadcasts program of BC compositions
and arrangements. --MM April 11, p. 5.

July. Leaves London, arrives Holland.

July 26, 28, 29. Holland. Plays at Kurhaus Hotel, Scheveningen.
--De Jazzwereld (The Hague) Sept. , p. 3.

July 31. Holland. Plays at Hamdorff Hotel, Laren.

Aug. 6. Holland. Plays at Kurhaus Hotel, Scheveningen. --MM
Aug. 15, p. 3.

Aug. 19. Arrives Copenhagen, remains three weeks. --Copenhagen
daily press, Aug. 20.

Aug. 20, 27. Copenhagen. Concerts with Kai Ewans band, Tivoli park. --Ibid. , Aug. 21, 28.

Sept. 9-13. Stockholm. Sept. 9, 11, concerts with the Swedish Orchestra at Royal Djurgarden Circus. --Orkester Journalen, Oct. , pp. 7-13.

Sept. 14. Copenhagen. Concert at Concert Palace. --Rosenkrantz, Politiken, Sept. 15.

Sept. 15. Concert on Danish radio with Kai Ewans band. --B. T. (newspaper) Sept. 16.

Sept. 16-Sept. 29. Plays at National Scala accompanied by Richard Johansen band. --Copenhagen daily press, Sept. 17.

Oct. 2. Returns to London, remaining until March 1937.

Oct. 13. Plays radio concert with BBC dance band. --MM Oct. 17, p. 14.

Fall. Arranges for first film, one tune, "Okay for Sound," Gaumont British, released 1937.

1937   Jan. 10. Leads British band, concert, Hippodrome Th, London. -- MM Jan. 16, p. 1; DB, Feb. , p. 5.

Feb. Plays with British band daily for one week, Locarno Bm, Streatham, London. --Musical News and Dance Band (London), March, p. 23.

March 16. Leaves London for Holland to negotiate summer engagement, remains two weeks. --MM March 20, p. 1.

April 6. Arrives in Paris, remaining until May 11.

May 11. Arrives London, remains two weeks, to line up musicians for summer engagement in Holland.

May 17. Leads British band in BBC weekly swing series on radio. --Met May, p. 38.

May 27. In Holland, putting together band for summer.

June 4-Sept. 7. Leads international, interracial band, Kurhaus Hotel, Scheveningen. --De Jazzwereld (The Hague), May, p. 4 and Sept. , p. 7. Personnel. Sam Dasberg, Cliff Woodridge (t), George Chisholm (tb), Louis Stephenson, Bertie King, Jimmy Williams (reeds), Justo Barretto or Freddy Johnson (p), Len Harrison (b), Ray Webb (g), Robert Mommarché (d). --Photo in McCarthy, Big Band Jazz, p. 314 and Doctor Jazz, Dec. 1971/Jan. 1972, p. 15; Met Sept. , pp. 66-67.

Sept. Leaves Holland for France, remains until April 1938.

Oct. 15-ca. April 20, 1938. Leads band at Boeuf sur le Toit, club, Paris. --MM Oct. 30, p. 1, and March 26, 1938, p. 6. Personnel. Louis Stephenson, Bertie King, Jean Luino (reeds), Yorke de Souza or Frank Etheridge (p), Len Harrison (b), Robert Mommarché or Jacques de Bourgarel (d). --MM Oct. 30, p. 1.

Dec. 17. Leads band, concert, Salle de l'Ecole Normale de Musique, Paris. --Jazz Hot (Paris), Dec. 1937-Jan. 1938, p. 13. Personnel. Jacques Raymond (t), Jesus Pia (ts), Michel Warlop (vn), Garland Wilson (p), Len Harrison (b), Tommy Benford (d). --Ibid.

1938   Feb. 19. Leads band from Paris for Italian students' ball, Zurich. --M. Cook, AN March 19, p. 19.

April 20 ca. Closes at Boeuf sur le Toit, there since Oct. 15, 1937.

April 24. Leaves Paris for London to embark for U. S.

April 27. Sails on Normandie from Southampton, arrives N. Y. May 2.

Summer. Forming new big band. Met Nov. , p. 64.

Nov. 25-Dec. 1. Leads new band, Howard Th, Wash. , D. C. --AA Nov. 26, pp. 10-11.

1939   March 25. Leads band at annual Beaux Arts ball, Yale U.

March 29. Opens with band at Savoy Bm, Harlem, there intermittently for months at a time until Jan. 1941, using "Melancholy Lullaby" as theme song. --AN July 8, pp. 16-17; BB, July 8, p. 13. Personnel. Lincoln Mills, Louis Bacon, Archie Johnson (t), Tyree Glenn, Vic Dickenson, Jimmy Archey (tb), Ernie Powell, Cass McCord, Jimmy Powell, Carl Frye (reeds), Eddie Heywood, Jr. (p), Hayes Alvis (b), Arnold Adams (g), Ted Fields (d). --AN April 15, p. 21. Foregoing personnel refers to 1939 and into 1940, with these changes from time to time: Bobby Woodlen, Joe Thomas (t) replace Bacon and Johnson; Sammy Davis (reeds) in, Frye out; Ulysses Livingston (g) replaces Adams; Henry "Chick" Morrison (d) replaces Ted Fields. --DB Sept. , p. 24.

July, early. Leaves Savoy to tour. --AN July 8, pp. 16-17; BB July 8, p. 13.

July 7-13. Starts tour at Apollo Th, Harlem. --Ibid.

July-Aug. Touring. --Ibid.

Oct. -Nov. Back in Savoy, out Dec. to Feb. 1940. --Burley in AN Oct. 21, p. 20.

Dec. 2-8. Leads band, Roseland Bm, Brooklyn, N. Y. --Burley in AN Dec. 2, p. 20.

Dec. 15. Leads band, Apollo Th, Harlem, with others, in benefit show. --AN Dec. 23, p. 13.

Dec. 22-28. Leads band, Howard Th, Wash., D.C. --BB Dec. 23,
band routes; AA Dec. 30, p. 14.

Dec. 24. Leads band, Tuxedo Club, Harrisburg, Pa. --AA ibid.

Dec. 31. Leads band, Celeron Park, N.Y., pier bm. --AA ibid.,
and BB Dec. 30, band routes. Both wrongly give this as Jamestown University, probably because the Chautauqua adult education
program is there. See advt. for this engagement, Jamestown
Evening Journal, Dec. 30, p. 10.

Band routes. BB April 1-July 8, Sept. 30-Oct. 28, Dec. 9-30.
--DB May-Oct. 15, Dec. 15.

1940   Jan. or Feb. Leads band at Savoy Bm, Pittsburgh. --BB April 27,
p. 11.

Jan.-Feb. Touring.

Feb. 23. Leads band in Savoy Bm, Harlem, to Feb. 27 or 28,
when BC is taken to alimony jail to end of March, while vocalist
Roy Felton fronts band. --Burley in AN March 9 and April 6, p.
20.

March. Band tours, fronted by Roy Felton.

April 6. BC leads band, Golden Gate Bm, Harlem. --MM May 4,
p. 4.

June. Leads band on midwestern tour, several weeks. --DB June 15,
p. 9. Personnel. Russell Smith, Shad Collins, Bill Coleman (t),
Milt Robinson, Sandy Williams, Fernando Arbello (tb), Carl Frye,
Stafford Simon, Sammy Davis, George Dorsey (reeds), Sonny White
(p), Hayes Alvis (b), Ulysses Livingston (g), Keg Purnell (d). --
Ibid.

July 26. Leads band, N.Y. World's Fair, Negro Week. --MM Aug.
7, p. 9.

Sept. 19-25. Leads band, Strand Bm, Philadelphia. --BB Sept. 21,
band routes.

Oct. 4-10. Leads band to reopen West End Th, Harlem. --AN Sept.
28, advt., p. 21; review, Oct. 12, p. 20. Personnel. Freddie
Webster, Bob Williams (t), Madison Vaughan (tb), George Irish,
George James (reeds), Everett Barksdale (g) replacing Livingston,
Ann Robinson (v). --DB Oct. 15, p. 9. These are new members
only, and all are in personnel given for Famous Door in next item.

Nov. 18-Dec. 2. Leads band, Famous Door, 52d St., N.Y. Per-
sonnel. Russell Smith, Bob Williams, Freddie Webster (t), Fer-
nando Arbello, Milt Robinson, Madison Vaughan (tb), Chauncey
Haughton, Stafford Simon, George James, George Irish (reeds),
Sonny White (p), Hayes Alvis (b), Everett Barksdale (g), Keg
Purnell (d), Ann Robinson, Roy Felton (v). --George Simon, Met
Nov., p. 16.

Dec.   Leads band at Savoy, into Jan. 1941.

Band routes.   BB Sept. 21. --DB Jan. 1-Feb. 15.

1941   Jan. 28-March 2.   Leads band, Nick's, club, N.Y. --AN Feb. 1, p.
       16; BB Feb. 8, p. 11; New Yorker, "Goings On About Town,"
       Feb. 1-March 1.   Personnel.   Lincoln Mills, Sidney de Paris,
       Tom Lindsay (t), Vic Dickenson, Jimmy Archey, Joe Britton (tb),
       Fred Mitchell, Al Gibson, Bill White, Jim Johnson (reeds), Sonny
       White (p), Charlie Drayton (b), Chris I. Cruickson (d). --DB Feb.
       15, p. 4.

       March 15.   Leads band, Princeton U. junior prom. --Daily Prince-
       tonian, March 15, p. 1.

       March-May.   Touring midwest. --DB Feb. 15, p. 4.

       March 30.   Plays at reunion of F. Henderson bands, Café Society,
       N.Y. --W. C. Allen, p. 407.

       June 21.   BC Featured with Vaughn Monroe band, CBS broadcast,
       Frank Dailey's Meadowbrook, club, Cedar Grove, N.J. --PC
       June 28, p. 21; NYT radio programs, 5 p.m., June 21, p. 30.

       July, early, to Sept.   Touring south, with Maxine Sullivan. --BB
       July 5, p. 14; DB July 15, p. 29.   Personnel.   Lincoln Mills,
       Sidney de Paris, Bobby Johnson (t), Jimmy Archey, Joe Britton,
       Milt Robinson (tb), Howard Johnson, Frank Powell, Al Sears, Al
       Gibson (reeds), Sonny White (p), Charlie Drayton (b), Willie Lewis
       (g), Shep Shepherd (d), Roy Felton (v), Maxine Sullivan (featured
       v). --DB ibid.

       Sept. or Oct.   Gives up big band on return from tour, re-forms big
       band Feb. 1942.

       Sept.   BC named in F. Henderson's "dream band." --W. C. Allen,
       p. 490.

       Oct.   Leads small combo, several weeks, Ritz Carlton Hotel, Bos-
       ton. --Met Oct., p. 11; DB Nov. 1, p. 2.   Personnel.   "Little"
       Benny Harris or Rostelle Reese (t), Eddie Barefield (cl), Sonny
       White (p), Charlie Drayton (b), Willie Lewis (g), Shep Shepherd
       (d). --Met ibid.; MM Nov. 8, p. 6.

       Oct. 23 ca.-Dec. 10.   Leads small combo, Kelly's Stable, club,
       52d St., N.Y. --DB Nov. 1, p. 2; BB Dec. 20, p. 11; New
       Yorker, Oct. 25, p. 4, and Dec. 13, p. 4.   Personnel.   Rostelle
       Reese (t), Al Gibson (reeds), Sonny White (p), Charlie Drayton
       (b), Willie Lewis (g), Eddie Dougherty (d).   Changes probably in
       Nov.: John Collins (g) replaces Lewis, Dizzy Gillespie (t) re-
       places Reese.

       Nov. 5.   Leads sextet (from Kelly's Stable), concert, Museum of
       Modern Art, N.Y., with Maxine Sullivan, harpsichordist Sylvia
       Marlowe, dancer Baby Lawrence. --N.Y. Herald Tribune, Nov. 6,
       p. 17; New Yorker, Nov. 1, p. 4.

Dec. 10-Feb. 4, 1942. Leads small combo, Famous Door, 52d St.,
N.Y. --BB Dec. 20, p. 11; DB Feb. 15, p. 2. Personnel.
Dizzy Gillespie (t), Al Gibson (reeds), Sonny White (p), Charlie
Drayton (b), Kenny Clarke (d). --Met Jan. 1942, pp. 11, 17.
Change: Gillespie left briefly, probably in late Dec., for another
engagement, and may have been replaced by "Tatti" Smith. --OW
Jan., p. 4. Jimmy Hamilton (reeds) replaces Gibson. --DB Feb.
1, 1942, p. 3.

Band routes. BB Feb. 22, May 10, July 5, Nov. 8-22, Dec. 6-27.
DB Feb. 15, March 15, Aug. 15-Dec. 1.

1942   Joins ASCAP.

Feb.   Assembles a new big band.

Feb. 4.   Leaves Famous Door; see entry 1941, Dec. 10.

Feb.   Begins to arrange for Mark Warnow's Lucky Strike Hit Parade
Orchestra. --DB Feb. 15, p. 2.

March 14.   Leads band (one-nighter?), Golden Gate Bm, Harlem.
--DB April 1, p. 1. Personnel. Lincoln Mills, Courtney Wil-
liams, Nelson Bryant (t), Claude Jones, John "Rocks" McConnell,
Alton "Slim" Moore (tb), George Dorsey, Frank Powell, Al Gib-
son, Fred Mitchell (reeds), Jimmy Phipps (p), Charlie Drayton
(b), John Collins (g), Specs Powell (d). --DB April 1, p. 1.
Changes in early spring: Sidney de Paris (t) replaces Bryant,
DB April 15, p. 3; add Dan Minor (tb). --DB May 15, p. 7.

April 10-16.   Leads band, Apollo Th, Harlem; start of tour, featuring Billie Holiday, into May. --DB April 15, p. 3. Personnel.
As above, entry for March 14. --MM June 6, p. 5.

April 27-May 3.   Leads band, Gaiety Th, N.Y. --BB May 9, p. 18;
NYT April 28, p. 24.

May 8.   Leads band, opening at Strand Th, Toledo, O., with Billie
Holiday. --Toledo Times, May 7.

May.   Leads band, Strand Th, Syracuse, N.Y., with Billie Holiday.
--Syracuse Post-Standard, May 9; DB June 15, p. 20.

June-July.   Touring east (without Billie Holiday).

June 7.   Leads band, opening at Tic-Toc Club, Boston, one or two
weeks. --OW June, p. 24.

June 14.   Leads band, Wagenbach's Hofbrau, Lawrence, Mass.

July 3-9.   Leads band, Apollo Th, Harlem. --AN July 4, p. 17.

Sept.   Leads band on tour westward, arriving Hollywood in Nov.

Sept. 11-17.   Leads band, Royal Th, Baltimore. --DB Sept. 1, band
routes.

Oct. Touring midwest.

Oct. 16 to mid-Nov. Leads band, Rainbow Rendezvous, Salt Lake
City. --BB Oct. 3, p. 24; OW Nov., advt., inside front cover.

Nov. BC arrives in Hollywood, settles in L. A. area for good.

Nov. 14-20. Leads band, Lincoln Th, L. A. --BB Nov. 14, band
routes.

Nov. 20. Leads band, opening at Billy Berg's Swing Club, L. A.,
to mid-Jan. 1943. --Met Dec., p. 21; DB Dec. 1, p. 13.
Personnel. George Treadwell, Hal Mitchell, William "Chiefie"
Scott (t), Earl Hardy, J. J. Johnson, John "Shorty" Haughton,
Slim Moore (tb), Ted Barnett, Carroll "Stretch" Ridley, Gene
Porter, Eddie De Verteuil (reeds), Teddy Brannon (p), Curly
Russell (b), Johnny Smith (g), Alvin Burroughs (d), Savannah
Churchill (v). --DB Nov. 15, p. 11. Changes by Jan. 1943:
Eddie Davis (reeds) in, Barnett out; Hardy (tb) out; Buddy Rich
(d) in, Burroughs out. --"The Lamplighter, " L. A. Daily News,
Jan. 2, 1943, p. 5. Add Hal Schaefer (p), briefly, late 1942.

Band routes. BB Jan. 10-March 28, May 9, June 13-20, Oct. 3-
Nov. 14, Dec. 5-26. DB March 15-July 1, Sept. 1, Oct. 1-
Nov. 1.

1943   Jan. BC works on his first Hollywood film, Stormy Weather.

Jan., middle. Band closes at Swing Club.

Jan., middle, to mid-Feb. Leads band, Hollywood Club, Hollywood.
--DB Feb. 1, p. 6.

March 17-23. Leads band, Orpheum Th, L. A. --DB March 15,
band routes.

April. Leads band, Sweet's Bm, Oakland, several days, perhaps
two weeks. --BB April 3, 10, 17, band routes; DB April 1, band
routes.

April 7 ca., to May, late. Leads band, Hollywood Club. --BB April
24-May 8, band routes; DB April 15-May 15, band routes. Per-
sonnel. Gerald Wilson, Snooky Young, Walter Williams, Fred
Trainer (t), Shorty Haughton, J. J. Johnson, Slim Moore (tb),
Kirt Bradford, Willard Brown, Gene Porter, Eddie Davis (reeds),
Teddy Brannon (p), Curly Russell (b), Oscar Bradley (d), Savan-
nah Churchill (v). Met, April, pp. 17, 33. Changes: add Frank
Comstock (tb and arranging). Uan Rasey, Teddy Buckner (t) in,
Young, Trainer out; Bumps Myers (reeds) replaces Davis. --DB
June 15, p. 2. Add Freddie Webster (t). DB Sept. 1, p. 6.
Add Art Pepper (reeds) playing April-Sept. April 10, aircheck:
see Discography.

May, late, to July, early. Leads band, Casa Mañana, club, Hollywood. --Met July, p. 20; BB May 22-June 5, June 19-July 10,
band routes; DB June 1-July 1, band routes.

July, early, to Aug. , early.   Leads band, Hollywood Casino. --DB
    Aug. 1, p. 6.

Aug. , early, to mid-Sept.   Leads band, Terrace Club, Hermosa
    Beach, California. --DB Aug. 15-Sept. 15, all p. 6.

Sept. , last week.   Leads band, Orpheum Th, L. A. --Met Nov. , p.
    26.

Sept. , late, to Dec.   Touring Pacific states and south, into spring
    1944. --DB Sept. 15, p. 6.

Band routes.   BB Jan. 2, Jan. 23-Feb. 13, April 3-May 8, May 22-
    June 5, June 19-Sept. 4, Sept. 18-Nov. 6, Nov. 20.   DB Jan.
    15-July 1, Aug. 1-Dec. 1.

1944   Jan. to spring.   Continues tour (begun Sept. 1943) to east.

Jan. 28-Feb. 3.   Leads band, Apollo Th, Harlem. --Met March, p.
    32.

Feb. 24-March 1.   Leads band, Loew's State Th, N. Y. --BB March
    4, p. 28.

March or April.   End of tour, band back in California.

May 16-22.   Leads band, Orpheum Th, L. A. --L. A. Examiner,
    May 17, pt. 2, p. 3.

June 1-July, end.   Leads band, Swing Club, Hollywood. --Met June,
    p. 11, and July, p. 13. Personnel.   Milton Fletcher, Tom
    "Sleepy" Grider, Fatso Ford, Edwin Davis (t), Shorty Haughton,
    Slim Moore, J. J. Johnson (tb), Porter Kilbert, Bumps Myers,
    Gene Porter, Willard Brown (reeds), Gerald Wiggins (p), Charlie
    Drayton (b), Jimmy Edwards (g), Max Roach (d). --Met July, p.
    14.

July 31-March 1945.   Leads band on tour to east and back to west.
    Band routes in BB July 29, 1944 to Jan. 20, 1945, and DB Sept.
    1, 1944 to March 1, 1945.   Some specific engagements reviewed
    in press: Kansas City, DB Dec. 1, 1944, p. 8; N. Y. , DB Dec.
    15, 1944, p. 3; Newark, Var Jan. 31, 1945, p. 34; Philadelphia,
    Var Feb. 14, 1945, p. 18; N. Y. , BB March 3, 1945, p. 21.
    Personnel, on tour ca. December 1944-January 1945.   Fats Ara-
    dando, Harold Bruce, Red Kelly (t), Charles Greenlea, Buster
    Scott (tb), Harold Clark, Porter Kilbert, Bumps Myers, Leo
    Parker, Howard Smith (reeds), Garland Finney (p), Tommy Moul-
    trie (b), Stanley Williams (d).   Add Jean Starr (t, v), 1944 and
    early 1945. --Var Jan. 31, 1945 p. 34.

Band routes.   BB June 3, July 29, Aug. 12-Sept. 30, Oct. 14, Oct.
    28-Nov. 11, Dec. 9-23.   DB Jan. 1-March 1, May 15-Oct. 15,
    Nov. 15-Dec. 15.

1945   Jan. -March.   Continues touring--see 1944, July 31.

March 22-28.   Leads band, Trocadero, club, Hollywood. --DB March
15, April 15, p. 6.

April 20-May 18.   Leads band, Casa Mañana, Culver City. --DB
May 1, p. 2.

June 26-July 1.   Leads band, Orpheum Th, L. A. --BB July 7,
pp. 35-36.

July 3-8.   Leads band, Plantation, club, L. A. --DB July 1, band
routes.

Aug.   BC wins court case to retain ownership of house in L. A.
despite restrictive covenant. --DB Sept. 1, p. 6.

Aug. 10-Feb. 13, 1946.   Leads band on tour to east. --DB band
routes, Aug. 1, 1945-Jan. 28, 1946.   Some specific engagements
reviewed in press: N. Y., AN Sept. 15, p. 9-B, and Dec. 22, p.
25; Detroit, Detroit Free Press, Feb. 6, 1946, p. 10.

Band routes.   BB Jan. 6-20.   DB Jan. 1-April 1, May 1, June 1,
July 1, Aug. 1, Sept. 1-Oct. 1, Nov. 15-Dec. 15.

1946   Jan.-Feb. 13.   Continues touring--see 1945, Aug. 10.

March 19-25.   Leads band, Orpheum Th, L. A. --BB March 30, p.
46.

March 26-May 21.   Leads band, Trianon, Bm, South Gate, L. A.
--Var April 17, p. 58 to May 15, p. 57, L. A. residencies.

April 12.   Leads some of his band, concert, UCLA, on first anniversary of death of Franklin D. Roosevelt. --DB May 6, p. 16;
California Daily Bruin, April 15, 1946, p. 1.

June 3-8.   Leads band, Swing Club, Hollywood. --DB June 3, July
1, band routes.   Personnel.   Fred Trainer, Calvin Strickland,
Walter Williams, Ira Pettiford (t), Candy Ross, Johnny Morris,
Al Grey, Charley Johnson (tb), Bob Graettinger, Joe Epps, Harold
Clark, Bumps Myers, Willard Brown (reeds), Sonny White (p),
Tommy Moultrie (b), Jimmy Cannady (g), Percy Brice (d), Lucy
Elliott, Ross (v), Graettinger, Cannady (arranging). --BB June
22, p. 22.   Changes as of August in Apollo Th, N. Y.: add Mar-
tin "Fuzzy" Gower (reeds), omit Graettinger, Epps; add Reunald
Jones (t), Trainer out. --Bérard, pp. 14-15.

July 19-Oct. 19.   Leads band on tour east, disbands in Boston.
Some specific engagements reviewed in press: N. Y., AN Aug. 3,
p. 17; Philadelphia, PT advt., Aug. 31, p. 12; Louisville, Var
Oct. 2, p. 20.

Oct. 8 ca.-19.   Leads band, Rio, club, Boston. --Boston Globe,
advts., Oct. 8, p. 16, and Oct. 19, p. 10.

Oct. 19.   BC gives up regular big band permanently on finishing engagement at Rio this day. --DB Nov. 18, p. 5; BB Dec. 14, p.
17.

Oct. 23 ca. BC returns home to California without a band.

Band routes. DB Jan. 1-28, March 25, April 8-22, June 3-Aug. 26, Sept. 23-Oct. 7.

1947   Neighbors threaten, on basis of a restricted covenant, to force BC out of his house in Hollywood; threat fades when such discriminatory agreements are ruled unenforceable.

March. Leads big band, for first time since disbanding, El Patio Th, L. A. --DB March 12, p. 19. Personnel (partial). Fred Trainer, Harry Parr Jones (t), Henry Coker (tb), Lucky Thompson (reeds), Eddie Beal (p), Charlie Drayton (b), Irving Ashby (g), Lee Young (d). --Ibid.

July 2. Leads band, Swing Club, Hollywood, several weeks. --DB July 2, p. 10. Personnel. Harry Parr Jones (t), Henry Coker (tb), Lucky Thompson (reeds), Dodo Marmarosa (p), Tommy Moultrie (b), Henry Tucker Green (d). --Ibid., some errors corrected by BC.

July, late. Leads band, Million Dollar Th, L. A., one week. --Var July 30, p. 44. Personnel. Some of sidemen as for July 2. Wardell Gray (reeds) replaces Thompson. --Ibid.

1948   July, late, into Aug. Leads band, Casbah, club., L. A. --DB Aug. 11, 25, p. 8. Personnel. Gerald Wilson (t), Henry Coker (tb), Bumps Myers (reeds), Gerald Wiggins (p), Charlie Drayton or Benny Booker (b), Lee Young (d).

Aug. 10-16. Leads band, Million Dollar Th, L. A. --DB July 28, Aug. 11, band routes. Personnel. Some of sidemen from previous entry: Coker, Myers, Wiggins.

Sept. 23-Oct. 13. Leads band, Cafe Society Uptown, San Francisco. --DB Nov. 3, p. 7. Personnel. Teddy Buckner (t), Henry Coker (tb), Bumps Myers (reeds), Gerald Wiggins (p), Benny Booker (b), Jesse Price (d). --Ibid.

Band routes. DB July 28, Aug. 11.

1949   June. Appendectomy.

1950   April. Leads band, Million Dollar Th, L. A. --DB May 5, p. 15. Personnel. Ernie Royal (t), Britt Woodman (tb), Bumps Myers (reeds), Gerald Wiggins (p), Ulysses Livingston (g), Lee Young (d). --Ibid.

Dec. 9 ca.-Dec. 21. Leads band, Blue Note, club, Chicago. -- Chicago Tribune, advts., Dec. 9, pt. 2, p. 5, and Dec. 20, pt. 3, p. 4; DB Dec. 29, p. 21. Personnel. Rostelle Reese (t), J. J. Johnson (tb), Al Williams (p), Johnny Williams (b), Joe Harris (d).

Dec., late. Leads band at High Hat, club, Boston. Personnel.
Same as previous entry.

Band routes. DB Dec. 29.

1951 Feb. 3-ca. 28. Leads band, Black Hawk, club, San Francisco.
      --DB March 9, p. 9, and March 23, p. 13. Personnel. Bumps
      Myers (reeds), Sheldon Smith (p), Charlie Drayton (b), Al Bartee
      or Roy Porter (d). --Ibid.

      May 12. Leads band, U. of Oregon, Eugene. --DB June 15, p. 8,
      L.A. sec. Personnel. Maxwell Davis (reeds), Moe Dieffenbach
      (p), Ulysses Livingston (g), Billy Hadnott (b), Bill Douglas (d).
      --Ibid.

      Aug.-Sept. Leads band, Club Royal, San Diego, two weeks to a
      month. --DB Nov. 30, p. 8. Personnel. Gerald Wiggins (p),
      Ulysses Livingston (g), Charlie Drayton (b), George Jenkins (d),
      Ruth Olay (v).

      Sept. 12-Oct. 9. Leads band, Tiffany, club, L.A. --DB Oct. 19,
      p. 6; PC Oct. 13, p. 17. Personnel. Herbie Harper (tb), War-
      dell Gray (reeds), Ernie Freeman (p), Harry Babasin (b), George
      Jenkins (d). --Ibid.

      Nov. to Jan. or Feb., 1952. Leads trio, Astor's Lounge, L.A.
      --DB Nov. 30, p. 1, and Jan. 25, 1952, p. 13. Personnel.
      Gerald Wiggins (p), George Jenkins (d). --Ibid.

      Band routes. DB Oct. 5-19, Nov. 30-Dec. 28.

1952 Jan., late, or Feb. Closes at Astor's Lounge--see previous entry.

      April or May to late June. Leads band, Sardi's, club, L.A. --DB
      June 4, p. 8, and June 18, p. 13. Personnel. Keg Johnson (tb),
      Bumps Myers or Ben Webster (reeds), Gerald Wiggins or Fred
      Otis (p), Charlie Drayton (b), George Jenkins (d). --Ibid., June 4.

      Sept. 13. BC makes his first appearance with JATP, Carnegie Hall,
      N.Y. --DB Sept. 24, p. 1.

      Band routes. DB Jan. 11.

1953 Spring. Leads band, touring West Coast. --MM Aug. 8, p. 3.
      Personnel. George Washington (tb), Ernie Powell (reeds), Ernie
      Freeman (p), George Bledsoe (b), Al Bartee (d). --Ibid.

      April 1. Amalgamation of black and white musicians' unions in L.A.
      BC plays important role since 1950.

      Sept. 19. Plays with JATP, Carnegie Hall, N.Y. --AN Sept. 12,
      p. 23, and NYT Sept. 20, sec. 2, p. 7.

      Nov., early. BC makes his first tour abroad with JATP, in Far
      East. --Var Nov. 11, p. 51.

1954   Feb. 5-March 9.   BC tours Europe with JATP.

        Oct.   Leads quartet, Keyboard Lounge, Beverly Hills, two weeks.
        --DB Dec. 1, p. 3.   Personnel.   Sir Charles Thompson (p), Red
        Callender (b), Bill Douglas (d).

        Nov.   Leads trio, Melody Room, Hollywood, two weeks. --Ibid.

1955   May 26-Oct. 13.   Leads band, opening of interracial hotel, Moulin
        Rouge, Las Vegas. --DB June 29, p. 38, and Nov. 16, p. 31.

1956   Jan., early.   Heart attack, seven weeks in L.A. hospital.

        Summer, ca.   Elected chairman of Local 47 committee on arrangers.
        --DB Aug. 8, p. 39.

1957   Elected to Board of Governors and Executive Committee of National
        Academy of Recording Arts and Sciences, also to Board of L.A.
        chapter.

1958   Elected to Executive Board of Composers and Lyricists Guild of
        America. --DB Dec. 25, pp. 12-13.

        Starts composing for television, M Squad.

        Oct. 5.   Plays for first time at a "jazz festival": Monterey Jazz
        Festival, its first. --DB Nov. 13, p. 50.

1959   Oct. 3.   BC conducts Basie band in BC's Kansas City Suite, at first
        L.A. Jazz Festival. --DB Nov. 12, pp. 18-19.

1960   June 17-18.   Plays, leads BC All-Stars, L.A. Jazz Festival. --DB
        Aug. 4, pp. 14-16.

        July 29-Aug. 7.   Leads quartet at The Embers, club, Melbourne,
        Australia; one concert in Sydney.   Personnel.   Paul Moer (p),
        Curtis Counce (b), Frankie Capp (d).

        Nov., early, to Dec. 7.   Tours Europe with JATP. --DB Dec. 8,
        p. 11; MM Dec. 3, pp. 3, 9.

1961   Nov., late, to Dec. 2.   Plays radio show and four days in night
        club, Cologne, W. Germany; visits London. --MM Dec. 9, p. 13;
        Jazzer (Kiel), Dec. 1961, p. 1.

1962   April 16-May 12.   Conducts big band accompanying Peggy Lee, Basin
        St. East, club, N.Y. --DB April 26, p. 54; New Yorker, April
        14, May 12, p. 8.

        July 7-8.   Plays and conducts BC Festival Orch. at first Las Vegas

Jazz Festival, featuring own composition Las Vegas Suite (never recorded). --DB Aug. 16, p. 19; MM Sept. 29, suppl. p. 10.

Sept. 21-23. BC musical director, Monterey Jazz Festival. Opening night BC conducts Dizzy Gillespie orch. in The New Continent, by Lalo Schifrin. --DB Nov. 8, pp. 13-15.

1963 Fall. Participates in course on recording arts, at UCLA extension division, conducted in cooperation with NARAS. --DB Nov. 21, p. 11.

1966 Nov. -Dec. , early. Tours Europe with JATP. --DB Jan. 26, 1967, pp. 27, 40, 45.

1967 March 26-July, early. Tours U. S. and Canada with JATP, opening at Carnegie Hall, N. Y. --DB March 9, p. 15.

1968 Jan. Substitutes on alto sax for Russell Procope (who substitutes for ill Harry Carney) in Ellington band, about three days, Harrah's, club, Reno.

Feb. Leads quintet, Donte's, club, L. A. , three weekends. --DB Feb. 8, p. 14, and Feb. 22, p. 24. Personnel. Billy Byers (tb), Jimmy Jones (p), Red Mitchell (b), Joe Harris (d). --Ibid.

July 5-6. First appearance at Newport Jazz Festival, solos with bands led by Gillespie (July 5) and Ellington (July 6). --DB June 27, p. 10, and Sept. 5, p. 18; Christian Science Monitor, July 12, p. 6.

Oct. 19. Featured soloist, and accompanies Carmen McRae, concert, Royce Hall, UCLA. --LAT Oct. 22, sec. 4, p. 15. Personnel. Norman Simmons (p), Chuck Domanico (b), Frank Severino (d). --Ibid.

Oct. 23-Nov. , early. BC in London with group from Newport Jazz Festival. --DB Oct. 31, p. 10; LAT Oct. 20, Calendar sec. , p. 40.

Nov. Plays in Ronnie Scott Club, London, ten days. --BB Nov. 23, p. 16.

Nov. 9. Plays with Henri Chaix band, "Jazz in der Aula," in Kantonsschule, Baden, Switzerland. --Badener Tagblatt, Nov. 8.

Nov. 10. Plays with Henri Chaix band at Vieilles Pierres, Geneva.

Nov. 11. Plays at C. N. P. -Capitole Th, Bordeaux.

1969 April 5. Conducts and solos with large orchestra and choir his own extended composition (with lyrics) in honor of the late Martin Luther King, Jr. , Pauley Pavilion, UCLA. --LAT April 7, pt. 4, p. 16; DB May 29, p. 33.

1970   Jan. 26-30. Plays and conducts seminars, Baldwin Wallace College,
        Berea, O.

        Feb. 2-3. Leads quartet, conducts seminars, Princeton U. --NYT
        Feb. 5, p. 34. Personnel. Roland Hanna (p), Ron Carter (b),
        Grady Tate (d). --Ibid.

        May 16-17. Plays and participates in seminar at National College
        Jazz Festival, U. of Ill. , Urbana. --DB July 9, p. 13.

1971   May 30. Conducts and plays with Louis Bellson band, big-band
        "festival," Disneyland. --DB Aug. 19, p. 44.

        June 1-24. Touring Denmark, Sweden, France.

        Sept. 4-6. Plays at Dick Gibson's jazz party, Colorado Springs.

1972   Feb. 13-14. Plays (Feb. 13) and conducts seminars (Feb. 14),
        Eisenhower College, Seneca Falls, N. Y. Personnel. Hank Jones
        (p), George Duvivier (b), Ron Zito (d).

        July 2-3. Newport Jazz Festival, N. Y. July 2 leads Swing Mas-
        ters, Carnegie Hall; July 3 jam session, Radio City Music Hall.
        --NYT July 3, p. 7, and July 5, p. 31. Personnel. July 2,
        Swing Masters: see Discography.

        July 4. Guest of honor, New Amsterdam Musical Association (est.
        1900), Harlem.

        Sept. 2-4. Dick Gibson jazz party, Colorado Springs.

        Oct. 6-8. Plays concert and named Fellow, Duke Ellington Fellow-
        ship Program, Yale U. --DB Dec. 7, pp. 11, 38.

        Oct. 24, ca. , to Nov. 8 ca. Touring Europe, Norman Granz man-
        agement. --DB Dec. 7, p. 10.

1973   April 18-19. Leads seminars and concert (April 19), Princeton U.
        Personnel. Hank Jones (p), Milt Hinton (b), Ron Zito (d). --NYT
        April 23, p. 41.

        May 21-June, early. Touring Denmark, France.

        July 18-28. Touring Japan. Personnel. Gildo Mahones (p), Larry
        Gales (b), Duffy Jackson (d).

        Sept. 1-3. Dick Gibson jazz party, Colorado Springs.

        Sept. 17. Leads quartet, L. A. County Museum of Art. --LAT Sept.
        20, pt. 4, p. 16. Personnel. Gildo Mahones (p), Larry Gales
        (b), Duffy Jackson (d). --Ibid.

        Sept. -Dec. Visiting professor, fall term, Princeton U. : workshops,
        seminars, concerts on Oct. 22, Dec. 3. Personnel. Oct. 22,
        McCarter Th. Clark Terry (t), Hank Jones (p), Bucky Pizzarelli

(g), Milt Hinton (b), Grady Tate (d). Personnel. Dec. 3, Alexander Hall: see Discography.

Nov. 10. Participates in workshop and concert conducted by Willie Ruff, Yale U.

Dec., mid. Leads local combo, Bourbon St., club, Toronto. --IM Jan. 1974, p. 21.

1974   Jan. 19. Receives "Jazzboree" award; leads quartet, concert, Paramount Th, Oakland. Personnel. Gildo Mahones (p), Larry Gales (b), Paul Humphrey (d). --Philip Elwood, San Francisco Examiner, Jan. 21, p. 27.

June 11. Receives honorary degree, Doctor of Humanities, Princeton U. --NYT June 12, p. 49; DB Nov. 7, p. 10.

Aug. 31-Sept. 2. Dick Gibson jazz party, Colorado Springs.

Nov. 6-7. Leads sextet in concert (Nov. 7), and seminars, Cornell U. Personnel. Jimmy Nottingham (t), Al Grey (tb), Roland Hanna (p), Milt Hinton (b), Alan Dawson (d).

Nov. Conducts band accompanying Maria Muldaur on U.S. tour. --NYT Nov. 20, p. 54, on Nov. 18 concert, Avery Fisher Hall, N.Y. Personnel. Sweets Edison, Snooky Young (t), Frank Rosolino (tb), Plas Johnson, Sahib Shihab, Tony Ortega (reeds), Marty Harris (p), John Collins (g), John B. Williams, Jr. (b), Earl Palmer (d).

Dec. 22. Conducts band accompanying Maria Muldaur, Troubadour, club, L.A. Personnel. Changes from Nov.: J. J. Johnson (tb) replaces Rosolino, Bud Shank (reeds) replaces Ortega, Mundell Lowe (g) replaces Collins.

1975   June 28. Leads band (also accompanies Maria Muldaur), Newport Jazz Festival, Carnegie Hall, N.Y. --NYT June 30, p. 40.

July. Plays at European festivals, Nice and Montreux.

Aug. 25-30. Leads quartet, Playboy Club, L.A. --LAT Aug. 27, pt. 4, p. 11. Personnel. Gildo Mahones (p), Larry Gales (b), Jimmie Smith (d). --Ibid.

Aug. 31-Sept. 2. Dick Gibson jazz party, Colorado Springs.

Sept. 9. Leads quartet, Ratso's, club, Chicago. --Chicago Daily News, Sept. 10, p. 24. Personnel. Jodie Christian (p), David Shipp (b), Jo Jones (d). --Ibid.

Oct. 26-Nov. 22. Touring Europe with Earl Hines. --Dance, World of Earl Hines, pp. 126, 310.

Dec. 16-Jan. 22, 1976. Leads quintet touring Middle East under auspices of U.S. Dept. of State and USIA. --LAT Jan. 31, 1976, p. 1, and Feb. 8, Calendar sec., pp. 73-75. Personnel. Sweets

Edison (t), Gildo Mahones (p), John B. Williams, Jr. (b), Earl
Palmer (d), Millicent Browne (v).

1976   Jan. 1-22.   Continues tour of Middle East.   See previous entry.

April 14-16.   Plays with student jazz band with Willie Ruff, Duke U.
--The Chronicle, student paper, April 21, p. 9.

May 29-June 6.   Tours Europe with show, "A Night in New Orleans."

June 8-July 3.   Leads quartet, Michael's Pub, N.Y., BC's first
club date in N.Y. since 1942 on 52d St. --NYT June 11, p. C4.
Personnel.   Ray Bryant (p), Milt Hinton (b), Grady Tate (d).
--Ibid.

July 5-17.   Plays with local rhythm section, Buena Vista Village
Lounge, Disney World, Fla. --Orlando Sentinel-Star, advt., July
11, p. 9-F.

July 27.   Honored in testimonial dinner by Hollywood Press Club.
--BB July 31, p. 41.

Aug.   Accepts three-year term on music advisory panel of NEA.

Sept.   Accepts four-year term on advisory council of Princeton U
Music department.

Sept. 4-6.   Dick Gibson jazz party, Colorado Springs.

Sept. 7-8.   Leads quartet, Donte's, club, L.A. --LAT advt. Sept.
5, Calendar sec., p. 76.

Sept. 17.   Plays at Monterey Jazz Festival in tributes to F. Henderson and Armstrong.   Receives award from American Music Con-
ference. --DB July 15, p. 6.

Oct. 13-15.   Gives interview on career for Jazz Oral History Project conducted by Smithsonian Institution on behalf of NEA.

1977   Jan.   Awarded prize for Pablo record, The King, by Académie du
Disque Français.

Feb. 15.   Leads band for dance, Palladium, L.A.

March 11-April 12.   Visiting lecturer, Princeton U.: workshops,
seminars, concerts Alexander Hall March 18 (leading quintet) and April 8 (solos with student P.U. Jazz Ensemble).   Personnel.   March
18. Joe Newman (t), Bucky Pizzarelli (g), Roland Hanna (p), Richard
Davis (b), Richard Pratt (d).   Personnel.   April 8: see Discography.

April 19-29.   Tours Japan with BC All Stars.   Personnel.   April 29:
see Discography.

May 2-7.   Plays at Kool festival, Hawaii.

May 17-June 11.   Leads quartet, Michael's Pub, N.Y. --NYT May

21, p. 11.   Personnel.   Ray Bryant (p), Richard Davis (b), Ronnie Bedford (d).   --Ibid.

June 23-July 2.   Tours England.   --Jazz Journal International, Aug.,
pp. 22-23.

July 7-12.   Plays at Nice festival, Grande Parade du Jazz.

July 13-14.   Plays at Montreux festival.   Personnel.   See Discography, July 13, 14.

July 15.   Plays at Northsea festival, The Hague.

July 16-18.   Plays at San Sebastian (Spain), Biarritz and Montauban
(France).

Sept. 3-5.   Dick Gibson jazz party, Colorado Springs.

1978   Feb. 19.   Inducted into Black Film Makers Hall of Fame, Oakland.
--Oakland Tribune, Feb. 19, special sec.; San Francisco Examiner, Feb. 20, p. 22.

March 20.   Plays with Jon Hendricks at Meadows Playhouse, Las
Vegas.

April 13-21.   Tours Japan.   Personnel.   See Discography, April 15.

April 28-May 12.   Tours Canada and Europe with "A Night in New
Orleans. "

May 14.   Leads quintet, concert, Jazz Heritage Series of Smithsonian
Institution, at National Museum of Natural History, Wash., D. C.
--Washington Post, May 15, p. B8.   Personnel.   Joe Kennedy,
Jr. (vn), Ray Bryant (p), Larry Ridley (b), Freddie Waits (d).
--Ibid.

May 16-27.   Leads quartet, Rick's Café Américain, Chicago. --Chi-
cago Tribune, May 19, sec. 2, p. 5.   Personnel.   Jodie Christian (p), John Bany (b), Barrett Deems (d).   --Ibid.

May 25.   Award made to BC by Center for Afro-American Studies,
UCLA.

June 18.   Leads ensemble at White House tribute to jazz.   Personnel.
Roy Eldridge, Clark Terry (t), Illinois Jacquet (ts), Teddy Wilson
(p), Milt Hinton (b), Jo Jones (d). --Washington Post, June 19,
p. B1.

June 23.   Plays in concert, Denver, produced by Dick Gibson.

Sept. 2-4.   Dick Gibson jazz party, Colorado Springs.

Sept. 10-11.   Plays at festival, Sao Paolo, Brazil. --LAT Oct. 8,
Calendar sec., pp. 92-94.

Sept. 14-17.   Gives master classes and concert, Capital U.   Con-
servatory of Music, Columbus, O.

Sept. 19-23. Leads quartet, Hong Kong Bar, Century Plaza Hotel,
L. A. --LAT Sept. 21, pt. 4, p. 26. Personnel. Gildo Mahones
(p), Andy Simpson (b), Jimmie Smith (d). --Ibid.

Oct. 20. Plays with youth band, Yale U. School of Music.

Oct. 21. Plays fund-raising concert, Wooster School, Danbury,
Conn.

Oct. 26. Leads band, inauguration of new president, California Institute of Technology, Pasadena. Personnel. Conte Candoli,
Bobby Bryant (t), Frank Rosolino (tb), Abe Most, Teddy Edwards
(reeds), Gildo Mahones (p), John Collins (g), Monte Budwig (b),
Jimmie Smith (d).

Oct. 27-29. Conducts seminars, two concerts (Oct. 28) SUNY Buffalo. In each concert BC solos with student band, then leads and
plays with Al Tinney Trio. Personnel, both ensembles: see
Discography.

1979   June 1-15. Tours Japan. Personnel. See Discography, June 2.

Aug. 30. Plays at Chicago festival. --Chicago Tribune, Aug. 31,
sec. 4, p. 6.

Sept. 1-3. Dick Gibson jazz party, Colorado Springs.

Sept. -Dec. Visiting professor, fall term, Princeton U., teaching in
regular course and giving two concerts, Alexander Hall: Oct. 12,
leads a sextet; Nov. 10, solos with student ensemble. Personnel,
Oct. 12. Dizzy Gillespie (t), Joe Kennedy, Jr. (vn), Barry Harris (p), Larry Ridley (b), Yusef Ali (d). Personnel, Nov. 10:
see Discography.

1980   Jan. 25-26. Plays in concert, Paramount Th, Denver, produced by
Dick Gibson.

April. Album of BC records appears, Giants of Jazz series, published by Time-Life Records.

June 8. Receives Golden Score award from American Society of
Music Arrangers in ceremony, Ambassador Hotel, L. A.

June 11-13. Plays at Stockholm Jazz and Blues Festival with several local groups. Personnel: see Discography.

June 20. Leads quartet, "Tonight Show," NBC-TV, L. A. Personnel.
Teddy Wilson (p), Ray Brown (b), Shelly Manne (d).

June 21. Leads quintet, Playboy festival, Hollywood Bowl. --LAT
June 23, pt. 6, pp. 1-2. Personnel. Sweets Edison (t), Teddy
Wilson (p), Ray Brown (b), Shelly Manne (d). --Ibid.

June 26. Plays with New McKinney Cotton Pickers, honoring Don
Redman, Detroit Institute of Arts. --Detroit News, June 26, p.
11B.

June 27-28. Leads quartet, One Step Down, club, Wash., D.C.
--Washington Star, June 27, sec. C, p. 11. Personnel. Gus
Simms (p), Tommy Cecil (b), Bernard Sweetney (d).

July 3. Leads band, Newport festival, Avery Fisher Hall. --NYT
July 5, p. 12. Personnel. Jimmy Maxwell, Doc Cheatham (t),
Curtis Fuller (tb), Budd Johnson, Cecil Payne (reeds), Joe Kennedy, Jr. (vn), Ray Bryant (p), Major Holley (b), Oliver Jackson
(d).

July 9-24. Leads BC All-Stars (personnel--see July 3 above) in
European festivals: France, Holland.

Aug. 10-15. Leads combo, Tivoli garden, Slukefter Jazz Club,
Copenhagen. Personnel. Kenny Drew (p), Jesper Lundgaard (b),
Ed Thigpen (d).

Sept. 3-7. Leads quintet in three concerts in Japan: Tokyo, Osaka,
Yokohama. Aurex festival also features groups led by Benny
Goodman, Freddie Hubbard, Dizzy Gillespie. Personnel. Sweets
Edison (t), Teddy Wilson (p), Milt Hinton (b), Shelly Manne (d),
Helen Humes (v).

Oct. 10. Plays at New Haven, Conn., with Yale Jazz Ensemble
(undergraduates), Willie Ruff and Dwike Mitchell in two concerts:
for elementary school pupils and for the general public.

Oct. 28. Leads big band in celebrating, over several evenings, 40th
anniversary of Palladium Bm, L.A.

1981   March 24-25. Member of ad hoc group convened by the Smithsonian
Institution Division of Performing Arts, in Washington, D.C., to
discuss its jazz program.

April 14-18. Leads quartet, Sweet Basil's, N.Y. --NYT April 17,
p. C15. Personnel. Norman Simmons (p), George Duvivier (b),
Ronnie Bedford (d).

April 28-May 3. Concerts in Denmark, Sweden.

May 5-8. Leads combo, Tivoli garden, Slukefter Jazz Club, Copenhagen.

May 25-June 13. Leads quartet, Lyte's, Royal York Hotel, Toronto.
Personnel. Carol Britto (p), Dave Field (b), Don Vickery (d).

July 1-21. Tours Japan. Personnel. Bill Berry, Pete Candoli (t),
George Bohanon (tb), Frank Wess (ts, flute), Jack Nimitz (bar.
sax), Kenny Barron (p), Joe Kennedy, Jr. (violin), George Duvivier (b), Frankie Capp (d).

Aug. 22-23. Leads quartet, Ojai Festival, Ojai, California. Personnel. Roger Kellaway (p), Chuck Domanico (b), John Guerin (d).

Aug. 26. Plays at concert, tribute to Lionel Hampton, Hollywood
Bowl. Personnel. Includes Harry Edison, Teddy Wilson.

Sept. 5-7.   Dick Gibson jazz party, Colorado Springs.

Sept. 26.   Leads sextet, concert, UCLA. (Portions later broadcast
over National Public Radio's "Jazz Alive.") Personnel.   Bill
Berry (cornet), George Bohanon (tb), Roger Kellaway (p), Chuck
Domanico (b), John Guerin (d).

Nov. 8.   Leads quintet, Bach Dancing and Dynamite Society, Half
Moon Bay, California. --San Francisco Examiner, Nov. 13, p.
E5. Personnel.   Tee Carson (p), Eddie Duran (g), Dean Reilly
(b), Benny Barth (d).

Nov. 20-21.   Plays in concert, Paramount Th, Denver, produced by
Dick Gibson. Personnel.   Red Rodney (t), Bill Watrous, Al Grey
(tb), Plas Johnson, Buddy Tate (ts), Dick Hyman, Jay McShann
(p), Slam Stewart (b), Gus Johnson (d).

Nov. 28.   Leads quintet, concert, Smithsonian Institution, Washington, D. C. Personnel.   Kenny Barron (p), Joe Kennedy, Jr. (violin), George Duvivier (b), Ronnie Bedford (d).

Dec. 1-5.   Leads quartet, Sweet Basil's, N. Y. --NYT Dec. 4, p.
C15. Personnel.   Kenny Barron (p), George Duvivier (b), Ronnie
Bedford (d).

Dec. 15-20.   Leads quartet, Parisian Room, L. A. Personnel.   Gildo
Mahones (p), Larry Gales (b), Harold Jones (d).

1982   Jan. 4-23.   Leads quartet, Lyte's, Royal York Hotel, Toronto.
Personnel.   Carol Britto (p), Dave Young (b), Don Vickery (d).

DISCOGRAPHY

29

INTRODUCTION*

In possessing such a wide range of talents, Carter has done little to "co-operate" with the discographer. It is easy to develop a workable format for the artist who is primarily a player (extracting the data, of course, may be anything but simple). Documenting the contributions of a composer/arranger is more complex. Carter is unique in the depth of his contributions to every domain discographers seek to cover. Moreover, his career encompasses many musical styles, all types of media, and is extraordinary in its longevity and sustained creativity.

Scope. This discography could not be confined to Carter's playing. Therefore a section has been devoted to his arrangements and compositions, with indexes to show who recorded them and a chronology of their creation.

Nor could any stylistic limitations be imposed, such as attempting to isolate the "jazz" component of his work. Aside from the inevitable arbitrariness of such a distinction, the exclusion of the non-jazz elements would severely distort the total picture of Carter's career. The symbiosis between jazz and popular music is well known and jazz musicians--Carter more than most--have always moved between the two realms. In fact, it would be safe to say that since the 1940s he has devoted more time to arranging and composing for television, films, and popular singers than to his activity as a jazz instrumentalist. Carter himself, unlike some purists, does not view this as an invidious distinction.

We include many private recordings because they provide important documentation of periods in Carter's career when he made few commercial studio recordings (particularly late 1960s and 1970s). Such performances, indeed, may yet become more widely available.

Sources. Rust's and Jepsen's general jazz discographies provide the basis for much of the information in this discography. More specialized artist-discographies and bio-discographies also proved helpful, as did two previous surveys of Carter's recordings: Jörgen Grunnet Jepsen's "Benny Carter Diskografi 1949-1959," Orkester Journalen, December 1959, pp. 56-57; January 1960, p. 34; February 1960, pp. 38-39, and a Carter discography in the Japanese Swing Journal, June 1979, pp. 222-227. The late Walter C. Allen's Hendersonia must be singled out not only for the information provided on Carter's recordings with Henderson but as a model for the presentation of arranging and composing data. Many collectors and researchers helped with the more ephemeral material, such as airchecks, transcriptions, and private recordings.

---

*This introduction is abbreviated from Edward Berger's article in the Journal of Jazz Studies. He invites additions to and corrections of this discography. Portions of the notes on the music are adapted from those in The Giants of Jazz: Benny Carter (Time-Life).

Special problems arose in the documentation of Carter's "popular" music because discographical coverage of this field is far less advanced than of jazz. Consequently, chance played a large role in the discovery of his participation as an instrumentalist on some sessions.

The identification of recorded arrangements by Carter was also problematical. The arranger is truly the stepchild of the recording session. Though his reworking of a composition often becomes an act of greater creativity and musical interest than the piece on which it is based, he is too often viewed as a journeyman.

Aural identification of arrangements is difficult but may be a starting point taken in conjunction with the arranger's known associations. Certainly Carter's arrangements have distinctive stylistic features, not the least of which are his innovative reed voicings. But, as other arrangers have attested, many copied his style--often rather successfully--so that after a time the presence of a flowing reed passage no longer guarantees that it is a Carter arrangement. Furthermore, the special demands of a particular bandleader or contractor often required Carter to treat a piece in a style different from his own. This results in the elimination, or at least the dilution, of some of Carter's trademarks, making it more difficult, even for him, to recognize his own work, especially after many years.

Musician as Source. The artist himself may be the single most valuable source in a project of this kind. Carter's cooperation has been complete. He opened his home to the project. His record collection, scores, memorabilia, and business files provided answers to many problems, as well as clues to a number of items which would otherwise have been overlooked. He submitted to hundreds of hours of interviews and listening, which helped immeasurably in identifying solos and arrangements. Carter's respect for scholarship and research methods led him to divulge even such information as his use of pseudonyms.

This was not the first time Carter willingly submitted to discographical grilling. In 1935 in Paris, Charles Delaunay enlisted Carter's help for his pioneering Hot Discography. It was Delaunay, on a visit to the United States in 1980, who revealed the extent of Carter's assistance. Carter himself never mentioned it, perhaps to avoid the appearance of impatience with this new inquisition.

As far as his credibility as a source is concerned, Carter is not one to claim credit for a solo, arrangement or composition unless he is certain that it is his work. Jelly Roll Morton claimed to have invented jazz in 1902. The Carter interviewer considers himself a success if he gets his subject to admit that he played the saxophone.

SECTION ONE: CARTER AS INSTRUMENTALIST

This section is a chronological listing of all known recordings on which
Carter plays.   Issued and unissued performances of the following types are
included: studio recordings, airchecks, private recordings, transcriptions
and some television broadcasts.   Carter's playing in films is listed here
only when such material has appeared on record (e. g. , soundtrack albums).
Other film work is documented in the filmography.

Each session includes the following data.

1.   Session number appears in brackets at the left and is assigned
sequentially to each session, beginning with 1.   If sets of recordings made
on one date have significant changes in personnel they are assigned different
session numbers (e. g. , the trio portion of a Jazz At The Philharmonic concert).

2.   Date of recording is followed by place of recording (city).   Following the date a brief description of the type of recording may appear, including a more precise location (e. g. , airchecks, Savoy Ballroom).   If no
additional descriptive information is present, the session is a studio recording.   The leader and/or group appears on the next line.   For recent Carter-
led sessions, the appropriate LP title(s) are given in parentheses.

3.   Personnel.   Carter always appears first, with abbreviations sum-
marizing his role(s) on the date (i. e. , instruments played, arrangements
and/or compositions contributed).

4.   Tune titles, Carter's solos, and matrix numbers.   Each title is
followed by an indication (using initials) of vocalists and/or arrangers, etc.
pertinent to that title.   Next is a notation of Carter's precise participation
on that particular piece.   The solo description consists of the number of
measures followed by an instrument abbreviation.   If Carter's solo is continued after a brief interlude (e. g. , bridge) by the ensemble or another
soloist, Carter's passages are separated by a + symbol.   If Carter returns
after a longer interval, the + does not appear between the solo statements.
Where Carter is not the only soloist on a given instrument, his solo is
identified.   The abbreviation "acc. " following the instrument means that
Carter's playing is accompanying a vocalist or another soloist (i. e. , obbligato).   An "e" is used to indicate titles on which Carter plays in the
ensemble but does not solo.   The absence of any solo indication means that
we have not heard the item.   The abbreviations "arr" and "comp" following
the solo description identify the piece as a Carter arrangement or composition.   With the advent of the LP, the release of longer performances became feasible.   After 1952 the number of measures of Carter's solos is no
longer indicated; only the instrument is given.

5.   Basic record issue information appears directly below the individual tune titles.   Issues are preceded by the type of disc (78: 45: LP: or

T: for transcription). Where helpful, the country of origin of a record issue is indicated by an abbreviation in parentheses after the label name.
These listings do not attempt to include every issue of every title, but
concentrate on the original issue, major reissues, and those issues (usually
recent) not covered in the standard comprehensive discographies. An absence of record issues indicates that the recordings exist or are likely to
exist on private tapes. Artist and title indexes to Section One refer to
session numbers.

6. Annotations follow many of the sessions; these annotations concentrate on the commercially issued recordings rather than the less widely-
circulated material.

Armed Forces Radio Service Transcriptions. From 1942 to 1952
Benny Carter participated in approximately thirty AFRS productions including Jubilee shows, Downbeat shows, the Basic Library of Popular Music
and the V-Disc program.

Most of the information for the AFRS listings comes from two major
sources: 1) Dr. Ranier E. Lotz, who is carrying out extensive research
on the AFRS series and provided drafts of his worksheets for the Jubilee
programs involving Carter. 2) Jerry Valburn, who supplied tapes of many
of the AFRS shows as well as information about the various series.

Jubilee. Jubilee shows were half-hour transcriptions distributed
overseas for broadcast to United States personnel. Many were especially
recorded before a live audience, but occasionally material from other
sources was included (e. g. , portions of the 1947 "Just Jazz" concerts).
Most of the shows featuring Carter were recorded in Los Angeles with
comedian Ernie "Bubbles" Whitman as m. c. Later shows originated from
the McCornack Hospital in Pasadena, with Gene Norman as host. Musicians donated their services. The Jubilee shows were often extensively
edited, with some segments reappearing in later programs. Some were
repeated in their entirety, although assigned a new program number. Where
specific dates are given in the discography, they come from Dr. Lotz, who
has examined AFRS books prior to 1946. He points out that these are not
actual recording dates, but probably the dates the transcriptions were edited.
He surmises that they are reasonably close to the date of recording and in
some cases the same. In any case, these dates should be considered as
"not later than" rather than exact.

Basic Library of Popular Music. According to Jerry Valburn, the
AFRS was allowed to take material off the air for inclusion in this transcription series, which served as the source for other programs.

Downbeat shows. These half-hour transcriptions derived from several sources. Those featuring Carter seem to have drawn primarily from
the Basic Library, although some regular commercial studio items are
present.

V-Discs. These were 12-inch 78 rpm discs playable on standard
phonographs and distributed directly to the military posts. Some performances were recorded especially for V-Discs; others came from commercial
recordings and other AFRS productions. Most of the Carter V-Discs contain performances from Jubilee transcriptions.

Discographical information about these recordings is highly speculative for several reasons. 1) Original documentation for many of these programs no longer exists. 2) A performance from one source was often used

for other types of programs (e. g. , Jubilee recordings used in Downbeat shows, commercial recordings reissued on V-Disc, etc.). 3) Dubbed applause and announcements may disguise the original source of the material. 4) A performance may reappear in various programs under different titles (e. g. , "Jump Tune," "No Title Jump," "Untitled Jump," and possibly "Jay Jay's Jump" for the Carter orchestra recording of "Polishin' Brass"). On the other hand, several different versions of the same tune may be included on different AFRS programs. 5) The approximately 15 LPs containing Carter AFRS material which have appeared to date include some wrong discographical data.

ABBREVIATIONS

Instruments

tp - trumpet

tb - trombone

cl - clarinet

ss - soprano saxophone

as - alto saxophone

ts - tenor saxophone

bs - baritone saxophone

p - piano

g - guitar

b - bass

d - drums

vib - vibraphone

v - vocal

ldr - leader

dir - director

Carter's role and solos:

instruments - abbreviated as above

e - ensemble (no solo)

acc - Carter plays accompaniment to vocalist or other soloist (obbligato)

arr - arranger

comp - composer

Record issues (countries of origin)

E - England

F - France

G - Germany

I - Italy

J - Japan

Sw - Sweden

CARTER AS INSTRUMENTALIST

---
[1]   January 24, 1928   New York
        CHARLIE JOHNSON'S PARADISE ORCHESTRA

Carter (as, cl, arr) Jabbo Smith, Sidney de Paris (tp) Charlie Irvis (tb) Edgar Sampson (as, violin) Ben Whittet (cl, as) Benny Waters (ts, as) Charlie Johnson (p) Bobby Johnson (banjo) Cyrus St. Clair (tuba) George Stafford (d) McNette Moore (v)

YOU AIN'T THE ONE   v-MM   (e) arr   41639-1
78: UNISSUED   LP: VICTOR 430687, PIRATE MPC521,
RCA (F) 741.065

YOU AIN'T THE ONE   v-MM   (e) arr   41639-2
78: VICTOR 21247   LP: MELODEON MLP7327, RCA (F)
741.065

CHARLESTON IS THE BEST DANCE AFTER ALL   (8as) arr   41640-1
78: VICTOR 21491   LP: MELODEON MLP7326, RCA (F)
741.065, RCA (F) PM42406

CHARLESTON IS THE BEST DANCE AFTER ALL   (8as) arr   41640-2
78: UNISSUED   LP: VICTOR "X" LVA3026, VICTOR 430687,
ONLY FOR COLLECTORS OFC10, RCA (F) 741.065

HOT TEMPERED BLUES   (e)   41641-1
78: UNISSUED   LP: VICTOR "X" LVA3026, VICTOR
430687, RCA (F) 741.065

HOT TEMPERED BLUES   (e)   41641-2
78: VICTOR 21247   LP: ONLY FOR COLLECTORS OFC10,
RCA (F) 741.065

*   *   *

This session is generally considered to be Carter's first, but he recalls making a recording much earlier (probably 1924) with blues singer Clara Smith. Carter, who would have been 17 at the time, remembers that he was contacted by Charles Matson, who played piano on the date. In an attempt to identify the recording more precisely, Carter perused Clara Smith titles of that time, and sessions with unidentified alto saxophone accompaniments were played for him (he was not yet doubling on clarinet). He could not recognize any of these titles or recordings. If indeed he played on one of them it may never have been issued, or perhaps he substituted for a saxophonist whose name remains as the accompanist.

Although Carter's playing on this 1928 date is limited to an eight-bar statement on "Charleston," we get our first extended look at Carter's incipient arranging style. The two Carter arrangements are not, however, his first on record. "PDQ Blues," recorded by Fletcher Henderson on April 28, 1927, is probably by Carter. While obviously drawing on past elements (e.g., the trumpet section breaks à la Armstrong/Oliver), Carter's special treatment of the reeds is evident in both arrangements. "Charleston," in particular, has a full chorus of the section displaying some of the characteristic lines and voicings--although with the prevailing choppier phrasing--which would mark his later work. His brief solo appearance (the eight-bar bridge within Jabbo Smith's solo trumpet chorus) is also unmistakably Carter in tone. He has difficulty in the second measure of his solo in take 2, possibly one reason the first take was chosen for issue.

---

[2]   Mid November, 1928   New York
         HENDERSON'S HAPPY SIX ORCHESTRA

Carter (as) Rex Stewart (cornet) Charlie Green (tb) Buster Bailey (cl) Fletcher Henderson (p) Charlie Dixon or Clarence Holiday (banjo) Coleman Hawkins (bass sax)

OLD BLACK JOE'S BLUES   (2as)   3491-A
78:   CAMEO 9033   LP: COLUMBIA CL1683

*   *   *

This is Carter's first recording with the Henderson group, although he was not to become a regular member of the band until 1930.

---

[3]   December 12, 1928   New York
         FLETCHER HENDERSON AND HIS ORCHESTRA

Carter (as, v, arr) Rex Stewart, Bobby Stark (tp) Charlie Green (tb) Buster Bailey (cl, as) Coleman Hawkins (ts) Fletcher Henderson (p) Clarence Holiday (banjo) June Cole (tuba) Kaiser Marshall (d)

COME ON, BABY   (8+8as) (v) arr   147421-3
78:   COLUMBIA 14392-D   LP: COLUMBIA CL1684

EASY MONEY   (e) arr   147422-2
78:   COLUMBIA 14392-D   LP: COLUMBIA CL1683

*   *   *

Carter's brief solo contribution to this date is in two parts and shows a growing confidence and forceful attack, with an ambitious break at the end of the first eight measures. He has some intonation problems during the second eight-bar spot.

His first recorded vocal is also his only attempt at scat-singing and makes up in energetic good humor what it lacks in technique.

Walter C. Allen lists Charlie Green with a question mark; Carter, after hearing these recordings, believes the trombonist is Green.

[4]   September 18, 1929 New York
         THE CHOCOLATE DANDIES

Carter (as, cl, v) Rex Stewart, Leonard Davis (tp) J. C. Higginbotham (tb)
Don Redman (as, cl, v) Coleman Hawkins (ts) Fats Waller (p) Bobby Johnson
(banjo) Cyrus St. Clair (tuba) George Stafford (d)

THAT'S HOW I FEEL TODAY   (16+8as)   402965-C
78: OKEH 8728 LP: PARLOPHONE (E) PMC7038,
SWAGGIE S1249, ODEON (J) EMI OR-8065

SIX OR SEVEN TIMES v-BC, DR (16as) (vocal duet   402966-D
     with DR) (16as trades with DR-v)+(16as trades
     with ensemble)
78: OKEH 8728 LP: FOLKWAYS FP69, FOLKWAYS
FJ2808, PARLOPHONE (E) PMC7038, SWAGGIE S1249,
ODEON (J) EMI OR-8065, TIME-LIFE STL-J10

                          *   *   *

This was the first of Carter's several associations with recording groups
named "Chocolate Dandies." He himself was to lead sessions under this
now anachronistic designation in 1930, 1933, and as late as 1946. Here,
Don Redman is in charge.

     The riff which opens and closes "Six Or Seven Times" later became
the basis of Count Basie's "One O'Clock Jump." The piece includes a six-
teen-bar conversation between Carter and Redman, with Redman's scat-singing replies to Carter's alto statements. (For a discussion of Carter's solo
on this piece, see chapter 3.)

[5]   November 5, 1929 New York
         McKINNEY'S COTTON PICKERS

Carter (as) Joe Smith, Leonard Davis, Sidney de Paris (tp) Claude Jones
(tb) Don Redman (as, v, arr) Coleman Hawkins, Theodore McCord (cl, ts)
Fats Waller (p) Dave Wilborn (banjo) Billy Taylor (tuba) Kaiser Marshall (d)
John Nesbitt (arr)

PLAIN DIRT arr-JN (e)   57064-2
78: VICTOR V-38097 LP: RCA (F) 741.088, RCA
(F) 42407, RCA (J) RA-47

GEE, AIN'T I GOOD TO YOU v-DR, arr-DR (16as)   57065-1
78: VICTOR V-38097 LP: RCA LPV520, RCA (E)
RD7561, RCA (F) 741.088, RCA (F) PM42407, RCA
(J) RA-47

[6]   November 6, 1929 New York
         McKINNEY'S COTTON PICKERS

Carter (as, cl) Joe Smith, Leonard Davis, Sidney de Paris (tp) Claude Jones
(tb) Don Redman (as, v, arr) Coleman Hawkins, Theodore McCord (cl, ts) Fats
Waller (p) Dave Wilborn (banjo) Billy Taylor (tuba) Kaiser Marshall (d)

I'D LOVE IT (32as)   57066-2

78: VICTOR V-38133 LP: RCA LPV520, RCA (E)
RD7561, RCA (F) 741.088, TIME-LIFE STL-J10, RCA
(F) PM42407

THE WAY I FEEL TODAY v-DR (e)   57067-1
78: VICTOR V-38102 LP: RCA LPV520, RCA (E)
RD7561, RCA (F) 741.109, RCA (F) PM42407, RCA
(J) RA-47

MISS HANNAH v-DR (16cl)   57068-2
78: VICTOR V-38102 LP: RCA LPV520, RCA (E)
RD7561, RCA (F) 741.109, RCA (F) PM42407, RCA
(J) RA-47

---

[7]	November 7, 1929 New York
	McKINNEY'S COTTON PICKERS

Carter (as) Joe Smith, Leonard Davis, Sidney de Paris (tp) Claude Jones
(tb) Don Redman (as, v, arr) Coleman Hawkins, Theodore McCord (cl, ts)
Fats Waller (p) Dave Wilborn (banjo) Billy Taylor (tuba) Kaiser Marshall (d)

PEGGY (e)   57139-3
78: VICTOR V-38133 LP: RCA (E) RD7561, RCA
LPV520, RCA (F) 741.109, RCA (F) PM43258

WHEREVER THERE'S A WILL, BABY v-DR (e)   57140-2
78: VICTOR 22736 LP: RCA (E) RD7561, RCA
LPV501, RCA (F) 741.109, TIME-LIFE STL-J06,
RCA (F) PM43258

WHEREVER THERE'S A WILL, BABY v-DR (e)   57140-3
78: UNISSUED LP: RCA (J) RA-5314, RCA (F)
741.109, RCA (F) PM43258

        NOTE: RCA (J) RA-47 contains one of the two takes of "Wherever..."

*   *   *

The personnel for these three sessions [5, 6, 7] is an augmented recording
version of the regular McKinney's Cotton Pickers, for which Don Redman
was then musical director; Carter would replace him two years later.
Carter credits Redman's leadership for the precise execution of the Cotton
Pickers and remembers him as "one of the sweetest and most generous men
I ever knew." Whenever they recorded together, the self-effacing Redman
usually delegated the alto or clarinet solos to Carter.

        Carter's alto chorus on "I'd Love It" is his longest recorded solo
outing to date and already shows some of the characteristics that have been
the cornerstones of his style to the present. There are hints of the long,
graceful lines to come, and a clear demonstration of his uncanny ability to
conceive a solo as a whole.

        Carter's clarinet solo on "Miss Hannah" is his first on record. He
recalls taking up the clarinet when he joined Charlie Johnson's band at
Small's Paradise: "In fact, that may have been one of the conditions of the
job, because in those days everybody doubled."

There have been several attempts in recent years to re-create the unique feel of the McKinney's Cotton Pickers. Carter, himself, who was in charge of one such effort in 1975, comments on the difficulty of the task: "The entire rhythmic conception was different then; it's so hard to find players familiar with that approach to rhythm. It takes four people thinking alike."

[8]   October 3, 1930   New York
         FLETCHER HENDERSON AND HIS ORCHESTRA

Carter (cl, as, v, arr) Russell Smith, Bobby Stark, Rex Stewart (tp) Jimmy Harrison (tb, v) Claude Jones (tb) Harvey Boone (as) Coleman Hawkins (ts) Fletcher Henderson (p) Clarence Holiday (g) John Kirby (b) Walter Johnson (d) John Nesbitt (arr)

CHINATOWN, MY CHINATOWN   arr-JN (16cl)   150857-1
78: COLUMBIA 2329-D LP: COLUMBIA CL1684,
TIME-LIFE STL-J10

SOMEBODY LOVES ME   v-BC, JH, CJ (e) (v in   150858-3
      vocal trio) arr
78: COLUMBIA 2329-D LP: COLUMBIA CL1684,
SMITHSONIAN P2-13710

                          *   *   *

Carter's first recording session as a regular member of the Fletcher Henderson orchestra includes a high-speed clarinet ride through "Chinatown." The almost reckless abandon of this solo is not typical of his clarinet work, and when he heard it almost 50 years later his first response was, "Did I do that?" In later years he preferred to play clarinet on slower "mood" pieces to which he applied a rounded, full, lower register tone, once described by Whitney Balliett as "the ideal sound for the instrument."

(For a discussion of Carter's arrangement of "Somebody Loves Me," see chapter 3.)

[9]   November 3, 1930   New York
         McKINNEY'S COTTON PICKERS

Carter (as) Rex Stewart, Buddy Lee, Langston Curl (tp) Ed Cuffee (tb) Don Redman (cl, as, v) Prince Robinson (cl, ts) Todd Rhodes (p, celeste) Dave Wilborn (banjo, g) Ralph Escudero (tuba) Cuba Austin (d)

TALK TO ME   v-DR (8as)   64605-1
78: VICTOR 22640 LP: RCA LPV520, RCA (F)
FPM1-7007, RCA (F) PM43258

TALK TO ME   v-DR (8as)   64605-2
78: UNISSUED LP: PIRATE MPC518, RCA (F)
FPM1-7007, RCA (F) PM43258

ROCKY ROAD   v-DR (8as)   64606-1
78: VICTOR 22932 LP: RCA LPV520, RCA (E)
RD7561, RCA (F) FPM1-7007, RCA (F) PM43258

[10]   November 4, 1930 New York
          McKINNEY'S COTTON PICKERS

Carter (cl, as, arr) Rex Stewart, Buddy Lee, Langston Curl (tp) Ed Cuffee
(tb) Don Redman (cl, as) Prince Robinson (cl, ts) Todd Rhodes (p, celeste)
Dave Wilborn (banjo, g) Ralph Escudero (tuba) Cuba Austin (d) Bill Coty (v)

LAUGHING AT LIFE   v-Coty (e)   64607-1
78: UNISSUED LP: GAPS 080, RCA (F) FPM1-7007,
RCA (F) PM43258

LAUGHING AT LIFE   v-Coty (e)   64607-2
78: VICTOR 23020 LP: RCA (F) FPM1-7007, RCA
(F) PM43258

NEVER SWAT A FLY   v-Coty (8cl)+(16cl over ensemble)+   64608-1
      (8cl over ensemble) arr
78: VICTOR 23020 LP: RCA (E) RD7561, RCA (F)
FPM1-7007, RCA (F) PM43258

NEVER SWAT A FLY   v-Coty (8cl)+(16cl over ensemble)+   64608-2
      (8cl over ensemble) arr
78: UNISSUED LP: GAPS 080, RCA (F) FPM1-7007,
RCA (F) PM43258

[11]   November 5, 1930 New York
          McKINNEY'S COTTON PICKERS

Carter (as) Rex Stewart, Buddy Lee, Langston Curl (tp) Ed Cuffee (tb) Don
Redman (cl, as) Prince Robinson (cl, ts) Todd Rhodes (p) Dave Wilborn
(banjo, g, v) Ralph Escudero (tuba) Cuba Austin (d) George Bias (v)

I WANT YOUR LOVE   v-DW (4as)   63195-1
78: UNISSUED LP: RCA(F) FPM1-7007, RCA (F)
PM43258

I WANT YOUR LOVE   v-DW (4as)   63195-2
78: VICTOR 22683 LP: RCA (F) FPM1-7007, RCA
(F) PM43258

HELLO! v-DW (e)   63196-2
78: VICTOR 23031 LP: RCA (F) FXM1-7059, RCA
(F) PM43258

AFTER ALL, YOU'RE ALL I'M AFTER v-GB (8as)   64609-2
78: VICTOR 23024 LP: RCA (F) FXM1-7059, RCA
(F) PM43258

I MISS A LITTLE MISS v-GB (e)   64610-2
78: VICTOR 23024 LP: GAPS 080, RCA (F) FXM1-
7059, RCA (F) PM43258

                          *   *   *

Exactly one year after his first recordings with McKinney's Cotton Pickers,
Carter sat in with the band for three more sessions [9, 10, 11]. He replaced George Thomas who was injured in, and later died as a result of,
an auto accident.

The November 4 session includes one of only two McKinney recordings of Carter arrangements ("Never Swat A Fly"). The other took place almost a year later, after Carter had become musical director of the group.

---

[12]   December 2, 1930 New York
          FLETCHER HENDERSON AND HIS ORCHESTRA

Carter (cl, as, arr) Russell Smith, Bobby Stark, Rex Stewart (tp) Jimmy Harrison, Claude Jones (tb) Harvey Boone (as) Coleman Hawkins (ts) Fletcher Henderson (p) Clarence Holiday (g) John Kirby (tuba) Walter Johnson (d)

KEEP A SONG IN YOUR SOUL (16as) arr   150997-2
78: COLUMBIA 2352-D LP: COLUMBIA CL1684,
SMITHSONIAN P2-13710, TIME-LIFE STL-J10

WHAT GOOD AM I WITHOUT YOU (4cl)+(cl coda)   150998-2
78: COLUMBIA 2352-D LP: GAPS 090

                           *   *   *

(For a discussion of Carter's arranging masterpiece, "Keep A Song In Your Soul," see chapter 3.)

---

[13]   December 4, 1930 New York
          THE CHOCOLATE DANDIES

Carter (as, v, arr, comp) Rex Stewart (tp) Jimmy Harrison (tb) Coleman Hawkins (ts) Horace Henderson (p) Benny Jackson (g) John Kirby (b)

GOODBYE BLUES (16as)(v) arr, comp   404566-A
78: COLUMBIA 35679 45: ODEON SOF3553 LP:
PARLOPHONE PMC7038, SWAGGIE S1249, CBS (F)
68227, ODEON (J) EMI OR-8065, ELECTROLA 1C
054-06 312

          NOTE: Rust lists Bobby Stark (tp) for Stewart; Allen's Hendersonia
          suggests Stewart. Carter agrees that it is Stewart.

---

[14]   December 8, 1930 New York
          FLETCHER HENDERSON AND HIS ORCHESTRA

Carter (as, cl) probably regular Henderson personnel

WE'RE FRIENDS AGAIN   E 35668
78: BRUNSWICK, UNISSUED

WHAT GOOD AM I WITHOUT YOU   E 35669
78: BRUNSWICK, UNISSUED

---

[15]   December 31, 1930 New York
          THE CHOCOLATE DANDIES

Carter (cl, as, arr, comp) Bobby Stark (tp) Jimmy Harrison (tb, v) Coleman Hawkins (ts) Horace Henderson (p) Benny Jackson (g) John Kirby (tuba)

CLOUDY SKIES (8as)+(4as over ensemble)   404596-B
78: COLUMBIA 35679 45: ODEON SOF3553 LP:
PARLOPHONE (E) PMC7038, SWAGGIE S1249, CBS
(F) 68227, ODEON (J) EMI OR-8065, ELECTROLA 1C
054-06 316

GOT ANOTHER SWEETIE NOW v-JH (e) arr   404597-B
78: COLUMBIA 36009 LP: PARLOPHONE (E)
PMC7038, SWAGGIE S1249, CBS (F) 68227, ODEON
(J) EMI OR-8065, ELECTROLA 1C 054-06 313

BUGLE CALL RAG (12as) (16cl) arr   404598-B
78: COLUMBIA 2543-D 45: ODEON SOF3553 LP:
PARLOPHONE (E) PMC7038, FOLKWAYS FP75,
FOLKWAYS FJ2811, SWAGGIE S1249, CBS (F) 68227,
ODEON (J) EMI OR-8065, TIME-LIFE STL-J06,
ELECTROLA 1C 054-06 318

DEE BLUES (12cl)(12cl) comp   404599-B
78: COLUMBIA 2543-D 45: ODEON SOF3553 LP:
PARLOPHONE (E) PMC7038, SWAGGIE S1249, CBS
(F) 68227, ODEON (J) EMI OR-8065, COLUMBIA
CG33557, TIME-LIFE STL-J10, ELECTROLA 1C
054-06 316

                    *   *   *

Perhaps the most famous of the Chocolate Dandies dates, this session's
personnel is again drawn from the Henderson orchestra.   Carter's sketchy
arrangements were designed to provide a loose framework for the solos,
which are the main focus of the session.   One of the sides, "Dee Blues,"
was completely impromptu; musicians were told that another number was
needed and the blues was a natural choice.

     There are excellent contributions on all four titles by Jimmy Harri-
son including the vocal on his own tune "Got Another Sweetie Now."   The
great trombonist, a close friend of Carter, died seven months later of
stomach cancer.   Carter's clarinet work is superb on "Bugle Call Rag"
where he plays the "Ole Miss" strain, and on "Dee Blues" where he opens
and closes the record.   The former also contains the first of many examples of Carter's soloing on two instruments in the same piece.

---

[16]   February 5, 1931 New York
         FLETCHER HENDERSON AND HIS ORCHESTRA

Carter (cl, as, arr) Russell Smith, Rex Stewart, Bobby Stark (tp) Jimmy
Harrison (tb, v) Claude Jones (tb) Harvey Boone (as) Coleman Hawkins (ts)
Fletcher Henderson (p) Clarence Holiday (g) John Kirby (tuba, b) Walter
Johnson (d) Lois Deppe (v) Bill Challis (arr)

I'VE FOUND WHAT I WANTED IN YOU v-LD (e)   151274-2
78: COLUMBIA 2414-D LP: GAPS 090

MY GAL SAL arr-Challis (e)   151275-1
78: COLUMBIA 2586-D LP: COLUMBIA CL1684

MY PRETTY GIRL v-LD (32cl acc) arr   151276-2

78: COLUMBIA 2586-D LP: JAZZ PANORAMA
LP4, JOKER SM3077

SWEET AND HOT v-JH (e) arr   151277-2
78: COLUMBIA 2414-D LP: COLUMBIA CL1684

---

[17]   March 30, 1931 New York
         CHICK WEBB AND HIS ORCHESTRA

Carter (cl, as, arr, comp) Shelton Hemphill, Louis Hunt (tp) Louis Bacon (tp,
v) Jimmy Harrison (tb) Hilton Jefferson (cl, as) Elmer Williams (cl, ts) Don
Kirkpatrick (p) John Trueheart (banjo, g) Elmer James (b) Chick Webb (d)

HEEBIE JEEBIES (e) arr   F-36432-
78: VOCALION 1607, BRUNSWICK 6898 LP: DECCA
DL79222, MCA (F) 510. 014, MCA 1303

BLUES IN MY HEART v-LB (e) arr, comp   F-36433-A
78: BRUNSWICK 6156, BRUNSWICK 6898 LP:
JAZUM 46

SOFT AND SWEET (e) arr   F-36434-
78: VOCALION 1607 LP: DECCA DL79222, MCA
(F) 510. 014, MCA 1303

        NOTE: Title appears on Brunswick 6156 as "I'm Left With The
        Blues In My Heart. "

                         *   *   *

This session took place during Carter's brief tenure with Webb. Although
he does not solo, Carter makes his presence felt through his arrangements.
This recording of "Blues In My Heart" is one of the first of what is Carter's most widely recorded composition (over 50 versions to date). It
was ante-dated only by the "King Carter And His Royal Orchestra" version,
recorded a week earlier. Although his name appears as leader, Carter did
not participate in the King Carter date.

---

[18]   September 8, 1931 Camden, N. J.
         McKINNEY'S COTTON PICKERS

Carter (cl, as, arr) Rex Stewart, Joe Smith, Doc Cheatham (tp) Ed Cuffee
(tb) Quentin Jackson (tb, v) Hilton Jefferson (cl, alt) Prince Robinson (ts) Todd
Rhodes (p) Dave Wilborn (g) Billy Taylor (b) Cuba Austin (d)

DO YOU BELIEVE IN LOVE AT SIGHT v-QJ (e) arr   68300-1
78: UNISSUED LP: RCA 430272, RCA (E) RD7561,
RCA (F) FXM1-7059

DO YOU BELIEVE IN LOVE AT SIGHT v-QJ (e) arr   68300-2
78: VICTOR 22811 LP: RCA (F) FXM1-7059

WRAP YOUR TROUBLES IN DREAMS v-QJ (32cl acc)   70495-1
78: VICTOR 22811 LP: GAPS 080, RCA (F)
FXM1-7059

WRAP YOUR TROUBLES IN DREAMS   v-QJ (32cl acc)   70495-2
78:   UNISSUED   LP: RCA (F) FXM1-7059

* * *

Carter's first and only recording session as musical director of McKinney's
Cotton Pickers features the second of the two Carter arrangements recorded
by that group.   The bridge of the first chorus is a characteristic Carter
reed passage.   Carter's own solo work is restricted to some lovely clarinet
behind the vocal chorus.   Chilton, Davies and Wright question the identity of
the vocalist; when the recordings were played for Doc Cheatham, however,
he confirmed that the vocals are, indeed, by Jackson.

---

[19]   ca. June 23, 1932   New York
           BENNY CARTER AND HIS ORCHESTRA

Carter (as) Louis Bacon, Frankie Newton, Unknown (tp) Dicky Wells (tb)
Wayman Carver (as, flute) Chu Berry (ts) Unknown (p) Unknown (g) Richard
Fullbright (b) Sid Catlett (d) Unknown Female (v)

TELL ALL YOUR DAY DREAMS TO ME   v-unknown (32as)   1765-1
78:   CROWN 3321, VARSITY 6004

* * *

The first record made by a regular Carter orchestra is a highly sought-
after collector's item, but certainly not on musical grounds.   Carter cannot
remember making this record and the identity of the vocalist is a mystery
to him.   It is quite obviously not a Carter arrangement, and although the
alto solo chorus is unmistakably his, the style sounds like the Carter of a
few years before.   This could almost have been a deliberate attempt to fit
in with an arrangement and vocal which must have sounded nostalgic even
then, and in no way foreshadowed the innovative and influential Carter orchestra recordings of the next year.

        Rust lists Teddy Wilson as pianist, but this does not seem possible,
given Wilson's activities at the time.   He did not join Carter until October
1933.   The other personnel are highly speculative.

---

[20]   October 5, 1932   New York
           KING CARTER AND HIS ORCHESTRA

Carter (as, arr, comp) Louis Bacon, Frankie Newton, Unknown (tp) Dicky
Wells, Unknown (tb) Wayman Carver (as, flute) Chu Berry, Unknown (ts)
Unknown (p) Unknown (g) Richard Fullbright (b) Sid Catlett (d)

HOT TODDY   arr, comp   73772-
78:   VICTOR-UNISSUED

JAZZ COCKTAIL   arr, comp   73773-
78:   VICTOR-UNISSUED

BLACK JAZZ   73774-
78:   VICTOR-UNISSUED

        NOTE: A test pressing of one of these titles is rumored to exist.

[21]	March 14, 1933 New York

BENNY CARTER AND HIS ORCHESTRA

Carter (cl, as, tp, v, arr, comp) Shad Collins, Leonard Davis, Bill Dillard (tp)
George Washington, Wilbur de Paris (tb) Howard Johnson (as) Chu Berry
(ts) Nicholas Rodriguez (p) Lawrence Lucie (g) Ernest Hill (b) Sid Catlett
(d) Spike Hughes (arr)

SWING IT   (v)(32as) arr   265090-2
78:   COLUMBIA CB-628   LP: FAMILY (I) SFR736,
PRESTIGE 7643, REGAL (E) 1108, WORLD RECORDS
(E) SHB42

SYNTHETIC LOVE   (16+8tp)(v)(16cl) arr, comp   265091-3
78:   COLUMBIA CB-636   LP: FAMILY (I) SFR736,
PRESTIGE 7643, REGAL (E) 1108, WORLD RECORDS
(E) SHB42

SIX BELLS STAMPEDE   arr-SH (e)   265092-2
78:   COLUMBIA CB-628   LP: MUSIC FOR PLEASURE
(E) MFP1085, FAMILY (I) SFR736, PRESTIGE 7643,
REGAL (E) 1038, WORLD RECORDS (E) SHB42

LOVE, YOU'RE NOT THE ONE FOR ME   (v)(4+4+8as)   265093-2
       arr, comp
78:   COLUMBIA CB-636   LP: FAMILY (I) SFR736,
PRESTIGE 7643, REGAL (E) 1108, WORLD RECORDS (E)
SHB42

*   *   *

The first real recording dates for the Carter band were set up for British
Columbia by John Hammond, with the purpose of releasing the sides in England.   Hammond describes contracting for the Carter sessions (as well as
those by Fletcher Henderson, Benny Goodman, and others) during a trip to
England "in the spring of 1933" (Hammond, p. 105).   This first Carter orchestra session, however, seems to have antedated that trip which, according to Hammond, took place after the Spike Hughes dates (April/May 1933)
(Hammond, p. 108).   It is possible that these recordings were already "in
the can" and released after the Hammond agreement with British Columbia.

       Three of the four pieces contain Carter vocals; he sounds most na-
tural and convincing on "Swing It."

       "Synthetic Love" opens with Carter's first recorded trumpet solo.
He stays close to the melody, which he delivers in a bright, full tone--even
at low volume--reminiscent of Doc Cheatham.   Cheatham had given Carter
encouragement and technical advice in his return to the instrument, which
was his first love and remains his favorite.   "Six Bells," composed and
arranged by Spike Hughes, is a preview of the sessions with the Carter band
led by Hughes a month later.

[22]	April 18, 1933 New York

SPIKE HUGHES AND HIS NEGRO ORCHESTRA

Carter (cl, as, v) Shad Collins, Leonard Davis, Bill Dillard (tp) Dicky Wells,
Wilbur de Paris, George Washington (tb) Wayman Carver, Howard Johnson

(cl, as) Coleman Hawkins (ts) Nicholas Rodriguez (p) Lawrence Lucie (g)
Ernest Hill (b) Kaiser Marshall, Sid Catlett (d) Spike Hughes (arr, comp)

NOCTURNE (8cl)   13257-A
78: DECCA F-3563 LP: DECCA (E) ACE OF CLUBS
ACL1153, LONDON LL1387, DECCA (SW) LK4173

SOMEONE STOLE GABRIEL'S HORN (v)(8as)   13258-A
78: DECCA F-3563 LP: DECCA (E) ACE OF CLUBS
ACL1153

PASTORALE (16as)   13259-A
78: DECCA F-3606 LP: DECCA (E) ACE OF CLUBS
ACL1153, LONDON LL1387, DECCA (SW) LK4173

BUGLE CALL RAG (16as)   13260-A
78: DECCA F-3606 LP: DECCA (E) ACE OF CLUBS
ACL1153, LONDON LL1387, DECCA (SW) LK4173

        NOTE: Catlett (d) on last two titles.

[23]	May 18, 1933 New York
	SPIKE HUGHES AND HIS NEGRO ORCHESTRA

Carter (cl, as) Henry Allen, Leonard Davis, Bill Dillard (tp) Dicky Wells,
Wilbur de Paris, George Washington (tb) Wayman Carver (cl, as, flute)
Howard Johnson (cl, as) Coleman Hawkins, Chu Berry (ts) Luis Russell (p)
Lawrence Lucie (g) Ernest Hill (b) Sid Catlett (d) Spike Hughes (arr, comp)

ARABESQUE (e)   13352-A
78: DECCA F-3639 LP: DECCA (E) ACE OF CLUBS
ACL1153, LONDON LL1387, DECCA (SW) LK4173

FANFARE (24cl)   13353-A
78: DECCA F-3639 LP: DECCA (E) ACE OF CLUBS
ACL1153, LONDON LL1387, DECCA (SW) LK4173

SWEET SORROW BLUES (e)   13354-A
78: DECCA F-5101 LP: DECCA (E) ACE OF CLUBS
ACL1153, LONDON LL1387, DECCA (SW) LK4173

MUSIC AT MIDNIGHT (12as)(8cl)   13355-A
78: DECCA F-3836 LP: DECCA (E) ACE OF CLUBS
ACL1153, LONDON LL1387, DECCA (SW) LK4173

SWEET SUE, JUST YOU (32as)   13356-A
78: DECCA F-3972 LP: DECCA (E) ACE OF CLUBS
ACL1153, LONDON LL1387, DECCA (SW) LK4173,
TIME-LIFE STL-J06, SMITHSONIAN P15470

        NOTE: Personnel for last title: Carter, Allen, Wells, Carver,
        Hawkins, Berry, Lucie, Rodriguez, Hughes (b), Catlett.

[24]	May 19, 1933 New York
	SPIKE HUGHES AND HIS NEGRO ORCHESTRA

Carter (cl, as, ss) Henry Allen, Howard Scott, Leonard Davis or Bill Dillard (tp) Dicky Wells, Wilbur de Paris, George Washington (tb) Wayman Carver (as, flute) Howard Johnson (cl, as) Coleman Hawkins, Chu Berry (ts) Nicholas Rodriguez (p) Lawrence Lucie (g) Ernest Hill (b) Sid Catlett (d) Spike Hughes (arr, comp)

AIR IN D FLAT   (e)   13359-A
78: DECCA F-5101 LP: DECCA (E) ACE OF CLUBS
ACL1153, LONDON LL1387, DECCA (SW) LK4173

DONEGAL CRADLE SONG   (e)   13360-A
78: DECCA F-3717 LP: DECCA (E) ACE OF CLUBS
ACL1153, LONDON LL1387, DECCA (SW) LK4173,
TIME-LIFE STL-J06

FIREBIRD   (e) [on soprano]   13361-A
78: DECCA F-3717 LP: DECCA (E) ACE OF CLUBS
ACL1153, LONDON LL1387, DECCA (SW) LK4173

MUSIC AT SUNRISE   (e)   13362-A
78: DECCA F-3836 LP: DECCA (E) ACE OF CLUBS
ACL1153

HOW COME YOU DO ME LIKE YOU DO v-HA (e)   13363-A
78: DECCA F-3972 LP: DECCA (E) ACE OF CLUBS
ACL1153, LONDON LL1387, DECCA (SW) LK4173,
SMITHSONIAN P15470

> NOTE: Personnel on last title: Allen (also v), Wells, Carver, Hawkins, Berry, Rodriguez, Lucie, Hughes (b), Catlett.

*   *   *

Spike Hughes had been impressed by the musicianship of the Carter orchestra at a rehearsal and the band became the nucleus for these three sessions [22, 23, 24] of his music. Soloists like Henry Allen and Coleman Hawkins were added. Carter is not heavily featured as a soloist but as Raymond Horricks observes, "No one else but Carter ... would have been capable of leading a saxophone section on to produce such a unique variety of tonal blends. Throughout all these sessions, the composer and rehearsal leader complemented each other perfectly, so that their names became inseparable" (Liner notes to London LL1387).

The label of the original issue of "Someone Stole Gabriel's Horn" lists Monette Moore as vocalist; Carter filled in when she failed to appear.

[25]   October 10, 1933   New York
         THE CHOCOLATE DANDIES

Carter (as, tp, arr, comp) Max Kaminsky (tp) Floyd O'Brien (tb) Chu Berry (ts) Teddy Wilson (p) Lawrence Lucie (g) Sid Catlett, Mezz Mezzrow (d) Ernest Hill (b)

BLUE INTERLUDE   (32as) arr, comp   265156-2
78: DECCA 18255 45: IL JAZZ (I) LP: PRESTIGE
7643, PARLOPHONE (E) PMC7038, SWAGGIE S1249

I NEVER KNEW   (8as)(8as)(8tp[2nd 8-bar solo]) arr   265157-1
78: COLUMBIA   2875-D LP: PRESTIGE 7643,
PARLOPHONE (E) PMC7038, SWAGGIE S1249, TIME-
LIFE STL-J10

ONCE UPON A TIME   (32tp)(10tp) arr, comp   265158-1
78: OKEH 41568, DECCA 18255 LP: PRESTIGE
7643, PARLOPHONE (E) PMC7038, SWAGGIE S1249,
FOLKWAYS FP71, FOLKWAYS FJ2809, TIME-LIFE
STL-J10

KRAZY KAPERS   (8as)(32as) arr, comp   265159-2
78: OKEH 41568 LP: PRESTIGE 7643, PARLO-
PHONE (E) PMC7038, SWAGGIE S1249, TIME-LIFE
STL-J10

> NOTES: Il Jazz 45rpm disc has no issue number. Carter's solo
> on "I Never Knew" is reproduced vocally by The Cats And The Fid-
> dle on their June 27, 1939 recording "Gangbusters" (reissued on
> Bluebird AXM2-5531). An alternate take of "Once Upon A Time" is
> known to exist.

                         *   *   *

This reincarnation of the Chocolate Dandies bore a clearer Carter stamp
than the other recordings made under that name. With the exception of Max
Kaminsky and Floyd O'Brien, all of the personnel were regular members of
Carter's orchestra. Furthermore, three of the four tunes recorded on the
date were Carter's own compositions, and his arrangements were far more
structured than the loose framework he provided for the 1930 Chocolate
Dandies. The producer, John Hammond, was a great admirer of those 1930
recordings and hoped to recapture their spirit.

Perhaps most significant about the session is the presence of Teddy
Wilson, who had arrived the day before from Chicago to join the Carter orchestra. His playing here shows why Carter was so eager to have him.
He already displays--fully formed--many of the components of his style:
the dancing right-hand lines, with bouncing tremolos and sparkling runs,
complemented by a lightly striding left. More importantly, he shares with
Carter the rare ability to create an improvised solo with a logical sense of
direction, without losing the spark of spontaneity.

In spite of the obvious maturity of his playing, Wilson cites the two
major influences in the further development of his style after his arrival in
New York as his study of classical music, and "...being around Benny
Carter. He played that flowing saxophone every night and that came out in
my playing." (Interview with Phil Schaap, March 5, 1980.) Keg Johnson,
whom Carter had recruited along with Wilson in Chicago, joined the trombone section.

Carter, who had given listeners a taste of his trumpet with a cautious
solo on his March 14 date, now felt confident enough to feature himself extensively on the instrument. The result, "Once Upon A Time," is one of
the great Carter trumpet solos; indeed it is one of the greatest trumpet
solos in jazz history. The ending shows an Armstrong influence, with soar-
ing half-valve effects and a pronounced vibrato. The tune, written for this
session, is a typical Carter composition: an attractive and deceptively
simple melody with interesting chord changes. It is also typical of Carter

in another sense: he never recorded or played it again. It thus joins a
long line of Carter melodies which, because they were never plugged, did
not attain the popularity they deserved.

On "Krazy Kapers," the supposed replacement of Sid Catlett, who
probably had another engagement, by the ubiquitous Mezz Mezzrow is dis-
puted by John Hammond who states, "Mezzrow tried to play drums, but I
asked him to leave the studio." (The Giants of Jazz: Benny Carter, p.
36.)

---

[26]   October 16, 1933   New York
         BENNY CARTER AND HIS ORCHESTRA

Carter (cl, as, arr, comp) Eddie Mallory, Bill Dillard, Dick Clark (tp) J. C.
Higginbotham, Fred Robinson, Keg Johnson (tb) Wayman Carver (as, flute)
Glyn Paque (as) Johnny Russell (ts) Teddy Wilson (p) Lawrence Lucie (g)
Ernest Hill (b) Sid Catlett (d)

DEVIL'S HOLIDAY (8as) arr, comp   265160-1
78: COLUMBIA 2898-D LP: MUSIC FOR PLEASURE
(E) MFP1085, PRESTIGE 7643, FAMILY (I) SFR736,
REGAL (E) 1038, WORLD RECORDS (E) SHB42

LONESOME NIGHTS (e) arr, comp   265161-1
78: OKEH 41567 LP: MUSIC FOR PLEASURE
(E) MFP1085, PRESTIGE 7643, FAMILY (I) SFR736,
REGAL (E) 1038, WORLD RECORDS (E) SHB42

SYMPHONY IN RIFFS (e) arr, comp   265162-2
78: COLUMBIA 2898-D LP: PARLOPHONE (E)
PMC1222, PRESTIGE 7643, FAMILY (I) SFR736,
REGAL (E) 1108, WORLD RECORDS (E) SHB42

BLUE LOU (4+4as) arr   265163-2
78: OKEH 41567 LP: MUSIC FOR PLEASURE
(E) MFP1085, PRESTIGE 7643, FAMILY (I) SFR736,
REGAL (E) 1038, WORLD RECORDS (E) SHB42,
TIME-LIFE STL-J20

*   *   *

These are the only recordings of the 1932-33 Carter band at its peak. Unlike the March 14 session, there are no distracting vocals and, of course,
the band personnel includes the great Teddy Wilson. Also, the saxophone
section has been expanded from three to four. Carter takes full advantage
of the addition by providing several innovative four-part saxophone choruses.
Carter's solo contributions on the four pieces total only 16 measures, yet
because of his writing, this session must be counted among his most significant.

The impact of these influential arrangements, "Symphony In Riffs"
and "Lonesome Nights," can be gauged by the large number and variety of
bands which recorded them precisely as Carter wrote them. Over a 25-
year period "Symphony In Riffs" was recorded by Tommy Dorsey, Gene
Krupa, Glenn Miller, Artie Shaw and Glen Gray (by some of these more
than once). "Lonesome Nights" (later called "Take My Word") was made by
Benny Goodman, Charlie Barnet, Bunny Berigan, Artie Shaw and Cab Callo-

way. "Lonesome Nights" also inspired two similar pieces, "Puddin' Head Serenade," recorded by Andy Kirk (March 31, 1936 and April 10, 1936) and "I'm Alone With You," recorded by Jimmie Lunceford (December 14, 1939). No doubt other bands had these Carter compositions in their books, but never recorded them. Even the lesser known title "Devil's Holiday" was recorded in its original arrangement by the bands of Charlie Barnet, Bunny Berigan and Charlie Spivak.

The session also affords a good opportunity to assess the importance of Carter as lead alto player. A comparison of the intricate saxophone choruses in "Lonesome Nights" as played by the bands named above with the original version demonstrates the difference Carter's presence in the section makes in the tonal blending and precision of execution.

The final number of the session "Blue Lou" is the first recording of the Edgar Sampson classic.

The musicians who played in this band all recall it with reverence. Trumpeter Bill Coleman, who was asked to join soon after his return from Europe with Lucky Millinder, missed playing on these recordings because he was spending a few days in New Jersey and could not be reached. He joined soon afterward and remarks, "The salary was not great, but the other musicians, like myself, admired and loved Benny to the point where they would have worked with him for the pleasure of playing his arrangements, if a job actually could not pay. We all hated to see this band of Benny's break up and I considered and still do consider it the best band I ever played with." (Coleman, interview, Jazz Oral History Project, 1978.) Ernest Hill, the bass player for these recordings, told Johnny Simmen, "It was a new pleasure every night to go on that bandstand and play Benny's music." (Liner notes to Prestige 7643.)

(For an analysis of "Lonesome Nights," see chapter 3.)

---

[27]   November 6, 1933   New York
          MEZZ MEZZROW AND HIS ORCHESTRA

Carter (as, tp, v, arr, comp) Max Kaminsky, Freddy Goodman, Ben Gusick (tp) Floyd O'Brien (tb, arr) Mezz Mezzrow (cl, as, arr) Johnny Russell (ts) Teddy Wilson (p) Clayton Duerr (g) Pops Foster (b) Jack Maisel (d)

FREE LOVE (e) arr, comp   14272-A
78: BRUNSWICK 7551 LP: FAMILY (I) SFR736

DISSONANCE arr-MM (e)   14273-A
78: BRUNSWICK 7551 LP: FAMILY (I) SFR736,
COLUMBIA KG31564, TAX (SW) M-8031

SWINGIN' WITH MEZZ   arr-MM, FO (18tp)(4tp)   14274-A
78: BRUNSWICK 6778 LP: FAMILY (I) SFR736,
TAX (SW) M-8031   /

LOVE, YOU'RE NOT THE ONE FOR ME   (v) arr, comp   14275-A
78: BRUNSWICK 6778 LP: FAMILY (I) SFR736,
TAX (SW) M-8031

* . *   *

In 1933 Mezz Mezzrow tried to form an interracial band, not just for recording (which was already fairly common), but for public performance.
Although this project failed, Mezzrow did succeed in leading two mixed recording sessions--this one and one on May 7, 1934.

Although Carter acknowledges that the fact that Mezz always "took
care of all the boys' needs" may have taken him further in musical circles
than his talent warranted, he respected Mezzrow as a musician with a sin-
cere and spirited, if not highly polished, style.

Carter's solo work is limited to the trumpet on "Swingin' With Mezz,"
a solo which drew praise from Louis Armstrong, himself.   In Really the
Blues (p. 269), Mezzrow quotes a letter he received from Louis Armstrong
in which Armstrong writes about the recordings made on this date:

> Say Gate ... how wonderful your records are.   Everybody en-
> joys them very much.   All of them are perfect.   My favorite one
> is Love your not the one for me and the one where your trumpet
> player hits that F right square in the face Yea man.   By the way
> who is that fellow?   Who ever he is hes mess (Mezz) I aint no
> playin Hes perfect....

Mezzrow claims these remarks were made about "Dissonance"; however, it is undoubtedly Carter's solo on "Swingin' With Mezz" to which
Armstrong was referring.

---

[28]   March 23, 1934   New York
         CHARLIE BARNET AND HIS ORCHESTRA

Carter (tp, as) includes Charlie Barnet (ts, v) Helen Heath, Jackie Martin (v)
Toots Camarata (tp) Red Norvo (vib)

BUTTERFINGERS   v-HH   14985-
78:   UNISSUED

INFATUATION   v-HH (e)   14986-
78:   BANNER 33015   LP: AJAX LP104

I LOST ANOTHER SWEETHEART   v-JM (e)   14987-1
78:   BANNER 33033   LP: AJAX LP104

EMALINE   v-CB (e)   14888-1
78:   BANNER 33033   LP: AJAX LP104

         NOTE: Personnel is uncertain.

---

[29]   March 29, 1934   New York
         CHARLIE BARNET AND HIS ORCHESTRA

Carter (tp, as) includes Charlie Barnet (ts, v) Helen Heath, Jackie Martin
(v) Toots Camarata (tp) Red Norvo (vib)

BUTTERFINGERS   v-HH (e)   14985-
78:   BANNER 33015   LP: AJAX LP104

BABY, TAKE A BOW   v-JM (e)   15020-
78:   BANNER 33029   LP: AJAX LP104

THIS IS OUR LAST NIGHT TOGETHER   v-JM (e)   15021-
78: BANNER 33029 LP: AJAX LP104

---

[30]   May 7, 1934 New York
        MEZZ MEZZROW AND HIS ORCHESTRA

Carter (as) Max Kaminsky, Reunald Jones, Chelsea Quealey (tp) Floyd
O'Brien (tb, arr) Mezz Mezzrow (cl, as, arr) Bud Freeman (ts) Willie 'The
Lion' Smith (p) John Kirby (b) Chick Webb (d) Alex Hill (arr)

OLD FASHIONED LOVE   arr-AH (e)   82392-1
78: VICTOR 25202 LP: VICTOR (F) 130. 219, RCA
(F) 741. 046, RCA (F) PM42406

APOLOGIES   arr-MM (24as)   82393-1
78: VICTOR 25019 LP: RCA (F) 130. 219, RCA
(F) 741. 046, TIME-LIFE STL-J10, RCA (F) PM42406

SENDIN' THE VIPERS   arr-MM (16as)   82394-1
78: VICTOR 25019 LP: RCA (F) 130. 219, RCA
(F) 741. 046, RCA (F) PM42406

35TH AND CALUMET   arr-FO (24as)   82395-1
78: VICTOR 25202 LP: RCA (F) 130. 219, RCA
(F) 741. 046, RCA (F) PM42406

                        *   *   *

The second of the two Mezzrow sessions is the only known collaboration on
record between Carter and Willie "The Lion" Smith and Carter and Bud
Freeman.   "The Lion" had helped Carter many years earlier to adjust from
the C-melody to the alto saxophone.

        The personnel was noteworthy as Mezzrow points out (p. 269) with a
number of leaders and future leaders present: Smith, Carter, Freeman,
Kirby and Webb.

        Carter's growling entrance on "Apologies" is unlike anything he had
played before on record.   Perhaps it was an early subconscious attempt to
shed the "urbane" label that was already becoming a cliché in describing his
playing.   His reaction 45 years later was, "Is that me?"   The piece, which
is derived from "Dippermouth Blues," ends abruptly with Webb's drum solo
chorus ending four bars short of the expected twelve.   The record had already well exceeded the normal three-minute average for 78's.

---

[31]   September 25, 1934 New York
        FLETCHER HENDERSON AND HIS ORCHESTRA

Carter (as) Russell Smith, Irving Randolph, Henry Allen (tp) Keg Johnson,
Claude Jones (tb) Buster Bailey (cl) Hilton Jefferson, Russell Procope (as)
Ben Webster (ts) Fletcher Henderson, Horace Henderson (p, arr) Lawrence
Lucie (g) Elmer James (b) Walter Johnson (d) Russ Morgan (arr)

WILD PARTY   arr-RM, p-HH (e)   38723-A
78: DECCA 342 LP: DECCA DL9228, DECCA (E)
ACE OF HEARTS AH61, WORLD RECORDS SHB42,
MCA (F) 510. 060, MCA 1318

RUG CUTTER'S SWING   arr-HH, p-FH (e)   38724-A
78: DECCA 342, LP: DECCA DL9228, DECCA (E)
ACE OF HEARTS AH61, WORLD RECORDS SHB42,
MCA (F) 510. 060, MCA 1318

HOTTER THAN 'ELL   arr-HH, p-FH (e)   38725-A
78: DECCA 555 LP: DECCA DL9228, DECCA
(E) ACE OF HEARTS AH61, WORLD RECORDS
SHB42, MCA (F) 510. 060, MCA 1318

LIZA   p-FH and HH (32as[1st solo; 2nd alto solo--8 bars--   38728-A
        is Procope])
78: DECCA 555 LP: DECCA DL9228, DECCA (E)
ACE OF HEARTS AH61, WORLD RECORDS SHB42,
MCA (F) 510. 060, MCA 1318

                        *   *   *

Carter was reunited with his old employer, Fletcher Henderson, for this
date.   It also brought him together with two alto players, Hilton Jefferson
and Russell Procope, whose styles in some ways closely resembled his own.
This similarity is particularly striking in Jefferson's solo on "Wild Party."

[32]   October 19, 1934 New York
          ALEX HILL AND HIS HOLLYWOOD SEPIANS

Carter (tp, arr) Joe Thomas (tp) Claude Jones (tb) Albert Nicholas (cl)
George James (as) Gene Sedric (ts) Garnet Clark (p) Eddie Gibbs (g) Billy
Taylor (b) Harry Dial (d) Alex Hill (v, arr)

SONG OF THE PLOW   v-AH, arr-AH (e)   16141-1
78: VOCALION 2848, BRUNSWICK 02078   LP:
JAZZ DOCUMENT 7999

LET'S HAVE A JUBILEE   v-AH (16tp) arr   16142-1
78: VOCALION 2848, VOCALION S-70   LP:
JAZZ DOCUMENT 7999

                        *   *   *

For many years, discographers disagreed about Carter's presence on this
and an earlier (September 10) Alex Hill session.   Carter seems to have
played only on the later date.   He confirmed the muted trumpet which opens
"Let's Have A Jubilee" as his.   He also identified the arrangement of this
Alex Hill composition as his.   Irving Mills commissioned him to make this
arrangement, which was first recorded on October 4, 1934 by the Mills
Blue Rhythm Band.

[33]   December 13, 1934 New York
          BENNY CARTER AND HIS ORCHESTRA

Carter (cl, as, arr, comp) Russell Smith, Otis Johnson, Irving Randolph (tp)
Benny Morton, Keg Johnson (tb) Ben Smith, Russell Procope (as) Ben Web-
ster (ts) Teddy Wilson (p) Clarence Holiday (g) Elmer James (b) Walter
Johnson (d) Charles Holland (v)

SHOOT THE WORKS   (e) arr, comp   16412-1
78: VOCALION 2898   LP: TAX (SW) M-8031

DREAM LULLABY   (16cl with ensemble) (8cl with   16413-1
      ensemble) arr, comp
78: VOCALION 2898   LP: TAX (SW) M-8031,
TIME-LIFE STL-J21

EVERYBODY SHUFFLE   (4+4as)(16as) arr, comp   16414-1
78: VOCALION 2870   LP: TAX (SW) M-8031

SYNTHETIC LOVE   v-CH (e) arr, comp   16415-1
78: VOCALION 2870

                          *   *   *

These are the last recordings of the band Carter had formed in 1932.   With
engagements slacking off and no prospects for steady work for his men,
within a few weeks of this session Carter reluctantly disbanded.   The legend
of this band has grown steadily; many of its illustrious alumni have called
it the finest unit in which they ever played.   By this session, Carter was
already putting together personnels on a job-to-job basis, drawing from the
Fletcher Henderson band to fill some slots.

      For this occasion, Carter supplied three new originals; the final
number was his "Synthetic Love," previously recorded at the March 14,
1933, date.   This time, Carter modestly relegated the vocal to Charles
Holland.

      The most important solo voices are those of Ben Webster on tenor,
Benny Morton on trombone and Irving Randolph on trumpet.   The two uptempo arrangements, "Shoot The Works" and "Everybody Shuffle," were obviously not attempts at the type of innovative ensemble writing of a "Lonesome Nights."   Rather they feature brief sax-section passages and well-
balanced brass and reed riffs, which serve to complement the excellent
solos.

      "Dream Lullaby" is the first of several similar wistful, melancholy
compositions by Carter, who seemed attracted to dreams and lullabies--
e. g., "Melancholy Lullaby," "Lullaby To A Dream," "Lullaby In Blue."   It
particularly foreshadowed "Just A Mood," one recording of which also featured Carter's clarinet (late April 1936).

[34]   December 28, 1934 New York
          BUSTER BAILEY & HIS SEVEN CHOCOLATE DANDIES

Carter (as) Henry Allen (tp) J. C. Higginbotham (tb) Buster Bailey (cl)
Charlie Beal (p) Danny Barker (g) Elmer James (b) Walter Johnson (d)
Fletcher Henderson (arr)

CALL OF THE DELTA (8as)   16445-1
78: VOCALION 2887   LP: RARITIES 17

CALL OF THE DELTA (8as)   16445-2
78: COLUMBIA 35677   LP: MERITT 13/14

SHANGHAI SHUFFLE   (8as)(16as)   16446-1
78: VOCALION 2887   LP: RARITIES 17

[35]   January 2, 1935 New York
    BOB HOWARD AND HIS ORCHESTRA

Carter (tp, as) Buster Bailey (cl) Teddy Wilson (p) Clarence Holiday (g)
Elmer James (b) Cozy Cole (d) Bob Howard (v)

IT'S UNBELIEVABLE   v-BH (16+8tp)   39217-A
78: BRUNSWICK 02097 LP: RARITIES 48

IT'S UNBELIEVABLE   v-BH (16+8tp)   39217-B
78: DECCA 347 LP: RARITIES 48

WHISPER SWEET   v-BH (4tp)(16tp)   39218-A
78: BRUNSWICK RL-221 LP: RARITIES 48

WHISPER SWEET   v-BH (4tp)(16tp)   39218-B
78: DECCA 347 LP: RARITIES 48

THROWIN' STONES AT THE SUN v-BH (e)   39219-A
78: DECCA 343, BRUNSWICK RL-221 LP:
RARITIES 48

YOU FIT INTO THE PICTURE   v-BH (16+8as)(16tp)   39220-A
78: DECCA 343, BRUNSWICK 02111 LP:
RARITIES 48

[36]   February 25, 1935 New York
    BOB HOWARD AND HIS ORCHESTRA

Carter (tp) Ben Webster (ts) Teddy Wilson (p) Clarence Holiday (g) Elmer
James (b) Cozy Cole (d) Bob Howard (v)

THE GHOST OF DINAH   v-BH (e)   39387-A
78: DECCA 400 LP: RARITIES 48

PARDON MY LOVE   v-BH (2tp)(16tp)   39388-A
78: DECCA 400 LP: RARITIES 48

PARDON MY LOVE   v-BH (2tp)(16tp)   39388-B
78: UNISSUED LP: RARITIES 61

[37]   March 4, 1935 New York
    BOB HOWARD AND HIS ORCHESTRA

Carter (tp, as) Rex Stewart (cornet) Barney Bigard (cl) Teddy Wilson (p)
Clarence Holiday (g) Elmer James (b) Cozy Cole (d) Bob Howard (v)

STAY OUT OF LOVE   v-BH (e)   39390-A
78: DECCA 439 LP: RARITIES 48

I'LL NEVER CHANGE   v-BH (8tp)   39391-A
78: DECCA 439 LP: RARITIES 48

WHERE WERE YOU ON THE NIGHT OF JUNE   39392-A
      THE THIRD v-BH (e)
78: DECCA 407 LP: CORAL CJE100, RARITIES 48

(LOOK'S LIKE I'M) BREAKIN' THE ICE   v-BH (16+8as)   39393-A
78: DECCA 407 LP: RARITIES 48

> NOTE: Coral CJE100 contains only excerpt (Wilson's solo) of
> "Where were you..."

[38]   May 7, 1935 New York
          BOB HOWARD AND HIS ORCHESTRA

Carter (tp) Russell Procope (cl, as) Teddy Wilson (p) Clarence Holiday (g)
Billy Taylor (b) Cozy Cole (d) Bob Howard (v)

CORINNE CORINNA   v-BH and impromptu v by   39518-A
     musicians (24tp)
78: DECCA 484 LP: RARITIES 48

EV'RY DAY   v-BH (4tp)(16+8tp)   39519-A
78: DECCA 460 LP: RARITIES 48

A PORTER'S LOVE SONG TO A CHAMBERMAID   39520-A
     v-BH (32tp with ensemble)
78: DECCA 460 LP: RARITIES 48

I CAN'T DANCE (I GOT ANTS IN MY PANTS)   39521-A
     v-BH (8tp)(16+8tp)
78: DECCA 484 LP: RARITIES 48

[39]   May 8, 1935 New York
          WILLIE BRYANT AND HIS ORCHESTRA

Carter (tp) Robert Cheek, Richard Clark (tp) Edgar Battle (tp, valve tb, arr)
John "Shorty" Haughton, Robert Horton, Eddie Durham (tb) Glyn Paque (cl,
as) Stanley Payne (as) Ben Webster, Johnny Russell (ts) Teddy Wilson (p)
Arnold Adams (g) Louis Thompson (b) Cozy Cole (d) Willie Bryant (v) Alex
Hill (arr)

RIGAMAROLE (e)   89817-1
78: VICTOR 25038 LP: RCA (F) FXM1-7084,
BLUEBIRD AXM2-5502, RCA (J) RA-56

LONG ABOUT MIDNIGHT v-WB, arr-AH (e)   89818-1
78: VICTOR 25045 LP: RCA (F) FXM1-7084,
BLUEBIRD AXM2-5502, RCA (J) RA-56

THE SHEIK (OF ARABY) (32tp)   89819-2
78: VICTOR 25038 LP: RCA (F) FXM1-7084,
BLUEBIRD AXM2-5502, RCA (J) RA-56, TIME-
LIFE STL-J20

JERRY THE JUNKER v-WB (e)   89820-1
78: VICTOR 25045 LP: RCA (F) FXM1-7084,
BLUEBIRD AXM2-5502, RCA (J) RA-56

*   *   *

[34-39] While Carter's own orchestra was breaking up, he took part in the
date under the leadership of his former Henderson colleague Buster Bailey.

The first of four sessions featuring singer/comedian Bob Howard followed five days later; the other Howard recordings came after Carter had followed several of his former sidemen into Willie Bryant's orchestra in February 1935.

On the Bob Howard recordings, and with Willie Bryant, Carter played trumpet almost exclusively. "I jumped at the chance to play trumpet in somebody's section; it was a lot of fun for me."

Teddy Wilson, who preceded Carter in the Bryant band, recalls that the band "improved a great deal because after awhile Benny Carter joined as the musical director and Willie's band really began to sound like something after Benny took over." (Interview with Phil Schaap, March 5, 1980.) Carter, who was not formally named "musical director," did arrange for the band and was heavily featured as a soloist. Unfortunately, at his one recording session with Bryant, none of his arrangements were recorded, and he solos on only one title.

---

[40]   January 17, 1936   Paris
          WILLIE LEWIS AND HIS ORCHESTRA

Carter (tp, as, arr, comp) Alex Renard (tp) Bobby Martin (tp, v) Billy Burns (tb) George Johnson (as) Willie Lewis (as, v) Joe Hayman, Coco Kiehn (ts) Herman Chittison (p) John Mitchell (g) June Cole (b) Ted Fields (d)

I'VE GOT A FEELING YOU'RE FOOLING v-WL   CPT-2450
    (8as) arr
78: PATHE PA-803   LP: PATHE CO54-11416,
ON THE LOOSE 5

STAY OUT OF LOVE v-WL (32tp acc) arr   CPT-2451-1
78: PATHE PA-816   LP: PATHE CO54-11416,
ON THE LOOSE 5

RHYTHM IS OUR BUSINESS v-BM (4tp break +   CPT-2452-1
    32tp) arr
78: PATHE PA-803   LP: PATHE CO54-11416,
ON THE LOOSE 5

JUST A MOOD (16as) arr, comp   CPT-2453-1
78: PATHE PA-816   LP: PATHE CO54-11416,
ON THE LOOSE 5

ALL OF ME (32+coda tp) arr   CPT-2454-1
78: PATHE PA-817   LP: PATHE CO54-11416,
ON THE LOOSE 5

STAR DUST (24tp+coda [last chorus; muted tp in CPT-2455-1
    1st chorus is probably Martin]) arr
78: PATHE PA-817   LP: PATHE CO54-11416,
ON THE LOOSE 5, TIME-LIFE STL-J10

*   *   *

Carter's first recording date in Europe finds him still featured primarily on trumpet and includes some of his finest work of the period on that instrument. The Willie Lewis orchestra, for which Carter had left the United

States in May of 1935, was, as Carter puts it, "almost a society band."
French writer Charles Delaunay, who met Carter at that time, was less
charitable. "It was simply not a good band," he recalls. He describes its
home base, the posh Chez Florence, as rather hostile to the small coterie
of jazz fans anxious to see Carter. "It was very difficult to get in if the
maître d' didn't know you. You practically had to be the Duke of Windsor!"

The music recorded at this session was, indeed, atypical of the
Lewis' Chez Florence repertoire, and Carter doubts that most of these arrangements were ever played in the club.

Carter's writing for reeds is his most ambitious since the October
16, 1933, "Lonesome Nights"/"Symphony In Riffs" date. "Stay Out Of
Love" and "Rhythm Is Our Business" both have short saxophone ensemble
passages but the real reed showcases are "All Of Me" and "Stardust." The
former opens with a dazzling chorus by the sax section; Carter was to incorporate this chorus for an expanded section in a 1940 recording of the
same tune.

Judging by the saccharine opening of "Stardust," one might suspect
the arrangement was geared to the Chez Florence clientele, but another fine
reed chorus intervenes. Carter's writing is full of brief asides and double-
time passages, while still preserving the melody. The brass play the first
eight bars of the last chorus to allow Carter, who had been leading the
saxes, to switch to trumpet for his solo.

Carter's trumpet work here ranks among his best on record. In the
brisk "Rhythm Is Our Business" he is at his most Armstrong-like. Despite
an occasional fluff on "All Of Me," he shows more of the high note trumpet
facility that attracted Armstrong himself to Carter's playing on the Mezzrow
date two years earlier. He ends the piece with a spectacular series of ascending arpeggios, culminating in an effortless climb to high E-flat (F concert).

His solo on "Stardust" is even more impressive. Here he takes
subtle liberties with the time, in places anticipating the melody and else-
where falling daringly behind, only to catch up with a flurry of 16th notes.
The full tone is, again, reminiscent of Armstrong's, as is the use of glis-
sandi.

Carter's composition, "Just A Mood," was used as the Lewis orchestra's theme for broadcast to England. The recording here features Carter
on alto; he made another version several months later in England on clarinet.

---

[41]   April 15, 1936 London
         BENNY CARTER AND HIS ORCHESTRA

Carter (tp, as, ts, cl, v, arr, comp) Max Goldberg, Tommy McQuater, Duncan
Whyte (tp) Ted Heath, Bill Mulraney (tb) Andy McDevitt (cl, as) E. O. Pog-
son (as) Buddy Featherstonhaugh (ts) Pat Dodd (p) George Elliot (g) Al Burke
(b) Ronnie Gubertini (d)

SWINGIN' AT MAIDA VALE   (16cl)(16+8as) arr, comp   S-103-2
78: VOCALION S-4 LP: DECCA (E) ACE OF
CLUBS ACL1167, EVEREST FS225, TIME-LIFE STL-J10

SWINGIN' AT MAIDA VALE   (16cl)(16+8as) arr, comp   S-103-3
78: UNISSUED-TEST EXISTS

NIGHTFALL   (8cl)(32ts) arr, comp   S-104-2
78: VOCALION S-4 LP: DECCA (E) ACE OF
CLUBS ACL1167, EVEREST FS225

BIG BEN BLUES   (v)(12as)+(12as alternating with   S-105-2
      ensemble) arr, comp
78: VOCALION S-7 LP: DECCA (E) ACE OF
CLUBS ACL1176, ON THE LOOSE 1

THESE FOOLISH THINGS   (4as intro)(16tp)(8cl)   S-106-1
      (8as)(2as) arr
78: VOCALION S-5 LP: ON THE LOOSE 1,
INTERCORD (G) 158001

THESE FOOLISH THINGS   (4as intro)(16tp)(8cl)   S-106-3
      (8as)(2as) arr
78: UNISSUED-TEST EXISTS

*   *   *

After nine months in France, Carter accepted Henry Hall's invitation to become arranger for the BBC dance orchestra. Five of Carter's arrangements for it were recorded commercially (see Arrangement section) and,
within the constraints imposed by the musical format and instrumentation,
they represent skillful marriages of jazz and dance music.   But Carter's
major impact on the British jazz scene came from a series of records
made for Vocalion, which signed him within 24 hours of his arrival there.

     Within the month Carter led the first of these sessions, giving notice
of his intent to produce first-rate swing music using only British musicians.
The players were Britain's finest.   Carter found them to be excellent readers, but as soloists they lacked real individuality.   So many were Scots that
the press dubbed them "Benny Carter and His Highland Swing."

     Carter frequently soloed on two and sometimes three instruments in
the same piece, which elicited accusations of grandstanding from some writers, notably John Hammond.   The English press, and certainly the musicians themselves, had nothing but praise for these records, and felt it only
natural that Carter should be so prominent.   Moreover, there were plenty
of opportunities for solo work by the sidemen.

     For his first British session Carter prepared four new arrangements,
three of which were his own compositions.

     "Swingin' At Maida Vale" refers to the section of London where the
BBC studios were located and where Carter lived.   The British soloists include the future bandleader Ted Heath on trombone, trumpeter Duncan Whyte,
and a very Hawkins-like Buddy Featherstonhaugh.

     "Nightfall," a lovely melancholy melody which Carter states on clari-
net, also features his first recorded solo on tenor.   Carter has no trouble
adjusting to the unfamiliar horn which he borrowed from Featherstonhaugh.

     "Big Ben Blues" includes a humorous vocal parody of blues lyrics by
Carter.   "These Foolish Things" finds him switching deftly from alto to
trumpet to clarinet and back to alto.   The third take of "These Foolish
Things" is slower than the issued version; there is a minor fluff in the
trumpet solo which may have contributed to the choice of take 1.

---

[42]   Late April, 1936 London
         BENNY CARTER AND HIS ORCHESTRA

Carter (tp, as, cl, arr, comp) Tommy McQuater, Duncan Whyte (tp) Andy Mc-
Devitt (cl) Buddy Featherstonhaugh (ts) Pat Dodd (p) George Elliot (g) Al
Burke (b) Ronnie Gubertini (d)

WHEN DAY IS DONE   arr   S-107-1
78: UNISSUED

WHEN DAY IS DONE   (32tp)(32as)(tp coda) arr   S-107-2
78: VOCALION S-11 LP: DECCA (E) ACE OF
CLUBS ACL1167

WHEN DAY IS DONE   (32tp)(32as)(tp coda) arr   S-107-3
78: UNISSUED LP: ON THE LOOSE 5

I'VE GOT TWO LIPS   (32cl with ensemble)(32as) arr   S-108-3
78: VOCALION S-9 LP: DECCA (F) ACE OF
CLUBS ACL1167, EVEREST FS225

I'VE GOT TWO LIPS   (32cl with ensemble)(32as) arr   S-108-2
78: UNISSUED LP: ON THE LOOSE 1

JUST A MOOD   (4cl)(16cl)(4cl) arr, comp   S-109
78: UNISSUED-TEST EXISTS

JUST A MOOD   (4cl)(16cl)(4cl) arr, comp   S-109-2
78: VOCALION S-11 LP: DECCA (F) ACE OF
CLUBS ACL1167, EVEREST FS225

SWINGIN' THE BLUES   (24as)(24tp [2nd solo; 1st   S-110-1
     is McQuater]) arr, comp
78: VOCALION S-5 LP: ON THE LOOSE 1

                        *   *   *

The information on take 1 of "When Day Is Done" comes from an article by
Carter entitled "My Nine Lives," which appeared in the May-June issue of
Swing Music (page 71).   Carter writes: "You may also be interested to
know that we made two masters on "When Day Is Done" in one of which I
played a piano chorus.   Whether that one will be selected for release hasn't
yet been decided. "

---

[43]   Mid June, 1936 London
         BENNY CARTER AND HIS ORCHESTRA

Carter (tp, cl, as, ts, p, arr, comp) Max Goldberg, Tommy McQuater (tp) Leslie
Thompson (tp, tb) Lew Davis, Ted Heath (tb) Freddy Gardner, Andy Mc-
Devitt (cl, as) Buddy Featherstonhaugh (ts) Billy Munn (p) Albert Harris (g)
Wally Morris (b) George Elrick (d) Elisabeth Welch (v)

SCANDAL IN A FLAT   (8ts) arr, comp   S-115-2
78: VOCALION S-14 LP: DECCA (E) ACE OF
CLUBS ACL1176, ON THE LOOSE 2

ACCENT ON SWING   (4as)+(8as with ensemble)   S-116-1
     arr, comp

78: VOCALION S-14 LP: DECCA (E) ACE OF
CLUBS ACL1167, EVEREST FS225

YOU UNDERSTAND (16p)(20) arr, comp   S-117-2
78: VOCALION S-27 LP: DECCA (E) ACE OF
CLUBS ACL1176, EVEREST FS221, ON THE LOOSE 2

GIN AND JIVE (32as) (8cl[2nd solo]) arr, comp   S-118
78: UNISSUED-TEST EXISTS

IF ONLY I COULD READ YOUR MIND (32ts)   S-119-1
    (8cl) arr, comp
78: VOCALION S-27 LP: DECCA (E) ACE OF
CLUBS ACL1167, EVEREST FS225

I GOTTA GO v-EW (20tp)(10as) arr, comp   S-120-1
78: UNISSUED-TEST EXISTS

I GOTTA GO v-EW (20ts)(10as) arr, comp   S-120-2
78: VOCALION S-16 LP: ON THE LOOSE 2

> NOTE: "You Understand" was included by mistake on Everest FS221,
> which is an Ellington reissue. The Carter recording appears in
> place of a track labelled "I'm Crazy 'Bout My Baby." The Carter
> piece immediately precedes Ellington's on the Decca anthology
> ACL1176, which apparently was the source of the Everest issue.

*   *   *

The full orchestra returns for these recordings which feature Carter on no
less than five instruments.

The trumpet soloist on "Accent On Swing" is Tommy McQuater, who
was one of the few original solo voices among the British musicians. His
brash exuberance, though occasionally bordering on the uncontrollable, lent
excitement to a number of these British sides. Carter, himself, in a letter
to a friend in January 1937, singles out McQuater. "There are quite a few
good players over here but not yet on a par with our boys. There is one
though I think is very good and that is Tommy McQuater, the trumpet player. His style is quite individual to a degree and he has a terrific attack at
times. "

"Accent On Swing" also contains Carter's first writing featuring the
British saxophone section, a 16-bar passage in the last chorus.

"You Understand, " one of Carter's favorites of his British recordings, includes his first piano work on record.

The unissued uptempo Carter original, "Gin And Jive," has Carter
on alto and briefly on clarinet in the final chorus; the earlier clarinet work
is by McDevitt. It may have been withheld because of a number of reed
squeaks in Featherstonhaugh's opening tenor solo. It was rerecorded at the
January 11-16, 1937, session and that version was issued. This arrangement became a staple of the Carter 1939 band's book at the Savoy as "Savoy
Stampede, " under which title it was recorded on June 29 (along with another
piece premiered in England, "Scandal In A Flat").

[44]   June 20, 1936   London
          BENNY CARTER AND HIS SWING QUARTET

Carter (tp, as, ts, comp) Gene Rodgers (p) Bernard Addison (g) Wally Morris
(b) George Elrick (d) Elisabeth Welch (v)

WHEN LIGHTS ARE LOW   v-EW (32as)(16tp acc) comp   S-121-1
78: VOCALION S-16 LP: DECCA (E) ACE OF
CLUBS ACL1167, EVEREST FS225

WALTZING THE BLUES   (24ts)(24as)(24tp) comp   S-122-1
78: VOCALION S-19 LP: DECCA (E) ACE OF
CLUBS ACL1167, EVEREST FS225, TIME-LIFE STL-J10

WALTZING THE BLUES   (24ts)(24as)(24tp) comp   S-122-2
78: UNISSUED-TEST EXISTS

TIGER RAG   (96ts)(16tp)   S-123-1
78: VOCALION S-19 LP: ON THE LOOSE 2

                              *   *   *

For his first small-group recordings in Europe Carter took advantage of the
presence of two visiting Americans--pianist Gene Rodgers, who was part of
the touring "Radcliffe and Rodgers" act, and Bernard Addison, the guitarist
from the early 1930s Carter orchestra who was then accompanying the Mills
Brothers.

        The two Carter originals on this date became classics but in quite
different ways.   This is the first recording of "When Lights Are Low."
This piece, composed by Carter (with lyrics by Spencer Williams), has en-
dured for some forty-five years as a favorite of jazzmen from Lionel
Hampton to Miles Davis and Eric Dolphy.

        "Waltzing The Blues," on the other hand, has been one of the most
controversial recordings in the history of jazz.   It is the first recorded attempt at playing the blues in 3/4 or waltz time and foreshadowed other efforts which expanded the notion of "acceptable" jazz time signatures by such
artists as Max Roach, Sonny Rollins, Dave Brubeck and Don Ellis.   Coin-
cidentally, a tune with the same title, composed by Clarence Gaskill, had
been recorded in 1923 by the Victor Arden-Phil Ohman orchestra (Victor
19017), but this was a straight waltz and had nothing to do with the blues or
jazz.   Carter's recording was prompted by Leonard Feather who, as early
as 1933, had proposed a jazz record in 3/4 time (Vocalion announcement
no. 8, mid-September 1936).   Carter, after experimenting with the idea on
piano, decided it was worth a try.   The result was a tune based on a 24-
bar blues chorus rather than the more conventional twelve.   Carter takes
one chorus each on tenor, alto, and trumpet, separated by piano and guitar
solo choruses.   The unissued test of take 2 follows the same pattern.
Carter's solos are quite different here, with no obvious flaws to account for
its rejection in favor of take 1.

        The British music press heralded the recording with headlines such
as "REVOLUTION IN JAZZ!!," "Benny Carter's Hot Waltz Record," and
"What's It All About?"   The Melody Maker ran a forum of reviews and de-
bates on the merits of the experiment (September 12, 1936).   The jury of
critics, who wrote under pseudonyms, was anything but unanimous.   "Ro-
phone," hot records critic for the Melody Maker: "Benny has started some-

thing which others were either too scared or too unobservant to start. "
"Pick-Up, " the commercial records critic for the Melody Maker: "This is
all very exciting, but if it is to be seriously regarded as a dance record,
hot or cold, it fails lamentably. " "Swing-High, " reviewer of hot records
in Rhythm: "I have never been more completely at a loss for words than
when I first heard the record. It just didn't seem possible that after 25
years of jazz records somebody could have produced one so completely and
radically different. " Leonard Hibbs in Swing Music: "No jazz swing, no
waltz swing (by Viennese standards) but a record of the utmost interest because of Benny Carter's three perfect solos. "

The severest indictment came from "Mike" (the noted writer and
composer Spike Hughes and a great Carter admirer): "Waltzing The Blues
is an idea that has as much prospect of posterity as a mule. And it isn't
even as useful ... what the hell's the matter with the blues anyway that 4-
in-a-bar is no longer enough?" Hughes also thought "Waltzing The Blues"
was a misnomer, suggesting that "blue-ing the waltz" was "nearer the
mark. " (Melody Maker, October 3, 1936, p. 5.)

Not to be outdone, John Hammond called it "affected, 'clever' in the
most odious sense of the word" and defended the blues as "simple folk music, far too pure for defilement at the hands of sophisticates. " (Rhythm,
November 1936, p. 13.)

Carter himself characteristically disclaims any attempt to "revolu-
tionize jazz" and was quite surprised by the controversy. Although he still
feels today that "three is almost a more natural swing feeling than four, "
Carter never continued the 3/4 experiment; it was almost 30 years before
he recorded another piece in waltz time.

In the face of the strong reactions on all sides to "Waltzing The
Blues, " the commercial recordings critic for Rhythm, "Swing-Low, " in-
jected a welcome note of sanity into the debate: "As to whether the record
proves anything or not I really do not care, as it has got me under its
spell to such an extent that I only wish to be left alone to enjoy it. "

"Tiger Rag" is Carter's most extensive tenor feature on record. He
plays three effortless, rollicking choruses and then caps the performance
with a brief appearance on trumpet.

---

[45]   August 2, 1936 Hilversum, Holland Airchecks
        BENNY CARTER WITH AVRO ORCHESTRA

Carter (cl, as, comp) Unknown (tp, b, d) Klaas Van Beeck (p)

NIGHTFALL (8cl)(32as) comp

SOPHISTICATED LADY (32+16as)

    NOTE: Piano and bass accompaniment only on second title.

---

[46]   August 26, 1936 Copenhagen
        BENNY CARTER WITH KAI EWANS' ORCHESTRA

Carter (tp, as, cl, arr, comp) Axel Skouby, Olaf Carlsson, Kurt Pederson (tp)
Peter Rasmussen, Palmer Traulsen (tb) Kai Ewans (as) Aage Voss (cl, as)

Knut Knutsson, Anker Skjoldborg (ts) Christian Jensen (p) Ulrik Neumann
(g) Kelof Nielsen (b) Eric Kragh (d) Leo Mathiesen (arr)

BLUE INTERLUDE   (32as)(16tp)(8cl)(8as with   OCS-435-2
    ensemble + coda) arr, comp
78: HMV X-4699   LP: ON THE LOOSE 2

BUGLE CALL RAG   arr-LM (4tp break)(4tp break+   OCS-436-2
    8tp+4tp break+8tp)(32as)
78: HMV X-4698   LP: ON THE LOOSE 2

---

[47]   August 29, 1936   Copenhagen
        BENNY CARTER WITH KAI EWANS' ORCHESTRA

Carter (tp, as, cl, v, arr, comp) Axel Skouby, Olaf Carlsson, Kurt Pederson
(tp) Peter Rasmussen, Palmer Traulsen (tb) Kai Ewans (as, v) Aage Voss
(cl, as) Knut Knutsson, Henry Hagemann-Larsen (ts) Christian Jensen (p)
Ulrik Neumann (g) Kelof Nielsen (b) Eric Kragh (d) Leo Mathiesen (arr)

MEMPHIS BLUES   v-KE, arr-LM (12tp)(12cl)   OCS-450-2
78: HMV X-4698   LP: ON THE LOOSE 2

WHEN LIGHTS ARE LOW (v)(32as)(8tp) arr, comp   OCS-451-2
78: HMV X-4699   LP: ON THE LOOSE 2

                        *   *   *

Carter's visit to Holland was arranged by Danish bandleader/musician/entre-
preneur Kai Ewans.   His activities in Copenhagen included two concerts as
well as two recording sessions [46, 47] with Evans's orchestra.

        "Blue Interlude" is a new arrangement of the composition Carter first
recorded with the Chocolate Dandies in 1933.

        On this second recording of "When Lights Are Low," Carter himself
does the vocal. His alto chorus here departs far more from the melody than
that on the British recording made two months earlier.   Soon after this
recording Kai Ewans adopted "When Lights Are Low" as the theme song of
his orchestra.   It became so closely associated with the popular bandleader
that as late as 1978, after he had retired to the United States, people still
whistled the tune to him whenever he was spotted in Copenhagen.

---

[48]   September 12, 1936   Stockholm
        BENNY CARTER MED SONORA SWING BAND

Carter (as, tp, arr) Thore Ehrling (tp) Uno Gorling (tb) Charles Redland (cl)
Zilas Gorling (ts) Stig Holm (p) Olle Sahlin (g) Thore Jederby (b) Sture
Aberg (d)

SOME OF THESE DAYS   (32as)(56tp)+(8tp with   1879-A
    ensemble)[1st tp solo - muted - is by
    Ehrling] arr
78: SONORA 3188 LP: SONORA SOLP106, ON
THE LOOSE 2

SOME OF THESE DAYS   (32as)(48tp)+(8tp with   1879-B

ensemble) [1st tp solo - muted - is by
    Ehrling] arr
78: UNISSUED LP: SONORA SOLP106, ON THE
LOOSE 2

---

[49]   Same Session
        BENNY CARTER MED ALL STAR ORCHESTRA

Carter (cl, as, tp, arr) Gosta Petersson, Thore Ehrling, Rune Ander (tp) Uno
Gorling, George Vernon (tb) Tony Mason, Olle Thalen (as) Zilas Gorling
(ts) Evert Haden (p) Olle Sahlin (g) Thore Jederby (b) Gosta Heden (d)

GLOAMING arr   1880-A
78: UNISSUED

GLOAMING (16+8tp [2nd chorus; 1st chorus   1880-B
      bridge by Ehrling])(4+4cl) arr
78: SONORA 3188 LP: SONORA SOLP106, ON
THE LOOSE 2

                        *   *   *

Carter's brief stay in Sweden included two concerts and this recording session [48, 49] with Swedish musicians. Because of the large number of local
musicians who wanted to play with him, the two tunes were recorded with
somewhat different personnels.

        "Some Of These Days," made with a nine-piece group, is capped by
some spectacular Carter trumpet, still very much in the Armstrong mold.
On both takes Carter begins the last chorus with an interpolation of "Dark
Eyes," one of the very few instances of his use of "quotes" (a device he
generally dislikes). On the A take (issued), Carter solos on trumpet for the
entire final chorus; on the B take the bridge of that chorus is taken by Sahlin on guitar.

        The attractive "Gloaming," recorded by the larger ensemble, was
composed by the trumpet player Thore Ehrling. The Nordiska Music Pub-
lishing Company had commissioned Carter to do an arrangement of a piece
by a Swedish composer. The company sent Carter one work by each of the
four leading writers of dance music and Carter selected "Gloaming." The
trumpet on the bridge of the first chorus is the composer's; the rest of the
trumpet work and the clarinet solo are by Carter.

        In general the rhythm sections on Carter's Scandinavian recordings
seem to be a little less rigid than those with which he recorded in Britain.
According to the Swedish press, however, the fans in Stockholm may have
been somewhat less sophisticated, applauding in the wrong places at Carter's
concerts. When asked about this report Carter responded, "Wherever they
applauded I was glad to accept it."

---

[50]   October 13, 1936 London
        ELISABETH WELCH

Carter (tp, cl, as) Gene Rodgers (p) Ivor Mairants (g) Wally Morris (b) Elisabeth Welch (v)

POOR BUTTERFLY v-EW (32as acc)(32as)(16as acc)   S-124-1
78: VOCALION 526 LP: ON THE LOOSE 2

DROP IN NEXT TIME YOU'RE PASSING v-EW   S-125-1
    (32as)(32as acc)(16tp acc)
78: VOCALION 515 LP: ON THE LOOSE 2,
TAX (SW) M-8031

THE MAN I LOVE v-EW (28cl acc)(16tp)   S-126-2
78: VOCALION 515 LP: ON THE LOOSE 2,
TAX (SW) M-8031

THAT'S HOW THE FIRST SONG WAS BORN v-EW   S-127-1
    (8tp)(32tp acc)(8tp)(10tp acc)
78: VOCALION 526 LP: ON THE LOOSE 2

---

[51]   October 19, 1936 London
          BENNY CARTER AND HIS SWING QUINTET

Carter (cl, as) Tommy McQuater (tp) Gerry Moore (p) Albert Harris (g)
Wally Morris (b) Al Craig (d)

THERE'LL BE SOME CHANGES MADE (8cl)   S-130-1
78: UNISSUED-TEST EXISTS

THERE'LL BE SOME CHANGES MADE (18cl)   S-130-2
78: VOCALION S-46 LP: DECCA (E) ACE OF
CLUBS ACL1167, DECCA (E) ACE OF CLUBS ACL1105

JINGLE BELLS (16cl)(32as)(8cl)   S-131-1
78: VOCALION S-39 LP: ON THE LOOSE 3,
TIME-LIFE STL-J10

JINGLE BELLS (16cl)(32as)(8cl)   S-131-2
78: UNISSUED LP: ON THE LOOSE 3

ROYAL GARDEN BLUES (12cl)(24as)   S-132-1
78: VOCALION S-46 LP: DECCA (E) ACE OF
CLUBS ACL1167, EVEREST FS225

CARRY ME BACK TO OLD VIRGINNY (8as)(32as)   S-133-1
78: VOCALION S-39 LP: ON THE LOOSE 3

*   *   *

Soon after his return to England, Carter participated in two small-group
sessions [50, 51]. For the first, he was part of a drumless quartet providing the accompaniment for the vocals of Elisabeth Welch, who has recently had a comeback in New York. For jazz fans, the most interesting
moments are provided by Carter's alto on the first two titles, as well as
Gene Rodgers's piano.

The quintet date features some excellent Red Allen-style solos by
McQuater. Guitarist Albert Harris, who later became a noted teacher and
composer in Hollywood, contributes some polished solos.

The first take of "Jingle Bells" is slightly faster than the originally
issued second take. The question has been raised whether both trumpet solo

choruses are by the same trumpeter.   In both takes the first chorus is open
and the second muted.   In take 2 there is practically no pause between the
two choruses, necessitating a rather deft application of the straight mute by
McQuater.

---

[52]   Between January 11 and 16, 1937   London
        BENNY CARTER AND HIS ORCHESTRA

Carter (tp, as, v, arr, comp) Leslie Thompson, Tommy McQuater, possibly
Max Goldberg (tp) Lew Davis, Bill Mulraney (tb) Freddy Gardner, Andy
McDevitt (cl, as) George Evans, Buddy Featherstonhaugh (ts) Eddie Macauley
(p) Albert Harris (g) Wally Morris (b) Al Craig (d)

GIN AND JIVE   (32as)(8as) arr, comp   S-140-1
78: UNISSUED-TEST EXISTS

GIN AND JIVE   (32as)(8as) arr, comp   S-140-2
78: VOCALION S-57, VOCALION S-58, LP:
DECCA (E) ACE OF CLUBS ACL1167, EVEREST
FS225

NAGASAKI   (v)(32as) arr   S-141-1
78: VOCALION S-69 LP: ON THE LOOSE 3

NAGASAKI   (v)(32as) arr   S-141-2
78: UNISSUED-TEST EXISTS

THERE'S A SMALL HOTEL   (16tp)(v) arr   S-142-1
78: VOCALION S-58 LP: ON THE LOOSE 3

THERE'S A SMALL HOTEL   (16tp) arr   S-142-2
78: VOCALION S-57 LP: ON THE LOOSE 3

I'M IN THE MOOD FOR SWING   (16tp) arr, comp   S-143-1
78: UNISSUED-TEST EXISTS

I'M IN THE MOOD FOR SWING   (16tp) arr, comp   S-143-2
78: VOCALION S-69 LP: ON THE LOOSE 3

        NOTE: "Gin And Jive" later recorded by Carter under title "Savoy
        Stampede. "

---

[53]   Same Session
        INFORMAL POST-SESSION

Carter (p, comp) possibly Max Goldberg (tp) Freddy Gardner (as, v) Al Craig
(d)

RAMBLING IN C v-FG? (16p) comp   S-144
78: UNISSUED-TEXT EXISTS LP: ON THE
LOOSE 5

STARS AND YOU (18p) comp   S-145
78: UNISSUED-TEST EXISTS

                            *   *   *

[52, 53] Immediately following his successful Hippodrome concert, Carter returned to the studio with the English big band for his last recordings in London. Another try at "Gin And Jive," which had been rejected at the mid-June 1936 session, yielded an acceptable take.

Carter demonstrates his vocal dexterity on the tongue-twisting lyrics of "Nagasaki." The arrangement is similar, but not identical, to one Carter had done two years earlier for Charlie Barnet (recorded January 21, 1935).

Both takes of "Small Hotel" were issued simultaneously, an unusual procedure explained by Leonard Feather who produced the session. After the first take, which included both a trumpet solo and a vocal chorus by Carter, Feather suggested that the recording might be improved if Carter substituted an alto solo for the vocal. On the second take Carter did eliminate the vocal, but assigned the saxophone solo to Freddy Gardner. This was Carter's expression of pique at the disparagement of his singing. "It was a way of putting me down," Feather recalls. "To cover all sides we issued both takes." A Vocalion Swing Records press leaflet issued in mid-February 1937 (No. 16) describes the recordings at some length, but deliberately fails to note that the alto solo on the instrumental version is not by Carter. For years, it was thought to be his by many listeners. Vocalion concluded its pitch by advising the music lover, "If you prefer to have the vocal version of 'Small Hotel' all you have to do is ask for record S. 58 instead of S. 57," to which Carter asked many years later, "I wonder what they did with all those surplus copies of S. 58?"

Carter recorded both "Gin And Jive" and "I'm In The Mood For Swing" again after his return to the United States. In a similar arrangement, the latter was recorded by an illustrious Lionel Hampton group at Carter's first session back in New York.

The final two items were recorded informally after the session ended [53]. These demos of two Carter compositions, neither of which was recorded again, were discovered on a test pressing in Carter's own collection. He identified the piano work as his own, and the alto as that of Freddy Gardner, whom he also believes sings the scat vocal in "Rambling in C." There is a brief passage of muted trumpet in the first title, and the muted trumpet opens the second. It does not sound like McQuater and Carter suggested that it might be Max Goldberg.

---

[54]   March 24, 1937 Laren, Holland
          BENNY CARTER AND THE RAMBLERS

Carter (tp, as, ts, cl, arr) George Van Helvoirt, Jack Bulterman (tp) Marcel Thielemans (tb) Wim Poppink, Andre Van Der Ouderaa (cl, as) Sal Doof (ts) Freddy Johnson (p) Jack Pet (b) Kees Kranenburg (d) Theo Uden Masman (dir)

BLACK BOTTOM   (8as)(16+8tp)(32cl)(8as)(cl coda)   AM 368-1
78: DECCA F-42121, VOCALION S-94 LP:
DECCA (F) 154.062, ON THE LOOSE 3

RAMBLER'S RHYTHM   (24as)(32tp)(8as)   AM 369-2
78: DECCA F-44076, DECCA F-42110, VOCALION
S-94, LP: DECCA (F) 154.062, ON THE LOOSE 3

NEW STREET SWING   (32as)(4+4+8cl)+(8cl with   AM 370-1
     ensemble)

78: DECCA F-42165, DECCA F-42110, VOCALION
S-81, LP: DECCA (F) 154.062, ON THE LOOSE 3

I'LL NEVER GIVE IN   (16+8tp)(12ts) arr   AM 371-2
78: DECCA F-42121, DECCA F-42110, VOCALION
S-81, LP: DECCA (F) 154.062, ON THE LOOSE 3

                              *   *   *

During a brief, exploratory visit to Holland to conclude an agreement for his
summer's engagement in Scheveningen, Carter recorded with this Dutch radio
band.   He was also reunited with his boyhood friend Freddy Johnson.

        The session was held in a makeshift studio at the Hamdorff Hotel in
Laren, where Carter had played one night the previous summer.

        The first three tunes were from the Rambler's book and were com-
pleted in the morning.   According to trumpeter Jack Bulterman (reported by
Evert Kaleveld in the liner notes to On The Loose 3), Carter's arrangement
of Freddy Johnson's "I'll Never Give In" was not ready.   Carter seems to
have spent the lunch hour in the studio "writing the arrangement, by hand,
for all instruments.   But at the convened time, one hour later, everyone
had his part ready waiting for him."

        The Ramblers provide excellent backing for perhaps the most im-
pressive showcase to date for Carter's talents as a multi-instrumentalist.
He takes all the solos here, except for an occasional spot for Johnson's
piano.   Playing four instruments, and switching as many as four times in
a single piece with only a few measures between solos, Carter might be
accused of gimmickry were it not for the technical mastery, coherence, and
beauty of each of these solo statements.

---

[55]   April 28, 1937   Paris
          COLEMAN HAWKINS AND HIS ALL STAR JAM BAND

Carter (as, tp, arr) André Ekyan (as) Alix Combelle (cl, ts) Coleman Hawkins
(ts) Stephane Grappelly (p) Django Reinhardt (g) Eugene D'Hellemmes (b)
Tommy Benford (d)

HONEYSUCKLE ROSE   (8as) arr   OLA 1742-1
78: SWING 1, HMV B-8754   45: HMV 7EG8393,
HMV (F) 7EMF26, LP: PATHE FELP174,
ODEON CLP1890, PATHE CHTX240-551,
PRESTIGE 7633, PATHE (F) C054-16004, TIME-
LIFE STL-J06, WORLD RECORDS SM643

CRAZY RHYTHM   (32as[2nd solo]) arr   OLA 1743-1
78: SWING 1, HMV B-8754   45: HMV 7EG8393,
HMV (F) 7EMF26, LP: PATHE FELP174,
ODEON CLP1890, PATHE CHTX240-551,
PRESTIGE 7633, PATHE (F) C054-16004, TIME-LIFE
STL-J06, WORLD RECORDS SM643

OUT OF NOWHERE   (32tp)   OLA 1744-1
78: HMV K-8511, HMV B-8812   45: HMV
7EG8393 LP: PATHE FELP174, ODEON CLP1890,
PATHE CHTX240-551, PRESTIGE 7633, PATHE
(F) C054-16004, WORLD RECORDS SM643

SWEET GEORGIA BROWN   (32tp[theme])(32tp)   OLA 1745-1
‾‾‾‾‾‾‾‾‾‾‾‾‾‾‾   (64tp with ensemble)
78: HMV K-8511, HMV B-8812 45: HMV 7EG8393,
LP: PATHE FELP174, ODEON CLP1890, PATHE
CHTX240-551, PRESTIGE 7633, PATHE (F)
C054-16004, TIME-LIFE STL-J06, WORLD
RECORDS SM643

                              *   *   *

Carter's first recorded meeting in Europe with Coleman Hawkins turned out
to be a landmark session.   The idea for the sax quartet was Charles Delaunay's who, along with Hugues Panassié, launched their new Swing label
with this date.   Delaunay recalls that Carter, who was supposed to furnish
four arrangements, arrived with none and sketched out the ensemble passages of "Honeysuckle Rose" and "Crazy Rhythm" on the spot.   The final
title was in the nature of an informal jam.   Part of Delaunay's plan was to
pair Carter and Hawkins with their French counterparts André Ekyan and
Alix Combelle.

     "Honeysuckle Rose" is basically all Hawkins, set off by Django's
tasteful fills and some lovely sax ensemble passages, with Carter's incom-
parable lead alto quite prominent.   Carter also solos on the bridge in the
last chorus.

     The Frenchmen rise to the occasion in "Crazy Rhythm, " Ekyan and
Combelle turning in, according to Delaunay, among their best performances
ever.   As Dan Morgenstern notes (liner notes to Prestige 7633), Carter
pays Combelle the supreme compliment of incorporating a figure from the
latter's bridge into his own.   (For an analysis of Carter's solo, see chapter 3.) Hawkins's solo is one of his greatest on record; after one sensational chorus, apparently all he was allotted, Django is heard urging him
to continue, which he does without breaking stride.   It is difficult to believe
Combelle's contention that Carter "advised" Hawkins how this tune should be
played (Delaunay, Django Reinhardt, p. 85).

     For the last pieces Carter switches to trumpet.   On "Out Of No-
where" he sets the stage for yet another Hawkins milestone, this time in
his rhapsodic ballad vein.

‾‾‾
[56]   August 17, 1937 The Hague
          BENNY CARTER AND HIS ORCHESTRA
‾‾‾

Carter (tp, as, cl, arr, comp) Sam Dasberg, Cliff Woodridge, Rolf Goldstein
(tp) George Chisholm, Harry Van Oven (tb) Louis Stephenson (as) Bertie
King, Jimmy Williams (ts) Freddy Johnson (p) Ray Webb (g) Len Harrison
(b) Robert Montmarche (d)

SKIP IT   (12as) arr, comp   AM 393-3
‾‾‾‾‾‾‾ DECCA F-42136, VOCALION S-126 LP:
DECCA (F) 154. 062, ON THE LOOSE 4, TAX
(SW) M-8031, TIME-LIFE STL-J10

LAZY AFTERNOON   (16tp)(34as) arr, comp   AM 394-2
‾‾‾‾‾‾‾‾‾‾‾‾‾‾ DECCA F-42130, DECCA F-42165,

VOCALION S-118, LP: DECCA (F) 154.062,
ON THE LOOSE 4, TAX (SW) M-8031

I AIN'T GOT NOBODY   (8cl)(16as) arr   AM 395-1
78: DECCA F-42125, VOCALION S-110, LP:
ON THE LOOSE 4

I AIN'T GOT NOBODY   (8cl)(16as) arr   AM 395-2
78: BRUNSWICK 03311 LP: DECCA (F)
154.062, ON THE LOOSE 4, TAX (SW) M-8031

BLUES IN MY HEART   (34as) arr, comp   AM 396-1
78: DECCA F-42128, VOCALION S-104 LP:
DECCA (F) 154.062, ON THE LOOSE 4, TAX
(SW) M-8031

*   *   *

Carter played in the summers of 1936 and 1937 in the Dutch seaside resort
of Scheveningen. For the second engagement he assembled an international,
interracial band with members from six countries. With some changes,
this was the group which recorded for Dutch Decca.

Since his arrival in Europe, Carter had hardly exercised his talent
for fashioning dazzling saxophone choruses. Having played several months
with his international band, Carter apparently felt he could now offer them
an arranging challenge. "Skip It" is a tour de force for the reeds. It is
a good example of Carter's skill at creating the most intricate reed passages
without ever sounding as if he were simply engaging in musical exercises.

Carter's lovely ballad, "Lazy Afternoon, " is another of his compositions which deserve to become more popular. It obviously made an impression on one of the reed men in this band, Bertie King, who, almost 20
years later, made the only other recording of it. The two versions of "I
Ain't Got Nobody" are quite similar. Rust lists Brunswick 03311(-2) as
"never issued" but Harold Flakser has shown us a copy.

The arrangement of "Blues In My Heart" is a novel, almost "sym-
phonic" treatment, which only hints at the melody.

[57]	August 18, 1937 The Hague
	BENNY CARTER AND HIS ORCHESTRA

Carter (tp, as, cl) George Chisholm (tb) Coleman Hawkins (ts) Jimmy Williams (cl, ts) Freddy Johnson (p) Ray Webb (g) Len Harrison (b) Robert
Montmarche (d)

SOMEBODY LOVES ME   (32tp)(8tp) arr   AM 397-1
78: DECCA F-42128, VOCALION S-104 LP:
DECCA (F) 154.062, ON THE LOOSE 4, TAX
(SW) M-8031

MIGHTY LIKE THE BLUES   (16tp)(12cl) arr   AM 398-3
78: DECCA F-42125, VOCALION S-110, BRUNS-
WICK 03311, LP: DECCA (F) 154.062, NEW
WORLD RECORDS NW174, ON THE LOOSE 4,
TAX (SW) M-8031

PARDON ME, PRETTY BABY   (32tp)(32as)   AM 399-1
        (32tp[4-bar trades with Hawkins]) arr
78: DECCA F-42130, VOCALION S-126   LP:
DECCA (F) 154.062, ON THE LOOSE 4, TAX
(SW) M-8031, TIME-LIFE STL-J10

MY BUDDY   (16as)(32tp) arr   AM 400-1
78: DECCA F-42136, VOCALION S-118   LP:
DECCA (F) 154.062, ON THE LOOSE 4, TIME-
LIFE STL-J10

                    *   *   *

For this session the orchestra pared down to an octet, making four sides
with guest Coleman Hawkins. The performances have a loose feeling.
Carter supplied an occasional arranged passage for cohesion, but the date
was meant to display the solo talents of the principals.

     Leonard Feather, visiting Holland, produced this and the previous
session for English Vocalion. Looking back, he recalls that there was an
"undeclared sense of rivalry" between Carter and Hawkins. Hawkins felt it
more, he adds, and was "not too eager" to record as a sideman. Charles
Delaunay, who produced the earlier Paris encounter between the saxophonists, and also saw them in Holland, remembers that Hawkins loved the
competition of a jam session, but Carter took part only on rare occasions.
"I always had the feeling that he preferred writing to playing," says Delaunay. Carter denies there was competition between him and Hawkins.
"We may have felt stimulated by each other's company, especially in Europe, but only to make the best music we could, and not in a combative
sense." Furthermore, on this session, Carter played mostly trumpet,
blunting direct comparison.

     In its own way, this relaxed date was as successful as the Paris
session four months earlier. It never became as well known, perhaps because the records were never as widely distributed, nor the reissues as
extensive.

[58]   March 7, 1938   Paris
          BENNY CARTER AND HIS ORCHESTRA

Carter (tp, as, arr, comp) Fletcher Allen (as) Bertie King (ts, cl) Alix Combelle (ts) Yorke De Souza (p) Django Reinhardt (g) Len Harrison (b) Robert
Montmarche (d)

I'M COMING VIRGINIA   (23as) arr   OSW 4-1
78: SWING 20 LP: ODEON CLP1907, PATHE
(F) C 054-16007, PRESTIGE 7633, TIME-LIFE
STL-J10, WORLD RECORDS SM645

FAREWELL BLUES   (32as[2nd solo; 1st is Allen]) arr   OSW 5-1
78: SWING 36 LP: PATHE CHTX240-551, ODEON
CLP1907, PATHE (F) C 054-16007, PRESTIGE 7633,
WORLD RECORDS SM645

BLUE LIGHT BLUES   (12tp with ensemble)(24tp with   OSW 6-1
        ensemble) comp
78: SWING 20 LP: ODEON CLP1907, PATHE

(F) C 054-16008, PRESTIGE 7633, WORLD
RECORDS SM646

> NOTE: "Blue Light Blues" as "Playin' The Blues" on Swing 20.

*   *   *

Carter's final European recordings were again for the Delaunay-Panassié
Swing label and featured the same instrumentation as the famous April 1937
date which inaugurated the label.   Two of the musicians from that session,
Combelle and Reinhardt, were present along with a couple from Carter's
Scheveningen band.

'I'm Coming Virginia" takes full advantage of the reed section from
the start with a ravishing ensemble chorus, which embellishes but never
obscures the melody.   The last chorus is an even more daring reed show.
After modulating from F to E-flat, the sax quartet, spurred on by Django's
fills, cascades through Carter's masterful reworking of the theme.

The other two tunes are less elaborate, concentrating on the solos.

---

[59]   July 21, 1938   New York
          LIONEL HAMPTON AND HIS ORCHESTRA

Carter (cl, as, arr, comp) Harry James (tp) Dave Matthews (as) Herschel
Evans, Babe Russin (ts) Billy Kyle (p) John Kirby (b) Jo Jones (d) Lionel
Hampton (vib, v)

I'M IN THE MOOD FOR SWING (32as) arr, comp   024065-1
78:   VICTOR 26011 LP: CAMDEN CAL402,
RCA (F) 730.641, BLUEBIRD AXM6-5536, TIME-
LIFE STL-J10, RCA (F) PM42406

SHOE SHINER'S DRAG (12as)(12cl) arr   024066-1
78:   VICTOR 26011 LP: CAMDEN CAL402, RCA
(F) 730.641, BLUEBIRD AXM6-5536, TIME-LIFE
STL-J10

ANY TIME AT ALL v-LH (e) arr   024067-1
78:   VICTOR 26039 LP: CAMDEN CAL517, RCA
(F) 741.077, BLUEBIRD AXM6-5536

MUSKRAT RAMBLE (16cl) arr   024068-1
78:   VICTOR 26017 LP: CAMDEN CAL402, RCA
(F) 730.641, BLUEBIRD AXM6-5536

*   *   *

By 1938 Carter felt that he needed a change musically.   Although satisfied
with many of his recordings of the preceding two years, he realized that he
had reached the limit of the talents available abroad.

His desire to hear his music performed by top American jazzmen
was soon gratified.   Within two months of his return to the United States,
he took part in one of Lionel Hampton's all-star dates for Victor and the
first tune recorded was Carter's composition 'I'm In The Mood For Swing, "
which he had recorded in England using a similar arrangement.   The con-

trast between the two recordings, particularly in the rhythm sections, is
startling.   Carter's own solo is a marvel; he makes excellent use of space,
allowing each idea to be absorbed.   During the transition from the bridge
to the final eight bars of his solo, Carter lays out almost two full measures, creating a sense of anticipation.   His ornate reentry draws a faintly
audible exclamation from someone in the studio.

In "Shoe Shiner's Drag, " which Hampton suggested he arrange, Carter incorporates elements of Jelly Roll Morton's classic recording, without
re-creating it.   Morton's blues figure opens and closes the piece which
features solos by Carter on alto, James, and Evans.   Carter reappears,
playing the clarinet chorus allotted to Omer Simeon on Morton's recording,
followed by Hampton's vibes and a brief spot by Russin.   The bass line
carried by the tuba on the Morton recording is played here by the horns
behind Carter's clarinet and Hampton's vibraphone solo.

In Hampton's vocal feature, "Anytime At All, " Carter has written
some lovely reed figures for the opening chorus.

"Muskrat Ramble" resembles "Shoe Shiner's Drag" in many ways:
a New Orleans standard given a modern treatment.

| [60] | July 29, 1938   New York |
| | TEDDY WILSON AND HIS ORCHESTRA |

Carter (as) Jonah Jones (tp) Ben Webster (ts) Teddy Wilson (p) John Kirby
(b) Cozy Cole (d) Nan Wynn (v)

NOW IT CAN BE TOLD   v-NW (32as)   23305-1
78: BRUNSWICK 8199   LP: TAX (SW) M-8032

LAUGH AND CALL IT LOVE   v-NW (4as)(8as)   23306-2
78: BRUNSWICK 8207   LP: TAX (SW) M-8032

ON THE BUMPY ROAD TO LOVE   v-NW (32as)   23307-1
78: BRUNSWICK 8207   LP: TAX (SW) M-8032,
TIME-LIFE STL-J10

A-TISKET, A-TASKET   v-NW (32as)   23308-1
78: BRUNSWICK 8199   LP: TAX (SW) M-8032

                                *   *   *

The first of Carter's several appearances on Teddy Wilson's all-star dates
for Brunswick yielded several excellent, and often overlooked, alto solos,
particularly those on the last two titles.   British critic Benny Green once
wrote that Carter's perfectly paced, flowing effort on the unlikely title
"Bumpy Road" managed to convince him that the "forgotten jingle ... was
the ideal jazz vehicle. "   (Liner notes to Pablo 2310-732.)

| [61] | October 31, 1938   New York |
| | TEDDY WILSON AND HIS ORCHESTRA |

Carter (as, arr) Harry James (tp) Benny Morton (tb) Edgar Sampson (as)
Lester Young, Herschel Evans (ts) Teddy Wilson (p) Al Casey (g) Walter
Page (b) Jo Jones (d) Billie Holiday (v)

EVERYBODY'S LAUGHING   v-BH (e)   23642-1
78: BRUNSWICK 8259   LP: SONY (J) SOPH67,
COLUMBIA JG34840

HERE IT IS TOMORROW AGAIN   v-BH (e) arr   23643-1
78: BRUNSWICK 8259   LP: SONY (J) SOPH67,
COLUMBIA JG34840

---

[62]   November 9, 1938   New York
          TEDDY WILSON AND HIS ORCHESTRA

Carter (as, arr) Harry James (tp) Benny Morton (tb) Edgar Sampson (as)
Lester Young, Herschel Evans (ts) Teddy Wilson (p) Al Casey (g) Walter
Page (b) Jo Jones (d) Billie Holiday (v)

SAY IT WITH A KISS   v-BH (e) arr   23687-1
78: BRUNSWICK 8270   LP: COLUMBIA CL2427,
COLUMBIA KG32127, SONY (J) SOPH67, COLUMBIA
JG34840

APRIL IN MY HEART   v-BH (20as) arr   23688-1
78: BRUNSWICK 8265   LP: RARETONE (I)
RTR24011 SONY (J) SOPH67

APRIL IN MY HEART   v-BH arr   23688-2
78: UNISSUED-TEST EXISTS

I'LL NEVER FAIL YOU   v-BH (e) arr   23689-1
78: BRUNSWICK 8265   LP: RARETONE (I)
RTR24011, SONY (J) SOPH67

THEY SAY   v-BH (12as) arr   23690-1
78: BRUNSWICK 8270   LP: TIME-LIFE STL-
J10, SONY (J) SOPH67, TWO FLAT DISC 5006

THEY SAY   v-BH (12as) arr   23690-2
78: UNISSUED   LP: COLUMBIA CL2427,
COLUMBIA KG32127, SONY (J) SOPH67

*   *   *

These two sessions [61, 62] were Carter's first recordings with Billie
Holiday, whom he had known for four or five years. While most of the
Wilson-Holiday sessions were impromptu affairs, for these Wilson asked
Carter to provide arrangements.

    For the personnel Wilson drew heavily on the Count Basie band,
which Billie had left in February of that year. Carter's arrangements are
good examples of his ability to provide a vocalist with tasteful accompaniment which is unobtrusive without being bland. The reed figures which
cushion the vocal in "They Say" are unmistakably Carter's, but do not de-
tract from the lyric. Singers to the present day are aware of Carter's
knack. In a 1976 Down Beat blindfold test Sarah Vaughan listened to a
Carter arrangement for pop singer Maria Muldaur. She was unable to
identify the vocalist, but instantly spotted the arrangement as Carter's.

    Carter remembers that recording with Billie Holiday was never
"just another gig, " but rather a special musical occasion marked by the

empathy that existed between the players and the vocalist who truly appreciated and understood their work.

---

[63]	November 22, 1938 New York
	BLUE LU BARKER ACC. BY DANNY BARKER'S FLY CATS

Carter (tp) Buster Bailey (cl) Sam Price (p) Danny Barker (g) Wellman Braud (b) Blue Lu Barker (v)

I FEEL LIKE LYING IN ANOTHER WOMAN'S   64767-
HUSBAND'S ARMS   v-BLB
78:   UNISSUED

GIVE ME SOME MONEY   v-BLB   64768-
78:   UNISSUED

I GOT WAYS LIKE THE DEVIL   v-BLB (12tp acc)   64769-
        (12tp)+(24tp acc)
78:   DECCA 7560   LP: JAZZ ARCHIVES JA47

THAT MADE HIM MAD   v-BLB (4tp intro)+(16tp   64770-A
        acc)
78:   DECCA 7538   LP: JAZZ ARCHIVES JA47

                        *   *   *

Rust lists Carter as the trumpeter on a previous Blue Lu Barker date (6-11-38) but it is definitely not Carter; it is probably Red Allen. This confusion with Red Allen is also apparent on the Jazz Archives LP; although it is entitled Red Allen and the Blues Singers vol. 2 it contains these two Blue Lu Barker items on which Carter is the trumpeter.

---

[64]	January 20, 1939 New York
	NAT GONELLA WITH JOHN KIRBY'S ORCHESTRA

Carter (as) Nat Gonella (tp, v) Buster Bailey (cl) Billy Kyle (p) Brick Fleagle (g) John Kirby (b) Jack Maisel (d)

YOU MUST HAVE BEEN A BEAUTIFUL BABY   64909-A
        v-NG (20as)
78:   PARLOPHONE F-1353 LP: HISTORIA (G)
H639, WORLD RECORDS (E) SH369

JUST A KID NAMED JOE   v-NG (as intro)(8as)   64910-A
78:   PARLOPHONE F-1376 LP: HISTORIA (G)
H639, WORLD RECORDS (E) SH369

JEEPERS CREEPERS   v-NG (16as)   64911-A
78:   PARLOPHONE F-1376 LP: HISTORIA (G)
H639, WORLD RECORDS (E) SH369

I MUST SEE ANNIE TONIGHT   v-NG (4+4as   64912-A
        [horns trade])(4+8as[horns trade])
78:   PARLOPHONE F-1353 LP: HISTORIA (G)
H639, WORLD RECORDS (E) SH369

                        *   *   *

The British trumpeter and vocalist led this session of top American jazzmen while on a visit to New York. Carter's solo on the first title is quite
"modern. " He discards the melody entirely and, using a restrained attack,
plays long lines incorporating a dazzling series of runs halfway into his
chorus.

---

[65]   January 30, 1939 New York
            TEDDY WILSON AND HIS ORCHESTRA

Carter (as, cl) Roy Eldridge (tp) Ernie Powell (ts) Teddy Wilson (p) Danny
Barker (g) Milt Hinton (b) Cozy Cole (d) Billie Holiday (v)

WHAT SHALL I SAY v-BH (4as intro)(32cl acc)   24044-1
78: BRUNSWICK 8314 LP: SONY (J) SOPH68,
TWO FLAT DISC 5007

IT'S EASY TO BLAME THE WEATHER v-BH   24045-1
      (16cl)(8as)(2as break)
78: BRUNSWICK 8314 LP: SONY (J) SOPH68,
TWO FLAT DISC 5007

IT'S EASY TO BLAME THE WEATHER v-BH   24045-2
78: UNISSUED-TEST EXISTS

MORE THAN YOU KNOW v-BH (16as)   24046-1
78: BRUNSWICK 8319 LP: RARETONE (I)
RTR24011, SONY (J) SOPH68

MORE THAN YOU KNOW v-BH (16as)   24046-2
78: UNISSUED LP: COLUMBIA CL2428,
COLUMBIA KG32127, SMITHSONIAN P13708

SUGAR v-BH (16+8as)   24047-1
78: BRUNSWICK 8319 LP: FOLKWAYS FJ2804,
FOLKWAYS FP59, COLUMBIA CL2428, COLUM-
BIA KG32127, SONY (J) SOPH67

                              *   *   *

Although Carter does not arrange, he plays a greater role as a soloist here
than on the previous dates with Billie Holiday. The first two titles have
some lovely Carter clarinet accompaniment, with his alto contributing
melodic solos to "More Than You Know" and "Sugar. "

---

[66]   April 17, 1939 New York Airchecks, Savoy Ballroom
            BENNY CARTER AND HIS ORCHESTRA

Carter (as, tp, arr, comp) Collective Personnel for Savoy Ballroom Airchecks:
Lincoln Mills, Louis Bacon, Joe Thomas, Archie Johnson, Bobby Woodlen
(tp) Tyree Glenn (tb, vib) Vic Dickenson, Jimmy Archey (tb) Jimmy Powell,
Carl Frye (as) Ernie Powell, Castor McCord (ts) Sammy Davis, Eddie Heywood (p) Ulysses Livingston, Arnold Adams (g) Hayes Alvis (b) Henry Morrison, Ted Fields, Keg Purnell (d)

MELANCHOLY LULLABY (16as)+(8as with ensemble)+
      (8as) arr, comp

I'M COMING VIRGINIA   (24as) arr

GIN AND JIVE   (32as) arr, comp

MORE THAN YOU KNOW   (32tp)(8tp) arr

HONEYSUCKLE ROSE (incomplete)   (32as[inter-
        rupted by signoff]) arr

>   NOTE: The personnel given above is a general one for the period
>   of the band's residencies at the Savoy in 1939. It covers the air-
>   checks recorded on April 22, April 29, May 6, May 8, May 13,
>   May 20, May 27, June 10, June 12, June 17, July 24, October 9,
>   October 14, October 23 and October 28. The personnel is not re-
>   peated for each session; only pertinent vocalist and arranger credits
>   are noted.

*   *   *

A few months after his return from Europe, Carter put together an orchestra of top musicians. He fondly remembers them as "terrific guys, fine
musicians and great friends--I loved every one of them. There was no
drinking, no drugs and no trouble."

        The band spent long periods during 1939 and 1940 in residence at the
Savoy Ballroom in Harlem. These airchecks from that legendary venue
are the earliest recorded examples of the orchestra, antedating its first
commercial sides by two months.

        Carter wrote "Melancholy Lullaby" specifically as a theme song, and
used it to open many of his appearances and broadcasts into the mid-forties.
Leonard Feather has called the melody "the loveliest of all the big band
themes." It was also admired by some of the top bandleaders; Glenn
Miller, Jimmy Dorsey, Gene Krupa and Artie Shaw all recorded or played
it over the air.

        The opening and closing sax ensemble passages of "I'm Coming Vir-
ginia" are based on the arrangement recorded by Carter in Paris on March
7, 1938.

        "Gin And Jive" also derives from his European period; this arrange-
ment was first recorded in London in June 1936.

        Carter's commercial recording of "More Than You Know" (Novem-
ber 1, 1939) was to become one of his most celebrated trumpet solos. In
this earlier version, some of the ideas which went into that classic are already apparent.

---

[67]   April 20, 1939 New York
          LEONARD FEATHER'S ALL STAR JAM BAND

Carter (tp, as) Bobby Hackett (cornet, g) Pete Brown (as, tp) Joe Marsala (cl)
Billy Kyle (p) Hayes Alvis (b) Cozy Cole (d)

TWELVE BAR STAMPEDE   (12tp)(24as)   65437-A
78: DECCA 18111 LP: BRUNSWICK (G) 87527,
MCA (F) 510.071, TIME-LIFE STL-J10, MCA 1324

FEATHER BED LAMENT   (12tp)   65438-A
78: DECCA 18111 LP: BRUNSWICK (G) 87527,
MCA (F) 510.071, MCA 1324

MEN OF HARLEM   (16tp)(16as)   65439-A
78: DECCA 18118 LP: BRUNSWICK (G) 87527,
MCA (F) 510.071, TIME-LIFE STL-J10, MCA 1324

OCEAN MOTION   (32tp)   65440-A
78: DECCA 18118 LP: BRUNSWICK (G) 87527,
MCA (F) 510.071, STASH ST104, MCA 1324

> NOTE: On MCA (F) 510.071 and MCA 1324 LPs titles for "Men
> Of Harlem" and "Ocean Motion" are reversed.

* * *

Leonard Feather, who had played an important role in Carter's British
recordings, was by now settled in the United States. This date was his
idea, and he wrote the tunes as well.

The personnel is a discographer's nightmare because of the multi-
instrumental talents of these versatile artists. Carter plays trumpet and
alto which is, of course, not unusual for him. Bobby Hackett plays his
lyrical cornet, but he also plays guitar, which was his original instrument.
Pete Brown, a truly original alto stylist, is heard here on trumpet as well.

This was Carter's only session with Brown, Marsala and Hackett.
On this date Brown set down some of his greatest playing on record. His
infectious bounce on alto seems to have rubbed off on Carter, especially in
"Twelve Bar Stampede." The tune ends with Carter, Hackett and Brown
riffing on brass.

In "Men Of Harlem," a jaunty melody which Feather based on the
traditional Welsh air "Men Of Harlech," Carter and Brown both solo on alto
and trumpet. Carter's alto statement is almost perfectly symmetrical in
structure, with its deliberately placed highest note (high F, concert A-flat)
occurring exactly midway. In a rare appearance on trumpet, Brown conveys
the same irrepressible jump feeling that he does on alto.

The solo sequence for this session is as follows: "Twelve Bar
Stampede"--Carter (tp), Brown (as), Kyle (p), Marsala (cl), Carter (as),
Hackett (cornet), Marsala (cl); "Feather Bed Lament"--Brown (as), Kyle
(p), Marsala (cl), Carter (tp), Marsala (cl); "Men Of Harlem"--Brown (as),
Carter (tp), Marsala (cl), Kyle (p), Carter (as), Brown (tp); "Ocean Mo-
tion"--Kyle (p), Marsala (cl), Brown (as), Carter (tp).

---

[68]   April 22, 1939 New York Airchecks, Savoy Ballroom
         BENNY CARTER AND HIS ORCHESTRA

Carter (as, tp, cl, arr, comp) Louis Bacon (v) for Collective Personnel for the
Period See 4/17/39.

MELANCHOLY LULLABY   (16as)+(8as with ensemble)+
       (8as) arr, comp

TEA FOR TWO   (16as) (4as with ensemble) arr

SCANDAL IN A FLAT   (16as) arr, comp

I AIN'T GOT NOBODY   (16as) arr

I'M IN THE MOOD FOR SWING   (32as)(16tp) arr, comp

BETWEEN THE DEVIL AND THE DEEP BLUE SEA
      v-LB (8tp) arr

HONEYSUCKLE ROSE   (32as)(32tp)(8cl arr

STAR DUST   (32tp)(20tp+coda) arr

MELANCHOLY LULLABY (incomplete)   (16as)+(8as
      with ensemble)+(8as) arr, comp

                          *   *   *

For his repertoire, Carter continues to mix material he had recorded in
Europe with newer scores.   Except for adaptations from earlier arrangements, like "Stardust," the distinctive saxophone ensemble passages which
marked Carter's past work are strangely absent during this period.   Carter
offers two explanations for this apparent change in his arranging style.
First, he was forced to put together a book for his new band rather quickly
and could not afford the time required to write and rehearse complex saxophone choruses.   Second, he felt at the time that his band might have wider
popular appeal without them.   Such figures began to reappear more consistently after 1940.

[69]	April 25, 1939 New York
	JERRY KRUGER AND HER ORCHESTRA

Carter (tp, arr) Ernie Powell (ts) Eddie Heywood (p) Hayes Alvis (b) Henry
Morrison (d) Jerry Kruger (v)

RAIN, RAIN, GO AWAY v-JK (8tp) arr   WM-1021-A
78: VOCALION 4927 LP: CBS (F) 65384

SUMMERTIME v-JK (16tp) arr   WM-1022-A
78: VOCALION 4927 LP: CBS (F) 65384,
NOSTALGIA BOOK CLUB 1005

                          *   *   *

Rust lists Buck Clayton (tp) and Lester Young (ts) but George Simon (writing at the time under the pseudonym Gordon Wright, Metronome, August
1939, p. 24) reports Carter and Ernie Powell (of Carter's band) on those
instruments.   Carter confirms this contemporary review, adding that the
arrangements were likely his and that the drummer was probably Henry
Morrison, also in his band then.

[70]	April 29, 1939 New York Airchecks, Savoy Ballroom
	BENNY CARTER AND HIS ORCHESTRA

Carter (tp, cl, as) for Collective Personnel for the Period See 4/17/39
Mercedes Carter (v) Andy Gibson (arr)

WHEN IRISH EYES ARE SMILING   arr-AG (32tp)

WE'VE COME A LONG WAY TOGETHER   v-MC (8cl)

BLUE SKIES   (32as)(8as with ensemble)

---

[71]   May 6, 1939   New York   Airchecks, Savoy Ballroom
          BENNY CARTER AND HIS ORCHESTRA

Carter (as, cl, arr, comp) for Collective Personnel for the Period See 4/17/39 Mercedes Carter (v)

MELANCHOLY LULLABY   (16as)+(8as with ensemble)+
        (8as) arr, comp

I'M COMING VIRGINIA   v-MC (24as) arr

HAVE MERCY   v-MC (2as break)(18+9as)

SUGARFOOT STOMP (incomplete)   (24cl)(12as[inter-
        rupted by signoff])

SOLID MAMA   (e)

---

[72]   May 8, 1939   New York   Airchecks, Savoy Ballroom
          BENNY CARTER AND HIS ORCHESTRA

Carter (as) for Collective Personnel for the Period See 4/17/39 Mercedes Carter (v) Phil Lang (arr)

HAVE MERCY   v-MC (2as break)(18+9as)

PLYMOUTH ROCK   arr-PL (e)

---

[73]   May 13, 1939   New York   Airchecks, Savoy Ballroom
          BENNY CARTER AND HIS ORCHESTRA

Carter (as, tp, arr, comp) for Collective Personnel for the Period See 4/17/39 Mercedes Carter (v)

THE LADY'S IN LOVE WITH YOU   v-MC (4as)(16as)

A HOME IN THE CLOUDS   v-MC (16tp)(8tp)(8tp)
        arr, comp

I CRIED FOR YOU   v-MC (16tp)(8tp) arr

PATTY CAKE   v-MC (e) arr

                    *   *   *

This is one of two airchecks by Carter of "A Home in The Clouds, " the tune that was first recorded by Benny Goodman (February 9, 1939, with a vocal by Martha Tilton). The composer credits for this tune are somewhat vague, with Carter's name mysteriously omitted from many issues.

[74]   May 20, 1939 New York Airchecks, Savoy Ballroom
          BENNY CARTER AND HIS ORCHESTRA

Carter (as, cl, arr, comp) for Collective Personnel for the Period See 4/17/
39 Mercedes Carter (v)

LIEBESTRAUM   (e)
LP: TAX (SW) M-8004, HOT 'N SWEET (F)
HOL6426

MY HEART HAS WINGS   v-MC (16as) arr
LP: TAX (SW) M-8004, HOT 'N SWEET (F)
HOL6426

LADY BE GOOD   (32as) arr
LP: TAX (SW) M-8004, HOT 'N SWEET (F)
HOL6426

BIG WIG IN THE WIGWAM   v-MC (4+16+8cl)
LP: TAX (SW) M-8004, HOT 'N SWEET (F)
HOL6426

MELANCHOLY LULLABY (incomplete) (16as)+
          (8as with ensemble)+(8as [interrupted by signoff])
LP: TAX (SW) M-8004, HOT 'N SWEET (F)
HOL6426

[75]   May 27, 1939 New York Airchecks, Savoy Ballroom
          BENNY CARTER AND HIS ORCHESTRA

Carter (as, arr) for Collective Personnel for the Period See 4/17/39 Mercedes Carter (v)

HOW STRANGE   v-MC (16as) arr

TEA FOR TWO   v-MC (2as)(16as)(4as) arr

[76]   June 10, 1939 New York Airchecks, Savoy Ballroom
          BENNY CARTER AND HIS ORCHESTRA

Carter (as, tp, arr) for Collective Personnel for the Period See 4/17/39

BLUE EVENING   (32as)+(32as[Carter covers when
          vocalist - probably Mercedes Carter - misses cue]) arr

BYE BYE BLUES   (12+12tp)

[77]   June 12, 1939 New York Aircheck, Savoy Ballroom /
          BENNY CARTER AND HIS ORCHESTRA

Carter (as) for Collective Personnel for the Period See 4/17/39

CLEMENTINE   (24as)

[78]	June 17, 1939 New York Aircheck, Savoy Ballroom

BENNY CARTER AND HIS ORCHESTRA

Carter (tp) for Collective Personnel for the Period See 4/17/39

STRANGE ENCHANTMENT   (16+8tp)

[79]	June 29, 1939 New York

BENNY CARTER AND HIS ORCHESTRA

Carter (as, arr, comp) Joe Thomas, Lincoln Mills, Bobby Woodlen (tp)
Jimmy Archey, Vic Dickenson (tb) Tyree Glenn (tb, vib) Jimmy Powell,
Carl Frye (as) Ernie Powell, Castor McCord (ts) Eddie Heywood (p)
Ulysses Livingston (g) Hayes Alvis (b) Henry Morrison (d) Phil Lang (arr)

PLYMOUTH ROCK arr-PL (12as)   WM-1046-A
78: VOCALION 4984 LP: TAX (SW) M-8004

SAVOY STAMPEDE   (32as) arr, comp   WM-1047-A
78: VOCALION 5112 LP: EPIC LG3127, TAX
(SW) M-8004

MELANCHOLY LULLABY   (16as)+(8as with ensemble)   WM-1048-A
     (8as) arr, comp
78: VOCALION 4984 LP: TAX (SW) M-8004,
TIME-LIFE STL-J10

SCANDAL IN A FLAT   (4+16as) arr, comp   WM-1049-A
78: VOCALION 5112 LP: TAX (SW) M-8004

                              *   *   *

For his new band's first commercial recording session, Carter chose four
tunes from his Savoy repertoire and for which there also exist earlier airchecks.

        "Savoy Stampede" is the new title for "Gin And Jive," which he
recorded in England.   "Scandal In A Flat" also premiered in England, but
the arrangement differs from the 1936 version, as well as from that used
on the three Savoy airchecks.

        The Carter band theme, "Melancholy Lullaby," features Carter play-
ing the melody straight (as befits a "signature") as well as Eddie Heywood
and Tyree Glenn.

[80]	July 24, 1939 New York Airchecks, Savoy Ballroom

BENNY CARTER AND HIS ORCHESTRA

Carter (as, tp, cl, arr, comp) for Collective Personnel for the Period See
4/17/39 Dell St. John (v) Phil Lang (arr)

MELANCHOLY LULLABY (incomplete)   (16as)+(8as
     with ensemble)+(8as[interrupted by signoff])
     arr, comp

PLYMOUTH ROCK arr-PL (12as)

A HOME IN THE CLOUDS v-DSJ (16tp)(8tp)(8tp)
    arr, comp

LADY BE GOOD (16as with ensemble)+(8as)+(8as
    with ensemble) arr

SCANDAL IN A FLAT (16as) arr, comp

I'M IN THE MOOD FOR SWING (32as)(16tp)
    arr, comp

BLUE EVENING v-DSJ (32as) arr

HONEYSUCKLE ROSE (32as)(8cl) arr

BYE BYE BLUES (32tp with ensemble)

MELANCHOLY LULLABY (incomplete) (8as)+(8as
    with ensemble)+(8as[interrupted by signoff])
    arr, comp

---

[81]   August 15, 1939 New York
     ETHEL WATERS ACCOM. BY EDDIE MALLORY & HIS
     ORCHESTRA

Carter (as) Eddie Mallory (tp) Tyree Glenn (tb, vib) Castor McCord (cl, ts)
Reginald Beane (p) Danny Barker (g) Milt Hinton (b) Ethel Waters (v)

BREAD AND GRAVY v-EW (e)   041552
78: BLUEBIRD B-10415 LP: RCA (F) 741. 067

DOWN IN MY SOUL v-EW (e)   041553
78: BLUEBIRD B-11284 LP: RCA (F) 741. 067

GEORGIA ON MY MIND v-EW (e)   041554
78: BLUEBIRD B-11028 LP: RCA (F) 741. 067

STOP MYSELF FROM WORRYIN' OVER YOU v-EW (e)   041555
78: BLUEBIRD B-11284 LP: RCA (F) 741. 067

OLD MAN HARLEM v-EW (e)   041556
78: BLUEBIRD B-11028 LP: RCA (F) 741. 067

PUSH OUT v-EW with chorus by the band (28as)   041557
78: BLUEBIRD B-10415 LP: RCA (F) 741. 067,
RCA (F) PM42406

---

[82]   August 31, 1939 New York
     BENNY CARTER AND HIS ORCHESTRA

Carter (as, cl, arr, comp) Joe Thomas, Lincoln Mills, Eddie Mullens (tp)
Jimmy Archey, Vic Dickenson, Tyree Glenn (tb) Jimmy Powell, Carl Frye
(as) Ernie Powell, Castor McCord (ts) Eddie Heywood (p) Ulysses Livingston (g) Hayes Alvis (b) Henry Morrison (d) Dell St. John (v)

WHEN LIGHTS ARE LOW v-DSJ (16as with   WM-1069-A

ensemble)+(8as) arr, comp
78:   UNISSUED LP: COLUMBIA CL2162

THE FABLE OF A FOOL   (32as)(4as) arr, comp   WM-1070-A
78:   VOCALION 5294 LP: TAX (SW) M-8031

RIFF ROMP   (16+8as)(8cl) arr, comp   WM-1071-A
78:   VOCALION 5294 LP: TAX (SW) M-8031,
TIME-LIFE STL-J10

*   *   *

Carter's second Vocalion session yielded his first U.S. recording of his
"When Lights Are Low" for which he provided a lively new arrangement.
Oddly enough, judging from the recorded evidence, Carter never played this
melody over the air from the Savoy, although there are many airchecks of
far less worthy tunes.   "I knew lots of song pluggers, of course, and they
came to the Savoy regularly.   I would play tunes to help a friend and try
for a hit, but I should also have done more of what other leaders did, promote my own tunes. "   "When Lights Are Low" was not helped by this version, however, which was not issued on 78.

"Fable Of A Fool" was mistakenly listed on the original label as
"The Favor Of A Fool" and appears that way on subsequent issues and in
reference sources.

The final Carter original of the date is an uptempo flag waver "Riff
Romp, " which effectively juxtaposes brass and reed figures, and includes
a trombone choir on the bridge of the third chorus.   Another interesting
feature of Carter's writing for brass is the difficult but perfectly executed
ascending run by the trumpets which caps this performance.

[83]	September 11, 1939 New York
	LIONEL HAMPTON AND HIS ORCHESTRA

Carter (as, arr, comp) Dizzy Gillespie (tp) Coleman Hawkins, Ben Webster,
Chu Berry (ts) Clyde Hart (p) Charlie Christian (g) Milt Hinton (b) Cozy
Cole (d) Lionel Hampton (vib, v)

WHEN LIGHTS ARE LOW   (8as) arr, comp   041406-1
78:   VICTOR 26371   LP: RCA (F) 731. 048,
SMITHSONIAN COLLECTION OF CLASSIC JAZZ,
BLUEBIRD AXM6-5536, RCA (F) PM42417

WHEN LIGHTS ARE LOW   (8as) arr, comp   041406-2
78:   UNISSUED LP: BLUEBIRD AXM6-5536,
RCA (F) PM42406, RCA (F) PM42417

ONE SWEET LETTER FROM YOU v-LH (e) arr   041407-1
78:   VICTOR 26393 LP: RCA CAMDEN CAL517,
RCA (F) 731. 048, BLUEBIRD AXM6-5536, RCA
(F) PM42417

HOT MALLETS   (8as)   041408-1
78:   VICTOR 26371 LP: RCA LPM2318, RCA
CAMDEN CAL517, RCA (F) 731. 048, BLUEBIRD
AXM6-5536, RCA (F) PM42417

EARLY SESSION HOP   (8as) arr   041409-1
78:   VICTOR 26393   LP: RCA LPV501, RCA
(F) 731.048, BLUEBIRD AXM6-5536, RCA (F)
PM42417, TIME-LIFE STL-J21

>   NOTE: On RCA LPM2318 track listed as "When Lights Are Low"
>   is actually "Hot Mallets."

                          *   *   *

"When Lights Are Low" finally received its due with this all-star recording, Carter's first with Dizzy Gillespie, and a rare summit meeting of the
three leading tenor voices of the day.

     The tenor soloist on "When Lights Are Low" is Hawkins.   He
launches his solo on take 1 with a 4-bar break, whereas take 2 has a brief
ensemble introduction.   Hampton is even more imaginative on the second
take, which was probably rejected because of some audible fluffs by Gillespie in the final ensemble.   In his autobiography, Gillespie recalls the date,
for which he believes he got the call because the "name" trumpet players
were all on the road.   "Milt Hinton and Cozy Cole probably told Hamp
there's a new trumpet player in Cab's band ... they brought me down to
this record date, and talk about giants, man, this was superroyalty ...
man, I was so scared ... all them kings were in there, and I was just a
young dude."   (Gillespie, p. 102.)

     The rhythmic accompaniment of "When Lights Are Low" is singled
out by André Hodeir as "the apex of the ascending curve that symbolizes
the evolution of swing."   (Jazz: Its Evolution And Essence, New York,
1961, pp. 215-17.)

     (For an analysis and transcription of Carter's solo on "When Lights
Are Low" see chapter 3.)

     Gillespie, apparently recovered from his bout of nerves, opens "Hot
Mallets," with a solo which he, and several other musicians on the date,
believe was a departure for him and a harbinger of things to come.   Hampton describes it as "the first time I heard be-bop played on a trumpet."
(Gillespie, To Be Or Not To Bop, p. 105.)   Carter's fluid alto solo occurs
on the bridge of Gillespie's chorus.

---

[84]   September 22, 1939 New York
          ETHEL WATERS ACC. BY EDDIE MALLORY AND HIS
          ORCHESTRA

Carter (as) Eddie Mallory (tp) Garvin Bushell (cl) Reginald Beane (p)
Charles Turner (b) Ethel Waters (v)

BABY, WHAT ELSE CAN I DO   v-EW (e)   042717
78: BLUEBIRD B-10517   LP: RCA (F) 741.067

I JUST GOT A LETTER   v-EW (16as)   042718
78: BLUEBIRD B-10517   LP: RCA (F) 741.067,
RCA (F) 42406

---

[85]   October 9, 1939 New York   Airchecks, Savoy Ballroom
          BENNY CARTER AND HIS ORCHESTRA

Carter (as, tp, arr, comp) for Collective Personnel for the Period See 4/17/
39 Dell St. John (v)

<u>MELANCHOLY LULLABY</u>   (16as)+(8as with ensemble)+
    (8as) arr, comp

<u>SAVOY STAMPEDE</u>   (32as)(16tp [last chorus]) arr, comp

<u>SCANDAL IN A FLAT</u>   (4+16as) arr, comp

<u>RUSSIAN LULLABY</u> (16as)

<u>THERE'S ONLY ONE IN LOVE</u> v-DSJ (incomplete) (e)

<u>BYE BYE BLUES</u> (incomplete) (32tp with ensemble)

---

[86]   October 14, 1939 New York Airchecks, Savoy Ballroom
           BENNY CARTER AND HIS ORCHESTRA

Carter (as, tp, arr, comp) for Collective Personnel for the Period See 4/17/
39 Dell St. John (v) Fred Norman (arr) Phil Lang (arr)

<u>MELANCHOLY LULLABY</u>   (16as)+(8as with ensemble)+
    (8as) arr, comp

<u>CHINA BOY</u> probably arr-FN (32as)

<u>IT'S FUNNY TO EVERYONE BUT ME</u> v-DSJ (16as)

<u>PLYMOUTH ROCK</u> arr-PL (12as)

<u>I'LL SEE YOU IN MY DREAMS</u>   (32tp)

<u>WHAT'S NEW</u> v-DSJ (e) arr

<u>STRANGE ENCHANTMENT</u>   (16+8tp)

<u>LAST NIGHT</u> v-DSJ (e)

<u>RIFF ROMP</u>   (32as) arr, comp

<u>MELANCHOLY LULLABY</u> (incomplete) (16as)+(8as
      with ensemble)+(8as [interrupted by signoff])
         arr, comp

---

[87]   October 23, 1939 New York Airchecks, Savoy Ballroom
           BENNY CARTER AND HIS ORCHESTRA

Carter (as, arr) for Collective Personnel for the Period See 4/17/39 Dell
St. John (v) Fred Norman (arr)

<u>BLUE ORCHIDS</u>   (32as)(8as with ensemble) arr

<u>CHINA BOY</u> probably arr: FN (32as)

<u>WHAT'S NEW</u> v-DSJ (e) arr

[88]	October 28, 1939 New York Airchecks, Savoy Ballroom
	BENNY CARTER AND HIS ORCHESTRA

Carter (as, arr) for Collective Personnel for the Period See 4/17/39 Dell St. John, Roy Felton (v)

LILACS IN THE RAIN v-DSJ (16as) arr

VAGABOND DREAMS v-RF (20as) arr

[89]	November 1, 1939 New York
	BENNY CARTER AND HIS ORCHESTRA

Carter (tp, as, arr, comp) Irving Randolph, Lincoln Mills, Joe Thomas, Eddie Mullens (tp) Jimmy Archey, Vic Dickenson (tb) Tyree Glenn (tb, vib) Jimmy Powell, Carl Frye (as) Ernie Powell, Sammy Davis (ts) Eddie Heywood (p) Ulysses Livingston (g) Hayes Alvis (b) Keg Purnell (d) Roy Felton (v)

SHUFFLEBUG SHUFFLE   (16as) arr, comp   WM-1109-
78: VOCALION 5508 LP: TAX (SW) M-8004

VAGABOND DREAMS v-RF (20as) arr   WM-1110-1
78: VOCALION 5224 LP: TAX (SW) M-8004

LOVE'S GOT ME DOWN AGAIN v-RF (8as) arr   WM-1111-1
78: VOCALION 5224 LP: TAX (SW) M-8004,
NOSTALGIA BOOK CLUB 1005

MORE THAN YOU KNOW v-RF (32tp)(8tp+coda) arr   WM-1112-1
78: VOCALION 5508 LP: TAX (SW) M-8004,
TIME-LIFE STL-J10

*   *   *

"More Than You Know" is one of Carter's most impressive trumpet features, and is a milestone in his stylistic development on that instrument. He hinted at this treatment in an earlier aircheck version (April 17, 1939). "More Than You Know" can be viewed as exemplifying the second of three stages in his trumpet playing. The earliest, best demonstrated by "Once Upon A Time" (October 10, 1933), was a more direct approach, very much in the Armstrong mold. In "More Than You Know" the phrasing is more ornate, containing intricate filigrees and multinoted runs. He treats the chord changes differently as well, assimilating them with subtle arpeggio figures rather than attacking them head on.

        The solo is in two parts, separated by Roy Felton's vocal. The first chorus again shows Carter's ability to achieve a full tone even at low volume, a skill he credits to the early technical advice of Doc Cheatham. His range has become even more commanding than two or three years before, as shown by the climb to high F to end the piece.

        His tone retains its characteristic delicate vibrato; this tone would change over the next five years before the recording of the third of the Carter trumpet display pieces, "I Surrender Dear" (May 21, 1944).

[90]	December 14, 1939 New York
	VARSITY SEVEN

Carter (tp, as) Danny Polo (cl) Coleman Hawkins (ts) Joe Sullivan (p)
Ulysses Livingston (g, v) Artie Bernstein (b) George Wettling (d) Jeanne
Burns (v)

IT'S TIGHT LIKE THAT v-JB (24tp with ensemble)   US-1158-1
78: VARSITY 8147 LP: STORYVILLE SLP703,
PHOENIX LP3

EASY RIDER v-JB, UL (8tp with ensemble)   US-1159-1
78: VARSITY 8147 LP: STORYVILLE SLP703,
PHOENIX LP3

SCRATCH MY BACK (24as)   US-1160-1
78: VARSITY 8135 LP: STORYVILLE SLP703,
PHOENIX LP3, TIME-LIFE STL-J06

SAVE IT, PRETTY MAMA v-JB (16tp)(4tp with   US-1161-1
     ensemble)+(4tp with ensemble)
78: VARIETY 8135 LP: STORYVILLE SLP703,
PHOENIX LP3

---

[91]   December 21, 1939 New York
          LIONEL HAMPTON AND HIS ORCHESTRA

Carter (tp) Edmond Hall (cl) Coleman Hawkins (ts) Joe Sullivan (p) Freddie
Green (g) Artie Bernstein (b) Zutty Singleton (d) Lionel Hampton (vib)

DINAH (32tp)   046024-1
78: VICTOR 26557 LP: RCA LPM2318, RCA
(F) 731.048, BLUEBIRD AXM6-5536, RCA (F)
PM42417, TIME-LIFE STL-J06

DINAH (32tp)   046024-2
78: UNISSUED LP: RCA LPV501, RCA (F)
741.077, BLUEBIRD AXM6-5536, RCA (F) PM42417

MY BUDDY (e)   046025-1
78: VICTOR 22608 LP: RCA (F) 731.048,
BLUEBIRD AXM6-5536, RCA (F) PM42417

SINGIN' THE BLUES (8tp with ensemble)   046026-1
78: VICTOR 26557 LP: RCA (F) 741.049,
BLUEBIRD AXM6-5536, RCA (F) PM42417

---

[92]   January 3, 1940 New York
          COLEMAN HAWKINS' ALL STAR OCTET

Carter (tp) J. C. Higginbotham (tb) Danny Polo (cl) Coleman Hawkins (ts)
Gene Rodgers (p) Lawrence Lucie (g) Johnny Williams (b) Walter Johnson
(d)

WHEN DAY IS DONE (16tp)(8tp with ensemble)   046156-1
78: BLUEBIRD B-10693 LP: RCA (F) 730.625,
TIME-LIFE STL-J06

THE SHEIK OF ARABY (32tp)(8tp with ensemble)   046157-1

78: BLUEBIRD B-10770 LP: RCA LPV501,
RCA (F) 730.625, QUINTESSENCE JAZZ SERIES
QJ25131, TIME-LIFE STL-J06

MY BLUE HEAVEN (32tp)(8tp with ensemble)   046158-1
78: BLUEBIRD B-10770 LP: RCA LPM1393,
RCA (F) 730.625

BOUNCING WITH BEAN (32tp)(16tp with ensemble)   046159-1
78: BLUEBIRD B-10693 LP: RCA (F) 730.625,
TIME-LIFE STL-J06

---

[93]   January 15, 1940   New York
          VARSITY SEVEN

Carter (tp, comp) Danny Polo (cl) Coleman Hawkins (ts) Joe Sullivan (p)
Ulysses Livingston (g) Artie Shapiro (b) George Wettling (d) Joe Turner (v)

HOW LONG, HOW LONG BLUES v-JT (8tp)   US-1284-1
     (8tp with ensemble)
78: VARSITY 8173 LP: STORYVILLE SLP703,
PHOENIX LP3

SHAKE IT AND BREAK IT v-JT (16tp)(16tp with   US-1285-1
     ensemble)
78: VARSITY 8179 LP: STORYVILLE SLP703,
PHOENIX LP3

A PRETTY GIRL IS LIKE A MELODY (16tp with   US-1286-1
     ensemble)(16tp)+(16tp with ensemble)
78: VARSITY 8179 LP: STORYVILLE SLP703,
PHOENIX LP3

POM POM (16tp) comp   US-1287-1
78: VARSITY 8173 LP: STORYVILLE SLP703,
PHOENIX LP3

---

[94]   January 30, 1940   New York
          BENNY CARTER AND HIS ORCHESTRA

Carter (tp, as, arr, comp) Russell Smith, Lincoln Mills, Joe Thomas (tp)
Jimmy Archey, Vic Dickenson, Gene Simon (tb) Jimmy Powell, Carl Frye
(as) Stanley Payne, Coleman Hawkins (ts) Eddie Heywood (p) Ulysses Livingston (g) Hayes Alvis (b) Keg Purnell (d) Roy Felton (v)

SLEEP (24as) arr   M-1126-1
78: VOCALION 5399 LP: COLUMBIA KG32945,
CBS (E) 88134, TAX (SW) M-8004, TIME-LIFE
STL-J10

AMONG MY SOUVENIRS v-RF (32as)(17tp) arr   M-1127-1
78: VOCALION 5458 LP: TAX (SW) M-8004

FISH FRY (32tp) arr, comp   M-1128-1
78: VOCALION 5458 LP: TAX (SW) M-8004,
TIME-LIFE STL-J10

SLOW FREIGHT   (8tp)(16+8tp)(8tp)[tp on bridge   M-1129-1
        of 3rd chorus is Joe Thomas] arr
78: VOCALION 5399 LP: TAX (SW) M-8004,
TIME-LIFE STL-J10

   NOTE: Alternate takes are known to exist of these titles.

                          *   *   *

The Carter band was given a boost on its next Vocalion date by the presence of Coleman Hawkins.

   The first tune, "Sleep," is the highlight of the session. Carter takes
Fred Waring's theme song, originally a waltz, and turns it into an uptempo
swinger. The arrangement is distinguished by Carter's imaginative use of
complementary riffs to introduce and back each soloist. After Hawkins's
driving solo, muted brass back Heywood, swelling reeds, Thomas, and a
new brass figure appears behind Carter's own solo. The last chorus includes a brief trombone choir passage and some exciting drumming by Keg
Purnell, who added some punch to the Carter rhythm section. Carter remembers arranging "Sleep" specifically for this session. Because of the
blistering tempo, he remarks, "Had we been able to play it every night for
a week or so before, it would have felt more comfortable, not just for the
soloist but for those playing parts."

   Carter's original "Fish Fry" remained in his band's book for the
next six years. On this first recording, Hawkins contributes a rough-edged
solo. Carter's full chorus of muted trumpet contains two fluffs, one just
before the bridge and one on it. These imperfections do not seem to faze
him as he delivers a solo which is both heated and relaxed.

   One in a long tradition of railroad songs in jazz, "Slow Freight" was
originally composed and arranged by Buck Ram, but Down Beat reported
that "since most of the swing records followed Carter's interpretation he
was delegated to revise the stock." (September 1, 1940, p. 18) One of
Carter's added touches was the electric guitar simulating a train whistle.
Carter plays the soulful muted trumpet which opens and closes the piece
as well as the muted solos before and after Hawkins's bridge on the second
chorus. The open trumpet solo on the bridge of the third chorus is by Joe
Thomas.

[95]   February 2, 1940 New York
          THE QUINTONES

Carter (as) The Quintones (v) Joe Thomas (tp) Coleman Hawkins (ts) Eddie
Heywood (p) Hayes Alvis (b) Keg Purnell (d) Buck Ram (dir)

HONEY BUNNY BOO v-Q (e)   WM-1130-A
78: VOCALION 5596

THE FIVE LITTLE QUINTS v-Q (e)   WM-1131-A
78: VOCALION 5409

HARMONY IN HARLEM v-Q (e)   WM-1132-A
78: VOCALION 5596

MIDNIGHT JAMBOREE v-Q (e)   WM-1133-A
78: VOCALION 5409

NOTE: This personnel is listed by Rust as probable; the presence of Hawkins has been questioned, and the lack of any alto solos makes confirmation of Carter's participation impossible.

---

[96]   February 7, 1940   New York
         METRONOME ALL-STAR BAND

Carter (as) Charlie Spivak, Harry James, Ziggy Elman (tp) Jack Teagarden, Jack Jenney (tb) Benny Goodman (cl) Toots Mondello (as) Eddie Miller, Charlie Barnet (ts) Jess Stacy (p) Charlie Christian (g) Bob Haggart (b) Gene Krupa (d) Fletcher Henderson (arr)

KING PORTER STOMP (e)   26489-A
78: COLUMBIA 35389   LP: COLUMBIA CL2528,
HARMONY HL7044, QUEEN-DISC Q009, SONY (J)
SONP50419

KING PORTER STOMP (e)   26489-B
LP: PHONTASTIC NOST7610

---

[97]   Same Session
         METRONOME ALL-STAR NINE

Carter (as) Harry James (tp) Jack Teagarden (tb) Benny Goodman (cl) Eddie Miller (ts) Jess Stacy (p) Charlie Christian (g) Bob Haggart (b) Gene Krupa (d)

ALL STAR STRUT   (12as)   26490-A
78: COLUMBIA 35389   LP: COLUMBIA CL2528,
HARMONY HL7044, COLUMBIA G30779, QUEEN-
DISC Q009, SONY (J) SONP50419

ALL STAR STRUT   26490-B
78: UNISSUED LP: SONY (J) SONP50419

---

[98]   February 14, 1940   New York
         FREDDIE RICH AND HIS ORCHESTRA

Carter (as, arr) Nat Natoli, Red Solomon, Roy Eldridge (tp) Larry Altpeter (tb) Sid Stoneburn, Sid Perlmutter (cl, as) Babe Russin, Frank Chase, Stafford Simon (ts) Clyde Hart (p) Ken Binford (g) Hayes Alvis (b) Johnny Williams (d) Rosemary Calvin (v)

TILL WE MEET AGAIN   (8as) arr   26514-A
78: VOCALION   5507

A HOUSE WITH A LITTLE RED BARN   v-RC   26515-A
     (e) arr
78: VOCALION 5420

I'M FOREVER BLOWING BUBBLES   (32as) arr   26516-
78: VOCALION 5507

HOW HIGH THE MOON   v-RC (8as)   26517-
78: VOCALION 5420

---

[99]   May 5, 1940   New York   Airchecks, NBC's 'Chamber Music
                 Society of Lower Basin St. '
          CARTER WITH THE CHAMBER MUSIC SOCIETY OF
          LOWER BASIN ST.

Carter (as, tp) Henry Levine (tp) Jack Epstein (tb) Alfie Evans (cl) Rudolph
Adler (ts) Tony Colucci (g) Henry Patent (b) Nat Levine (d) Franklyn Marks
(arr)

HONEYSUCKLE ROSE   (2as break+32+32+18
        with ensemble)
LP: JOKER (I) SM3115, SAGA (E) 6927, KINGS
OF JAZZ (I) KLJ20027, HOT 'N SWEET (F) HOL6426

STAR DUST   (4tp intro+32+32+coda)
LP: JOKER (I) SM3115, SAGA (E) 6927, HOT 'N
SWEET (F) HOL6426

       NOTE: Personnel from Hot 'N Sweet LP; Carter recalled arranger.

---

[100]   May 20, 1940   New York
          BENNY CARTER AND HIS ORCHESTRA

Carter (as, cl, arr, comp) Bill Coleman, Shad Collins, Russell Smith (tp)
Sandy Williams, Milton Robinson (tb) Carl Frye, George Dorsey (as) Staf-
ford Simon, Sammy Davis (ts) Sonny White (p) Ulysses Livingston (g) Hayes
Alvis (b) Keg Purnell (d)

NIGHT HOP   (16as with ensemble)+(8as)   67781-A
        arr, comp
78:   DECCA 3294   LP: DECCA DL79242, MCA 1323

POM POM   (8cl)(8cl) arr, comp   67782-A
78:   DECCA 3262   LP: DECCA DL79242, MCA (F)
510. 178-180, MCA 1323

O.K. FOR BABY   (16as) arr, comp   67783-A
78:   DECCA 3294   LP: BRUNSWICK (F) 87. 505,
DECCA DL79242, MCA (F) 510. 178-180, TIME-
LIFE STL-J10, MCA 1323

SERENADE TO A SARONG   (8+8as) arr, comp   67784-A
78:   DECCA 3262   LP: DECCA DL79242,
MCA 1323

                    *   *   *

The Carter orchestra's first sides for Decca are among the best recorded
representations of the band of the period.   Several important personnel
changes have taken place.   Shad Collins and Bill Coleman, both of whom
had played in Carter's 1933 orchestra, are in the trumpet section and
Sammy Davis has replaced Ernie Powell as principal tenor soloist.   Perhaps most significant is the addition on piano of Sonny White, formerly
Billie Holiday's accompanist.   White was to remain with Carter, with a
few interruptions, until 1946.

       Leonard Feather reported in the Melody Maker (June 1940) that
"Carter went into the studio not knowing what numbers he was going to do,

which resulted in the usual clambake with the supervisor. Finally they picked out four Carter originals which all came out very well. "

In spite of the apparent informality of the session, this latest edition of the Carter orchestra sounds even tighter and better drilled than the Savoy band of the previous year.

"Night Hop" and "O. K. For Baby" are relaxed swingers. The latter is notable for the excellent balance between the reeds and the brass, and the dynamic shadings in the sections.

"Pom Pom" is a big-band version of the Carter tune previously recorded by smaller ensembles including the Varsity Seven and Joe Sullivan's Cafe Society Orchestra. Carter's very personal clarinet tone is well captured.

"Serenade To A Sarong" is an impressionistic mood piece with an "Oriental" flavor, with brief contributions by Carter's alto and Sandy Williams's growling trombone.

This session is yet another example of Carter's reluctance to promote his own music. He never again recorded, or possibly even played, these four excellent pieces. "O. K. For Baby" did, however, become part of the Jimmie Lunceford band's book in an arrangement by Lonnie Wilfong and was also recorded by Les Brown among others. "Pom Pom" was revived six years later by Eddie Heywood, who recorded it with a small group.

This was guitarist Ulysses Livingston's last session as a regular member of the Carter orchestra. Livingston combined music with a career as a quality control engineer for Hughes Aircraft, which included work on the NASA "Survivor" program. He remains close friends with Carter and remembers the thrill of playing Carter's music: "His arrangements were enlightening; a revelation. He was the first to include flatted fifths, augmented ninths and other features that became popular later. We used to eagerly put in extra rehearsal time to get things to sound the way he wanted. " Livingston also recalls the circumstances of his leaving the band: "No one ever wanted to leave Benny. In 1940, during a period when the band wasn't working too regularly, I got an offer from the Gale agency to join Ella Fitzgerald. When Benny found out about it he said, 'Ulysses, it's a great opportunity--you've got to take it. ' I said, 'No way, I'm not leaving. ' So Benny told me, 'In that case, you're fired!' So I had to go, but that was the only way I would have left Benny Carter. "

| [101] | May 25, 1940 New York |
| | THE CHOCOLATE DANDIES |

Carter (as, p) Roy Eldridge (tp) Coleman Hawkins (ts) Bernard Addison (g) John Kirby (b) Sid Catlett (d)

SMACK (64as)(8as)   R2995
78: COMMODORE 533 LP: MAINSTREAM
56037, ATLANTIC SD2-306, COMMODORE
XFL14936, LONDON 6.24056, TIME-LIFE
STL-J10

SMACK (64as)(8as)   R2995-4

78: UNISSUED LP: ATLANTIC SD2-306,
COMMODORE XFL14936, LONDON 6.24056

I SURRENDER DEAR   (4p intro+piano acc)   R2996
78: COMMODORE 1506 LP: MAINSTREAM
56037, ATLANTIC SD2-306, COMMODORE
XFL14936, LONDON 6.24056

I SURRENDER DEAR   (4p intro+piano acc)   R2996-
78: UNISSUED LP: ATLANTIC SD2-306,
COMMODORE XFL14936, LONDON 6.24056

I CAN'T BELIEVE THAT YOU'RE IN LOVE WITH   R2997
     ME (64as)
78: COMMODORE 1506 LP: MAINSTREAM 56037,
MAINSTREAM 56017, ATLANTIC SD2-306, COM-
MODORE XFL14936, LONDON 6.24056, SMITH-
SONIAN COLLECTION OF CLASSIC JAZZ

I CAN'T BELIEVE THAT YOU'RE IN LOVE WITH   R2997-1
     ME (32as)
78: UNISSUED LP: COMMODORE XFL14936,
LONDON 6.24056

      NOTES: Second version of "I Surrender Dear" is a composite of
      alternate takes (possibly 1 and 2). Smithsonian LP contains only
      excerpt of R2997.

*   *   *

Carter's only appearance on the Commodore label was another Leonard
Feather production. Milt Gabler, the founder of the label, recalls that
"you never saw him [Carter] on 52nd Street blowing, sitting in. He was
always too busy with his big bands or writing and arranging." (Giants of
Jazz, p. 47.)

      Feather's intent was to bring together some of the illustrious Fletch-
er Henderson alumni and, since Henderson himself was unable to be present,
it was decided to go without a piano.

      These were Carter's first small-group recordings with Roy El-
dridge, who has always maintained that his own style derived as much from
the influence of saxophonists Carter and Hawkins in particular, as from
trumpeters.

      The first tune was dedicated to Fletcher Henderson whose nickname
was "Smack." It is unusual for that time--an improvised performance from
the beginning, based on chord changes sketched out by Feather. Carter's
opening two choruses follow the same general pattern in both takes. His
playing is more rhythmic than usual, as he builds excitement by hitting the
beat head on. There is a pronounced difference, however, between the 8-
bar bridges played by Carter after Hawkins's solo chorus in the two takes.
In the first version, Carter's return is a dramatic departure from the hot
choruses preceding it. He plays a descending melodic figure with a detached coolness, which foreshadows later styles. In the alternate take,
Carter's first two measures hint at a similar approach but he then takes a
different direction.

"I Surrender Dear" is a ballad feature for Hawkins and Eldridge, with Carter providing a piano introduction and accompaniment.

In his remarkable solo on "I Can't Believe" (issued take) Carter elaborates upon the prescient ideas suggested in "Smack." Beginning with the last eight measures of his first solo chorus, Carter seems to discard the chord changes, melody line, and even the AABA 32-bar song structure itself. He plays a 16-bar melodic statement which begins with a descending figure similar to that present on his bridge in "Smack" (issued version) and carries it over into his second chorus. In the 9th measure of that chorus he introduces yet another repeated descending figure which carries through the transition to the bridge. Here he adds to the startling effect by deliberately falling behind the beat. He recovers in the middle of the bridge and finishes the chorus in more conventional fashion.

The recently discovered alternate take of "I Can't Believe" is completely different, with the tempo almost half that of the issued version.

---

[102]   June 1940   New York
          BUSTER BAILEY AND HIS SEXTET

Carter (as) Charlie Shavers (tp) Buster Bailey (cl) Billy Kyle (p) John Kirby (b) Zutty Singleton (d) Judy Ellington (v)

SEEMS LIKE A MONTH OF SUNDAYS   v-JE (e)   US-1841-1
78: VARSITY 8358 LP: RARITIES 17, STORY-
VILLE SLP701, SAVOY SJL2246

FABLE OF A ROSE   v-JE (4as)(4as)   US-1842-1
78: VARSITY 8358 LP: RARITIES 17, STORY-
VILLE SLP701, SAVOY SJL2246

PINETOP'S BOOGIE WOOGIE   (12+12as)   US-1843-1
78: VARSITY 8365 LP: RARITIES 17, STORY-
VILLE SLP701, SMITHSONIAN P2-14584, STORY-
VILLE (G) 6.28474, SAVOY SJL2246

ECCENTRIC RAG   (16as)   US-1844-1
78: VARSITY 8365 LP: RARITIES 17, STORY-
VILLE SLP701, SMITHSONIAN P2-14584, SAVOY
SJL2246

*   *   *

This personnel is essentially the John Kirby sextet with Carter and Singleton substituting for Russell Procope and O'Neil Spencer. Although the arrangements are less structured than the sextet's usual recordings, the session naturally has a Kirby-like feel.

---

[103]   October 15, 1940   New York
          BILLIE HOLIDAY ACC. BY BENNY CARTER AND
          HIS ALL STAR ORCHESTRA

Carter (as, cl, arr) Bill Coleman (tp) Benny Morton (tb) Georgie Auld (ts) Sonny White (p) Ulysses Livingston (g) Wilson Myers (b) Yank Porter (d) Billie Holiday (v)

ST. LOUIS BLUES   v-BH (12cl acc)(12cl) arr   28874-1
78: OKEH 6064, COLUMBIA 30229 LP: SONY
(J) SOPH69

ST. LOUIS BLUES   v-BH (12cl acc)(12cl) arr   28874-2
78: OKEH 6064 LP: COLUMBIA CL2428,
COLUMBIA KG32127, COLUMBIA CG30782,
SONY (J) SOPH69

LOVELESS LOVE   v-BH (e) arr   28875-1
78: OKEH 6064, COLUMBIA 30229 LP: SONY
(J) SOPH69

LOVELESS LOVE   (e) arr   28875-2
78: UNISSUED LP: COLUMBIA CG30782

> NOTE: Both takes of "St. Louis Blues" appear on various copies
> of Okeh 6064. One take of each title on Two Flat Disc 5007.

[104]	October 15, 1940 New York
	BENNY CARTER AND HIS ALL STAR ORCHESTRA

Carter (cl) Bill Coleman (tp) Benny Morton (tb) Georgie Auld (ts) Sonny
White (p) Ulysses Livingston (g) Wilson Myers (b) Yank Porter (d) Joe
Turner (v)

JOE TURNER BLUES   v-JT (12cl acc)   28876-1
78: OKEH 6001

JOE TURNER BLUES   v-JT (12cl acc)   28876-2
78: UNISSUED LP: MERITT 10

BEALE STREET BLUES   v-JT (e)   28877-1
78: OKEH 6001

BEALE STREET BLUES   v-JT (e)   28877-2
78: UNISSUED LP: MERITT 10

                         *   *   *

[103, 104] Carter's role here was to provide accompaniment for two great
jazz vocalists, Billie Holiday and Joe Turner. His playing is confined to
the tasteful clarinet obbligatos and one solo clarinet chorus on "St. Louis
Blues. "

[105]	October 23, 1940 New York
	BENNY CARTER AND HIS ORCHESTRA

Carter (as, arr) Russell Smith, Jonah Jones, Bobby Williams (tp) Milton
Robinson, Madison Vaughan (tb) Chauncey Haughton (as) George James (as,
bs) George Irish, Stafford Simon (ts) Sonny White (p) Everett Barksdale (g)
Hayes Alvis (p) Keg Purnell (d) Roy Felton, The Mills Brothers (v)

BY THE WATERMELON VINE, LINDY LOU   v-RF, MB   68284-A
       (16as) arr
78: DECCA 3545 LP: MCA CORAL 62100

THE LAST KISS YOU GAVE ME   v-RF (8as) arr   68285-A
78: DECCA 3588

BOOGIE WOOGIE SUGAR BLUES   (18as)(4+2as) arr   68286-A
78: DECCA 3588

I'VE BEEN IN LOVE BEFORE   v-RF (16as) arr   68287-A
78: DECCA 3545

                              *   *   *

This session, his second for Decca, ended in a dispute which led Carter
to break with that label. At his first Decca session (May 20, 1940) Carter
had enjoyed a free rein in choice of material: four excellent big-band
sides resulted. But by this date, some five months later, the company
had formed definite ideas about how the band was to sound and what it
should play. Vocals were given high priority, with three of the four tunes
featuring Roy Felton. The Mills Brothers were brought in for one sentimental ballad dating back to 1914. The final straw, however, was the single
instrumental number, a boogie-woogie interpretation of Clyde McCoy's
"Sugar Blues, " complete with laughing saxophone and trumpet. "Someone
at the studio had the idea that this would make the band more commercially
successful, " Carter recalls. "I went along at first, but the results were
just not what I wanted my orchestra to sound like. " Carter failed in an
attempt to prevent the record's release. Less than a month later he signed
with Bluebird.

---

[106]   November 13, 1940   New York
          UNA MAE CARLISLE AND HER JAM BAND

Carter (tp) Everett Barksdale (g) Slam Stewart (b) Zutty Singleton (d) Una
Mae Carlisle (p, v)

WALKIN' BY THE RIVER   v-UMC (4tp intro)(32tp)   057641-1
78: BLUEBIRD B-11033 LP: RCA (F) FXM1-7124,
RCA (F) PM42406

---

[107]   November 19, 1940   New York
          BENNY CARTER AND HIS ORCHESTRA

Carter (cl, as, arr, comp) Russell Smith, Sidney De Paris, Bobby Williams
(tp) Milton Robinson, Madison Vaughan, Benny Morton (tb) Chauncey Haughton (as) George James (as, bs) George Irish, Stafford Simon (ts) Sonny White
(p) Everett Barksdale (g) Hayes Alvis (b) Keg Purnell (d) Roy Felton (v)

ALL OF ME   (14cl) arr   057656-1
78: BLUEBIRD B-10962 LP: RCA (F) 430.686,
RCA (F) 741.073, RCA (J) RA-57, TIME-LIFE
STL-J10, RCA (F) PM42406, RCA (F) PM43259

THE VERY THOUGHT OF YOU   v-RF (16as) arr   057657-1
78: BLUEBIRD B-10962 LP: RCA (F) 430.686,
RCA (F) 741.073, RCA (F) PM42406

COCKTAILS FOR TWO   (32as)(10as) arr   057658-1
78: BLUEBIRD B-10998 45: HMV (F) 7EMF26

LP: RCA (F) 430. 686, RCA (F) 741. 073, RCA
(J) RA-57, RCA (F) PM42406

TAKIN' MY TIME (32as) arr, comp   057659-1
78: BLUEBIRD B-10998 LP: RCA (F) 430. 686,
RCA (F) 741. 073, RCA (F) PM42406

*　　*　　*

This was the first of four sessions by Carter for RCA's Bluebird label
over a one-year period. Aside from the personnel changes, the date is
significant because of a shift to the two-alto, two-tenor, one-baritone reed
section which was rapidly becoming the big band standard. The first tune,
"All Of Me, " takes full advantage of the added depth of the baritone with a
typically supple sax section chorus, an expanded version of the one Carter
had recorded four years earlier with the Willie Lewis band in Paris.
Carter's burnished, rounded clarinet tone is almost in the New Orleans
tradition.

The standards, "The Very Thought Of You" and "Cocktails For Two, "
both have Carter alto solos which elegantly paraphrase the melodies.

---

[108]　　January 16, 1941　New York
　　　　　METRONOME ALL STAR BAND

Carter (as) Harry James, Ziggy Elman, Cootie Williams (tp) Tommy Dorsey, J. C. Higginbotham (tp) Benny Goodman (cl) Toots Mondello (as) Coleman Hawkins, Tex Beneke (ts) Count Basie (p) Charlie Christian (g) Artie
Bernstein (b) Buddy Rich (d)

BUGLE CALL RAG (e)   060331-1
78: VICTOR 27314 LP: RCA (F) 731. 089,
RCA (F) PM42046

ONE O'CLOCK JUMP (12as)   060332-1
78: VICTOR 27314 LP: RCA (F) 731. 089,
RCA (F) PM42046

---

[109]　　January 21, 1941　New York
　　　　　BENNY CARTER AND HIS ORCHESTRA

Carter (as, arr, comp) Russell Smith, Sidney De Paris, Jonah Jones (tp)
Vic Dickenson, Jimmy Archey, Joe Britton (tb) George Dorsey, Bill White
(as) George Irish, Fred Mitchell (ts) Sonny White (p) Herb Thomas (g) Ted
Sturgis (b) J. C. Heard (d) Roy Felton (v)

CUDDLE UP, HUDDLE UP (16as) arr, comp   060351-1
78: BLUEBIRD B-11197 LP: RCA (F) 430. 686,
RCA (F) 741. 073, RCA (F) PM42406

EV'RY GOODBYE AIN'T GONE arr, comp   060352-1
78: UNISSUED

BABALU (intro+16as) arr   060353-1
78: BLUEBIRD B-11090 LP: RCA (F) 430. 686,
RCA (F) 741. 073, RCA (F) PM42406, RCA (J) RA-57

THERE I'VE SAID IT AGAIN v-RF (8as) arr   060354-1
78: BLUEBIRD B-11090 LP: RCA (F) 430.686,
RCA (F) 741.073, RCA (F) PM42406

*   *   *

"Cuddle Up" is reminiscent of "O.K. For Baby" (May 20, 1940) with all
sections beautifully integrated. The arrangement features declamatory
brass, a rich 16-measure reed passage, and a brief trombone choir.

[109A]   March 22, 1941 Cedar Grove, N.J. Airchecks, CBS
                          Broadcast "Matinee at the Meadowbrook"
           BENNY CARTER WITH THE GENE KRUPA ORCHESTRA

Includes Carter (as, arr) Gene Krupa (d)

THERE'LL BE SOME CHANGES MADE   (36+20as)

ROCKIN' CHAIR   (intro+32+28+coda tp) arr

---

[110]   April 1, 1941 New York
          BENNY CARTER AND HIS ORCHESTRA

Carter (tp, as, arr, comp) Doc Cheatham, Lincoln Mills, Sidney De Paris
(tp) Vic Dickenson, Jimmy Archey, Joe Britton (tb) Ernie Purce, Eddie
Barefield (as) Fred Williams, Ernie Powell (ts) Sonny White (p) Herb
Thomas (g) Charles Drayton (b) Al Taylor (d) Maxine Sullivan (v)

MIDNIGHT v-MS (16as) arr   063700-1
78: BLUEBIRD B-11288 LP: RCA (F) 430.686,
RCA (F) 741.073, RCA (F) PM42406

MY FAVORITE BLUES (24tp) arr, comp   063701-1
78: BLUEBIRD B-11288 LP: RCA LEJ-2, RCA
(F) 430.686, RCA (F) 741.073, RCA (F) PM42406,
RCA (J) RA-57

LULLABY TO A DREAM (32tp)(2tp) arr, comp   063702-2
78: UNISSUED LP: RCA (F) 741.073, RCA (F)
PM42406, RCA (J) RA-57

WHAT A DIFFERENCE A DAY MADE v-MS (e) arr   063703-1
78: BLUEBIRD B-11197 LP: RCA (F) 430.686,
RCA (F) 741.073, RCA (F) PM42406

*   *   *

For his third Bluebird date, Carter drew on the talents of Maxine Sullivan
(who was soon to tour with the orchestra). Some veterans of Carter's various orchestras have returned, including trumpeters Doc Cheatham and Lincoln Mills, and tenorman Ernie Powell.

Carter plays trumpet for the two originals. The medium-fast "My
Favorite Blues" opens with Carter's muted solo followed by Vic Dickenson.
A brief reed passage leads into Sonny White's piano and Ernie Powell's
tenor spot.

Carter plays his lovely piece "Lullaby To A Dream" on open horn, with Eddie Barefield taking the lead alto part.

[111]	June 26, 1941 New York

ARTIE SHAW AND HIS ORCHESTRA

Carter (as) Henry Allen (tp) J. C. Higginbotham (tb) Artie Shaw (cl, arr) Sonny White (p) Jimmy Shirley (g) Billy Taylor (b) Shep Shepherd (d) Laura Newell (harp) 12 violins, violas and violincellos, Lena Horne (v)

CONFESSIN' (16+8as [trades with Higginbotham])   066146-1
78: UNISSUED LP: CAMDEN CAL584, RCA
VPM6062, RCA (F) FXM1-7336, BLUEBIRD
AXM2-5576

LOVE ME A LITTLE LITTLE v-LH (8+8as)   066147-1
78: VICTOR 27509 LP: RCA LPM1570, RCA
(F) FXM1-7336, BLUEBIRD AXM2-5576

BEYOND THE BLUE HORIZON   066148-1
78: UNISSUED LP: BLUEBIRD AXM2-5576

DON'T TAKE YOUR LOVE FROM ME v-LH (e)   066149-1
78: VICTOR 27509 LP: RCA VPM6039, RCA
(F) FXM1-7336, RCA (J) RA-5445/6, BLUEBIRD
AXM2-5576

*   *   *

Carter's only appearance on record with Artie Shaw came at a time when Shaw was experimenting with strings. Here he added some top jazz solo talents.

In the liner notes to French RCA FXM1-7336, Jean-Pierre Daubresse attributes the arrangements from this session to Carter. Mr. Shaw, however, has verified that he, Shaw, was actually the arranger (letter dated 5/31/77).

[112]	October 16, 1941 New York

BENNY CARTER AND HIS ORCHESTRA

Carter (as, arr, comp) Nathaniel Williams, Emmett Berry, Rostelle Reese (tp) Jimmy Archey, Benny Morton, John McConnell (tb) Ernie Purce, George James (as) Ernie Powell, Al Gibson (ts) Sonny White (p) Willie Lewis (g) Charles Drayton (b) Shep Shepherd (d)

SUNDAY (8+32as) arr   066792-1
78: BLUEBIRD B-11341 45: HMV (F) 7EMF26
LP: RCA (F) 430.686, RCA (F) 741.073, RCA
(J) RA-57, RCA (F) PM42406, TIME-LIFE STL-
J10, RCA (F) PM43259

ILL WIND (20as)(14as) arr   066793-2
78: UNISSUED LP: RCA (J) RA-5335, RCA (F)
741.073, RCA (J) RA-57, RCA (F) PM42406, TIME-
LIFE STL-J10

BACK BAY BOOGIE   (24as) arr, comp   066794-1
78:   BLUEBIRD B-11341   LP: RCA (F) 430. 686,
RCA (F) 741. 073, RCA (J) RA-57, RCA (F)
PM42406, TIME-LIFE STL-J10

TREE OF HOPE   (2as break)(8as) arr, comp   066795-1
78:   UNISSUED   LP: RCA (F) 741. 073, RCA
(F) PM42406

                              *   *   *

Carter's last Bluebird date was strictly instrumental.   "Sunday" has an excellent Carter alto solo, in which he cleverly alternates melody with playing
on the changes.

          His alto really sings the melody of "Ill Wind, " allowing each note to
ripen before moving on.   The arrangement uses an interesting sequence of
ensemble voicings.   A rich reed passage leads to an unexpected and effec-
tive moment of silence, before a more forceful swinging bridge is carried
by the brass.

          "Back Bay Boogie" is based on a riff Carter used to play with his
sextet at the Ritz Carlton Hotel in Boston--hence the title.   The arrangement is a showstopper and Carter used it often in situations calling for the
frantic uptempos that came into vogue during World War II.   The boogie
motif is supplied by pianist White.   In subsequent air checks and transcriptions of this piece Carter adhered closely to the pattern of his forceful
solo here.

---

[113]   December 31, 1941   New York
            METRONOME ALL STAR BAND

Carter (as) Harry James, Cootie Williams, Roy Eldridge (tp) J. C. Higgin-
botham, Lou McGarity (tb) Benny Goodman (cl) Toots Mondello (as) Vido
Musso, Tex Beneke (ts) Count Basie (p) Freddie Green (g) Doc Goldberg (b)
Gene Krupa (d)

ROYAL FLUSH   (8as [2nd solo])   32079-1
78:   COLUMBIA 36499   LP: SONY (J)
SONP50419

ROYAL FLUSH   (8as [2nd solo])   32079-2
78:   UNISSUED   LP: COLUMBIA CL2528, HAR-
MONY HL7044, QUEEN-DISC Q009, SONY (J)
SONP50419

DEAR OLD SOUTHLAND   (16as)   32080-1
78:   UNISSUED   LP: HARMONY HL7044,
QUEEN-DISC Q009, SONY (J) SONP50419

---

[114]   January 16, 1942   New York
            METRONOME ALL STAR LEADERS

Carter (as) Cootie Williams (tp) J. C. Higginbotham (tb) Benny Goodman (cl)
Charlie Barnet (ts) Count Basie (p) Alvino Rey (g) John Kirby (b) Gene
Krupa (d)

I GOT RHYTHM   (16+8as)   32261-1
78:   COLUMBIA C-601   LP: COLUMBIA
CL2528, HARMONY HL7044, QUEEN-DISC
Q009, SONY (J) SONP50419

I GOT RHYTHM   (16+8as)   32261-2
78:   COLUMBIA 36499   LP: SONY (J) SONP50419

I GOT RHYTHM   (16+8as)   32261-3
78:   UNISSUED   LP: SONY (J) SONP50419,
TAX (SW) M-8039

---

[115]   February 9, 1942   New York
           MARK WARNOW AND HIS ORCHESTRA

Carter (cl, as, arr) Russ Case, Ivor Lloyd, Nat Natoli (tp) Cliff Heather,
Larry Altpeter (tb) Sid Trucker, Ezell Watson, Bernie Ladd, Reggie Mer-
rill, Babe Russin (reeds) Arnold Fidus, Bernard Ocke, Max Pilzer, Jules
Sherter, Max Silverman, Waldo Mayo, M. Polikoff, Leo Kahn (violin)
Bernie Lazaroff (p) Ben Mortell (g) R. Berman (harp) Sam Shoobe (b) John
Williams (d) The Hit Paraders, Joan Edwards, Barry Wood (v)

THESE FOOLISH THINGS   v-BW arr   071783-1
78:   VICTOR 27867

TI-PI-TIN   v-HP, JE, BW (e)   071784-1
78:   VICTOR 27865

ALL THE THINGS YOU ARE   v-JE   071785-1
78:   VICTOR 27866

THE MUSIC GOES ROUND AND ROUND   v-HP   071786-1
      (e) arr
78:   VICTOR 27868

                         *   *   *

Carter's tenure as arranger for Mark Warnow's Hit Parade network broadcasts included this one commercial recording session. The string arrangements were Carter's first since his work for Henry Hall in England. As
Carter recalls, the Hit Parade scores had to be turned out on short notice:
"You didn't know until a few days before the broadcast what the hit of the
week would be. " He adds, "In every arrangement the introduction would
have to start with part of the melody of the song, so that it would be immediately recognizable. "

---

[116]   December 18, 1942   Los Angeles   AFRS Jubilee #4
           BENNY CARTER AND HIS ORCHESTRA

Carter (as, arr) George Treadwell, Hal Mitchell, Chiefie Scott (tp) Earl
Hardy, J. J. Johnson, John "Shorty" Haughton, Alton Moore (tb) Ted
Barnett, Stretch Ridley, Gene Porter, Eddie De Verteuil (reeds) Ted Bran-
non (p) Johnny Smith (g) Curly Russell (b) Alvin Burroughs (d) Savannah
Churchill (v)

STOMPIN' AT THE SAVOY

ALL I NEED IS YOU   v-SC

I CAN'T GET STARTED   arr

OL' MAN RIVER   (32as) arr

> NOTE: Tentative listing of personnel based on Carter's opening at
> the Swing Club in Los Angeles, November 1942 (Down Beat, Novem-
> ber 15, 1942, p. 11).

---

[117]   Probably Late 1942   Los Angeles   AFRS Basic Library
                      of Popular Music P-8
          BENNY CARTER AND HIS ORCHESTRA

Carter (as, arr) Carter Band Personnel Probably Similar to 12-18-42 Jubilee #4 Listing, Savannah Churchill (v)

WHY DON'T YOU DO RIGHT   v-SC

ILL WIND   v-SC arr?

> NOTE: This may be Carter's arrangement of "Ill Wind" as first
> recorded October 16, 1941.

[117A]   January 1, 1943 (New Year's Eve) Hollywood   Aircheck
          BENNY CARTER AND HIS ORCHESTRA

Includes Carter (as)

ONE O'CLOCK JUMP   (24as)

---

[118]   January 23, 1943   Los Angeles
          FATS WALLER AND HIS RHYTHM

Carter (tp, comp) Alton Moore (tb) Gene Porter (cl, ts) Irving Ashby (g)
Fats Waller (p, v) Slam Stewart (b) Zutty Singleton (d) Ada Brown (v)

MOPPIN' AND BOPPIN'   (16+8tp)(16+8tp with   D6-V6-6215
           ensemble) comp
78: 20TH CENTURY FOX TCF202, VICTOR 40-
4003 LP: HMV C3737, SOUNTRAK STK103, RCA
(J) RA-80, RCA (F) PM42361

AIN'T MISBEHAVIN'   v-FW (12tp)+(8tp acc)   D6-V6-6216
78: 20TH CENTURY FOX TCF203, VICTOR 40-
4003, LP: HMV C3737, CAMDEN CAL473,
SOUNTRAK STK103, RCA (J) RA-80, RCA (F)
PM42361, TIME-LIFE STL-J15

THAT AIN'T RIGHT   v-FW, AB (8tp with ensemble)   VP 471
           (8tp acc)(12tp acc)
78: 20TH CENTURY FOX TCF201 LP: SWAGGIE
S1227, ALAMAC QSR2438, JAZZ ANTHOLOGY
JA5104, RCA (J) RA-80

> NOTE: "That Ain't Right" appears as "It Ain't Right" on Swaggie LP.

                                *   *   *

These recordings, which were among Waller's last, are from the soundtrack of the film Stormy Weather.   Carter's only other recordings with
Waller were the 1929 Chocolate Dandies and McKinney's sessions.

        Carter recalls their composition "Moppin' And Boppin'": "Fats had
part of the tune, I think the beginning, and he asked me to finish it with
him. " This was not their first collaboration; in 1927 a tune called "Nobody
Knows How Much I Love You" was registered with the U. S. copyright office.   Carter and Waller were the composers, Bud Allen the lyricist.   Andy
Razaf recorded it January 17, 1928, under the pseudonym Johnny Thompson,
with Fats supplying piano accompaniment.

---

[119]   January-February 1943 Los Angeles
           SOUNDTRACK OF FILM STORMY WEATHER

Carter (as, arr) Large Orchestra With Strings and Vocal Chorus, Lena
Horne, Bill 'Bojangles' Robinson (v) David Raksin (arr)

STORMY WEATHER v-LH (e) arr
LP: SOUNTRAK STK103

STORMY WEATHER vocal chorus (5as)(5as) arr
      [last 29 measures]
LP: SOUNTRAK STK103

I CAN'T GIVE YOU ANYTHING BUT LOVE
      v-LH, BR, chorus (e) arr [instrumental
      section only]
LP: SOUNTRAK STK103

AIN'T THAT SOMETHIN' v-BR (e) arr
LP: SOUNTRAK STK103

GOOD FOR NOTHIN' JOE v-LH (e) arr
LP: SOUNTRAK STK103

---

[120]   January-February 1943 Los Angeles
           BENNY CARTER WITH CAB CALLOWAY AND HIS ORCHESTRA

Carter (as) Shad Collins, Jonah Jones, Russell Smith, Lammar Wright (tp)
Tyree Glenn, Quentin Jackson, Keg Johnson (tb) Andy Brown (cl, as) Hilton
Jefferson (as) Al Gibson, Illinois Jacquet (ts) Greely Walton (bs) Benny
Payne (p) Danny Barker (g) Milt Hinton (b) J. C. Heard (d) Cab Calloway
(leader)

BODY AND SOUL (32as [1st solo])
78: 20TH CENTURY FOX TCF207/TCF211
LP: SPOTLITE SPJ148

                                *   *   *

This performance was originally issued in two parts on a limited Twentieth
Century-Fox 12-inch pressing. It took place on the sound stage during the

filming of the picture Stormy Weather but was not intended for use in the
film.   Personnel is from the Spotlite LP.   The soloists are, in order:
Jacquet (ts), Carter (as), Jefferson (as).

---

[121]	March 24, 1943 Los Angeles Radio Show, "Blueberry Hill"
	BENNY CARTER AND HIS ORCHESTRA

Carter (tp, as, arr, comp) Gerald Wilson, Snooky Young, Walter Williams,
Fred Trainer (tp) John "Shorty" Haughton, J. J. Johnson, Alton Moore
(tb) Kirt Bradford, Willard Brown, Gene Porter, Eddie Davis (reeds) Ted
Brannon (p) Curly Russell (b) Oscar Bradley (d) The Charioteers (v)

FISH FRY   (32tp) arr, comp
LP: IAJRC 17

I CAN'T GET STARTED   (32as) arr

JOSHUA FIT DE BATTLE OF JERICHO   v-C (e)

AIN'T THAT SOMETHIN' (incomplete) (e)

> NOTE: "Fish Fry" announced as "Blueberry Hill Fish Fry," and
> listed on IAJRC LP as "Blueberry Hill Jamboree."

*   *   *

This show was the pilot for what was to be the civilian version of the Jubilee series.   It was aired over the CBS network.

The source for the tentative personnel is a Leonard Feather report
on a Benny Carter engagement in April-May 1943 at the Hollywood Club
(Metronome, April 1943, pp. 17, 33).

---

[122]	March-April 1943 Los Angeles Soundtrack of Film
	The Gang's All Here
	ALICE FAYE WITH BENNY GOODMAN AND HIS ORCHESTRA

Carter (as, arr) Benny Goodman (cl) Lee Castaldo, Ray Linn, Bobby Guyer
(tp) Miff Mole, Charlie Castaldo (tb) Hymie Schertzer, Leonard Kaye (as)
Jon Walton, Bob Taylor (ts) Joe Rushton (bs) Jess Stacy (p) Bart Roth (g)
Gus Van Camp (b) Louis Bellson (d) strings, Alice Faye (v)

NO LOVE, NO NOTHIN' v-AF (14as) arr
LP: CLASSIC INTERNATIONAL FILMUSICALS
3003

---

[123]	April 10, 1943 Los Angeles Airchecks, Hollywood Club
	BENNY CARTER AND HIS ORCHESTRA

Carter (as, tp, v, arr, comp) Gerald Wilson, Snooky Young, Walter Williams,
Fred Trainer (tp) Alton Moore, John "Shorty" Haughton (tb) J. J. Johnson
(tb, arr) Kirt Bradford, Willard Brown, Gene Porter, Eddie Davis (reeds)
Ted Brannon (p) Curly Russell (b) Oscar Bradley (d) Savannah Churchill (v)

MELANCHOLY LULLABY (incomplete) (4+4as)
       arr, comp

I'VE HEARD THAT SONG BEFORE v-SC (6tp)

BLUE SKIES v-SC with "Benny Carter Quartet"
    (Carter and three others) (4+4+4as)(v)

WITHOUT A SONG probably arr-JJJ (e)

ONE O'CLOCK JUMP probably arr-JJJ (20as)

ILL WIND (10+10+14as) arr

BACK BAY BOOGIE (incomplete) (24as) arr, comp

> NOTE: Personnel from Leonard Feather report in Metronome (April 1943, pp. 17, 33). Eddie Davis not same as Eddie "Lockjaw" Davis.

---

[124]   May or Later 1943 Los Angeles AFRS Basic Library
                    of Popular Music P-33
            BENNY CARTER AND HIS ORCHESTRA

Carter (as, tp, arr, comp) Carter Band Personnel Probably Similar to 10-25-43 Capitol Recording Session, Savannah Churchill (v) Frank Comstock (arr)

SLEEP (24as) arr
LP: ALAMAC QSR2449

I USED TO LOVE YOU v-SC, arr-FC (16+8as)
LP: ALAMAC QSR2449

ILL WIND (20as)(14as) arr
LP: PALM CLUB 12, ALAMAC QSR2449, SWING
TREASURY ST109, HOT 'N SWEET (F) HOL6426

FISH FRY (32tp) arr, comp
LP: PALM CLUB 12, ALAMAC QSR2449, HOT
'N SWEET (F) HOL6426

> NOTE: The tenor saxophone soloist is probably Bumps Myers, who joined Carter in May 1943.

---

[125]   October 25, 1943 San Francisco
            BENNY CARTER AND HIS ORCHESTRA

Carter (as, arr, comp) Claude Dunson, Vernon 'Jake' Porter, Teddy Buckner, Freddie Webster (tp) Alton Moore, J. J. Johnson, John "Shorty" Haughton (tb) Porter Kilbert (as) Willard Brown (as, bs) Gene Porter, Bumps Myers (ts) Ted Brannon (p) Ulysses Livingston (g) Curly Russell (b) Oscar Bradley (d) Savannah Churchill (v) Frank Comstock (arr)

POINCIANA arr-FC (16as with ensemble)   93
        (8as)(as coda)
78: CAPITOL 144 T: VA TRANSCRIPTION
HERE'S TO VETERANS 335, LP: CAPITOL
(E) LC6649, HITS H1002, CAPITOL (G) 1 C
056-85610 M

JUST A BABY'S PRAYER AT TWILIGHT   94
    v-SC, arr-FC (e)
78: CAPITOL 165 LP: CAPITOL (G) 1 C
056-85610 M

HURRY HURRY v-SC, arr-FC (8as) comp   95
78: CAPITOL 144 45: IL JAZZ (I)

LOVE FOR SALE (16as) arr   96
78: CAPITOL 100 LP: CAPITOL M11057,
CAPITOL (G) 1 C 056-85610 M

> NOTE: I1 Jazz 45 rpm has no issue number; Capitol M11057 also
> issued under number 5C 052-80850.

*   *   *

In 1942 Ella Mae Morse and Freddie Slack helped to put Capitol Records
on firm ground with a huge hit "Cow Cow Boogie," which Carter had composed with Don Raye and Gene DePaul. A year later Carter himself made
his first recordings for the label.

The personnel is entirely different from Carter's East Coast orchestra, although his old friend, guitarist Ulysses Livingston, has returned.

Some of the influential modernists, such as J. J. Johnson and Freddie Webster, are beginning to make their presence felt. One of the most
important additions was tenor saxophonist Bumps Myers, who was to become a mainstay of the orchestra over the next three years. Myers was
a consistent and exciting soloist as well as one of Carter's closest friends.

Carter was now busy enough to hire Frank Comstock to help arrange
for the orchestra. Comstock deeply admired Carter and brought so sym-
pathetic an understanding of Carter's style to his work that his arrangements were often credited to Carter. Carter did not attempt to dictate to
his arranger. "I left it up to him. He knew the band and he used to sit
in with us occasionally." Although Carter hired Comstock because of the
increasing demands on his time by film assignments, he had a secondary
motive. "I was also hoping someone would come up with a hit for the band
--a big seller. My thinking wasn't too bad because the arrangements he
[Comstock] made really were bigger sellers than anything I had done."

---

[126]   1943 Los Angeles Soundtrack of Film Thousands Cheer
      LENA HORNE WITH BENNY CARTER AND HIS ORCHESTRA

Carter (as, arr) Lena Horne (v)

HONEYSUCKLE ROSE v-LH (e) arr
LP: MCA2-11002, HOLLYWOOD SOUNDSTAGE SS409

---

[127]   1943 Los Angeles AFRS Basic Library of Popular Music P-34
      BENNY CARTER AND HIS ORCHESTRA

Carter (as, arr) Carter Band Personnel May Be Similar to 10-25-43 Capitol
Session, Savannah Churchill (v) Frank Comstock (arr)

SWANEE RIVER arr-FC (16+8as)
LP: PALM CLUB 12, ALAMAC QSR2449, HOT
'N SWEET (F) HOL6426

ALL OF ME (14as) arr
LP: PALM CLUB 12, ALAMAC QSR2449, HOT
'N SWEET (F) HOL6426

HONEYSUCKLE ROSE possibly arr: FC (32as)
LP: PALM CLUB 12, ALAMAC QSR2449

MIDNIGHT v-SC (16as) arr
LP: ALAMAC QSR2449

[128]   1943 Los Angeles AFRS Basic Library of Popular Music P-40
         BENNY CARTER AND HIS ORCHESTRA

Carter (as) Carter Band Personnel May Be Similar to 12-25-43 Capitol Session, Savannah Churchill (v) Frank Comstock (arr)

PRELUDE TO A KISS arr-FC (16as)
LP: ALAMAC QSR2449

I HEARD YOU CRIED LAST NIGHT v-SC (8+12as)
LP: ALAMAC QSR2449

ON THE ALAMO arr-FC (16as)(32as)
LP: ALAMAC QSR2449

[129]   1943 Los Angeles AFRS Basic Library of Popular Music P-86
         BENNY CARTER AND HIS ORCHESTRA

Carter (as) Rex Stewart (cornet) Remainder of Carter Band Personnel May
Be Similar to 12-25-43 Capitol Session

BOY MEETS HORN (e)
T: AFRS DOWNBEAT #218 LP: BLACK JACK
LP3010, SPOTLITE SPJ147

                              *   *   *

This is a feature for Rex Stewart who, according to John Chilton, gigged
with Carter in July 1943. The Downbeat show includes a brief interview
with Carter (added later) in which he discusses his career and the formation of his band. He mentions touring the country, "winding up at the
present time at the Orpheum Theater here in Los Angeles. " Carter first
played at the Orpheum March 17-23, 1943, and returned for the last week
in September.

[130]   May 21, 1944 Los Angeles
         BENNY CARTER AND HIS ORCHESTRA

Carter (as, tp, arr) John Carroll, Karl George, Edwin Davis, Milton Fletcher (tp) Alton Moore, J. J. Johnson, John "Shorty" Haughton, Bart Varsalona
(tb) Porter Kilbert (as) Willard Brown (as, bs) Gene Porter, Bumps Myers

(ts) Gerald Wiggins (p) W. J. Edwards (g) Charles Drayton (b) Max Roach
(d) Dick Gray (v)

I CAN'T ESCAPE FROM YOU   (6as) arr   254
78: CAPITOL 40048   LP: CAPITOL (E)
LC6649, CAPITOL M11057, CAPITOL (G)
1 C 056-85610 M

I'M LOST   v-DG (8as) arr   255
78: CAPITOL 165

I CAN'T GET STARTED   (32as)(4as) arr   256
78: CAPITOL 48015   LP: CAPITOL (E)
LC6649, CAPITOL M11057, CAPITOL (G)
1 C 056-85610 M

I SURRENDER DEAR   (32tp)(40tp)(tp coda) arr   257
78: CAPITOL 200   LP: CAPITOL H235,
CAPITOL M11057, CAPITOL (G) 1 C 056-
85610 M, TIME-LIFE STL-J10

NOTE: Capitol M11057 also issued under number 5C 052-80850.

* * *

"I Can't Escape From You" is one of the great Carter sax section features,
with a full chorus allotted to the reeds.   Although comparable to "Lonesome
Nights" or "Skip It" in concept, this arrangement has harmonic and rhythmic
innovations which give it a modern flavor.

This is Carter's first commercial recording of "I Can't Get Started,"
which he has consistently chosen as a ballad feature at concerts down to the
1980s.   In later versions it evolved into something of a set piece--a dazzling technical display with a spectacular coda.   Here the melody is more
explicit, although the last eight measures of Carter's solo foreshadow the
later virtuoso approach.

"I Surrender Dear" marks the final step in the evolution of Carter's
trumpet style from the Armstrong influence of his early work to the more
ornamented approach suggested by "More Than You Know."   The tone has
become drier and Carter makes greater use of tonguing.   The piece is in
two parts.   After Carter's decorative exposition of the melody at moderate
tempo in the first chorus, the pace doubles.   Carter's trumpet soars over
the ensemble and climaxes in a break.   His crisply-played ascending two-
note figures come to a slightly premature end, before the ensemble returns.
A fat-toned trumpet coda and flight to high E-flat end the record.   In subsequent performances he usually re-created the sensational solo he had improvised at this session.   "That was what you tried to do when a record
achieved some degree of success," he explains.   "If you varied it too much,
people would come up to you and say, 'Oh, but that's not the way you played
it on the record!'"

These are the first commercial recordings of Max Roach with the
Carter orchestra.   Carter recalls that Roach brought excitement to the
band, but occasionally the men had trouble picking up after one of his drum
solos.   "We were on the edge of our seats," Carter recalls.   "You never
knew where 'one' was!"

[131]	June 12, 1944 Los Angeles AFRS Jubilee #83

BENNY CARTER AND HIS ORCHESTRA

Carter (as, tp, arr) Milton Fletcher, Sleepy Grider, Fatso Ford, Edwin Davis (tp) John "Shorty" Haughton, Alton Moore, J. J. Johnson (tb) Porter Kilbert, Bumps Myers, Gene Porter, Willard Brown (reeds) Gerald Wiggins (p) Jimmy Edwards (g) Charles Drayton (b) Max Roach (d) Savannah Churchill (v)

JAY JAY'S JUMP

THEN YOU'VE NEVER BEEN BLUE   v-SC

I SURRENDER DEAR   arr

OL' MAN RIVER   arr

> NOTES: Tentative listing of personnel from Carter engagement at the Swing Club, Los Angeles, June 1944 reported by Barry Ulanov (Metronome, July 1944, p. 14). "Jay Jay's Jump" may be the same as "Polishin' Brass," arranged and composed by J. J. Johnson. "I Surrender Dear" probably features Carter on tp. From this show on Ernie "Bubbles" Whitman serves as m. c. for the Jubilee series.

[132]	July 11, 1944 Los Angeles AFRS Jubilee #87

BENNY CARTER AND HIS ORCHESTRA

Carter (as, tp, arr) Carter Band Personnel Probably Similar to 6-12-44 Jubilee #83, Savannah Churchill (v) Frank Comstock (arr)

SWEET GEORGIA BROWN   (32tp)(16as) arr

I LOST MY SUGAR IN SALT LAKE CITY   v-SC
      (4as intro)

STAR DUST   (32tp)(28tp+coda) arr

ROSE ROOM   arr-FC (16as)
LP: JAZZ SOCIETY AA502, JAZZ ANTHOLOGY
JA5123, KAYDEE KD2, SWEET 'N HOT (F) HOL6426

[133]	September 11, 1944? New York Recorded for V-Disc--Unissued

BENNY CARTER AND HIS ORCHESTRA

Carter (as, tp, arr) Bumps Myers (ts) Probably Regular Band Personnel

AMONG MY SOUVENIRS   (32as)(16tp) arr   32633

*   *   *

The date given above is listed on the sleeve of the acetate and is probably only approximate. Band routes show the Carter orchestra on tour at this time, but probably not in New York. There is a brief tenor solo at the end which is quite likely Bumps Myers.

---

[134]   Possibly January or November 1944   New York   Aircheck,
                                                           Apollo Theater
             BENNY CARTER AND HIS ORCHESTRA

Carter (as, arr, comp) Probably Regular Carter Band Personnel for the
Period

BACK BAY BOOGIE   arr, comp

---

[135]   1944   Los Angeles   AFRS Basic Library of Popular Music P-238
             BENNY CARTER AND HIS ORCHESTRA

Carter (as, arr) Carter Band Personnel May Be Similar to 6-12-44 Jubilee
#83, Savannah Churchill (v)

TWO AGAIN   v-SC (16as) arr
T: AFRS DOWNBEAT #218

I NEVER MENTION YOUR NAME   v-SC (e) arr
T: AFRS DOWNBEAT #218

I LOST MY SUGAR IN SALT LAKE CITY
        v-SC (4as intro)
T: AFRS DOWNBEAT #215

        NOTE: On dubbed narrative to Downbeat #218 Carter notes that he
        used "Two Again" as a theme song for some time.

---

[136]   February 26, 1945   New York
             TIMMIE ROGERS AND HIS ORCHESTRA

Carter (as) William Johnson, Talib Dawud, Felix Barboza, Loyal Walker
(tp) Alton Moore, John "Shorty" Haughton, George Washington, J. J. Johnson (tb) Porter Kilbert, Jewell Grant (as) Harold Clark, Don Byas (ts) Willard Brown (bs) Rufus Webster (p) Herman Mitchell (g) Charles Drayton (b)
Max Roach (d) Timmie Rogers (v)

DADDY-O   v-TR (e)   W1256
78:   REGIS 7001

GOOD DEAL   v-TR (e)   W1258
78:   REGIS 7001

CAPACITY
78:   UNISSUED

IF YOU CAN'T SMILE AND SAY YES DON'T
        CRY AND SAY NO
78:   UNISSUED

---

[137]   February 27, 1945   New York
             SAVANNAH CHURCHILL AND HER ALL STAR ORCHESTRA

Carter (as, tp, arr) William Johnson, Talib Dawud, Felix Barboza, Loyal
Walker (tp) Alton Moore, John "Shorty" Haughton, George Washington, J. J.

Johnson (tb) Porter Kilbert, Jewell Grant, Harold Clark, Willard Brown,
Don Byas (reeds) Rufus Webster (p) Herman Mitchell (g) Charles Drayton
(b) Max Roach (d) Savannah Churchill (v)

ALL ALONE   v-SC (e) arr   W1261
78: MANOR 1004 LP: BLUE STAR (F) 116

DADDY DADDY   v-SC (12tp acc) arr   W1262
78: MANOR 1004 LP: BLUE STAR (F) 116

> NOTE: Label of Manor 1004 states "trombone solo by Jay Jay"
> ("Daddy Daddy") and "tenor solo Don Byas" ("All Alone").

---

[138]   March 19, 1945 Los Angeles AFRS Jubilee #125
            BENNY CARTER AND HIS ORCHESTRA

Carter (as, tp, arr) Irving Lewis, Fred Trainer, Gerald Wilson, Emmett
Berry, Paul Cohen (tp) J. J. Johnson, George Washington, Louis Taylor
(tb) Porter Kilbert, Jewell Grant (as) Bumps Myers, Harold Clark (ts)
John Taylor (bs) Rufus Webster (p) Herman Mitchell (g) Charles Drayton
(b) Max Roach (d) Timmie Rogers (v)

SWEET GEORGIA BROWN   (32tp)(16as) arr
LP: PALM CLUB 12, JAZZ SOCIETY AA502,
JAZZ ANTHOLOGY JA5123, GOLDEN ERA
LP15058, SWEET 'N HOT (F) HOL6426, JOYCE
LP5007

DADDY-O   v-TR (e)
LP: JOYCE LP5007

JUST YOU, JUST ME   (8as)(16tp)(8tp) arr
LP: PALM CLUB 12

> ADDITIONAL ISSUES: All on Jubilee #219; "Sweet Georgia Brown"
> on AFRS Downbeat.

*   *   *

This tentative personnel is based on Carter's recording session for Capitol
on April 9, 1945. The presence of Bumps Myers and J. J. Johnson is
confirmed by Carter's announcement of the soloists following "Sweet Georgia
Brown" on the AFRS Downbeat show. This announcement is not present on
the Jubilee show.

---

[139]   March 26, 1945 Los Angeles AFRS Jubilee #126
            BENNY CARTER AND HIS ORCHESTRA

Carter (as, tp, v, arr, comp) Carter Band Personnel Probably Similar to 3-19-
45 (Jubilee #125) Barney Bigard (cl) Timmie Rogers, Betty Roche (v)
Arthur Treacher, Nat King Cole (spoken v)

JUBILEE JUMP   (8tp [2nd solo])
LP: EXTREME RARITIES 1007, JAZZ SOCIETY
AA502, JAZZ ANTHOLOGY JA5123, KAYDEE KD2,
HOT 'N SWEET (F) HOL6426, JOYCE LP5007

TROUBLE, TROUBLE   v-BR (e)
LP: JOYCE LP5007

COMEDY SKETCH   v-AT, NKC (spoken v)
LP: JOYCE LP5007

GOOD DEAL   v-TR (e)
LP: JOYCE LP5007

TEA FOR TWO   (e)
LP: SUNBEAM SB214, BLACK JACK LP3003,
JOYCE LP5007, SPOTLITE SPJ147

BACK BAY BOOGIE   (4as break)+(24as) arr, comp
LP: SUNBEAM SB214, JOYCE LP5007

>   NOTE: "Tea For Two" is a feature for Bigard.

>   ADDITIONAL ISSUES: "Jubilee Jump" on Jubilee #131 and #207;
>   "Tea For Two" on Jubilee #207 and #292; "Trouble..." and "Back
>   Bay Boogie" on Jubilee #207.

---

[140]	March 30, 1945 Los Angeles
	CAPITOL INTERNATIONAL JAZZMEN

Carter (as, comp) Bill Coleman (tp) Buster Bailey (cl) Coleman Hawkins (ts)
Nat King Cole (p) Oscar Moore (g) John Kirby (b) Max Roach (d) Kay Starr
(v)

YOU CAN DEPEND ON ME   (16as)   599
78:   CAPITOL 283   45:   IL JAZZ (I) LP:
CAPITOL M11031, CAPITOL (G) 1 C 056-
85610 M

IF I COULD BE WITH YOU   v-KS (18as)   600
78:   CAPITOL 10031 LP: CAPITOL (E)
LC6520, CAPITOL M11031

STORMY WEATHER   v-KS (8as)   601
78:   CAPITOL 283 LP: CAPITOL (G) 1 C
056-85610 M

RIFFAMAROLE   (24as) comp   602
78:   CAPITOL 10031   45:   IL JAZZ (I)   LP:
TULIP TLP105, CAPITOL M11031

>   NOTE: Il Jazz 45 rpm has no issue number; Capitol M11031 also
>   issued under number 5C 052-80806.

*   *   *

Capitol took advantage of the presence in Los Angeles of this dream personnel.   The group derived its name from the long periods of time Carter,
Hawkins and Coleman had spent in Europe.

Considering the magnitude of talent, the results are less than spectacular.   Hawkins is the dominant soloist on the two instrumentals.   Carter

sounds as if he is distracted in the middle of his solo on "You Can Depend On Me, " and falls into a predictable pattern on his boppish blues original "Riffamarole. " Cole's piano is superb throughout.

Bill Coleman has fond memories of this date, once calling it "one of the greatest thrills of my life, " because it was his first chance to record with both Hawkins and Carter.

Nat Cole was also glad to participate because, as producer Dave Dexter recounts in his autobiography, the pianist was "being castigated by the Eastern critics ... for deserting jazz to become a pop singer. " (Dexter, Playback, p. 98.)

---

[141]   Early 1945?   Los Angeles   AFRS Jubilee?
          BENNY CARTER AND HIS ORCHESTRA

Carter (as, tp, arr) Carter Band Personnel Unknown but Probably Includes J. J. Johnson (tb) Bumps Myers (ts) Frank Comstock (arr)

SOMEBODY LOVES ME   (8as) arr
T: AFRS DOWNBEAT # ?

MOONGLOW   arr-FC (16+8as)
T: AFRS DOWNBEAT # ?

ROSE ROOM   arr-FC (16as)
T: AFRS DOWNBEAT # 215

STAR DUST   (32tp)(28tp+coda) arr
T: AFRS DOWNBEAT # 97, AFRS DOWNBEAT # 215?
LP: SPOTLITE SPJ147

AFTER YOU'VE GONE   arr-FC (38as)
T: AFRS DOWNBEAT # ?

*   *   *

Although all of these recordings were included on AFRS Downbeat shows, their original source is not known. They may have been made for the Jubilee series and probably were not all done at the same time.

Carter has identified the trombone soloist on "Stardust" as J. J. Johnson, who probably left the band in early April 1945.

Although "Moonglow" is announced as a Carter arrangement, it is by Frank Comstock.

---

[142]   April 2, 1945 Los Angeles AFRS Jubilee #127
          BENNY CARTER AND HIS ORCHESTRA

Carter (as, tp) Carter Band Personnel Probably Similar to 3-19-45 (Jubilee #125) Timmie Rogers (v) Frank Comstock (arr)

ROSITA   arr-FC (32tp)(16as)
LP: JAZZ SOCIETY AA502, JAZZ ANTHOLOGY
JA5123, KAYDEE KD2

IF YOU CAN'T SMILE AND SAY YES DON'T
   CRY AND SAY NO   v-TR (e)

     NOTE: "Rosita" announced and listed on Jazz Society and Jazz
     Anthology LPs as "Slick Mix."

[143]	April 9, 1945 Los Angeles
	BENNY CARTER AND HIS ORCHESTRA

Carter (as, arr, comp) Irving Lewis, Fred Trainer, Gerald Wilson, Emmett
Berry, Paul Cohen (tp) Henry Coker, Alton Moore, George Washington,
Louis Taylor (tb) Jewell Grant, Porter Kilbert (as) Bumps Myers, Harold
Clark (ts) John Taylor (bs) Rufus Webster (p) Herman Mitchell (g) Charles
Drayton (b) Max Roach (d) Larry Stewart (v)

JUNE COMES AROUND   v-LS   610
78: UNISSUED

MALIBU (16+8as)(8as) arr, comp   611
78: CAPITOL 200   T: HERE'S TO VETERANS 26

     NOTE: Veterans transcription contains only excerpt of "Malibu."

               *   *   *

"Malibu" is one of Carter's most haunting melodies and his arrangement
highlights its stark simplicity. An errie background of swelling reeds and
muted brass back Carter's alto, which carries the theme. The only other
soloist is Henry Coker, who plays the eight-bar trombone bridge.

     Quincy Jones cites this record as one which made him want to be-
come an arranger. "I dug his record of 'Malibu' when I was in high school
and he's been my idol ever since."

[144]	April 16, 1945 Los Angeles AFRS Jubilee #129
	BENNY CARTER AND HIS ORCHESTRA

Carter (as, arr) Carter Band Personnel Probably Similar to 4-9-45 Recording
Date for Capitol, Barney Bigard (cl) Judy Carroll (v)

UNIDENTIFIED TITLE   (e)

EELIBUJ BLUES   (e)
LP: SPOTLITE SPJ147

PLAY ME THE BLUES   v-JC (e)

OL' MAN RIVER   (16as) arr
LP: SWING TREASURY 109

        NOTES: Carter believes that the first title may have been an original
        by one of the band members. "Eelibuj" features Bigard.

        ADDITIONAL ISSUES: All on Jubilee #220.

---

[145]   April 30, 1945   Los Angeles   AFRS Jubilee #131
           BENNY CARTER AND HIS ORCHESTRA

Carter (as, arr) Carter Band Personnel Probably Similar to 4-9-45 Recording Date for Capitol, Judy Carroll (v)

SOMEBODY LOVES ME   (8as) arr
LP: JAZZ SOCIETY AA502, JAZZ ANTHOLOGY
JA5123, PROBABLY MUSIDISC CCV2521

DARLING   v-JC (e)

SLEEP   (24as) arr
LP: JAZZ SOCIETY AA502, JAZZ ANTHOLOGY
JA5123, SWEET 'N HOT (F) HOL 6426

> ADDITIONAL ISSUES: "Somebody..." and "Sleep" on Jubilee #246;
> Jubilee #131 also includes version of "Jubilee Jump" from #126
> (March 26, 1945).

---

[146]   May 8, 1945   Los Angeles   AFRS Jubilee #132
           BENNY CARTER AND HIS ORCHESTRA

Carter (tp, as, arr, comp) Carter Band Personnel Probably Similar to 4-9-45
Recording Date for Capitol Except from Here on Percy Brice (d) Replaces
Max Roach, Helen Humes (v)

FISH FRY   (32tp) arr, comp
LP: SUNBEAM SB214

UNLUCKY WOMAN   v-HH (e)
LP: SUNBEAM SB214

FIESTA IN BRASS   (e)

> NOTE: "Unlucky Woman" listed on Sunbeam LP as "Blues"; although
> the m.c. announces that Humes is backed on this title by Carter,
> Carter does not believe that the trumpet accompaniment is his.

> ADDITIONAL ISSUES: "Unlucky Woman" on Jubilee #136 and #222.

---

[147]   June 4, 1945   Los Angeles   AFRS Jubilee #136
           BENNY CARTER AND HIS ORCHESTRA

Carter (as, tp, arr) Carter Band Personnel Probably Similar to 5-8-45 (Jubilee #132), Helen Humes (v) Frank Comstock (arr)

SUNDAY   (8as)(32as) arr
LP: JAZZ SOCIETY AA502, JAZZ ANTHOLOGY
JA5123

HABANERA   arr-FC (16as)
LP: JAZZ SOCIETY AA502, JAZZ ANTHOLOGY
JA5123

I CRIED FOR YOU   v-HH (tp acc)

EARLY BOYD (8as)
LP: JAZZ SOCIETY AA502, JAZZ ANTHOLOGY
JA5123, EXTREME RARITIES 1007

ADDITIONAL ISSUES: All on Jubilee #222.

| [148] | September 24, 1945 Los Angeles AFRS Jubilee #149 |

Carter (as) Unidentified Orchestra with Strings, Dick Haymes (v)

I'M GONNA LOVE THAT GAL v-DH

IT MIGHT AS WELL BE SPRING v-DH

NOTE: Carter's presence not confirmed.

ADDITIONAL ISSUES: Both titles on Jubilee #223.

---

[149]	November 16-22, 1945 Chicago Live Recording or
	Aircheck, Regal Theater
	BENNY CARTER AND HIS ORCHESTRA

Carter (as, tp, v, arr, comp) Probably Regular Band Personnel for the Period

THE HONEYDRIPPER (v)(8tp)

MALIBU (16+8as)(8as) arr, comp

| [150] | December 12, 1945 New York |
| | BENNY CARTER AND HIS ORCHESTRA |

Carter (as, tp, arr, comp) Louis Gray, Wallace Jones, Lewis Botton, Idrees
Sulieman (tp) Alton Moore, Charley Johnson, Al Grey, Johnny Morris (tb)
Joe Epps, Porter Kilbert (as) Willard Brown (as, bs) Bumps Myers, Harold
Clark (ts) Rufus Webster (p) James Cannady (g) Thomas Moultrie (b) Percy
Brice (d) Frank Comstock (arr)

CUTTIN' TIME (32as) arr, comp   838
78: UNISSUED LP: CAPITOL M11057,
CAPITOL (G) 1 C 056-85610 M

BUNBELINA arr, comp   839
78: UNISSUED

PRELUDE TO A KISS arr-FC (16as)   847
78: CAPITOL 40048 LP: PICKWICK
SPC3281, PICKWICK PTP2072, CAPITOL
M11057, CAPITOL (G) 1 C 056-85610 M

JUST YOU, JUST ME (6as)(16tp)(8tp) arr   848
78: UNISSUED LP: CAPITOL M11057,
CAPITOL (G) 1 C 056-85610 M

NOTE: Capitol M11057 also issued under number 5C 052-80850.

* * *

There is some confusion over the first title from this session. The Capitol files show this tune as "Forever Blue" and the Capitol Jazz Classics
LP lists that title. Carter, however, remembers writing "Forever Blue"
and does not believe that this is it. Furthermore, the title does not seem
to correspond to this uptempo non-blues swinger. This same composition
and arrangement was performed on an AFRS Jubilee show where it is announced as "Cuttin' Time." In any case, this arrangement and "Just You,
Just Me" show a marked be-bop influence, particularly in the brass writing.
The trumpet and tenor soloists on "Cuttin' Time" are Idrees Sulieman (who
was Leonard Graham at the time) and Bumps Myers. On "Just You, Just
Me" Carter has some reed trouble which may have prevented the record's
release. Although the notes to the Capitol Jazz Classics LP state that
Sulieman is the trumpet soloist on "Just You, Just Me," it is certainly
Carter, with Myers again featured on tenor.

---

[151]   January 5, 1946 New York
           BENNY CARTER AND HIS ORCHESTRA

Carter (as, v, arr, comp) Probably Louis Gray, Wallace Jones, Lewis Botton,
Idrees Sulieman (tp) Charley Johnson, Al Grey, Johnny Morris (tb) Joe
Epps, Porter Kilbert (as) Willard Brown (as, bs) Bumps Myers, Harold
Clark (ts) Rufus Webster (p) James Cannady (g) Thomas Moultrie (b) Percy
Brice (d) Bixy Harris (v) Gil Fuller (arr)

JUMP CALL (32as) arr, comp   166
78: DELUXE 1008 LP: AUDIOLAB 1505,
EMBER CJS802, JAZZ SELECTION 602

PATIENCE AND FORTITUDE v-BH, arr-GF   167
      (16as)(v)
78: DELUXE 1008

---

[152]   January 7, 1946 New York
           BENNY CARTER AND HIS ORCHESTRA

Carter (as, tp) Emmett Berry, Shorty Rogers, Joe Newman (tp) Neal Hefti
(tp, arr) Trummy Young, Alton Moore, Sandy Williams, Dicky Wells (tb)
Russell Procope (as) Willard Brown (as, bs) Tony Scott (cl, as) Flip Phillips,
Don Byas (ts) Sonny White (p) Al Casey (g) John Simmons (b) J. C. Heard
(d) James Cannady (arr)

DIGA DIGA DOO arr-JC (32as)   168
78: DELUXE 1028 LP: AUDIOLAB 1505,
EMBER CJS802, JAZZ SELECTION 606

WHO'S SORRY NOW arr-NH (32tp)   169
78: DELUXE 1009 LP: AUDIOLAB 1505,
EMBER CJS802, JAZZ SELECTION 606

SOME OF THESE DAYS arr-NH (8as with ensemble)+   170
      (8as)
78: DELUXE 1012 LP: AUDIOLAB 1505,
EMBER CJS802

[153]   January 8, 1946   New York
         BENNY CARTER AND HIS ORCHESTRA

Carter (as, arr, comp) Emmett Berry, Shorty Rogers, Joe Newman, Neal
Hefti (tp) Al Grey, Trummy Young, Alton Moore, Sandy Williams (tb) Rus-
sell Procope (as) Willard Brown (as, bs) Tony Scott (cl, as) Dexter Gordon,
Don Byas (ts) Sonny White (p) Freddie Green (g) John Simmons (b) J. C.
Heard (d) Maxine Sullivan (v) Frank Comstock (arr)

I'M THE CARING KIND   v-MS (8as) arr, comp   171
78: DELUXE 1012 LP: AUDIOLAB 1549,
AUDIOLAB 1505, EMBER CJS802

LOOKING FOR A BOY   v-MS (e) arr   172
78: DELUXE 1009 LP: AUDIOLAB 1505,
EMBER CJS802

ROSE ROOM   arr-FC (16as)   173
78: DELUXE 1028   45: DELUXE DEP282 LP:
AUDIOLAB 1505, EMBER CJS802

       NOTE: Although Audiolab 1549 is a Billy Eckstine release, it mis-
       takenly contains "I'm The Caring Kind."

                        *   *   *

The first of these three Deluxe sessions [151-153] was done with the regular Carter orchestra, but for the second and third dates an all-star group
of New York musicians was brought in.   Carter cites two reasons for this
curious shift in personnel: "The producers wanted some big names on the
date.   Also, they went to Gil Fuller, Neal Hefti, and Budd Johnson for arrangements.   Not all of the players in my band could just walk into the
studio and read, and these arrangements were all new to us."

       Gil Fuller, one of the pioneer bebop arrangers, provided the chart
for "Patience And Fortitude." With appropriately boppish ensemble accents
spurring him on, Carter here, more than in any other solo to date, shows
that he was absorbing some of the rhythmic and harmonic features of the
new style without abandoning his own. "I certainly paid attention to what
the younger musicians in my band and others were playing and tried to understand it.   But I made no attempt to incorporate anything in particular
into my own playing. I'm sure what I heard must have affected me, but
the change was purely subconscious."

       Carter's vocal exchanges with Bixie Harris are among his more
successful attempts at singing on record.

       The first arrangement played on the all-star date was far removed
from the boppish flavor of "Patience And Fortitude." "Diga Diga Doo" is
definitely a product of the 1930s with solos by Dicky Wells, Flip Phillips,
Joe Newman, Carter, Sonny White, and J. C. Heard.

       Carter opens "Who's Sorry Now" on trumpet, and his rather nostalgic
reading of the melody is somewhat incongruent with Neal Hefti's arrangement.   The two tenor spots are by Phillips, and Al Casey solos on electric
guitar.

       Soloists on "Some Of These Days" are Trummy Young, Sonny White,
Carter, probably Emmett Berry, and Don Byas.

Maxine Sullivan interprets Carter's attractive composition "I'm The Caring Kind" as well as "Looking For A Boy." The latter features some excellent Carter sax ensemble writing in the first chorus. The six-man section, which includes no less than Don Byas and Dexter Gordon, blends together well. The tenor solo is by Gordon.

"Rose Room" is one of those Frank Comstock scores which capture the essence of Carter's reed section so faithfully. Even the original 78 label credits Carter as arranger of this piece which features solos by Emmett Berry, Carter, John Simmons, Don Byas and Trummy Young.

[154]	March 31, 1946 Los Angeles Airchecks from Club
	'The Streets of Paris'
	BENNY CARTER

Carter (as) Miles Davis, Howard McGhee (tp) Al Grey, Possibly Britt Woodman (tb) Bumps Myers, Unknown (ts) Sonny White (p) James Cannady (g) Thomas Moultrie (b) Percy Brice (d)

JUST YOU, JUST ME   (32as with ensemble)(32as)

DON'T BLAME ME   (20as)(32as)

SWEET GEORGIA BROWN   (64as)

*   *   *

The personnel for this informal session is confusing. It seems to change after the first title, for which the soloists are announced. Following "Just You, Just Me" there is a presentation of the Esquire Gold alto sax award to Carter and for the final two tunes, other soloists seem to sit in. Tentative identifications of these were offered by Carter. "Just You, Just Me": all soloists named by announcer--Carter (as), Myers (ts), Davis (tp), Cannady (g), Carter (as) fades into Grey (tb), White (p). "Don't Blame Me": Carter (as) fades into ? (tb), White (p), ? (ts), Davis (tp) fades into Carter (as), Cannady (g). The tb soloist is probably not Grey; Carter has suggested Woodman. The ts solo is not by Myers. "Sweet Georgia Brown": tp over ensemble (may be Davis), Carter (as), Grey (tb), Myers (ts), Moultry (b) fades into Cannady (g), McGhee (tp); announcer interrupts after third chorus.

During his brief tenure with Carter, Miles Davis made no commercial recordings with the band but seems to have been present on several of the airchecks and AFRS programs. Carter remembers him as "very quiet," getting along well with the others in the band. He adds, "When Miles joined me it was quite clear that he was already thinking along different lines. But he was a good reader and certainly had no trouble with the book."

[155]	April 7, 1946
	ARNOLD ROSS QUARTET

Carter (as) Arnold Ross (p) Allan Reuss (g) Artie Bernstein (b) Nick Fatool (d)

THE MOON IS LOW   (32as)(32as)   HL145-1
78: UNISSUED-TEST EXISTS

THE MOON IS LOW (32as)(16as)   HL145-2
78: UNISSUED LP: EMARCY MG26029,
TRIP TLP5543

STAIRWAY TO THE STARS (16as)(16as)   HL146
78: KEYNOTE 648 LP: EMARCY MG26029,
TRIP TLP5543

BYE BYE BLUES (32as[theme])+(32as)(32as)   HL147
78: KEYNOTE 648 LP: EMARCY MG26029,
TRIP TLP5543

I DON'T KNOW WHY (16as[theme])(8as)
78: UNISSUED LP: EMARCY MG26029,
TRIP TLP5543

*   *   *

Although Arnold Ross was the nominal leader, Carter's alto is the major
focus of this excellent session. The instrumentation is significant because
these are Carter's first recordings with only a rhythm section since the
Swing Quartet date ten years earlier in England. His playing in this setting
was to change little throughout the 1950s and 1960s, when he recorded often
this way.

---

[156]   April 30, 1946 Southgate, California Airchecks
                          Trianon Ballroom
           BENNY CARTER AND HIS ORCHESTRA

Carter (as, tp, arr, comp) Probably 4 of These 5: Miles Davis, Fred Train-
er, Calvin Strickland, Walter Williams, Ira Pettiford (tp) Candy Ross (tb,
v) Johnny Morris, Al Grey, Charley Johnson (tb) Bob Graettinger, Joe
Epps, Harold Clark, Bumps Myers, Willard Brown (reeds) Sonny White (p)
James Cannady (g) Thomas Moultrie (b) Percy Brice (d) Lucy Elliott (v)
J. J. Johnson, Neal Hefti (arr)

I'M GONNA MAKE BELIEVE I'VE GOT
        MYSELF A SWEETHEART v-CR (8as)

I COVER THE WATERFRONT   (4tp intro)+(32tp)
     arr

I'M THE CARING KIND   v-LE (8as) arr, comp

POLISHIN' BRASS (incomplete) arr-JJJ (e)

WHO'S SORRY NOW arr-NH

        NOTE: "Polishin' Brass" announced as "Comin' On At The Tri-
    anon."

*   *   *

This probable personnel is based on a review of the band at a June 5 show
at the Swing Club in Los Angeles (Billboard, June 22, 1946, p. 22) and
photos in Carter's collection. Miles Davis was not listed in the review but
is known to have been with the band from January to May 1946.

[157]　May 5, 1946　Southgate, California　Airchecks,
Trianon Ballroom
BENNY CARTER AND HIS ORCHESTRA

Carter (as, tp, arr, comp) probably 4 of these 5: Miles Davis, Fred Train-
er, Calvin Strickland, Walter Williams, Ira Pettiford (tp) Candy Ross
(tb, v) Johnny Morris, Al Grey, Charley Johnson (tb) Bob Graettinger, Joe
Epps, Harold Clark, Bumps Myers, Willard Brown (reeds) Sonny White (p)
James Cannady (g) Thomas Moultrie (b) Percy Brice (d) Lucy Elliott (v)
J. J. Johnson (arr)

MY GUY'S COME BACK v-LE (16tp)

DREAM CASTLE (16+4as)(4as) arr, comp

BACK BAY BOOGIE (incomplete) (24as[inter-
    rupted]) arr, comp

NIGHT AND DAY v-LE (4as intro)(16as)(8tp) arr

IF I CAN'T HAVE YOU v-CR (e) arr, comp

POLISHIN' BRASS arr-JJJ (e)

WHERE OR WHEN (incomplete) (12as[inter-
    rupted by signoff]) arr

    NOTES: "Polishin' Brass" announced as "Comin' On At The Tri-
    anon." See note on personnel from preceding session.

[158]　April-May 1946　Los Angeles　AFRS Jubilee #184
BENNY CARTER AND HIS ORCHESTRA

Carter (as, tp, arr, comp) probably 4 of these 5: Miles Davis, Fred Train-
er, Calvin Strickland, Walter Williams, Ira Pettiford (tp) Candy Ross,
Johnny Morris, Al Grey, Charley Johnson (tb) Bob Graettinger, Joe Epps,
Harold Clark, Bumps Myers, Willard Brown (reeds) Sonny White (p) James
Cannady (g) Thomas Moultrie (b) Percy Brice (d) Kay Starr (v) Neal Hefti
(arr)

WHO'S SORRY NOW arr-NH (32as)
LP: QUEEN-DISC Q009

SHE'S FUNNY THAT WAY v-KS (tp acc)

ON THE SUNNY SIDE OF THE STREET v-KS
    (tp acc)

I CAN'T GET STARTED (32as)(4as) arr
LP: JAZZ SOCIETY AA502, JAZZ ANTHOLOGY
JA5123

JUMP CALL (32as) arr, comp
78: V-DISC 701 LP: JAZZ SOCIETY AA502,
JAZZ ANTHOLOGY JA5123, SPOTLITE SPJ147

    NOTES: "She's Funny..." announced and sung as "He's..." "Jump

Call" as "Melodrama In A V-Disc Record Room" on V-Disc 701.
See note on personnel from 4-30-46 session.

ADDITIONAL ISSUES: "Jump Call" on Jubilee #186.

*   *   *

Carter believes the trumpet soloist on "Jump Call" is Miles Davis. Although the style is rather different from that of Davis's recordings of the
period with Charlie Parker, it has often been pointed out that the Parker
recordings may not be representative. Carter recalls that Davis was far
more technically proficient at that time than he is usually given credit for.
Furthermore, he states that Davis did solo often with the band, and could
easily have been featured here and on "Just You, Just Me" from the next
session.

---

[159]   April-May 1946 Los Angeles AFRS Jubilee #186
         BENNY CARTER AND HIS ORCHESTRA

Carter (as, arr) See Personnel and Notes for Previous Jubilee Session, Lucy
Elliott (v)

JUST YOU, JUST ME (8as)(8as) arr
LP: SPOTLITE SPJ147

LOVER MAN v-LE

NOTE: This Jubilee show also includes the version of "Jump Call"
from Jubilee #184.

---

[160]   Same Show

Carter (as) Charlie Parker, Willie Smith (as) Nat King Cole (p) Oscar
Moore (g) Johnny Miller (b) Buddy Rich (d)

BODY AND SOUL (56as)
LP: SOUNDS 1206

CHEROKEE (e)
LP: SOUNDS 1206

*   *   *

[159, 160] Only one of two instances of Parker and Carter together on
record, this session is disappointing in that the medley format precluded
any interaction between the soloists, although they come together briefly on
"Cherokee." "Body And Soul" is Carter's feature in a two-part medley;
the first part was Smith's solo on "Tea For Two."

    The Spotlight LP credits Miles Davis with the trumpet solo on "Just
You, Just Me." Carter agrees. The solo sounds somewhat more characteristic of the style Davis displayed on other recordings of the period.

---

[161]   May-June 1946 Los Angeles AFRS Jubilee #191
         BENNY CARTER AND HIS ORCHESTRA

Carter (as, tp, arr, comp) Fred Trainer, Calvin Strickland, Walter Williams, Ira Pettiford (tp) Candy Ross, Johnny Morris, Al Grey, Charley Johnson (tb) Bob Graettinger, Joe Epps, Harold Clark, Bumps Myers, Willard Brown (reeds) Sonny White (p) James Cannady (g) Thomas Moultrie (b) Percy Brice (d) Lucy Elliott, Herb Jeffries (v) Calvin Jackson, J. J. Johnson (arr)

MR. COED   arr-CJ (e)
LP: PALM CLUB 12, QUEEN-DISC Q009

I'M THE CARING KIND   v-LE (8as) arr, comp

FRIM FRAM SAUCE   v-LE (16tp with ensemble)

SHE'S FUNNY THAT WAY   v-HJ (e)

POLISHIN' BRASS   arr-JJJ (e)
LP: PALM CLUB 12, EXTREME RARITIES
1007, SPOTLITE SPJ147

> NOTES: Personnel from Carter engagement at Swing Club, Los Angeles, June 5, 1946 (Billboard, June 22, 1946, p. 22) and photos in Carter collection. "Polishin' Brass" on Palm Club as "Jump Tune, " on Extreme Rarities as "No Title Jump, " and on Spotlite as "untitled original. "

[162]	Ca. July 1946 Los Angeles AFRS Jubilee #193
	BENNY CARTER AND HIS ORCHESTRA

Carter (as, cl, tp, arr, comp) Carter Band Personnel Probably Similar to May-June 1946 Jubilee #191 Listing, The Delta Rhythm Boys (v) James Cannady, Frank Comstock (arr)

CUTTIN' TIME   (32as) arr, comp
LP: EXTREME RARITIES 1007

ON THE SUNNY SIDE OF THE STREET   v-DRB (e)

STAR DUST   arr-JC (e)

PRELUDE TO A KISS   arr-FC (16as)
78:   V-DISC 823   LP: QUEEN-DISC Q009

I COVER THE WATERFRONT   (4tp intro)+(32tp) arr
LP: EXTREME RARITIES 1007

HELLO, GOODBYE, FORGET IT   v-DRB (e)

BACK BAY BOOGIE   (24as)(48cl) arr, comp
78:   V-DISC 678   LP: QUEEN-DISC Q009

> NOTES: Presence of Bumps Myers, Candy Ross and Sonny White confirmed by announcement of soloists on "I Cover The Waterfront. " "Stardust" is a feature for James Cannady on pedal steel guitar. The introduction to this performance is included on Spotlite SPJ147, but the version which follows on that LP is from an AFRS Downbeat show.

[163]   Ca. July 1946 Los Angeles AFRS Jubilee #203
          BENNY CARTER AND HIS ORCHESTRA

Carter (as, tp, v, arr, comp) Carter Band Personnel Probably Similar to May-
June 1946 Jubilee #191 Listing, Lucy Elliott (v) Gil Fuller, J. J. Johnson
(arr)

LOVE FOR SALE (4as)(32as) arr
LP: JAZZ ANTHOLOGY JA5123, JAZZ SOCIETY
AA502

I GOT IT BAD AND THAT AIN'T GOOD v-LE (16as)
LP: QUEEN-DISC Q009

PATIENCE AND FORTITUDE v-LE, BC arr-GF (v)(16as)
LP: QUEEN-DISC Q009

WITHOUT A SONG probably arr: JJJ (e)
LP: JAZZ SOCIETY AA502, JAZZ ANTHOLOGY
JA5123

OOFDAH (24tp [1st solo; 2nd is Walter Williams])
        arr, comp
LP: JAZZ SOCIETY AA502, JAZZ ANTHOLOGY
JA5123

          ADDITIONAL ISSUES: "Love For Sale," "Without A Song" and
          "Oofdah" on Jubilee #297; "I Got It Bad" on Jubilee #295.

[164]   Ca. July 1946 Los Angeles AFRS Jubilee #205
          BENNY CARTER AND HIS ORCHESTRA

Carter (as, tp, arr, comp) Carter Band Personnel Probably Similar to May-
June 1946 Jubilee #191, Vivian Garry (v)

I SURRENDER DEAR   (32tp)(40tp+coda) arr
LP: QUEEN-DISC Q009

I'M IN THE MOOD FOR LOVE v-VG (as acc)

MALIBU (16as)(8as)(8as) arr, comp

WHAT IS THIS THING CALLED LOVE (16+8as)

          NOTE: Presence of Sonny White, Thomas Moultry and Percy Brice
          confirmed by announcement by Vivian Garry before "I'm In The
          Mood For Love." Candy Ross and Harold Clark announced as solo-
          ists by m.c. on "What Is This Thing Called Love."

          ADDITIONAL ISSUES: Jubilee #292 contains all except "What Is
          This Thing...." In its place "Tea For Two" (featuring Barney
          Bigard) is repeated from Jubilee #126.

[165]   August 23, 1946 New York
          BENNY CARTER AND HIS CHOCOLATE DANDIES

Carter (as, cl, arr, comp) Buck Clayton (tp) Al Grey (tb) Ben Webster (ts)
Sonny White (p) John Simmons (b) Sid Catlett (d, v)

SWEET GEORGIA BROWN   (32cl)   D6VB 2694
78: SWING 258 LP: PRESTIGE 7604, PATHE
C054-16026, RCA (F) 75.594

OUT OF MY WAY v-SC (e) arr   D6VB 2695
78: SWING 226 LP: PRESTIGE 7604, PATHE
C054-16026, RCA (F) 75.594

WHAT'LL IT BE   (8as)(32as) comp   D6VB 2696
78: SWING 226 LP: PRESTIGE 7604, PATHE
C054-16026, RCA (F) 75.594

CADILLAC SLIM   (32as [trades with Webster])   D6VB 2697
    +(32as)
78: SWING 258 LP: PRESTIGE 7604, PATHE
C054-16026, RCA (F) 75.594, TIME-LIFE STL-J10

                    *   *   *

The last of Carter's Chocolate Dandies sessions took place while Carter
was in New York leading his band at the Apollo Theater.   Charles Delaunay and Hugues Panassié were anxious to revive their Swing label, and
Delaunay traveled to the United States to arrange for several sessions in a
variety of styles.

        Panassié was a great admirer of Mezz Mezzrow, and insisted that
he be hired to supervise the sessions, one of which featured some of the
leading exponents of bebop.   When Delaunay questioned Mezzrow's participation in a session centered around a music for which he had little sym-
pathy, Mezzrow quickly countered with an authentic-sounding legality:
Delaunay could not supervise these dates because he was a Frenchman.

        The sides have an informal air; the only writing seems to be the
introduction and background to Catlett's vocal feature "Out Of My Way."
Al Grey's solos on "Out Of My Way" and "Cadillac Slim" are probably his
first on record.   Grey, who had joined Carter's orchestra a few months
earlier, recalls the importance of his stay with Carter: "...the biggest
thing about him from my point of view was that he taught me how to
phrase." (Dance, The World of Count Basie, p. 205.)

        Carter's clarinet chorus on "Sweet Georgia Brown" is his last re-
cording on that instrument.   "I was more concerned with devoting time to
the trumpet which I preferred to the clarinet and even to the alto," he
recalls.   Whitney Balliett writes, "One of the persistent sorrows of jazz
is Carter's abandonment of the clarinet...," adding that his recordings
"suggest that Carter might easily have been the jazz clarinetist." (Balliett,
Such Sweet Thunder, p. 20.)

        The highlight of the session is "Cadillac Slim," an "I Got Rhythm"
variant credited to Catlett.   The melody is very similar to Billy Strayhorn's
"Raincheck," recorded by the Ellington band in 1941.   Ben Webster may
have been the link since he was prominent in the Ellington recording as
well.   Webster's solo generates an electricity reminiscent of his famous
solo on "Cottontail," and is followed by an inspired series of 4-bar exchanges with Carter.   Carter flies through the first 16 measures of his

chorus. As on several other recordings, when he reaches the bridge, he adopts a cooler, more detached approach, before resuming the rapid pace. Pianist White shares the next chorus with Grey, who makes the most of his eight bars. Clayton's piercing, yet warm sound and relaxed phrasing are complemented by Catlett's accompaniment. Throughout the session his rim shots, fills and bass drum explosions, perfectly timed, constantly spur the soloists.

---

[166]   August 1946   New York
           BENNY CARTER AND HIS ORCHESTRA

Carter (as, arr, comp) Paul Cohen, Ira Pettiford, Walter Williams (tp) Al Grey, Candy Ross (tb) Bumps Myers (ts) Willard Brown (as, bs) Sonny White (p) James Cannady (g) Thomas Moultrie (b) Percy Brice (d) Lucy Elliott (v)

RE-BOP BOOGIE   (24as) arr, comp   236
78: DELUXE 1044   45: DELUXE DEP282 LP:
PARLOPHONE GEP8568

TWELVE O'CLOCK JUMP   (32as) arr, comp   237
78: DELUXE 1041 LP: PARLOPHONE GEP8566,
AUDIOLAB 1505, EMBER CJS802

YOUR CONSCIENCE TELLS YOU SO v-LE (8as) arr, comp   238
78: DELUXE 1041 45: DELUXE DEP282 LP:
PARLOPHONE GEP8568

MEXICAN HAT DANCE (4as)   239
78: DELUXE 1044 45: DELUXE DEP282 LP:
PARLOPHONE GEP8568, AUDIOLAB 1505, EMBER CJS802

> NOTE: Ember CJS802 and Audiolab 1505 lists "Re-bop Boogie" but track is actually "Twelve O'Clock Jump" which appears twice.

*   *   *

Carter's final Deluxe date was made with his regular orchestra. The strange hybrid, "Re-bop Boogie, " and "Twelve O'Clock Jump" again show the rhythmic influence of the new music on Carter's writing, particularly for the brass. The last tune was arranged by Budd Johnson.

---

[167]   1946   Los Angeles
          ERNIE ANDREWS WITH THE CALVIN JACKSON ORCHESTRA

Carter (as) Manny Klein (tp) Calvin Jackson (p) Dave Barbour (g) Red Callender (b) Jackie Mills (d) Ernie Andrews, The Air Crew (v)

BABY I'M GONE   (8as)
78: G & G 1028, EXCLUSIVE 55X

---

[168]   Ca. 1946 Los Angeles   AFRS Jubilee #207
          BENNY CARTER AND HIS ORCHESTRA

Carter (as) For General Personnel for This Period See May-June 1946 Jubilee #191 Listing, Jimmy Durante (v.)

WHO WILL BE WITH YOU WHEN I'M FAR AWAY   v-JD (e)

CHICAGO (incomplete)   (32as)

    NOTE: Rest of show repeats Jubilee #126.

---

[169]   March 1947 Pasadena, California   AFRS Jubilee #230,
                    from McCornack Hospital
        BENNY CARTER AND THE ALL STARS FROM BLACK &
        WHITE RECORDS

Carter (as) Gerald Wilson (tp) Murray McEachern (tb) Barney Bigard (cl)
Phil Moore (p) Al Hendrickson (g) Red Callender (b) Hal West (d)

STOMPIN' AT THE SAVOY   (88as)
LP: QUEEN-DISC Q009

                        *   *   *

The m.c. for this session is Lena Horne and the announcer is Gene Norman; hereafter Norman serves as m.c. The date is established when Lena
Horne says that "Carter is leading a band at the El Patio Theater in a
review called Sumpin's Jumpin'."

---

[170]   Probably Early 1947 Pasadena, California   AFRS Jubilee #246,
                      Possibly from McCornack Hospital
        BENNY CARTER AND HIS ORCHESTRA

Carter (as, arr, comp) Unknown Personnel Probably Including Henry Coker
(tb) Dexter Gordon (ts) Sonny White (p) Dave Barbour (g) Peggy Lee (v) The
Pied Pipers (v) Frank Comstock (arr)

JUMP CALL   (32as) arr, comp
LP: EXTREME RARITIES 1007, SPOTLITE SPJ147

SUGAR   v-PL (e)

MY GAL SAL   v-PP (e)
LP: SPOTLITE SPJ147

PRELUDE TO A KISS   arr-FC (16as)

        NOTES: "Jump Call" listed on Extreme Rarities LP as "Bugle Call
        Rag." This show concludes with a repeat of "Somebody Loves Me"
        from Jubilee #131.

                        *   *   *

Because Carter no longer maintained a big band after October 1946, it is
impossible to establish a consistent personnel for this session and others
from this period. Carter certainly used some of the musicians who had
been with him for the past several years, but he also drew on other available talent to put together groups for varying periods of time. This may
explain the likely presence of Dexter Gordon on this date. Although Carter
cannot recall Gordon playing with him at this time, several sources maintain that the solo on "Jump Call" and the brief tenor passage on "My Gal

Sal" are by Gordon, who was then on the West Coast. These recordings
were played for Bob Porter and Michael Cuscuna, two Dexter Gordon spe-
cialists, who concur that it is he.

---

[171]   April 22, 1947 Los Angeles
           LUCKY THOMPSON AND HIS LUCKY SEVEN

Carter (as, arr, comp) Neal Hefti (tp) Lucky Thompson (ts) Bob Lawson (bs)
Dodo Marmarosa (p) Barney Kessel (g) Red Callender (b) Lee Young (d)

JUST ONE MORE CHANCE (e)   D7VB510-
78: VICTOR 20-2504 LP: RCA LPV544, RCA (F)
741. 106

FROM DIXIELAND TO BEBOP (e)   D7VB511'J'
78: UNISSUED-TEST EXISTS

FROM DIXIELAND TO BEBOP (e)   D7VB511'K'
78: UNISSUED-TEST EXISTS

FROM DIXIELAND TO BEBOP (e)   D7VB511-
78: VICTOR 20-3142 LP: RCA LPV544, RCA (F)
741. 106

BOULEVARD BOUNCE (32+16as) arr, comp   D7VB512'B'
78: UNISSUED-TEST EXISTS

BOULEVARD BOUNCE (32+16as) arr, comp   D7VB512'D'
78: UNISSUED-TEST EXISTS

BOULEVARD BOUNCE (32+16as) arr, comp   D7VB512'H'
78: UNISSUED LP: RCA LPV544, RCA (F) 741. 106

BOPPIN' THE BLUES (24as)   D7VB513-
78: VICTOR 20-2504, VICTOR 20-3142 LP: RCA
LPV3046, RCA LPV519, RCA (F) 741. 106

*   *   *

Carter does not solo on "Just One More Chance, " an extended ballad feature
for Thompson, nor on the humorous three-minute capsule history of jazz,
"From Dixieland To Be-bop. "

        Carter's own "Boulevard Bounce, " however, is a feature for him and
is particularly interesting because of the existence of three complete takes,
none of which, oddly enough, was issued on 78.

        He has no trouble negotiating the bebop head on the last title, and
his brief solo is in the spirit of the piece.

        (For an analysis of Carter's solo on the "H" take of "Boulevard
Bounce" see chapter 3.)

---

[172]   April 29, 1947 Pasadena, California Concert, Civic Auditorium
           GENE NORMAN'S 'JUST JAZZ'

Carter (as) Howard McGhee (tp) Vic Dickenson (tb) Wardell Gray (ts) Erroll
Garner (p) Irving Ashby (g) Red Callender (b) Jackie Mills (d)

ONE O'CLOCK JUMP   MM 914
78:   MODERN 20-641   T: AFRS JUBILEE 262
LP: MODERN LP1207, CROWN CLP5004, VOGUE
CMDGN766, CROWN CST293, CROWN CST420,
UNITED SUPERIOR US7722

TWO O'CLOCK JUMP   MM 915
78:   MODERN 20-641   LP: MODERN LP1207,
CROWN CLP5004, VOGUE CMDGN766, CROWN
CST293, CROWN CST420, UNITED SUPERIOR US7722

THREE O'CLOCK JUMP   (84as)   MM 916
78:   MODERN 20-642   LP: MODERN LP1207, CROWN
CLP5004, VOGUE CMDGN766, CROWN CST293,
CROWN CST420, UNITED SUPERIOR US7722

FOUR O'CLOCK JUMP   MM 917
78:   MODERN 20-642   LP: MODERN LP1207,
CROWN CLP5004, VOGUE CMDGN766, CROWN
CST420, UNITED SUPERIOR US7722

[173]	Same Concert

Carter (as) Chuck Peterson (tp) Vic Dickenson (tb) Charlie Barnet (ts)
Dodo Marmarosa (p) Irving Ashby (g) Red Callender (b) Jackie Mills (d)

PERDIDO (part one)   MM 1000
78:   MODERN 20-660   T: AFRS JUBILEE 261
LP: CROWN CP5008, VOGUE (E) E2296, JAZZ
SELECTION 633, SWING HOUSE SWH10

PERDIDO (part two)   (96as)   MM 1001
78:   MODERN 20-660   T: AFRS JUBILEE 261
LP: CROWN CP5008, VOGUE (E) E2296, JAZZ
SELECTION 633, SWING HOUSE SWH10

NOTE: Jepsen lists mx MM 1002 "Just You, Just Me" as by this
same group, but it is by Erroll Garner with rhythm section only.

*   *   *

[172, 173] In a jam atmosphere which foreshadowed his appearances with
Jazz at the Philharmonic, Carter turns in two genuinely exciting solos.
His playing has none of the forced frenzy of some of his JATP work; his
solos here are shorter and perhaps the novelty of the concept had yet to
wear off.

The first four titles comprise one continuous performance which was
divided for release on 78.

"Perdido" was also one performance, divided into two parts when
originally issued.   The 78 version is also edited: Vic Dickenson's solo,
which opens the tune, has been eliminated and Barnet's solo has been cut
from five choruses to three.   This edited version may be on some of the
LP's, except the Swing House, which contains the complete performance.

[174]   May 29, 1947 Los Angeles
           THE HOLLYWOOD HUCKSTERS

Carter (as) Charlie Shavers (tp) Benny Goodman (cl, v) Dave Cavanaugh (ts,
arr) Joe Koch (bs) Red Norvo (vib, xylophone) Jimmy Rowles (p) Irving
Ashby (g) Red Callender (b) Lee Young (d) Stan Kenton (v)

I APOLOGIZE   (4as)   2006
78: CAPITOL 48013   45: CAPITOL 7-1230 LP:
CAPITOL EAP 2-441, CAPITOL T441, CAPITOL (J)
EMI CR8811

THEM THERE EYES   (16as)   2007
78: CAPITOL 40022 LP: CAPITOL EBF 322,
CAPITOL H322, CAPITOL (E) LC6563, CAPITOL (J)
EMI CR8811

HAPPY BLUES v-BG, SK (12as)   2008
78: CAPITOL 40022   45: CAPITOL 7-1230 LP:
BANDSTAND 7106, CAPITOL (J) EMI CR8811

                          *   *   *

Dave Dexter brought this unusual personnel together. When asked why he
did not participate in the vocal repartee between Goodman and Kenton on
"Happy Blues, " Carter replied, "Because it was just a put-on; they would
have asked me to sing only if it were serious!"

[175]   May 31, 1947 Los Angeles Aircheck, Bocage Hotel?
           BENNY CARTER AND THE KING COLE TRIO

Carter (as) Nat King Cole (p) Oscar Moore (g) Johnny Miller (b)

COCKTAILS FOR TWO   (32+24as)

[176]   Early June 1947 Pasadena, California Gene Norman's 'Just Jazz, '
                           Civic Auditorium
           BENNY CARTER AND THE ALL STARS

Carter (as) Chuck Peterson (tp) Vic Dickenson (tb) Charlie Barnet (ts) Dodo
Marmarosa (p) Irving Ashby (g) Red Callender (b) Jackie Mills (d)

HOW HIGH THE MOON   (64as)
T: AFRS JUBILEE 262 LP: SWING TREASURY ST109

[177]   June 16, 1947 Los Angeles
           JULIA LEE AND HER BOY FRIENDS

Carter (as) Bobby Sherwood (tp) Vic Dickenson (tb) Dave Cavanaugh (ts) Red
Norvo (xylophone) Julia Lee (p, v) Jack Marshall (g) Red Callender (b) Sam
'Baby' Lovett (d) Joe Alexander (v)

MAMA DON'T ALLOW IT v-JL (16as)   2061
78: CAPITOL 1589 45: CAPITOL F1589 LP:
CAPITOL (E) LC6563, CAPITOL (J) EMI CR8811, CHARLY CRB1039

DOUBTFUL BLUES   v-JL (e)   2062
78: CAPITOL 40056

AIN'T IT A CRIME   v-JL (e)   2063
78: CAPITOL 838   LP: CAPITOL (E) LC6563

KNOCK ME A KISS   v-JL, JA   (e)   2064
78: UNISSUED   LP: CHARLY CRB1039

---

[178]   June 18, 1947 Los Angeles
           JULIA LEE AND HER BOY FRIENDS

Carter (as) Red Nichols (cornet) Vic Dickenson (tb) Dave Cavanaugh (ts)
Red Norvo (xylophone) Julia Lee (p, v) Jack Marshall (g) Red Callender (b)
Sam 'Baby' Lovett (d)

COLD HEARTED DADDY   v-JL (e)   2065
78: CAPITOL 15300   LP: CAPITOL (E) CL13323

MY SIN   v-JL (16as)   2066
78: CAPITOL 40056   LP: CAPITOL T1057

WHEN YOU'RE SMILING   v-JL (16as)   2067
78: CAPITOL 40082   LP: CAPITOL T1057, CAPITOL
(G) 1 C 056-85610 M

I WAS WRONG   v-JL (8as)   2068
78: CAPITOL 40028   LP: CAPITOL T1057, CAPITOL
T2038, TULIP TLP103, CAPITOL (G) 1 C 056-85610 M

---

[179]   Ca. July 1947 Pasadena, California AFRS Jubilee #248,
                  Probably from McCornack Hospital
           BENNY CARTER AND HIS ORCHESTRA

Carter (as, arr, comp) Unknown Personnel Probably Including Henry Coker
(tb) Lucky Thompson (ts) Sonny White (p) The Pied Pipers (v)

FISH FRY   (16as) arr, comp

LINDA   v-PP (e)

SAME OLD DREAM   v-PP (e)

JUST YOU, JUST ME (incomplete)   (8as) arr
LP: SPOTLITE SPJ147

                        *   *   *

The trombone and tenor solos on "Just You, Just Me" sound like Coker and
Thompson, who were working with Carter on and off during this time.

        This show also includes a version of Carter's composition "Lonely
Woman" sung by Peggy Lee, accompanied by piano and guitar.

---

[180]   September 22, 1947 Los Angeles
           JOE ALEXANDER WITH DAVE CAVANAUGH'S MUSIC

Carter (as, comp) Ernie Royal (tp) Clint Neagley (tb) Dave Cavanaugh, Babe
Russin (ts) Joe Koch (bs) Juan Panalle (p) Jack Marshall (g) Harry Babasin
(b) Lee Young (d) Joe Alexander (v)

FOR YOU   v-JA   2263
78: CAPITOL 40055

WHEN I CLOSE MY EYES   v-JA   2264
78: CAPITOL 40055

I'M A THREE TIME LOSER   v-JA comp   2265
78: CAPITOL 40079

SO LONG DARLING   v-JA (12as)   2266
78: CAPITOL 15274

---

[181]   October 14, 1947 Los Angeles
          TEN CATS AND A MOUSE

Carter (ts) Dave Barbour (tp) Billy May, Bobby Sherwood (tb) Paul Weston
(cl) Eddie Miller (as) Dave Cavanaugh (bs) Red Norvo (p) Hal Derwin (g)
Frank Devol (b) Peggy Lee (d)

JA-DA   (16ts [trades with tb])   2343
78: CAPITOL 15015

THREE O'CLOCK JUMP   (12ts)   2344
78: CAPITOL 15015

*   *   *

In this Capitol novelty the musicians switch instruments.   Carter on tenor
was nothing new, of course.

---

[182]   Same Date
          RED NORVO'S NINE

Carter (as, arr, comp) Bobby Sherwood (cornet) Dave Cavanaugh, Eddie
Miller (ts) Arnold Ross (p) Dave Barbour (g) Billy Hadnott (b) Jesse Price
(d) Red Norvo (vib)

HOLLYRIDGE DRIVE   (16as) arr, comp   2345
78: CAPITOL 15083   45: CAPITOL 6F-1225, LP:
CAPITOL (J) EMI CR8811, CAPITOL (G) 1 C 056-85609 M

UNDER A BLANKET OF BLUE   (8as)   2346
78: CAPITOL 15083   45: CAPITOL 6F-1225, LP:
CAPITOL H322, CAPITOL T795, CAPITOL (E)
CL13405, CAPITOL (E) LC6563, CAPITOL (J)
EMI CR8811, CAPITOL (G) 1 C 056-85609 M

*   *   *

Carter's lovely composition and small-group arrangement "Hollyridge Drive"
was named for the Beverly Hills street on which he lived.

[183]   October 20, 1947 Los Angeles
KAY STARR WITH DAVE CAVANAUGH'S MUSIC

Carter (as) Uan Rasey, Joe Triscari, George Seaburg, Irv Stumph (tp)
Hoyt Bohannon, Lloyd Ulyate, Lou McGarity, Ed Kusby (tb) Clint Neagley
(as) John Hamilton, Jack Crowlet, Dave Cavanaugh (ts) Joe Koch (bs) Arnold Ross (p) George Van Eps (g) Billy Hadnott (b) Lee Young (d) Dan Lube
(viola)

MANY HAPPY RETURNS v-KS (e)   2348
78: CAPITOL 15137

YOU'VE GOTTA SEE MAMA EV'RY NIGHT OR YOU   2349
      CAN'T SEE MAMA AT ALL v-KS (e)
78: CAPITOL 497 LP: CAPITOL T211, CAPITOL
T1468, CAPITOL (E) CL13047

WAS THAT THE HUMAN THING TO DO v-KS (e)   2350
78: CAPITOL 40066

THEN I'LL BE TIRED v-KS (e)   2351
78: CAPITOL 40066

        NOTE: Last title by smaller group (no brass, possibly fewer reeds).

[184]   November 11, 1947 Los Angeles
JULIA LEE AND HER BOY FRIENDS

Carter (as, tb, comp) Geechie Smith (tp) Dave Cavanaugh (ts) Julia Lee (p, v)
Jack Marshall (g) Red Callender (b) Sam 'Baby' Lovett (d)

PAGAN LOVE SONG v-JL (e [on tb])   2441
78: CAPITOL 1149

ALL I EVER DO IS WORRY v-JL (8tb)   2442
78: CAPITOL 15106

TAKE IT OR LEAVE IT v-JL (4+4as) comp   2443
78: CAPITOL 57-70006 LP: CHARLY CRB1039

THAT'S WHAT I LIKE v-JL (e)   2444
78: CAPITOL 15060 LP: CAPITOL (G)
1 C 056-85610 M, CHARLY CRB1039

KING SIZE PAPA v-JL (4+4as) comp   2445
78: CAPITOL 40082 LP: CAPITOL T2038, CAPITOL
(E) CL13055, CAPITOL (E) LC6535, CHARLY CRB1039

BLUES FOR SOMEONE v-JL (e)   2446
78: CAPITOL 57-70051

I'M FOREVER BLOWING BUBBLES v-JL (32as)   2447
78: CAPITOL 1149

BREEZE, BLOW MY BABY BACK TO ME (e)   2448
78: CAPITOL 1589 45: CAPITOL F1589

---
[185]   November 13, 1947 Los Angeles
           JULIA LEE AND HER BOY FRIENDS

Carter (as, tb, comp) Vic Dickenson (tb) Dave Cavanaugh (ts) Julia Lee (p, v)
Jack Marshall (g) Billy Hadnott (b) Sam 'Baby' Lovett (d)

I DIDN'T LIKE IT THE FIRST TIME v-JL (16as) comp   2458
78: CAPITOL 15367 LP: CAPITOL (E) LC6535, CHARLY CRB1039

CRAZY WORLD v-JL (12as [trades with Dickenson -   2460
     Carter starts])
78: CAPITOL 15060 LP: CAPITOL T2038

TELL ME DADDY v-JL (12as)   2461
78: CAPITOL 15144 LP: CAPITOL (E) LO6535

CHRISTMAS SPIRITS v-JL (e)   2462
78: CAPITOL 15203

                        *   *   *

These two sessions [184, 185] comprise Carter's total recorded output on
trombone.   "I had been playing trombone occasionally and had written some
things for my band where I played in the trombone section.   Dave Dexter
suggested that I play it on these dates. " Carter can be heard riffing with
the ensemble on trombone in "Pagan Love Song, " and he takes an 8-bar
solo on "All I Ever Do Is Worry. "

     Vic Dickenson joined the group for the second session, and he and
Carter play a trombone-duet chorus on "Crazy World, " with Carter leading
and Dickenson providing the more intricate fills.   Carter achieves a full
sound on the instrument, especially on "All I Ever Do Is Worry. " He himself notes that he became more proficient on the horn after this date but
never again recorded on it.   Trombonist Al Grey, who played in the Carter
orchestra, recalls Carter's initial efforts: "One day he decided to pick up
the trombone.   Though I was only a newcomer, I thought I sounded pretty
good.   So he played, and I was soon saying to myself, 'Well, well, you'd
better take note here!'" (Dance, The World of Count Basie, p. 205.)

     These sessions also marked the first use by Carter of the pseudonym
"Johnny Gomez" under which he co-composed "King Size Papa" and "I Didn't
Like It The First Time" (subtitled "The Spinach Song").   Apparently Carter
preferred not to have his name attached to these tunes, whose double-entendre lyrics were somewhat risqué for that time.

---
[186]   November 25, 1947 Los Angeles
           FREDDIE SLACK AND HIS ORCHESTRA

Carter (as, arr, comp) Chuck Peterson, Jim Salco, Jack Trainer, Gerald
Wilson (tp) Hoyt Bohannon, Tommy Pederson (tb) Jewell Grant (as) Bumps
Myers, Vido Musso (ts) Chuck Gentry (bs) Freddie Slack (p) Ulysses Liv-
ingston (g) Harry Babasin (b) Henry Green (d)

BOOGIE MINOR (e) arr, comp   2596
78: CAPITOL 10134 LP: CAPITOL (E) H83,
CAPITOL (E) LC6529

ST. LOUIS BLUES (e) arr   2597
78: UNISSUED LP: CAPITOL H323, BIG BAND
ARCHIVES 1202

CHOPSTICK BOOGIE (e) arr   2598
78: CAPITOL 10132 LP: CAPITOL (E) H83,
CAPITOL (E) LC6529, BIG BAND ARCHIVES 1202

*   *   *

These three Carter arrangements are centered around the boogie-woogie
piano stylings of the leader. Of particular interest are the excellent brass
and reed figures in "St. Louis Blues."

---

[187]   1947 Los Angeles
           ANITA O'DAY WITH RALPH BURNS AND HIS ORCHESTRA &
           BENNY CARTER AND HIS ORCHESTRA

Carter (as, arr, comp) 12 Piece Orchestra Including Ray Linn (tp) Ray Sims
(tb) Ralph Burns (p, arr) Don Lamond (d) Anita O'Day (v)

HOW HIGH THE MOON v-AO (e)   SRC 657
78: SIGNATURE 15185 LP: SIGNATURE LSP8,
CORAL CRL56073, BOB THIELE MUSIC BBM1-0595,
RCA (J) PG-86

I AIN'T GETTIN' ANY YOUNGER v-AO (e) arr, comp   SRC 658
78: SIGNATURE 15217 LP: SIGNATURE LSP8,
CORAL CRL56073, BOB THIELE MUSIC BBM1-0595,
RCA (J) PG-86

MALAGUENA v-AO (e)   SRC 659
78: SIGNATURE 15181 LP: SIGNATURE LSP8,
CORAL CRL56073, BOB THIELE MUSIC BBM1-0595,
RCA (J) PG-86

KEY LARGO v-AO (e) arr, comp   SRC 660
78: SIGNATURE 15185 LP: CORAL CRL56073,
BOB THIELE MUSIC BBM1-0595, RCA (J) PG-86

NOTE: First three titles--Ralph Burns And His Orchestra; last
title--Benny Carter And His Orchestra.

*   *   *

Two Carter compositions were premiered at this session. The boppish
blues "I Ain't Gettin' Any Younger" was later recorded by Woody Herman.
The alto solo on this version is not by Carter.

The Latin-flavored "Key Largo" was recorded by a variety of artists, including Sarah Vaughan. Carter believes he may have written the
bridge with co-composer Karl Suessdorf providing the "A" section. Carter's
arrangement for O'Day has some lush reed background figures with Carter
prominent on lead alto.

---

[188]   1947 Los Angeles
           LEE RICHARDSON ACC. BY BENNY CARTER'S ALL STARS

Carter (as) Lee Richardson (v) Others Unknown

IT'S TOO SOON TO KNOW   801
78: DELUXE 3196, DELUXE 3197

AM I ASKING FOR TOO MUCH   802
78: DELUXE 3195

WHEN I THINK OF YOU   803
78: DELUXE 3196

A FOOL FOR YOU   804
78: DELUXE 3197

[189]   Late 1947 or Early 1948   Pasadena, California AFRS Jubilee
                                        #276, from McCornack Hospital
              BENNY CARTER AND HIS ORCHESTRA

Carter (as, arr, comp) Mary Lou Williams (p) Unknown Carter Band Personnel Probably Including Henry Coker (tb) Bumps Myers (ts)

LOVER   (32as)

HOLLYRIDGE DRIVE   (16as) arr, comp

ROLL 'EM   (e)
LP: SPOTLITE SPJ147

CONGOROO   (32as) arr, comp

     NOTES: Mary Lou Williams plays only on "Roll 'Em." "Hollyridge
     Drive" is by a small group from the orchestra.

[190]   January 1948 Los Angeles
              BENNY CARTER AND HIS ORCHESTRA

Carter (as, arr) Lew Obergh (tp) Henry Coker (tb) Bumps Myers (ts) Cyril
Haynes (p) Jack Marshall (g) Dallas Bartley (b) Henry Green (d) Bob Decker, Emma Lou Welch, The Enchanters (v)

BABY, YOU'RE MINE FOR KEEPS v-ELW (8as) arr
78: REINA 101

YOU'LL NEVER BREAK MY HEART AGAIN v-ELW, E
        (8as) arr
78: REINA 101

AN OLD LOVE STORY v-ELW, E (8as) arr
78: REINA 102

CHILPANCINGO v-BD, E (12as) arr
78: REINA 102

REINA v-BD, E (4as intro)(16as) arr
78: REINA 103

LET US DRINK A TOAST TOGETHER   arr
78:   REINA 103

*   *   *

This session was similar in concept, but on a smaller scale, to the work
Carter was to do for amateur songwriter Bob Friedman some 25 years later.   Here Harry Atwood hired Carter to provide an appropriate showcase
for his compositions and issued the sides on his own label.

These recordings are of little jazz interest except for good alto and
guitar solos on "Chilpancingo."

[191]   March 30, 1948   Pasadena, California   AFRS Jubilee # 284, from
                            McCornack Hospital
           BENNY CARTER AND HIS ORCHESTRA

Carter (as, arr, comp) Unknown Personnel

CONGOROO   arr, comp

ORIGINAL JELLY ROLL BLUES

BOP BOUNCE   arr, comp

*   *   *

The date is from an AFRS script for this show, which was a jazz retrospective, tracing the history of the music.   Along with the Carter band were
Peggy Lee, Pete Daley's Chicagoans and the Deep River Boys.   Also included were recordings by Jelly Roll Morton of "King Porter Stomp" and
"Winin' Boy Blues."

The script originally listed "Sleep" which was crossed out in favor
of "Little Bo Bop Has Lost Her Beep."   Rainer E. Lotz lists the title as
"Bop Bounce."   It is not known whether these are the same composition.

On the script "Congoroo" is crossed out and the title "Bamboula" is
substituted.   These are probably the same composition.

[192]   December 14, 1948   Los Angeles
           CLARENCE CLUMP WITH ORCHESTRA [Clump is pseudonym for
           Carter]

Carter (v, comp) Possibly Henry Coker (tb) Unknown (as) Possibly Dave
Cavanaugh (ts) Unknown (p, g, b, d) Clarence Clump (v)

HAPPY GO LUCKY YOU AND BROKEN HEARTED ME   (v)   3800-2D-5
78:   CAPITOL 15363

I DON'T WANT IT NO MORE   (v) comp   3801-3D-4
78:   CAPITOL 15363

*   *   *

After many years Carter revealed his identity as the mysterious Clarence Clump on these humorous sides put together by Carter and Dave Dexter. Although bearing a standard Capitol label and issue-number, the disc must have had a limited pressing and appears in very few Capitol catalogs.

Carter sings the first title with mock seriousness, using a British accent. A tenor saxophone is audible: Carter suggests Dave Cavanaugh.

Carter sings the double-entendre lyrics to "I Don't Want It No More" with no special accent. There are brief alto (not Carter), tenor and trombone (Carter suggests Henry Coker) solos and an impromptu vocal group. Capitol files show the session as non-union and no personnel records were kept.

Carter used a double pseudonym on this last title; not only did he sing it under the name "Clarence Clump," but again he used "Johnny Gomez" to mask his role as co-composer.

[193]   May 1949   Los Angeles
         BENNY CARTER AND HIS ALL STARS

Carter (as, comp) Possibly Chuck Peterson (tp) Vic Dickenson (tb) Ben Webster (ts) Dodo Marmarosa (p) John Simmons or Charles Drayton (b) Jackie Mills (d)

COTTONTAIL   (e)   MM1767
78: MODERN 858   LP: RIVERBOAT (F) 900.267

TIME OUT FOR THE BLUES   (e)   MM1768
78: MODERN 858   LP: CROWN CLP5009, RIVERBOAT
(F) 900.267, TIME-LIFE STL-J21

SURF BOARD   (e) comp   MM1813
78: MODERN 865   LP: IAJRC 15, RIVERBOAT (F) 900.267

YOU ARE TOO BEAUTIFUL   (e)   MM1814
78: MODERN 865   LP: CROWN CLP5009, RIVERBOAT
(F) 900.267

*   *   *

This date has several puzzling aspects. First, Carter remembers it as a Ben Webster session. This possibility is given credence by the fact that Webster is the featured soloist on all sides, with Carter himself not soloing at all. The records may have been issued under Carter's name in error, someone mistaking "Benny" for "Ben."

Dubbed applause is audible on the original issues of "Time Out For The Blues" and "Cottontail," a re-creation by Webster of his famous 1940 solo.

[194]   July 8, 1949   Los Angeles
         KITTY WHITE ACC. BY DAVE CAVANAUGH'S ORCH.

Carter (as, comp) Parr Jones, Vernon Smith, Mickey Mangano (tp) George Washington (tb) Marvin Johnson (as) Dave Cavanaugh, Maxwell Davis (ts)

Chuck Waller (bs) Charlie Davis (p) Billy Hadnott (b) Jackie Mills (d) Kitty White (v)

I'M PLAYING WITH FIRE   v-KW (e)   4654
78:   CAPITOL 57-70061   LP: CAPITOL (E) CL13549

A MAN IS GOOD   v-KW   4655
78:   CAPITOL 57-70032

OO-WEE   v-KW (e)   4656
78:   CAPITOL 57-70061

IT PAYS TO ADVERTISE   comp   4657
78:   CAPITOL 57-70032   LP: CAPITOL (E) CL13549

---

[195]   September 22, 1949 Los Angeles
           JOE ROBINSON WITH BENNY CARTER'S ORCHESTRA

Carter (as, arr, comp) Teddy Buckner (tp) Bumps Myers (ts) Chuck Waller (bs) Gerald Wiggins (p) Gene Phillips (g) Charles Drayton (b) Jackie Mills (d) Joe Robinson (v)

ROLL WITH THE BOOGIE   v-JR (e) arr, comp   D9VB747-1
78:   VICTOR 22-0054   45:   VICTOR 50-0038

IF I CAN'T HAVE YOU   v-JR (e) arr, comp   D9VB748-1
78:   VICTOR 22-0054   45:   VICTOR 50-0038

SUSPICIOUS OF MY WOMAN   v-JR (e) arr, comp   D9VB749-1
78:   VICTOR 22-0067   45:   50-0052

SUSPICIOUS OF MY WOMAN   v-JR (e) arr, comp   D9VB749-2
78:   UNISSUED

DON'T SCREAM, DON'T SHOUT   v-JR (e) arr   D9VB750-1
78:   VICTOR 22-0067   45:   50-0052

DON'T SCREAM, DON'T SHOUT   arr   D9VB750-2
78:   UNISSUED

                          *   *   *

Carter used his "Johnny Gomez" pseudonym for his compositions "Roll With The Boogie" and "Suspicious Of My Woman." He wrote the ballad "If I Can't Have You" under his own name, assuming the role of lyricist as well.

All titles except "Suspicious ..." have good solos by Bumps Myers.

---

[196]   1949 Los Angeles
           DEBBIE ANDREWS

Carter (as) Debbie Andrews (v) Others Unknown

I LOST YOU   v-DA
78:   MERCURY 8282

I AIN'T GOT NOBODY   v-DA
78: MERCURY 8282

---

[197]   October 21, 1950 Los Angeles
           AL HIBBLER WITH THE ELLINGTONIANS

Carter (as) Mercer Ellington (mellophone, arr) Harry Carney (bs) Billy Strayhorn (p, arr) Dave Barbour (g) Wendell Marshall (b) Charlie Smith (d) Al
Hibbler (v)

STORMY WEATHER v-AH arr-BS (e)   M4019
78: MERCER 1956 LP: MERCER LP1004, BRUNSWICK
BL54036

CHERRY v-AH arr-ME (e)   M4020
78: MERCER 1956 LP: MERCER LP1004, BRUNSWICK
BL54036

STAR DUST v-AH (e)   M4021
78: MERCER 1965 LP: MERCER LP1004, BRUNSWICK
BL54036

HONEYSUCKLE ROSE v-AH (e)   M4022
78: MERCER 1965 LP: MERCER LP1004, BRUNSWICK
BL54036, JAZZ SELECTION JS652

---

[198]   November 6, 1950 New York
           THE THREE FLAMES WITH ORCH. UNDER THE DIRECTION OF
           BENNY CARTER

Carter (as) The Three Flames: Tiger Haynes (g) Roy Testamark (p, v)
Bill Pollard (b, v) Unknown vib. and d.

SKY FULL OF SUNSHINE   v-TF (as, arr)   44616
78: COLUMBIA 39078

SUCCOTASH BABY v-TF (4as intro)(12as acc)(8as acc)   44618
78: COLUMBIA 39078

STICK AROUND v-TF   ZSP5445
78 AND/OR 45: COLUMBIA 39259

GO WAY GAL v-TF   ZSP5447
78 AND/OR 45: COLUMBIA 39259

> NOTE: Last two titles may be from same session; Carter's pres-
> ence not confirmed.

---

[199]   December 27, 1951 Los Angeles
           BEN WEBSTER SEXTET

Carter (as, comp) Maynard Ferguson (tp) Ben Webster (ts) Gerald Wiggins
(p) John Kirby (b) George Jenkins (d)

RANDALL'S ISLAND (e) comp   4720

78: MERCURY 8265 LP: EMARCY MG36050, EMARCY
MG26006, MERCURY (F) MEP 14076, TRIP TLP5555

OLD FOLKS (e)   4721
78: MERCURY 8298 LP: EMARCY MG26006, MERCURY
(F) MEP14076

KING'S RIFF (24as) comp   4722
78: MERCURY 8298 LP: EMARCY MG36050, EMARCY
MG26006, MERCURY (F) MEP14076, TRIP TLP5555

*   *   *

Carter provided two blues--the boppish "Randall's Island" and the basic
"King's Riff"--for this session showcasing the talents of his good friend
Ben Webster.

        The date was one of the last for John Kirby, who was in poor health
and whom Carter had assisted after Kirby's move to the West Coast.

---

[200]   April 23, 1952 Los Angeles   AFRS Jubilee #366
           BENNY CARTER QUINTET

Carter (as, tp?, comp) Unknown TP and Rhythm Section

LADY BE GOOD

CRUISIN' comp

---

[201]   June or July 1952 Los Angeles
           JAM SESSION (NORMAN GRANZ)

Carter (as, comp) Charlie Shavers (tp) Johnny Hodges, Charlie Parker (as)
Flip Phillips, Ben Webster (ts) Oscar Peterson (p) Barney Kessel (g) Ray
Brown (b) J. C. Heard (d)

JAM BLUES (84as [1st as solo])   802-2
LP: CLEF MGC4001, CLEF MGC601, VERVE MGV8002,
VERVE MGV8049, VERVE VE-2-2508, VERVE (F) 2683-043,
VERVE (J) MV2530, BOOK OF THE MONTH CLUB BOMC10-5604

WHAT IS THIS THING CALLED LOVE (96as [2nd as solo])   803-3
        (horns trade 4 bars at end for 3 choruses, Carter 1st)
LP: CLEF MGC4002, CLEF MGC602, VERVE MGV8002,
VERVE MGV8050, VERVE V8486, VERVE VE-2-2508,
VERVE (E) 2683-043

ISN'T IT ROMANTIC (32as)   804-4
LP: CLEF MGC4001, CLEF MGC601, VERVE MGV8002,
VERVE MGV8049, VERVE VE-2-2508, VERVE (E) 2683-043,
VERVE (J) MV2530, BOOK OF THE MONTH CLUB BOMC10-5604

FUNKY BLUES (24as [3rd as solo])   805-2
LP: CLEF MGC4002, CLEF MGC602, VERVE MGV8002,
VERVE MGV8050, VERVE V8486, VERVE VE-2-2508,
VERVE (E) 2683-043

NOTE: "Isn't It Romantic" is Carter's feature in ballad medley.

*   *   *

In one of his most intriguing jam session productions, Norman Granz brought together Carter, Parker and Hodges for the only recordings including all three of the shapers of the jazz alto saxophone.   As is Granz's stated preference, the date was a loose affair, with the blues a common meeting ground much of the time.

The air of competition which pervades many such gatherings and which one might expect, given the extraordinary personnel, did not materialize, at least as far as Carter was concerned.   "I don't recall any sense of rivalry at the date.   I wouldn't say we felt 'pitted' against each other; more like 'combined.'"   He then added with a smile, "It all went very smoothly--how else could it go with three so-called giants?"

In many spots Carter's playing seems stylistically closer to Parker's than it does to that of his own contemporary, Hodges.   This is particularly evident in the standard "What Is This Thing Called Love."   Hodges, who solos first among the altoists, uses the melody as a base, paraphrasing, reshaping and changing its emphasis, whereas Carter and Parker go directly to the changes.   Indications of Carter's assimilation of new developments are evident, including an increased use of tonguing, and some boppish rhythmic figures.   Carter notes the difference in approach between himself and Hodges: "What Johnny had was so uniquely his that he felt no need to change.   I'm sure my own style was not so set."

As for any direct effect Parker may have had on him, he adds, "I never took any of the published Parker solos and practiced them endlessly as many of the younger saxophonists have done.   But I have looked at them, and I've always tried to keep listening."

Carter has continued his efforts to keep abreast of musical developments.   His record collection includes items by Sun Ra and Muhal Richard Abrams among others, and during the 1980 Newport Jazz Festival he made a special point of attending a concert by the World Saxophone Quartet.

---

[202]   July 26, 1952   Los Angeles
          BENNY CARTER AND HIS ORCHESTRA

Carter (as, arr, comp) Ernie Royal (tp) Milt Bernhart (tb) Ben Webster (ts) Bob Lawson (bs) Gerald Wiggins (p) Ulysses Livingston (g) Curtis Counce (b) George Jenkins (d)

LULLABY IN BLUE (32+2as) arr, comp 78: VICTOR 20-5389 45: RCA 47-5389 LP: RCA (F) PM42406	E2VB6903-1
MAMA LOU arr, comp 78: UNISSUED	E2VB6904-1
ROCKIN' ALONG (32as) arr, comp 78: UNISSUED T: HERE'S TO VETERANS 335 LP: HITS H1002	E2VB6905-1
CRUISIN' (36as) arr, comp	E2VB6906-1

78: VICTOR 20-5389 T: HERE'S TO VETERANS 335
45: RCA 47-5389, LP: RCA (F) PM42406

> NOTES: "Rockin' Along" on Hits LP as "Rock Alone." RCA LP
> lists -2 for matrices 6903 and 6906.

* * *

Until the recent two-record French RCA Benny Carter issue, Carter's 1952
RCA dates were not readily available. The sides vary from highly commercial production numbers, replete with choruses, strings and echo, to some
forays into near-R&B.

The personnel comes from the RCA files in New York. The French
RCA LP lists New York as the place of recording and suggests a different
personnel with a full big-band instrumentation (a personnel actually present
on the October 2, 1952, session). Carter, however, remembers the location as Los Angeles, and aural evidence confirms the personnel and instrumentation shown above.

"Lullaby In Blue" is an attractive mood piece stated by Carter's alto
with little embellishment and a lot of echo.

"Rockin' Along" is a riff tune which, although originally unissued,
somehow made its way onto LP via a Veteran's Administration transcription.
The sound quality is poor, and the alto break with which Carter opens his
solo is marred by a very conspicuous reed squeak.

"Cruisin'," another uptempo riff tune, this time based on the blues,
is more successful.

[203]   August 18, 1952 Los Angeles
         BENNY CARTER AND HIS ORCHESTRA

Carter (as, arr) Rubin Zarchy, Ray Linn, Manny Klein (tp) Bill Schaefer,
Pullman Pederson (tb) Phil Shuken, Jess Carneol, Ted Nash, Sal Franzella
(reeds) Paul Smith (p) Al Hendrickson (g) Phil Stephenson (b) Milt Holland
(d) Harry Bluestone, Mischa Russell, Nick Pisani, Felix Slatkin, Erno Neu-
feld, Ben Gill (violins) Eleanor Slatkin (cello) Paul Robyn, William Hyman-
son (viola) Gail Laughton (harp) Ray Linn, Burton Dole, Maxwell Smith, Gil
Mershon, Sue Allen, Delores Dahl, Gloria Wood, Dorothy McArty (v)

WISH YOU WERE HERE vocal group arr   E2VB6957-1
78: UNISSUED

WANNA GO HOME vocal group (8as) arr   E2VB7304-1
78: VICTOR 20-5005 45: RCA 47-5005 LP:
RCA (F) PM42406

GEORGIA ON MY MIND (32as)(4as+ coda) arr   E2VB7305
78: UNISSUED LP: RCA (F) PM42406

YOU BELONG TO ME (32as) arr   E2VB7306-1
78: VICTOR 20-5005 45: RCA 47-5005 LP:
RCA (F) PM42406

* * *

This is one of Carter's most "commercial" dates. His alto echoes through an ethereal background of strings and voices.

Once again the French RCA LP gives New York as the location and September 1952 as the date. Carter recalls Los Angeles, and the RCA files list the personnel and date as above.

"Georgia On My Mind" was not issued until 1980 when it was included on the French RCA two-record set. The liner notes list October 2, 1952 as the recording date but RCA files and the general sound of the piece indicate this session as its source.

---

[204]   September 13, 1952   New York   Concert, Carnegie Hall
           JAZZ AT THE PHILHARMONIC

Carter (as) Roy Eldridge, Charlie Shavers (tp) Lester Young, Flip Phillips (ts) Hank Jones, Oscar Peterson (p) Barney Kessel (g) Ray Brown (p) Buddy Rich (d)

JAM SESSION BLUES   (108as)
LP: CLEF MG VOL. 15, VERVE MG VOL. 8, VERVE (J)
MV9073/75

COCKTAILS FOR TWO   (32as)
LP: CLEF MG VOL. 15, VERVE MG VOL. 8

PERDIDO   (e)
LP: CLEF MG VOL. 15, VERVE MG VOL. 8, VERVE (E)
2615-040, VERVE (E) 2332-060

COTTONTAIL   (32as)
LP: CLEF MG VOL. 15, VERVE MG VOL. 8, VERVE
MGV 8368

THE TRUMPET BATTLE   (128as)
LP: CLEF MG VOL. 15, VERVE MG VOL. 8, VERVE (J)
MV9073/75

> NOTE: "Cocktails..." is Carter's feature in ballad medley; Jones plays piano on medley, Peterson elsewhere.

*   *   *

Carter has always been ambivalent about the often combative atmosphere of Norman Granz's extravaganzas. The idea of several horns, without arrangements, playing endless crowd-pleasing solo choruses in an artificial recreation of a jam session is basically antithetical to his musical philosophy. "I found playing these long solos somewhat unpleasant. I've always felt that after I've said what I had to say there's no point in milking the audience for applause. Sometimes after I'd finish a solo, Norman would be waiting in the wings and would say, 'You were just getting started, Benny!'"

Consequently, on some JATP recordings Carter sounds bored and detached. On others he actually seems to be subtly mocking the JATP concept by going overboard in achieving the required frenzy. Such is the impression given by his solo on "Jam Session Blues."

Carter seems more at home in the ballad medley portion of the JATP format, and his "Cocktails For Two" here is a typically virtuoso performance.

Jepsen gives the date of this recording as October 11, 1952, but may be confusing it with an October 11 concert--also at Carnegie--featuring Nat King Cole, the Stan Kenton Orchestra, Sarah Vaughan and others (see New York Times, October 11, 1952, p. 17 and New Yorker, October 4, 1952, p. 12 and October 11, 1952, p. 12). Down Beat and New Yorker for September and October 1952 show the JATP concert as September 13. Also, a review in the New York Times, September 15, p. 15, mentions the identical personnel as on this recording.

---

[205]   September 1952   New York
           BENNY CARTER WITH THE OSCAR PETERSON TRIO AND
           BUDDY RICH (ALONE TOGETHER)

Carter (as) Oscar Peterson (p) Barney Kessel (g) Ray Brown (b) Buddy Rich (d) Horns and String Section-Joe Glover (arr, cond)

ISN'T IT ROMANTIC   arr-JG (32+16as+ coda)   871-7
78: CLEF 89026 LP: NORGRAN MGN1058, VERVE
MGV8148

SOME OTHER SPRING   arr-JG (intro+32+16as)   872-4
45: NORGRAN EPN45   LP: NORGRAN MGN1058, VERVE
MGV8148

THESE THINGS YOU LEFT ME   arr-JG (34as)(10as+ coda)   873-1
45: NORGRAN EPN45   LP: NORGRAN MGN1058, VERVE
MGV8148

[205A]   September 1952   New York
           BENNY CARTER WITH THE OSCAR PETERSON TRIO AND
           BUDDY RICH (ALONE TOGETHER)

Carter (as) Oscar Peterson (p) Barney Kessel (g) Ray Brown (b) Buddy Rich (d)

GONE WITH THE WIND   (64as)+(16as trades with piano)   874-5
     (32as+ coda)
78: NORGRAN 111 LP: NORGRAN MGN1058, VERVE
MGV8148, VERVE (E) 2683-043

I GOT IT BAD AND THAT AIN'T GOOD   (48as)   875-2
45: CLEF EPC187 LP: NORGRAN MGN1058, VERVE
MGV8148, VERVE (E) 2683-043

LONG AGO AND FAR AWAY   (64as)(36as)   876-9
45: CLEF EPC187 LP: NORGRAN MGN1058, VERVE
MGV8148, VERVE (E) 2683-043

I'VE GOT THE WORLD ON A STRING   (48as)   877-3
78: NORGRAN 111 LP: NORGRAN MGN1058, VERVE
MGV8148, VERVE (E) 2683-043

[205B]   September 1952 New York
          BENNY CARTER WITH THE OSCAR PETERSON TRIO AND
          BUDDY RICH (ALONE TOGETHER)

Carter (as, arr, comp) Oscar Peterson (p) Barney Kessel (g) Ray Brown (b)
Buddy Rich (d) Horns and String Section-Joe Glover (arr, cond)

ROUND MIDNIGHT (32+16as+coda) arr   878-5
45: NORGRAN EPN45 LP: NORGRAN MGN1058, VERVE
MGV8148, VSP 38

ALONE TOGETHER arr-JG (72+16as)   879-3
45: NORGRAN EPN46 LP: NORGRAN MGN1058, VERVE
MGV8148

BEWITCHED, BOTHERED AND BEWILDERED (48as+coda) arr   880-4
78: NORGRAN 120 45: BLUE STAR (F) GM8512 LP:
NORGRAN MGN1058, VERVE MGV8148

COCKTAILS FOR TWO (32+12as+coda) arr   881-6
78: NORGRAN 120 45: BLUE STAR (F) GM8512 LP:
NORGRAN MGN1058, VERVE MGV8148

KEY LARGO (64as)(12as) arr, comp   882-7
78: CLEF 89026 LP: NORGRAN MGN1058, VERVE MGV8148

[206]   Probably September 1952 New York
          BENNY CARTER QUINTET (COSMOPOLITE)

Carter (as) Oscar Peterson (p) Barney Kessel (g) Ray Brown (b) J. C.
Heard (d)

STREET SCENE (48as)   938
78: CLEF 89044 LP: NORGRAN MGN1070, VERVE
MGV8160, VERVE (J) MV2635

IMAGINATION (36as)(12as+coda)   939-2
78: CLEF 89065 LP: NORGRAN MGN1070, VERVE
MGV8160, VERVE (J) MV2635

PICK YOURSELF UP (64as)(36as)   940
78: CLEF 89044 LP: NORGRAN MGN1070, VERVE
MGV8160, VERVE (J) MV2635

I GET A KICK OUT OF YOU (52as)   941-3
78: CLEF 89065 LP: NORGRAN MGN1070, VERVE
MGV8160, VERVE (J) MV2635

[207]   October 2, 1952 New York
          BENNY CARTER AND HIS ORCHESTRA

Carter (as, arr, comp) Doc Cheatham, Taft Jordan, Dick Vance (tp) Tyree
Glenn, Claude Jones, Frank Rehak (tb) Eddie Barefield (as) Art Drelinger,
Lucky Thompson (ts) Willard Brown (bs) Billy Taylor (p) Rene Hall (g) Joe
Benjamin (b) Chris Colombus (d)

LOVE IS CYNTHIA (28as)+(10as with ensemble) arr   E2VB7382-1
78: VICTOR 20-5133 45: VICTOR 47-5133, HMV 7M189,
LP: RCA (F) PM42406

SUNDAY AFTERNOON (32as)(16as) arr, comp   E2VB7383-1
78: VICTOR 20-5133 45: 47-5133, LP: RCA (F)
PM42406

*   *   *

On "Love Is Cynthia," an Alfred Newman melody from the film The Snows
Of Kiliminjaro, Carter re-creates the melodic solo he played on the film's
soundtrack.

| [208] | Same Date |
| | SAVANNAH CHURCHILL |

Carter (as) as above add Savannah Churchill (v) and vocal group

WALKIN' BY THE RIVER v-SC (as acc)   E2VB7384-1
78: VICTOR 20-5031

IF I DIDN'T LOVE YOU SO v-SC (as acc)   E2VB7385-1
78: VICTOR 20-5031

| [209] | August 3, 1953 Los Angeles |
| | JAM SESSION (NORMAN GRANZ) |

Carter (as) Harry Edison (tp) Willie Smith (as) Stan Getz, Wardell Gray (ts)
Buddy DeFranco (cl) Count Basie (organ, p) Arnold Ross (p) Freddie Green
(g) John Simmons (b) Buddy Rich (d)

APPLE JAM (as [1st solo])   1259-6
LP: CLEF MGC4003, VERVE MGV8051, VSP 31,
VERVE (E) 2304-421

LADY BE GOOD (as [1st solo])   1260-2
LP: CLEF MGC4004, VERVE MGV8052, VERVE (J)
MV2518, BOOK OF THE MONTH CLUB BOMC20-5605

BLUES FOR THE COUNT (as [1st solo])   1261-2
LP: CLEF MGC4004, VERVE MGV8052, BOOK OF THE
MONTH CLUB BOMC20-5605

I HADN'T ANYONE TILL YOU (as)   1262-4
LP: CLEF MGC4003, VERVE MGV8051, VERVE (E)
2304-421

   NOTES: Last title is Carter's feature in ballad medley; Ross is
   pianist. Beginning with this session, the number of measures of
   Carter's solos is no longer given.

*   *   *

Although similar to the JATP in format, this studio session manages to
avoid some of the crowd-pleasing excesses of Granz's live productions.

Consequently Carter is able to turn in some thoughtful solos without fear of
being accused of malingering.   Particularly interesting is his playing on
"Blues For The Count," which benefits from Basie's excellent organ accompaniment.

This is Carter's first recording with Harry "Sweets" Edison; the two
became very close and collaborated many times over the next three decades.

---

[210]   September 10, 1953 Los Angeles
           BUDDY RICH AND HIS ALL STARS

Carter (as, arr, comp) Harry Edison (tp) Milt Bernhart (tb) Georgie Auld (ts)
Bob Lawson (bs) Jimmy Rowles (p) John Simmons (b) Buddy Rich (d)

LET'S FALL IN LOVE   (as) arr   1266
78: CLEF 89094 LP: NORGRAN EPN37, VERVE (E)
2683-035

ME AND MY JAGUAR   (e) arr, comp   1267
78: CLEF 89094 LP: NORGRAN EPN37, VERVE (E)
2683-035

JUST BLUES (as)   1268
LP: NORGRAN EPN37, VERVE (E) 2683-035

---

[211]   Early September 1953 Los Angeles
           LOUIS BELLSON ORCHESTRA

Carter (as) Harry Edison, Maynard Ferguson, Conrad Gozzo, Ray Linn (tp)
Hoyt Bohannon, Herb Harper, Tommy Pederson (tb) Willie Smith (as)
Wardell Gray, Bumps Myers (ts) Bob Lawson (bs) Jimmy Rowles (p) Barney
Kessel (g) John Simmons (b) Louis Bellson (d)

CAXTON HALL SWING (e)   1250
78: CLEF 89093 LP: NORGRAN MGN14, NORGRAN
MGN1046, VERVE MGV8137

FOR EUROPEANS ONLY (e)   1251
78: NORGRAN 108 LP: NORGRAN MGN14, NORGRAN
MGN1046, VERVE MGV8137

PHALANGES (e)   1252
78: CLEF 89093 LP: NORGRAN MGN14, NORGRAN
MGN1046, VERVE MGV8137

SKIN DEEP (e)   1253
78: UNISSUED 45: NORGRAN EPN104 LP: NORGRAN
MGN14, NORGRAN MGN1046, VERVE MGV8137

---

[212]   September 19, 1953 New York Concert, Carnegie Hall
           JAZZ AT THE PHILHARMONIC

Carter (as) Charlie Shavers, Roy Eldridge (tp) Bill Harris (tb) Willie Smith
(as) Lester Young, Ben Webster, Flip Phillips (ts) Oscar Peterson (p) Herb
Ellis (g) Ray Brown (b) J. C. Heard, Gene Krupa (d)

COOL BLUES (as)
LP: CLEF MG VOL. 16, VERVE MG VOL. 9, BARCLAY GLP6918

FLAMINGO (as)
LP: CLEF MG VOL. 16, VERVE MG VOL. 9, BARCLAY GLP6918

ONE O'CLOCK JUMP (as)
LP: CLEF MG VOL. 16, VERVE MG VOL. 9, BARCLAY GLP6920

FLYING HOME (e)
LP: CLEF MG VOL. 16, VERVE MG VOL. 9, BARCLAY GLP6920

> NOTES: "Flamingo" is Carter's feature in ballad medley. Young
> does not play on "Cool Blues." Krupa is the drummer on "Flying
> Home"; Heard on other titles.

---

[213]   Same Concert
          GENE KRUPA TRIO

Carter (as) Oscar Peterson (p) Gene Krupa (d)

INDIANA (as)
LP: CLEF MG VOL. 16, VERVE MG VOL. 9

SOMEBODY LOVES ME (as)
LP: CLEF MG VOL. 16, VERVE MG VOL. 9

LAURA (as)
LP: CLEF MG VOL. 16, VERVE MG VOL. 9, VERVE (J)
MV9073/75

STOMPIN' AT THE SAVOY (as)
LP: CLEF MG VOL. 16, VERVE MG VOL. 9, VERVE (J)
MV9073/75

                    *   *   *

[212, 213] Carter's 17 12-bar choruses on "Cool Blues" constitute one of
his longest solos on record. His wild performance is the epitome of the
JATP spirit, and the crowd responds appropriately. Carter's effort seems
to have adversely affected his tone, which is harsher than usual for the rest
of the concert.

On this JATP tour Carter was featured in a new context, as a member (with Oscar Peterson) of the Gene Krupa trio. This setting seems more
to his liking, although Krupa's bass drum is overbearing at times.

Jepsen lists this date as September 23, but contemporary reports indicate September 19 (New York Amsterdam News advertisement, September
12, 1953, p. 23, and article in New York Times, September 20, 1953, section 2, p. 7).

---

[214]   Late September 1953 Location Unknown
          JAZZ AT THE PHILHARMONIC

Carter (as) Roy Eldridge, Charlie Shavers (tp) Bill Harris (tb) Willie Smith (as) Lester Young, Ben Webster, Flip Phillips (ts) Oscar Peterson (p) Herb Ellis (g) Ray Brown (b) Gene Krupa (d)

CONCERT BLUES (as)
LP: CLEF MG VOL. 16

*   *   *

This item was added as a "bonus" ten-inch LP to Clef MG volume 16 and is not from the same concert as the rest of that volume.

---

[215]   Between November 4 and 9, 1953 Tokyo Concert, Nichigeki
                                          Theater
          JAZZ AT THE PHILHARMONIC

Carter (as) Roy Eldridge, Charlie Shavers (tp) Willie Smith (as) Flip Phillips, Ben Webster (ts) Oscar Peterson (p) Herb Ellis (g) Ray Brown (b) J. C. Heard (d)

JAM SESSION BLUES (as)
LP: VERVE (J) MV9061, VERVE 2660-112, PABLO LIVE 2620-104, VERVE (J) MV9076/78

J. C. HEARD DRUM SOLO (e)
LP: VERVE (J) MV9061, VERVE 2660-112, PABLO LIVE 2620-104, VERVE (J) MV9076/78

COTTONTAIL (e)
LP: VERVE (J) MV9061, VERVE 2660-112, PABLO LIVE 2620-104, VERVE (J) MV9076/78

FLAMINGO (as)
LP: VERVE (J) MV9061, VERVE 2660-112, PABLO LIVE 2620-104, VERVE (J) MV9076/78

> NOTE: "Flamingo" is Carter's feature in ballad medley. "Jam Session Blues" appears as "Tokyo Blues" and "J. C. Heard Drum Solo" as "Up" on Pablo Live set.

---

[216]   Same Concert
          GENE KRUPA TRIO

Carter (as) Oscar Peterson (p) Gene Krupa (d)

COCKTAILS FOR TWO (as)
LP: VERVE (J) MV9061, VERVE 2660-112, PABLO LIVE 2620-104, VERVE (J) MV9076/78

INDIANA (as)
LP: VERVE (J) MV9061, VERVE 2660-112, PABLO LIVE 2620-104, VERVE (J) MV9076/78

DON'T BE THAT WAY (as)
LP: VERVE (J) MV9061, VERVE 2660-112, PABLO LIVE 2620-104, VERVE (J) MV9076/78

STOMPIN' AT THE SAVOY (as)
LP: VERVE (J) MV9061, VERVE 2660-112, PABLO LIVE
2620-104, VERVE (J) MV9076/78

[217]	Same Concert

Carter (as) Roy Eldridge, Charlie Shavers (tp) Willie Smith (as) Flip Phillips, Ben Webster (ts) Oscar Peterson (p) Herb Ellis (g) Ray Brown (b) Ella
Fitzgerald (v)

PERDIDO (e)
LP: VERVE (J) MV9063, VERVE 2660-112, PABLO LIVE
2620-104, VERVE (J) MV9076/78

[218]	Between November 4 and 9, 1953 Tokyo Concert, Nichigeki Theater
	JAZZ AT THE PHILHARMONIC

Carter (as) Roy Eldridge, Charlie Shavers (tp) Willie Smith (as) Flip Phillips, Ben Webster (ts) Oscar Peterson (p) Herb Ellis (g) J. C. Heard (d)

COTTONTAIL (e)
UNISSUED

FLAMINGO (as)
UNISSUED

J. C. HEARD DRUM SOLO (e)
UNISSUED

    NOTE: "Flamingo" is Carter's feature in ballad medley.

[219]	Between November 4 and 9, 1953 Tokyo Concert, Nichigeki Theater
	JAZZ AT THE PHILHARMONIC

Carter (as) Roy Eldridge, Charlie Shavers (tp) Willie Smith (as) Flip Phillips, Ben Webster (ts) Oscar Peterson (p) Herb Ellis (g) J. C. Heard (d)

FLAMINGO (as)
UNISSUED

J. C. HEARD DRUM SOLO (e)
UNISSUED

    NOTE: "Flamingo" is Carter's feature in ballad medley.

                          *   *   *

[215-219] The date given for the concert on the Pablo Live issue, November 18, 1953, is certainly incorrect. Carter's passport shows him leaving
Japan November 15 for Honolulu. A Variety report from Tokyo (November
11, 1953, p. 51) describes the opening on November 4 of a six-day engagement at the Nichigeki Theater. The commercially issued recording and the
two unissued portions of concerts listed after it are probably from this

period, although their correct order is not known. Variety also reports a
projected two days of dates in Osaka and Nagoya, probably November 10-12,
and a November 13-14 engagement for servicemen at the U.S. Ernie Pyle
Theater.   This schedule would coincide with the November 15 departure
from Japan shown in Carter's passport.

The Japanese Verve issues contain an informal "After Hours Session"
on which Carter does not seem to play.

His playing with the trio and on his ballad feature is far superior to
the Carnegie Hall September JATP recordings.   The interaction among
Krupa, Peterson and Carter is more balanced, and his tone is back to normal.

---

[220]   December 8, 1953   Los Angeles
           BEN WEBSTER AND HIS ORCHESTRA

Carter (as) Harry Edison (tp) Ben Webster (ts) Oscar Peterson (p) Herb
Ellis (g) Ray Brown (b) Alvin Stoller (d)

THAT'S ALL   1362-2
UNISSUED

THAT'S ALL   (e)   1362-5
78: NORGRAN 103   LP: NORGRAN MGN1001, VERVE
MGV8020, VERVE (E) 2683-049, VERVE (J) MV2554,
VERVE UMV2081

PENNIES FROM HEAVEN   (e)   1363-2
78: NORGRAN 115 LP: NORGRAN MGN1001, VERVE
MGV8020, METRO 2356-075, VERVE (J) MV2554, VERVE
UMV2081, TIME-LIFE STL-J21

JIVE AT SIX   (as)   1365-2
78: NORGRAN 103   LP: NORGRAN MGN1001, VERVE
MGV8020, METRO 2356-075, VERVE (J) MV2554, VERVE
UMV2081

JIVE AT SIX   1365-5
UNISSUED

DON'T GET AROUND MUCH ANYMORE   (e)   1366-3
78: UNISSUED 45: NORGRAN EPN15 LP: NORGRAN
MGN1001, VERVE MGV8020, VERVE (E) 2683-049, VERVE
(J) MV2554, VERVE UMV2081

---

[221]   December 31, 1953   Los Angeles
           BENNY CARTER AND HIS ORCHESTRA (COSMOPOLITE)

Carter (as, arr, comp) Gerald Wiggins (p) Red Callender (b) Bill Douglas (d)
Horn and String Sections

I'LL BE AROUND   (as) arr   1482-5
45: NORGRAN EPN18 LP: NORGRAN MGN1070,
VERVE MGV8160, VERVE (J) MV2635

BEAUTIFUL LOVE (as) arr   1483
45: NORGRAN EPN18 LP: NORGRAN MGN1070, VERVE
MGV8160, VERVE (J) MV2635

BLUE STAR (as) arr, comp   1484-2
45: NORGRAN EPN18 LP: NORGRAN MGN1070, VERVE
MGV8160, VERVE (J) MV2635

FLAMINGO (as) arr   1485-4
78: CLEF 89109 45: NORGRAN EPN18 LP: NORGRAN
MGN1070, VERVE MGV8160, VERVE (J) MV2635

    NOTE: Two takes (-1, -5) were made of "Beautiful Love."

[221A]   January 4, 1954 Los Angeles
        BENNY CARTER AND HIS ORCHESTRA (COSMOPOLITE)

Carter (as, arr, comp) Gerald Wiggins (p) Red Callender (b) Bill Douglas (d)
Horn and String Sections

WITH A SONG IN MY HEART (as) arr   1490
45: NORGRAN EPN17 LP: NORGRAN MGN1070, VERVE
MGV8160, VERVE (J) MV2635

CAN'T WE BE FRIENDS (as) arr   1491-3
78: CLEF 89109 45: NORGRAN EPN18 LP: NORGRAN
MGN1070, VERVE MGV8160, VERVE (J) MV2635

SYMPHONY (as) arr   1492
45: NORGRAN EPN17 LP: NORGRAN MGN1070, VERVE
MGV8160, VERVE (J) MV2635

I'M SORRY (as) arr, comp   1493-3
45: NORGRAN EPN17 LP: NORGRAN MGN1070, VERVE
MGV8160, VERVE (J) MV2635

    NOTE: Two takes (-2, -7) were made of "With A Song" and three
    of "Symphony" (-5, -6, -8). "I'm Sorry" appears on LP as "Sorry."

*   *   *

[221]-[221A] Among his most successful recordings with strings, these dates
epitomize the facet of Carter's playing which critics like to call "urbane."
Coming at a time when listeners had become accustomed to a less "legiti-
mate" alto sound, they also show why some critics labeled his tone "saccharine."

    Carter's arrangements here are skillfully crafted; he never has to
compete with the strings, as some jazz soloists have had to do in similar
settings.

    Two lovely original ballads, "Blue Star" and "I'm Sorry" are intro-
duced here, and Carter lavishes his fullest and purest tone on them.

    Uptempo delights include "Symphony" and "With A Song in My Heart."

[221B]   June 23, 1954 Los Angeles
          BENNY CARTER (PLAYS PRETTY/MOONGLOW)

Carter (as) Don Abney (p) George Duvivier (b) Louis Bellson (d)

                                                                  1780-1
MOONGLOW (as)
45: NORGRAN EPN87 LP: NORGRAN MGN1015, VERVE
MGV2025

                                                                  1781-2
MY ONE AND ONLY LOVE (as)
45: NORGRAN EPN87 LP: NORGRAN MGN1015, VERVE
MGV2025

                                                                  1782-3
OUR LOVE IS HERE TO STAY (as)
45: NORGRAN EPN87 LP: NORGRAN MGN1015, VERVE
MGV2025

                                                                  1783-5
THIS CAN'T BE LOVE (as)
45: NORGRAN EPN88 LP: NORGRAN MGN1044, VERVE
MGV8135

                                                                  1784-3
TENDERLY (as)
45: NORGRAN EPN87 LP: NORGRAN MGN1015, VERVE
MGV2025

                                                                  1785-2
UNFORGETTABLE (as)
45: NORGRAN EPN88 LP: NORGRAN MGN1015, VERVE
MGV2025

                                                                  1786-5
RUBY (as)
45: NORGRAN EPN88 LP: NORGRAN MGN1015, VERVE
MGV2025

                                                                  1787
MOON SONG (as)
45: NORGRAN EPN88 LP: NORGRAN MGN1015, VERVE
MGV2025

          NOTE: Two takes (-3, -4) were made of "Moon Song."

[222]   June 25, 1954 Los Angeles
          ART TATUM-BENNY CARTER-LOUIS BELLSON

Carter (as, comp) Art Tatum (p) Louis Bellson (d)

                                                                  1788-1
MY BLUE HEAVEN (as)
45: CLEF EPC320 LP: CLEF MGC643, VERVE MGV8013,
METRO 2682-024, PABLO 2310-733, PABLO 2625-706

                                                                  1789-2
BLUES IN B FLAT (as)
45: CLEF EPC319 LP: CLEF MGC643, VERVE MGV8013,
METRO 2682-024, PABLO 2310-732, PABLO 2625-706,
TIME-LIFE STL-J10

                                                                  1790-1
BLUES IN C (as)
LP: VERVE MGV8227, METRO 2682-024, PABLO 2310-732,
PABLO 2625-706

A FOGGY DAY (as)   1791-2
LP: VERVE MGV8227, METRO 2682-024, PABLO 2310-732,
PABLO 2625-706

BLUES IN MY HEART (as) comp   1792-1
45: CLEF EPC318 LP: CLEF MGC643, VERVE MGV8013,
METRO 2682-024, PABLO 2310-733, PABLO 2625-706

STREET OF DREAMS (as)   1793-2
45: CLEF EPC320 LP: CLEF MGC643, VERVE MGV8013,
METRO 2682-024, PABLO 2310-732, PABLO 2625-706

IDAHO (as)   1794-2
45: CLEF EPC320 LP: CLEF MGC643, VERVE MGV8013,
METRO 2682-024, PABLO 2310-733, PABLO 2625-706

YOU'RE MINE, YOU (as)   1795-1
LP: VERVE MGV8227, METRO 2682-024, PABLO 2310-733,
PABLO 2625-706

UNDECIDED (as)   1796-2
LP: VERVE MGV8227, METRO 2682-024, PABLO 2310-732,
PABLO 2625-706

UNDER A BLANKET OF BLUE (as)   1797-2
LP: VERVE MGV8227, METRO 2682-024, PABLO 2310-732,
PABLO 2625-706

MAKIN' WHOOPEE (as)   1798-1
UNISSUED

MAKIN' WHOOPEE (as)   1798-2
LP: VERVE MGV8227, METRO 2682-024, PABLO 2310-733,
PABLO 2625-706

OLD FASHIONED LOVE (as)   1799-1
45: CLEF EPC318 LP: CLEF MGC643, VERVE MGV8013,
METRO 2682-024, PABLO 2310-733, PABLO 2625-706

'S WONDERFUL (as)   1800-2
45: CLEF EPC319 LP: CLEF MGC643, VERVE MGV8013,
METRO 2682-024, PABLO 2310-732, PABLO 2625-706

HANDS ACROSS THE TABLE (as)   1801-1
45: CLEF EPC319 LP: CLEF MGC643, VERVE MGV8013,
METRO 2682-024, PABLO 2310-733, PABLO 2625-706

*   *   *

Carter and Tatum were brought together in the studio for the first and only
time by Norman Granz. This marathon session (14 tunes in one day) points
up the many similarities between their styles. Both have flawless technique
and are most at home with the more sophisticated standards, which they re-
shape with elegant multinoted embellishments. But both men have another,
more earthy side, and perhaps most surprising are their superb collabora-
tions on the blues, especially the "Blues in B Flat."

If Tatum was ever criticized it was for his alleged inability to subordinate his great solo gifts to a secondary accompanying role. Carter, however, found his backing solid and imaginative. Nor did the absence of a bass bother Carter, who recalls, "With Art Tatum, no bass was needed. It would only get in the way." He adds that the only inhibiting factor in playing with the pianist was "the feeling of awe he generated, and the question of whether you could keep up with what he was doing."

---

[223]   August 2, 1954   Los Angeles
         MEL TORME

Carter (as, arr) large orchestra, George Cates (dir) Matty Matlock (cl) Mel Torme (v)

TUTTI FRUTTI v-MT (as) arr   L7770
LP: CORAL CRL57044, VOCALION VL73905

IT DON'T MEAN A THING IF IT AIN'T GOT THAT SWING   L7771
      v-MT (e) arr
LP: CORAL CRL57044, VOCALION VL73905

ROSE O'DAY v-MT (e)   L7772
LP: CORAL CRL57044, VOCALION VL73905

HOLD TIGHT v-MT (e)   L7773
LP: CORAL CRL57044, VOCALION VL73905

I'SE A MUGGIN' v-MT (e)   L7774
LP: CORAL CRL57044

---

[224]   August 3, 1954   Los Angeles
         MEL TORME

Carter (as) large orchestra, George Cates, Sonny Burke (dir) Conrad Gozzo (tp) Georgie Auld (ts) Al Pellegrini (p) Mel Torme (v) Billy May (arr)

ALL OF YOU v-MT arr-BM (e)   L7775
LP: CORAL CRL57044

SPELLBOUND v-MT (e)   L7776
LP: CORAL CRL57044

CEMENT MIXER v-MT (e)   L7777
LP: CORAL CRL57044

FLAT FOOT FLOOGIE v-MT (e)   L7778
LP: CORAL CRL57044

THE HUT-SUT SONG v-MT (e)   L7779
LP: CORAL CRL57044

        NOTE: Burke (dir) on "Cement Mixer" and "Flat Foot"; Cates on
        others.

---

[225]   September 14, 1954   New York
         NEW JAZZ SOUNDS

Carter (as) Dizzy Gillespie (tp) Bill Harris (tb) Oscar Peterson (p) Herb
Ellis (g) Ray Brown (b) Buddy Rich (d)

LAURA (as)   1955-1
LP: NORGRAN MGN1015, VERVE MGV2025

THAT OLD BLACK MAGIC (as)   1956-2
LP: NORGRAN MGN1044, VERVE MGV8135, VERVE (J)
MV2549

ANGEL EYES (as)   1957-3
LP: NORGRAN MGN1044, VERVE MGV8135, VERVE (J)
MV2549

THE SONG IS YOU (as)   1958-8
LP: NORGRAN MGN1044, VERVE MGV8135, VERVE (J)
MV2549

MARRIAGE BLUES (as)   1959-1
LP: NORGRAN MGN1044, VERVE MGV8135, VERVE (J)
MV2549

JUST ONE OF THOSE THINGS (as)   1960-1
LP: NORGRAN MGN1044, VERVE MGV8135, VERVE (J)
MV2549

     NOTE: Gillespie plays on last two titles only.

                         *   *   *

Carter's first recorded collaboration with Dizzy Gillespie since the famous
"Hot Mallets" session of 1939 with Lionel Hampton was not planned.   Gilles-
pie dropped by the studio during this session and, as the liner notes (Verve
MGV8135) report, asked to sit in.   Although the two titles with Gillespie
are the highlights, the date as a whole is also consistently inspired, with
Harris's gruff trombone contrasting well with Carter's smooth alto.

[225A]   September 20, 1954 New York   Studio Session for Norgran--
                              Unissued
          BENNY CARTER TRIO

Carter (as) Teddy Wilson (p) Jo Jones (d)

LITTLE GIRL BLUE   1988-5

JUNE IN JANUARY   1989-4

JEEPERS CREEPERS   1990-2

ROSETTA   1991-2

BIRTH OF THE BLUES   1992-1

WHEN YOUR LOVER HAS GONE   1993-3

THE MOON IS LOW   1994-1

THIS LOVE OF MINE   1995-3

[225B]   November 12, 1954   Los Angeles
          BENNY CARTER

Carter (as) Oscar Peterson (p) Herb Ellis (g) Ray Brown (b) Bobby White (d)

DON'T YOU THINK   2042-1
UNISSUED

WILL YOU STILL BE MINE   2043-2
UNISSUED

A FOGGY DAY (as)   2044-1
LP: NORGRAN MGN1035, VERVE MGV8126, COLUMBIA
(E) 33CX10072, VERVE (J) KL5021

WE'LL BE TOGETHER AGAIN   2045-2
UNISSUED

YOU TOOK ADVANTAGE OF ME (as)   2046-1
LP: NORGRAN MGN1035, VERVE MGV8126, COLUMBIA
(E) 33CX10072, VERVE (J) KL5021

POINCIANA (as)   2047-2
LP: NORGRAN MGN1035, VERVE MGV8126, COLUMBIA
(E) 33CX10072, VERVE (J) KL5021

PRISONER OF LOVE (as)   2048-1
LP: NORGRAN MGN1035, VERVE MGV8126, COLUMBIA
(E) 33CX10072, VERVE (J) KL5021

FRENESI (as)   2049-2
LP: NORGRAN MGN1044, VERVE MGV2025, VERVE
MGV8135, COLUMBIA (E) 33CX10049

[226]   December 23, 1954 Los Angeles
          BIG DAVE (CAVANAUGH) AND HIS ORCHESTRA

Carter (as) Dave Cavanaugh, Plas Johnson, Ted Romersa, Mort Friedman
(reeds) Don Robertson (p) Jack Marshall (g) Mike Rubin (b) Roy Harte (d)
The Hard Tops, (i. e.) Buck Stapleton, Allan Copeland, Harold Dickenson,
Tom Kenny, Charles Schrouder (v)

ROCK AND ROLL PARTY v-HT   13339
45?: CAPITOL 3028

YOUR KIND OF LOVE v-HT   13340
45?: CAPITOL 3028

[227]   1954 Los Angeles
          PEGGY LEE WITH ORCH. CONDUCTED BY JOSEPH LILLEY

Carter (as, arr) Peggy Lee (v) Large Orchestra with Strings

LOVE, YOU DIDN'T DO RIGHT BY ME v-PL (as) arr   L7706
78: DECCA 29250

SISTERS   v-PL (e)   L7707
78: DECCA 29250

---

[228]   Ca. 1954   Los Angeles
            PEGGY LEE

Carter (as) Unknown Rhythm Section, Peggy Lee (v)

BOUQUET OF BLUES   (as)
45: DECCA 9-29373

---

[229]   January 7, 1955   Los Angeles
            LORD BUCKLEY & THE ROYAL COURT ORCH. UNDER THE
            DIRECTION OF HIS GRACE, SIR HARRY M. G.

Carter (as) Maury Harris (tp) Milt Bernhart (tb) Ted Nash (ts?) Edwin Cole
(p) Red Callender (b) Lou Singer (d) Harry Geller (dir) Lord Buckley (v)

FRIENDS, ROMANS, COUNTRYMEN   v-LB (as acc)   F2PB-0402
LP: RCA LPM3246, RCA LPV580

HIAWATHA   v-LB (e)   F2PB-0403
LP: RCA LPM3246

BOSTON TEA PARTY   v-LB (e)   F2PB-0404
LP: RCA LPM3246

BAA BAA BLACK SHEEP   v-LB (e)   F2PB-0405
UNISSUED?

> NOTE: On the first title musical accompaniment is present through-
> out only on RCA LPV580; apparently, the music track was omitted
> on the original issue, except for brief passages at the beginning and
> end of this piece.

---

[230]   March 23, 1955   Los Angeles
            ROY ELDRIDGE-BENNY CARTER QUINTET (URBANE JAZZ)

Carter (as, comp) Roy Eldridge (tp) Bruce MacDonald (p) John Simmons (b)
Alvin Stoller (d)

I STILL LOVE HIM SO   (as) comp   2296-1
LP: VERVE MGV8202, ARS G413

THE MOON IS LOW   (as)   2297-1
LP: VERVE MGV8202, ARS G413

THE MOON IS LOW   (as)   2297-3
78: CLEF 89143

CLOSE YOUR EYES   (as)   2298-4
78: CLEF 89143   LP: VERVE MGV8202, ARS G413

I MISSED MY HAT   (as)   2299-2
LP: VERVE MGV8202, ARS G413

POLITE BLUES (as)   2300-1
LP: VERVE MGV8202, ARS G413

I REMEMBER YOU (as)   2301-2
LP: VERVE MGV8202, ARS G413

   NOTE: "I Remember You" is Carter's feature in ballad medley.

*   *   *

Carter and Eldridge are both in top form and each seems inspired by the
other. "I Still Love Him So" is a Carter ballad which is a favorite of
Eldridge's. The trumpeter first recorded it in Paris in 1951 and redid it
in 1976 for Pablo.

   The LP version of "The Moon Is Low" is more than twice as long as
the 78 and is far superior, with space for both Carter and Eldridge to
stretch out as well as two full choruses of 8-bar trades between the two
horns. Both versions have the same riff in the out-chorus, but on the 78
Eldridge has some problems executing it.

[231] - reassigned

[232]   May 4, 1955   New York
         EARL BOSTIC

Carter (as) Elmon Wright, John Coles (tp) Earl Bostic (as) Benny Golson (ts)
Frank Flynn (vib) Stash O'Laughlin (p) Ulysses Livingston (g) George Tucker
(b) Granville Hogan (d) String Section

DREAM (e)   K9626
45: KING 4815 LP: KING LP515, PARLOPHONE (E)
R4061, POLYDOR 623229

BEYOND THE BLUE HORIZON (e)   K9627
45: KING 4829 LP: KING LP515, PARLOPHONE (E)
R4208, POLYDOR 623229

EAST OF THE SUN (e)   K9628
45: KING 4815 LP: KING LP515, PARLOPHONE (E)
R4061, POLYDOR 623229

FOR ALL WE KNOW (e)   K9629
45: KING 4829 LP: KING LP558, PARLOPHONE (E) R4208

[233]   August 23, 1955 Los Angeles
         BILLIE HOLIDAY AND HER ORCHESTRA

Carter (as) Harry Edison (tp) Jimmy Rowles (p) Barney Kessel (g) John
Simmons (b) Larry Bunker (d) Billie Holiday (v)

I DON'T WANT TO CRY ANYMORE v-BH (as acc)   2438-2
45: CLEF EPC368 LP: VERVE MGV8026, VERVE (J)
MV2595, VERVE (E) 2304-114, VERVE VE-2-2515

PRELUDE TO A KISS v-BH (as)   2439-2
LP: CLEF MGC713, VERVE MGV8096, VERVE (J)
MV2596, VERVE (E) 2304-114, VERVE VE-2-2515

GHOST OF A CHANCE v-BH (as acc)   2440-1
45: CLEF EPC369 LP: VERVE MGV8026, VERVE (J)
MV2595, VERVE (E) 2304-114, VERVE VE-2-2515

WHEN YOUR LOVER HAS GONE v-BH (e)   2441-3
LP: CLEF MGC713, VERVE MGV8096, VERVE (J)
MV2596, VERVE (E) 2304-114, VERVE VE-2-2515

PLEASE DON'T TALK ABOUT ME WHEN I'M GONE   2443-2
      v-BH (as)
LP: CLEF MGC713, VERVE MGV8096, VERVE (J)
MV2596, VERVE 2-V6S-8816, VERVE (E) 2304-114,
VERVE VE-2-2515

IT HAD TO BE YOU v-BH (as acc)   2444-1
45: CLEF EPC368 LP: VERVE MGV8026, VERVE (J)
MV2595, VERVE (E) 2304-114, VERVE VE-2-2515

NICE WORK IF YOU CAN GET IT v-BH (as acc)   2445-5
LP: CLEF MGC713, VERVE MGV8096, VERVE (J)
MV2596, VERVE (E) 2304-114, VERVE VE-2-2515

[233A]   August 25, 1955 Los Angeles
          BILLIE HOLIDAY AND HER ORCHESTRA

Carter (as) Harry Edison (tp) Jimmy Rowles (p) Barney Kessel (g) John
Simmons (b) Larry Bunker (d) Billie Holiday (v)

COME RAIN OR COME SHINE v-BH (as acc)   2446-3
LP: CLEF MGC669, VERVE MGV8026, VERVE (J)
MV2595, VERVE (E) 2304-114, VERVE VE-2-2515

WHAT'S NEW v-BH (as)   2448-3
LP: CLEF MGC669, VERVE MGV8096, VERVE (J)
MV2596, VERVE 2-V6S-8816, VERVE (E) 2304-115,
VERVE VE-2-2529

A FINE ROMANCE v-BH (as acc)   2449-8
45: CLEF EPC368 LP: VERVE MGV8026, VERVE (J)
MV2595, VERVE (E) 2304-115, VERVE VE-2-2529

I GET A KICK OUT OF YOU v-BH (as)   2451-3
45: CLEF EPC369 LP: VERVE MGV8026, VERVE (J)
MV2595, VERVE (E) 2304-115, VERVE VE-2-2529

ISN'T IT A LOVELY DAY v-BH (as)   2453-3
LP: CLEF MGC669, VERVE MGV8026, VERVE (J)
MV2595, VERVE (E) 2304-115, VERVE VE-2-2529

---

[234]   December 2, 1955 Los Angeles
          SESSION AT MIDNIGHT

Carter (as, tp) Shorty Sherock, Harry Edison (tp) Murray McEachern (tb, as)
Gus Bivona (cl) Willie Smith (as) Plas Johnson, Babe Russin (ts) Jimmy
Rowles (p) Al Hendrickson (g) Mike Rubin (b) Irv Cottler (d)

MOTEN SWING   (as [2nd solo])
LP: CAPITOL T707, CAPITOL (DENMARK) 6E-052-81006

MAKING THE SCENE   (tp [2nd solo])
LP: CAPITOL T707, CAPITOL (DENMARK) 6E-052-81006

SWEET GEORGIA BROWN   (as)
LP: CAPITOL T707, CAPITOL (DENMARK) 6E-052-81006

BLUE LOU (tp [Edison, Carter, Sherock trade fours in that
        order]) (as [McEachern, Carter, Smith trade fours in
        that order])
LP: CAPITOL T707, CAPITOL (DENMARK) 6E-052-81006

STOMPIN' AT THE SAVOY   (as [1st solo])
LP: CAPITOL T707, CAPITOL (DENMARK) 6E-052-81006

SESSION AT MIDNIGHT   (as [2nd solo])
LP: CAPITOL T707, CAPITOL (DENMARK) 6E-052-81006

[235]   - reassigned

[236]   1955 Los Angeles
         ALFRED NEWMAN AND HIS ORCHESTRA

Carter (as, arr) Large Orchestra with Strings, Alfred Newman (conductor)

TO AVA   (as) arr
LP: DECCA DL8123

                        *   *   *

This is another recording of the theme written by Alfred Newman which
Carter played in the film The Snows of Kiliminjaro. It is known variously
as "To Ava" (after Ava Gardner who starred), "Blue Mountain," and "Love
Is Cynthia."

[237]   February 25, 1957 Los Angeles
            QUINCY JONES' ALL STARS

Carter (as) Herb Geller, Charlie Mariano, Art Pepper (as) Lou Levy (p)
Red Mitchell (b) Shelly Manne (d) Quincy Jones (dir) Jimmy Giuffre, Lennie
Niehaus (arr, comp)

BE MY GUEST   arr&comp-LN (as [4th 16b solo, 4th in trades])
LP: ABC PARAMOUNT ABC186, HMV CLP1157, ABC (J)
YW8511

DANCIN' PANTS   arr&comp-JG (as [2nd solo])
LP: ABC PARAMOUNT ABC186, HMV CLP1157, ABC (J)
YW8511

KING'S ROAD BLUES   arr&comp-LN (as [1st solo])
LP: ABC PARAMOUNT ABC186, HMV CLP1157, ABC
(J) YW8511

*   *   *

Quincy Jones directed this date which brings Carter together with three of
the younger West Coast alto men.   The catchy originals by Niehaus and
Giuffre provide an excellent basis for a comparison of the alto styles.

[238]   Ca. February 1957   Los Angeles
          STARS FOR DEFENSE DIXIELAND JAMBOREE

Carter (as) Charlie Teagarden, Red Nichols, Dick Cathcart, Conrad Gozzo,
Frank Beach, John Best (tp) Jack Teagarden (tb, v) Moe Schneider, King
Jackson, Murray McEachern, Warren Smith, Bill Schaefer (tb) Chuck Gen-
try, Wayne Songer, Matty Matlock, Eddie Miller, Babe Russin (reeds) Stan
Wrightsman, Al Pellegrini (p) Al Hendrickson, Nappy Lamare (g) Morty Corb
(b) Phil Stevens (tuba) Jack Sperling, Nick Fatool (d)

SOUTH RAMPART STREET PARADE   (e)
T: STARS FOR DEFENSE   LP: BLACK JACK LP3009,
FANFARE LP-2-102

BASIN STREET BLUES   v-JT (e)
T: STARS FOR DEFENSE   LP: FANFARE LP-2-102

MILENBERG JOYS   (as)
T: STARS FOR DEFENSE   LP: BLACK JACK LP3009,
FANFARE LP-2-102

    NOTE: The Fanfare LP contains two versions of "South Rampart
    Street Parade," designated no. 1 and no. 2.   The liner notes list
    no. 2 from this session and no. 1 as from a 1949 session but aural
    evidence indicates the reverse.

[239]   June 3, 1957   Los Angeles   TV Show Soundtrack
          BOBBY TROUP'S STARS OF JAZZ

Carter (as) Pete Jolly (p) Unknown (g, b, d)

THIS CAN'T BE LOVE   (as)
LP: CALLIOPE CAL320

LAURA   (as)
LP: CALLIOPE CAL320

TAKE THE A TRAIN   (as)
LP: CALLIOPE CAL320

[240]   June 11, 1957   Los Angeles
          BENNY CARTER (JAZZ GIANT)

Carter (as, arr) Frank Rosolino (tb) Ben Webster (ts) Andre Previn (p) Barney
Kessel (g) Leroy Vinnegar (b) Shelly Manne (d)

OLD FASHIONED LOVE (as) arr
LP: CONTEMPORARY C3555/S7028

BLUE LOU (as) arr
LP: CONTEMPORARY C3555/S7028

                              *   *   *

This is the first of four sessions comprising Carter's Jazz Giant, one of his
finest LPs of the 1950s. The album was to have been completed on August
6, but Carter became ill at the last moment. (The session, which was continued without him, resulted in the Barney Kessel album Let's Cook, Contemporary S7603.)

       Carter's arrangements consist primarily of opening and closing riffs
which allow maximum space for the string of superb solos.

---

[241]   July 22, 1957 Los Angeles
           BENNY CARTER (JAZZ GIANT)

Carter (as, tp, arr, comp) Frank Rosolino (tb) Ben Webster (ts) Jimmy Rowles
(p) Barney Kessel (g) Leroy Vinnegar (b) Shelly Manne (d)

A WALKIN' THING (as) arr, comp
LP: CONTEMPORARY C3555/S7028

I'M COMING VIRGINIA (tp) arr
LP: CONTEMPORARY C3555/S7028

                              *   *   *

The second Jazz Giant session opens with the first recording of a catchy
Carter original, "A Walkin' Thing. "

       "I'm Coming Virginia" is Carter's first trumpet feature on record in
over ten years. After 1946 he found that the increasing demands of arranging and composing for films precluded his devoting sufficient time to the instrument. Lester Koenig of Contemporary Records was a great admirer of
Carter's trumpet, however, and Carter recalls, "He was always after me to
record on trumpet and I finally acquiesced. " His solo, while containing none
of the bravura of an "I Surrender Dear," shows excellent control and the
typically bright singing tone, delicate vibrato, and varied dynamics which
have always distinguished Carter's trumpet work.

---

[242]   October 7, 1957 Los Angeles
           BENNY CARTER (JAZZ GIANT)

Carter (as, tp, arr, comp) Frank Rosolino (tb) Ben Webster (ts) Andre Previn
(p) Barney Kessel (g) Leroy Vinnegar (b) Shelly Manne (d)

HOW CAN YOU LOSE (tp)(as) arr, comp
LP: CONTEMPORARY C3555/S7028

---

[243]   December 6 and 12, 1957 Los Angeles
           HENRI RENE & HIS ORCHESTRA--BENNY CARTER, SOLO
           SAXOPHONE

Carter (as) John Towner Williams (p) Al Hendrickson (g) Joe Mondragon (b)
Lou Singer or Irv Cottler (d) 12 violins, 4 violas, Henri Rene (dir)

FRANKIE (as)
LP: RCA LPM1583

TAB (as)
LP: RCA LPM1583

PAT (as)
LP: RCA LPM1583

DINO (as)
LP: RCA LPM1583

JOHNNY (as)
LP: RCA LPM1583

> NOTE: Despite the label designations, Carter solos only on the titles
> listed above.

*   *   *

There is little of jazz interest in this "easy listening" date. Carter's role
as featured soloist is to play the themes and occasional obbligatos behind the
strings. Henri Rene's music is supposed to depict some of the singing idols
of women of the day and was issued under the dated title "Music For The
Weaker Sex."

[243A] 1957 Los Angeles
         SOUNDTRACK OF FILM THE SUN ALSO RISES

Carter (C-melody sax) with P/B/D

I LOVE YOU (C-melody sax)
LP: KAPP KDL7001

SWINGIN' DOWN THE LANE (C-melody sax)
LP: KAPP KDL7001

YOU DO SOMETHING TO ME (C-melody sax)
LP: KAPP KDL7001

THE CARTER CHARLESTON (C-melody sax)
LP: KAPP KDL7001

> NOTE: First three tunes played in medley; accordion added on last.

---

[244]   April 21, 1958 Los Angeles
         BENNY CARTER (JAZZ GIANT)

Carter (as) Andre Previn (p) Barney Kessel (g) Leroy Vinnegar (b) Shelly
Manne (d)

AIN'T SHE SWEET (as)
LP: CONTEMPORARY C3555/S7028

BLUES MY NAUGHTY SWEETIE GAVE TO ME   (as)
LP: CONTEMPORARY C3555/S7028

* * *

To finish the Jazz Giant album, Carter recorded two selections with just the
rhythm section. His alto solos are perhaps the strongest on the album.

[245]   September 1958 Los Angeles
           FRANK DEVOL AND HIS ORCHESTRA

Carter (as) Large Orchestra, Frank Devol (dir) Albert Harris (comp)

CIRCE (as)
LP: COLUMBIA CL1287

MORPHEUS (as)
LP: COLUMBIA CL1287

* * *

Carter is featured soloist on these pieces written by Albert Harris. Harris,
guitarist on several of Carter's 1936-1937 British recordings, moved to
Hollywood, where he has become a composer of note.

[246]   September or Early October 1958
           SOUNDTRACK OF FILM THE FIVE PENNIES

Carter (as, arr) Collective Personnel: Red Nichols (tp, cornet) Louis Arm-
strong (tp, v) Bobby Goodrich, Clyde Hurley, Dick Cathcart (tp) Warren
Smith, Pete Beilman, Elmer Schneider (tb) Heinie Beau (cl) Wayne Songer
(as) Eddie Miller (ts) Joe Rushton (bs) Stan Wrightsman, Gene Plummer (p)
George Van Eps, Allan Reuss (g) Morty Corb (b) Jack Sperling, Nick Fatool,
Shelly Manne (d) Danny Kaye (v)

AFTER YOU'VE GONE (as acc)
LP: DOT DLP9500

BILL BAILEY, WON'T YOU PLEASE COME HOME   v-LA, DK
      (e) arr
LP: DOT DLP9500

BATTLE HYMN OF THE REPUBLIC   v-LA (e)
LP: DOT DLP9500, DOT DLP25878

JUST THE BLUES (e) arr
LP: DOT DLP9500, DOT DLP25878

* * *

Carter does not solo on his only recordings with Louis Armstrong. He arranged and conducted (but did not play) on a session for him in 1955.

    Carter may play in the ensemble on other selections on the sound-
track album, but is clearly audible on the four listed above.

In addition to the two arrangements listed, Carter arranged the following tunes in the film which do not appear on the soundtrack album: "Washington And Lee Swing," "Runnin' Wild," "Tiger Rag" and "Sleepy Time."

[247]   October 24, 1958 Los Angeles
          BOBBY TROUP AND HIS STARS OF JAZZ

Carter (as) Collective Personnel: Buddy Childers, Conte Candoli, Pete Candoli, Ollie Mitchell, Al Porcino, Ray Triscari, Stu Williamson (tp) Shorty Rogers (tp, arr) Milt Bernhart, Harry Betts, Bob Enevoldsen, John Halliburton, Dick Nash, Frank Rosolino, Kenny Shroyer (tb) Paul Horn, Bud Shank (fl, as) Bob Cooper, Plas Johnson, Richie Kamuca (ts) Bill Holman (ts, bs) Chuck Gentry (bs) Jimmy Rowles (p, arr) Red Norvo (vib) Barney Kessel (g) Monty Budwig, Joe Mondragon (b) Mel Lewis, Shelly Manne (d) Bobby Troup (v)

PLEASE BE KIND v-BT (as)
LP: RCA LPM1959

AS LONG AS I LIVE v-BT (e)
LP: RCA LPM1959

IS YOU IS OR IS YOU AIN'T MY BABY v-BT (e)
LP: RCA LPM1959

PERDIDO v-BT
UNISSUED

> NOTE: Personnel listed is for three sessions; Carter plays on this one only.

[248]   November 2, 1958 Los Angeles
          BENNY CARTER QUARTET WITH EARL HINES (SWINGIN' THE
          TWENTIES)

Carter (as, tp) Earl Hines (p) Leroy Vinnegar (b) Shelly Manne (d)

MARY LOU (as)
LP: CONTEMPORARY M3561/S7561, VOGUE (E) LAC12225,
CONTEMPORARY (F) CHTX240.630

IF I COULD BE WITH YOU (tp)
LP: CONTEMPORARY M3561/S7561, VOGUE (E) LAC12225,
CONTEMPORARY (F) CHTX240.630

IN A LITTLE SPANISH TOWN (as)
LP: CONTEMPORARY M3561/S7561, VOGUE (E) LAC12225,
CONTEMPORARY (F) CHTX240.630

JUST IMAGINE (as)
LP: CONTEMPORARY M3561/S7561, VOGUE (E) LAC12225,
CONTEMPORARY (F) CHTX240.630

SWEET LORRAINE (as)
LP: CONTEMPORARY M3561/S7561, VOGUE (E) LAC12225,
CONTEMPORARY (F) CHTX240.630

A MONDAY DATE (as)
LP: CONTEMPORARY M3561/S7561, VOGUE (E) LAC12225,
CONTEMPORARY (F) CHTX240. 630

SOMEONE TO WATCH OVER ME (tp)
LP: CONTEMPORARY M3561/S7561, VOGUE (E) LAC12225,
CONTEMPORARY (F) CHTX240. 630

ALL ALONE (tp)
LP: CONTEMPORARY M3561/S7561, VOGUE (E) LAC12225,
CONTEMPORARY (F) CHTX240. 630

WHO'S SORRY NOW (as)
LP: CONTEMPORARY M3561/S7561, VOGUE (E) LAC12225,
CONTEMPORARY (F) CHTX240. 630

THOU SWELL (as)
LP: CONTEMPORARY M3561/S7561, VOGUE (E) LAC12225,
CONTEMPORARY (F) CHTX240. 630

LAUGH, CLOWN, LAUGH (as)
LP: CONTEMPORARY M3561/S7561, VOGUE (E) LAC12225,
CONTEMPORARY (F) CHTX240. 630

MY BLUE HEAVEN (as)
LP: CONTEMPORARY M3561/S7561, VOGUE (E) LAC12225,
CONTEMPORARY (F) CHTX240. 630

*   *   *

Carter's first recording with Hines is a generally successful date, featuring
updated versions of 1920s standards. Lester Koenig again persuaded Carter
to play trumpet, which he does effectively on three tunes.

[249]   1958 Los Angeles
         DON EVANS WITH ORCH. UNDER THE DIRECTION OF BENNY
         CARTER

Carter (as, arr, comp) Unknown Rhythm Section, Don Evans (v)

HOW LONG IS A MOMENT v-DE (as) arr, comp
45: DOME 100-2

    NOTE: Dome is Carter's own label.

[250]   1958 Los Angeles
         THE SMART SET

Carter (as) Includes Dick Cathcart (tp) Ted Nash (as, flute) Bob Enevoldsen
(ts) Red Norvo (vib) The Smart Set (v) Jimmy Joyce (arr)

THE LONESOME ROAD v-SS (e)
LP: WARNER BROS. W1258

CARELESS v-SS (e)
LP: WARNER BROS. W1258

IT'S ALL RIGHT WITH ME   v-SS (e)
LP: WARNER BROS. W1258

I HEAR MUSIC   v-SS (e)
LP: WARNER BROS. W1258

FIVE FOOT TWO, EYES OF BLUE   v-SS (e)
LP: WARNER BROS. W1258

---

[251]   1958 Los Angeles
           KITTY WHITE

Carter (as) Jimmy Rowles (p) Bill Pitman (g) Larry Bunker (vib) Red Callender (b) Alvin Stoller (d) Carlos Vidal (bongos, conga) Kitty White (v)

PLEASE BE PATIENT   v-KW (as)
LP: ROULETTE R52020

FOREVER YOUNG   v-KW (as)
LP: ROULETTE R52020

SO HELP ME   v-KW (as)
LP: ROULETTE R52020

IT WAS SO BEAUTIFUL   v-KW (as)
LP: ROULETTE R52020

---

[252]   Ca. 1958 Los Angeles
           KITTY WHITE WITH BENNY CARTER AND HIS ORCHESTRA

Carter (as, arr) Gale Robinson (French horn) Unknown (tb, p, g, b, d) Kitty
White (v)

THE OLD MAN AND THE SEA   v-KW (as acc) arr
45:   GNP 141X

I AM YOUR DREAM   v-KW (as) arr
45:   GNP 141X

---

[253]   Late 1958 or Early 1959 Los Angeles
           BENNY CARTER AND HIS ORCHESTRA (ASPECTS/JAZZ
           CALENDER)

Carter (as, arr, comp) Conrad Gozzo, Shorty Sherock, Pete Candoli, Uan
Rasey (tp) Tommy Pederson, George Roberts, Herb Harper (tb) Buddy Collette, Bill Green, Justin Gordon, Chuck Gentry (reeds) Arnold Ross (p)
Bobby Gibbons (g) Joe Comfort (b) Shelly Manne (d) Larry Bunker (vib,
bongos)

JUNE IN JANUARY   (as) arr
LP: UNITED ARTISTS UAL4017/UAS5017, UNITED ARTISTS
UAL4080/UAS5080, UNITED ARTISTS (J) GXF3039

FEBRUARY FIESTA   (as) arr
LP: UNITED ARTISTS UAL4017/UAS5017, UNITED ARTISTS
UAL4080/UAS5080, UNITED ARTISTS (J) GXF3039

I'LL REMEMBER APRIL   (as) arr
LP: UNITED ARTISTS UAL4017/UAS5017, UNITED ARTISTS
UAL4080/UAS5080, UNITED ARTISTS (J) GXF3039

SEPTEMBER SONG   (as) arr
LP: UNITED ARTISTS UAL4017/UAS5017, UNITED ARTISTS
UAL4080/UAS5080, UNITED ARTISTS (J) GXF3039

ONE MORNING IN MAY   (as)
LP: UNITED ARTISTS UAL4017/UAS5017, UNITED ARTISTS
UAL4080/UAS5080, UNITED ARTISTS (J) GXF3039

AUGUST MOON   (as) comp
LP: UNITED ARTISTS UAL4017/UAS5017, UNITED ARTISTS
UAL4080/UAS5080, UNITED ARTISTS (J) GXF3039

> NOTE: Carter with p, g, b, d, vib on last two titles. See comments
> for next session.

---

[254]   Late 1958 or Early 1959   Los Angeles
             BENNY CARTER AND HIS ORCHESTRA (ASPECTS/JAZZ
             CALENDER)

Carter (as, arr, comp) Al Porcino, Stu Williamson, Ray Triscari, Joe Gordon
(tp) Frank Rosolino, Tommy Pederson, Russ Brown (tb) Buddy Collette, Bill
Green, Jewell Grant, Plas Johnson (reeds) Gerald Wiggins (p) Barney Kessel
(g) Joe Comfort (b) Shelly Manne (d)

MARCH WIND   (as) arr, comp
LP: UNITED ARTISTS UAL4017/UAS5017, UNITED ARTISTS
UAL4080/UAS5080, UNITED ARTISTS (J) GXF3039

JUNE IS BUSTIN' OUT ALL OVER   (as) arr
LP: UNITED ARTISTS UAL4017/UAS5017, UNITED ARTISTS
UAL4080/UAS5080, UNITED ARTISTS (J) GXF3039

SLEIGH RIDE IN JULY   (as) arr
LP: UNITED ARTISTS UAL4017/UAS5017, UNITED ARTISTS
UAL4080/UAS5080, UNITED ARTISTS GXF3039

SOMETHING FOR OCTOBER   (as) arr, comp
LP: UNITED ARTISTS UAL4017/UAS5017, UNITED ARTISTS
UAL4080/UAS5080, UNITED ARTISTS GXF3039

SWINGIN' IN NOVEMBER   (as) arr, comp
LP: UNITED ARTISTS UAL4017/UAS5017, UNITED ARTISTS
UAL4080/UAS5080, UNITED ARTISTS (J) GXF3039

ROSES IN DECEMBER   (as) arr
LP: UNITED ARTISTS UAL4017/UAS5017, UNITED ARTISTS
UAL4080/UAS5080, UNITED ARTISTS (J) GXF3039

                              *   *   *

[253, 254] Jazz Calendar is a good representation of Carter's big-band writing during the period when he was recording almost exclusively with smaller
groups. He also supplied original compositions for those months without appropriate tunes.

Dates for Carter's three United Artists LPs range from 1959 to 1962 in various sources.   Carter believes they were all recorded in a one-year period, ca. 1958.   Hal Schaefer, who was with United Artists at the time, concurs.   Schaefer conceived the theme for the Aspects/Jazz Calendar session (originally entitling it A Year of Joy--12 Swinging Months) and the Can Can album (as well as playing piano on the latter).   He joined United Artists in April 1958 and was not involved in Carter's last album for the label, Sax à la Carter.

---

[255]   Late 1958 or 1959   New York
           BENNY CARTER--HAL SCHAEFER (CAN CAN)

Carter (as) Hal Schaefer (p) John Drew (p) Gus Johnson (d) Teddy Charles (vib)

ANYTHING GOES (as)
LP: UNITED ARTISTS UAL3055/UAS6055, UNITED
ARTISTS UAL4073/UAS5073

ALL THROUGH THE NIGHT (as)
LP: UNITED ARTISTS UAL3055/UAS6055, UNITED
ARTISTS UAL4073/UAS5073

WALTZ DOWN THE AISLE (as)
LP: UNITED ARTISTS UAL3055/UAS6055, UNITED
ARTISTS UAL4073/UAS5073

BUDDIE BEWARE (as)
LP: UNITED ARTISTS UAL3055/UAS6055, UNITED
ARTISTS UAL4073/UAS5073

YOU'RE THE TOP (as)
LP: UNITED ARTISTS UAL3055/UAS6055, UNITED
ARTISTS UAL4073/UAS5073

---

[256]   Late 1958 or 1959   New York
           BENNY CARTER--HAL SCHAEFER (CAN CAN)

Carter (as) Hal Schaefer (p) Joe Benjamin (b) Gus Johnson (d) Ted Sommer (percussion)

I LOVE PARIS (as)
LP: UNITED ARTISTS UAL3055/UAS6055, UNITED
ARTISTS UAL4073/UAS5073

C'EST MAGNIFIQUE (as)
LP: UNITED ARTISTS UAL3055/UAS6055, UNITED
ARTISTS UAL4073/UAS5073

IT'S ALL RIGHT WITH ME (as)
LP: UNITED ARTISTS UAL3055/UAS6055, UNITED
ARTISTS UAL4073/UAS5073

ALLEZ-VOUS EN (as)
LP: UNITED ARTISTS UAL3055/UAS6055, UNITED
ARTISTS UAL4073/UAS5073

I AM IN LOVE   (as)
LP: UNITED ARTISTS UAL3055/UAS6055, UNITED
ARTISTS UAL4073/UAS5073

                              *   *   *

[255, 256]   Although there has been some dispute over the place of recording, both Carter and Hal Schaefer recall that this date and the final one for
United Artists (session [267]) were made in New York.

---

[257]   January 5, 1959   Los Angeles
           HELEN HUMES

Carter (tp) Frank Rosolino (tb) Teddy Edwards (ts) Andre Previn (p) Leroy
Vinnegar (b) Shelly Manne (d) Helen Humes (v)

BILL BAILEY, WON'T YOU PLEASE COME HOME   v-HH (tp)
45: CONTEMPORARY 366   LP: CONTEMPORARY M3571/S7571,
VOGUE (E) LAC12245

WHEN THE SAINTS GO MARCHING IN   v-HH (tp)
45: CONTEMPORARY 366   LP: CONTEMPORARY M3571/S7571,
VOGUE (E) LAC12245

AIN'T MISBEHAVIN'   v-HH (tp acc)
CONTEMPORARY M3571/S7571, VOGUE (E) LAC12245

BILL   v-HH (e)
45: CONTEMPORARY M3571/S7571, VOGUE (E) LAC12245

---

[258]   January 9 and 12, 1959   Los Angeles
           BARBARA DANE

Carter (tp) Herb Harper or John Halliburton (tb) Plas Johnson (ts) Earl Hines
(p) Leroy Vinnegar (b) Shelly Manne (d) Barbara Dane (v)

LIVIN' WITH THE BLUES   v-BD (tp acc)
LP: DOT DLP3177, DOT SDLP25177, DOT DLP25878

HOW LONG, HOW LONG BLUES   v-BD (tp acc)
LP: DOT DLP3177, DOT SDLP25177

IF I COULD BE WITH YOU   v-BD (tp)
LP: DOT DLP3177, DOT SDLP25177

IN THE EVENIN'   v-BD (tp acc)
LP: DOT DLP3177, DOT SDLP25177

BYE BYE BLACKBIRD   v-BD (tp)
LP: DOT DLP3177, DOT SDLP25177

A HUNDRED YEARS FROM TODAY   v-BD (tp acc)
LP: DOT DLP3177, DOT SDLP25177

MECCA FLAT BLUES   v-BD (tp acc)
LP: DOT DLP3177, DOT SDLP25177

WHY DON'T YOU DO RIGHT   v-BD (e)
LP: DOT DLP3177, DOT SDLP25177

PORGY   v-BD (tp acc)
LP: DOT DLP3177, DOT SDLP25177

SINCE I FELL FOR YOU   v-BD (tp acc)
LP: DOT DLP3177, DOT SDLP25177

*   *   *

[257, 258] In a supporting role, Carter turns in some of his best trumpet work of the period on these sessions featuring vocalists Helen Humes and Barbara Dane.

---

[259]   January 26, 1959   Los Angeles
            EARL BOSTIC

Carter (as) Earl Bostic (as) Bill Green, Plas Johnson (ts) Buddy Collette (reeds) Sir Charles Thompson (p) Rene Hall (g) Herb Gordy (b) Earl Palmer (d) Elmer Schmidt (vib)

THAT OLD BLACK MAGIC (e)   K10231
45:   KING 5454, KING EP452 LP: KING LP640,
KING LP786, PARLOPHONE (E) PMC1119

WHILE WE'RE YOUNG (e)   K10232
45:   KING EP454 LP: KING LP640, PARLOPHONE
(E) PMC1119

MOONLIGHT IN VERMONT (e)   K10233
45:   KING EP452 LP: KING LP640, PARLOPHONE
(E) PMC1119

FULL MOON AND EMPTY ARMS (e)   K10234
45:   KING 5454, KING EP453 LP: KING LP640,
PARLOPHONE (E) PMC1119

I THINK OF YOU (e)   K10235
45:   KING EP453 LP: KING LP640, PARLOPHONE
(E) PMC1119

AUTUMN SERENADE (e)   K10236
45:   KING EP454 LP: KING LP640, PARLOPHONE
(E) PMC1119

---

[260]   January 27, 1959   Los Angeles
            HELEN HUMES

Carter (tp) Frank Rosolino (tb) Teddy Edwards (ts) Andre Previn (p) Leroy Vinnegar (b) Mel Lewis (d) Helen Humes (v)

'TAIN'T NOBODY'S BIZNESS IF I DO v-HH (tp)
45:   CONTEMPORARY 368 LP: CONTEMPORARY
M3571/S7571, VOGUE (E) LAC12245

AMONG MY SOUVENIRS   v-HH (e)
CONTEMPORARY M3571/S7571, VOGUE (E) LAC12245

I GOT IT BAD AND THAT AIN'T GOOD   v-HH (tp acc)
CONTEMPORARY M3571/S7571, VOGUE (E) LAC12245

A GOOD MAN IS HARD TO FIND   v-HH (e)
CONTEMPORARY M3571/S7571, VOGUE (E) LAC12245

---

[261]   February 10, 1959   Los Angeles
           HELEN HUMES

Carter (tp) Frank Rosolino (tb) Teddy Edwards (ts) Andre Previn (p) Leroy
Vinnegar (b) Shelly Manne (d) Helen Humes (v)

TROUBLE IN MIND   v-HH (tp acc)
45: CONTEMPORARY 368   LP: CONTEMPORARY
M3571/S7571, VOGUE (E) LAC12245

YOU CAN DEPEND ON ME   v-HH (tp)
CONTEMPORARY M3571/S7571, VOGUE (E) LAC12245

STAR DUST   v-HH (tp)
CONTEMPORARY M3571/S7571, VOGUE (E) LAC12245

WHEN I GROW TOO OLD TO DREAM   v-HH (tp)
CONTEMPORARY M3571/S7571, VOGUE (E) LAC12245

---

[262]   March 1959   Los Angeles
           THE MUSIC FROM M SQUAD

Carter (as, ss, arr, comp) Collective Personnel: Pete Candoli, Frank Beach,
Don Fagerquist, Maury Harris (tp) Frank Rosolino, Pete Carpenter, Joe
Howard, George Roberts (tb) John Towner Williams (p, arr, comp) Red
Mitchell, Joe Mondragon (b) Alvin Stoller (d) Stanley Wilson (cond)

M SQUAD THEME   (as)
LP: RCA LPM/LSP2062

THE CHASE   (as)
LP: RCA LPM/LSP2062

THE SEARCH   (e) arr, comp
LP: RCA LPM/LSP2062

PHANTOM RAIDERS   (as) arr, comp
LP: RCA LPM/LSP2062

LONELY BEAT   (ss)
LP: RCA LPM/LSP2062

THE JUKE BOX   (as) arr, comp
LP: RCA LPM/LSP2062

THE MUGGER   (as) arr, comp
LP: RCA LPM/LSP2062

THE DISCOVERY (as)
LP: RCA LPM/LSP2062

THE LATE SPOT (as)
LP: RCA LPM/LSP2062

THE CHA-CHA CLUB (as)
LP: RCA LPM/LSP2062

A LADY SINGS THE BLUES (as) arr
LP: RCA LPM/LSP2062

THE END (as)
LP: RCA LPM/LSP2062

                    *   *   *

This album features music performed on the soundtrack of the TV series,
for which Carter composed, arranged and played. Of particular interest is
Carter's only recorded solo on soprano saxophone in "Lonely Beat."

[263]   July 28, 1959 Los Angeles
           SOUNDTRACK OF FILM ON THE BEACH

Carter (as) Large Orchestra

ON THE BEACH-SOUNDTRACK ALBUM
LP: ROULETTE R25098

     NOTE: Carter plays in the orchestra but does not solo on this album.

[264]   Probably November-December 1959 Los Angeles
           SAM COOKE

Carter (as) Vocal Group and Orchestra Including: Pete Candoli, Conte Can-
doli (tp) Conrad Gozzo, Milt Bernhart (tb) Jewell Grant (as) Jackie Kelso,
Plas Johnson (ts) Ernie Freeman (p) Red Callender (b) Earl Palmer (d) Sam
Cooke (v) Rene Hall (arr)

LOVER MAN v-SC (as acc)
LP: KEEN A2004, UP FRONT UPF160, RCA APL1-0899,
TRIP TLX9517, RCA (E) HY1030

'TAIN'T NOBODY'S BIZNESS IF I DO v-SC (as acc)
LP: KEEN A2004, UP FRONT UPF160, RCA APL1-0899,
TRIP TLX9517, TRIP TOP 16-2, RCA (E) HY1030

SOLITUDE v-SC (as acc)
LP: KEEN A2004, UP FRONT UPF160, RCA APL1-0899,
TRIP TLP8030, RCA (E) HY1030

LOVER, COME BACK TO ME v-SC (as acc)
LP: KEEN A2004, UP FRONT UPF160, RCA APL1-0899,
TRIP TLP8030, TRIP TOP 16-2, RCA (E) HY1030

COMES LOVE v-SC (as acc)
LP: KEEN A2004, TRIP TLP8030

GOOD MORNING HEARTACHE   v-SC (e)
LP: KEEN A2004, UP FRONT UPF160, RCA APL1-0899,
TRIP TLX9517, TRIP TOP 16-2, RCA (E) HY1030

LET'S CALL THE WHOLE THING OFF   v-SC (e)
LP: KEEN A2004, UP FRONT UPF160, RCA APL1-0899,
TRIP TLX9517, SPRINGBOARD SPX6003, RCA (E) HY1030

GOD BLESS THE CHILD   v-SC (e)
LP: KEEN A2004, UP FRONT UPF160, TRIP TLP8030,
TRIP TOP 16-2

CRAZY IN LOVE WITH YOU   v-SC (e)
LP: KEEN A2004, UP FRONT UPF160, RCA APL1-0899,
TRIP TLP8030, RCA (E) HY1030

THEY CAN'T TAKE THAT WAY FROM ME   v-SC (e)
LP: KEEN A2004, RCA APL1-0899, TRIP TLP8030, RCA
(E) HY1030

I GOT A RIGHT TO SING THE BLUES   v-SC (e)
LP: KEEN A2004, RCA APL1-0899, TRIP TLP8030, TRIP
TOP 16-2, RCA (E) HY1030

SHE'S FUNNY THAT WAY   v-SC (e)
LP: KEEN A2004, TRIP TLP8030

> NOTES: Strings, vocal group present on "Good Morning Heartache,"
> "God Bless The Child," "Crazy In Love With You" and "She's Funny
> That Way." "Lover Man" as "Lover Girl" on Up Front and Trip;
> "Crazy In Love" as "Crazy She Calls Me" on RCA.

                          *   *   *

Rene Hall put together this album as a tribute to Billie Holiday, who died
several months earlier. Carter wrote the liner notes for the original issue,
Keen A2004.

---

[265]   1959 Los Angeles Soundtrack from Film The Gene Krupa Story
         GENE KRUPA

Carter (as) Pete Candoli, Conrad Gozzo, Ray Triscari, Joe Triscari (tp)
Ed Kusby, Murray McEachern, Tommy Pederson, George Roberts (tb)
Heinie Beau (as, cl) Jerry Casper, Dave Harris (ts) Dave Pell (bs) Jimmy
Rowles (p) Barney Kessel (g) Morty Corb (b) Gene Krupa, Shelly Manne (d)
Jerry Williams, John Williams (percussion) Ruby Lane, Anita O'Day (v)
Leith Stevens (arr)

MAIN TITLE   (e)
LP: VERVE MGV15010, HMV CLP1352, HMV CSD1296

SPIRITUAL JAZZ   (e)
LP: VERVE MGV15010, HMV CLP1352, HMV CSD1296

CHEROKEE . (as)
LP: VERVE MGV15010, HMV CLP1352, HMV CSD1296

INDIANA MONTAGE (e)
LP: VERVE MGV15010, HMV CLP1352, HMV CSD1296

OAHU DANCE/CHEROKEE (FINALE) (e)
LP: VERVE MGV15010, HMV CLP1352, HMV CSD1296

I LOVE MY BABY v-RL (e)
LP: VERVE MGV15010, HMV CLP1352, HMV CSD1296

MEMORIES OF YOU v-AO (e)
LP: VERVE MGV15010, HMV CLP1352, HMV CSD1296

[266]   Same Session

Carter (as) Red Nichols (c) Moe Schneider (tb) Heinie Beau (cl) Eddie Miller
(ts) Jess Stacy (p) Barney Kessel (g) Morty Corb (b) Gene Krupa (d)

ROYAL GARDEN BLUES (e)
LP: VERVE MGV15010, HMV CLP1352, HMV CSD1296

INDIANA JAM SESSION (as)
LP: VERVE MGV15010, HMV CLP1352, HMV CSD1296

WAY DOWN YONDER IN NEW ORLEANS (e)
LP: VERVE MGV15010, HMV CLP1352, HMV CSD1296

[267]   Probably 1959
         BENNY CARTER QUARTET (SAX ALA CARTER)

Carter (as, ts) Jimmy Rowles (p) Leroy Vinnegar (b) Mel Lewis (d)

FAR AWAY PLACES (as)
LP: UNITED ARTISTS UAL4094/UAS5094

AND THE ANGELS SING (as)
LP: UNITED ARTISTS UAL4094/UAS5094

EVERYTHING I HAVE IS YOURS (as)
LP: UNITED ARTISTS UAL4094/UAS5094

I UNDERSTAND (as)
LP: UNITED ARTISTS UAL4094/UAS5094

ALL OR NOTHING AT ALL (as)
LP: UNITED ARTISTS UAL4094/UAS5094

I'LL NEVER SMILE AGAIN (as)
LP: UNITED ARTISTS UAL4094/UAS5094

IF I LOVED YOU (as)
LP: UNITED ARTISTS UAL4094/UAS5094

I SHOULD CARE (as)
LP: UNITED ARTISTS UAL4094/UAS5094

FOR ALL WE KNOW (as)
LP: UNITED ARTISTS UAL4094/UAS5094

GHOST OF A CHANCE (as)
LP: UNITED ARTISTS UAL4094/UAS5094

THE ONE I LOVE (as)
LP: UNITED ARTISTS UAL4094/UAS5094

MOON OF MANAKOORA (as) (ts [Carter dubbed tenor part])
LP: UNITED ARTISTS UAL4094/UAS5094

---

[268]   March 1, 1960 Los Angeles
           NAT KING COLE

Carter (as) Large Orchestra with Strings and Vocal Group, Nat King Cole
(v) Nelson Riddle (arr, cond)

WILD IS LOVE v-NKC (e)
LP: CAPITOL (S) WAK1392

HUNDREDS AND THOUSANDS OF GIRLS v-NKC (as [2 bars])
LP: CAPITOL (S) WAK1392

TELL HER IN THE MORNING v-NKC (e)
LP: CAPITOL (S) WAK1392

PICK UP v-NKC (e)
LP: CAPITOL (S) WAK1392

BEGGAR FOR THE BLUES v-NKC (e)
LP: CAPITOL (S) WAK1392

STAY WITH IT v-NKC (e)
LP: CAPITOL (S) WAK1392

WILD IS LOVE FINALE v-NKC (e)
LP: CAPITOL (S) WAK1392

---

[269]   November 21, 1960 Stockholm Concert, Konserthuset
           JAZZ AT THE PHILHARMONIC

Carter (as, comp) Dizzy Gillespie (tp) J. J. Johnson (tb) Cannonball Adderley
(as) Lalo Schifrin (p) Art Davis (b) Chuck Lampkin (d)

BERNIE'S TUNE (as [1st solo])
LP: VERVE MGV8539, VERVE (E) VLP9045, BARCLAY
GLP3638, VERVE 2V6S-8823

SWEDISH JAM (as [2nd solo]) comp
LP: VERVE MGV8539, VERVE (E) VLP9045, BARCLAY
GLP3638, VERVE 2V6S-8823

---

[270]   Same Session

Carter (as, comp) Roy Eldridge (tp) Coleman Hawkins, Don Byas (ts) Lalo
Schifrin (p) Art Davis (b) Jo Jones (d)

INDIANA (as)
LP: VERVE V6-8541, VERVE (E) VLP9047, BARCLAY GLP3640

TAKE THE A TRAIN (as)
LP: VERVE V6-8541, VERVE (E) VLP9047, BARCLAY GLP3640

THE NEARNESS OF YOU (as)
LP: VERVE V6-8541, VERVE (E) VLP9047, BARCLAY GLP3640

A JAZZ PORTRAIT OF BRIGITTE BARDOT (as) comp
LP: VERVE V6-8541, VERVE (E) VLP9047, BARCLAY GLP3640

> NOTE: "The Nearness Of You" is Carter's feature in the ballad medley.

*   *   *

[269, 270] This version of JATP features Carter with two different generations of stars. Obviously inspired, he turns in his best recorded JATP work. Some stylistic adjustment in his playing with the different groups is evident. With the modernists his tone is slightly more strident. Also, his lines are less symmetrical; each phrase seems stimulated by the one preceding, rather than fitting into a larger scheme as on "Indiana" or "Take The A Train."

This is Carter's only recording with Cannonball Adderley, who named him, along with Charlie Parker, as his major influence.

Jepsen gives November 22 as the concert date, but Carter's passport shows he left Sweden on November 21. Also, the reproduction of a poster on the cover of Verve V8541 shows the date as November 21.

---

[271]   Probably Same Date and Location
           JAZZ AT THE PHILHARMONIC

Carter (as) Lalo Schifrin (p) Art Davis (b) Jo Jones (d)

THE NEARNESS OF YOU (as)
LP: UNISSUED

> NOTE: This piece is part of a ballad medley probably recorded at a different concert performance of JATP on the same day as the issued items.

---

[272]   1960 Los Angeles
           ELLA FITZGERALD-HAROLD ARLEN SONGBOOK

Carter (as) Large Orchestra, Ella Fitzgerald (v) Billy May (arr, dir)

BLUES IN THE NIGHT v-EF (as)
LP: VERVE MGV4057, VERVE V6-4046, VERVE SELECT
DOUBLE (E) 2683-064

LET'S FALL IN LOVE v-EF (as)
LP: VERVE MGV4057, VERVE V6-4046, VERVE SELECT
DOUBLE (E) 2683-064

THIS TIME THE DREAM'S ON ME   v-EF (as)
LP: VERVE MGV4057, VERVE V6-4046, VERVE SELECT
DOUBLE (E) 2683-064

> NOTE: Carter plays in the ensemble on other tunes from this ses-
> sion.

---

[273]   April 14-15, 1961 Los Angeles
           PEGGY LEE ACC. BY QUINCY JONES' ORCHESTRA

Carter (as, arr) Frank Beach, Bob Fowler, Conrad Gozzo, Manny Klein, Al
Porcino, Jack Sheldon (tp) Vernon Friley, Lewis McGreery, Frank Rosolino
(tb) Bob Knight (bass tb) Bill Green (as) Plas Johnson, Bill Perkins (ts)
Jack Nimitz (bs) Lou Levy, Jimmy Rowles (p) Dennis Budimir (g) Max Ben-
nett (b) Stan Levey (d) Chano Pozo (conga, bongos) Peggy Lee (v) Quincy
Jones (arr)

BOSTON BEANS v-PL (e)
LP: CAPITOL (S) T1671

KANSAS CITY BLUES v-PL (e)
LP: CAPITOL (S) T1671

BASIN STREET BLUES v-PL (e)
LP: CAPITOL (S) T1671

GOING TO CHICAGO BLUES v-PL (e)
LP: CAPITOL (S) T1671

NEW YORK CITY BLUES v-PL (e)
LP: CAPITOL (S) T1671

LOS ANGELES BLUES v-PL (e)
LP: CAPITOL (S) T1671

SAN FRANCISCO BLUES v-PL (e) arr
LP: CAPITOL (S) T1671

I LOST MY SUGAR IN SALT LAKE CITY v-PL (e)
LP: CAPITOL (S) T1671

ST. LOUIS BLUES v-PL (e)
LP: CAPITOL (S) T1671

FISHERMAN'S WHARF v-PL (e)
LP: CAPITOL (S) T1671

THE GRAIN BELT BLUES v-PL (e)
LP: CAPITOL (S) T1671

THE TRAIN BLUES v-PL (e)
LP: CAPITOL (S) T1671

ORANGE BLUES v-PL (e)
LP: CAPITOL (S) T1671

[274]   June 6, 1961 Los Angeles
           ALFRED NEWMAN

Carter (as, arr) Horns / 24 Violins / Rhythm Section, Alfred Newman (cond, comp)

LAURA (as) arr
LP: CAPITOL ST1652, ANGEL S36066

THE BAD AND THE BEAUTIFUL (as) arr
LP: CAPITOL ST1652, ANGEL S36066

[275]   October 30-31, 1961 New York
           COUNT BASIE AND HIS ORCHESTRA

Carter (as, arr, comp) Sonny Cohn, Al Aarons, Thad Jones, Snooky Young (tp)
Henry Coker, Quentin Jackson, Benny Powell (tb) Frank Wess (as) Frank
Foster, Budd Johnson (ts) Charlie Fowlkes (bs) Count Basie (p) Sam Herman
(g) Ed Jones (b) Sonny Payne (d)

THE BASIE TWIST (e) arr, comp   16356
45: ROULETTE 4403 LP: ROULETTE R25176

THE TROT (e) arr, comp   16357
45: ROULETTE 4403 LP: ROULETTE R52086,
COLUMBIA (E) 33SX1496, ROULETTE RE118, VOGUE 500021

THE LEGEND (e) arr, comp
LP: ROULETTE R52086, COLUMBIA (E) 33SX1496,
ROULETTE RE118, VOGUE 500021

GOIN' ON (e) arr, comp
LP: ROULETTE R52086, COLUMBIA (E) 33SX1496,
ROULETTE RE118, VOGUE 500021

[276]   November 1-2, 1961 New York
           COUNT BASIE AND HIS ORCHESTRA

Carter (as, arr, comp) Sonny Cohn, Al Aarons, Thad Jones, Snooky Young
(tp) Henry Coker, Quentin Jackson, Benny Powell (tb) Frank Wess (as) Frank
Foster, Budd Johnson (ts) Charlie Fowlkes (bs) Count Basie (p) Sam Herman
(g) Ed Jones (b) Sonny Payne (d) Dizzy Gillespie (cowbell)

EASY MONEY (e) arr, comp
LP: ROULETTE R52086, COLUMBIA (E) 33SX1496,
ROULETTE RE118, VOGUE 500021

WHO'S BLUE (e) arr, comp
LP: ROULETTE R52086, COLUMBIA (E) 33SX1496,
ROULETTE (E) 2683-013, ROULETTE RE118, VOGUE 500021

AMOROSO (e) arr, comp
LP: ROULETTE R52086, COLUMBIA (E) 33SX1496,
ROULETTE RE118, VOGUE 500021

THE SWIZZLE   (e) arr, comp
LP: ROULETTE R52086, COLUMBIA (E) 33SX1496,
ROULETTE RE118, VOGUE 500021

TURNABOUT   (e) arr, comp
LP: ROULETTE R52086, COLUMBIA (E) 33SX1496,
ROULETTE (E) 2683-013, ROULETTE RE118, VOGUE 500021

   NOTE: Gillespie plays cowbell on "Amoroso" only.

*   *   *

[275, 276] This collaboration with Basie--The Legend--is less celebrated
than Carter's Kansas City Suite of the previous year (on which Carter did
not play). The Legend is just as successful musically, however. While the
arrangements are unmistakably Carter's, he has obviously tailored them to
the Basie style, with more riffs than usual and plenty of space for the leader's piano fills. The Basie band also proves itself amenable to some of the
arranger's trademarks, the reed section capturing the distinctive Carter
sound on "Easy Money" and "Turnabout."

   Carter plays on the album only because Basie asked him to fill in
for Marshall Royal at the last minute. He agreed, provided that he not be
called upon to solo and that Frank Wess play lead alto.

[277]   November 13, 1961   New York
             BENNY CARTER AND HIS ORCHESTRA (FURTHER DEFINITIONS)

Carter (as, arr) Phil Woods (as) Coleman Hawkins, Charlie Rouse (ts) Dick
Katz (p) John Collins (g) Jimmy Garrison (b) Jo Jones (d)

HONEYSUCKLE ROSE   (as) arr
LP: IMPULSE A(S)#12, HMV (E) CLP1624/CSD1480, IM-
PULSE (J) YP8519, WORLD RECORD CLUB (E) T864, KING
(J) SH3002

THE MIDNIGHT SUN WILL NEVER SET   (as) arr
LP: IMPULSE A(S)#12, HMV (E) CLP1624/CSD1480, IM-
PULSE AS9258, IMPULSE (J) YP8519, WORLD RECORD CLUB
(E) T864, KING (J) SH3002

CHERRY   (as) arr
LP: IMPULSE A(S)#12, HMV (E) CLP1624/CSD1480, IM-
PULSE (J) YP8519, WORLD RECORD CLUB (E) T864, KING
(J) SH3002

CRAZY RHYTHM   (as) arr
LP: IMPULSE A(S)#12, HMV (E) CLP1624/CSD1480, IM-
PULSE (J) YP8519, WORLD RECORD CLUB (E) T864, KING
(J) SH3002

[278]   November 15, 1961   New York
             BENNY CARTER AND HIS ORCHESTRA (FURTHER DEFINITIONS)

Carter (as, arr, comp) Phil Woods (as) Coleman Hawkins, Charlie Rouse (ts)
Dick Katz (p) John Collins (g) Jimmy Garrison (b) Jo Jones (d)

DOOZY (as) arr, comp
LP: IMPULSE A(S)#12, HMV (E) CLP1624/CSD1480, IM-
PULSE (J) YP8519, WORLD RECORD CLUB (E) T864, KING
(J) SH3002

BLUE STAR (as) arr, comp
LP: IMPULSE A(S)#12, HMV (E) CLP1624/CSD1480, IM-
PULSE (J) YP8519, WORLD RECORD CLUB (E) T864, KING
(J) SH3002

COTTONTAIL (as) arr
LP: IMPULSE A(S)#12, HMV (E) CLP1624/CSD1480, IM-
PULSE ASH9272-3, IMPULSE (J) YP851, WORLD RECORD
CLUB (E) T864, KING (J) SH3002

BODY AND SOUL (as) arr
LP: IMPULSE A(S)#12, HMV (E) CLP1624/CSD1480, IM-
PULSE ASH9253-3, IMPULSE (J) YP8519, WORLD RECORD
CLUB (E) T864, KING (J) SH3002

                    *   *   *

[277, 278] Further Definitions is considered by many not only Carter's finest overall album, but one of the greatest jazz records of the last 30 years.
Intended as a "retrospective" of the epic 1937 Hawkins Paris date, the session pairs Carter and Hawkins with two leading voices of a later generation
of reed players.   The instrumentation is the same as on the earlier date.

       Carter and Hawkins are superb throughout, but perhaps their most
outstanding contributions come on the ballads, "Blue Star" and "The Midnight
Sun" and Hawkins's work on "Body And Soul."

       There are arranging delights in every piece, with a perfect balance
between solo and ensemble passages.   The sax quartet blends perfectly and
the sound of Carter's lead alto has never been captured more clearly.

       Two of the pieces have a particularly "retrospective" flavor: on
"Cottontail" Carter has included the original Ellington saxophone chorus, and
"Body And Soul" opens with a sax ensemble reading of the first eight meas-
ures of Hawkins's classic 1939 solo.

[279]   1961 New York
          PEARL BAILEY WITH LOUIS BELLSON AND HIS ORCHESTRA

Carter (as, arr) Louis Bellson (d, arr) Pearl Bailey (v)

TIRED v-PB (e) arr
LP: ROULETTE R25144

THAT'S GOOD ENOUGH FOR ME v-PB (e)
LP: ROULETTE R25144

IT TAKES TWO TO TANGO v-PB (e)
LP: ROULETTE R25144

ROW ROW ROW ROW v-PB (e) arr
LP: ROULETTE R25144

MA, HE'S MAKIN' EYES AT ME   v-PB (e)
LP: ROULETTE R25144

TOOT TOOT TOOTSIE   v-PB (e) arr
LP: ROULETTE R25144, ROULETTE RE101

ST. LOUIS BLUES   v-PB (e)
LP: ROULETTE R25144

LEGALIZE MY NAME   v-PB (e)
LP: ROULETTE R25144

FIFTEEN YEARS   v-PB (e)
LP: ROULETTE R25144

AC-CENT-UATE THE POSITIVE   v-PB (e)
LP: ROULETTE R25144

CHERRY'S AT TOP OF THE TREE   v-PB (e)
LP: ROULETTE R25144

OLD, TIRED AND TORN   v-PB (e)
LP: ROULETTE R25144

---

[280]   1961   Los Angeles
          SOUNDTRACK OF FILM THE FLOWER DRUM SONG

FLOWER DRUM SONG-SOUNDTRACK ALBUM
LP: DECCA DL79098, MCA 2069

> NOTE: Carter played in the orchestra and assisted in the orchestration of parts of this production.

---

[281]   1961   Los Angeles
          DAVE PELL--TRIBUTE TO JOHN KIRBY

Carter (as) Ray Linn (tp) Dave Pell (cl) John Towner Williams (p, arr, comp)
Lyle Ritz (b) Frankie Capp (d) Harry Betts (arr) Marty Paich (arr, comp)
Med Flory (arr)

ROSE ROOM (original Kirby sextet arr)   (as [re-creation
        of Procope solo])
LP: CAPITOL (S) T1687

ROYAL GARDEN BLUES (original arr adapted by HB)   (as)
LP: CAPITOL (S) T1687

ANITRA'S DANCE (original arr transcribed by MP)   (as)
LP: CAPITOL (S) T1687

IT FEELS SO GOOD (original arr transcribed by MF)   (as)
LP: CAPITOL (S) T1687

TOOTSIE ROLL   arr&comp-MP (as)
LP: CAPITOL (S) T1687

DOUBLE WALK   arr&comp-JTW (as)
LP: CAPITOL (S) T1687

UNDECIDED   arr-JTW (as)
LP: CAPITOL (S) T1687

BLUE SKIES (original arr adapted by HB)   (as)
LP: CAPITOL (S) T1687

COQUETTE (original arr transcribed by MF)   (as)
LP: CAPITOL (S) T1687

OPUS 5 (original arr adapted by HB)   (as)
LP: CAPITOL (S) T1687

20TH CENTURY CLOSET   arr-JTW (as)
LP: CAPITOL (S) T1687

THEN I'LL BE HAPPY   (as)
LP: CAPITOL (S) T1687

*   *   *

Dave Pell organized this session as a tribute to Carter's close friend John
Kirby.   The repertoire includes several of the Kirby sextet's arrangements,
as well as some originals by Marty Paich and John Williams played in the
Kirby style.   The group is quite successful in capturing the flavor of the
Kirby band.   On "Rose Room," Carter plays Russell Procope's original solo
note-for-note, coming close to Procope's distinctive timbre and vibrato.
This is the only instance of Carter attempting such a re-creation on record.

[282]   April 10, 1962   Los Angeles
             BBB & CO

Carter (as, tp, comp) Shorty Sherock (tp) Barney Bigard (cl) Ben Webster (ts)
Jimmy Rowles (p) Dave Barbour (g) Leroy Vinnegar (b) Mel Lewis (d)

OPENING BLUES   (as)
LP: SWINGVILLE/STATUS 2032, PRESTIGE (F) FELP15002,
PRESTIGE (J) SMJ7572, PRESTIGE MPP2513

LULA   (as) comp
LP: SWINGVILLE/STATUS 2032, PRESTIGE (F) FELP15002,
PRESTIGE (J) SMJ7572, PRESTIGE MPP2513

WHEN LIGHTS ARE LOW   (tp [8-bar sequence in 1st chorus:
         Carter, Sherock, Carter]) (as) comp
LP: SWINGVILLE/STATUS 2032, PRESTIGE (F) FELP15002,
PRESTIGE (J) SMJ7572, PRESTIGE MPP2513

YOU CAN'T TELL THE DIFFERENCE WHEN THE SUN GOES
         DOWN BLUES   (as)
LP: SWINGVILLE/STATUS 2032, PRESTIGE (F) FELP15002,
PRESTIGE (J) SMJ7572, PRESTIGE MPP2513

*   *   *

This date does not live up to the potential of its personnel. The repertoire lacks a focus, with most of the session taken up by the two extended blues.

---

[283]   May 1963   Paris
          STANLEY WILSON ORCH. WITH BENNY CARTER, GUEST SOLOIST

Carter (as, arr, comp) Maurice Van Der (p) Pierre Culloz (g) Pierre Michelot (b) Lionel Galli (violin) Christian Garros (d) Strings / Horns / Vocal Choir Directed by Christiene Legrand, Stanley Wilson (arr)

UNDER PARIS SKIES vocal group (as) arr
LP: CHARTER CLS105

IF YOU LOVE ME, REALLY LOVE ME (as)
LP: CHARTER CLS105

COMME CI, COMME CA vocal group (as)
LP: CHARTER CLS105

DOMINO (as) arr
LP: CHARTER CLS105

CHERCHEZ LA FEMME   arr-SW (as) comp
LP: CHARTER CLS105

MY PLACE vocal group (as)
LP: CHARTER CLS105

IF YOU GO (as) arr
LP: CHARTER CLS105

DANCE WITH ME vocal group (as) arr
LP: CHARTER CLS105

I WISH YOU LOVE (as)
LP: CHARTER CLS105

---

[284]   May 1963   Paris Studio recording-Unissued
          STANLEY WILSON ORCH. WITH BENNY CARTER, GUEST SOLOIST

Carter (as, arr) Maurice Van Der (p) Pierre Culloz (g) Pierre Michelot (b) Christian Garros (d) Orchestra Including 20 Strings, Stanley Wilson, John Towner Williams (arr)

THE VERY THOUGHT OF YOU   arr-SW (as)

HE NEEDS ME   arr-JTW (as)

NEVER MORE   arr-SW (as)

WHAT KIND OF FOOL AM I   (as) arr

ROOM WITH A VIEW   arr-JTW (as)

THE BRITISH GRENADIERS   arr-JTW (e)

POOR LITTLE RICH GIRL (as) arr

SHOW ME THE WAY TO GO HOME (as) arr

THESE FOOLISH THINGS arr-SW (as)

SERENADE TO A WEALTHY WIDOW arr-SW (as)

GREENSLEEVES arr-JTW (e)

ROSES OF PICARDY (as) arr

---

[285]　　　May 1963　Paris
　　　　BENNY CARTER (BENNY CARTER IN PARIS/AUTUMN LEAVES)

Carter (as, arr, comp) Maurice Van Der (p) Pierre Michelot (b) Christian Garros (d) Christiene Legrand, Alice Herald, Jeanette Beaucamont (vocal group)

AROUND THE WORLD IN 80 DAYS vocal group (as) arr
LP: 20TH CENTURY FOX TFM3134, MOVIETONE 71020/S72020

I'LL CLOSE MY EYES (as)
LP: 20TH CENTURY FOX TFM3134, MOVIETONE 71020/S72020

CUANDO CALIENTE EL SOL vocal group (as) arr
LP: 20TH CENTURY FOX TFM3134, MOVIETONE 71020/S72020

SMILE (as)
LP: 20TH CENTURY FOX TFM3134, MOVIETONE 71020/S72020

BLACK KNIGHT vocal group (as) arr
LP: 20TH CENTURY FOX TFM3134

AUTUMN LEAVES (as)
LP: 20TH CENTURY FOX TFM3134, MOVIETONE 71020/S72020

CHEROKEE vocal group (as) arr
LP: 20TH CENTURY FOX TFM3134, MOVIETONE 71020/S72020

WALTZ GAY (as) comp
LP: 20TH CENTURY FOX TFM3134, MOVIETONE 71020/S72020

VOUS QUI PASSEZ SANS ME VOIR vocal group (as) arr
LP: 20TH CENTURY FOX TFM3134, MOVIETONE 71020/S72020

BAGATELLE (as) comp
LP: 20TH CENTURY FOX TFM3134, MOVIETONE 71020/S72020

THE GYPSY vocal group (as) arr
LP: 20TH CENTURY FOX TFM3134, MOVIETONE
71020/S72020

BLUES FOR BENNY (as)
LP: 20TH CENTURY FOX TFM3134

*   *   *

[283, 284, 285] Carter traveled to Paris in order to record three albums.
Two were to be part of a series conceived by Stanley Wilson called "The
World Of Sights And Sounds" for Panel Productions, founded by Carter and
Wilson. Two albums in the series were recorded, but only the first, Stop
One: Paris was released. (The second was to be Stop Two: London.)

The sessions featured arrangements of songs of the country named.
Of greater jazz interest was the Paris session with rhythm section alone,
although some may find the presence of a vocal group on half the tracks
distracting.

---

[286]   May 1963 Paris
          KPM MUSIC LIBRARY

Carter (as, arr, comp) 19 Piece Orchestra Including: Maurice Van Der (p)
Pierre Culloz (g) Pierre Michelot (b) Christian Garros (d)

LONELY AFFAIR - A (as) arr, comp
78: KPM (E) 155

LONELY AFFAIR - B   arr, comp
78: KPM (E) 155

LONELY AFFAIR - C arr, comp
78: KPM (E) 155

LONELY AFFAIR - D arr, comp
78: KPM (E) 155

BE COOL - A (as) arr, comp
78: KPM (E) 156

BE COOL - B arr, comp
78: KPM (E) 156

BE COOL - C arr, comp
78: KPM (E) 156

DISCOVERY arr, comp
78: KPM (E) 156

HEELS UP arr, comp
78: KPM (E) 156

JAZZ WALTZ - A (as) arr, comp
78: KPM (E) 157

JAZZ WALTZ - B arr, comp
78: KPM (E) 157

JAZZ WALTZ - C   arr, comp
78: KPM (E) 157

METROPOLE   arr, comp
78: KPM (E) 157

GOTTA GO HOME   arr, comp
78: KPM (E) 157

BLUE YONDER - A   arr, comp
78: KPM (E) 158

BLUE YONDER - B   arr, comp
78: KPM (E) 158

SHOW BREAK - 1   arr, comp
78: KPM (E) 158

SHOW BREAK - 2   arr, comp
78: KPM (E) 158

IMMINENT   arr, comp
78: KPM (E) 158

CATFISH ROW   arr, comp
78: KPM (E) 158

CATFISH ROW - LINK 1   arr, comp
78: KPM (E) 158

CATFISH ROW - LINK 2   arr, comp
78: KPM (E) 158

ONE WAY OUT   arr, comp
78: KPM (E) 158

VINHO VERDE   (as) arr, comp
78: KPM (E) 159

*   *   *

These recordings were made for the Keith Prowse Music Recorded Library
Catalog (London) which furnishes music for films and TV productions.   Several versions of some pieces were recorded to provide a variety of tempos
and moods.   Also, a number of very short transitional passages and endings
were included.

Carter probably does not play except where noted as a soloist but,
for completeness, all titles have been listed.

| [287] | August 1964   Los Angeles |
| | BENNY CARTER |

Carter (as, arr, comp) Skeets Herfurt, Bill Green (as) Harry Klee, Jack Du-
mont, Paul Horn (as) Plas Johnson, Babe Russin, Carrington Visor (ts)
Bill Hood, Chuck Gentry (bs) Gerald Wiggins (p) John Collins (g) Joe Comfort (b) Alvin Stoller (d) Lalo Schifrin (arr)

TICKLE TOE   (as) arr
LP: VEE-JAY VJLP2501

ALTO EGO   (as) arr, comp
UNISSUED

WATERMELON MAN   arr-LS (as)
UNISSUED

SHANGRI-LA   (as) arr
UNISSUED

RIGHT HERE WITH YOU   (as) arr
UNISSUED

MEMORIES OF YOU   (as) arr
UNISSUED

FAIRY TALES   (as) arr
UNISSUED

THE GREAT LIE   (as) arr
UNISSUED

GIRL FROM IPANEMA   (as) arr
UNISSUED

I WANNA BE AROUND   (as) arr
UNISSUED

DON'T GET AROUND MUCH ANYMORE   (as) arr
UNISSUED

ON GREEN DOLPHIN STREET   (as) arr
UNISSUED

                              *   *   *

This ambitious project featuring Carter leading ten reeds was produced by
Lee Young for Vee Jay Records.   The only item ever released appeared on
an anthology compiled by Leonard Feather (Encyclopedia Of Jazz, Jazz Of
The 60's, Vol. 1--Giants Of The Saxophones).

[287A]   Ca. 1964   Studio Recording--Unissued
           BENNY CARTER

Carter (as, ss, comp) Ten Piece Band Including Rex Stewart, Teddy Buckner
(tp) Ben Webster (ts) Rozelle Gayle (p)

DUKE STEPS OUT

HOW COME YOU DO ME LIKE YOU DO

QUEER NOTIONS

BLUES IN MY HEART   comp

[288]   March 30-April 1, 1965 Los Angeles
          PEARL BAILEY

Carter (as, arr, comp) Large Orchestra Including Harry Edison (tp) Pearl
Bailey (v) Louis Bellson (arr)

PLEASURES AND PALACES v-PB (e) arr
LP: ROULETTE (S)R25300

TAKE BACK YOUR MINK v-PB (e) arr
LP: ROULETTE (S)R25300

WHAT IS A MAN v-PB (e) arr
LP: ROULETTE (S)R25300

I SHOULDA QUIT WHEN I WAS AHEAD v-PB (e) arr
LP: ROULETTE (S)R25300

WHO'S TIRED v-PB (e) arr
LP: ROULETTE (S)R25300

PUSHING FORTY v-PB arr-LB (e)
LP: ROULETTE (S)R25300

THE GENTLEMAN IS A DOPE v-PB arr-LB (e)
LP: ROULETTE (S)R25300

A MAN IS A NECESSARY EVIL v-PB (e) arr
LP: ROULETTE (S)R25300

LOOK AT THAT FACE v-PB (e) arr
LP: ROULETTE (S)R25300

BIG NOBODY v-PB (e) arr
LP: ROULETTE (S)R25300

YOU'D BETTER THINK IT OVER v-PB (e) arr, comp
LP: ROULETTE (S)R25300

HEY THERE v-PB (e) arr
LP: ROULETTE (S)R25300

[289]   March 2, 1966 Los Angeles
          BENNY CARTER (ADDITIONS TO FURTHER DEFINITIONS)

Carter (as, arr, comp) Bud Shank (as) Buddy Collette, Teddy Edwards (ts)
Bill Hood (bs) Don Abney (p) Barney Kessel (g) Ray Brown (b) Alvin Stoller
(d)

IF DREAMS COME TRUE (as) arr
LP: IMPULSE A(S)9116, HMV (E) CLP/CSD3576,
IMPULSE (J) YP8520

FANTASTIC, THAT'S YOU (as) arr
LP: IMPULSE A(S)9116, HMV (E) CLP/CSD3576,
IMPULSE (J) YP8520

COME ON BACK   (as) arr, comp
LP: IMPULSE A(S)9116, HMV (E) CLP/CSD3576,
IMPULSE (J) YP8520

PROHIBIDO   (as) arr, comp
LP: IMPULSE A(S)9116, HMV (E) CLP/CSD3576,
IMPULSE (J) YP8520

---

[290]   March 4, 1966   Los Angeles
           BENNY CARTER (ADDITIONS TO FURTHER DEFINITIONS)

Carter (as, arr, comp) Bud Shank (as) Bill Perkins, Teddy Edwards (ts) Bill
Hood (bs) Don Abney (p) Mundell Lowe (g) Al McKibbon (b) Alvin Stoller (d)

DOOZY   (as) arr, comp
LP: IMPULSE A(S)9116, HMV (E) CLP/CSD3576,
IMPULSE (J) YP8520

WE WERE IN LOVE   (as) arr, comp
LP: IMPULSE A(S)9116, HMV (E) CLP/CSD3576,
IMPULSE (J) YP8520

TITMOUSE   (as) arr, comp
LP: IMPULSE A(S)9116, HMV (E) CLP/CSD3576,
IMPULSE (J) YP8520

ROCK BOTTOM   (as) arr, comp
LP: IMPULSE A(S)9116, HMV (E) CLP/CSD3576,
IMPULSE (J) YP8520

*   *   *

[289, 290]   This album does not equal Further Definitions (1961) but affords
many pleasant moments.   Aside from some excellent new material, Carter
updates the 1961 "Doozy." Here it is taken at a faster tempo and a middle
ensemble-section consisting of three 12-bar choruses and an 8-bar bridge
has been added.

---

[291]   Between June 28 and July 1, 1967
           CONCERT TOUR, JAZZ AT THE PHILHARMONIC

Carter (as) Clark Terry (tp) Zoot Sims, Paul Gonsalves (ts) Oscar Peterson
(p) Sam Jones (b) Bobby Durham (d)

NOW'S THE TIME   (as)
LP: PABLO (E) 2335-721, PABLO 2625-704

WEE DOT   (as)
LP: PABLO (E) 2335-721, PABLO 2625-704

I CAN'T GET STARTED   (as)
LP: PABLO (E) 2335-721, PABLO 2625-704, TIME-LIFE
STL-J10

NOTE: Carter with rhythm section only on last title.

[292]	Same Tour

Carter (as) Johnny Hodges (as) Coleman Hawkins (ts) Oscar Peterson (p)
Sam Jones (b) Louis Hayes (d)

C-JAM BLUES (as)
LP: PABLO (F) 2335-722, PABLO 2625-704

[293]	Same Tour
	BENNY CARTER WITH THE DUKE ELLINGTON ORCH.

Carter (as) Cat Anderson, Mercer Ellington, Herb Jones, Cootie Williams
(tp) Buster Cooper, Chuck Connors, Lawrence Brown (tb) Russell Procope,
Johnny Hodges (as) Jimmy Hamilton, Paul Gonsalves (ts) Harry Carney (bs)
Duke Ellington (p) John Lamb (b) Rufus Jones (d)

SATIN DOLL (as)
LP: PABLO (E) 2335-723, PABLO 2625-704

PRELUDE TO A KISS (as)
LP: PABLO (E) 2335-723, PABLO 2625-704

                    *   *   *

[291, 292, 293] This material, issued as the "World's Greatest Jazz Concert," was recorded on a tour produced by Norman Granz. It was billed as
a JATP event, and it is not known at which concert or concerts the issued
recordings were made. Performances were given in various cities in the
United States and Canada.

    As usual, Carter is more at home with the ballad portion, playing
one of his best versions of "I Can't Get Started." Carter has chosen to ex-
plore many lovely ballads over the years but always returns to Vernon Duke's
standard. Oscar Peterson's daring uptempo introduction works perfectly.
Carter embellishes the melody without obscuring it; he departs from it tem-
porarily to create a complementary inlay of perfectly executed runs and arpeggios, returning just in time to keep the melodic thread intact. Despite
the many times he has played this piece, Carter once again provides a stun-
ning coda, moving one of the players to exclaim, "Play it, Benny!"

    During the preceding jam numbers, "Now's The Time" and "Wee Dot,"
Carter has some reed trouble. He plays with atypical abandon on the way-
up "Wee Dot." Yielding to his stated preference, he takes a brief three
choruses, unheard of at a JATP concert. His restraint catches the other
musicians off guard; they continue to riff in anticipation of the other half of
his solo.

    "C-Jam Blues" marks the last time Carter and Coleman Hawkins re-
corded together. The tenor saxophonist's health was failing and his playing
sounds weak and disjointed. Carter recalls touring with him: "We had a
lot of nice conversation and a lot of laughs together. But it was very difficult to get him to eat; he was drinking more than he was eating. After the
concert in Toronto, he had dinner brought up to the hotel room, and on the
next day the food was there, practically untouched."

    Carter's masterful collaboration with Johnny Hodges on "Prelude To
A Kiss" is historic. It is their only recording together, with the exception

of the 1952 Norman Granz studio-date. Hodges, on his home ground, is the
more aggressive voice, but the piece provides valuable insights into the contrasting tonal and melodic approaches of the two architects of the swing alto
style. (Alto solo sequence: Hodges (8b), Carter (8b), Hodges (8b), Carter
(8b), Hodges (8b), Carter (4b), Hodges [ending].)

---

[294]   May 28, 1968 Los Angeles
           ELLA FITZGERALD WITH BENNY CARTER'S MAGNIFICENT
           SEVEN

Carter (as, arr) Harry Edison (tp) Georgie Auld (ts) Jimmy Jones (p) John
Collins (g) Bob West (b) Panama Francis (d) Ella Fitzgerald (v)

NO REGRETS v-EF
LP: CAPITOL ST2960, CAPITOL SL6751

I'VE GOT A FEELING YOU'RE FOOLING   v-EF
LP: CAPITOL ST2960, CAPITOL SL6751

DON'T BLAME ME
LP: CAPITOL ST2960, CAPITOL SL6751

DEEP PURPLE v-EF
LP: CAPITOL ST2960, CAPITOL SL6751

RAIN v-EF
LP: CAPITOL ST2960, CAPITOL SL6751

YOU'RE A SWEETHEART v-EF (e)
LP: CAPITOL ST2960, CAPITOL SL6751

ON GREEN DOLPHIN STREET v-EF
LP: CAPITOL ST2960

HOW AM I TO KNOW v-EF
LP: CAPITOL ST2960

JUST FRIENDS
LP: CAPITOL ST2960

I CRIED FOR YOU v-EF
LP: CAPITOL ST2960

SEEMS LIKE OLD TIMES v-EF (e)
LP: CAPITOL ST2960

YOU STEPPED OUT OF A DREAM v-EF
LP: CAPITOL ST2960

---

[295]   May 29, 1968 Los Angeles
           ELLA FITZGERALD WITH BENNY CARTER'S MAGNIFICENT
           SEVEN

Carter (as, arr) Harry Edison (tp) Georgie Auld (ts) Jimmy Jones (p) John
Collins (g) Bob West (b) Louis Bellson (d) Ella Fitzgerald (v)

IF I GIVE MY HEART TO YOU   v-EF
LP: CAPITOL ST2960

ONCE IN A WHILE   v-EF
LP: CAPITOL ST2960

EBB TIDE   (as)
LP: CAPITOL ST2960

THE LAMP IS LOW   v-EF
LP: CAPITOL ST2960

WHERE ARE YOU   v-EF
LP: CAPITOL ST2960

THINKING OF YOU   v-EF (as acc)
LP: CAPITOL ST2960

MY MOTHER'S EYES   v-EF
LP: CAPITOL ST2960

TRY A LITTLE TENDERNESS   v-EF
LP: CAPITOL ST2960

I GOT IT BAD AND THAT AIN'T GOOD   (as)
LP: CAPITOL ST2960

EVERYTHING I HAVE IS YOURS   v-EF
LP: CAPITOL ST2960

I NEVER KNEW I COULD LOVE ANYBODY LIKE I'M LOVING
       YOU   v-EF
LP: CAPITOL ST2960

GOODNIGHT, MY LOVE   v-EF
LP: CAPITOL ST2960

[296]   June 3, 1968   Los Angeles
           ELLA FITZGERALD WITH BENNY CARTER'S MAGNIFICENT
           SEVEN

Carter (as, arr) Harry Edison (tp) Georgie Auld (ts) Jimmy Jones (p) John
Collins (g) Bob West (b) Louis Bellson (d) Ella Fitzgerald (v)

CANDY   v-EF
LP: CAPITOL ST2960, CAPITOL SL6751

ALL I DO IS DREAM OF YOU   v-EF
LP: CAPITOL ST2960, CAPITOL SL6751

SPRING IS HERE
LP: CAPITOL ST2960, CAPITOL SL6751

720 IN THE BOOKS   v-EF
LP: CAPITOL ST2960, CAPITOL SL6751

IT HAPPENED IN MONTEREY   v-EF
LP: CAPITOL ST2960, CAPITOL SL6751

WHAT CAN I SAY AFTER I'M SORRY   v-EF (e)
LP: CAPITOL ST2960, CAPITOL SL6751

FOUR OR FIVE TIMES   v-EF (e)
LP: CAPITOL ST2960

MAYBE   v-EF
LP: CAPITOL ST2960

TAKING A CHANCE ON LOVE
LP: CAPITOL ST2960

ELMER'S TUNE   v-EF
LP: CAPITOL ST2960

AT SUNDOWN   v-EF
LP: CAPITOL ST2960

IT'S A WONDERFUL WORLD   v-EF (e)
LP: CAPITOL ST2960

                              *   *   *

[294, 295, 296]   This album, 30 By Ella, presents a large number of standards in medley form.   Two medleys were recorded at each of the three sessions; the first six and last six tunes listed each comprise a medley.   Although Carter plays only where indicated, the complete contents of each medley has been noted.   Carter also worked out the transitions between the
pieces.   Each medley included one instrumental featuring one of the band
members.

[297]   November 9, 1968   Baden, Switzerland   Broadcast of Concert,
                           Jazz in der Aula
             BENNY CARTER WITH HENRI CHAIX AND HIS ORCHESTRA

Carter (as, arr, comp) Jo Gagliardi (tp) Andre Faist (tb) Roger Zufferey (as)
Michel Pilet (ts) Marc Erbetta (bs) Henri Chaix (p) Alain Du Bois (b) Ro-
mano Cavicchiolo (d)

SWINGIN' IN NOVEMBER   (as) arr, comp

BLUE LOU   (as)

EASY MONEY   (as) arr, comp

ROSE ROOM   (as)

SWINGIN' THE BLUES   (as)

I CAN'T GET STARTED   (as)

TITMOUSE   (as) arr, comp

MARCH WIND   (as) arr, comp

PERDIDO   (as)

BODY AND SOUL (as)

C-JAM BLUES (as)

'S WONDERFUL (as)

UNDECIDED (as)

---

[298]   1968 Los Angeles
          NANCY WILSON

Carter (as, arr) Large Orchestra with Strings, Nancy Wilson (v) Jimmy
Jones (arr)

I'M YOUR SPECIAL FOOL v-NW (e)
LP: CAPITOL ST148

PRISONER OF MY EYES v-NW (e) arr
LP: CAPITOL ST148

PLAYER PLAY ON v-NW (e)
LP: CAPITOL ST148

ONLY LOVE v-NW (e)
LP: CAPITOL ST148

LOOKING BACK v-NW (e)
LP: CAPITOL ST148

IF WE ONLY HAVE LOVE v-NW (e)
LP: CAPITOL ST148

IN A LONG WHITE ROOM v-NW (e)
LP: CAPITOL ST148

YOU'D BETTER GO v-NW (e)
LP: CAPITOL ST148

QUIET SOUL v-NW (e)
LP: CAPITOL ST148

WHAT DO YOU SEE IN HER v-NW (e)
LP: CAPITOL ST148

WE COULD LEARN TOGETHER v-NW (e)
LP: CAPITOL ST148

        NOTE: Strings on "Only Love" and "If We Only Have Love."

---

[299]   1968 Los Angeles
          NANCY WILSON

Carter (as) John Audino, Bobby Bryant, Pete Candoli, Harry Edison, Clyde
Reesinger (tp) Chuck Cooper, Ed Kusby, Lew McCreary, Dick Nash, Tommy
Pederson, Kenny Shroyer (tb) Chuck Gentry, Justin Gordon, Bill Green,
Arthur Herbert, Plas Johnson (reeds) Jimmy Jones (p, arr) Donn Trenner (p)

Bob Bain, Mundell Lowe (g) Buster Williams, Carol Kaye (b) Shelly Manne (d) Larry Bunker, Gene Estes, Victor Feldman (percussion) Nancy Wilson (v)

OUT OF THIS WORLD   v-NW (e)
LP: CAPITOL ST2970

THIS BITTER EARTH   v-NW (e)
LP: CAPITOL ST2970

BY MYSELF   v-NW (e)
LP: CAPITOL ST2970

WHEN THE SUN COMES OUT   v-NW (as acc)
LP: CAPITOL ST2970

ALONE WITH MY THOUGHTS OF YOU   v-NW (e)
LP: CAPITOL ST2970

IT ONLY TAKES A MOMENT   v-NW (e)
LP: CAPITOL ST2970

PEACE OF MIND   v-NW (e)
LP: CAPITOL ST2970

ON THE OTHER SIDE OF THE TRACKS   v-NW (e)
LP: CAPITOL ST2970

BELOW, ABOVE   v-NW (e)
LP: CAPITOL ST2970

THE RULES OF THE ROAD   v-NW (e)
LP: CAPITOL ST2970

BLACK IS BEAUTIFUL   v-NW (e)
LP: CAPITOL ST2970

---

[300]   September 4-6, 1971   Colorado Springs   Recorded Live for
                                   BASF-Unissued
              COLORADO JAZZ PARTY

Carter (as) Clark Terry (tp) Carl Fontana (tb) Victor Feldman (p) Lyn Christie (b) Alan Dawson (d)

TERRY CLOTH

WHEN I FALL IN LOVE

THE SHADOW OF YOUR SMILE

MY FOOLISH HEART

A TIME FOR LOVE

RIFFTIDE

[301]	As Above

Carter (as) Dick Hyman (p) Larry Ridley (b) Duffy Jackson (d)

ALL THE THINGS YOU ARE

WHAT'S NEW

STOMPIN' AT THE SAVOY

[302]	As Above

Carter (as) Joe Newman (tp) Vic Dickenson (tb) James Moody, Bob Wilber
(reeds) Dick Hyman (p) Larry Ridley (b) Alan Dawson (d)

IN A LITTLE SPANISH TOWN

BODY AND SOUL

IT'S THE TALK OF THE TOWN

LAURA

YOU'VE CHANGED

TANGERINE

LESTER LEAPS IN

[303]	As Above

Carter (as) Teddy Wilson (p) Milt Hinton (b) Cliff Leeman (d)

ROSETTA

I CAN'T GET STARTED

'S WONDERFUL

MAKIN' WHOOPEE

*   *   *

[300-303]   Although portions of the Jazz Party were released on BASF
25099, Carter refused to allow any of his own work to be issued: "I wasn't
told about the recording until I arrived, and I simply didn't want to be repre-
sented that way on record. "

[304]	July 2, 1972 New York Broadcast, Newport Jazz Festival
	Concert, Carnegie Hall
	BENNY CARTER AND THE SWINGMASTERS

Carter (as, arr, comp) Harry Edison, Joe Thomas, Taft Jordan, Carl War-
wick, Jimmy Nottingham (tp) Tyree Glenn, Benny Morton, Dicky Wells,
Quentin Jackson (tb) Earle Warren, Howard Johnson (as) Buddy Tate, Budd

Johnson (ts) Haywood Henry (bs, cl) Teddy Wilson (p) Bernard Addison (g) Milt Hinton (b) Jo Jones (d)

HONEYSUCKLE ROSE   (as) arr

DOOZY   (as) arr, comp

BLUES FOR BEGINNERS   (e) arr, comp

THE JUKE BOX   (as) arr, comp

I CAN'T GET STARTED   (as) arr

SLEEP   (as) arr

YOU ARE   (as) arr, comp

*   *   *

This emotional reunion of many of the swing era's seminal figures, including former Carter band members Joe Thomas, Tyree Glenn, Dicky Wells and Teddy Wilson, was a high point of the first Newport Jazz Festival in New York.

[305]   July 3, 1972   New York   Newport Jazz Festival Concert,
                              Radio City Music Hall
               MIDNIGHT JAM SESSION

Carter (as) Bobby Hackett (tp) Vic Dickenson (tb) Bud Freeman (ts) Red Norvo (vib) Teddy Wilson (p) Jim Hall (g) Larry Ridley (b) Bobby Rosengarden, Gene Krupa (d)

IN A MELLOTONE   (as)

BLUES   (as)

HONEYSUCKLE ROSE   (as)

> NOTES: This session was probably recorded, but was not included on the commercially issued LPs of the Festival. Krupa plays on last tune only.

[306]   October 7, 1972   New Haven, Conn.
               CONCERT, YALE UNIVERSITY

Carter (as) Harry Edison (tp) Duke Ellington (p) Ray Brown (b) Jo Jones (d) Joe Williams (v)

TAKE THE A TRAIN   (as)

SATIN DOLL   (as)

ROCKS IN MY BED   v-JW (as)

JUST SQUEEZE ME   v-JW (as)

EVERYDAY I HAVE THE BLUES v-JW (as)

>   NOTE: This concert was to benefit the Duke Ellington Fellowship
>   Program--"Conservatory Without Walls." Tapes may exist.

---

[307]   November 7, 1972 Malmo, Sweden   Concert Recording
          JAZZ AT THE PHILHARMONIC

Carter (as) Roy Eldridge (tp) Al Grey (tb) Eddie "Lockjaw" Davis (ts) Oscar
Peterson (p) Niels Pedersen (b) Louis Bellson (d)

JIM DOGS BLUES (as)
LP: UNIQUE JAZZ (I) 002

THE NEARNESS OF YOU (as)
LP: UNIQUE JAZZ (I) 002

UNDECIDED (as)
LP: UNIQUE JAZZ (I) 002

>   NOTES: Date and location of this bootleg JATP issue from con-
>   temporary reports in Orkester Journalen. Carter with rhythm only
>   on "Nearness Of You."

---

[308]   April 19, 1973 Princeton, New Jersey Concert, Princeton
                          University
          BENNY CARTER AND HIS ALL STARS

Carter (as) Hank Jones (p) Milt Hinton (b) Ron Zito (d)

NIGHT IN TUNISIA (as)

UNDECIDED (as)

ROBBINS NEST (as)

THE SHADOW OF YOUR SMILE (as)

HONEYSUCKLE ROSE (as)

IN A MELLOTONE (as)

A DAY IN THE LIFE OF A FOOL (MANHA DE CARNIVAL) (as)

ALL THE THINGS YOU ARE (as)

ONE GOOD BLUES (as)

SWEET GEORGIA BROWN (as)

HOW HIGH THE MOON (as)

---

[309]   October 22, 1973 Princeton, New Jersey Concert, Princeton
                            University
          BENNY CARTER AND HIS ALL STARS

Carter (as, comp) Clark Terry (tp, flugelhorn, v) Hank Jones (p) Bucky Pizzarelli (g) Milt Hinton (b) Grady Tate (d, v)

UNDECIDED (as)

THE SHADOW OF YOUR SMILE   (as)

SATIN DOLL (as)

WHEN LIGHTS ARE LOW   (as) comp

BLUES

BLUE MONK   (e)

MY GAL   v-CT (as)

BLUE MONK   (e)

TAKE THE A TRAIN   (as)

PERDIDO (as)

BLUE STAR   (as) comp

DOOZY   (as) comp

IN A MELLOTONE   (as)

SWEET GEORGIA BROWN   (as)

> NOTE: "Blues"/"Blue Monk"/"My Gal"/"Blue Monk" played in medley.

---

[310]   November 10, 1973 New Haven, Conn.   Yale University
            BENNY CARTER AND HIS ORCHESTRA

Carter (as, arr, comp) Earle Warren (as) Billy Mitchell, Charlie Rouse (ts) Cecil Payne (bs) Dwike Mitchell (p) Willie Ruff (b) Grady Tate (d)

DOOZY   (as) arr, comp

PROHIBIDO   (as) arr, comp

I CAN'T GET STARTED   (as)

ROCK BOTTOM   (as) arr, comp

IF DREAMS COME TRUE   (as) arr

> NOTE: Carter with rhythm only on "I Can't Get Started."

---

[311]   December 3, 1973 Princeton, New Jersey Concert, Princeton
                             University
            BENNY CARTER AND HIS ORCHESTRA

Carter (as, arr, comp) Jon Faddis, Joe Newman, Victor Paz, Ernie Royal
(tp) Eddie Bert, Dickie Harris, Quentin Jackson, Jimmy Knepper (tb) George
Dorsey (as) Jerry Dodgion (as, flute) Budd Johnson, Billy Mitchell (ts) George
Barrow (bs) Roland Hanna (p) Wally Richardson (g) Major Holley (b) Mousie
Alexander (d) Ray Barretto (conga) Hale Smith (v)

DOOZY   (as) arr, comp

WHEN LIGHTS ARE LOW   (as) arr, comp

YOU ARE   (e) arr, comp

SOUVENIR   (as) arr, comp

HONEYSUCKLE ROSE   (as) arr

BLUES FOR BEGINNERS   v-HS (as) arr, comp

COALITION   (as) arr, comp

I CAN'T GET STARTED   (as) arr

COTTONTAIL   (e) arr

A KISS FROM YOU   (e) arr, comp

A WALKIN' THING   (as) arr, comp

SLEEP   (as) arr

THE NEARNESS OF YOU   (as)

THE JUKE BOX   (as) arr, comp

> NOTES: "Souvenir" announced as "That's How It Goes"; title changed
> later. "A Kiss From You" formerly entitled "Lydia." "The Near-
> ness Of You" is Carter's feature in ballad medley.

---

[312]   November 7, 1974 Ithaca, New York Concert, Cornell University
          BENNY CARTER AND HIS ALL STARS

Carter (as) Jimmy Nottingham (tp, flugelhorn) Al Grey (tb) Roland Hanna (p)
Milt Hinton (b) Alan Dawson (d)

IN A MELLOTONE   (as)

ON GREEN DOLPHIN STREET   (as)

MISTY   (as)

UNDECIDED   (as)

PERDIDO   (as)

STOMPIN' AT THE SAVOY   (as)

BROADWAY (as)

I CAN'T GET STARTED (as)

COTTONTAIL (as)

---

[313]   December 22, 1974   Los Angeles   Broadcast of Concert,
                              The Troubadour
           MARIA MULDAUR

Carter (as, arr, comp) Snooky Young, Harry Edison (tp) J. J. Johnson (tb)
Bud Shank (as, cl, flute) Plas Johnson (ts) Sahib Shihab (bs) Marty Harris
(p, electric p) Mundell Lowe (g) John B. Williams (b) Earl Palmer (d) Maria
Muldaur (v)

SQUEEZE ME v-MM (e) arr

ANY OLD TIME v-MM (e) arr

GEE, AIN'T I GOOD TO YOU v-MM (e) arr

SWEETHEART v-MM (e) arr

DOOZY (e) arr, comp

IT DON'T MEAN A THING IF IT AIN'T GOT THAT SWING
        v-MM (e)

LOVER MAN v-MM (as) arr

WALKIN' ONE AND ONLY v-MM (e) arr

DON'T YOU MAKE ME HIGH v-MM (e) arr

I'M A WOMAN v-MM (e) arr

IT AIN'T THE MEAT IT'S THE MOTION v-MM (e) arr

---

[314]   July 16, 1975   Montreux, Switzerland   Montreux Jazz Festival
                              Concert
           JAZZ AT THE PHILHARMONIC

Carter (as) Roy Eldridge (tp) Clark Terry (tp, flugelhorn) Zoot Sims (ts)
Tommy Flanagan (p) Joe Pass (g) Keter Betts (b) Bobby Durham (d)

FOR YOU (as)
LP: PABLO 2310-748

AUTUMN LEAVES (as)
LP: PABLO 2310-748

IF I HAD YOU (as)
LP: PABLO 2310-748

I NEVER KNEW (as)
LP: PABLO 2310-748

SUNDAY (as)
LP: PABLO 2625-707

*   *   *

Those listening to Carter at live performances in the early 1970s noticed a
change in his style. His tone acquired a new edge, his attack became more
forceful. The clearest evidence of change on record is Carter's remarkable
solo on "Autumn Leaves." At several points Carter descends into the lower
register for a decidedly non-"urbane" honk. He also plays behind the beat,
exploring the chord changes with almost mockingly deliberate arpeggios.
Once again, Carter seems to have assimilated those features of more recent
styles necessary to keep his own sound current.

[314A]   July 17, 1975 Nice, France
          INTERNATIONAL JAZZ FESTIVAL - LA GRANDE PARADE DU
          JAZZ

Carter (as) Bobby Hackett (tp) Vic Dickenson (tb) Barney Bigard (cl) Joe
Venuti (violin) Teddy Wilson, Earl Hines (p) Red Norvo (vib) George Duvivier (b) Bobby Rosengarden (d)

FOR YOU (as)

MONDAY DATE (as)

ROSETTA (as)

> NOTE: Wilson plays on first title, Hines on second. Both play on
> "Rosetta," with Hines soloing first.

[314B]   July 18, 1975 Nice, France
          INTERNATIONAL JAZZ FESTIVAL - LA GRANDE PARADE DU
          JAZZ

Carter (as) Bobby Hackett (tp) Teddy Wilson (p) Larry Ridley (b) David Lee
(d)

BODY AND SOUL (as)

WHAT IS THIS THING CALLED LOVE (as)

[314C]   July 21, 1975 Nice, France
          INTERNATIONAL JAZZ FESTIVAL - LA GRANDE PARADE DU
          JAZZ

Carter (as) Bob Wilber (ss) Earle Warren (as) Teddy Wilson (p) Major
Holley (b) Panama Francis (d)

THE JEEP IS JUMPIN' (as)

I GOT IT BAD AND THAT AIN'T GOOD (as)

PERDIDO (as)

NOTE: Carter with rhythm section only on "I Got It Bad"; "Perdido" fades during Carter's solo.

[314D]   Same Date
          INTERNATIONAL JAZZ FESTIVAL - LA GRANDE PARADE DU
          JAZZ

Carter (as) Harry Edison, Clark Terry (tp) Zoot Sims (ts) Teddy Wilson (p) Major Holley (b) Ray Mosca (d)

LADY BE GOOD (as)

---

[315]   September 9, 1975   Chicago   Club Date, Ratso's
          BENNY CARTER

Carter (as) Jody Christian (p) Dave Shipp (b) Jo Jones (d)

IN A MELLOTONE (as)

ALL THE THINGS YOU ARE (as)

MISTY (as)

THREE LITTLE WORDS (as)

AUTUMN LEAVES (as)

AS TIME GOES BY (as)

BYE BYE BLACKBIRD (as)

I FOUND A NEW BABY (as)

---

[316]   September 10, 1975   Chicago   TV Show Soundstage, WTTW-TV
                                         Studios
          A TRIBUTE TO JOHN HAMMOND

Carter (as) Benny Morton (tb) Teddy Wilson (p) George Benson (g) Milt Hinton (b) Jo Jones (d) Red Norvo (vib) Helen Humes (v)

RIFF INTERLUDE (as)

JOHN'S IDEA (as)

SONG OF THE WANDERER v-HH (as)

---

[317]   December 18, 1975   Istanbul, Turkey   Concert, Park Hotel-U.S.
                                         State Dept. Tour
          BENNY CARTER QUINTET

Carter (as) Harry Edison (tp) Gildo Mahones (p) John B. Williams (b) Earl Palmer (d)

IN A MELLOTONE (as)

UNDECIDED   (as)

MISTY   (as)

HONEYSUCKLE ROSE   (as)

STOMPIN' AT THE SAVOY   (as)

TAKE THE A TRAIN   (as)

> NOTE: All titles except "Honeysuckle Rose" and "Stompin' At The Savoy" aired over Turkish TV and radio.

---

[318]   December 21, 1975 Ankara, Turkey Concert, Turkish-American
                                Assoc.-U.S. State Dept. Tour
           BENNY CARTER QUINTET

Carter (as) Harry Edison (tp) Gildo Mahones (p) John B. Williams (b) Earl Palmer (d)

IN A MELLOTONE   (as)

UNDECIDED   (as)

MISTY   (as)

HONEYSUCKLE ROSE   (as)

STOMPIN' AT THE SAVOY   (as)

PERDIDO   (as)

---

[319]   Same Concert

Carter (as, p) Harry Edison (tp) Tuna Otenel (as, p) Selcuk Sun (b) Erol Pekcan (d)

JUMPIN' WITH SYMPHONY SID   (as)

> NOTE: For this piece Carter and Edison were joined by some Turkish musicians.   Carter plays piano accompaniment while Otenel solos on alto.

---

[320]   December 22, 1975 Ankara, Turkey Broadcast, Turkish Radio/
                                Television-U.S. State Dept. Tour
           BENNY CARTER QUINTET

Carter (as) Harry Edison (tp) Gildo Mahones (p) John B. Williams (b) Earl Palmer (d)

BLUES   (e)

UNDECIDED   (as)

IN A MELLOTONE   (as)

I CAN'T GET STARTED (as)

PERDIDO (incomplete) (e)

---

[321]   December 22, 1975 Ankara, Turkey Concert, Turkish-American
                              Assoc.-U.S. State Dept. Tour
          BENNY CARTER QUINTET

Carter (as) Harry Edison (tp) Gildo Mahones (p) John B. Williams (b) Earl
Palmer (d) Millicent Browne (v)

IN A MELLOTONE (as)

UNDECIDED (as)

HONEYSUCKLE ROSE (as)

STOMPIN' AT THE SAVOY (as)

MISTY (as)

PERDIDO (as)

EVERYDAY I HAVE THE BLUES v-MB (as)

---

[322]   December 24, 1975 Tehran, Iran Concert, City Theater-U.S.
                              State Dept. Tour
          BENNY CARTER QUINTET

Carter (as) Harry Edison (tp) Gildo Mahones (p) John B. Williams (b) Earl
Palmer (d)

IN A MELLOTONE (as)

UNDECIDED (as)

HONEYSUCKLE ROSE (as)

MISTY (as)

PERDIDO (as)

JINGLE BELLS (as)

---

[323]   December 25, 1975 Tehran, Iran Concert, City Theater-U.S.
                              State Dept. Tour
          BENNY CARTER QUINTET

Carter (as) Harry Edison (tp) Gildo Mahones (p) John B. Williams (p) Earl
Palmer (d)

IN A MELLOTONE (as)

UNDECIDED (as)

HONEYSUCKLE ROSE   (as)

SUPERSWEET   (as)

I CAN'T BELIEVE THAT YOU'RE IN LOVE WITH ME   (as)

MISTY   (as)

PERDIDO   (as)

---

[324]   December 30, 1975 Islamabad, Pakistan Concert, Liaquat
                            Memorial Hall-U.S. State Dept. Tour
          BENNY CARTER QUINTET

Carter (as) Harry Edison (tp) Gildo Mahones (p) John B. Williams (b) Earl
Palmer (d) Millicent Browne (v)

IN A MELLOTONE   (as)

UNDECIDED   (as)

MISTY   (as)

HONEYSUCKLE ROSE   (as)

SUPERSWEET   (as)

EVERYDAY I HAVE THE BLUES   v-MB (as)

PERDIDO   (e)

---

[325]   December 31, 1975 Lahore, Pakistan Concert, Foreman Christian
                            College-U.S. State Dept. Tour
          BENNY CARTER QUINTET

Carter (as) Harry Edison (tp) Gildo Mahones (p) John B. Williams (b) Earl
Palmer (d) Millicent Browne (v)

SUPERSWEET   (as)

EVERYDAY I HAVE THE BLUES   v-MB (as)

TAKE THE A TRAIN   (as)

> NOTE: Due to a power failure, only part of this concert was re-
> corded.

---

[326]   January 1, 1976 Karachi, Pakistan Concert, American Center-
                            U.S. State Dept. Tour
          BENNY CARTER QUINTET

Carter (as) Harry Edison (tp) Gildo Mahones (p) John B. Williams (b) Earl
Palmer (d) Millicent Browne (v)

IN A MELLOTONE   (as)

UNDECIDED (as)

MISTY (as)

PERDIDO (as)

SUPERSWEET (as)

EVERYDAY I HAVE THE BLUES v-MB (as)

TAKE THE A TRAIN (as)

>   NOTE: This concert was filmed for Karachi television.

[327]   January 2, 1976 Karachi, Pakistan Concert, Pakistan-American
                              Cultural Center-U. S. State Dept. Tour
           BENNY CARTER QUINTET

Carter (as) Harry Edison (tp) Gildo Mahones (p) John B. Williams (b) Earl
Palmer (d) Millicent Browne (v)

IN A MELLOTONE (as)

UNDECIDED (as)

I CAN'T GET STARTED (as)

PERDIDO (as)

SUPERSWEET (as)

EVERYDAY I HAVE THE BLUES v-MB (as)

TAKE THE A TRAIN (as)

>   NOTE: This concert was filmed for Karachi television.

[328]   January 3, 1976 Karachi, Pakistan Broadcast, Karachi TV-U. S.
                              State Dept. Tour
           BENNY CARTER QUINTET

Carter (as, comp) Harry Edison (tp) Gildo Mahones (p) John B. Williams (b)
Earl Palmer (d) Millicent Browne (v)

UNDECIDED (as)

IN A MELLOTONE (as)

BLUE STAR (as) comp

SUPERSWEET (as)

ONLY TRUST YOUR HEART (as) comp

WHEN LIGHTS ARE LOW v-MB (as) comp

ALL THAT JAZZ v-MB (as) comp

PERDIDO (as)

[329]	January 5, 1976 Kuwait Concert/Seminar, Aldar Gallery-U. S. State Dept. Tour

BENNY CARTER QUINTET

Carter (as) Harry Edison (tp) Gildo Mahones (p) John B. Williams (b) Earl Palmer (d) Millicent Browne (v)

UNDECIDED (as)

HONEYSUCKLE ROSE (as)

EVERYDAY I HAVE THE BLUES v-MB (as)

WHEN THE SAINTS GO MARCHING IN (as)

MISTY (as)

SUPERSWEET (e)

JUMPIN' AT THE WOODSIDE (as)

IN A MELLOTONE (as)

PERDIDO (as)

> NOTE: Williams became ill after the first number and no bass is present thereafter.

[330]	January 6, 1976 Kuwait Concert, Kuwait Hilton-U. S. State Dept. Tour

BENNY CARTER QUINTET

Carter (as) Harry Edison (tp) Gildo Mahones (p) John B. Williams (b) Earl Palmer (d) Millicent Browne (v)

IN A MELLOTONE (as)

UNDECIDED (as)

MISTY (as)

PERDIDO (as)

SUPERSWEET (as)

EVERYDAY I HAVE THE BLUES v-MB (as)

TAKE THE A TRAIN (as)

[331]	January 11, 1976 Damascus, Syria Concert, Al Hamra Theatre-U. S. State Dept. Tour

BENNY CARTER QUINTET

Carter (as) Harry Edison (tp) Gildo Mahones (p) John B. Williams (b) Earl
Palmer (d) Millicent Browne (v)

IN A MELLOTONE   (as)

UNDECIDED   (as)

MISTY   (as)

PERDIDO   (as)

SUPERSWEET   (as)

EVERYDAY I HAVE THE BLUES   v-MB (as)

TAKE THE A TRAIN   (as)

> NOTE: Concert filmed for television.

---

[332]   January 13, 1976 Irbid, Jordan Concert, Irbid Trade School-U.S.
                              State Dept. Tour
            BENNY CARTER QUINTET

Carter (as) Harry Edison (tp) Gildo Mahones (p) John B. Williams (b) Earl
Palmer (d) Millicent Browne (v)

UNDECIDED   (as)

MISTY   (as)

PERDIDO   (as)

SUPERSWEET   (as)

EVERYDAY I HAVE THE BLUES   v-MB (as)

TAKE THE A TRAIN   (as)

---

[333]   January 14, 1976 Amman, Jordan Concert, Greek Orthodox
                              Club-U.S. State Dept. Tour
            BENNY CARTER QUINTET

Carter (as) Harry Edison (tp) Gildo Mahones (p) John B. Williams (b) Earl
Palmer (d) Millicent Browne (v)

IN A MELLOTONE   (as)

MISTY   (as)

PERDIDO   (as)

SUPERSWEET   (as)

EVERYDAY I HAVE THE BLUES   v-MB (as)

TAKE THE A TRAIN   (as)

[334]   January 14, 1976   Amman, Jordan   Concert, University of Jordan-
                             U.S. State Dept. Tour
          BENNY CARTER QUINTET

Carter (as) Harry Edison (tp) Gildo Mahones (p) John B. Williams (b) Earl
Palmer (d) Millicent Browne (v)

IN A MELLOTONE   (as)

MISTY   (as)

PERDIDO   (as)

SUPERSWEET   (as)

EVERYDAY I HAVE THE BLUES   v-MB (as)

[335]   January 16, 1976   Cairo, Egypt   Concert, American University of
                             Cairo-U.S. State Dept. Tour
          BENNY CARTER QUINTET

Carter (as) Harry Edison (tp) Gildo Mahones (p) John B. Williams (b) Earl
Palmer (d) Millicent Browne (v)

UNDECIDED   (as)

IN A MELLOTONE   (as)

MISTY   (as)

PERDIDO   (as)

SUPERSWEET   (as)

EVERYDAY I HAVE THE BLUES   v-MB (as)

[336]   Same Concert

Carter (as) Harry Edison (tp) Said Salama (ts) Gildo Mahones (p) John B.
Williams (b) Bib Hanein (timbales) Salah Ragab (d)

CARAVAN   (as)

> NOTE: For this piece Carter was joined by members of the Cairo
> University jazz band.

[337]   January 19, 1976   Alexandria, Egypt   Concert, Sayed Darwish
                             Theatre-U.S. State Dept. Tour
          BENNY CARTER QUINTET

Carter (as) Harry Edison (tp) Gildo Mahones (p) John B. Williams (b) Earl
Palmer (d) Millicent Browne (v)

IN A MELLOTONE   (as)

UNDECIDED (as)

MISTY (as)

PERDIDO (as)

SUPERSWEET (as)

EVERYDAY I HAVE THE BLUES v-MB (as acc)

I CAN'T BELIEVE THAT YOU'RE IN LOVE WITH ME   (as)

[338]   February 11, 1976 Los Angeles
            BENNY CARTER (THE KING)

Carter (as, comp) Milt Jackson (vib) Tommy Flanagan (p) Joe Pass (g) John
B. Williams (b) Jake Hanna (d)

A WALKIN' THING   (as) comp
PABLO 2310-768

MY KIND OF TROUBLE IS YOU   (as) comp
PABLO 2310-768

EASY MONEY   (as) comp
PABLO 2310-768

BLUE STAR   (as) comp
PABLO 2310-768

I STILL LOVE HIM SO   (as) comp
PABLO 2310-768

GREEN WINE   (as) comp
PABLO 2310-768

MALIBU   (as) comp
PABLO 2310-768

BLUES IN D FLAT   (as) comp
PABLO 2310-768

ALL THAT JAZZ   comp
UNISSUED

                            *   *   *

The King, in a sense, was Carter's "comeback" date; it had been ten years
since his last album as a leader.   This session is valuable if only because
it documents a number of fine Carter compositions, some of which had previously existed only in obscure versions ("Green Wine," and "My Kind Of
Trouble Is You").   Also included were new interpretations of earlier classics
("Malibu," "Blue Star").

[339]   April 27, 1976 Los Angeles
            CARTER, GILLESPIE, INC.

Carter (as, comp) Dizzy Gillespie (tp, comp) Tommy Flanagan (p) Joe Pass (g) Al McKibbon (b) Mickey Roker (d, v)

SWEET AND LOVELY   (as)
PABLO 2310-781

BROADWAY   (as)
PABLO 2310-781

THE COURTSHIP   (as) comp
PABLO 2310-781

CONSTANTINOPLE   (as)
PABLO 2310-781

NOBODY KNOWS THE TROUBLE I'VE SEEN   v-MR
PABLO 2310-781

NIGHT IN TUNISIA   (as)
PABLO 2310-781

                              *   *   *

This session is an intriguing and highly enjoyable reunion.   Although Gillespie takes the initiative (he set the tempos and suggested most of the music), Carter sounds much more at ease than on his own date two months earlier.

     Most of the tracks are impromptu with the solo routines and endings in some cases evolving on the spot.

     Carter supplied a new composition, "The Courtship," an insinuating 38-bar melody.

     (For an analysis of Carter's solo on "A Night In Tunisia" see chapter 3.)

----

[340]   May 6, 1976   Los Angeles
          BASIE JAM #2 AND #3

Carter (as, comp) Clark Terry (tp) Al Grey (tb) Eddie "Lockjaw" Davis (ts) Count Basie (p) Joe Pass (g) John Heard (b) Louis Bellson (d)

MAMA DON'T WEAR NO DRAWERS   (as) comp
LP: PABLO 2310-786

DOGGIN' AROUND   (as)
LP: PABLO 2310-786

KANSAS CITY LINE   (as) comp
LP: PABLO 2310-786

JJJJUMP   (as) comp
LP: PABLO 2310-786

BYE BYE BLUES   (as)
LP: PABLO 2310-840

MOTEN SWING   (as)
LP: PABLO 2310-840

I SURRENDER DEAR   (as)
LP: PABLO 2310-840

SONG OF THE ISLANDS   (as)
LP: PABLO 2310-840

                            *   *   *

Carter's exuberant playing is one of the highlights of this informal gathering.
He credits Count Basie's ideal backing with spurring on the soloists: "He
stays out of the way and feeds you perfectly.   His choice of chords, spac-
ing, and, above all, taste set him apart."

---

[341]   June 19, 1976   New York   Club Date, Michael's Pub
           BENNY CARTER QUARTET

Carter (as, tp, comp) Ray Bryant (p) Milt Hinton (b) Grady Tate (d)

THREE LITTLE WORDS   (as)

EASY MONEY   (as) comp

MISTY   (as)

IN A MELLOTONE   (as)(tp)

ALL THE THINGS YOU ARE   (as)

LAURA (as)

BLUES   (tp)

IT DON'T MEAN A THING IF IT AIN'T GOT THAT SWING   (as)

MEMORIES OF YOU   (as)

OVER THE RAINBOW   (tp)

EASY MONEY   (as) comp

WHAT ARE YOU DOING THE REST OF YOUR LIFE   (as)

THESE FOOLISH THINGS   (features Hinton)

DON'T BLAME ME   (tp)

TAKE THE A TRAIN   (as)

MEAN TO ME   (as)

        NOTE: "Memories Of You"/"Over The Rainbow" and "What Are You
        Doing"/"These Foolish Things"/"Don't Blame Me" are medleys.

---

[342]   June 24, 1976   New York   Club Date, Michael's Pub
           BENNY CARTER QUARTET

Carter (as, tp, comp) Ray Bryant (p) Milt Hinton (b) Grady Tate (d)

THREE LITTLE WORDS (as)

ROBBINS NEST (as)(tp)

I CAN'T GET STARTED (as)

EASY MONEY (as)(tp) comp

BLUE LOU (as)

WAVE (as)

POOR BUTTERFLY (tp)(as)

ON GREEN DOLPHIN STREET (as)

I COVER THE WATERFRONT (tp)

MOONGLOW (tp)(as)

ALL THE THINGS YOU ARE (as)(tp)

BUT NOT FOR ME (tp)

SWEET GEORGIA BROWN (tp)

BLUES IN MY HEART (tp) comp

---

[343]   July 3, 1976 New York Club Date, Michael's Pub
         BENNY CARTER QUARTET

Carter (as, tp, comp) Ray Bryant (p) Milt Hinton (b) Grady Tate (d, v)

EASY MONEY (as) comp

ALL THE THINGS YOU ARE (as)

WAVE (as)

BLUES IN MY HEART (tp)(as) comp

UNDECIDED (incomplete) (as)

HERE'S THAT RAINY DAY (as)

DON'T BLAME ME (tp)

I'LL NEVER BE THE SAME (features Bryant)

THESE FOOLISH THINGS (features Hinton)

BODY AND SOUL v-GT (tp)

> NOTE: "Don't Blame Me"/"I'll Never Be The Same"/"These Foolish
> Things" played in medley.

[344]   September 17, 1976   Monterey, California   Airchecks?, Monterey
                                  Jazz Festival Concert
           BENNY CARTER - TRIBUTE TO FLETCHER HENDERSON

Carter (as) Gene Coe, Blue Mitchell, Cat Anderson, Bill Berry (tp) Britt
Woodman, Benny Powell, Jimmy Cleveland, Tricky Lofton (tb) Russell Pro-
cope (cl) Marshall Royal, Unknown (as) Richie Kamuca, Don Menza (ts) Jack
Nimitz (bs) Dave Frishberg (p) Mundell Lowe (g) Monty Budwig (b) Frankie
Capp (d)

WRAPPIN' IT UP

BIG JOHN SPECIAL

CHRISTOPHER COLUMBUS

KING PORTER STOMP

          NOTE: These tunes were scored by Mundell Lowe based on the
          original Fletcher/Horace Henderson arrangements.

[345]   Same Concert
           TRIBUTE TO LOUIS ARMSTRONG

Carter (tp) Harry Edison, Doc Cheatham, Dizzy Gillespie, Clark Terry, Jon
Faddis (tp) Dave Frishberg (p) Mundell Lowe (g) Monty Budwig (b) Frankie
Capp (d)

CONFESSIN'   (tp)

STRUTTIN' WITH SOME BARBECUE   (e)

[346]   November 30, 1976   New York Studio Recording for Pablo--Unissued
           BENNY CARTER

Carter (as, tp, comp) Ray Bryant (p) Milt Hinton (b) Grady Tate (d)

A TEA VISTA   (as) comp

JOHNNY   (as) comp

STROLL   (as) comp

BODY AND SOUL   (tp)

MISTY   (as)

[347]   Same Date   Studio recording for Pablo--Unissued
           BENNY CARTER

Carter (as, tp, arr, comp) Harry Edison (tp) Eddie "Lockjaw" Davis (ts) Ray
Bryant (p) Milt Hinton (b) Grady Tate (d)

SUMMER NIGHT   (as) arr, comp

THREE LITTLE WORDS (as)

BLUES (tp)

>   NOTE: "Summer Night" also known as "Wonderland."

---

[348]   March 18, 1977 Princeton, N.J.   Concert, Princeton University
         BENNY CARTER SEXTET

Carter (as, comp) Joe Newman (tp) Roland Hanna (p) Bucky Pizzarelli (g)
Richard Pratt (d)

UNDECIDED (as)

EASY MONEY (as) comp

HERE'S THAT RAINY DAY (as)

SOUTH SIDE SAMBA (as) comp

GREEN WINE (as) comp

YESTERDAYS (as)

SATIN DOLL (as)

ST. THOMAS (as)

BLUE STAR (as) comp

ON GREEN DOLPHIN STREET (as)

THE COURTSHIP (as) comp

PERDIDO (as)

IN A MELLOTONE (as)

---

[349]   April 8, 1977 Princeton, N.J.   Concert, Princeton University
         BENNY CARTER WITH THE PRINCETON UNIVERSITY JAZZ
         ENSEMBLES

Carter (as, arr, comp) Ernie Rivera, Randy Rydell, Steve Silliman, Bill Ash,
Bill McHenry (tp) Bob Gibbons, Myles Connors, Barry Welch, Dave Preston
(tb) Brian Ewart, Mike Zelner, Gary Monheit, Rob Kaminsky, Rick Sonnen-
feld (reeds) John Novaria (p) Steve Wexler (g) Todd Beany (b) John Pittenger
(d)

SOUVENIR (as) arr, comp

COTTONTAIL (as) arr

>   NOTE: "Souvenir" previously entitled "That's How It Goes."

---

[350]   Same Concert

Carter (as, arr, comp) John Dolan, Tom Orlofsky, Ben Ballard, Doug Abbott,
Bob McKillip (tp) Ben Monderer, Tony Maoicco, Jim Huffman, Ken Marantz
(tb) Art Fogartie, Leslie Ritts, Tim McNally, Jon Healy, Steve Mathews
(reeds) Jeff Presslaff (p) Joe Defrisco (b) Jon Stroup (d) Frank Foster
(arr, comp)

WHEN LIGHTS ARE LOW   (as) arr, comp

I CAN'T GET STARTED   (as) comp

DOOZY   (as) arr, comp

WHO, ME?   arr&comp-FF (as)

---

[351]   April 29, 1977 Tokyo Concert, Koseinenkin Kaikan Hall
           BENNY CARTER ALL STARS

Carter (as, tp, arr, comp) Cat Anderson (tp) Joe Newman (tp, v) Britt Woodman (tb) Budd Johnson (ts, ss) Cecil Payne (bs, flute) Nat Pierce (p, arr)
Mundell Lowe (g) George Duvivier (b) Harold Jones (d)

SQUATTY ROO   (as) arr
LP: PABLO LIVE 2308-216, PABLO LIVE (J) MTF1815,
PABLO 2310-853

THEM THERE EYES   (as) arr
LP: PABLO LIVE 2308-216, PABLO LIVE (J) MTF1815

IN A SENTIMENTAL MOOD   (e) arr
UNISSUED

SOUTH SIDE SAMBA   (as) arr, comp
UNISSUED

NUAGES   (e) arr
UNISSUED

WHEN IT'S SLEEPY TIME DOWN SOUTH   (e) arr
LP: PABLO LIVE 2308-216, PABLO LIVE (J) MTF1815,
MAXELL JAZZ II SAMPLER

CONFESSIN'   (tp) arr
LP: PABLO LIVE 2308-216, PABLO LIVE (J) MTF1815,
MAXELL JAZZ II SAMPLER

WHEN YOU'RE SMILING v-JN (e) arr
LP: PABLO LIVE 2308-216, PABLO LIVE (J) MTF1815,
MAXELL JAZZ II SAMPLER

CHINATOWN, MY CHINATOWN   (e) arr
UNISSUED

THINGS AIN'T WHAT THEY USED TO BE   (as) arr
UNISSUED

ALL MY LOVE   (e) arr
UNISSUED

GIRL TALK   arr-NP (e)
UNISSUED

SOUVENIR   (as) arr, comp
UNISSUED

JITTERBUG WALTZ   (as) arr
UNISSUED

GOD BLESS THE CHILD   (as) arr
UNISSUED

IT DON'T MEAN A THING IF IT AIN'T GOT THAT SWING   (as) arr
LP: PABLO LIVE 2308-216, PABLO LIVE (J) MTF1815, PABLO
2310-853

COTTONTAIL   (e) arr
UNISSUED

> NOTES: "Sleepy Time"/"Confessin'"/"When You're Smiling" played
> as medley in tribute to Louis Armstrong. "Souvenir" previously
> known as "That's How It Goes."

*   *   *

Carter's triumphant tour of Japan resulted in this live recording, which includes his first trumpet playing on a commercial release since 1962.   Carter remarks, "I was being very careful, like treading on eggs!"   In spite of
the layoff, on "Confessin'" he achieves a lovely tone without straining.
"That's what Cuban Bennett used to do and what Doc Cheatham does.   I think
it's the way the instrument should be played."

Carter put together an interesting book for this small "big band."   At
the request of the Japanese he included several pieces in tribute to some of
the departed jazz creators.   Of particular interest is "Chinatown," which
features a transcription played by the three trumpets (Carter, Newman and
Anderson) of Louis Armstrong's famous November 3, 1931 solo.

[352]	July 13, 1977 Montreux, Switzerland Montreux Jazz Festival
	Concert
	BENNY CARTER FOUR (BENNY CARTER FOUR, MONTREUX '77)

Carter (as, tp) Ray Bryant (p) Niels Pedersen (b) Jimmie Smith (d)

THREE LITTLE WORDS   (as)
LP: PABLO LIVE 2308-204, TIME LIFE STL-J10, PABLO
2310-853

IN A MELLOTONE   (as)(tp)
LP: PABLO LIVE 2308-204, PABLO 2310-853

WAVE   (as)
LP: PABLO LIVE 2308-204, PABLO 2310-853

UNDECIDED   (as)
LP: PABLO LIVE 2308-204

BODY AND SOUL (tp)(as)
LP: PABLO LIVE 2308-204

ON GREEN DOLPHIN STREET (as)
LP: PABLO LIVE 2308-204

HERE'S THAT RAINY DAY (as)
LP: PABLO LIVE 2308-204

*   *   *

Carter has always amazed his followers with his ability to maintain his com-
mand of the alto even after long layoffs. Such is his mastery that he does
not usually practice regularly; he prepares only for a specific engagement.
In the mid-1970s, as he returned to a more active playing schedule, under-
taking several extended club dates and concert tours, his playing became
awesome.

Norman Granz caught Carter at just such a peak at the 1977 Montreux
Jazz Festival and the result is the Carter album of the 1970s. With him is
Ray Bryant, with whom Carter first played at a New York club in 1976.
The two achieved instant rapport, and Carter has since called on Bryant
whenever possible for concerts, recordings and tours.

Every track is superb. On two tunes Carter plays trumpet as well,
muted on "Mellotone" and open on "Body And Soul." Despite some fluffs on
the latter, it is a striking statement which prompted contemporary trumpet
star Freddie Hubbard to exclaim in a Downbeat blindfold test, "What!! Are
you kiddin'? Benny Carter! Oh, man, he should play more trumpet. That
is unbelievable!!" (April 20, 1978, p. 35.)

One witness reported that in the usually noisy musicians' lounge at
Montreux, there was complete silence, as those who had played or were
waiting to go on watched Carter's set on the TV monitor. When he returned
after the performance he received a standing ovation from his peers. As
Gary Giddins wrote in his review of this record, "excepting pianists and Joe
Venuti, I don't think any septuagenarian jazzman has ever played with such
unimpeded authority." (Village Voice, February 6, 1978, p. 56.)

[353]   July 14, 1977 Montreux, Switzerland Montreux Jazz Festival
                         Concert
           COUNT BASIE JAM

Carter (as) Roy Eldridge (tp, v) Vic Dickenson, Al Grey (tb) Zoot Sims (ts)
Count Basie (p) Ray Brown (b) Jimmie Smith (d)

ROOKIE BLUES (as)
LP: PABLO LIVE 2308-209

SHE'S FUNNY THAT WAY (e)
LP: PABLO LIVE 2308-209

THESE FOOLISH THINGS (as)
LP: PABLO LIVE 2308-209

KIDNEY STEW v-RE (e)
LP: PABLO LIVE 2308-209

I GOT IT BAD AND THAT AIN'T GOOD   (e)
LP: PABLO LIVE 2308-209

JUMPIN' AT THE WOODSIDE   (e)
LP: PABLO LIVE 2308-209

FREEPORT JUMP   (as)
LP: PABLO LIVE 2620-105

---

[354]   April 15, 1978 Tokyo Concert, Nakano Sun Plaza Hotel
           BENNY CARTER ALL STAR ORCHESTRA

Carter (as, tp, arr, comp) Al Aarons, Ernie Royal (tp) Joe Newman (tp, v)
Britt Woodman (tb) Budd Johnson (ts, arr) Buddy Collette (ts, cl, flute) Cecil
Payne (bs, flute) Nat Pierce (p, arr) Mundell Lowe (g) George Duvivier (b,
arr, comp) Gus Johnson (d)

SWEET GEORGIA BROWN   arr-NP (as)

THEM THERE EYES   (as) arr

LOVER MAN   arr-NP (as)

DOOZY   (e) arr, comp

EKE'S BLUES   arr&comp-GD (as)

IT DON'T MEAN A THING IF IT AIN'T GOT THAT SWING   (as) arr

THINGS AIN'T WHAT THEY USED TO BE   (as) arr

WHEN IT'S SLEEPY TIME DOWN SOUTH   (e) arr

CONFESSIN'   (tp) arr

WHEN YOU'RE SMILING   v-JN (e) arr

BROADWAY (incomplete)   arr-NP (e)

BODY AND SOUL   (tp)

GIRL TALK   arr-NP (e)

ROSETTA   arr-BJ (as)

COTTONTAIL   (e) arr

> NOTE: "Sleepy Time"/"Confessin'"/"When You're Smiling" played as
> medly in tribute to Louis Armstrong; "Body And Soul"/"Girl Talk"
> part of medley.

---

[355]   Ca. April 19, 1978 Tokyo Concert, Nakano Sun Plaza Hotel
           BENNY CARTER ALL STAR ORCHESTRA

Carter (as, tp, arr) Joe Newman (tp, v) Al Aarons, Ernie Royal (tp) Britt
Woodman (tb) Budd Johnson (ts, arr) Buddy Collette (ts, cl, flute) Cecil Payne

(bs, flute) Nat Pierce (p, arr) Mundell Lowe (g) George Duvivier (b, arr, comp)
Gus Johnson (d)

SWEET GEORGIA BROWN   arr-NP (as)

THEM THERE EYES   (as) arr

EKE'S BLUES   arr&comp-GD (as)

IT DON'T MEAN A THING IF IT AIN'T GOT THAT SWING   (as) arr

THINGS AIN'T WHAT THEY USED TO BE   (as) arr

WHEN IT'S SLEEPY TIME DOWN SOUTH   (e) arr

CONFESSIN'   (tp) arr

WHEN YOU'RE SMILING   v-JN (e) arr

BROADWAY   arr-NP (as)

DON'T BLAME ME   (tp)

I CAN'T GET STARTED   (as)

GIRL TALK   arr-NP (e)

ROSETTA   arr-BJ (as)

COTTONTAIL   (e) arr

> NOTE: "Sleepy Time"/"Confessin'"/"When You're Smiling" played as
> medley in tribute of Louis Armstrong; "Don't Blame Me"/"I Can't
> Get Started"/"Girl Talk" part of medley.

[356]   May 14, 1978 Washington, D.C.   Concert, Smithsonian Institution
                              Jazz Heritage Series
          BENNY CARTER

Carter (as, comp) Joe Kennedy (violin) Ray Bryant (p) Larry Ridley (b) Freddie Waits (d)

ON GREEN DOLPHIN STREET   (as)

EASY MONEY   (as) comp

MISTY   (as)

WAVE   (as)

PERDIDO   (as)

IN A MELLOTONE   (as)

ALL THE THINGS YOU ARE   (as)

COTTONTAIL   (as)

[357]   June 18, 1978 Washington, D.C.   NPR Broadcast of White House
                      Concert
           TRIBUTE TO THE 25TH ANNIVERSARY OF THE NEWPORT JAZZ
           FESTIVAL

Carter (as) Roy Eldridge, Clark Terry (tp) Illinois Jacquet (ts) Teddy Wilson
(p) Milt Hinton (b) Jo Jones (d)

IN A MELLOTONE (as)

LADY BE GOOD (as)

[358]   October 28, 1978 Buffalo, N.Y.   Concert (1st), State University
                      of N.Y.
           BENNY CARTER WITH THE UNIV. OF BUFFALO JAZZ
           ENSEMBLE, SAM FALZONE, DIR.

Carter (as, arr, comp) Tony Gorruso, Norm Friedman, Ken Koleff, Mitch
Robinson (tp) Craig Brown, Wallace Kotarski, Bruce Caldwell (tb) Sam Fal-
zone, David Markiewicz, Steve Rosenthal, Mike Stalteri, Phil Lamacchia,
Jonathan Schnepps, Michael Colquhoun, Robert Sowyrda (reeds) Randolph
Noel, Kevin Doyle (p) Tony Logan, Rick Harris (g) Hans Halt (b) Charles
Fadale (d)

WHEN LIGHTS ARE LOW (as) arr, comp

LYDIA (e) arr, comp

I CAN'T GET STARTED (as) arr

HONEYSUCKLE ROSE (as) arr

[359]   Same Concert
           BENNY CARTER WITH THE AL TINNEY TRIO

Carter (as) Al Tinney (p) Lou Hackney (b) Jerry McClam (d)

IN A MELLOTONE (as)

WHAT'S NEW (as)

ON GREEN DOLPHIN STREET (as)

TWELVE BAR BLUES (as)

UNDECIDED (as)

TAKE THE A TRAIN (as)

[360]   Same Date--2nd Concert
           BENNY CARTER WITH THE UNIV. OF BUFFALO JAZZ
           ENSEMBLE, PHIL SIMS, DIR.

Carter (as, arr, comp) Mike Reade, Mitch Robinson, Chris Conlon, Jerry
Saratini (tp) Phil Sims, Craig Brown, Walter Koslowski, Wallace Kotarski,

James Ford, Denis Bourden (tb) Chuck Briem, Gary White, Jeff Hackworth, Carl Kesselman, Daven Skrzynski (reeds) David Billowus, Leslie Glassman (p) Rick Harris (g) Manuel Guevara (b) Bob Chaplin (d)

WHEN LIGHTS ARE LOW (as) arr, comp

A WALKIN' THING (as) arr, comp

BLUES FOR BEGINNERS (as) arr, comp

I CAN'T GET STARTED (as) arr

HONEYSUCKLE ROSE (as) arr

---

[361]   Same Concert
          BENNY CARTER WITH THE AL TINNEY TRIO

Carter (as) Al Tinney (p) Lou Hackney (b) Jerry McClam (d)

IN A MELLOTONE (as)

ON GREEN DOLPHIN STREET (as)

LOVER MAN (as)

PERDIDO (as)

BODY AND SOUL (as)

CHEROKEE (as)

ALL THE THINGS YOU ARE (as)

---

[362]   March 14, 1979
          OSCAR PETERSON

Carter (as) Clark Terry (tp) Zoot Sims (ts) Oscar Peterson (p) Milt Jackson (vib) John Heard (b) Grady Tate (d)

THEME FOR CELINE (as)
PABLO TODAY 2312-103

THE HAPPY HOUR (as)
PABLO TODAY 2312-103

PARTY TIME U.S.A. (as)
PABLO TODAY 2312-103

ELLIOT (as)
PABLO TODAY 2312-103

THEME FOR SUSANNAH (as)
PABLO TODAY 2312-103

> NOTE: The music for this album, The Silent Partner, is based on Oscar Peterson's score for the film of the same name.

[363]   June 2, 1979   Tokyo   Concert, Kosei Nenkin Hall
          BENNY CARTER JAZZ ALL STAR ORCHESTRA

Carter (as, arr, comp) Cat Anderson, Joe Newman (tp) Jimmy Cleveland (tb)
Budd Johnson (ts, arr) Cecil Payne (bs, flute) Joe Kennedy (violin) Ray Bryant
(p) George Duvivier (b) Harold Jones (d)

SHAVERS' TUNE   arr-BJ (as)
PADDLE WHEEL (J) GP3199

SOUTH SIDE SAMBA   (as) arr, comp
PADDLE WHEEL (J) GP3199

I CAN'T GET STARTED   (as)
PADDLE WHEEL (J) GP3199

        NOTE: "I Can't Get Started" is Carter's feature in ballad medley.

[364]   October 12, 1979   Princeton, N.J.   Concert, Princeton University
          BENNY CARTER SEXTET

Carter (as) Dizzy Gillespie (tp) Joe Kennedy (violin) Barry Harris (p) Larry
Ridley (b) Yusef Ali (d) Stanley Jordan (g)

AIN'T MISBEHAVIN'   (as)

STRAIGHT, NO CHASER   (as)

GEE, AIN'T I GOOD TO YOU   (as)

BROADWAY   (as)

PERDIDO   (as)

ON GREEN DOLPHIN STREET   (as)

ALL THE THINGS YOU ARE   (as)

CARAVAN   (as)

BLUES   (as)

        NOTE: Jordan plays on "All The Things You Are" and "Blues" only.

[365]   November 10, 1979   Princeton, N.J.   Concert, Princeton University
          BENNY CARTER WITH THE PRINCETON UNIVERSITY JAZZ
          ENSEMBLE

Carter (as, comp) Tony Branker (tp, arr) Bill Ash, John Dolan, John Hill,
Burns Stanfield (tp) Matt Geymann, Doug Green, Ben Monderer, Jon Rein-
gold (tb) Mike Connor, Tom Falin, Amy Leenhouts, Tim McNally, Steve
Ratner (reeds) Emery Snyder (p) Steve Wexler (b, arr) Jeff Penny (d) James
Capolupo (dir)

FEASANT PHEATHERS   arr-SW (as) comp

THE COURTSHIP   arr-SW (as) comp

ORNITHOLOGY   arr-TB (as)

---

[366]   Same Concert
           BENNY CARTER WITH THE PRINCETON UNIVERSITY JAZZ
           SEXTET

Carter (as) Tony Branker, John Dolan (tp) Ben Monderer (tb) Emery Snyder (p) Steve Wexler (b) Jeff Penny (d)

NIGHT IN TUNISIA   (as)

MISTY (Carter with rhythm)   (as)

WHAT IS THIS THING CALLED LOVE   (as)

---

[367]   June 11, 1980 Stockholm TV Broadcast, Stockholm Jazz and
                          Blues Festival
           BENNY CARTER WITH ARNE DOMNERUS & HIS ORCH.

Carter (as) Jan Allan (tp) Arne Domnerus (as) Claes Rosendahl (ts) Bengt Hallberg (p) Rune Gustafsson (g) Georg Riedel (b) Egil Johansen (d)

EASY MONEY   (as) comp

MISTY   (as)

HONEYSUCKLE ROSE   (as)

JEEP'S BLUES   (as)

     NOTE: Carter with rhythm on first title.

---

[368]   June 12, 1980 Stockholm TV Broadcast, Stockholm Jazz and
                          Blues Festival
           BENNY CARTER WITH KUSTBANDET

Carter (as) 12-Piece Swedish Band

UNKNOWN TITLES

---

[369]   June 13, 1980 Stockholm TV Broadcast, Stockholm Jazz and
                          Blues Festival
           BENNY CARTER QUARTET

Carter (as) Tommy Flanagan (p) Red Mitchell (b) Rune Carlsson (d)

THREE LITTLE WORDS   (as)

SOMETIMES I'M HAPPY   (as)

HERE'S THAT RAINY DAY   (as)

ON THE SUNNY SIDE OF THE STREET   (as)

BLUES   (as)

PERDIDO   (as)

*   *   *

At this concert Carter literally performed a musical miracle. The festival
was held outdoors and, although the musicians were under cover, the audience was being drenched by a rainstorm. After playing "Here's That Rainy
Day," Carter picked up the tempo, segued into "Sunny Side Of The Street,"
and during his solo the rain stopped. A Swedish newspaper ran a photo of
Carter with the caption, "The Man Who Stopped The Rain!"

---

[370]   June 20, 1980 Los Angeles Television Broadcast, The Tonight Show
           PLAYBOY JAZZ FESTIVAL GROUP

Carter (as) Teddy Wilson (p) Ray Brown (b) Shelly Manne (d)

BLUE LOU   (as)

I CAN'T BELIEVE THAT YOU'RE IN LOVE WITH ME   (as)

> NOTE: This group, with the addition of Harry "Sweets" Edison, per-
> formed the next day at the Playboy Jazz Festival in the Hollywood
> Bowl.

[370A]   June 26, 1980 Detroit National Public Radio Broadcast of Concert,
                          Detroit Institute of Arts
           TRIBUTE TO DON REDMAN

Carter (as) Doc Cheatham (tp, v) Dave Wilborn (v) with Rhythm Section

GEE, AIN'T I GOOD TO YOU   v-DC (as acc)

HONEYSUCKLE ROSE   (as)

MISTY   (as)

I WANT A LITTLE GIRL   v-DW, DC (as)

[370B]   Same Concert
           NEW McKINNEY'S COTTON PICKERS

Carter (as, arr) Doc Cheatham (tp) Dave Wilborn, Orrin Foslien (v) with the
New McKinney's Cotton Pickers

CHERRY   v-DW (e)

NEVER SWAT A FLY   v-OF (e) arr

MISS HANNAH   v-DW (e)

PLAIN DIRT   (e)

HELLO v-DW (e)

> NOTE: Carter plays lead alto on these titles. "Never Swat" is a McKinney's arrangement which Carter believes is his own, although it is usually credited to Redman.

[370C]   Same Concert
         RE-CREATION OF DON REDMAN ORCHESTRA

Includes Carter (as) Doc Cheatham (tp) Orchestra Conducted by Dave Hutson, Dave Wilborn (v)

HOW'M I DOIN' v-DW (as)

DOWN, DOWN, DOWN (e)

HOW DO YOU CALL A MAN A TWO TIMIN' MAN...   V-DW (e)

I GOTCHA (e)

REDMAN BLUES (as)

---

[371]   August 17, 1980   Copenhagen   Studio Recording for Sonet
          BENNY CARTER

Carter (as) Kenny Drew (p) Jesper Lundgaard (b) Ed Thigpen (d)

UNKNOWN TITLES

---

[372]   September 3, 1980   Tokyo   Aurex Jazz Festival
          GENTLEMEN OF SWING

Carter (as) Harry Edison (tp) Teddy Wilson (p) Milt Hinton (b) Shelly Manne (d)

HONEYSUCKLE ROSE (as)
LP: EAST WORLD (J) EWJ80188

MISTY (as)
LP: EAST WORLD (J) EWJ80188

SOMETIMES I'M HAPPY (as)
LP: EAST WORLD (J) EWJ80188

[372A]   September 7, 1980   Yokohama, Japan   Aurex Jazz Festival
          GENTLEMEN OF SWING

Carter (as) Harry Edison (tp) Teddy Wilson (p) Milt Hinton (b) Shelly Manne (d)

IN A MELLOTONE (as)
LP: EAST WORLD (J) EWJ80188

IDAHO (as)
LP: EAST WORLD (J) EWJ80188

HONEYSUCKLE ROSE   (as)
UNISSUED

[372B]   September 1980
            KEI ISHIGURO

Carter (as) Norrio Maeda (p) Yasur Arakawa (b) Takeshi Inomata (d) Kei
Ishiguro (v)

MISTY NIGHT v-KI (as)
LP: VICTOR (J) SJX30032

MY DEAR OLD LOVE v-KI (as)
LP: VICTOR (J) SXJ30032

---

[373]   February 4-5, 1981   Los Angeles
           TERESA BREWER

Carter (as) Oscar Brashear (flugelhorn) Mike Lang (p) Chuck Domanico (b)
Shelly Manne (d) Teresa Brewer (v)

SOPHISTICATED LADY   (feature for Carter) (as)
LP: COLUMBIA FC37363

SOLITUDE v-TB (as)
LP: COLUMBIA FC37363

COME SUNDAY v-TB (as)
LP: COLUMBIA FC37363

DUKE'S PLACE v-TB (as)
LP: COLUMBIA FC37363

IT DON'T MEAN A THING IF IT AIN'T GOT THAT SWING v-TB (as)
LP: COLUMBIA FC37363

DON'T GET AROUND MUCH ANYMORE v-TB (as)
LP: COLUMBIA FC37363

I'M BEGINNING TO SEE THE LIGHT v-TB (as)
LP: COLUMBIA FC37363

---

[374]   April 18, 1981 New York Club Date, Sweet Basil
           BENNY CARTER QUARTET

Carter (as, v, comp) Norman Simmons (p) George Duvivier (b) Ronnie Bedford
(d)

IN A MELLOTONE   (as)

BLUE STAR   (as) comp

UNDECIDED   (as)

ALL THE THINGS YOU ARE   (as)

EASY MONEY (as) comp

WHAT IS THIS THING CALLED LOVE (as)

MISTY (as)

SOUTH SIDE SAMBA (as) comp

SOUVENIR (as) comp

ALL THAT JAZZ (as)(v) comp

---

[375]   July 1981 Japan (13 Concerts--see note below)
          BENNY CARTER ALL STARS

Carter (as, tp, arr, comp) Bill Berry (cornet) Pete Candoli (tp, v) George Bohanon (tb) Frank Wess (ts, flute) Jack Nimitz (bs) Kenny Barron (p) Joe Kennedy (violin) George Duvivier (b, arr) Frankie Capp (d)

THINGS AIN'T WHAT THEY USED TO BE (as) arr

MOOD INDIGO (as) arr

I'M BEGINNING TO SEE THE LIGHT (as) arr

THE COURTSHIP (as) arr, comp

WHEN IT'S SLEEPY TIME DOWN SOUTH (e) arr

CONFESSIN' (tp) arr

WHEN YOU'RE SMILING v-PC (e) arr

CHINATOWN (e) arr

EKE'S BLUES GD-comp & arr (tp)(as)

AIN'T MISBEHAVIN' (tp)

MISTY (as)

SOUTH SIDE SAMBA (as) arr, comp

COTTONTAIL (e) arr

> NOTE: Carter gave 13 concerts during a three week tour of Japan;
> all performances exist on tape. The usual program consisted of the
> tunes listed here, although some variations occurred from concert to
> concert. Schedule: July 3-Yokohama, July 4-Tokyo (two concerts),
> July 7-Kushiro, July 9-Tokushima, July 10-Tsuruoka, July 11-Tokyo,
> July 12-Toyama, July 14-Osaka, July 15-Shimonoseki, July 16-Shizu-
> oka, July 17-Tokyo, July 20-Mito.
>
> "Sleepy Time," "Confessin'," "When You're Smiling" played as medley
> in tribute to Louis Armstrong.
>
> "Chinatown" includes a transcription, played by the three trumpets,

of Louis Armstrong's 11/3/31 solo.

"Ain't Misbehavin'" and "Misty" are Carter features in a medley.

---

[376]   July 17, 1981 Tokyo   Television Show
           NANCY WILSON WITH BENNY CARTER, GUEST SOLOIST

Carter (as) Nancy Wilson (v) with Large Studio Orchestra

I'M BEGINNING TO SEE THE LIGHT v-NW (as)

BUT BEAUTIFUL v-NW (as acc)

---

[377]   July 18, 1981 Tokyo
           BENNY CARTER WITH THE KAZUO YASHIRO TRIO
           (STREET OF DREAMS)

Carter (as, comp) Kazuo Yashiro (p) Kohji Tohyama (b) Ikuo Shiozaki (g)

AFTER YOU'VE GONE (as)
LP: LOB (J) LDC-1030

EASY LIVING (as)
LP: LOB (J) LDC-1030

WHEN LIGHTS ARE LOW (as) comp
LP: LOB (J) LDC-1030

MARI (as)
LP: LOB (J) LDC-1030

LIKE SOMEONE IN LOVE (as)
LP: LOB (J) LDC-1030

STREET OF DREAMS (as)
LP: LOB (J) LDC-1030

ROSETTA (as)
LP: LOB (J) LDC-1030

CHIYO (as)
LP: LOB (J) LDC-1030

---

[378]   September 26, 1981 Los Angeles   National Public Radio Broadcast /
                                             of Concert, UCLA
           BENNY CARTER SEXTET

Carter (as, comp) Bill Berry (cornet) George Bohanon (tb) Roger Kellaway
(p) Chuck Domanico (b) John Guerin (d)

WHEN LIGHTS ARE LOW (as) comp

BLUE STAR (as) comp

SOUTH SIDE SAMBA (as) comp

[379]   November 28, 1981 Washington, D. C.   Concert, Smithsonian
                                          Institution
         BENNY CARTER

Carter (as, comp) Joe Kennedy (violin) Kenny Barron (p) George Duvivier (b)
Ronnie Bedford (d)

EASY MONEY (as) comp

ON GREEN DOLPHIN STREET (as)

BLUE STAR (as) comp

LIKE SOMEONE IN LOVE (as)

SOUTH SIDE SAMBA (as) comp

HONEYSUCKLE ROSE (as)

MISTY (as)

TAKE THE A TRAIN (as)

COTTONTAIL (as)

AUTUMN LEAVES (as)

    NOTE: Concert videotaped for Public Television.

[380]   December 4, 1981 New York Club Date, Sweet Basil
         BENNY CARTER QUARTET

Carter (as, comp) Kenny Barron (p) George Duvivier (b) Ronnie Bedford (d)

ON GREEN DOLPHIN STREET (as)

EASY MONEY (as) comp

LOVER MAN (as)

IN A MELLOTONE (as)

TAKE THE A TRAIN (as)

BROADWAY (as)

BLUE STAR (as) comp

PERDIDO (as)

ALL OF ME (as)

THERE IS NO GREATER LOVE (as)

MEAN TO ME (as)

ALL THE THINGS YOU ARE (as)

MOOD INDIGO (as)

HONEYSUCKLE ROSE (as)

---

[381]   December 5, 1981 New York Club Date, Sweet Basil
           BENNY CARTER QUARTET

Carter (as, comp) Kenny Barron (p) George Duvivier (b) Ronnie Bedford (d)

EASY MONEY (as) comp

UNDECIDED (as)

LOVER MAN (as)

ON GREEN DOLPHIN STREET (as)

IN A MELLOTONE (as)

HONEYSUCKLE ROSE (as)

TAKE THE A TRAIN (as)

MALIBU (as) comp

ON GREEN DOLPHIN STREET (as)

MISTY (as)

ALL OF ME (as)

SOUTH SIDE SAMBA (as) comp

BLUE STAR (as) comp

ALL THE THINGS YOU ARE (as)

THE COURTSHIP (as) comp

MEAN TO ME (as)

PERDIDO (as)

BLUES (as)

INDEX OF ARTISTS

Note: Numbers refer to Session Numbers, not page numbers.

INDEX OF TUNE TITLES

Note: Numbers refer to Session Numbers, not page numbers.

255

CARTER AS ARRANGER AND COMPOSER

This section presents Benny Carter's recorded work as an arranger and composer. It is divided into three parts: 1) master list of arrangements and compositions, 2) index of artists, 3) chronological index.

1. Master list of arrangements and compositions. This is an alphabetical listing by title of all known recorded Carter arrangements and compositions. Arrangements and compositions are merged into a single list. Each title is followed by the composer credits (Benny Carter is abbreviated as "BC"). Unless otherwise noted, Carter is presumed to have composed the music to a piece, not its lyric. For Carter compositions with lyrics, the lyricist is specified; for non-Carter compositions no distinction between lyricist and composer is made.

Date provided for each recording include 1) date, 2) leader and/or group (if Carter is the leader "BC" appears), 3) vocalist (if any)--if the leader is the vocalist a "v" appears after the name; other vocalists appear in parentheses, 4) instrumentation (an approximate listing which is given only for the first recording of Carter arrangements), 5) record issues--these are not comprehensive; usually only the most recent LP is shown. An asterisk following the date of recording indicates that Carter played on the session, and the reader may refer to Section One of the discography for record issue information (which is not repeated here).

Each Carter arrangement of a piece is listed under that title in chronological order by the date of its first recording, which is underscored. Subsequent recordings of the same arrangement appear chronologically (without underscoring) under the first recording of that arrangement. Within each title, new arrangements are separated by one space; multiple recordings of the same arrangement have no spaces between them.

All recordings listed under titles which Carter did not compose are, of course, his arrangements. Under titles which Carter did compose, however, all recordings of that piece are listed, including many which he did not arrange. Such recordings (i. e. "head" arrangements of Carter's compositions, or Carter's compositions arranged by others) are set off by one space and marked with a ●.

2. Index of artists. This is an alphabetical listing of artists or groups who have recorded Carter arrangements or compositions. The titles recorded appear in chronological order under each leader's name. "See" and "see also" references are provided from all vocalists, co-leaders and some prominent accompanists or groups, to the leader under whose name the recording was issued. Following the tune title an "a" and/or "c" identifies the recording as a Carter arrangement or composition (or both). Multiple recordings by the same artist of a Carter arrangement or composition are indicated by listing the additional recording dates directly under the title. No record issues are given, as this information appears in the master list. Film soundtrack recordings are listed by title in a separate section following the artist index. Only recordings of Carter film arrangements and compositions which have been issued on disc are included here (see filmography for more comprehensive film lists).

Carter himself does not appear in this index; the number of recordings of his arrangements and compositions by his own groups would make such a list unwieldy. Moreover, by perusing Section One of the discography the reader can readily locate the Carter arrangements and compositions recorded on Carter-led dates. Similarly, arrangements and compositions recorded by vocalists on Carter-led sessions are not enumerated; rather, the vocalist's name appears in the index with a list of recording dates at which he or she performed a Carter arrangement or composition (e. g. , Maxine Sullivan--see BC 4/1/44). The reader is thus referred to the appropriate session(s) in Section One.

3. Chronological index. This is a year-by-year listing of Carter arrangements and compositions (indicated by "a" and/or "c"). The year under which a given title appears is the year of the first recording of that arrangement or composition. Readers should note that this is only an approximate indication of the period to which a work belongs; the actual date of creation may, of course, be much earlier. In the few instances where the creation of an arrangement or composition is known to greatly antedate its first recording, this is noted. Similarly, for an arrangement by Carter of an earlier composition, the original year of composition is noted.

MASTER LIST OF ARRANGEMENTS AND COMPOSITIONS

A TEA VISTA (BC)
- 11/30/76*   BC

ACCENT ON SWING (BC)
mid 6/36   BC   3tp/2tb/3as/1ts/p/g/b/d

AFTER YOU'VE GONE (T. Layton/H. Creamer)
9/61   Jonah Jones with Glen Gray & the Casa Loma
                   Orch. 6tp/4tb/2as/2ts/1bs/p/g/b/d   Capitol T1713

1962   Sarah Vaughan (v) 4tp/4tb/5reeds/p/g/b/d/vib/v
                   Roulette R(S)52092, Roulette (E) 2682-043

AGAIN (D. Cochran/L. Newman)
8/30/74   Yujiro Ishihara (v) 2tp/1tb/1as/2ts/1bs/p/g/b/d/
                   14violins/4violas/4celli/v Continental (J) CO1
                   NOTE: Instrumental tracks recorded 8/30/74,
                   Los Angeles; vocal added later in Japan.

AIN'T I (BC)
11/65   film soundtrack: A Man Called Adam   1tp/1tb/
                   1ts/p/b/d   Reprise 6180

AIN'T MISBEHAVIN' (Waller/Brooks/Razaf)
2/15-16/79   Ella Fitzgerald with Count Basie's Orch.   4tp/
                   4tb/5reeds/p/g/b/d/v   Pablo Today 2312-132

AIN'T THAT SOMETHING?
Jan.-Feb. 1943*   film soundtrack: Stormy Weather (Bill Robinson-
                   v) large orch/v

ALL ALONE (I. Berlin)
2/27/45*   Savannah Churchill (v) & Her All Star Orch.
                   4tp/4tb/5reeds/p/g/b/d/v

ALL ALONE AND LONESOME (BC/lyrics: Paul Herrick)
1953   Ernie Andrews (v) with Benny Carter's Orch.
                   large orch/v 78: Trend 2502

ALL MY LOVE (P. Durand)
4/29/77*   BC   2tp/1tb/3reeds/p/g/b/d

ALL OF ME (G. Marks/S. Simons)
1/17/36*   Willie Lewis & His Orch.   2tp/1tb/2as/2ts/p/g/b/d

11/19/40*   BC 3tp/3tb/2as/2ts/1bs/p/g/b/d NOTE: The
                                saxophone chorus in this arrangement is based on
                                the one recorded by Willie Lewis.
1943*   (AFRS Basic Library P-34) BC

ALL THAT I CAN DO IS THINK OF YOU (Bob Friedman)
11/71-3/72   Carmen McRae (v) large orch/v Temponic
                                TB29562

ALL THAT JAZZ (BC/lyrics: Al Stillman)
11/65   film soundtrack: A Man Called Adam 1tp/1tb/
                                1ts/p/b/d Reprise 6180

   • 11/65   film soundtrack: A Man Called Adam (Mel
                                Torme-v) Reprise 6180

   • 11/65   film soundtrack: A Man Called Adam (Mel
                                Torme-v) Reprise 6180

   • 1/3/76*   BC (Millicent Browne-v)

   • 4/18/81*   BC (BC-v)

ALL THE TIME (Bob Friedman)
11/71-3/72   Carmen McRae (v) large orch/v Temponic
                                TB29562

ALL TORE DOWN (D. Wyatt)
1968   Don Wyatt (v) large orch with strings/v NOTE:
                                Recorded for Dome Records--unissued.

ALTO EGO (BC)
8/64*   BC 2ss/4as/3ts/2bs/p/g/b/d

ALWAYS ON MY MIND (Green/Newell)
1/63   Sarah Vaughan (v) 4fr. horns/p/g/b/d/tuba/v
                                Roulette R(S)52104

ALWAYS ON SUNDAY (Bob Friedman)
11/71-3/72   Joe Williams (v) large orch with strings/chorus/
                                v Temponic TB29561

AMONG MY SOUVENIRS (H. Nicholls/E. Leslie)
1/30/40*   BC (Roy Felton-v) 3tp/3tb/3as/2ts/p/g/b/d/v
9/11/44?*   BC

AMOROSO (BC)
11/1-2/61*   Count Basie & His Orch.   4tp/3tb/2as/2ts/1bs/p/
                                g/b/d

1/22-24/62   Louis Bellson Orch.   5tp/3tb/1fr. horn/1tuba/2as/
                                2ts/1bs/p/g/b/d/vib Roulette R52087, Roulette
                                (E) 2934-020

ANY OLD TIME (J. Rodgers)
12/22/74*   Maria Muldaur (v) 2tp/1tb/1as/1ts/1bs/p/g/b/d/v

ANY TIME AT ALL (Van Heusen/J. Dorsey)
7/21/38*   Lionel Hampton (v) & His Orch. 1tp/2as/2ts/p/
                                b/d/vib/v

APOLLO JUMPS (BC)
9/61   Jonah Jones with Glen Gray & the Casa Loma
                        Orch. 6tp/4tb/2as/2ts/1bs/p/g/b/d   Capitol
                        T1713

APRIL IN MY HEART (H. Carmichael/H. Melnardi)
11/9/38*   Teddy Wilson & His Orch. (Billie Holiday-v)
                        1tp/1tb/2as/2ts/p/g/b/d/v

AROUND THE WORLD IN EIGHTY DAYS (V. Young)
5/63*   BC 1as/p/b/d/vocal group

AS TIME GOES BY (H. Hupfeld)
8/30/74   Yujiro Ishihara (v) 2tp/1tb/1as/2ts/1bs/p/g/b/d/v
                        Continental (J) C01 NOTE: Instrumental tracks
                        recorded 8/30/74, Los Angeles; vocal added later
                        in Japan.

ASK (BC/lyrics: H. C. Mahr)
ca. 1958   Lois Peters (v) with the Ravenscroft Singers &
                        Orch. 5brass/4woodwinds/rhythm section/strings/
                        v 45: Decca 9-30269 [copyrighted as ASK, BE-
                        LIEVING THAT YOU WILL RECEIVE]

ASK, BELIEVING THAT YOU WILL RECEIVE see ASK

AUGUST MOON (BC)
 • late 1958 or   BC
early 1959*

AUTUMN LEAVES (J. Kosma)
10/57   "Mucho Calor" (features Art Pepper)   1tp/1as/
                        1ts/p/b/d/bongo/conga Andex A3002

BABALU (Margarita Lecuona)
1/21/41*   BC 3tp/3tb/3as/2ts/p/g/b/d

BABY, DON'T YOU QUIT NOW (J. Mercer/J. Rowles)
1968   Pearl Bailey (v) with the Louis Bellson Orch.
                        4tp/4tb/5reeds/p/g/b/d/v Project 3 PR5022SD,
                        Project 3 PR4003SD

BABY WON'T YOU PLEASE COME HOME (Warfield/Williams)
early 1950's   Ruby Lane (v) large orch with strings/v 45:
                        Colpix CP139

BABY, YOU'RE MINE FOR KEEPS (H. Atwood/L. Herscher)
1/48*   BC (Emma Lou Welch-v) 1tp/1tb/1as/1ts/p/g/
                        b/d/v

BACK BAY BOOGIE (BC)
10/16/41*   BC 3tp/3tb/3as/2ts/p/g/b/d
4/10/43*   BC
possibly Jan. or   BC
Nov. 1944*
3/26/45*   (AFRS Jubilee #126) BC
5/5/46*   BC
ca. 6/46*   (AFRS Jubilee #193) BC

BACK HOME AGAIN IN INDIANA see INDIANA

BACK IN YOUR OWN BACKYARD (A. Jolson/B. Rose/D. Dreyer)
     ca. 1951   Patti Page (v) with Herb Geller Orch. large
                                 orch/v 78: Mercury 5463

THE BAD AND THE BEAUTIFUL (D. Raksin)
     1961*   Alfred Newman large orch with horns/strings

BAGATELLE (BC)
     • 5/63*   BC

BAMBOULA see CONGOROO

THE BASIE TWIST (BC)
     10/30-31/61*   Count Basie & His Orch. 4tp/3tb/2as/2ts/1bs/p/
                                g/b/d

BAUBLES, BANGLES AND BEADS (R. Wright/G. Forrest)
     9/61   Jonah Jones with Glen Gray & the Casa Loma
                                Orch. 6tp/4tb/2as/2ts/1bs/p/g/b/d Capitol
                                T1713, Capitol (G) 1C 054-81710

BE ANYTHING (I. Gordon)
     2/60   Dakota Staton (v) large orch with strings/v Capi-
                                tol T1427

BE-BOP BOOGIE see RE-BOP BOOGIE

BE COOL (BC)
     5/63*   KPM Music Library 4tp/4tb/2fr. horns/5reeds/p/
                                g/b/d

     5/63*   KPM Music Library 4tp/4tb/2fr. horns/5reeds/p/
                                g/b/d

     5/63*   KPM Music Library 4tp/4tb/2fr. horns/flutes/p/
                                g/b/d

                                NOTE: See notes for this session in chronological
                                section of discography.

A BEAUTIFUL FRIENDSHIP (S. Styne/D. Kahn)
     2/19/64   Billy Eckstine (v) 1tp/1tb/2reeds/p/g/b/d/v/vocal
                                group Mercury SR60916, Mercury MG20916

BEAUTIFUL LOVE (Young/Van Alstyne/Gillespie/King)
     12/31/53*   BC horns/strings/p/b/d

BETWEEN 18th AND 19th ON CHESTNUT STREET (W. Osborne/D. Rodgers)
     1955   Freddie Slack 1tp/1tb/1ts/1bs/p/g/b/d Emarcy
                                MG36094, Wing MGW60003

BETWEEN THE DEVIL AND THE DEEP BLUE SEA (H. Arlen/T. Koehler)
     4/27/55   Ella Fitzgerald (v) with Benny Carter Orch. 3tp/
                                1tb/2as/2ts/p/g/b/d/v Decca DL8155, MCA
                                Coral CB20024, MCA Coral (G) 0082. 050-2

BEWITCHED, BOTHERED AND BEWILDERED (Rodgers/Hart)
    9/52*   BC with the Oscar Peterson Trio & Buddy Rich
                       horns/strings/p/g/b/d

BIG BEN BLUES (BC--words & music)
    4/15/36*   BC (v) 3tp/2tb/3as/2ts/p/g/b/d/v

BIG NOBODY (Wellington/Chaudet)
    Mar. 30-Apr. 1   Pearl Bailey (v) 4tp/4tb/5reeds/p/g/b/d/v
    1965*

BILL BAILEY, WON'T YOU PLEASE COME HOME (H. Cannon)
    Sept.-Oct. 1958*   film soundtrack: The Five Pennies (Louis Arm-
                      strong, Danny Kaye-v) probably 1tp/1tb/1cl/1as/
                      1ts/p/g/b/d/v

BLACK BUTTERFLY (Duke Ellington)
    8/14/79   Zoot Sims 4tp/4tb/2as/2ts/1bs/p/g/b/d Pablo
                      Today 2312-120 NOTE: This arrangement was
                      written for Sarah Vaughan, but at session Sims
                      substituted as featured soloist.

BLACK NIGHT (J. Williams)
    5/63*   BC 1as/p/b/d/vocal group

BLAZIN' (Sanders)
    5/16/29   Fletcher Henderson & His Orch. 3tp/2tb/3reeds/
                      p/banjo/tuba/d Columbia CL1684, Smithsonian
                      P2-13710

BLITZEN (L. Feather)
    1/22-24/62   Louis Bellson Orch. 5tp/3tb/1fr. horn/1tuba/2as/
                      2ts/1bs/p/g/b/d/vib Roulette R52087, Roulette
                      (E) 2934-020

BLUE EVENING (G. Jenkins/J. Bishop)
    6/10/39*   BC 3tp/3tb/2as/2ts/p/g/b/d
    7/24/39*   BC (Dell St. John-v)

BLUE FIVE JIVE (BC)
    9/6-11/60   Count Basie & His Orch. 4tp/3tb/2as/2ts/1bs/p/
                      g/b/d Roulette (S)R52056, Roulette RE124 NOTE:
                      See note on recording date under Kansas City Suite;
                      one of ten pieces comprising the Suite.

BLUE INTERLUDE (BC/lyrics: M. Kurtz/I. Mills)
    10/10/33*   The Chocolate Dandies 1tp/1tb/1as/1ts/p/g/b/d

   ● 12/19/34   Chuck Richards (v) 78: Vocalion 2877

    8/8/36   Benny Goodman & His Orch. (Martha Tilton-v)
                      3tp/2tb/2as/2ts/p/g/b/d/v Bluebird AXM2-5566

    8/26/36*   BC with Kai Ewans' Orch. 3tp/2tb/3as/2ts/p/g/b/d

   ● 10/27/38   Cab Calloway (v) & His Orch. Two Flat Disc
                      5008

   ● 12/2/38   Artie Shaw & His Orch. arr: Jerry Gray (air-
                      check) Hindsight 139

● 9/20/56   Bertie King Jazz Group   Nixa (E) NJT506

NOTE: Melody Maker (May 30, 1936) reports
that Carter was commissioned by Henry Hall to
arrange this tune. It may have been broadcast
by Hall and the B. B. C. Dance Orchestra and may
be the same as the arrangement recorded on 8/
26/36*. The Whiteman Archive at Williams College has a non-Carter arrangement of this title
from the Whiteman book.   There are no known
recordings.

BLUE LIGHT BLUES (BC)
● 3/7/38*   BC [also entitled PLAYIN' THE BLUES]

BLUE LOU (E. Sampson)
10/16/33*   BC 3tp/3tb/3as/1ts/p/g/b/d

6/11/57*   BC 1as/1tb/1ts/p/g/b/d

BLUE MOON (Rodgers/Hart)
1/15/35   Benny Goodman & His Orch.   3tp/2tb/2as/2ts/p/
g/b/d/v   Sunbeam SB140

BLUE MOUNTAIN (A. Newman)
10/2/52*   BC 3tp/3tb/2as/2ts/1bs/p/g/b/d (as Love Is
Cynthia)

1955*   Alfred Newman & His Orch.   (as To Ava)

NOTE: This piece was composed by Newman for
the film The Snows of Kiliminjaro (1952).   Carter
also solos on the soundtrack. [also entitled LOVE
IS CYNTHIA and TO AVA]

BLUE ORCHIDS (H. Carmichael)
10/23/39*   BC 3tp/3tb/2as/2ts/p/g/b/d

BLUE PRELUDE (J. Bishop/G. Jenkins)

11/56   Billy Daniels (v) accompanied by Benny Carter's
Orch. 4tp/4tb/2as/2ts/1bs/p/g/b/d/v Verve
MGV2072

THE BLUE ROOM (Rodgers/Hart)
ca. 12/40   Jean Omer & His Swing Orch. 3tp/2tb/4reeds/p/
g/b/d 78: Decca (Belgium) 9010

BLUE SKIES (I. Berlin)
11/56   Billy Daniels (v) accompanied by Benny Carter's
Orch. 4tp/4tb/2as/2ts/1bs/p/g/b/d/v Verve
MGV2072

BLUE STAR (BC)
12/31/53*   BC horns/strings/p/b/d
11/15/61*   BC 2as/2ts/p/g/b/d
● 10/22/73*   BC
● 1/3/76*   BC

- 2/11/76*   BC
- 3/18/77*   BC
- 4/18/81*   BC
- June–July 1981   Eddie Johnson   Nessa n-22
- 9/26/81*   BC
- 11/28/81*   BC
- 12/4/81*   BC
- 12/5/81*   BC

BLUE TRAIN   (BC)
<u>1965</u>   Pat Dorn Orch.   4tp/4tb/2as/2ts/1bs/p/g/b/d
                           45: Capitol test pressing (may have been issued
                           commercially)

BLUE YONDER   (BC)
<u>5/63*</u>   KPM Music Library   4tp/4tb/2fr. horns/5reeds/p/
                           g/b/d/xylophone

<u>5/63*</u>   KPM Music Library   4tp/4tb/2fr. horns/5reeds/p/
                           g/b/d

                           NOTE: See notes for this session in chronologi-
                           cal section of discography.

BLUEBERRY HILL FISH FRY   see   FISH FRY

BLUEBERRY HILL JAMBOREE   see   FISH FRY

BLUEBIRDS IN THE MOONLIGHT   (R. Rainger/L. Robin)
<u>10/9/39</u>   Glenn Miller & His Orch. (Marion Hutton-v)   4tp/
                           4tb/5reeds/p/g/b/d/v   RCA (E) LFM1-7512, RCA
                           AXM2-5534
11/17/39   Glenn Miller & His Orch. (Marion Hutton-v)
                           (broadcast)
11/25/39   Glenn Miller & His Orch. (Marion Hutton-v)
                           (aircheck)   RCA Victor LPT6701

BLUES FOR BEGINNERS   (BC)
7/2/72*   BC   5tp/4tb/3as/2ts/1bs/p/g/b/d
<u>12/3/73*</u>   BC   (Hale Smith-scat v)
10/28/78*   BC

BLUES FOR THE WEEPERS   (L. Magid/M. Rich)
<u>1965</u>   Lou Rawls (v)   2tp/4tb/2reeds/p/g/b/d/v   Capitol
                           T2273

BLUES IN D FLAT   (BC)
- 2/11/76*   BC

BLUES IN MY HEART   (BC/lyrics: I. Mills/M. Parish)
<u>3/23/31</u>   King Carter & His Royal Orch.   (Dick Rogers
                           [pseudonym for Dick Robertson]-v)   3tp/2tb/3reeds/
                           p/banjo/b/d/v   78: Columbia 2439-D

                           NOTE: May be same arrangement as 3/30/31*
                           Chick Webb.

<u>3/30/31*</u>   Chick Webb & His Orch. (Louis Bacon-v)   3tp/
                           1tb/2as/1ts/p/g/b/d/v

- 5/6/31   Cab Calloway & His Orch.   78:   Banner 32221

- 9/15/31   Mildred Bailey (v) with the Casa Loma Orch.
                               arr: Gene Gifford   78: Brunswick 6190

- 9/16/31   Bert Lown & His Hotel Biltmore Orch. (Elmer
                               Feldkamp-v)   The Old Masters TOM18

- 9/23/31   Washboard Rhythm Kings (Eddie Miles-v)   78:
                               Victor 23301

- ca. 9/31   Eubie Blake & His Orch. (Dick Robertson-v)   78:
                               Crown 3197

- 10/5/31   Greta Keller (v)   78:   Decca (F) F-2592

- 10/16/31   Fletcher Henderson & His Orch. (Les Reis-v)
                               Jazz Panorama LP4

- 1931-1934   Ethel Waters (v) with the Herman Chittison Trio
                               78: Victor 20-2459

- ca. 1931   Lee Sims   78: Brunswick 6212

- 2/10/32   Spike Hughes & His Orch. (Joey Shields-v)   arr:
                               Spike Hughes   78: Parlophone R-1175

- 2/12/32   Ray Noble & His Orch. (Al Bowlly-v)   arr: Ray
                               Noble   Monmouth-Evergreen MES7021, World
                               Records SM624

- 2/23/32   Guy Lombardo & His Royal Canadians (Carmen
                               Lombardo-v)   arr: Carmen Lombardo?   78:
                               Brunswick 20104 NOTE: Medley: "Between the
                               Devil and the Deep Blue Sea introducing Blues in
                               My Heart."

- ca. 1932   Jack Payne & His Orch.   78: Imperial (E) 2665

3/27/36   Henry Hall & the B.B.C. Dance Orch.   large
                               orch.   (B.B.C. broadcast, no known airchecks)

8/17/37*   BC   3tp/3tb/2as/2ts/p/g/b/d

- 7/3/40   Glenn Miller & His Orch.   (broadcast)
9/10/40   Glenn Miller & His Orch.   (broadcast)

- 1941-1942   Bob Chester & His Orch. (Betty Bradley-v)   (air-
                               check) Big Band International LP2708

- 1943-1944   Glenn Miller & the Army Air Force Band   RCA
                               VPM6080

- 1944-1946   Joe Sullivan   Folkways FA2851

- 2/14/45   Buddy Featherstonhaugh & the Radio Rhythm Club
                               Sextet   78: HMV (E) B9406

- 10/20/45   Lem Davis Sextet   Polydor (E) 2460 137 Select
             NOTE: On the Polydor LP the positions of "Blues
             in My Heart" and "It Was Meant to Be" are re-
             versed.

- 1/24/46   All Hall's Quintet 78: Wax 101 LP: Crystal
             12503

- 1946   Roy Milton & His Solid Senders   78: Roy Milton
             111, LP: Riverboat (F) 900. 264

- 4/6/50   Chris Powell (v) & His Blue Flames 78: Colum-
             bia 30216

- 10/6-9/50   Sidney Bechet avec Claude Luter et son Orch.
             Scepter SM537, Up Front 186

- ca. 1950   Pee Wee Crayton (v?) Crown CLP5171

- 1951   Johnny Moore (Billy Valentine?-v) 78: Hollywood
             425

- ca. 1951   Eddie "Lockjaw" Davis Quartet Roost LP2227

- 1/14/53   Sticks McGhee (v) & His Buddies 78: King
             4628

- 12/28/53   Art Tatum   Clef MGC612, Pablo 2625-703

- 6/25/54*   Art Tatum - BC

- 4/6/55   Bertie King Jazz Group   Jazz Today (E) JTL5

- 4/9/56   Sammy Price   Club Francais du Disque 72

- 5/24/56   Bill Coleman (v?) Columbia (F) ESDF1119

- 1956-1957   Sam Taylor 45: MGM 12325, MGM E3553

- 7/25/57   Lee Wiley (v) arr: Bill Finegan RCA LPM1566

- 8/57   George Shearing Quintet with Dakota Staton (v)
             Capitol T1003

- 1958   Mae Barnes (v) Vanguard VSD2016

- 1958   Ann Richards (v) arr: Warren Baker   Capitol
             T1087

- ca. 1958   Bobby Hackett   arr: Stan Applebaum   Capitol
             T1172

- 2/27/59   Arnott Cobb   Prestige LP7184

- 1959   Helen Merrill (v) arr: Jimmy Jones   Metrojazz
             E1010, Metrojazz (J) MM2086

- ca. 1959   John Buzon Trio Liberty LRP3108

- 1960   Plas Johnson arr: Gerald Wilson or Rene Hall
                                Capitol (S)T1503

- 1962   Jonah Jones   Capitol T1405

- 1962   Mark Murphy (v) Riverside RM441, Riverside
                                (J) SMJ6091

- 1964   Harry Edison with Benny Carter's Orch.   arr:
                                Dick Hazard   Vee Jay VJS3065

- ca. 1964*   BC

- 10/20/69   Count Basie & His Orch.   arr: Chico O'Farrill
                                BASF MPS MC25111

- 3/1-2/71   Joe Williams (v) & George Shearing   Sheba ST102

- 4/22/72   Miss Rhapsody [Viola Wells] (v)   Matchbox
                                SDM227, Savoy SJL2233

- 2/9/74   Earle Warren & the Anglo-American All Stars
                                RCA (E) LFL1-5066

- 11/74   Ellis Larkins   Halcyon HAL113

- 2/24/75   Sonny Criss   Muse 5068

- 5/2/75   Doc Cheatham   Black and Blue (F) 33. 090, Clas-
                                sic Jazz CJ113

- 5/29/76   Joe Turner (pianist)   Classic Jazz CJ138

- 5/30/76   Milt Buckner/Arnett Cobb/Panama Francis   Black
                                and Blue (F) 333. 093

- 6/24/76*   BC

- 7/21/77   Ellis Larkins   Classic Jazz CJ145

- 1/22/79   Jazz Gala '79, Cannes, France (Joe Williams-v)
                                arr: Jimmy Jones   Personal Choice PC51001

- 4/14/80   Milt Jackson Pablo Today D2312-124

                                NOTE: The Whiteman Archive at Williams Col-
                                lege has a non-Carter arrangement of this title
                                from the Whiteman book. There are no known
                                recordings.

BOBBY (Bob Friedman)
    11/71-3/72   Carmen McRae (v) large orch/v Temponic
                                TB29562

BODY AND SOUL (J. Green/R. Sour/E. Heyman/F. Eyton)
    2/60   Dakota Staton (v) large orch with strings/v
                                Capitol T1427

    11/15/61*   BC 2as/2ts/p/g/b/d

BODYGUARD (B. Blalock)
early 1950's   Bruce Blalock (Ketty Lester?-v) small group/v
                      45: Coral 9-61884

BOOGIE MINOR   (BC)
11/25/47*   Freddie Slack & His Orch.   4tp/2tb/2as/2ts/1bs/
                      p/g/b/d

BOOGIE WOOGIE SUGAR BLUES (C. Williams/L. Fletcher)
10/23/40*   BC 3tp/2tb/2as/2ts/p/g/b/d

BOP BOUNCE   (BC)
3/30/48*   (AFRS Jubilee #284) BC large orch NOTE:
                      May have been announced under title "Little Bo
                      Bop Has Lost Her Beep." See note for 3/30/48*
                      session.

BOULEVARD BOUNCE   (BC)
4/22/47*   Lucky Thompson & His Lucky Seven 1tp/1as/1ts/
                      1bs/p/g/b/d

BOY MEETS HORN (I. Mills/D. Ellington/R. Stewart)
9/61   Jonah Jones with Glen Gray & the Casa Loma
                      Orch. 6tp/4tb/2as/2ts/1bs/p/g/b/d Capitol
                      T1713

BRAZILIAN TWIST   (BC)
1965   Pat Dorn Orch. 4tp/4tb/2as/2ts/1bs/p/g/b/d
                      45: Capitol test pressing (may have been issued
                      commercially)

BUGLE CALL RAG (Pettis/Meyers/Schoebel)
12/31/30*   The Chocolate Dandies 1tp/1tb/1as/1ts/p/g/tuba

1955   Horace Heidt & His Musical Knights 3tp/3tb/
                      4reeds/p/g/b/d 45: Magnolia MS1069

BUNBELINA (BC)
12/12/45*   BC 4tp/4tb/3as/2ts/1bs/p/g/b/d

BUSTED (H. Howard)
7/16/63   Ray Charles (v), The Raelets (v. group) 4tp/4tb/
                      2as/2ts/1bs/p/g/b/d/v/vocal group 45: ABC
                      Paramount 590X, LP: ABC Paramount 465
                      NOTE: This record won a Grammy Award for
                      Charles. Carter received a certificate from the
                      National Academy of Recording Arts and Sciences
                      in recognition of his nomination for "best back-
                      ground arrangement" of 1963.

BUT NOW I KNOW (E. Townsend)
1957   Ernie Andrews (v) with Benny Carter's Orch.
                      large orch/v GNP 28, GNP-Crescendo 10008

BY THE WATERMELON VINE, LINDY LOU (T. S. Allen)
10/23/40*   BC (Roy Felton, The Mills Brothers-v) 3tp/2tb/
                      5 reeds/p/g/b/d/v/vocal group

BYE BYE BABY (L. Handman/W. Hirsch)
     10/24/36   Henry Hall & the B. B. C. Dance Orch. (George
                                 Elrick-v) large orch/v 78: Columbia (E)
                                 FB1400

THE CALL OF THE FAR AWAY HILLS (M. David/V. Young)
     8/30/74   Yujiro Ishihara (v) 2tp/1tb/1as/2ts/1bs/p/g/b/d/
                                 14violins/4celli/v Continental (J) C01 NOTE:
                                 Instrumental tracks recorded 8/30/74, Los Ange-
                                 les; vocal added later in Japan.

CALLING ALL BARS (L. Feather)
     5/18/40   Cab Calloway & His Orch. 3tp/3tb/3as/2ts/p/g/
                                 b/d CBS (F) 62950, Jazz Archives JA8

CAN'T BUY ME LOVE (J. Lennon/P. McCartney)
     ca. 1966   Keely Smith (v) large orch/v Reprise RS6142

CAN'T WE BE FRIENDS (K. Swift/P. James)
     1/4/54*   BC horns/strings/p/b/d

CARE (Bob Friedman)
     11/71-3/72   Joe Williams (v) large orch/strings/vocal chorus/
                                 v Temponic TB29561

CATFISH ROW (BC)
     5/63*   KPM Music Library 4tp/4tb/2fr. horns/5reeds/p/
                                 g/b/d NOTE: Two brief thematic transition pas-
                                 sages for this piece were recorded at the same
                                 session. Both were arranged and composed by
                                 Carter. See notes for this session in chronologi-
                                 cal section of discography.

CHAIN GANG (S. Cooke)
     1/3-4/68   Jackie Wilson (v) with the Count Basie Orch.
                                 4tp/4tb/2as/2ts/1bs/p/g/b/d/v Brunswick
                                 BL54134

CHAMPAGNE WALTZ (B. Oakland/C. Conrad/M. Drake)
     1960-1961   Stanley Wilson Orch. 28violins/4violas/9celli/3b/
                                 2harps Time S2041

CHARLESTON IS THE BEST DANCE AFTER ALL (C. Johnson/A. Porter)
     1/24/28*   Charlie Johnson's Paradise Orch. 2tp/1tb/3as/
                                 cl/1ts/p/banjo/tuba/d

CHARMAINE (E. Rapee/L. Pollack)
     1965   Lou Rawls (v) large orch with strings/vocal
                                 group/v Capitol T2401

CHERCHEZ LA FEMME (BC)
   • 5/63*   Stanley Wilson Orch. arr: Stanley Wilson
                                 horns/strings/rhythm section

CHEROKEE (R. Noble)
     5/63*   BC 1as/p/b/d/vocal group

CHERRY (D. Redman/R. Gilbert)
     11/13/61*   BC 2as/2ts/p/g/b/d

CHICKFEED   (BC)
   5/7/36   Henry Hall & the B. B. C. Dance Orch.   large
                      orch (B. B. C. broadcast, no known airchecks)

CHILPANCINGO   (H. Atwood/L. Herscher)
   1/48*   BC (Bob Decker, The Enchanters-v) 1tp/1tb/1as/
                      1ts/p/g/b/d/v/vocal group

CHINATOWN, MY CHINATOWN   (J. Schwartz/W. Jerome)
   4/29/77*   BC   3tp/1tb/2reeds/p/g/b/d
   July 1981*   BC

                      NOTE: This arrangement includes a transcrip-
                      tion, played by three trumpets, of Louis Arm-
                      strong's solo from his 11/3/31 recording of
                      "Chinatown. "

CHOPSTICK BOOGIE
   11/25/47*   Freddie Slack & His Orch.   4tp/2tb/2as/2ts/1bs/
                      p/g/b/d

CHRISTMAS IN NEW ORLEANS   (D. Sherman/J. Van Winkle)
   9/8/55   Louis Armstrong (v) with Benny Carter's Orch.
                      3tp/2tb/1cl/2as/2ts/p/b/d/v   78: Decca 29710,
                      45: Cid (F) UM95. 504

CHRISTMAS NIGHT IN HARLEM   (R. Scott/M. Parish)
   9/8/55   Louis Armstrong (v) with Benny Carter's Orch.
                      3tp/2tb/1cl/2as/2ts/p/b/d/v   78: Decca 29710,
                      45: Cid (F) UM95. 504

CIRIBIRIBIN   (Italian; U. S. version by R. Thaler/A. Pestalozza)
   9/61   Jonah Jones with Glen Gray & the Casa Loma
                      Orch.   6tp/4tb/2as/2ts/1bs/p/g/b/d   Capitol
                      T1713

CLAUDIA   (BC/lyrics: A. Stillman)
   11/65   film soundtrack: A Man Called Adam   4tp/4tb/
                      4reeds/p/g/b/d   Reprise 6180

   ● 11/65   film soundtrack: A Man Called Adam   1tb/p/b/d
                      Reprise 6180

CLOSE YOUR EYES   (B. Petkere)
   2/60   Dakota Staton (v)   large orch with strings/v
                      Capitol T1427

COALITION   (BC)
   12/3/73*   BC   3tp/4tb/3as/2ts/1bs/p/g/b/d/conga

COCKTAILS FOR TWO   (Johnson/Coslow)
   11/19/40*   BC   3tp/3tb/2as/2ts/1bs/p/g/b/d

   2/2/42   Mark Warnow & His Orch. (Barry Wood-v) 3tp/
                      2tb/4reeds/8violins/1harp/p/g/b/d/v   78: Victor
                      27868

   9/52*   BC with the Oscar Peterson Trio with Buddy Rich
                      horns/strings/p/g/b/d

COLD COLD HEART   (H. Williams)
   1965   Lou Rawls (v)   large orch with strings/vocal
                           group/v   Capitol T2401

COME ON BABY   (A. Gottler/S. Clare/M. Pinkard)
   12/12/28*   Fletcher Henderson & His Orch. (BC-v)   2tp/1tb/
                           3reeds/p/banjo/tuba/d/v

COME ON BACK   (BC)
   3/2/66*   BC   2as/2ts/1bs/p/g/b/d

COMES LOVE   (S. Stept/C. Tobias/L. Brown)
   11/56   Billy Daniels (v) accompanied by Benny Carter's
                           Orch.   4tp/4tb/2as/2ts/1bs/p/g/b/d/v   Verve
                           MGV2072

CON ALMA   (D. Gillespie/Russell)
   ca. 1970   Benard Ito (v)   large orch   45:   Mercury 72686

CONFESSIN'   (D. Dougherty/E. Reynolds/A. Neiburg)
   4/29/77*   BC   3tp/1tb/2reeds/p/g/b/d
   4/15/78*   BC
   4/19?/78*   BC
   July 1981*   BC

CONGOROO   (BC/Lucille Ostrow)   also recorded as BAMBOULA
   late 1947 or early   (AFRS Jubilee #276)   BC   large orch
   1948*
   3/30/48*   (AFRS Jubilee #284)   BC   NOTE: May have been
                           announced as "Bamboula."

CONGRATULATIONS TO SOMEONE   (A. Frisch/R. Alfred)
   2/60   Dakota Staton (v)   large orch with strings/v
                           Capitol T1427

COTTONTAIL   (D. Ellington)
   11/15/61*   BC   2as/2ts/p/g/b/d

   12/3/73*   BC   4tp/4tb/3as/2ts/1bs/p/g/b/d
   4/8/77*   BC with the Princeton University Jazz Ensemble

   4/29/77*   BC   2tp/1tb/3reeds/p/g/b/d
   4/15/78*   BC
   4/19?/78*   BC
   July 1981*   BC

THE COURTSHIP   (BC)
   ● 4/27/76*   BC, Gillespie, Inc.

   ● 3/18/77*   BC

   ● 11/10/79*   BC with the Princeton University Jazz Ensemble
                           arr: Steve Wexler

   July 1981*   BC   2tp/1tb/3reeds/1violin/p/b/d

   ● 12/5/81*   BC

COW COW BOOGIE (BC/D. Raye/G. DePaul)
- 5/21/42   Freddie Slack & His Orch. (Ella Mae Morse-v)
                                 Capitol T1802, AJAZ 281

- 10/19/42   Benny Goodman & His Orch. (Peggy Lee-v)
                                 (aircheck) Jazz Society AA510

- 11/13/42   Gene Krupa & His Orch. (Anita O'Day-v)
                                 (aircheck) Fanfare LP10-110

- 7/27/43   R. A. F. Dance Orch. [The Squadronaires] (Sid
                                 Colin-v) 78: Decca F8364

- 11/3/43   Ella Fitzgerald (v) with The Ink Spots (v) Decca
                                 DL4129, MCA-2-4016, MCA Coral (G) 0082 050-2

- 3/46   Dave Bowman & His Orch. 78: Signature 28126

- 11/15/46   Chico Cristobal & His Boogie Woogie Boys 78:
                                 Blue Star (F) 6

- ca. 1948   Ella Mae Morse (v) 78: Capitol 15188

- 1955   Ray McKinley's Dixie Six (Ray McKinley-v)
                                 Grand Award 33-333

- 1955   Freddie Slack & His Orch. (Thelma Gracen-v)
                                 arr: Freddie Slack Emarcy MG36094, Wing
                                 MGW60003

- ca. 1956   Dick Hyman MGM E3536

- 4/15/58   Art Simmons Wing MGW12150, Wing SEW12505

- 1/8/61   Sir Charles Thompson Columbia CL1663, Colum-
                                 bia CS8463

- 1962   David Swift, with Rene Hall's Orch. arr: Rene
                                 Hall Warner Brothers B1441

- 1975   Ray Stevens (v) arr: Ray Stevens Barnaby 4009

- 1976   Charlie Byrd, Barney Kessel, Herb Ellis Con-
                                 cord CJ23

- ca. 1976   Blind John Davis Alligator 4709

- date unknown   piano roll played by J. Lawrence Cook Q. R. S.
                                 Word Roll 7739

CRACK UP (Coleman/Leigh)
11/65   film soundtrack: A Man Called Adam 1tp/1tb/p/
                                 b/d Reprise 6180

CRAZY RHYTHM (Meyer/Kahn/Caesar)
4/28/37*   Coleman Hawkins & His All Star Jam Band 2as/
                                 2ts/p/g/b/d

   11/13/61*   BC   2as/2ts/p/g/b/d

CRUISIN'   (BC)
   • 4/23/52*   (AFRS Jubilee #366)   BC

   7/26/52*   BC   1tp/1tb/3reeds/p/g/b/d

CUANDO CALIENTE EL SOL   (C. and M. Rigual)
   5/63*   BC   1as/p/b/d/vocal group

CUDDLE UP, HUDDLE UP   (BC)
   1/21/41*   BC   3tp/3tb/3as/2ts/p/g/b/d

CUTTIN' TIME   (BC)
   12/12/45*   BC   4tp/4tb/2as/2ts/1bs/p/g/b/d   NOTE: Appears
                                on Capitol LP under title "Forever Blues."
   ca. 7/46*   (AFRS Jubilee #193)   BC

DADDY DADDY   (S. Churchill/I. Berman)
   2/27/45*   Savannah Churchill & Her All Star Orch.   4tp/4tb/
                                5reeds/p/g/b/d/v

DANCE WITH ME   (Rome/Hornez/Lopez)
   5/63*   Stanley Wilson Orch.   horns/strings/vocal group/
                                rhythm section

DAY DREAM   (B. Strayhorn)
   8/13/79   Sarah Vaughan (v)   1flute/1ts/9violins/3viola/
                                2celli/p/g/b/d/v   NOTE: Recorded for Pablo--
                                unissued.

DEBBIE'S DEBUT
   date unknown   Annie Malone (v)   ?/v   45: Kady 45102

DEDICATED TO YOU   (S. Chaplin/S. Cahn/H. Zaret)
   2/60   Dakota Staton (v)   large orch with strings/v
                                Capitol T1427

DEE BLUES   (BC)
   • 12/31/30*   The Chocolate Dandies

DEVIL'S HOLIDAY   (BC)   also appears as ON A HOLIDAY
   10/16/33*   BC   3tp/3tb/3as/1ts/p/g/b/d
   1/21/35   Charlie Barnet & His Orch.   RCA Bluebird AXM2-
                                5526   NOTE: Recorded as "On a Holiday."
   4/8/38   Bunny Berigan   (probably aircheck)   Jazz Archives
                                JA11
   6/2/38   Charlie Barnet & His Orch.   (aircheck)
   6/27/38   Bunny Berigan   (Thesaurus transcription 563)
                                IAJRC 5, Collector's Classics CC15, Forsgate
                                Products SAP7500

   1/7/47   Charlie Spivak & His Orch.   (AFRS One Night
                                Stand #1259)
   1/12/47   Charlie Spivak & His Orch.   (AFRS One Night
                                Stand #1273)

2/12/47   Charlie Spivak & His Orch.   (AFRS One Night
                                 Stand #1252) Swing Era LP1017

                                 NOTE: The arrangements for Charlie Spivak are
                                 probably the same as the five listed above them.
                                 The Whiteman Archive at Williams College has an
                                 arrangement of this title from the Whiteman book.
                                 Carter does not recognize it as his own arrange-
                                 ment.   There are no known recordings.

DIRTY HANDS, DIRTY FACE (J. Monaco/E. Leslie)
                                 NOTE: Melody Maker (May 30, 1936) reports
                                 that Carter was commissioned by Henry Hall to
                                 arrange this tune.   It may have been broadcast
                                 by Hall and the B. B. C. Dance Orchestra.   There
                                 are no known airchecks.

DISCOVERY   (BC)
    5/63*   KPM Music Library   4tp/4tb/2fr. horns/5reeds/p/
                                 g/b/d NOTE: See notes for this session in
                                 chronological section of discography.

DO I NEED YOU (D. Wyatt)
    1968   Don Wyatt (v)   large orch with strings/v   NOTE:
                                 Unissued

DO YOU BELIEVE IN LOVE AT SIGHT (G. Kahn/T. Fiorito)
    9/8/31*   McKinney's Cotton Pickers (Quentin Jackson-v)
                                 3tp/2tb/3reeds/p/g/b/d/v

DOMINO   (Raye/Plante/Ferrari)
    5/63*   Stanley Wilson Orch.   horns/strings/vocal group/
                                 rhythm section

DON'T BURN THE CANDLE AT BOTH ENDS (BC/lyrics: I. Gordon)
    • 12/8/47   Louis Jordan & His Tympany Five (Martha Davis-
                                 v) 78: Decca 24483

DON'T COME TOO SOON (BC under pseudonym "Johnny Gomez"/lyrics:
I. Gordon)
    • 4/49   Julia Lee (v) & Her Boy Friends 45: Capitol
                                 1111

DON'T EXPLAIN
    6/60   Dakota Staton (v)   large orch with strings/v
                                 Capitol T1597

DON'T GET AROUND MUCH ANYMORE (D. Ellington/B. Russell)
    8/64*   BC 2ss/4as/3ts/2bs/p/g/b/d

DON'T LEAD ME ON (J. Greene/J. Anz)
    1953   Ernie Andrews (v) with Benny Carter's Orch.
                                 large orch/v 78: Trend 68, LP: GNP 28
                                 NOTE: Although the discographies list two ver-
                                 sions of this title by Ernie Andrews, one from
                                 1953 (Trend 68) and one from 1957 (GNP 28), both
                                 discs contain the same performance, probably re-
                                 corded in 1953.

DON'T LEAVE ME NOW (Westray/Freed)
   6/60   Dakota Staton (v)   large orch/v   Capitol T1490

DON'T SCREAM, DON'T SHOUT (Gabriel Jones)
   9/22/49*   Joe Robinson (v) with Benny Carter's Orch.
                             1tp/1as/1ts/1bs/p/g/b/d/v

DON'T WORRY 'BOUT ME (R. Bloom/T. Koehler)
   2/15-16/79   Ella Fitzgerald (v) with Count Basie's Orch.
                             4tp/4tb/5reeds/p/g/b/d/v   Pablo Today 2312-132

DON'T YOU FEEL MY LEG see DON'T YOU MAKE ME HIGH

DON'T YOU MAKE ME HIGH (D. Barker/K. Harris)
   12/22/74*   Maria Muldaur (v)   2tp/1tb/1as/1ts/1bs/p/g/b/d/v

DOOZY (BC)
   11/15/61*   BC   2as/2ts/p/g/b/d

   1/22-24/62   Louis Bellson Orch.   5tp/3tb/1fr. horn/1tuba/2as/
                             2ts/1bs/p/g/b/d/vib   Roulette R52087, Roulette
                             (E) 2934-020

   3/4/66*   BC   2as/2ts/1bs/p/g/b/d
   11/10/73*   BC

   7/2/72*   BC   5tp/4tb/3as/2ts/1bs/p/g/b/d

  • 10/22/73*   BC

   12/3/73*   BC   4tp/4tb/3as/2ts/1bs/p/g/b/d
   4/8/77*   BC with the Princeton University Jazz Ensemble

   12/22/74*   Maria Muldaur   2tp/1tb/2as/1ts/1bs/p/g/b/d
                             NOTE: This is instrumental feature for band.
   4/15/78*   BC

DREAM CASTLE (BC)
   5/5/46*   BC   large orch

DREAM LULLABY (BC)
   12/13/34*   BC   3tp/2tb/1cl/2as/1ts/p/g/b/d

DU BIST DIE LIEBE (Olias/Schwabach/Neiburg)
   1965   Lou Rawls (v)   large orch/strings/vocal group/v
                             Capitol T2401

EARLY SESSION HOP (Teddy Wilson/B. Harding)
   9/11/39*   Lionel Hampton & His Orch.   1tp/1as/3ts/p/g/b/
                             d/vib

EASY MONEY (C. Austin)
   12/12/28*   Fletcher Henderson & His Orch.   2tp/1tb/2as/c1/
                             1ts/p/banjo/tuba/d

EASY MONEY (BC)
   11/1-2/61*   Count Basie & His Orch.   4tp/3tb/2as/2ts/1bs/p/
                             g/b/d

| 8/10/62 | Count Basie & His Orch.   NOTE: Recorded live in Stockholm--unissued. |
| 11/9/68* | BC with Henri Chaix & His Orch.   NOTE: Similar arrangement but performed by 1tp/1tb/2as/1ts/1bs/p/b/d |

- 2/11/76*   BC
- 6/19/76*   (two versions)   BC
- 6/24/76*   BC
- 3/18/77*   BC
- 4/18/81*   BC
- 11/28/81*   BC
- 12/4/81*   BC
- 12/5/81*   BC

ECHOES OF HARLEM   (D. Ellington)
9/61   Jonah Jones with Glen Gray & the Casa Loma
                            Orch.   6tp/4tb/2as/2ts/1bs/p/g/b/d   Capitol T1713

EVEN WHEN YOU CRY   (Q. Jones/M. Bergman/A. Bergman)
1/3-4/68   Jackie Wilson (v) with the Count Basie Orch.
                            4tp/4tb/2as/2ts/1bs/p/g/b/d/v   Brunswick
                            BL54134

EVERYBODY SHUFFLE   (BC)
10/13/33   Joe Venuti & His Orch.   3tp/2tb/4reeds/p/g/b/d
                            RCA (F) FPM1-7016
12/13/34*   BC

EVERYBODY'S SOMEBODY'S FOOL   (Hampton/Adams/Adams)
6/60   Dakota Staton (v)   large orch/v   Capitol T1490

EV'RY GOODBYE AIN'T GONE   (BC)
1/21/41*   BC   3tp/3tb/3as/2ts/p/g/b/d

THE FABLE OF A FOOL   (BC)
8/31/39*   BC   3tp/3tb/3as/2ts/p/g/b/d   NOTE: On most
                            issues as "Favor of a Fool."

FAIRY TALES   (G. Shearing)
8/64*   BC   2ss/4as/3ts/2bs/p/g/b/d

FALLING IN LOVE WITH LOVE   (Rodgers/Hart)
1962   Sarah Vaughan (v)   4tp/4tb/5reeds/p/g/b/d/vib/v
                            Roulette R(S)52092, Roulette (E) 2682-043

FANTASTIC, THAT'S YOU   (G. Cates/G. Douglas)
3/2/66*   BC   2as/2ts/1bs/p/g/b/d

FAREWELL BLUES   (Mares/Rappolo/Schoebel)
3/7/38*   BC   2as/2ts/p/g/b/d

THE FAVOR OF A FOOL   see   FABLE OF A FOOL

FEASANT PHEATHERS   (BC)
- 11/10/79*   BC with the Princeton University Jazz Ensemble

FEBRUARY FIESTA   (H. Schaefer)
late 1958 or early   BC   4tp/3tb/5reeds/p/g/b/d
1959*

FEUDIN' AND FIGHTIN'   (Dubin/Lane/Lane)
1964   Ray Charles (v) & the Raelets 5tp/3tb/2as/2ts/
                       1bs/p/g/b/d/v ABC Paramount 495

FIRST THINGS FIRST
6/60   Dakota Staton (v) large orch with strings/v 45:
                       Capitol 4465

FISH FRY   (BC)
1/30/40*   BC   3tp/3tb/2as/2ts/p/g/b/d
3/24/43*   BC
May or later 1943*   (AFRS Basic Library P-33) BC
5/8/45*   (AFRS Jubilee #132) BC
ca. 7/47*   (AFRS Jubilee #248) BC

FLAMINGO   (T. Grouya/E. Anderson)
12/31/53*   BC horns/strings/p/b/d

FLOWER DRUM SONG [film title]   (Rodgers/Hammerstein)
                       NOTE: Carter played in the orchestra and as-
                       sisted in the orchestration of parts of this 1961
                       production. The soundtrack is on Decca DL79098
                       (later labelled MCA2069).

A FOGGY DAY   (G. and I. Gershwin)
1/22-24/62   Louis Bellson Orch. 5tp/3tb/1fr. horn/1tuba/2as/
                       2ts/1bs/p/g/b/d/vib Roulette R25167

THE FOLKS WHO LIVE ON THE HILL   (J. Kern/O. Hammerstein II)
6/60   Dakota Staton (v) large orch with strings/v
                       Capitol T1597

FOR SALE - ONE BROKEN HEART   (Hoffman/Saronne)
early 1950's   Ruby Lane (v) large orch with strings 45: Col-
                       pix CP139

FOR YOUR PRECIOUS LOVE   (A. Brooks/R. Brooks/J. Butler)
1/3-4/68   Jackie Wilson (v) with the Count Basie Orch.
                       4tp/4tb/2as/2ts/1bs/p/g/b/d/v 45: Brunswick
                       BR55365, LP: Brunswick BL54134

FOREVER BLUE   (BC)
                       NOTE: This piece by Carter may have been re-
                       corded by his orchestra in 1945 but was never re-
                       leased. A recording for Capitol done on 12/12/45*
                       by Benny Carter was labelled "Forever Blues"
                       but is actually his composition "Cuttin' Time."

FREE LOVE   (BC/E. Sampson)
  11/6/33*   Mezz Mezzrow & His Orch.   3tp/1tb/2as/1ts/p/
                             g/b/d

FRIENDLESS   (BC/lyrics: P. Vandervoort)
  1/63   Sarah Vaughan (v) with orchestra directed by
                             Benny Carter 4tb/20strings/p/g/b/d/v Roulette
                             R(S)52104

FRIENDLY ISLANDS   (BC--words & music)
  ● 1959   Ethel Azama (v) arr: Paul Conrad Liberty
                             LRP3104

FUNKY BROADWAY   (A. Christian)
  1/3-4/68   Jackie Wilson (v) with the Count Basie Orch.
                             4tp/4tb/2as/2ts/1bs/p/g/b/d/v Brunswick
                             BL54134

THE GANG'S ALL HERE [film title]
                             NOTE: For Carter's work on this film see the
                             individual title "No Love, No Nothin.'"

A GARDEN IN THE RAIN   (C. Gibbons/J. Dyrenforth)
  1962   Sarah Vaughan (v) 4tp/4tb/5reeds/p/g/b/d/vib/v
                             Roulette R(S)52092, Roulette (E) 2682-043

GEE, AIN'T I GOOD TO YOU   (D. Redman/A. Razaf)
  1965   Lou Rawls (v) 2tp/4tb/2reeds/p/g/b/d/v Capitol
                             T2273

  12/22/74*   Maria Muldaur (v) 2tp/1tb/1as/1ts/1bs/p/g/b/d/v

GEORGIA ON MY MIND   (H. Carmichael)
  8/18/52*   BC 3tp/3tb/2as/2ts/1bs/p/g/b/d

GIN AND JIVE   (BC)   also entitled SAVOY STAMPEDE
  mid 6/36*   BC 2tp/2tb/2as/2ts/p/g/b/d
  1/11-16/37*   BC
  4/17/39*   BC
  6/29/39*   BC (as Savoy Stampede)
  10/9/39*   BC (as Savoy Stampede)

THE GIRL FROM IPANEMA   (Jobim/de Moraes/Gimbel)
  8/64*   BC 2ss/4as/3ts/2bs/p/g/b/d

  1964   Harry Edison with Benny Carter's Orch.   1tp/4tb/
                             14strings/1harp/p/g/b/d Vee-Jay VJS3065

THE GIRL UPSTAIRS   (A. Newman)
  1955   Alfred Newman & His Orch.   large orch with
                             strings Decca DL8123

GLOAMING   (T. Ehrling)
  9/12/36*   BC 3tp/2tb/3as/1ts/p/g/b/d

GO NOW   (BC)
  11/65   film soundtrack: A Man Called Adam 1tp/1tb/p/
                             b/d Reprise 6180

GOD BLESS THE CHILD   (A. Herzog, Jr./B. Holiday)
    4/29/77*   BC   2tp/1tb/3reeds/p/g/b/d

GOD BLESS YOU   (Bob Friedman)
    11/71-3/72   Joe Williams (v)   large orch with strings/v
                         Temponic TB29561

GOIN' ON   (BC)
    10/30-31/61*   Count Basie & His Orch.   4tp/3tb/2as/2ts/1bs/p/
                         g/b/d

GONNA BUILD A MOUNTAIN   (L. Bricusse/A. Newley)
    1965   Pat Dorn Orch.   4tp/4tb/2as/2ts/1bs/p/g/b/d
                         45: Capitol test pressing (may have been issued
                         commercially)

GOOD FOR NOTHIN' JOE   (R. Bloom)
    Jan.-Feb. 1943*   film soundtrack: Stormy Weather (Lena Horne-v)
                         large orch with strings/v

GOODBYE BLUES   (BC)
    12/4/30*   The Chocolate Dandies (BC-v) 1tp/1tb/1as/1ts/p/
                         g/b/v

GOT ANOTHER SWEETIE NOW   (J. Harrison)
    12/31/30*   The Chocolate Dandies (Jimmy Harrison-v) 1tp/
                         1tb/1as/1ts/p/g/tuba/v

GOT THAT FEELING   (Bob Friedman)
    11/71-3/72   Joe Williams (v)   large orch/v Temponic
                         TB29561

GOTTA GO HOME   (BC)
    5/63*   KPM Music Library 4tp/4tb/2fr. horns/5reeds/p/
                         g/b/d NOTE: See notes for this session in
                         chronological section of discography.

GREAT DAY   (V. Youmans/B. Rose/E. Eliscu)
    1962   Sarah Vaughan (v) 4tp/4tb/5reeds/p/g/b/d/vib/v
                         Roulette R(S)52092, Roulette (E) 2682-043

THE GREAT LIE   (Lester Young)
    8/64*   BC 2ss/4as/3ts/2bs/p/g/b/d

GREEN DOLPHIN STREET see ON GREEN DOLPHIN STREET

GREEN WINE   (BC/lyrics: L. Feather) see also VINHO VERDE
    ● 2/11/76*   BC

    ● 3/18/77*   BC

GUIDING LIGHT   (BC/lyrics: Romola Robinson) [copyrighted as MY GUID-
ING LIGHT]
    ● 1960   Dihann Carroll (v) arr: Al Cohn 45: United
                         Artists UA142X

GUMSHOE   (BC)
    1/22-24/62   Louis Bellson Orch. 5tp/3tb/1fr. horn/1tuba/2as/

2ts/1bs/p/g/b/d/vib   Roulette R52087, Roulette
(E) 2934-020

THE GUNS OF NAVARONE [film soundtrack]
                    NOTE: For Carter's work on this film see the
                    individual title "Yassu."

THE GYPSY   (B. Reid)
   5/63*   BC   1as/p/b/d/vocal group

THE GYPSY IN MY SOUL   (M. Jaffe/C. Boland)
   ca. 1959   Dean Jones (v)   ?/v   MGM K12462

HALLELUJAH   (V. Youmans/L. Robin/C. Grey)
   11/56   Billy Daniels (v) accompanied by Benny Carter's
                    Orch.   4tp/4tb/2as/2ts/1bs/p/g/b/d/v   Verve
                    MGV2072

HAPPY AS THE DAY IS LONG   (H. Arlen/T. Koehler)
   9/11/34   Fletcher Henderson & His Orch.   3tp/2tb/1cl/2as/
                    1ts/p/g/b/d   Decca DL9228, MCA 1318, Time-
                    Life STL-J10
   7/29/71   Time-Life series The Swing Era (Billy May-lead-
                    er)   Time-Life STL340   NOTE: In the Time-Life
                    series significant swing era performances are
                    "recreated" including imitations of the solos
                    present on the original recordings.

THE HAPPY ONES   (Bob Friedman)
   11/71-3/72   Carmen McRae (v)   large orch/v   Temponic
                    TB29562

A HARD DAY'S NIGHT   (J. Lennon/P. McCartney)
   ca. 1966   Keely Smith (v)   large orch with strings/v   Re-
                    prise RS6142

HARLEM ON PARADE   (BC/lyrics: Redd Evans)
   ● 1/23/42   Gene Krupa & His Orch. (Anita O'Day-v)   78:
                    Okeh 6607, LP: Ajax 167

A HEART MUST LEARN TO CRY   (D. Tiomkin/P. F. Webster)
   ca. 1966   Irma Curry (v)   large orch/v   45: Vee-Jay 669

HEEBIE JEEBIES   (B. Atkins)
   3/30/31*   Chick Webb & His Orch.   3tp/1tb/2as/c1/1ts/p/
                    g/b/d
   6/26/31   Mills Blue Rhythm Band (Chick Bullock-v)   RCA
                    (F) 741. 045

HEELS UP   (BC)
   5/63*   KPM Music Library   4tp/4tb/2fr. horns/5reeds/p/
                    g/b/d/xylophone   NOTE: See notes for this ses-
                    sion in chronological section of discography.

HELLS BELLS   (A. Kassel)
   date unknown   Annie Malone (v)   ?/v   45: Kady 45102

HERE IT IS TOMORROW AGAIN
    10/31/38*   Teddy Wilson & His Orch. (Billie Holiday-v)
                                 1tp/1tb/2as/2ts/p/g/b/d/v

HERE'S THAT RAINY DAY (J. Van Heusen/J. Burke)
    1971   Pearl Bailey (v) 4tp/4tb/5reeds/p/g/b/d/strings/v
                                 RCA LSP4529

HE'S GOT TWO LEFT HANDS see TWO LEFT HANDS

HEY LAWDY MAMA (Easton)
    6/60   Dakota Staton (v) 1tp/1reed/p/g/b/d/v   Capitol
                                 T1597

HEY THERE (Adler/Ross)
    Mar. 30-Apr. 1   Pearl Bailey (v) 4tp/4tb/5reeds/p/g/b/d/v
    1965*

HIGH SOCIETY LIMBO (BC)
    1965   Pat Dorn Orch. 4tp/4tb/2as/2ts/1bs/p/g/b/d 45:
                                 Capitol test pressing (may have been issued com-
                                 mercially)

HOBNOBBIN' (BC)
    4/8/77   Princeton University Jazz Ensemble 5tp/4tb/
                                 5reeds/p/g/b/d (private tape--concert) NOTE:
                                 This Carter composition was published in the
                                 Repertory Stage Band Series.

HOLD ME TIGHT, I'M FALLING
    ca. 5/36   Henry Hall & the B. B. C. Dance Orch.   large
                                 orch (B. B. C. broadcast, no known airchecks)

HOLLYRIDGE DRIVE (BC)
    10/14/47*   Red Norvo's Nine 1cornet/1as/2ts/p/g/b/d
    late 1947 or early   (AFRS Jubilee #276) BC
    1948*

A HOME IN THE CLOUDS (BC/B. Goodman/B. Henderson/K. Parker)
    ● 2/9/39   Benny Goodman & His Orch. (Martha Tilton-v)
                                 Jazum 19

    ● 5/1/39   Dick Todd (v), The Three Reasons (v. group)
                                 Victor AXM2-5509

    5/13/39*   BC (Mercedes Carter-v) 3tp/3tb/2as/2ts/p/g/b/
                                 d/v
    7/24/39*   BC (Dell St. John-v)

    ● 5/17/39   Ray Herbeck & His Music with Romance (Betty
                                 Bronson, Kirby Brooks-v) 78: Vocalion 4876

    ● 5/22/39   Shep Fields & His Rippling Rhythm (Hal Derwin-v)
                                 78: Bluebird B-10291

    ● 5/26/39   Jimmy Dorsey & His Orch. (Helen O'Connell-v)
                                 78: Decca 2522

● 3/69   Bobby Henderson   Chiaroscuro 122

● 3/69   Bobby Henderson   Halcyon (also labelled Chiaro-
                                scuro) 102

HONEYSUCKLE ROSE   (T. Waller/A. Razaf)
    4/28/37*   Coleman Hawkins & His All Star Jam Band   2as/
                                2ts/p/g/b/d

    4/17/39*   BC   3tp/3tb/2as/2ts/p/g/b/d
    4/22/39*   BC
    7/24/39*   BC

    1943*   Lena Horne (v) with Benny Carter's Orch.   large
                                orch/v

    11/13/61*   BC   2as/2ts/p/g/b/d

    1962   Sarah Vaughan (v)   4tp/4tb/5reeds/p/g/b/d/vib/v
                                Roulette R(S)52092, Roulette (E) 2582-043

    7/2/72*   BC   5tp/4tb/3as/2ts/1bs/p/g/b/d
    12/3/73*   BC
    10/28/78*   BC with the University of Buffalo Jazz Ensemble
                                directed by Sam Falzone
    10/28/78*   BC with the University of Buffalo Jazz Ensemble
                                directed by Phil Sims

    2/15-16/79   Ella Fitzgerald (v) with Count Basie's Orch.   4tp/
                                4tb/5reeds/p/g/b/d/v   Pablo Today 2312-132

HONGI TONGI HOKI POKI   (BC/lyrics: A. and C. Hanson)
    ● 1950   Gordon MacRae (v) with the Les Baxter Chorus
                                & Paul Weston & His Orch.   arr: Paul Weston
                                78: Capitol 1021

HOT LIPS   (H. Busse/H. Lange/L. Davis)
    9/61   Jonah Jones with Glen Gray & the Casa Loma
                                Orch.   6tp/4tb/2as/2ts/1bs/p/g/b/d   Capitol T1713

HOT TODDY   (BC)
    6/9/32   Cab Calloway & His Orch.   3tp/2tb/2ts/p/g/b/d
                                (unissued)
    9/21/32   Cab Calloway & His Orch.   Collector's Classics
                                20
    10/5/32*   BC
    1932   Cab Calloway (v) & His Orch. in film: The Big
                                Broadcast of 1932
                                NOTE: These are all probably the same arrange-
                                ment.

A HOUSE IS NOT A HOME   (B. Bacharach/H. David)
    1971   Pearl Bailey (v)   4tp/4tb/5reeds/p/g/b/d/strings/v
                                RCA LSP4529

A HOUSE WITH A LITTLE RED BARN   (M. Lewis/N. Hamilton)
    2/14/40*   Freddie Rich & His Orch. (Rosemary Calvin-v)
                                3tp/1tb/3as/3ts/p/g/b/d/v

HOW AM I TO KNOW? (J. King/D. Parker)
   <u>11/56</u>   Billy Daniels (v) accompanied by Benny Carter's
                     Orch. 1tp/4reeds/p/g/b/d/strings/v Verve
                     MGV2072

HOW CAN YOU LOSE? (BC)
   <u>10/7/57</u>*   BC 1tp/1tb/1as/1ts/p/g/b/d

   ● 10/24-25/60   Art Pepper Quintet Contemporary M3602, Con-
                     temporary S7602

HOW DEEP IS THE OCEAN (I. Berlin)
   <u>ca. 1958</u>   Lois Peters (v) 5brass/4reeds/rhythm section/
                     strings/v 45: Decca 9-30269

HOW HIGH THE MOON (M. Lewis/N. Hamilton)
   <u>2/14/40</u>*   Freddie Rich & His Orch. (Rosemary Calvin-v)
                     3tp/1tb/3as/3ts/p/g/b/d/v

HOW LONG IS A MOMENT (BC/lyrics: P. Zeller)
   <u>1958</u>*   Don Evans (v) with Orch. under direction of
                     Benny Carter 1as/p/g/b/d/v

HOW STRANGE (H. Stothart/E. Brent/G. Kahn)
   <u>5/27/39</u>*   BC (Mercedes Carter-v) 3tp/3tb/2as/2ts/p/g/b/
                     d/v

A HUNDRED YEARS FROM TODAY (V. Young/N. Washington)
   <u>1957</u>   Martha Davis (v) 4tp/4tb/2as/2ts/1bs/p/g/b/d/v
                     NOTE: Recorded for ABC Paramount--unissued.

HURRY HURRY (BC/lyrics: R. Larkin [pseudonym for Dave Dexter])
   ● 10/25/43*   BC (Savannah Churchill-v) arr: Frank Comstock

   ● 4/6/44   Christine Chatham & Her Orch. (Mabel Smith
                     [Big Maybelle]-v) 78: Decca 8660

   ● 5/26/44   Lucky Millinder & His Orch. (Wynonie Harris-v)
                     MCA (F) 510. 065, MCA 1319

   ● 1953-1955   Pee Wee Crayton (v) 78: Imperial 5297

   ● 1958   Ruth Olay (v) arr: Jerry Fielding Mercury
                     MG20390

I AIN'T GETTIN' ANY YOUNGER (BC/lyrics: A. Hanson) also entitled
I AIN'T GONNA WAIT TOO LONG
   <u>1947</u>*   Anita O'Day (v) 12 piece orch/v

   ● 12/30/48   Woody Herman (v) & His Orch. arr: Shorty
                     Rogers Capitol (E) CL13060 (as I Ain't Gonna
                     Wait Too Long)

   ● 1949   Martha Davis (v) Decca 48174

I AIN'T GONNA WAIT TOO LONG see I AIN'T GETTIN' ANY YOUNGER

I AIN'T GOT NOBODY (Spencer Williams)
     8/17/37*   BC   3tp/2tb/2as/2ts/p/g/b/d
     4/22/39*   BC

     1949   Debbie Andrews (v)   ?/v 78: Mercury 8282

                              NOTE: Melody Maker (May 30, 1936) reports
                              that Carter was commissioned by Henry Hall to
                              arrange this tune. It may have been broadcast
                              by Hall and the B. B. C. Dance Orchestra and may
                              be the same as the arrangement recorded on 8/17/
                              37*. There are no known airchecks.

I AM YOUR DREAM (Tiomkin/Webster)
     ca. 1958*   Kitty White (v) with Benny Carter & His Orch.
                              1tb/1fr. horn/1as/p/g/b/d/v

I BELIEVE IN YOU (F. Loesser)
     8/61   Peggy Lee (v)   4tp/4tb/5reeds/p/g/b/d/v   Capitol
                              T1772

     1962   Sarah Vaughan (v)   4tp/4tb/5reeds/p/g/b/d/vib/v
                              45: Roulette 4516, LP: Roulette R(S)52092,
                              Roulette (E) 2682-043

I CAN'T ESCAPE FROM YOU (L. Robin/R. Whiting)
     5/21/44*   BC   4tp/3tb/2as/2ts/1bs/p/g/b/d

I CAN'T GET STARTED (V. Duke/I. Gershwin)
     12/18/42*   (AFRS Jubilee #4) BC   4tp/3tb/2as/2ts/p/g/b/d
                              NOTE: Probably same arrangement as two below.
     5/21/44*   BC
     Apr.-May 1946*   (AFRS Jubilee #184) BC

     3/24/43*   BC   large orch

     2/60   Dakota Staton (v)   large orch with strings/v
                              Capitol T1427

     9/61   Jonah Jones with Glen Gray & the Casa Loma
                              Orch.   6tp/4tb/2as/2ts/1bs/p/g/b/d   Capitol T1713

     7/2/72*   BC   5tp/4tb/3as/2ts/1bs/p/g/b/d
     12/3/73*   BC
     4/8/77*   BC with the Princeton University Jazz Ensemble
     10/28/78*   BC with the University of Buffalo Jazz Ensemble
                              directed by Sam Falzone
     10/28/78*   BC with the University of Buffalo Jazz Ensemble
                              directed by Phil Sims
                              NOTE: Ending differs slightly on University of
                              Buffalo recordings.

I CAN'T GIVE YOU ANYTHING BUT LOVE (J. McHugh/D. Fields)
     Jan.-Feb. 1943*   film soundtrack: Stormy Weather (Lena Horne,
                              Bill Robinson-v)   large orch with strings/v/vocal
                              group

     1962   Sarah Vaughan (v)   4tp/4tb/5reeds/p/g/b/d/vib/v
                              Roulette R(S)52092, Roulette (E) 2682-043

I COVER THE WATERFRONT (G. Green/E. Heyman)
    4/30/46*   BC   large orch
    ca. July 1946*   (AFRS Jubilee #193) BC

I CRIED FOR YOU (G. Arnheim/A. Lyman/A. Freed)
    5/13/39*   BC (Mercedes Carter-v) 3tp/3tb/2as/2ts/p/g/b/
                         d/v

I DIDN'T LIKE IT THE FIRST TIME   (BC under pseudonym "Johnny Gomez"
/lyrics: I. Gordon)
    • 11/13/47*   Julia Lee (v) & Her Boy Friends arr: Dave
                         Cavanaugh 1tb/1as/1ts/p/g/b/d/v

I DIDN'T SAY YES (I DIDN'T SAY NO) (O. Harbach/J. Kern)
    1956   Abbey Lincoln (v) large orch/v 45: Liberty
                         F55035

I DON'T KNOW WHAT KIND OF BLUES I'VE GOT (D. Ellington)
    1964   Harry Edison with Benny Carter's Orch. 1tp/4tb/
                         14strings/1harp/p/g/b/d Vee-Jay VJS3065

I DON'T WANT IT NO MORE   (BC under pseudonym "Johnny Gomez"/lyrics:
B. Strother, B. Ide)
    • 12/14/48*   Clarence Clump (v) with Orch. NOTE: Clarence
                         Clump is a pseudonym for Benny Carter.

I GOT IT BAD (D. Ellington/P. F. Webster)
    8/14/79   Zoot Sims 4tp/4tb/2as/2ts/1bs/p/g/b/d Pablo
                         Today 2312-120 NOTE: This arrangement was
                         written for Sarah Vaughan, but at session Sims
                         substituted as featured soloist.

I GOT RHYTHM (G. and I. Gershwin)
    3/27/36   Henry Hall & the B.B.C. Dance Orch. large
                         orch (B.B.C. broadcast, no known airchecks)

I GOTTA GO (BC/lyrics: Spencer Williams)
    mid 6/36*   BC (Elisabeth Welch-v) 3tp/2tb/4reeds/p/g/b/d/v

I HAVEN'T GOT ANYTHING BETTER TO DO (P. Vance/L. Pockriss)
    1968   Carmen McRae (v) large orch with strings/v
                         Atlantic SD8165

I LET A SONG GO OUT OF MY HEART (D. Ellington/Mills/Nemo)
    8/14/79   Zoot Sims 4tp/4tb/2as/2ts/1bs/p/g/b/d Pablo
                         Today 2312-120 NOTE: This arrangement was
                         written for Sarah Vaughan, but at session Sims
                         substituted as featured soloist.

I LIKE A SHUFFLE BEAT (P. Vandervoort)
    1954   Jimmie Maddin (v) & His Orch. small orch/v
                         78: Skyway 104

I LONG FOR YOU (K. E. Beam)
    date unknown   Arthur Lee Simpkins (v) p/vib/g/b/d/v/vocal
                         group 45: Miranda 4-56-14

I LOST YOU
    1949   Debbie Andrews (v) ?/v 78: Mercury 8282

I LOVE YOU FOR THAT (Fischer/Carey)
    ca. 1951   Frankie Laine (v) & Patti Page (v) with Harry
                       Geller Orch. large orch/v 78: Mercury 5442

I NEVER KNEW (Fiorito/Kahn)
    10/10/33*   The Chocolate Dandies 2tp/1tb/1as/1ts/p/g/b/d

    5/7/36   Henry Hall & the B. B. C. Dance Orch. large
                       orch (B. B. C. broadcast, no known airchecks)

I NEVER LOVED A MAN see I NEVER LOVED A WOMAN

I NEVER LOVED A WOMAN (R. Shannon) [original title: I NEVER LOVED
A MAN]
    1/3-4/68   Jackie Wilson (v) with Count Basie's Orch. 4tp/
                       4tb/2as/2ts/1bs/p/g/b/d/v Brunswick BL54134

I NEVER MENTION YOUR NAME
    1944*   (AFRS Basic Library P-238) BC (Savannah
                       Churchill-v) large orch/v

I NEVER MET A STRANGER (D. Redman)
    1971   Pearl Bailey (v) 4tp/4tb/5reeds/p/g/b/d/strings/v
                       RCA LSP4529

I RESOLVE (Sourwine/Cunningham/Whitcup)
    date unknown   Arthur Lee Simpkins (v) p/vib/g/b/d/v/vocal
                       group 45: Miranda 4-56-13

I SAID NO (J. Styne/F. Loesser)
    9/29/70   Mrs. Miller (v) 2tp/2tb/2as/1ts/1bs/p/g/b/d/v
                       45: Mrs. Miller Records (no issue number)

I SHOULDA QUIT WHEN I WAS AHEAD (Livingston/Evans)
    Mar. 30-Apr. 1   Pearl Bailey (v) 4tp/4tb/5reeds/p/g/b/d/v
    1965*

I STILL LOVE HIM SO (BC) [also recorded under title I'D LOVE HIM SO]
    • 3/28/51   Roy Eldridge Quintet Inner City IC7012 (as I'd
                       Love Him So)

    • 3/23/55*   Roy Eldridge - Benny Carter Sextet

    • 1/16/76   Roy Eldridge Pablo 2310-766

    • 2/11/76*   BC

I STOLE DE WEDDING BELL (BC/lyrics: P. Vandervoort)
    1954   Jimmie Maddin (v) & His Orch. small orch/v
                       78: Skyway 104

I SURRENDER DEAR (H. Barris/G. Clifford)
    5/21/44*   BC 4tp/3tb/2as/2ts/p/g/b/d
    6/12/44*   (AFRS Jubilee #83?) BC
    ca. July 1946*   (AFRS Jubilee #205) BC
    2/17/72   Time-Life series The Swing Era (Billy May-lead-
                       er) Time-Life STL353 NOTE: This is a recre-
                       ation of Carter's 5/21/44* performance including

imitations of the solos.   Carter's trumpet solo
is played by Joe Graves.

I WANNA BE AROUND   (J. Mercer)
  8/64*   BC   2ss/4as/3ts/2bs/p/g/b/d

I WANT TO HOLD YOUR HAND   (Lennon/McCartney)
  ca. 1966   Keely Smith (v)   large orch with strings/v Re-
                             prise RS6142

I WAS MADE TO LOVE HER   (H. Cosby/L. Hardaway/S. Wonder/S. Moy)
  1/3-4/68   Jackie Wilson (v) with Count Basie's Orch.   4tp/
                             4tb/2as/2ts/1bs/p/g/b/d/v   Brunswick BL54134

I WON'T WORRY
  6/60   Dakota Staton (v)   large orch with strings/v
                             Capitol T1597

I'D LOVE HIM SO   see   I STILL LOVE HIM SO

I'D RATHER BE A ROOSTER   (BC/lyrics: P. Vance)
  ● ca. 1949   Scat Man Crothers (v)   78: London 17008

IF DREAMS COME TRUE   (E. Sampson/B. Goodman)
  3/2/66*   BC   2as/2ts/1bs/p/g/b/d
  11/10/73*   BC

IF I CAN'T HAVE YOU   (BC--words & music)
  5/5/46*   BC (Candy Ross-v)   large orch/v

  9/22/49*   Joe Robinson with Benny Carter's Orch.   1tp/1as/
                             1ts/1bs/p/g/b/d/v

IF I HAD MY LIVE TO LIVE OVER   (Tobias/Jaffe/Vincent)
  1965   Lou Rawls (v)   2tp/4tb/2reeds/p/g/b/d/v   Capitol
                             T2273

IF I HAD YOU   (I. Berlin)
  1/63   Sarah Vaughan (v)   4fr. horns/p/g/b/d/1tuba/v
                             Roulette R(S)52104

IF I LOVE AGAIN   (B. Oakland/J. P. Murray)
  6/60   Dakota Staton (v)   large orch/v   Capitol T1490

IF IT'S THE LAST THING I DO   (S. Cahn/S. Chaplin)
  1965   Lou Rawls (v)   2tp/4tb/2reeds/p/g/b/d/v   Capitol
                             T2273

IF ONLY I COULD READ YOUR MIND   (BC/L. Feather)
  mid 6/36*   BC   3tp/2tb/2as/2ts/p/g/b/d

IF YOU GO   (Parsons/Emer)
  5/63*   Stanley Wilson Orch.   horns/strings/rhythm sec-
                             tion

I'LL BE AROUND   (A. Wilder)
  12/31/53*   BC   horns/strings/p/b/d

I'LL BE HERE WITH YOU   (BC--words & music)
   • 1968   Billy Eckstine (v) arr: Jimmy Jones Motown
                            MS677

I'LL BE YOUR BRIDE AGAIN   (G. Steinman)
   ca. 1958   Lois Peters (v) with the Ravenscroft Singers &
                            Orch. 5brass/4woodwinds/rhythm section/strings/
                            v/vocal group 45: Decca 9-30269

I'LL CLOSE MY EYES   (B. Reid/B. Kaye)
   6/60   Dakota Staton (v) large orch/v Capitol T1490

I'LL NEVER BE THE SAME   (Kahn/Malneck/Signorelli)
   1/63   Sarah Vaughan (v) 4tp/4tb/2as/2ts/1bs/p/g/b/d/v
                            Roulette R(S)52104

I'LL NEVER FAIL YOU   (V. Mizzy/I. Taylor)
   11/9/38*   Teddy Wilson & His Orch. (Billie Holiday-v) 1tp/
                            1tb/2as/2ts/p/g/b/d/v

I'LL NEVER GIVE IN   (Freddy Johnson)
   3/24/37*   BC & the Ramblers 2tp/1tb/2as/2ts/p/b/d

I'LL NEVER LEAVE YOU
   1968   Don Wyatt (v) large orch with strings/v (unis-
                            sued)

I'LL NEVER PASS THIS WAY AGAIN   (Bob Friedman)
   11/71-3/72   Carmen McRae (v) large orch/v Temponic
                            TB29562

I'LL PLANT MY OWN TREE   (D. and A. Previn)
   1967   film soundtrack: Valley of the Dolls (unidentified
                            female-v) large orch with strings/v Twentieth
                            Century Fox S4196

I'LL REMEMBER APRIL   (DePaul/Johnson/Raye)
   late 1958 or early   BC 4tp/3tb/5reeds/p/g/b/d
   1959*

I'LL SEE YOU IN MY DREAMS   (I. Jones/G. Kahn)
   1965   Lou Rawls (v) large orch with strings/vocal
                            group/v Capitol T2401

ILL WIND   (Koehler/Arlen)
   10/16/41*   BC 3tp/3tb/3as/2ts/p/g/b/d
   probably late 1942*   (AFRS Basic Library of Popular Music P-8) BC
                            (Savannah Churchill-v)
                            NOTE: Probably same arrangement as the three
                            others.
   4/10/43*   BC
   May or later 1943*   (AFRS Basic Library P-33) BC

I'M A LUCKY GUY   (Bob Friedman)
   11/71-3/72   Joe Williams (v) large orch/v Temponic
                            TB29561

I'M A THREE TIME LOSER   (BC/lyrics: I. Gordon)
   • 9/22/47*   Joe Alexander (v)

I'M A WOMAN   (J. Lieber/M. Stoller)
   7/62   Peggy Lee (v) 1tp/1ts/p/g/b/d/v 45: Capitol
                           4888, LP: Capitol SM386, Capitol STC L576

I'M ALONE WITH YOU   see LONESOME NIGHTS

I'M ALWAYS DRUNK IN SAN FRANCISCO   (T. Wolf)
   1968   Carmen McRae (v) large orch with strings/v
                           Atlantic SD8165

I'M BEGINNING TO SEE THE LIGHT   (Ellington/Hodges/James)
   July 1981*   BC 2tp/1tb/3reeds/1violin/p/b/d

I'M COMING VIRGINIA   (D. Heywood)
   3/7/38*   BC 2as/2ts/p/g/b/d

   4/17/39*   BC 3tp/3tb/2as/2ts/p/g/b/d NOTE: Saxophone
                         arrangement similar to 3/7/38* above.
   5/6/39*   BC (Mercedes Carter-v)

   7/22/57*   BC 1tp/1tb/1ts/p/g/b/d

I'M FOREVER BLOWING BUBBLES   (J. Kenbrovin/J. Kellette)
   2/14/40*   Freddie Rich & His Orch.   3tp/1tb/3as/3ts/p/g/
                         b/d

I'M GETTING SENTIMENTAL OVER YOU   (G. Bassman/N. Washington)
   9/11/34   The Modernists [Benny Goodman & Orch.] (Tony
                         Sacco-v) 3tp/2tb/1cl/2as/1ts/p/g/b/d Sunbeam
                         SB135, Columbia Special Products P2A 12020

   2/15-16/79   Ella Fitzgerald (v) with Count Basie's Orch.
                         4tp/4tb/5reeds/p/g/b/d/v Pablo Today 2312-132

I'M GONNA LIVE TIL I DIE   (A. Hoffman/W. Kent/M. Curtis)
   1962   Sarah Vaughan (v) 4tp/4tb/5reeds/p/g/b/d/vib/v
                         Roulette R(S)52092, Roulette (E) 2682-043

I'M IN THE MOOD FOR SWING   (BC)
   1/11-16/37*   BC 3tp/2tb/2as/2ts/p/g/b/d
   4/22/39*   BC
   7/24/39*   BC

   7/21/38*   Lionel Hampton & His Orch. 1tp/2as/2ts/p/b/d/
                         vib
   5/30-31/79   Bob Wilber & the American All Stars featuring
                         Lars Erstrand Phontastic 7526

I'M LEFT WITH THE BLUES IN MY HEART   see BLUES IN MY HEART

I'M LOST   (Otis René)
   5/21/44*   BC (Dick Gray-v) 4tp/3tb/2as/2ts/1bs/p/g/b/d/v

   1964   Harry Edison with Benny Carter's Orch. 1tp/4tb/
                         14strings/1harp/p/g/b/d Vee-Jay VJS3065

I'M OUT OF STYLE   (BC/lyrics: Mack David)
   ● 12/17/40   Ginny Simms (v) with Eddie South & His Orch.
                         1tp/1cl/1as/1violin/p/g/b/d/v 78: OK 5990

I'M PUTTING ALL MY EGGS IN ONE BASKET   (Berlin)
   4/4/36   Henry Hall & the B.B.C. Dance Orch. (Dan
                        Donovan-v) 3tp/3tb/5reeds/p/g/b/d/6strings/v
                        World Records (E) SH172

I'M SORRY   (BC) [appears on LP as SORRY]
   1/4/54*   BC horns/strings/p/b/d

I'M SUCH A FOOL TO BE IN LOVE WITH YOU   (BC/lyrics: P. Vandervoort)
   ● 1950   Virgie Austin (v)   78: London 17009

I'M THE CARING KIND   (BC/lyrics: I. Gordon)
   1/8/46*   BC (Maxine Sullivan-v) 4tp/4tb/3as/3ts/1bs/p/g/
                        b/d/v
   4/30/46*   BC (Lucy Elliott-v)
   May-June 1946*   (AFRS Jubilee #191) BC (Lucy Elliott-v)

   ● ca. 1950   The Drifters (vocal group) 78: Coral 65037

I'M TICKLED TO DEATH I'M ME
   ca. 5/36   Henry Hall & the B.B.C. Dance Orch. large
                        orch (B.B.C. broadcast, no known airchecks)

IMMINENT   (BC)
   5/63*   KPM Music Library 4tp/4tb/2fr. horns/5reeds/p/
                        g/b/d NOTE: See notes for this session in
                        chronological section of discography.

IN A MELLOTONE   (D. Ellington)
   8/14/79   Zoot Sims 4tp/4tb/2as/2ts/1bs/p/g/b/d Pablo
                        Today 2312-120 NOTE: This arrangement was
                        written for Sarah Vaughan, but at session Sims
                        substituted as featured soloist.

IN A SENTIMENTAL MOOD   (D. Ellington/I. Mills/M. Kurtz)
   4/29/77*   BC 2tp/1tb/3reeds/p/g/b/d

   8/13/79   Sarah Vaughan (v) 1flute/2cl/1bass cl/3fr. horns/
                        1oboe/1ts/9violins/3viola/2celli/1harp/p/g/b/d/v
                        NOTE: Recorded for Pablo--unissued.

IN THE DARK   (L. Greene/W. Broonzy)
   1957   Ernie Andrews (v) with Benny Carter's Orch.
                        large orch/v GNP 28, GNP-Crescendo 10008

IN THE EVENING (WHEN THE SUN GOES DOWN)   (L. Carr)
   7/13/63   Ray Charles (v), The Raelets (v) 4tp/4tb/2as/2ts/
                        1bs/p/g/b/d/v/vocal group ABC 465

IN THE MIDNIGHT HOUR   (W. Pickett/S. Cropper)
   1/3-4/68   Jackie Wilson (v) with Count Basie's Orch.   4tp/
                        4tb/2as/2ts/1bs/p/g/b/d/v Brunswick BL54134

INDIANA   (Hanley/MacDonald)
   3/27/36   Henry Hall & the B.B.C. Dance Orch. large
                        orch (B.B.C. broadcast, no known airchecks)

6/60   Dakota Staton (v) 1tp/1reed/p/g/b/d/v Capitol
                             T1597

INTO EACH LIFE SOME RAIN MUST FALL (A. Roberts/D. Fiseer)
    1965   Lou Rawls (v) 2tp/4tb/2reeds/p/g/b/d/v Capitol
                             T2273

IT AIN'T THE MEAT, IT'S THE MOTION (H. Glover/L. Mann)
    12/22/74*   Maria Muldaur (v) 2tp/1tb/1as/1ts/1bs/p/g/b/d/v
    1974   Maria Muldaur (v) Reprise MS2194

IT DON'T MEAN A THING IF IT AIN'T GOT THAT SWING (D. Ellington/
I. Mills)
    8/2/54*   Mel Torme (v) 4tp/4tb/5reeds/p/g/b/d/v

    12/22/74*   Maria Muldaur (v) 2tp/1tb/1as/1ts/1bs/p/g/b/d/v

    4/29/77*   BC 2tp/1tb/3reeds/p/g/b/d
    4/15/78*   BC
    4/19?/78*   BC

    8/14/79   Zoot Sims 4tp/4tb/2as/2ts/1bs/p/g/b/d Pablo
                             Today 2312-120 NOTE: This arrangement was
                             written for Sarah Vaughan, but at session Sims
                             was substituted as featured soloist.

IT HAPPENS TO THE BEST OF FRIENDS (R. Bloom/M. Parish)
    8/16/34   Benny Goodman & His Music Hall Orch. (Ann
                             Graham-v) 3tp/2tb/2as/2ts/p/g/b/d/v Sunbeam
                             SB139

IT PAYS TO ADVERTISE (BC/lyrics: P. Vandervoort)
  • 7/8/49*   Kitty White (v) accompanied by Dave Cavanaugh's
                             Orch. arr: Dave Cavanaugh 3tp/1tb/2as/2ts/1bs/
                             p/b/d/v

IT'S ALL RIGHT WITH ME (C. Porter)
    1966   Pat Dahl (v) large orch with strings/v Audio
                             Fidelity AFLP2157

IT'S DE-LOVELY (C. Porter)
    11/56   Billy Daniels (v) accompanied by Benny Carter's
                             Orch. 4tp/4tb/2as/2ts/1bs/p/g/b/d/v Verve
                             MGV2072

IT'S IMPOSSIBLE (A. and D. Previn)
    1971   Pearl Bailey (v) 4tp/4tb/5reeds/p/g/b/d/strings/v
                             RCA LSP4529

IT'S MONDAY EVERY DAY (S. Robin)
    1965   Lou Rawls (v) 2tp/4tb/2reeds/p/g/b/d/v Capitol
                             T2273

IT'S SO FRIGHTNIN' (BC/lyrics: D. Overstreet Gray)
    1958   Don Evans (v) with orch. under the direction of
                             Benny Carter p/g/b/d/v 45: Dome 100-1

IT'S UP TO ME AND YOU   (Ella Fitzgerald)
   5/10/68   Ella Fitzgerald (v)   1fr. horn/20strings/1harp/p/
                              g/b/d/v   45: Capitol P2212

I'VE BEEN IN LOVE BEFORE   (F. Hollander/F. Loesser)
   10/23/40*   BC (Roy Felton-v)   3tp/2tb/5reeds/p/g/b/d/v

I'VE GOT A FEELING YOU'RE FOOLING   (N. Brown/A. Freed)
   1/17/36*   Willie Lewis (v) & His Orch.   3tp/2as/2ts/p/g/b/
                              d/v

I'VE GOT TWO LIPS   (L. Feather)
   late 4/36*   BC   2tp/1cl/1as/1ts/p/g/b/d

JJJJUMP   (BC/C. Basie/C. Terry)
   • 5/6/76*   Basie Jam #2

JACKSON COUNTY JUBILEE   (BC) [One of ten pieces comprising Carter's
Kansas City Suite.]
   9/6-11/60   Count Basie & His Orch.   4tp/3tb/2as/2ts/1bs/p/
                              g/b/d   Roulette (S)R52056, Roulette (E) 2683-013,
                              Roulette RE124   NOTE: See note on recording
                              date under Kansas City Suite.

JAM BLUES   (BC/C. Shavers/J. Hodges/C. Parker/F. Phillips/B. Webster/
O. Peterson/B. Kessel/R. Brown/J. C. Heard)
   • June or July 1952*   Jam Session (Norman Granz)

JAZZ COCKTAIL   (BC)
   9/21/32   Duke Ellington & His Orch.   3tp/3tb/4reeds/p/g/
                              b/d   Gaps 040, CBS (F) 88035
   9/23/32   Mills Blue Rhythm Band   78: Banner 32608, LP:
                              Swingfan (G) 1019
   10/5/32*   BC

A JAZZ PORTRAIT OF BRIGITTE BARDOT   (BC/C. Hawkins/R. Eldridge/
D. Byas)
   • 11/22/60*   Jazz at the Philharmonic

JAZZ WALTZ   (BC)
   5/63*   KPM Music Library   4tp/4tb/2fr. horns/5reeds/p/
                              g/b/d   NOTE: Two different brief thematic transi-
                              tion passages for this piece were recorded at the
                              same session.   Both were arranged and composed
                              by Carter.   Also see notes for this session in
                              chronological section of discography.

JITTERBUG WALTZ   (Waller)
   4/29/77*   BC   2tp/1tb/3reeds/p/g/b/d

JOHNNY   (BC)
   • 11/30/76*   BC

JOHNNY KLINGARINGDING   (L. Chase)
   1953-1954   Lincoln Chase (v) with Spencer-Hagen Orch.
                              small group/v   Liberty LRP3076

(THE) JUKE BOX   (BC)
   3/59*   The Music From M Squad   large orch

7/2/72*   BC 5tp/4tb/3as/2ts/1bs/p/g/b/d
12/3/73*   BC

                           NOTE: Composed for TV series M Squad.

JUMP CALL (BC) [also appears as MELODRAMA IN A V-DISC RECORD
ROOM]
    1/5/46*   BC 4tp/3tb/3as/2ts/1bs/p/g/b/d
    April-May 1946*   (AFRS Jubilee #184) BC NOTE: appears on V-
                           Disc 701 as Melodrama In A V-Disc Record
                           Room.
    probably early 1947*   (AFRS Jubilee #246) BC

JUNE COMES AROUND (H. Arlen)
    4/9/45*   BC 5tp/4tb/3as/2ts/1bs/p/g/b/d

JUNE IN JANUARY (Robin/Rainger)
    late 1958 or early   BC 4tp/3tb/5reeds/p/g/b/d
    1959*

JUNE IS BUSTIN' OUT ALL OVER (Rodgers/Hammerstein)
    late 1958 or early   BC 4tp/3tb/5reeds/p/g/b/d
    1959*

JUST A MOOD (BC)
    1/17/36*   Willie Lewis & His Orch. 2tp/1tb/2as/2ts/p/g/b/d
    late 4/36*   BC NOTE: Arrangement similar to Lewis re-
                           cording above.

  ● 9/7/36   Garland Wilson 78: Brunswick 03115

JUST A RIDE see SWINGIN' AT THE MAIDA VALE

JUST A-SITTIN' AND A-ROCKIN' (Ellington/Strayhorn/Gaines)
    2/15-16/79   Ella Fitzgerald (v) with Count Basie's Orch.
                           4tp/4tb/5reeds/p/g/b/d/v   Pablo Today 2312-
                           132

JUST IN TIME (J. Styne/B. Comden)
    11/56   Billy Daniels (v) accompanied by Benny Carter's
                           Orch. 1tp/4reeds/p/g/b/d/strings/v Verve
                           MGV2072

JUST SQUEEZE ME (Ellington/Gaines)
    1957   Ernie Andrews with Benny Carter's Orch. large
                           orch/v GNP 28, GNP-Crescendo 10008

JUST THE BLUES (L. Stevens/S. Fine)
    Sept.-Oct. 1958*   film soundtrack: The Five Pennies 2tp/2tb/
                           4reeds/p/b/d NOTE: Features Louis Armstrong,
                           tp.

JUST YOU, JUST ME (J. Greer/R. Klages)
    3/19/45*   (AFRS Jubilee #125) BC 4tp/4tb/2as/2ts/1bs/p/
                           g/b/d
    12/12/45*   BC
    Apr.-May 1946*   (AFRS Jubilee #186) BC
    ca. 7/47*   (AFRS Jubilee #248) BC

KANSAS CITY LINE   (BC/C. Basie/C. Terry/Eddie "Lockjaw" Davis)
  • 5/6/76*   Basie Jam #2

KANSAS CITY MOODS   (BC/A. De Haas)
  • 1/24/40   Jan Savitt & His Orch.   arr: Jack Pleis?
                         Sounds of Swing LP104
  10/25/45   Jan Savitt & His Orch.   (AFRS broadcast One
                         Night Stand ONS #817)

  • 9/26/41   Nat Gonella & His New Georgians   78:   Columbia
                         FB-2754

                         NOTE: Although he is listed as co-composer in
                         the copyright records, Carter ascribes primary
                         authorship of "Kansas City Moods" to De Haas,
                         who felt that Carter's name would increase the
                         chances of having the composition recorded.

KANSAS CITY SUITE
                         This is a collective title for a set of Carter com-
                         positions and arrangements recorded by Count
                         Basie and His Orchestra in 1960.   For further
                         details see the individual titles:

VINE STREET RUMBLE, KATY DO, MISS MISSOURI, JACKSON COUNTY
JUBILEE, SUNSET GLOW, THE WIGGLE WALK, MEETIN' TIME,
PASEO PROMENADE, BLUE FIVE JIVE, ROMPIN' AT THE RENO

                         Jepsen gives recording date as 11/17/60 and
                         location as New York.   Carter was present and
                         recalls that session was in Los Angeles.   Rou-
                         lette master tapes list dates as 9/6, 9/7, 9/10
                         and 9/11 (four sessions).   This is probably ac-
                         curate, because Carter was touring with Jazz at
                         the Philharmonic from early November to Decem-
                         ber 7, 1960.

KATY DO   (BC) [One of ten pieces comprising Carter's Kansas City Suite]
  9/6-11/60   Count Basie & His Orch.   4tp/3tb/2as/2ts/1bs/p/
                         g/b/d   Roulette (S)R52056, Roulette RE124
                         NOTE: See note on recording date under Kansas
                         City Suite.

KEEP A SONG IN YOUR SOUL   (T. Waller/A. Hill)
  12/2/30*   Fletcher Henderson & His Orch.   3tp/2tb/2as/1ts/
                         p/g/b/d

KEY LARGO   (BC, K. Suessdorf/lyrics: L. Worth)
  • 1947   Ellington Gang   Queen Disc Q041

  1947*   Anita O'Day (v)   12 piece orch/v

  • 1947   Jimmy Zito & His Orch.   (Nick Delane-v)   78:
                         Coast 8034

  9/52*   BC with the Oscar Peterson Trio & Buddy Rich
                         horns/strings/p/g/b/d

- 3/4/55   Arne Domnerus Quintet HMV (Sw) 7EGS17

- 2/56   Jane Fielding (v) with the Kenny Drew Quintet
                            arr: Kenny Drew Jazz West JWLP5

- 1960   Cal Tjader arr: Eddie Cano Fantasy 3309
                            (mono), Fantasy 8053 (stereo)

- ca. 1963   Sarah Vaughan (v) Roulette (E) 2682-032, New
                            World Records NW295

- date unknown   Tony Lovelle & Orch. 45: Acama X-121

KING SIZE PAPA (BC under pseudonym "Johnny Gomez"/lyrics: P. Vandervoort)
- 11/11/47*   Julia Lee (v) & Her Boy Friends arr: Dave
                            Cavanaugh

- 1956-1957   Julia Lee (v) Foremost 104

KING'S RIFF (BC)
- 12/27/51*   Ben Webster Sextet

A KISS FROM YOU (BC/lyrics: J. Mercer) [also recorded as LYDIA]
- ca. 1963   Stanley Wilson & His Orch. arr: Stanley Wilson
                            Decca 74481 (as Lydia)

12/3/73*   BC 4tp/4tb/3as/3ts/1bs/p/g/b/d
10/28/78*   BC with the University of Buffalo Jazz Ensemble
                            directed by Sam Falzone (as Lydia)

                            NOTE: This composition was originally written
                            for TV's Chrysler Theatre and called "Lydia."
                            When Johnny Mercer added the lyrics, the title
                            was changed.

KNOCK ME A KISS (A. Razaf)
6/60   Dakota Staton (v) 1tp/1reed/p/g/b/d/v Capitol
                            T1597

KRAZY KAPERS (BC)
10/10/33*   The Chocolate Dandies 1tp/1tb/1as/1ts/p/g/b/d

LADY BE GOOD (Gershwin)
5/20/39*   BC 3tp/3tb/3as/2ts/p/g/b/d
7/24/39*   BC

9/9/39   Roy Eldridge & His Orch. 2tp/1tb/1as/2ts/p/g/
                            b/d Jazz Archives JA14

LADY OH LADY (B. Blalock)
early 1950's   Bruce Blalock (v) small group 45: Coral 9-
                            61884

A LADY SINGS THE BLUES (Stanley Wilson)
3/59*   The Music From M Squad large orch

THE LADY'S IN LOVE WITH YOU (B. Lane/F. Loesser)
   1962   Sarah Vaughan (v) 4tp/4tb/5reeds/p/g/b/d/vib/v
                       Roulette R(S)52092, Roulette (E) 2682-043 Roulette
                       RE103

LASSE LASSE LITTEN (BC/I. Stevens)
   1968   Inger Stevens (v) large orch with strings/v 45:
                       Dome D506

THE LAST KISS YOU GAVE ME (H. Ruby)
   10/23/40*   BC (Roy Felton-v) 3tp/2tb/2as/2ts/1bs/p/g/b/d/v

LAURA (D. Raksin/J. Mercer)
   1961*   Alfred Newman large orch with horns/strings/
                       rhythm section

LAZY AFTERNOON (BC)
   8/17/37*   BC 3tp/2tb/2as/2ts/p/g/b/d

   ● 9/20/56   Bertie King Jazz Group Nixa (E) NJT506

THE LEGEND (BC)
   10/30-31/61*   Count Basie & His Orch. 4tp/3tb/2as/2ts/1bs/p/
                       g/b/d

LET IT BE ME
   ca. 6/36   Henry Hall & the B. B. C. Dance Orch. large
                       orch (B. B. C. broadcast, no known airchecks)

LET THEM TALK
   6/60   Dakota Staton (v) large orch with strings/v
                       Capitol T1597

LET US DRINK A TOAST TOGETHER (H. Atwood)
   1/48*   BC (Bob Decker and/or The Enchanters-v) 1tp/
                       1tb/1as/1ts/p/g/b/d/v

LET'S FALL IN LOVE (Arlen/Koehler)
   9/10/53*   Buddy Rich & His All Stars 1tp/1tb/1as/1ts/1bs/
                       p/b/d

LET'S HAVE A JUBILEE (A. Hill/I. Mills)
   10/4/34   Mills Blue Rhythm Band 3tp/2tb/3reeds/p/g/b/d
                       Jazz Archives JA10
   10/19/34*   Alex Hill (v) & His Hollywood Sepians

LILACS IN THE RAIN (P. DeRose/M. Parish)
   1/28/39*   BC (Dell St. John-v) 3tp/3tb/2as/2ts/p/g/b/d/v

LIMEHOUSE BLUES (P. Braham/D. Furber)
   9/11/34   Fletcher Henderson & His Orch. 3tp/2tb/1cl/2as/
                       1ts/p/g/b/d Decca DL9228, MCA 1318, Time-
                       Life STL-J21

   1/5/35   Benny Goodman & His Orch. (aircheck) Sunbeam
                       SB100

LITTLE BO BOP HAS LOST HER BEEP see BOP BOUNCE

LIVIN' IN THE SUNLIGHT (LOVIN' IN THE MOONLIGHT) (A. Sherman/A.
Lewis)
   1/1975   Geoff Muldaur (v) 3tp/2tb/1ss/2as/1ts/1bass sax/
                              p/celeste/banjo/tuba/d/vocal chorus/v Reprise
                              MS2220 NOTE: Vocal arrangement by Amos
                              Garrett.

LIZA (I. and G. Gershwin/G. Kahn)
   5/3/38   Chick Webb & His Orch.   3tp/3tb/2as/2ts/p/g/b/d
                              Decca DL79223, MCA 2-4107
   8/13/38   Chick Webb, Roy Eldridge accompanied by the
                              Saturday Night Swing Club Houseband (aircheck)
                              Jazz Archives JA33
   11/30/70   Time-Life series The Swing Era (Billy May-lead-
                              er) Time-Life STL342 NOTE: In this series,
                              significant swing era performances are "recreated"
                              including imitations of the solos present on the
                              original recordings.

THE LONE ARRANGER
   5/18/40   Cab Calloway & His Orch.   3tp/3tb/3as/2ts/p/g/
                              b/d Jazz Archives JA8, Merritt 12

LONELY AFFAIR   (BC)
   5/63*   KPM Music Library   4tp/4tb/2fr. horns/5reeds/p/
                              g/b/d

   5/63*   KPM Music Library   4tp/4tb/2fr. horns/5reeds/p/
                              g/b/d

                              NOTE: Two brief thematic transition passages
                              for this piece were recorded at the same session.
                              Both were arranged and composed by Carter.
                              Also see notes for this session in chronological
                              section of discography.

LONELY HOURS   (Glaser/Solomon)
   1/63   Sarah Vaughan (v)   4tp/4tb/2as/2ts/1bs/p/g/b/d/v
                              Roulette R(S)52104

LONELY WOMAN   (BC/lyrics: R. Sonin)
   ● ca. 7/47   Peggy Lee (v) T: AFRS Jubilee #248

   ● 12/6/47   Stan Kenton & His Orch. (June Christy-v) arr:
                              Pete Rugolo Creative World ST1037
   Nov. 25-Dec. 21   Stan Kenton & His Orch.   T: AFRS "One Night
   1947   Stand"

   ● 10/48   Charlie Ventura (Jackie Cain-v) arr: Roy Kral?
                              Savoy SJL2243

   ● 1952   Sylvia Syms (v) with Barbara Carroll Trio   At-
                              lantic 1243

   ● 5/9/55   June Cristy (v) and Stan Kenton   Capitol T656

   ● 4/8/56   Sarah Vaughan (v) arr: Hal Mooney Trip
                              TLP5517

- 9/21/59   Stan Kenton & His Orch.   arr: Bill Matthews
                     Capitol (S)T1394

- 4/9/62   Chris Connor (v) arr: Al Cohn?   Atlantic
                     SD8061

1966   Path Dahl (v) large orch with strings/v Audio
                     Fidelity AFLP2157

- 1976   Sylvia Syms (v) arr: Dick Hyman   Atlantic
                     SD18177

A LONESOME CUP OF COFFEE   (B. Russell)
1956   Abbey Lincoln (v) large orch/v 45: Liberty
                     F55035

LONESOME NIGHTS   (BC) also entitled TAKE MY WORD
10/16/33*   BC 3tp/3tb/3as/1ts/p/g/b/d
8/16/34   Benny Goodman & His Music Hall Orch.   Sunbeam
                     SB139, Columbia Special Products P2A 12020 (as
                     Take My Word)
ca. 7/20/36   Bunny Berigan & His Studio Orch.   Thesaurus
                     transcription 273   (as Take My Word)
5/6/37   California Ramblers (Charlie Barnet Orch.)
                     Ajax 106 (as Take My Word)
2/15/38   Artie Shaw & His Orch.   Thesaurus transcription
                     549, Alamac QSR2434 (as Take My Word)
8/28/40   Cab Calloway & His Orch.   CBS (F) 62950, Epic
                     EE22008, Merritt 12
1945?   Sam Donahue & His Navy Orch.   Big Band Land-
                     marks vol. 23-24 NOTE: May be same ar-
                     rangement as those above.

- ca. 1960   Lionel Hampton & His Orch.   arr: Bobby Plater
                     Glad Hamp LP1001
12/61   Lionel Hampton & His Orch.   Glad Hamp LP1005

                     NOTE: There are two recordings by Andy Kirk
                     and His Twelve Clouds of Joy of a Clyde Hart
                     composition and arrangement entitled "Puddin'
                     Head Serenade" which bears a marked resemblance
                     to "Lonesome Nights." The 3/31/36 version is
                     on Mainstream MRL399; the 4/10/36 on 78:
                     Decca 1208.   Another recording inspired by
                     "Lonesome Nights" is the Jimmie Lunceford
                     Orchestra's "I'm Alone with You," which even
                     contains a saxophone chorus based on Carter's.
                     This composition is credited to Buff Estes, who
                     was also the arranger.   The date is 12/14/39 and
                     it is on Columbia CL2715, and Columbia CS9515.

LOOK AT THAT FACE   (Newley/Bricusse)
Mar. 30-Apr. 1   Pearl Bailey (v) 4tp/4tb/5reeds/p/g/b/d/v
1965*

LOOK FOR ME, I'LL BE AROUND (Wood/Dee)
1/63   Sarah Vaughan (v) 4tb/20strings/p/g/b/d/v
                     Roulette R(S)52104

LOOK OUT FOR TOMORROW (BC/lyrics: P. Vandervoort)
 ● ca. 1949   Calvin Boze (v) & His All Stars 78: Aladdin
         3072

LOOKING FOR A BOY (G. and I. Gershwin)
 1/8/46*   BC (Maxine Sullivan-v) 4tp/4tb/3as/2ts/1bs/p/g/
         b/d/v

LOUIS ARMSTRONG MEDLEY
        See individual titles:
 WHEN IT'S SLEEPY TIME DOWN SOUTH, CONFESSIN', WHEN
 YOU'RE SMILING

LOU'S BLUES (BC)
 1/22-24/62   Louis Bellson Orch. 5tp/3tb/1fr. horn/1tuba/2as/
         2ts/1bs/p/g/b/d/vib Roulette R52087, Roulette
         (E) 2934-020

LOVE FOR SALE (Cole Porter)
 10/25/43*   BC 4tp/3tb/2as/2ts/1bs/p/g/b/d
 ca. 7/47*   (AFRS Jubilee #203) BC

LOVE IS A FEELING (Bob Friedman)
 11/71-3/72   Joe Williams (v) large orch/v Temponic
         TB29561

LOVE IS CYNTHIA see BLUE MOUNTAIN

LOVE, YOU DIDN'T DO RIGHT BY ME (I. Berlin)
 1954*   Peggy Lee (v) large orch with strings/v

LOVE, YOU'RE NOT THE ONE FOR ME (BC--words & music)
 3/14/33*   BC (v) 3tp/2tb/2as/1ts/p/g/b/d/v
 11/6/33*   Mezz Mezzrow & His Orch. (BC-v)

LOVELESS LOVE (W. C. Handy)
 10/15/40*   Billie Holiday (v) accompanied by Benny Carter
         Orch. 1tp/1tb/2reeds/p/g/b/d/v

LOVER COME BACK TO ME (S. Romberg/O. Hammerstein)
 4/27/55   Ella Fitzgerald (v) with Benny Carter Orch. 3tp/
         1tb/2as/2ts/p/g/b/d/v Decca DL4129, MCA Coral
         (G) 0082. 050-2

 1957   Ernie Andrews (v) with Benny Carter's Orch.
         large orch/v GNP 28, GNP-Crescendo 10008

LOVER MAN (J. Davis/R. Ramirez/J. Sherman)
 12/22/74*   Maria Muldaur (v) 2tp/1tb/1as/1ts/1bs/p/g/b/d/v

LOVE'S GOT ME DOWN AGAIN (Cahn/Chaplin)
 11/1/39*   BC (Roy Felton-v) 3tp/3tb/3as/2ts/p/g/b/d/v

THE LOVING ROOM (BC/lyrics: Al Stillman)
 1968   Inger Stevens (v) large orch with strings/v 45:
         Dome D506

LULA (BC/lyrics: P. Vandervoort)
 ● 4/10/62*   BBB & Co. 1tp/1cl/1as/1ts/p/g/b/d

LULLABY IN BLUE   (BC)
  7/26/52*   BC   1tp/1tb/3reeds/p/g/b/d

LULLABY TO A DREAM   (BC)
  4/1/41*   BC   3tp/3tb/2as/2ts/p/g/b/d

LUSH LIFE   (B. Strayhorn)
  8/13/79   Sarah Vaughan (v)   1flute/2cl/1bass c1/3fr. horns/
                                     1oboe/1ts/9violins/3viola/2celli/1harp/p/g/b/d/v
                                       NOTE: Recorded for Pablo--unissued.

LYDIA   see   A KISS FROM YOU

M SQUAD
                                       For Carter's contributions to the album The Mu-
                                       sic From M Squad (RCA LPM2062) which was
                                       based on the TV series, see 3/59* in chronologi-
                                       cal section of discography.

MA (SHE'S MAKING EYES AT ME)   (S. Clare/C. Conrad)
  1964   Ray Charles (v)   5tp/3tb/2as/2ts/1bs/p/g/b/d/v
                                       ABC Paramount ABC495

  9/29/70   Mrs. Miller (v)   2tp/2tb/2as/1ts/1bs/p/g/b/d/v
                                       45: Mrs. Miller Records (no issue number)

MAKE ME A PRESENT OF YOU   (J. Greene)
  1953   Ernie Andrews (v) with Benny Carter's Orch.
                                       large orch/v   78: Trend 68, LP: GNP 28
                                       NOTE: Although the discographies list two ver-
                                       sions of this title by Andrews, one from 1953
                                       (Trend 68) and one from 1957 (GNP 28), both
                                       discs contain the same performance, probably re-
                                       corded in 1953.

  6/60   Dakota Staton (v)   large orch/v   Capitol T1490

MALIBU   (BC)
  4/9/45*   BC   5tp/4tb/3as/2ts/1bs/p/g/b/d
  11/16-22/45*   BC
  ca. 7/46*   (AFRS Jubilee #205)   BC
  8/14/59   Glen Gray & His Casa Loma Orch.   Capitol
                                       (S)T1289, Time-Life STL348   NOTE: This is a
                                       recreation of Carter's 4/9/45 version including
                                       solos.   Carter's alto solo is played by Skeets
                                       Herfurt.

  ● 2/11/76*   BC

  ● 12/5/81*   BC

MAMA, A RAINBOW
  1971   Pearl Bailey (v)   4tp/4tb/5reeds/p/g/b/d/strings/v
                                       RCA LSP4529

MAMA DON'T WEAR NO DRAWERS   (BC/C. Basie/C. Terry)
  ● 5/6/76*   Basie Jam #2

MAMA LOU   (BC)
    7/26/52*   BC   1tp/1tb/3reeds/p/g/b/d

A MAN CALLED ADAM [film soundtrack]
                                Carter's compositions and arrangements for this
                                1966 film were released on a soundtrack album
                                of the same name and are listed under the follow-
                                ing individual titles, recorded in November, 1965:
                                ALL THAT JAZZ, GO NOW, AIN'T I, SOFT
                                TOUCH, CLAUDIA, CRACK UP, NIGHT WALK,
                                WHISPER TO ONE.   The film was about a trum-
                                peter, Adam Johnson (played by Sammy Davis,
                                Jr.), and the soundtrack featured Nat Adderley
                                as trumpet soloist along with contributions by Kai
                                Winding, Jimmy Cleveland (tb), Jerome Richard-
                                son, Lucky Thompson (ts), Junior Mance (p),
                                Everett Barksdale (g), Aaron Bell (b), and Herb
                                Lovelle (d) on the titles listed above.   In addi-
                                tion, two performances by Louis Armstrong and
                                his All Stars were included, "Someday Sweetheart"
                                and "Back of Town Blues."   The personnel for
                                these titles was Armstrong (tp, v), Tyree Glenn
                                (tb), Buster Bailey (cl), Billy Kyle (p), Buddy
                                Catlett (b), and Danny Barcelona (d), although
                                John Brown (b) and Jo Jones (d) appear on the
                                screen.

THE MAN I LOVE   (G. and I. Gershwin)
    1/63   Sarah Vaughan (v)   4tb/20strings/p/g/b/d/v
                                Roulette R(S)52104, Roulette RE103   NOTE:
                                Melody Maker (May 30, 1936) reports that Carter
                                was commissioned by Henry Hall to arrange this
                                tune.   It may later have been broadcast by Hall
                                and the B.B.C. Dance Orchestra.   There are no
                                known airchecks.

A MAN IS A NECESSARY EVIL   (W. Shelley)
    Mar. 30-Apr. 1   Pearl Bailey (v)   4tp/4tb/5reeds/p/g/b/d/v
    1965*

MARCH WIND   (BC)
    late 1958 or early   BC   4tp/3tb/5reeds/p/g/b/d
    1959*
    11/9/68*   BC with Henri Chaix & His Orch.   NOTE: Sim-
                                ilar arrangement but performed by 1tp/1tb/2as/
                                1ts/1bs/p/b/d

MARGIE   (Conrad/Robinson/Davis)
    1965   Lou Rawls (v)   large orch with strings/vocal
                                group/v   Capitol T2401

THE MASQUERADE IS OVER   (H. Magidson/A. Wrubel)
    11/5-6/56   Abbey Lincoln (v)   1tp/1tb/1fr. horn/3woodwinds/
                                p/g/b/d/v   Liberty LRP3025

    6/60   Dakota Staton (v)   large orch/v   Capitol T1490

ME AND MY JAGUAR   (BC)
  9/10/53*   Buddy Rich & His All Stars   1tp/1tb/1as/1ts/1bs/
                                   p/b/d

ME AND MY SHADOW   (Jolson/Dreyer/Rose)
  1965   Lou Rawls (v)   large orch with strings/vocal
                                   group/v   Capitol T2401

MEET ME AT NO SPECIAL PLACE   (J. R. Robinson)
  6/60   Dakota Staton (v)   large orch/v   Capitol T1490

MEETIN' TIME   (BC) [One of ten pieces comprising Carter's Kansas City
Suite.]
  9/6-11/60   Count Basie & His Orch.   4tp/3tb/2as/2ts/1bs/p/
                                   g/b/d   Roulette S(R)52056, Roulette RE124
                                   NOTE: See note on recording date under Kansas
                                   City Suite.

 • 12/20-21/63   Lambert, Hendricks & Bavan (v)   arr: Jon Hen-
                                   dricks   RCA LPM2861   NOTE: Lyrics added by
                                   Jon Hendricks for this recording.

MELANCHOLY LULLABY   (BC/lyrics: E. Heyman)
  4/17/39*   BC   3tp/3tb/3as/2ts/p/g/b/d
  4/22/39*   BC   (two versions)
  5/6/39*   BC
  5/20/39*   BC
  6/29/39*   BC
  7/24/39*   BC   (two versions)
  10/9/39*   BC
  10/14/39*   BC   (two versions)
  4/10/43*   BC
  8/3/70   Time-Life series The Swing Era (Billy May-lead-
                                   er)   Time-Life STL343   NOTE: This is a recrea-
                                   tion of Carter's 6/29/39 Vocalion recording in-
                                   cluding note-for-note imitations of the solos.
                                   Carter's solo is played by Skeets Herfurt.

 • ca. 8/39   Gene Krupa & His Orch.   (broadcast from Steel
                                   Pier, Atlantic City)
  2/2/40   Gene Krupa & His Orch.   (broadcast from Meadow-
                                   brook, Cedar Grove, N.J.)

 • 9/5/39   Jimmy Dorsey & His Orch. (Helen O'Connell-v)
                                   Ajax 164

 • 9/11/39   Glenn Miller & His Orch. (Ray Eberle-v)   RCA
                                   Camden CAL829, RCA (F) 900.028, RCA (E)
                                   LFM1-7503

 • 1939   Reggie Childs & His Orch. (Marion Kaye-v)   78:
                                   Varsity 8079

 • 1939   Ginny Simms (v)   78: Vocalion 5140

 • 1939   Artie Shaw Helen Forrest (v)   Hindsight
                                   149 (aircheck)

 • early 1950's?   Peggy Lee (v)   Capitol transcription

● 11/60   Arne Domnerus & His Orch.   Metronome
                           MLP15062

MELODRAMA IN A V-DISC RECORD ROOM   see   JUMP CALL

A MELODY FROM THE SKY   (L. Alter/S. Mitchell)
  11/56   Billy Daniels (v) accompanied by Benny Carter's
                           Orch.   1tp/4reeds/p/g/b/d/strings/v   Verve
                           MGV2072

MEMORIES OF YOU   (E. Blake/A. Razaf)
  8/64*   BC   2ss/4as/3ts/2bs/p/g/b/d

METROPOLE   (BC)
  5/63*   KPM Music Library   4tp/4tb/2fr. horns/5reeds/p/
                           g/b/d   NOTE: See notes for this session in
                           chronological section of discography.

MIDNIGHT   (Gomez/Parker)
  4/1/41*   BC (Maxine Sullivan-v)   3tp/3tb/3as/2ts/p/g/b/d/v
  1943*   (AFRS Basic Library P-34)   BC (Savannah
                           Churchill-v)

THE MIDNIGHT SUN WILL NEVER SET   (D. Cockran/H. Salvador/Q. Jones)
  11/13/61*   BC   2as/2ts/p/g/b/d

MIGHTY LIKE THE BLUES   (L. Feather)
  8/18/37*   BC   1tp/1tb/1cl/1ts/p/g/b/d

MILLIONS OF PEOPLE   (BC/lyrics: P. Herrick)
  1955   Larry Barbro (v) with Benny Carter Orch.
                           5brass/4reeds/p/b/d/v   45: Benida No 5033, 45:
                           Imperial X3003

MISS MISSOURI   (BC) [One of ten pieces comprising Carter's Kansas City
Suite.]
  9/6-11/60   Count Basie & His Orch.   4tp/3tb/2as/2ts/1bs/p/
                           g/b/d   Roulette (S)R52056, Roulette 2683-013,
                           Roulette RE124   NOTE: See note on recording
                           date under Kansas City Suite.

MR. LOVE   (Bob Friedman)
  11/71-3/72   Carmen McRae (v)   large orch/v   Temponic
                           TB29562

MOMENTS TO REMEMBER   (R. Allen/A. Stillman)
  9/8/55   Louis Armstrong (v) with Benny Carter's Orch.
                           3tp/2tb/1cl/2as/2ts/p/b/d/v   Vocalion VL73851,
                           MCA Coral 42026, MCA Coral 82051/2

MONA LISA   (R. Evans/J. Livingston)
  8/30/74   Yujiro Ishihara (v)   2tp/1tb/1as/2ts/1bs/p/g/b/d/v
                           Continental (J) C01   NOTE: Instrumental tracks
                           recorded 8/30/74, Los Angeles; vocal added later
                           in Japan.

MOOD INDIGO   (Ellington/Bigard)
  July 1981*   BC   2tp/1tb/3reeds/1violin/p/b/d

THE MOON IS LOW (N. Brown/A. Freed)
 1/22-24/62   Louis Bellson Orch. 5tp/3tb/1fr. horn/1tuba/2as/
            2ts/1bs/p/g/b/d/vib Roulette R52087, Roulette
            (E) 2934-020

MOONLIGHT ON THE GANGES (S. Myers/C. Wallace)
 1962   Sarah Vaughan (v) 4tp/4tb/5reeds/p/g/b/d/vib/v
            Roulette R(S)52092, Roulette (E) 2682-043

MOPPIN' AND BOPPIN' (BC/T. Waller/E. Kirkeby)
 • 1/23/43*   Fats Waller & His Rhythm

MORE THAN YOU KNOW (V. Youmans/B. Rose/E. Eliscu)
 4/17/39*   BC 3tp/3tb/2as/2ts/p/g/b/d
 11/1/39*   BC (Roy Felton-v)

THE MUGGER (BC)
 3/59*   The Music from M Squad large orch NOTE:
            Composed for TV series M Squad.

THE MUSIC GOES 'ROUND AND 'ROUND (E. Farley/M. Riley/R. Hodgson)
 2/9/42*   Mark Warnow & His Orch. (The Hit Paraders-v)
            3tp/2tb/6reeds/8violins/1harp/p/g/b/d/vocal group

MUSKRAT RAMBLE (Kid Ory)
 7/21/38*   Lionel Hampton & His Orch. 1tp/2as/2ts/p/b/d/
            vib

MY BUDDY (Donaldson/Kahn)
 8/18/37*   BC 1tp/1tb/1as/2ts/p/g/b/d
 date unknown   Electrecord Orch. (Roumania) Electrecord 0971
            NOTE: This recording is a recreation, including
            solos, of the 8/18/37* recording above.

 1965   Lou Rawls (v) large orch with strings/vocal
            group/v Capitol T2401

MY FAVORITE BLUES (BC)
 4/1/41*   BC 3tp/3tb/3as/2ts/p/g/b/d

MY FUNNY VALENTINE (R. Rodgers)
 early 1970's   The Airmen of Note (U. S. Air Force Jazz En-
            semble) (Sarah Vaughan-v) 4tp/4tb/5reeds/p/g/b/
            d/v NOTE: Promotional album: The Airmen of
            Note and Sarah Vaughan (no label and issue)

MY GIRL (W. Robinson/R. White)
 1/3-4/68   Jackie Wilson (v) with Count Basie's Orch. 4tp/
            4tb/2as/2ts/1bs/p/g/b/d/v Brunswick BL54134

MY GUIDING LIGHT see GUIDING LIGHT

MY HEART HAS WINGS
 5/20/39*   BC (Mercedes Carter-v) 3tp/3tb/3as/2ts/p/g/b/d/v

MY KIND OF TROUBLE IS YOU (BC/lyrics: P. Vandervoort)
 • 11/11/55   Helen Carr (v) Bethlehem BCP1027

- 1959   Felicia Sanders (v) Time S/2110

- 2/11/76*   BC

- 4/76   Milt Jackson & Strings arr: Jimmy Jones
                          Pablo 2310-774

2/15-16/79   Ella Fitzgerald (v) with Count Basie's Orch.
                          4tp/4tb/5reeds/p/g/b/d/v Pablo Today 2312-132

MY MELANCHOLY BABY (Burnett/Norton/Watson)
date unknown   Meg Myles (v) large orch/v 45: Capitol F3437

MY PRETTY GIRL (Fulcher)
2/5/31*   Fletcher Henderson & His Orch. (Lois Deppe-v)
                          3tp/2tb/2as/cl/1ts/p/g/b/d/v NOTE: Carter is
                          possibly the arranger.

MY TWILIGHT REVERIE (BC/lyrics: Kay Parker)
- 8/23/45   Fred Waring & the Pennsylvanians (unknown v)
                          arr: Hawley Ades, Roy Ringwald (aircheck)

MY WISH (B. Young/Una Mae Carlisle)
2/60   Dakota Staton (v) large orch with strings/v
                          Capitol T1427

NAGASAKI (H. Warren)
1/21/35   Charlie Barnet & His Orch.   3tp/1tb/2as/2ts/p/g/
                          b/d Bluebird AXM2-5526

1/11-16/37*   BC (v) 2tp/2tb/3as/2ts/p/g/b/d/v NOTE: This
                          arrangement is similar to the one recorded by
                          Barnet.

NEVER AGAIN (J. Moody)
ca. 1970   Benard Ito (v) large orch 45: Mercury 72686

NEVER SWAT A FLY (Desylva/Brown/Henderson)
11/4/30*   McKinney's Cotton Pickers (Bill Coty-v) 3tp/1tb/
                          3reeds/p/g/tuba/d/v
9/20/75   New McKinney's Cotton Pickers (Orrin Foslien-v)
                          Bountiful B38003
6/26/80*   New McKinney's Cotton Pickers (Orrin Foslien-v)

THE NEW CONTINENT (L. Schifrin)
                          This extended work was written and arranged by
                          Lalo Schifrin to feature Dizzy Gillespie. Carter
                          conducted the orchestra at the 1962 Monterey
                          Jazz Festival performance of the piece and during
                          a studio recording of it made in two sessions in
                          September 1962, one before and one after the
                          festival. The recording was originally released
                          on Limelight LS86022 (Dizzy Gillespie, The New
                          Continent) and reissued on Emarcy EMS2410
                          (Dizzy Gillespie, Composer's Concepts).

NIGHT AND DAY (C. Porter)
5/5/46*   BC (Lucy Elliott-v) large orch/v

NIGHT HOP   (BC)
   5/20/40*
   1981   BC   3tp/2tb/3as/2ts/p/g/b/d
                           Widespread Depression Orch.   Stash ST212
                           NOTE: Carter's 1940 arr. transcribed by John
                           Ellis.

NIGHT WALK   (BC)
   11/65   film soundtrack: A Man Called Adam   4tp/4tb/
                           4reeds/p/g/b/d   Reprise 6180

NIGHTFALL   (BC)
   4/15/36*   BC   3tp/2tb/3as/cl/2ts/p/g/b/d

   5/7/36   Henry Hall & the B. B. C. Dance Orch.   (B. B. C.
                           broadcast, no known airchecks) NOTE: May be
                           same as 4/15/36* arrangement above.

  • 8/2/36*   BC with the AVRO Orch.   (aircheck)

  • 1963   George Shearing arr: Julian Lee Capitol
                         (S)T2143

NO LOVE, NO NOTHIN'   (H. Warren/M. Gordon)
   Mar.-Apr. 1943*   Alice Faye (v) with Benny Goodman & His Orch.
                         3tp/2tb/6reeds/strings/p/g/b/d/v   NOTE: This
                         performance is from the film soundtrack: The
                         Gang's All Here.

NOBODY BUT ME   (B. Myles)
   1965   Lou Rawls (v)   2tp/4tb/2reeds/p/g/b/d/v   Capitol
                         T2273

NOBODY ELSE BUT ME   (Hammerstein/Kern)
   1962   Sarah Vaughan (v)   4tp/4tb/5reeds/p/g/b/d/vib/v
                         Roulette R(S)52092, Roulette (E) 2682-043

NOBODY KNOWS HOW MUCH I LOVE YOU   (BC, Fats Waller/lyrics: Bud
Allen)
  • 1/17/28   Andy Razaf (v)   78: Columbia 14285-D NOTE:
                         Issued under the pseudonym "Johnny Thompson";
                         Fats Waller plays piano.

NOTHING REALLY FEELS THE SAME   (Rachaels/Hart/Magid)
   1965   Lou Rawls (v)   large orch with strings/vocal
                         group/v   Capitol T2401

NOW AND THEN THERE'S A FOOL SUCH AS I   (B. Trader)
   1965   Lou Rawls (v)   large orch with strings/vocal
                         group/v   Capitol T2401

NUAGES   (D. Reinhardt)
   4/29/77*   BC   2tp/1tb/3reeds/p/g/b/d

O. K. FOR BABY   (BC)   also appears as OKAY FOR BABY
   5/20/40*   BC   3tp/2tb/3as/2ts/p/g/b/d

  • 12/23/40   Jimmie Lunceford & His Orch. arr: Lonnie
                         Wilfong   Tax m-8003, Swingfan (G) 1009

Nov. -Dec. 1940   Jimmie Lunceford & His Orch.   Lang-Worth
                          transcription, Circle CLP11

● 8/10/43   Les Brown & His Orch.   Fanfare 30-130 (air-
                          check) NOTE: Although the notes to the Fanfare
                          LP state that O.K. for Baby is from the Lunceford
                          book, the arrangement is not the same as that on
                          the Lunceford recordings.

● 8/45   Jack McVea & His All Stars 78: Apollo 761

● 6/19/46   Harry Parry 78: Parlophone (E) R3013

● 6/24/58   The Big Eighteen arr: Charlie Shirley RCA
                          LPM1983, RCA DPS2058

ODE TO BILLY JO   (B. Gentry)
    1/3-4/68   Jackie Wilson with Count Basie's Orch.   4tp/4tb/
                          2as/2ts/1bs/p/g/b/d/v Brunswick BL54134

OH LADY BE GOOD   see   LADY BE GOOD

OH! LOOK AT ME NOW   (J. Bushkin/J. DeVries)
    1963   Jo Stafford (v)   large orch/vocal group/v   Reprise
                          RS6090, Stanyan 10073

OKAY FOR BABY   see   O. K. FOR BABY

OL' MAN RIVER   (Kern/Hammerstein)
    10/3/33   Horace Henderson & His Orch. (Red Allen-v)
                          3tp/2tb/4reeds/p/g/b/d/v Prestige 7645
    3/31/73   New McKinney's Cotton Pickers (Dave Wilborn-v)
                          Bountiful B38001 NOTE: The New McKinney's
                          recording is based on Carter's 1933 arrangement,
                          but differs in places.

    12/18/42*   (AFRS Jubilee #4) BC large orch
    6/12/44*   (AFRS Jubilee #83?) BC
    4/16/45*   (AFRS Jubilee #129) BC NOTE: This
                          arrangement is probably the same as the
                          one above.

OL' MAN TIME   (C. Friend/J. Reynolds)
    7/13/63   Ray Charles (v), The Raelets (v. group) 4tp/4tb/
                          2as/2ts/1bs/p/g/b/d/v/vocal group ABC 465

OLD DEVIL MOON   (B. Lane/E. Y. Harburg)
    4/27/55   Ella Fitzgerald (v) with Benny Carter Orch.   3tp/
                          1tb/2as/2ts/p/g/b/d/v Decca DL4129, MCA
                          Coral CB20024, MCA Coral (G) 0082. 050-2

OLD FASHIONED LOVE   (James P. Johnson/C. Mack)
    6/11/57*   BC 1as/1tb/1ts/p/g/b/d

OLD FOLKS   (W. Robison/D. L. Hill)
    2/60   Dakota Staton (v)   large orch with strings/v
                          Capitol T1427

AN OLD LOVE STORY   (H. Atwood/L. Herscher)
<u>1/48</u>*   BC (Emma Lou Welch, The Enchanters-v) 1tp/
                               1tb/1as/1ts/p/g/b/d/v

THE OLD MAN AND THE SEA   (Tiomkin/Webster)
     <u>ca. 1958</u>*   Kitty White (v) with Benny Carter & the Orch.
                               1tb/1as/1fr. horn/p/g/b/d/v

ON A HOLIDAY   see   DEVIL'S HOLIDAY

ON CENSORSHIP   (background music: BC/narrative text: V. Lundberg)
     <u>1968</u>   Victor Lundberg (v) 2fr. horns/1woodwind/1harp/
                               10strings/p/g/b/d/narrative v Liberty LST7547

ON GREEN DOLPHIN STREET   (B. Kaper/N. Washington)
     <u>6/60</u>   Dakota Staton (v) large orch/v Capitol T1490

     <u>8/64</u>*   BC   2ss/4as/3ts/2bs/p/g/b/d

ONCE IN A WHILE   (M. Edwards/B. Green)
     <u>11/5/57</u>   Stringin' Along 2reeds/p/vib/g/b/d/string quartet
                               Andex LP3001 NOTE: Personnel includes Bob
                               Keene (cl) and session appears in Jepsen under
                               his name.

ONCE UPON A HAPPY TIME (THE BIG BAND DAYS)   (Bob Friedman)
     <u>11/71-3/72</u>   Joe Williams (v) large orch/v Temponic
                               TB29561

ONCE UPON A TIME   (BC)
     <u>10/10/33</u>*   The Chocolate Dandies 2tp/1tb/1ts/p/g/b/d

   ● <u>4/6/55</u>   The Bertie King Jazz Group Jazz Today (E)
                               JTL5

ONCE UPON A TIME (IT HAPPENED)   (BC/lyrics: J. Moen)
   ● <u>6/20/58</u>   Dean Martin (v) arr: Gus Levine 45: Capitol
                               4065

THE ONE I LOVE BELONGS TO SOMEONE ELSE   (I. Jones/G. Kahn)
     <u>1963</u>   Jo Stafford (v) large orch/vocal group/v Reprise
                               RS6090, Stanyan 10073

ONE SWEET LETTER FROM YOU   (Clare/Brown/Warren)
     <u>9/11/39</u>*   Lionel Hampton (v) & His Orch. 1tp/1as/3ts/p/g/
                               b/d/vib/v

ONE, TWO, BUTTON YOUR SHOE   (Burke/Johnston)
     <u>1/23/37</u>   Henry Hall & the B.B.C. Dance Orch. (George
                               Elrick-v) 3tp/3tb/5reeds/p/g/b/d/6strings/v 78:
                               Columbia (E) FB1627, LP: World Records (E)
                               SH172

ONE WAY OUT   (BC)
     <u>5/63</u>*
                               KPM Music Library 4tp/4tb/2fr. horns/5reeds/p/
                               g/b/d/perc NOTE: See notes for this session in
                               chronological section of discography.

ONLY TRUST YOUR HEART   (BC/S. Cahn)
- 8/19/64   The New Stan Getz Quartet (Astrud Gilberto-v)
                            Verve V8600, Verve 2352095 NOTE: This per-
                            formance of Only Trust Your Heart was included
                            in the soundtrack of the film The Hanged Man
                            (1966) in which Getz and Gilberto appeared.

- 1/3/76*   BC

ONLY YOU   (B. Ram/A. Rand)
9/8/55   Louis Armstrong (v) with Benny Carter's Orch.
                            3tp/2tb/1cl/2as/2ts/p/b/d/v Vocalion VL73851,
                            MCA Coral 52026, MCA Coral 82051/2

OOFDAH!   (BC)
ca. 7/46*   (AFRS Jubilee #203) BC   large orch

ORGAN GRINDER'S SWING   (Hudson/Mills/Parish)
2/15-16/79   Ella Fitzgerald (v) with Count Basie's Orch.   4tp/
                            4tb/5reeds/p/g/b/d/v Pablo Today 2312-132

OUT OF MY WAY   (Sid Catlett)
8/23/46*   BC (Sid Catlett-v) 1tp/1tb/1as/1ts/p/b/d/v

OUT OF NOWHERE   (Green/Heyman)
4/28/37*   Coleman Hawkins & His All Star Jam Band 1tp/
                            1as/1cl/1ts/p/g/b/d

PDQ BLUES   (Henry/Simpson)
4/28/27   Fletcher Henderson & His Orch.   3tp/2tb/3reeds/
                            p/banjo/tuba/d   78: Columbia 1002-D, LP: Only
                            For Collectors OFC23 NOTE: In an interview in
                            the May 1936 issue of the British periodical Mu-
                            sical News, Carter recalls his first attempts at
                            arranging.   He mentions three pieces which he
                            did for Charlie Johnson's Orchestra--"Do, Do,
                            Do" (from the musical Oh! Kay), "Moonlight on
                            the Ganges," and "Rhapsody in Blue." He then
                            states that he was approached by Fletcher Hender-
                            son to do an arrangement of "PDQ Blues." The
                            arranger for Henderson's recording of this title
                            (made on April 28, 1927) is not identified by
                            Walter C. Allen, who suggests in Hendersonia (p.
                            202) that it may be a stock.   Although Carter
                            does not recognize the recording today, it is quite
                            possible that this is his arrangement. If so, it
                            is his first on record, preceding by several
                            months the Charlie Johnson session of January
                            1928, at which two Carter arrangements were
                            recorded.

PAPA TREE TOP BLUES
1951   Little Miss Cornshucks [pseudonym for Mildred
                            Cummings] (v) small group/v Coral 65045

PARADISE   (N. H. Brown/G. Clifford)
1945   Sam Donahue & the Navy Band 4tp/4tb/6reeds/p/
                            g/b/d Big Band Landmarks vol. 24, Hep (E) 5

NOTE: This arrangement was originally done for Fletcher Henderson, probably in the early 1930's. Although the Henderson band never recorded it, Walter Allen notes in his chronology that the band in 1943 "was still using some of Fletcher's old charts from the Benny Goodman days, even a couple of tattered Benny Carter pieces like "Paradise," which Fletcher thought was a masterpiece, and which Chet Kruley and Leon Comegys recalled with respect." (Hendersonia, p. 424)

Note on Hep LP sleeve: "Paradise saxophone chorus, originally written for 4 saxes in the Fletcher Henderson band, was raised in key to accomodate [sic] 6 saxes by Sam Donahue."

PARDON ME, PRETTY BABY (V. Rose/R. Klages/J. Meskill)
   8/18/37*   BC 1tp/1tb/1as/1cl/1ts/p/g/b/d

PASEO PROMENADE (BC) [One of ten pieces comprising Carter's Kansas City Suite.]
   9/6-11/60   Count Basie & His Orch. 4tp/3tb/2as/2ts/1bs/p/ g/b/d Roulette (S)R52056, Roulette RE124
                      NOTE: See note on recording date under Kansas City Suite.

PATTY CAKE, PATTY CAKE, BAKER MAN (Waller)
   5/13/39*   BC (Mercedes Carter-v) 3tp/3tb/2as/2ts/p/g/b/d/v

THE PAWNBROKER (Q. Jones/J. Lawrence)
   1965   Sarah Vaughan (v) large orch with strings/v 45: Mercury 72417

PEACE (Rogers/Fields)
   1957   Ernie Andrews (v) with Benny Carter's Orch. large orch/v GNP 28 NOTE: This recording also has a vocal accompaniment by an unknown female singer.

PEOPLE (J. Styne/B. Merrill)
   2/19/64   Billy Eckstine (v) 1tp/1tb/2reeds/p/g/b/d/v/vocal group Mercury SR60916, Mercury MG20916

PHANTOM RAIDERS (BC)
   3/59*   The Music from M Squad large orch NOTE: Composed for TV series M Squad.

PHEASANT FEATHERS see FEASANT PHEATHERS

PICK YOURSELF UP (J. Kern/D. Fields)
   6/60   Dakota Staton (v) large orch Capitol T1490

PINKY (A. Newman)
   1961   Alfred Newman large orch with horns/strings/ rhythm section Capitol S(T)1652, Capitol SP8639, Angel S36066

PLAY BALL (BC/lyrics: P. Vandervoort)
  1954   Jimmy Maddin (v) & His Orch. small orch/v
                        78: Skyway 103

PLAYBOY THEME see CRACK UP

PLAYIN' THE BLUES see BLUE LIGHT BLUES

PLEASE DON'T TALK ABOUT ME WHEN I'M GONE (S. Stept/S. Clare)
  2/15-16/79   Ella Fitzgerald (v) with Count Basie's Orch.
                        4tp/4tb/5reeds/p/g/b/d/v NOTE: Recorded for
                        Pablo--unissued.

PLEASE PLEASE ME (Lennon/McCartney)
  ca. 1966   Keely Smith (v) large orch with strings/v Re-
                        prise RS6142

PLEASURES AND PALACES (F. Loesser)
  Mar. 30-Apr. 1   Pearl Bailey (v) 4tp/4tb/5reeds/p/g/b/d/v
  1965*

POINT OF NO RETURN (BC/lyrics: J. Moen)
  1968   Don Wyatt (v) large orch with strings/v NOTE:
                        Recorded for Capitol--unissued.

POLKA DOTS AND MOONBEAMS (J. Van Heusen/J. Burke)
  11/5/57   Stringin' Along 2reeds/p/vib/g/b/d/string quartet
                        Andex LP3001 NOTE: Personnel includes Bob
                        Keene (cl) and appears in Jepsen under his name.

POM POM (BC)
  ● 1/15/40*   Varsity Seven

  ● 4/29/40   Joe Sullivan & His Cafe Society Orch. Blu-Disc
                        T1005

  5/20/40*   BC 3tp/2tb/3as/2ts/p/g/b/d

  ● 2/29/46   Eddie Heywood & His Orch. Decca DL8202

POOR FOOL (BC/lyrics: P. Vandervoort)
  2/19/64   Billy Eckstine (v) 1tp/1tb/2reeds/p/g/b/d/v/vocal
                        group Mercury SR60919, Mercury MG20916

  ● date unknown   Ernie Freeman Orch. (Lawrence Stone-v) arr:
                        Ernie Freeman 45: Mambo 107

POOR LITTLE RICH GIRL (N. Coward)
  5/63*   Stanley Wilson Orch. 4tp/4tb/5reeds/p/g/b/d

THE POWER OF LOVE (A. Schroeder/C. Demetrius)
  1965   Lou Rawls (v) 2tp/4tb/2reeds/p/g/b/d/v Capitol
                        T2273

PRISONER OF MY EYES (I CAN NEVER LET YOU GO) (L. Pockriss/H.
Hackady)
  1968*   Nancy Wilson (v) 4tp/4tb/5reeds/p/g/b/d/v

PROHIBIDO (BC)
   3/2/66*   BC   2as/2ts/1bs/p/g/b/d
   11/10/73*   BC

PROTECT ME (H. Dietz/A. Schwartz)
   1968   Pearl Bailey (v) with Louis Bellson Orch.   4tp/
                           4tb/5reeds/p/g/b/d/v   Project 3 PR5022SD, Pro-
                           ject 3 PR4003SD

PUDDIN' HEAD SERENADE   see   LONESOME NIGHTS

QUEEN FOR A DAY   (B. Blalock)
   early 1950's   Bruce Blalock (Ketty Lester?-v)   small group/v
                           45: Coral 9-61884

RAIN, RAIN, GO AWAY   (J. Green/E. Heyman/M. David)
   4/25/39*   Jerry Kruger (v) & Her Orch.   1tp/2reeds/p/b/d/v

RAINBOW RHAPSODY   (BC)
   ● 7/16/42   Glenn Miller & His Orch.   arr: George Williams
                           4tp/4tb/5reeds/p/g/b/d Bluebird AXM2-5574
   1959   New Glenn Miller Orch. directed by Ray McKinley
                           RCA LSP1948 NOTE: This recording is a re-
                           creation, including solos, of the 1942 perform-
                           ance.
   late 1950's?   Don Raleigh & His Orch.   Palace PST621 NOTE:
                           This recording also appears on Parade SPS385,
                           A Tribute to Glenn Miller which does not identify
                           the orchestra. It may also be the version of
                           Rainbow Rhapsody included on Spinorama M83,
                           also entitled A Tribute to Glenn Miller.

                           NOTE: The Bluebird LP credits Carter with the
                           arrangement, but Carter recalls it was by George
                           Williams.

RAISIN' THE ROOF   (McHugh/Fields)
   ca. 4/29   Fletcher Henderson   2tp/2tb/2cl/as/1ts/p/banjo/
                           tuba   Columbia CL1684

RAMBLING IN C   (BC)
   ● 1/11-16/37*   BC

RANDALL'S ISLAND   (BC)
   ● 12/27/51*   Ben Webster Sextet

RE-BOP BOOGIE   (BC) [also entitled BE-BOP BOOGIE]
   8/46*   BC   3tp/2tb/3reeds/p/g/b/d

   12/16/47   Freddie Slack & His Orch.   1tp/1tb/1as/p/g/b/d
                           Capitol LC6529 (as Be-Bop Boogie)

RED RED RIBBON
   1957   Martha Davis (v)   4tp/4tb/2as/2ts/1bs/p/g/b/d/v
                           NOTE: Recorded for ABC Paramount--unissued.

RED ROSE WALTZ
   date unknown   Johnny Ridge [pseudonym for Art Kassel]   ?/v
                           45: Kady (no issue number)

REINA (H. Atwood)
   1/48*   BC (Bob Decker, The Enchanters-v) 1tp/1tb/1as/
                                   1ts/p/g/b/d/v/vocal group

RESPECT (O. Redding)
   1/3-4/68   Jackie Wilson (v) with Count Basie Orch.   4tp/
                                   4tb/2as/2ts/1bs/p/g/b/d/v Brunswick BL54134

RHUMBOOGIE (D. Raye/H. Prince)
   1955   Freddie Slack (v) 1tp/1tb/1ts/1bs/p/g/b/d/v
                                   Emarcy MG36094, Wing MGW60003

RHYTHM IS OUR BUSINESS (Lunceford/Cahn/Kaplan)
   1/17/36*   Willie Lewis & His Orch. (Bobby Martin-v) 2tp/
                                   1tb/2as/2ts/p/g/b/d/v

RHYTHM OF THE TAMBOURINE (D. Franklin)
   3/2/37   Fletcher Henderson & His Orch.   3tp/3tb/2cl/as/
                                   2ts/p/g/b/d Columbia CL1685

RIDING TO GLORY ON A TRUMPET (McCoy)
   1955   Horace Heidt & His Musical Knights (unknown v)
                                   3tp/3tb/4reeds/p/g/b/d/v 45: Magnolia MS1070

RIFF ROMP (BC)
   8/31/39*   BC 3tp/3tb/3as/2ts/p/g/b/d
   10/14/39*   BC

RIFFAMAROLE (BC)
  ● 3/30/45*   Capitol International Jazzmen

RIGHT HERE IN MY HEART (Bob Friedman)
   11/71-3/72   Joe Williams (v) large orch/v Temponic
                                   TB29561

RIGHT HERE WITH YOU
   8/64*   BC 2ss/4as/3ts/2bs/p/g/b/d

RISE AND SHINE   see   RISE 'N SHINE

RISE 'N SHINE (Youmans/DeSylva)
   ca. 5/36   Henry Hall & the B. B. C. Dance Orch.   large
                                     orch (B. B. C. broadcast, no known airchecks)

THE RIVER OF NO RETURN (K. Darby/L. Newman)
   8/30/74   Yujiro Ishihara (v) 2tp/1tb/1as/2ts/1bs/p/g/b/d/
                                     14violins/4violas/4celli/v/vocal group Continental
                                     (J) C01 NOTE: Instrumental tracks recorded
                                     8/30/74, Los Angeles; vocal added later in Japan.

ROCK ALONE   see   ROCKIN' ALONG

ROCK BOTTOM (BC)
   3/4/66*   BC 2as/2ts/1bs/p/g/b/d
   11/10/73*   BC

ROCK ME TO SLEEP (BC/lyrics: P. Vandervoort)
  ● 5/9/50   Helen Humes (v) accompanied by Marshall Royal
                                    & His Orch.   Discovery 519, Savoy SJL2242

- 11/14/50   Les Brown & His Orch. (Lucy Ann Polk-v)
                              Columbia CL539

- 1950   Peggy Lee (v) 78: Capitol 1428 45: F1428

1951   Little Miss Cornshucks [pseudonym for Mildred
                              Cummings] (v) small group/v Coral 65045

- ca. 1951   Rudy Render (v) with Maxwell Davis & His Orch.
                              arr: Maxwell Davis 78: London 17014

- 6/58   June Christy (v) accompanied by Bob Cooper's
                              Orch. arr: Bob Cooper Capitol T1076

6/60   Dakota Staton (v) large orch/v Capitol T1490

- 1963   Irene Kral (v) accompanied by Junior Mance Trio
                              Ava 33

- 1963   Maynard Ferguson Roulette (S)R52107? NOTE:
                              Although a "Rock Me to Sleep" is listed on the
                              jacket of this Maynard Ferguson LP, the disc
                              does not actually contain a track with this title.
                              Whether the tune was recorded but not issued,
                              and whether it is Carter's composition or a dif-
                              ferent song with the same title is not known.

ROCKIN' ALONG   (BC)   also appears as ROCK ALONE
   7/26/52*   BC 1tp/1tb/3reeds/p/g/b/d

ROCKIN' CHAIR   (H. Carmichael)
   3/22/41*   Gene Krupa & His Orch. featuring BC.
   6/7/41   Gene Krupa & His Orch. 4tp/3tb/2as/2ts/p/g/b/d
                          (NBC broadcast from Meadowbrook, Cedar Grove,
                          N.J.)
   7/2/41   Gene Krupa & His Orch. Columbia C2L29
   10/3/41   Gene Krupa & His Orch. (broadcast from Holly-
                          wood Palladium)
   4/15/49   Gene Krupa & His Orch. (AFRS One Night Stand
                          #1961) (possibly same arrangement)
   4/22/49   Gene Krupa & His Orch. (AFRS One Night Stand
                          #1936) (possibly same arrangement)
   8/2/71   Time-Life series The Swing Era (Billy May-lead-
                          er) Time-Life STL347 NOTE: This recording
                          is a recreation of the 7/2/41 Krupa performance.

   9/75   Maria Muldaur, Hoagy Carmichael (v) 2tp/1tb/
                          1as/1ts/1bs/p/g/b/d/v Warner Brothers MS2235

ROLL WITH THE BOOGIE   (BC under pseudonym "Johnny Gomez"/lyrics:
F. Cadrez)
   9/22/49*   Joe Robinson (v) with Benny Carter's Orch. 1tp/
                          1as/1ts/1bs/p/g/b/d/v

ROMPIN' AT THE RENO   (BC) [One of ten pieces comprising Carter's
Kansas City Suite.]
   9/6-11/60   Count Basie & His Orch. 4tp/3tb/2as/2ts/1bs/p/
                          g/b/d Roulette (S)R52056, Roulette (E) 2683-013,

Roulette RE124   NOTE: See note on recording
date under <u>Kansas City Suite</u>.

ROSES IN DECEMBER   (Oakland/Jessel/Magidson)
  <u>late 1958 or early</u>   BC   4tp/3tb/5reeds/p/g/b/d
  <u>1959*</u>

ROSES OF PICARDY   (H. Wood/F. Weatherly)
  <u>5/63*</u>   Stanley Wilson Orch.   4tp/4tb/5reeds/20strings/
                        p/g/b/d

'ROUND MIDNIGHT   (Hanighen/Williams/Monk)
  <u>9/52*</u>   BC with the Oscar Peterson Trio & Buddy Rich
                        horns/strings/p/g/b/d

  <u>1957</u>   Ernie Andrews (v) with Benny Carter's Orch.
                        large orch/v   GNP 28, GNP-Crescendo 10008

  <u>6/60</u>   Dakota Staton (v)   large orch with strings/v
                        Capitol T1597

ROW ROW ROW ROW
  <u>1961*</u>   Pearl Bailey (v)   large orch/v

RUBY   (M. Parish/H. Roemheld)
  <u>8/30/74</u>   Yujiro Ishihara (v)   2tp/1tb/1as/2ts/1bs/p/g/b/d/
                        14violins/4violas/4celli/v   Continental (J) C01
                        NOTE: Instrumental tracks recorded 8/30/74,
                        Los Angeles; vocal added later in Japan.

RUMBLE, RUMBLE, RUMBLE   (F. Loesser)
  <u>1947</u>   Betty Hutton (v) with Joe Lilley & His Orch.
                        large orch/v   78: Capitol 380

ST. LOUIS BLUES   (W. C. Handy)
  <u>10/15/40*</u>   Billie Holiday (v) accompanied by Benny Carter
                        Orch.   1tp/1tb/2reeds/p/g/b/d/v

  <u>11/25/47*</u>   Freddie Slack & His Orch.   4tp/2tb/2as/2ts/1bs/
                        p/g/b/d

SAN FRANCISCO BLUES
  <u>4/15-16/61*</u>   Peggy Lee (v) accompanied by Quincy Jones' Orch.
                        6tp/4tb/2as/2ts/1bs/p/g/b/d/v

SATIN LATIN   (Bob Friedman)
  <u>11/71-3/72</u>   Joe Williams (v)   large orch/v   Temponic
                        TB29561

SAVOY STAMPEDE   see   GIN AND JIVE

SAY IT WITH A KISS   (J. Mercer/H. Warren)
  <u>11/9/38*</u>   Teddy Wilson & His Orch. (Billie Holiday-v)
                        1tp/1tb/2as/2ts/p/g/b/d/v

SCANDAL IN A FLAT   (BC)
  <u>mid 6/36*</u>   BC   3tp/2tb/3as/1ts/p/g/b/d

  <u>4/22/39*</u>   BC 3tp/3tb/2as/2ts/p/g/b/d

7/24/39*   BC
10/9/39*   BC

6/29/39*   BC 3tp/3tb/2as/2ts/p/g/b/d NOTE: Differs
                            slightly from 4/22/39* arrangement.

THE SEARCH (BC)
  3/59*   The Music from M Squad large orch NOTE:
                            Composed for TV series M Squad.

SECOND HAND LOVE (BC/lyrics: P. Vandervoort under pseudonym "Paul
Vance")
  11/26/47   Kay Starr (v) 1cornet/3tb/1ts/p/g/b/d/v 78:
                            Capitol 15380

SEPTEMBER SONG (Anderson/Weill/DeSylva/Brown/Henderson)
  late 1958 or early   BC 4tp/3tb/5reeds/p/g/b/d
  1959*

  8/30/74   Yujiro Ishihara (v) 2tp/1tb/1as/2ts/1bs/p/g/b/d/
                            14violins/4violas/4celli/v Continental (J) C01
                            NOTE: Instrumental tracks recorded 8/30/74,
                            Los Angeles; vocal added later in Japan.

SERENADE TO A SARONG (BC)
  5/20/40*   BC 3tp/2tb/3as/2ts/p/g/b/d

SHANGRI-LA (Maxwell)
  8/64*   BC 2ss/4as/3ts/2bs/p/g/b/d

SHE DOESN'T LAUGH LIKE YOU (BC/lyrics: K. Suessdorf, L. Worth)
  ● ca. 1953   Jack Powers (v) & the Cheer Leaders 78: Click
                            JP-503

SHE HAD TO GO AND LOSE IT AT THE ASTOR
  9/29/70   Mrs. Miller (v) 2tp/2tb/2as/1ts/1bs/p/g/b/d/v
                            45: Mrs. Miller Records (no issue number)

THE SHIP THAT NEVER SAILED (A. Kassel)
  date unknown   Johnny Ridge [pseudonym for Art Kassel] (v) ?/v
                            45: Kady (no issue number)

SHOE SHINER'S DRAG (Jelly Roll Morton)
  7/21/38*   Lionel Hampton & His Orch. 1tp/2as/2ts/p/b/d/
                            vib

SHOOT THE WORKS (BC)
  12/13/34*   BC 3tp/2tb/3as/1ts/p/g/b/d

SHOW BREAK #1 (BC)
  5/63*   KPM Music Library 4tp/4tb/2fr. horns/5reeds/p/
                            g/b/d NOTE: See notes for this session in
                            chronological section of discography.

SHOW BREAK #2 (BC)
  5/63*   KPM Music Library 4tp/4tb/2fr. horns/5reeds/p/
                            g/b/d NOTE: See notes for this session in
                            chronological section of discography.

SHOW ME THE WAY TO GO HOME   (I. King)
    5/63*   Stanley Wilson Orch.   4tp/4tb/5reeds/20strings/
                               p/g/b/d

SHUFFLEBUG SHUFFLE   (BC)
    11/1/39*   BC   3tp/3tb/3as/2ts/p/g/b/d

SIGHS AND TEARS   (BC/lyrics: Mack David)
    ● 12/17/40   Ginny Simms (v) with Eddie South & His Orch.
                               78:   OK 5990

SKIP IT   (BC)
    8/17/37*   BC   3tp/2tb/2as/2ts/p/g/b/d

    ● 9/20/56   Bertie King Jazz Group   Nixa (E) NJT506

THE SKY IS CRYING   (BC/lyrics: P. Herrick)
    ● 2/1/50   Mary Ann McCall (v)   arr: Al Cohn   78:   Roost
                               511

SLEEP   (E. Lebieg)
    1/30/40*   BC   3tp/3tb/3as/2ts/p/g/b/d
    May or later 1943*   (AFRS Basic Library P-33)   BC
    4/30/45*   (AFRS Jubilee #131)   BC
    7/2/72*   BC
    12/3/73*   BC

SLEIGH RIDE IN JULY   (Burke/Van Heusen)
    late 1958 or early   BC   4tp/3tb/5reeds/p/g/b/d
    1959*

SLIDES AND HIDES   (BC/L. Bellson)
    1/18/65   Buddy Rich - Louis Bellson with the George Kawa-
                             guchi Orch.   4tp/6tb/5reeds/p/g/b/2d   Roost
                             SLP2263, Roulette (E) 2432-003   NOTE: Recorded
                             in Tokyo.

SLOW BUT SURE   (BC/lyrics: A. Hansen)
    ● early 1950's   Kay Brown (v)   arr: Van Alexander   45:   Crown
                               45x132

    ● ca. 1957   Ruth Olay (v)   Emarcy MG36125

SLOW FREIGHT   (Buck Ram)
    1/30/40*   BC   3tp/3tb/2as/2ts/p/g/b/d

SMACK DAB IN THE MIDDLE   (C. E. Calhoun)
    1964   Ray Charles (v) & the Raelets   5tp/3tb/2as/2ts/
                             1bs/p/g/b/d/v   ABC Paramount 495

SO IN LOVE   (C. Porter)
    6/60   Dakota Staton (v)   large orch with strings/v
                             Capitol T1597

SO LONG, MY LOVE   (Cahn/Spence)
    1/63   Sarah Vaughan (v)   4tp/4tb/2as/2ts/1bs/p/g/b/d/v
                             Roulette R(S)52104

SOFT AND SWEET   (E. Sampson)
   3/30/31*   Chick Webb & His Orch.   3tp/1tb/2as/c1/1ts/p/g/
                                           b/d

SOFT TOUCH   (BC)
   11/65   film soundtrack: A Man Called Adam   1tb/1ts/p/
                                           b/d   Reprise 6180

SOLITUDE   (D. Ellington/E. DeLange/I. Mills)
   2/60   Dakota Staton (v)   large orch with strings/v
                                           Capitol T1427

   1/63   Sarah Vaughan (v)   4tp/4tb/2as/2ts/1bs/p/g/b/d/v
                                           Roulette R(S)52104, Roulette RE103

   8/13/79   Sarah Vaughan (v)   1flute/1ts/9violins/3violas/
                                           2celli/p/g/b/d/v   NOTE: Recorded for Pablo--
                                         unissued.

SOME OF THESE DAYS   (S. Brooks)
   9/12/36*   BC med Sonora Swing Band   2tp/1tb/1cl/1ts/p/g/
                                           b/d

SOME OTHER SPRING   (Kitchings/Herzog)
   2/15-16/79   Ella Fitzgerald (v) with Count Basie's Orch.
                                           4tp/4tb/5reeds/p/g/b/d/v   NOTE: Recorded for
                                         Pablo--unissued.

SOMEBODY LOVES ME   (B. Macdonald/B. DeSylva/G. Gershwin)
   10/3/30*   Fletcher Henderson & His Orch.   3tp/2tb/2as/
                                           1ts/p/g/b/d/v(trio)

   8/18/37*   BC   1tp/1tb/1cl/1ts/p/g/b/d

   early 1945*   (AFRS Jubilee?)   BC
   4/30/45*   (AFRS Jubilee #131)   BC

SOMEONE TO WATCH OVER ME   (G. and I. Gershwin)
   12/20/65   Johnny Hodges with Lawrence Welk Orch.   4tb/
                                           3fr. horns/1as/p/g/b/d/vib/strings   Dot DLP25682

SOMETHING FOR OCTOBER   (BC)
   late 1958 or early   BC   4tp/3tb/5reeds/p/g/b/d
   1959*

SONG OF THE WANDERER   (N. Moret)
   1957   Ernie Andrews (v) with Benny Carter's Orch.
                                           large orch/v   GNP 28, GNP-Crescendo 10008

SOPHISTICATED LADY   (D. Ellington)
   8/13/79   Sarah Vaughan (v)   1flute/2cl/1bass cl/3fr. horns/
                                           1oboe/1ts/9violins/3violas/2celli/1harp/p/g/b/d/v
                                         NOTE: Recorded for Pablo--unissued.

SORRY   see   I'M SORRY

SOUTH SIDE SAMBA   (BC)
  ● 3/18/77*   BC

4/29/77*	BC 2tp/1tb/3reeds/p/g/b/d
6/2/79*	BC
July 1981*	BC
● 4/18/81*	BC
● 9/26/81*	BC
● 11/28/81*	BC
● 12/5/81*	BC

SOUVENIR (BC) originally entitled THAT'S HOW IT GOES
12/3/73*	BC 4tp/4tb/3as/2ts/1bs/p/g/b/d (as That's How It Goes)
4/8/77*	BC with the Princeton University Jazz Ensemble
4/29/77*	BC 2tp/1tb/3reeds/p/g/b/d NOTE: This arrangement is similar to the one above.
● 1978	Mundell Lowe Dobre DR1018
● 1978	The Capp/Pierce Juggernaut arr: Nat Pierce Concord CJ72
● 4/18/81*	BC

SPRING FEVER BLUES (L. Whenham)
1954	The Dream Dusters (v) with Jimmie Maddin (v) & His Orch. small orch/v/vocal group 78: Skyway 103

SQUATTY ROO (J. Hodges)
4/29/77*	BC 2tp/1tb/3reeds/p/g/b/d

SQUEEZE ME (T. Waller/C. Williams)
12/22/74*	Maria Muldaur (v) 2tp/1tb/1as/1ts/1bs/p/g/b/d/v
1974	Maria Muldaur (v) Reprise MS2194

STAR DUST (H. Carmichael/M. Parish)
1/17/36*	Willie Lewis & His Orch. 2tp/1tb/2as/2ts/p/g/b/d
4/22/39*	BC 3tp/3tb/2as/2ts/p/g/b/d NOTE: This is a slightly altered version of the 1/17/36 arrangement. The saxophone chorus has been retained.
7/11/44*	(AFRS Jubilee #87) BC large orch
early 1945?*	(AFRS Jubilee?) BC

STARS AND YOU (BC)
● 1/11-16/37*	BC 1tp/1as/p

STATE FAIR
	For Carter's work on this movie musical see the individual title THAT'S FOR ME.

STAY OUT OF LOVE (Gerlach/Freniere)
1/17/36*	Willie Lewis (v) & His Orch. 2tp/1tb/2as/2ts/p/g/b/d/v

STICK OR TWIST   (BC)
<u>early 1960's</u>   Laurie Johnson Orch.   8brass/5reeds/p/g/b/d
                                     NOTE: Test pressing--may have been issued.

STINKIN' FROM DRINKIN'   (BC/lyrics: P. Vandervoort)
 • ca. 1949   Calvin Boze (v) & His All Stars   78:   Aladdin
                                     3072

STORMY WEATHER   (H. Arlen/T. Koehler)
<u>Jan. -Feb. 1943*</u>   film soundtrack: <u>Stormy Weather</u> (Lena Horne-v)
                                     large orch with <u>strings/v</u>

<u>Jan. -Feb. 1943*</u>   film soundtrack: <u>Stormy Weather</u>   large orch
                                     with strings/vocal group   NOTE: Carter arranged
                                     last 29 measures.

STROLL   (BC)
 • <u>11/30/76*</u>   BC   1as/p/b/d

SUGAR BLUES   (C. McCoy)
<u>9/61</u>   Jonah Jones with Glen Gray & the Casa Loma
                                     Orch.   6tp/4tb/2as/2ts/1bs/p/g/b/d   Capitol T1713

SUMMER NIGHT   (BC/lyrics: Jimmy Kennedy) also known as WONDER-
LAND
 • ca. 1961   Harry Williams (v)   45: Pye (issue number un-
                                     known)

 • 1962   Mantovani & His Orch.   45:   Decca 11500

 • <u>11/30/76*</u>   BC   1tp/1as/1ts/p/b/d

SUMMERTIME   (G. Gershwin/D. Heyward)
<u>4/25/39*</u>   Jerry Kruger (v) & Her Orch.   1tp/2reeds/p/b/d/v

SUMMERTIME IN VENICE   (Pinchi/Sigman/Cicognini)
<u>8/30/74</u>   Yujiro Ishihara (v)   2tp/1tb/1as/2ts/1bs/p/g/b/d/
                                     14violins/4violas/4celli/v   Continental (J) C01
                                     NOTE: Instrumental tracks recorded 8/30/74,
                                     Los Angeles; vocal added later in Japan.

A SUNBONNET BLUE
<u>ca. 5/36</u>   Henry Hall & the B. B. C. Dance Orch.   large
                                     orch (B. B. C. broadcast, no known airchecks)

SUNDAY   (Miller/Cohn/Stein/Kruger)
<u>10/16/41*</u>   BC   3tp/3tb/3as/2ts/p/g/b/d
<u>6/4/45*</u>   (AFRS Jubilee #136)   BC

SUNDAY AFTERNOON   (BC)
<u>10/2/52*</u>   BC   3tp/3tb/2as/2ts/1bs/p/g/b/d

SUNSET EYES   (T. Edwards/D. Wayne)
<u>1957</u>   Ernie Andrews (v) with Benny Carter's Orch.
                                     large orch/v   GNP 28, GNP-Crescendo 10008

SUNSET GLOW   (BC) [One of ten pieces comprising Carter's <u>Kansas City</u>
<u>Suite.</u>]

9/6-11/60   Count Basie & His Orch.   4tp/3tb/2as/2ts/1bs/p/
                               g/b/d Roulette (S)R52056, Roulette RE124
                               NOTE: See note on recording date under
                               Kansas City Suite.
8/9/62   Count Basie & His Orch.   NOTE: Recorded
                               live in Stockholm--unissued.

SUPPER TIME   (I. Berlin)
    1971   Pearl Bailey (v) 4tp/4tb/5reeds/p/g/b/d/strings/v
                               RCA LSP4529

SURF BOARD   (BC)
  ● 5/49*   BC 1tp/1tb/1as/1ts/p/b/d

SUSPICIOUS OF MY WOMAN   (BC under pseudonym "Johnny Gomez"/B.
Austin)
    9/22/49*   Joe Robinson (v) with Benny Carter's Orch.   1tp/
                               1as/1ts/1bs/p/g/b/d/v

SWEDISH JAM   (BC/D. Gillespie/J. J. Johnson/J. Adderley)
  ● 11/22/60*   Jazz At The Philharmonic

SWEET AND HOT   (J. Yellen/H. Arlen)
    2/5/31*   Fletcher Henderson & His Orch.   (Jimmy Har-
                               rison-v) 3tp/2tb/2as/1ts/p/g/b/d/v

SWEET GEORGIA BROWN   (B. Bernie/M. Pinkard/K. Casey)
    7/11/44*   (AFRS Jubilee #87) BC large orch
    3/19/45*   (AFRS Jubilee #125) BC

SWEET LORRAINE   (Burwell/Parish)
    2/15-16/79   Ella Fitzgerald (v) with Count Basie's Orch.
                               4tp/4tb/5reeds/p/g/b/d/v   Pablo Today 2312-132

SWEET RHYTHM   (Maxey/Bechet)
    11/15/32   Cab Calloway & His Orch.   3tp/2tb/4reeds/p/g/b/
                               d/v   Collector's Classics 20

SWEETHEART   (K. Burgan)
    12/22/74*   Maria Muldaur (v) 2tp/1tb/1as/1ts/1bs/p/g/b/d/v
    1974   Maria Muldaur (v) Reprise MS2194

SWING IT   (Bretz/Weitz)
    3/14/33*   BC (v) 3tp/2tb/2as/1ts/p/g/b/d/v

SWINGIN' AT MAIDA VALE   (BC) originally entitled JUST A RIDE
    3/27/36   Henry Hall & the B.B.C. Dance Orch.   large
                               orch (B.B.C. broadcast, no known airchecks)

    4/15/36*   BC 3tp/2tb/3as/2ts/p/g/b/d NOTE: This ar-
                               rangement may be the same as or similar to the
                               3/27/36 version above.

SWINGIN' IN NOVEMBER   (BC)
    late 1958 or early   BC 4tp/3tb/5reeds/p/g/b/d
    1959*
    11/9/68*   BC with Henri Chaix & His Orch.   NOTE:

Similar arrangement but performed by 1tp/1tb/
2as/1ts/1bs/p/b/d

SWINGIN' THE BLUES   (BC)
  late 4/36*   BC 2tp/1cl/1as/1ts/p/g/b/d

SWINGIN' WITH RHYTHM AND BLUES   (J. Barnett/J. Durante)
  ca. 1957   Jimmy Durante, Peter Lawford (v) 4tp/4tb/2as/
                               2ts/1bs/p/g/b/d/v 45: Decca 9-29581

THE SWIZZLE   (BC)
  11/1-2/61*   Count Basie & His Orch.   4tp/3tb/2as/2ts/1bs/p/
                               g/b/d

SYMPHONY   (Alstone/Lawrence)
  1/4/54*   BC horns/strings/p/b/d

SYMPHONY IN RIFFS   (BC)
  10/16/33*   BC 3tp/3tb/3as/1ts/p/g/b/d
  4/28/37   Artie Shaw & His Orch.   Thesaurus Transcription
                               402, Alamac QSR2434
  7/8/38   Artie Shaw & His Orch.   (broadcast, aircheck?)
  7/25/38   Tommy Dorsey & His Orch.   RCA (F) FXM1-
                               7171, Historia (G) H628
  ca. 8/39   Gene Krupa & His Orch.   (broadcast from Steel
                               Pier, Atlantic City)
  9/20/39   Gene Krupa & His Orch.   Bandstand 7117, Colum-
                               bia Special Products JCL641, Ajax 121
  11/5/39   Gene Krupa & His Orch.   (broadcast, Sherman
                               Hotel, Chicago)
  2/5/40   Glenn Miller & His Orch.   (aircheck, NBC broad-
                               cast, Hotel Pennsylvania, New York)
  3/4/40   Glenn Miller & His Orch.   (aircheck, NBC broad-
                               cast, Hotel Pennsylvania, New York)
  6/22/40   Tommy Dorsey & His Orch. featuring Bunny
                               Berigan Fanfare 4-104 (aircheck)
  3/8/58   Glen Gray & His Casa Loma Orch.   Capitol
                               SM1022, Capitol (G) IC054-81 710 NOTE: This
                               recording is a recreation, including note-for-note
                               solos of the 9/20/39 Gene Krupa version and is
                               included in the Time-Life series The Swing Era
                               Time-Life STL344.
  date unknown   Electrecord Orch. (Roumania) Electrecord 0971
                               NOTE: This is a recreation, including solos, of
                               Carter's 10/16/33* recording.

  • 4/20/55   The Jazz Today Unit (Kenny Baker-leader, fea-
                               turing Bertie King) Jazz Today (E) JTL5 NOTE:
                               This arrangement is based on Carter's.

SYNTHETIC LOVE   (BC/lyrics: N. Washington)
  3/14/33*   BC (v) 3tp/2tb/2as/1ts/p/g/b/d/v
  12/13/34*   BC (Charles Holland-v)

TAKE BACK YOUR MINK   (F. Loesser)
  Mar. 30-Apr. 1   Pearl Bailey (v) 4tp/4tb/5reeds/p/g/b/d/v
  1965*

TAKE IT OR LEAVE IT (BC/lyrics: M. Hammond)
   • 11/11/47*   Julia Lee (v) & Her Boy Friends

TAKE MY WORD see LONESOME NIGHTS

TAKIN' MY TIME (BC)
   11/19/40*   BC   3tp/3tb/2as/2ts/1bs/p/g/b/d

TEA FOR TWO (V. Youmans/I. Caesar)
   4/22/39*   BC   3tp/3tb/2as/2ts/p/g/b/d
   5/27/39*   BC (Mercedes Carter-v)

TEACH ME TONIGHT (Cahn/DePaul)
   2/15-16/79   Ella Fitzgerald (v) with Count Basie's Orch.   4tp/
                      4tb/5reeds/p/g/b/d/v Pablo Today 2312-132

TENDER LOVING WORDS (Bob Friedman)
   11/71-3/72   Carmen McRae (v) large orch/v Temponic
                      TB29562

TENDERLY (W. Gross/J. Lawrence)
   9/61   Jonah Jones with Glen Gray & the Casa Loma
                      Orch. 6tp/4tb/2as/2ts/1bs/p/g/b/d Capitol
                      T1713

THAT AIN'T IT (BC/lyrics: P. Vandervoort)
   1950   Virgie Austin (v) small orch/v 78: London
                      17009

THAT OLD BLACK MAGIC (H. Arlen/J. Mercer)
   4/27/55   Ella Fitzgerald with Benny Carter Orch.   3tp/1tb/
                      2as/2ts/p/g/b/d/v Decca DL8155, MCA Coral
                      (G) 0082. 050-2

THAT'S FOR ME (Rodgers/Hammerstein)
   1962   film soundtrack: State Fair (Pat Boone-v) large
                      orch with strings/v Dot DLP9011

THAT'S HOW IT GOES see SOUVENIR

THEM THERE EYES (M. Pinkard/W. Tracey/D. Tauber)
   4/29/77*   BC   2tp/1tb/3reeds/p/g/b/d
   4/15/78*   BC
   4/19?/78*   BC

THERE I'VE SAID IT AGAIN (R. Evans/D. Mann)
   1/21/41*   BC (Roy Felton-v) 3tp/3tb/3as/2ts/p/g/b/d/v

THERE'LL NEVER BE ANOTHER YOU (H. Warren)
   early 1970's   The Airmen of Note (U. S. Air Force Jazz En-
                      semble) (Sarah Vaughan-v) 4tp/4tb/5reeds/p/g/b/
                      d/v NOTE: Promotional album: The Airmen of
                      Note and Sarah Vaughan (no label and issue)

THERE'S A SMALL HOTEL (Rodgers/Hart)
   1/11-16/37*   BC (v) 2tp/2tb/3as/2ts/p/g/b/d/v
   1/11-16/37*   BC

NOTE: Two versions recorded at same session, one with and one without vocal.

THESE FOOLISH THINGS   (J. Strachey/H. Link)
   4/15/36*   BC   3tp/2tb/3as/2ts/p/g/b/d

   2/9/42*   Mark Warnow & His Orch. (Barry Wood-v)   3tp/
                      2tb/6reeds/7violins/1harp/p/g/b/d/v

   1/63   Sarah Vaughan (v)   4tb/20strings/p/g/b/d/v
                      Roulette R(S)52104, Roulette RE103

THEY SAY   (E. Heyman/P. Mann/S. Weiss)
   11/9/38*   Teddy Wilson & His Orch. (Billie Holiday-v)   1tp/
                      1tb/2as/2ts/p/g/b/d/v

THINGS AIN'T WHAT THEY USED TO BE   (D. Ellington)
   4/29/77*   BC   2tp/1tb/3reeds/p/g/b/d
   4/15/78*   BC
   4/19?/78*   BC
   July 1981*   BC

THIS CAN'T BE LOVE   (Rodgers/Hart)
   11/5-6/56   Abbey Lincoln (v)   1tp/1tb/1fr. horn/3woodwinds/p/
                      g/b/d/v   Liberty LRP3025

THREE O'CLOCK IN THE MORNING   (J. Robledo/D. Terriss)
   1965   Lou Rawls (v)   large orch with strings/vocal
                      group/v   Capitol T2401, Capitol SM2948

THREE TIME LOSER (WITH A TWO TIME GIRL)   see   I'M A THREE
TIME LOSER

TICKLE TOE   (Lester Young)
   8/64*   BC   2ss/4as/3ts/2bs/p/g/b/d

TIGER RAG

                      NOTE: Melody Maker (May 30, 1936) reports that
Carter was commissioned by Henry Hall to arrange this tune. It may have been broadcast by Hall and the B. B. C. Dance Orchestra. There are no known airchecks.

TILL WE MEET AGAIN   (R. Whiting/R. Egan)
   2/14/40*   Freddie Rich & His Orch.   3tp/1tb/3as/3ts/p/g/b/d

TIME AFTER TIME   (J. Styne/S. Cahn)
   11/56   Billy Daniels (v) accompanied by Benny Carter's
                      Orch.   1tp/4reeds/p/g/b/d/strings/v   Verve
                      MGV2072

TIRED   (B. Lown/T. Kurrus)
   1961*   Pearl Bailey (v)   large orch/v

TITMOUSE   (BC)
   3/4/66*   BC   2as/2ts/1bs/p/g/b/d
   11/9/68*   BC with Henri Chaix & His Orch.

TO AVA   see   BLUE MOUNTAIN

TO THE DESTROYERS (background music: BC/narrative text: V. Lundberg)
    1968   Victor Lundberg (v) 2fr. horns/1woodwind/1harp/
                              10strings/p/g/b/d/narrative v Liberty LST7547

TONIGHT I SHALL SLEEP WITH A SMILE ON MY FACE (D. Ellington)
    8/13/79   Sarah Vaughan (v) 1flute/2cl/1bass cl/3fr. horns/
                              1oboe/1ts/9violins/3violas/2celli/1harp/p/g/b/d/v
                              NOTE: Recorded for Pablo--unissued.

TOOT TOOT TOOTSIE (T. Fiorito/R. A. King/G. Kahn/E. Erdman)
    1961*   Pearl Bailey (v) large orch/v

TRANSATLANTIC (BC)
                              NOTE: Melody Maker (May 30, 1936) reports that
                              Carter was commissioned by Henry Hall to arrange this tune. It may have been broadcast by Hall and the B. B. C. Dance Orchestra. There are no known airchecks.

TRAPPED IN THE WEB OF LOVE (Jeanne Burns)
    6/60   Dakota Staton (v) large orch/v Capitol T1490

TREE OF HOPE (BC)
    10/16/41*   BC 3tp/3tb/3as/2ts/p/g/b/d

THE TROLLEY SONG (H. Martin/R. Blane)
    1962   Sarah Vaughan (v) 4tp/4tb/5reeds/p/g/b/d/vib/v
                              Roulette R(S)52092, Roulette (E) 2682-043

THE TROT (BC)
    10/30-31/61*   Count Basie & His Orch. 4tp/3tb/2as/2ts/1bs/p/
                              g/b/d

TRUMPETS HAVE TRIPLETS (DeVol)
    1955   Horace Heidt & His Musical Knights 3tp/3tb/
                              4reeds/p/g/b/d 45: Magnolia MS1070

TURNABOUT (BC)
    11/1-2/61*   Count Basie & His Orch. 4tp/3tb/2as/2ts/1bs/p/
                              g/b/d

TUTTI FRUTTI (D. Fisher/S. Gaillard)
    8/2/54*   Mel Torme (v) 4tp/4tb/5reeds/p/g/b/d/v

TWELVE O'CLOCK JUMP (BC/S. Shepherd)
    8/46*   BC 3tp/2tb/1as/1ts/1bs/p/g/b/d

TWO AGAIN (T. Grouya)
    1944*   (AFRS Basic Library P-238) BC (Savannah
                              Churchill-v) large orch/v

TWO CIGARETTES IN THE DARK (P. Webster/L. Pollack)
    11/5-6/56   Abbey Lincoln (v) 1tp/1tb/1fr. horn/3woodwinds/p/
                              g/b/d/v Liberty LRP3025

TWO LEFT HANDS (BC/lyrics: I. Gordon) [registered with ASCAP as HE'S GOT TWO LEFT HANDS]

• 1947   Freddie Slack   (Charlotte Blackburn-v)   78:
                              Capitol 15035

TWO O'CLOCK JUMP   (H. James)
     9/61   Jonah Jones with Glen Gray & the Casa Loma
                              Orch.   6tp/4tb/2as/2ts/1bs/p/g/b/d   Capitol
                              T1713, Capitol (G) IC054-81 710

TWO TICKETS WEST   (R. Stevens/J. Zackery)
     1965   Lou Rawls (v) 2tp/4tb/2reeds/p/g/b/d/v   Capitol
                              T2273

UNDER PARIS SKIES   (Gannon/Drejac/Giraud)
     5/63*   Stanley Wilson Orch.   horns/strings/vocal group/
                              rhythm section

UPTIGHT (EVERYTHING'S ALL RIGHT)   (S. Moy/S. Wonder/H. Cosby)
     1/3-4/68   Jackie Wilson (v) with Count Basie Orch.   4tp/
                              4tb/2as/2ts/1bs/p/g/b/d/v   45: Brunswick 55365,
                              LP: Brunswick BL54134

VAGABOND DREAMS   (H. Carmichael/J. Lawrence)
     10/28/39*   BC (Roy Felton-v) 3tp/3tb/2as/2ts/p/g/b/d/v
     11/1/39*   BC (Roy Felton-v)

VALLEY OF THE DOLLS
                              For Carter's work on this film soundtrack see
                              the individual title I'LL PLANT MY OWN TREE.

THE VERY THOUGHT OF YOU   (R. Noble)
     11/19/40*   BC (Roy Felton-v) 3tp/3tb/2as/2ts/1bs/p/g/b/d/v

     2/60   Dakota Staton (v) large orch with strings/v
                              Capitol T1427

VINE STREET RUMBLE   (BC) [one of ten pieces comprising Carter's
Kansas City Suite.]
     9/6-11/60   Count Basie & His Orch.   4tp/3tb/2as/2ts/1bs/p/
                              g/b/d   Roulette (S)R52056, Roulette RE124   NOTE:
                              See note on recording date under Kansas City
                              Suite.

VINHO VERDE   (BC)
     5/63*   KPM Music Library 4tp/4tb/2fr. horns/5reeds/p/
                              g/b/d NOTE: Carter rewrote the melody to this
                              piece and called it "Green Wine" (with lyrics by
                              Leonard Feather) under which title he later re-
                              corded it.   See also notes for this session in
                              chronological section of discography.

VOUS QUI PASSEZ SANS ME VOIR   (C. Trenet/J. Hess)
     5/63*   BC 1as/p/b/d/vocal group

WALKIN' ONE AND ONLY   (D. Hicks)
     12/22/74*   Maria Muldaur (v) 2tp/1tb/1as/1ts/1bs/p/g/b/d/v

A WALKIN' THING   (BC)
     7/22/57*   BC 1tp/1as/1ts/p/g/b/d

- 4/1/64   Phineas Newborn   Contemporary S7615

- 5/68   Milt Jackson & the Hip String Quartet   arr: Tom
                      McIntosh   Verve V6-8761

12/3/73*   BC 4tp/4tb/3as/2ts/1bs/p/g/b/d/conga
10/28/78*   BC with the University of Buffalo Jazz Ensemble
                      directed by Phil Sims

- 2/11/76*   BC

WALTZ GAY   (BC)
  - 5/63*   BC

WALTZING THE BLUES   (BC)
  - 6/20/36*   BC

THE WANG WANG BLUES   (Mueller/Johnson/Busse/Wood)
    5/16/29   Fletcher Henderson & His Orch.   3tp/2tb/2cl/as/
                      1ts/p/banjo/tuba/d   Columbia CL1684

WANNA GO HOME   (J. Thomas/H. Biggs)
    8/18/52*   BC 3tp/2tb/5reeds/p/g/b/d/10strings/vocal group

WAY DOWN YONDER IN NEW ORLEANS   (Layton/Creamer)
    3/27/36   Henry Hall & the B.B.C. Dance Orch.   large
                      orch   (B.B.C. broadcast, no known airchecks)

WE JUST COULDN'T SAY GOODBYE   (H. Woods)
    9/75   Maria Muldaur (v) 2tp/1tb/1as/1ts/1bs/p/2g/b/d/
                      v/vocal group   Warner Brothers MS2235

WE SAW THE SEA   (I. Berlin)
    4/4/36   Henry Hall & the B.B.C. Dance Orch. (Dan
                      Donovan-v) large orch 78: Columbia (E)
                      FB1364

WE WERE IN LOVE   (BC--words & music)
    3/4/66*   BC   2as/2ts/1bs/p/g/b/d

  - ca. 1966   Irma Curry (v) arr: Ernie Freeman   45: Vee-
                      Jay 669

WEAK FOR THE MAN   (Jeanne Burns)
    6/60   Dakota Staton (v) large orch/v   Capitol T1490

THE WEEKEND OF A PRIVATE SECRETARY   (B. Hanighen/J. Mercer)
    9/29/70   Mrs. Miller (v) 2tp/2tb/2as/1ts/1bs/p/g/b/d/v
                      45: Mrs. Miller Records (no issue number)

WEST END BLUES   (King Oliver)
    9/61   Jonah Jones with Glen Gray & the Casa Loma
                      Orch. 6tp/4tb/2as/2ts/1bs/p/g/b/d   Capitol
                      T1713

WHAT A DIFFERENCE A DAY MADE   (S. Adams/M. Grever)
    4/1/41*   BC (Maxine Sullivan-v) 3tp/3tb/3as/2ts/p/g/b/d/v

WHAT ARE YOU DOING THE REST OF YOUR LIFE? (Bergman/Legrand)
    early 1970's   The Airmen of Note (U. S. Air Force Jazz Ensemble) (Sarah Vaughan-v) 4tp/4tb/5reeds/p/g/b/d/v NOTE: Promotional album: Airmen of Note Come Out Swinging (no label and issue)

WHAT IS A MAN? (Rodgers/Hart)
    Mar. 30-Apr. 1   Pearl Bailey (v) 4tp/4tb/5reeds/p/g/b/d/v
    1965*

WHAT KIND OF FOOL AM I? (A. Newley)
    5/63*   Stanley Wilson Orch. 4tp/4tb/5reeds/20strings/p/g/b/d

WHATCHA KNOW JOE? (Young)
    1963   Jo Stafford (v) large orch/vocal group/v Reprise RS6090, Stanyan 10073

WHAT'LL I DO? (I. Berlin)
    1/63   Sarah Vaughan (v) 4fr. horns/p/g/b/d/tuba/v 45: Roulette 4516, LP: Roulette R(S)52104

WHAT'LL IT BE? (BC)
    ● 8/23/46*   BC 1tp/1tb/1as/1ts/p/b/d

WHAT'S NEW? (B. Haggart/J. Burke)
    10/14/39*   BC (Dell St. John-v) 3tp/3tb/2as/2ts/p/g/b/d/v
    10/23/39*   BC (Dell St. John-v)

WHAT'S THE NAME OF THAT SONG? (V. Lawnhurst/T. Seymour)
    5/2/36   Henry Hall & the B. B. C. Dance Orch. (Dan Donovan-v) 3tp/3tb/5reeds/p/g/b/d/6strings/v 78: Columbia (E) FB1400
    1936   Henry Hall & the B. B. C. Dance Orch. (probably Dan Donovan-v) (B. B. C. broadcast, no known airchecks)

WHEN DAY IS DONE (DeSylva/Katscher)
    late 4/36*   BC 2tp/1cl/1as/1ts/p/g/b/d

WHEN IT'S SLEEPY TIME DOWN SOUTH (L. and O. Rene/C. Muse)
    4/29/77*   BC 2tp/1tb/3reeds/p/g/b/d
    4/15/78*   BC
    4/19?/78*   BC
    July 1981*   BC

WHEN IT'S TIME TO TELL (Bob Friedman)
    11/71-3/72   Carmen McRae (v) large orch/v Temponic TB29562

WHEN LIGHTS ARE LOW (BC/lyrics: Spencer Williams)
    ● 6/20/36*   BC (Elisabeth Welch-v) (with bridge)

    8/29/36*   BC (v) with Kai Ewans' Orch. 3tp/2tb/3as/2ts/p/g/b/d (with bridge)

    ● 1937   Teddy Joyce & His Orch. (unknown v) 78: Decca (E) F6063 (with bridge)

8/31/39*	BC (Dell St. John-v) 3tp/3tb/3as/2ts/p/g/b/d/v (with bridge)
9/11/39*	Lionel Hampton & His Orch. 1tp/1as/3ts/p/g/b/d/ vib (with bridge)
5/30-31/79	Bob Wilber & the American All Stars featuring Lars Erstrand Phontastic 7526
● 1940	Svenska Hotvintetten 78: Columbia DS1227
● 5/4/49	Putte Wickmans Orch. 78: Cupol 4225 (with bridge)
● 7/17/52	George Shearing Quintet 45: MGM x4072, LP: Verve 2683-069 (with bridge)
● 5/19/53	Miles Davis Quartet Prestige 7822 (without bridge)
● 9/5/55	Georg Riedel Sextet Metronome MEP152
● 1/19/56	Bud Shank - Bob Cooper Quartet Pacific Jazz PJ1219 (without bridge) NOTE: On this live recording, "When Lights Are Low" is announced as a Miles Davis composition.
● 10/26/56	Kenny Clarke arr: Andre Hodeir Epic LN3376 (without bridge)
● 10/26/56	Miles Davis New Quintet Prestige 7094 (without bridge)
● 1956	Pete Jolly Trio RCA LPM1367, RCA (J) RGP1085
● 4/29/57	Herbie Mann arr: A. K. Salim Epic LN3395 (without bridge)
● 4/57	Cal Tjader Quartet Fantasy S8084
● 6/58	June Christy (v) arr: Bob Cooper Capitol T1076, Capitol W1162 (with bridge)
● 7/58	Oscar Peterson Trio Verve MGV8287 (without bridge)
● 9/58	Chet Baker Riverside RLP12-281, Riverside RS1119, Riverside (J) SMJ6095, Jazzland 998 (without bridge)
● 1958	Nils Bertil Dahlander [Bert Dale] Verve MGV8253
● 1958	Oscar Peterson Trio Verve MGV8268 (without bridge)
● 3/10/59	Arne Domnerus & His Orch. arr: Georg Riedel Telefunken BLE14120
● 6/24/59	Billy Taylor Trio Atlantic SD1329

- 1959   Curtis Fuller Sextet arr: Curtis Fuller? United Artists UAS5041

- 1959   Bill Shepherd Orch. with the Beryl Scott Chorus arr: Bill Shepherd Roulette R25086 (with bridge)

- 1959   Dakota Staton (v) arr: Sid Feller Capitol T1241 (with bridge)

- late 1950's   Alice Babs & Ulrick Neuman (v) Dot DLP3128 (with bridge)

- 10/31/60   Dick Morgan Riverside RLP12-347 (without bridge)

- 1/2-4/61   Frans van Bergen CNR (Holland) LPT35006

- 8/21/61   Webster Young VGM 0005 (without bridge)

- 8/30/61   Eric Dolphy Inner City 3017 (without bridge)

- 9/6/61   Eric Dolphy Prestige 24027 (without bridge)

- 10/15-17/61 Buddy DeFranco Mercury MG20685, Mercury SR60685

- 1961   Vic Damone (v) arr: Jack Marshall Capitol T1646 (with bridge)

- 3/62   Art Blakey & the Jazz Messengers arr: Cedar Walton United Artists UAS5633 (without bridge)

- 4/10/62*   BBB & Co. (with bridge)

- 2/12-13/63   Howard Roberts Capitol ST1887 (with bridge)

- 1963   Tony Bennett (v) with Ralph Sharon Trio Columbia CL2175 (with bridge)

- ca. 1963   Sarah Vaughan (v) Roulette (E) 2682-032 (with bridge)

- 11/28/66   Richard "Groove" Holmes Prestige 7493

- ca. 1966   Harry Edison arr: Julian Lee Liberty LST7484 (with bridge)

- ca. 1968   Eric Delaney Saga (Eros) 8050 (with bridge)

- 7/29/71   Jaki Byard Swing (F) 05, Musica (F) 2008 (with bridge)

- 10/7/72   Joe Albany Revelation 16, Spotlight (E) JA3 (without bridge)

- 10/22/73*   BC (with bridge)

12/3/73*	BC 4tp/4tb/3as/2ts/1bs/p/g/b/d (with bridge)
4/8/77*	BC with the Princeton University Jazz Ensemble
10/28/78*	BC with the University of Buffalo Jazz Ensemble directed by Sam Falzone
10/28/78*	BC with the University of Buffalo Jazz Ensemble directed by Phil Sims

- 1973   Bobby Hackett, Vic Dickenson Hyannisport HR1002 (with bridge) NOTE: Rhythm section featured on this track--Hank Jones (p), Remo Palmieri (g), George Mraz (b), Jackie Williams (d)

- 2/12/74   Chuck Folds RCA LFL1-5064 (with bridge)

- 5/10/75   Conte Condoli - Frank Rosolino MPS (G) 68.167

- 1/3/76*   BC (Millicent Browne-v) (with bridge)

- 12/27/76   Chuck Wayne Quartet arr: Chuck Wayne? Progressive Records 7008 (with bridge)

- 1976   Elisabeth Welch (v) World Records SH233 (with bridge)

- 9/77   Cal Tjader Galaxy GXY5107 (with bridge)

- 1979   Kenny Burrell Concord CJ83 (without bridge)

- 1980   Joe Kennedy Black and Blue (F) 33.171 (with bridge)

- 1981   Pharoah Sanders Theresa TR112/113 (with bridge)

- 7/18/81*   BC (with bridge)

- 9/26/81*   BC (with bridge)

NOTE: Many recordings after 1953 follow the Miles Davis version, which does not include Carter's original bridge, but rather repeats the "A" section up a fourth. The presence or absence of the original bridge is noted for those recordings which have been verified by the authors.

WHEN TWILIGHT COMES (Bob Friedman)
  11/71-3/72   Carmen McRae (v) large orch/v Temponic TB29562

WHEN YOU'RE SMILING (L. Shay/J. Goodwin/M. Fisher)
  ca. 5/36   Henry Hall & the B.B.C. Dance Orch. large orch (B.B.C. broadcast, no known airchecks)

| 4/29/77* | BC (Joe Newman-v) 2tp/1tb/3reeds/p/g/b/d/v |
| 4/15/78* | BC (Joe Newman-v) |

```
        4/19?/78*                BC (Joe Newman-v)
        July 1981*               BC (Pete Candoli-v)
```

WHEN YOU'RE YOUNG (Bob Friedman/lyrics: S. Cahn)
     11/71-3/72   Joe Williams (v) large orch/v Temponic
                                 TB29561

WHERE OR WHEN (Rodgers/Hart)
     5/5/46*   BC large orch

WHISPER TO ONE (BC/lyrics: A. Stillman)
     • 11/65   film soundtrack: A Man Called Adam (Sammy
                                 Davis, Jr.-v) Reprise 6180

WHISPERING GRASS (D. Fisher/F. Fisher)
     2/60   Dakota Staton (v) large orch with strings/v
                                 Capitol T1427

     1965   Lou Rawls (v) 2tp/4tb/2reeds/p/g/b/d/v
                                 Capitol T2273

WHO'S BLUE?   (BC)
     11/1-2/61*   Count Basie & His Orch.   4tp/3tb/2as/2ts/1bs/p/
                                 g/b/d

WHO'S TIRED? (L. Bellson)
     Mar. 30-Apr. 1   Pearl Bailey (v) 4tp/4tb/5reeds/p/g/b/d/v
     1965*

WHO'S WHO   (BC)
     1/22-24/62   Louis Bellson Orch.   5tp/3tb/1fr. horn/1tuba/2as/
                                 2ts/1bs/p/g/b/d/vib Roulette R52087, Roulette
                                 (E) 2934-020

WHO'S YEHOODI? (M. Dennis)
     5/18/40   Cab Calloway (v) & His Orch. 3tp/3tb/3as/2ts/
                                 p/g/b/d/v Jazz Archives JA8

THE WIGGLE WALK (BC) [One of ten pieces comprising Carter's Kansas
City Suite.]
     9/6-11/60   Count Basie & His Orch. 4tp/3tb/2as/2ts/1bs/p/
                                 g/b/d Roulette (S)R52056, Roulette RE124
                                 NOTE: See note on recording under Kansas City
                                 Suite.

WILL YOU STILL BE MINE? (M. Dennis/T. Adair)
     6/60   Dakota Staton (v) 1tp/1reed/p/g/b/d/v Capitol
                                 T1597

THE WINE OF SWEET REMEMBRANCE (BC/lyrics: J. Flint)
     • 1967   Martha Mason (v) ?/v 45: Take V (no issue
                                 number)

WISH YOU WERE HERE (H. Rome)
     8/18/52*   BC 3tp/2tb/5reeds/p/g/b/d/10strings/vocal group

WITH A SONG IN MY HEART (Rodgers/Hart)
     1/4/54*   BC horns/strings/p/b/d

WITHOUT A WORD OF GOODBYE (BC/lyrics: P. Vandervoort)
- 1950's   Lawrence Stone (v) with Ernie Freeman's Orch.
                            arr: Ernie Freeman 45: Vita 45-V-115

WONDERLAND see SUMMER NIGHT

WOULDN'T IT BE LOVERLY (A. J. Lerner/F. Lowe)
2/19/64   Billy Eckstine (v) 1tp/1tb/2reeds/p/g/b/d/v/vocal
                            group Mercury SR60916, Mercury MG20916

YASSU (D. Tiomkin)
1961   film soundtrack: The Guns of Navarone large
                            orch with strings Columbia CL1655, Columbia
                            CS8455

YES INDEED (S. Oliver)
1963   Jo Stafford (v) large orch/vocal group/v Reprise
                            RS6090, Stanyan 10073

YOU AIN'T THE ONE (C. Johnson/A. Porter)
1/24/28*   Charlie Johnson's Paradise Orch. (Monette
                            Moore-v) 2tp/1tb/3as/cl/1ts/p/banjo/tuba/d/v

YOU ARE (BC/lyrics: F. Herbert)
7/2/72*   BC 5tp/4tb/3as/2ts/1bs/p/g/b/d

12/3/73*   BC 4tp/4tb/3as/2ts/1bs/p/g/b/d

YOU ARE NOT MY FIRST LOVE
1957   Martha Davis (v) 4tp/4tb/2as/2ts/1bs/p/g/b/d/v
                            NOTE: Recorded for ABC Paramount--unissued.

YOU BELONG TO ME (P. W. King/R. Stewart/C. Price)
8/18/52*   BC 3tp/2tb/5reeds/p/g/b/d/10strings

YOU CALL IT MADNESS (R. Colombo/C. Conrad/G. DuBois/P. Gregory)
6/60   Dakota Staton (v) large orch with strings/v
                            Capitol T1597

YOU GO TO MY HEAD (J. F. Coots/H. Gillespie)
11/56   Billy Daniels (v) accompanied by Benny Carter's
                            Orch. 1tp/4reeds/p/g/b/d/strings/v Verve
                            MGV2072

YOU TURNED THE TABLES ON ME (L. Alter/S. Mitchell)
11/56   Billy Daniels (v) accompanied by Benny Carter's
                            Orch. 4tp/4tb/2as/2ts/1bs/p/g/b/d/v Verve
                            MGV2072

YOU UNDERSTAND (BC/R. Sonin)
mid 6/36*   BC 3tp/2tb/2as/1ts/p/g/b/d

YOU'D BETTER THINK IT OVER (BC/lyrics: P. Vandervoort)
1957   Martha Davis (v) 4tp/4tb/2as/2ts/1bs/p/g/b/d/v
                            NOTE: Recorded for ABC Paramount--unissued.

Mar. 30-Apr. 1   Pearl Bailey (v) 4tp/4tb/5reeds/p/g/b/d/v
1965*

YOU'LL NEVER BREAK MY HEART AGAIN (H. Atwood/L. Herscher)
   1/48*   BC (Emma Lou Welch, The Enchanters-v) 1tp/
                       1tb/1as/1ts/p/g/b/d/v

YOU'LL NEVER GET THE CHANCE AGAIN (BC/lyrics: P. Vandervoort)
   • 1954   Helen Troy (v), Charles Schrouder (bass v) with
                       Van Alexander's Orch. arr: Van Alexander 45:
                       Vito VO-109X

YOUNG AND IN LOVE
   ca. 1959   Dean Jones (v) ?/v MGM K12462

YOUR CONSCIENCE TELLS YOU SO (BC/lyrics: D. Raye)
   • 4/24/46   Ella Mae Morse (v) with Freddie Slack 78:
                       Capitol 278

   8/46*   BC (Lucy Elliott-v) 3tp/2tb/1as/1ts/1bs/p/g/b/d/v

YOU'RE DRIVING ME CRAZY (W. Donaldson)
   1953-1954   Lincoln Chase (v) with Spencer-Hagen Orch.
                       small group/v Liberty LRP3076

   1/63   Sarah Vaughan (v) 4fr. horns/p/g/b/d/tuba/v
                       Roulette S(R)52104

YOU'RE GONE FOR A LONG LONG TIME
   1953   Ernie Andrews (v) with Benny Carter's Orch.
                       large orch/v 78: Trend 2502

YOU'RE GONNA MISS IT (BC under pseudonym "Johnny Gomez"/lyrics: P.
Vandervoort)
   • 7/21/50   Julia Lee (v) & Her Boy Friends (unissued)

YOU'RE MINE YOU (J. Green/E. Heyman)
   2/60   Dakota Staton (v) large orch with strings/v
                       Capitol T1427

YOU'RE MY EVERYTHING (H. Warren/M. Dixon/J. Young)
   11/56   Billy Daniels (v) accompanied by Benny Carter's
                       Orch. 1tp/4reeds/p/g/b/d/strings/v Verve
                       MGV2072

YOU'RE ON THE RIGHT TRACK BABY (BUT YOU'RE GOIN' THE WRONG
WAY) (BC/lyrics: I. Gordon)
   • 12/8/47   Louis Jordan & His Tympany Five (Louis Jordan,
                       Martha Davis-v) 78: Decca 24502

INDEX OF ARTISTS WHO HAVE RECORDED
CARTER ARRANGEMENTS AND/OR COMPOSITIONS

a = Carter arrangement c = Carter composition

THE AIRMEN OF NOTE (U.S. AIR FORCE JAZZ ENSEMBLE)
   early 1970's
My Funny Valentine (Sarah Vaughan-v) a
There'll Never Be Another You (Sarah Vaughan-
v) a
What Are You Doing the Rest of Your Life?
(Sarah Vaughan-v) a

ALBANY, JOE
   10/7/72
When Lights Are Low c

ALEXANDER, JOE
   9/22/47
I'm a Three Time Loser c

ALEXANDER, VAN see Helen Troy

ANDERSON, ERNESTINE see Bob Friedman

ANDREWS, DEBBIE
   1949
I Ain't Got Nobody a
I Lost You a

ANDREWS, ERNIE
   1953
All Alone and Lonesome a, c
Don't Lead Me On a
Make Me a Present of You a
You're Gone for a Long Long Time a
   1957
But Now I Know a
In the Dark a
Just Squeeze Me a
Lover Come Back to Me a
Peace a
'Round Midnight a
Song of the Wanderer a
Sunset Eyes a

ARMSTRONG, LOUIS
   9/8/55
Christmas in New Orleans a
Christmas Night in Harlem a
Moments to Remember a
Only You a
See also Soundtrack: The Five Pennies NOTE:
The liner notes to MCA 1334 suggest that two
1942 recordings by Armstrong, "Among My Sou-
venirs" and "Cash for Your Trash," are Carter
arrangements. Carter denies this.

THE ARMY AIR FORCE BAND   see   Glenn Miller

AUSTIN, VIRGIE
   1950   I'm Such a Fool to Be in Love with You   c
                           That Ain't It   a, c

AVRO ORCHESTRA   see   BC 8/2/36

AZAMA, ETHEL
   1959   Friendly Islands   c

B. B. C. DANCE ORCHESTRA   see   Henry Hall

BABS, ALICE
   late 1950's   When Lights Are Low   (with Ulrick Neuman)   c

BACON, LOUIS   see   Chick Webb

BAILEY, MILDRED
   9/15/31   Blues in My Heart   (with the Casa Loma Orch.)   c

BAILEY, PEARL
   1961   Row Row Row Row   a
                           Tired   a
                           Toot Toot Tootsie   a
   Mar. 30-Apr. 1   Big Nobody   a
   1965   Hey There   a
                           I Shoulda Quit When I Was Ahead   a
                           Look at That Face   a
                           A Man Is a Necessary Evil   a
                           Pleasures and Palaces   a
                           Take Back Your Mink   a
                           What Is a Man   a
                           Who's Tired   a
                           You'd Better Think It Over   a, c
   1968   Baby, Don't You Quit Now   (with Louis Bellson
                           Orch.)   a
                           Protect Me   (with Louis Bellson Orch.)   a
   1971   Here's That Rainy Day   a
                           A House Is Not a Home   a
                           I Never Met a Stranger   a
                           It's Impossible   a
                           Mama, a Rainbow   a
                           Supper Time   a

BAKER, CHET
   9/58   When Lights Are Low   c

BAKER, KENNY   see   Jazz Today Unit

BARBRO, LARRY
   1955   Millions of People   a, c

BARNES, MAE
   1958   Blues in My Heart   c

BARNET, CHARLIE
   1/21/35   Devil's Holiday   (as On a Holiday)   a, c
   6/2/38

Nagasaki a
See also California Ramblers

BASIE, COUNT
 9/6-11/60   Blue Five Jive a, c
                              Jackson County Jubilee   a, c
                              Katy Do   a, c
                              Meetin' Time   a, c
                              Miss Missouri a, c
                              Paseo Promenade   a, c
                              Rompin' at the Reno   a, c
                              Sunset Glow   a, c
                              8/9/62
                              Vine Street Rumble   a, c
                              The Wiggle Walk   a, c
 10/30-31/61   The Basie Twist   a, c
                              Goin' On a, c
                              The Legend a, c
                              The Trot a, c
 11/1-2/61   Amoroso a, c
                              Easy Money a, c
                              8/10/62
                              The Swizzle a, c
                              Turnabout a, c
                              Who's Blue? a, c
 10/20/69   Blues in My Heart   c
 5/6/76   JJJJump c
                              Kansas City Line c
                              Mama Don't Wear No Drawers c
                              See also Ella Fitzgerald, Jackie Wilson

BAXTER, LES see Gordon MacRae

BECHET, SIDNEY
 10/6-9/50   Blues in My Heart (with Claude Luter) c

BELLSON, LOUIS
 1/22-24/62   Amoroso a, c
                              Blitzen a
                              Doozy a, c
                              A Foggy Day a
                              Gumshoe a, c
                              Lou's Blues a, c
                              The Moon Is Low a
                              Who's Who a, c
                              See also Pearl Bailey, Buddy Rich

BENNETT, TONY
 1963   When Lights Are Low (with Ralph Sharon Trio) c

BERIGAN, BUNNY
 7/20/36   Lonesome Nights (as Take My Word) a, c
 4/8/38   Devil's Holiday a, c
                              6/27/38
                              See also Tommy Dorsey

THE BIG EIGHTEEN
 6/24/58   O. K. For Baby c

BIG MAYBELLE [MABEL SMITH] see Christine Chatham

BLACKBURN, CHARLOTTE   see   Freddie Slack

BLAKE, EUBIE
    ca. 9/31   Blues in My Heart   (Dick Robertson-v)   c

BLAKEY, ART
    3/62   When Lights Are Low   c

BLALOCK, BRUCE
    early 1950's   Bodyguard   (Ketty Lester?-v)   a
                               Lady Oh Lady   c
                               Queen for a Day   (Ketty Lester?-v)   c

BOONE, PAT   see   Soundtrack: State Fair

BOWLLY, AL   see   Ray Noble

BOWMAN, DAVE
    3/46   Cow Cow Boogie   c

BOZE, CALVIN
    ca. 1949   Look Out for Tomorrow   c
                               Stinkin' from Drinkin'   c

BRADLEY, BETTY   see   Bob Chester

BRONSON, BETTY   see   Ray Herbeck

BROOKS, KIRBY   see   Ray Herbeck

BROWN, KAY
    early 1950's   Slow But Sure   c

BROWN, LES
    8/10/43   O. K. for Baby   c
    11/14/50   Rock Me to Sleep   (Lucy Ann Polk-v)   c

BROWNE, MILLICENT   see   BC 1/3/76

BUCKNER, MILT
    5/30/76   Blues in My Heart   (with Arnett Cobb/Panama
                               Francis)   c

BULLOCK, CHICK   see   Mills Blue Rhythm Band

BURNS, RALPH   see   Anita O'Day

BURRELL, KENNY
    1979   When Lights Are Low   c

BUZON, JOHN
    ca. 1959   Blues in My Heart   c

BYARD, JAKI
    7/29/71   When Lights Are Low   c

BYRD, CHARLIE
    1976   Cow Cow Boogie   (with Barney Kessel, Herb
                               Ellis)   c

CAIN, JACKIE see Charlie Ventura

CALIFORNIA RAMBLERS (CHARLIE BARNET ORCHESTRA)
   5/6/37   Lonesome Nights (as Take My Word) a, c

CALLOWAY, CAB
   5/6/31   Blues in My Heart c
   6/9/32   Hot Toddy a, c
                          9/21/32
                          1932 (Soundtrack: The Big Broadcast of 1932)
  11/15/32   Sweet Rhythm a
  10/27/38   Blue Interlude c
   5/18/40   Calling All Bars a
                          The Lone Arranger a
                          Who's Yehoodi a
   8/28/40   Lonesome Nights a, c

CALVIN, ROSEMARY see Freddie Rich

CANDOLI, CONTE
   5/10/75   When Lights Are Low (with Frank Rosolino) c

CAPITOL INTERNATIONAL JAZZMEN
   3/30/45   Riffamarole c

CAPP, FRANKIE
   1978   Souvenir (with Nat Pierce) c

CARMICHAEL, HOAGY see Maria Muldaur

CARR, HELEN
  11/11/55   My Kind of Trouble Is You c

CARROLL, BARBARA see Sylvia Syms

CARROLL, DIHANN
   1960   Guiding Light c

CARTER, BENNY, CHORALE see Bob Friedman

CARTER, KING
   3/23/31   Blues in My Heart (Dick Robertson-v) a?, c
                          NOTE: Although his name appears as leader,
                          Carter was not present. King Carter and His
                          Royal Orchestra was an Irving Mills - sponsored
                          unit.

CARTER, MERCEDES
                          See chronological section of discography for vari-
                          ous arrangements and compositions recorded by
                          this vocalist with the Carter Orchestra in 1939.

CASA LOMA ORCHESTRA see Mildred Bailey, Glen Gray

CATLETT, SID see BC 8/23/46

CAVANAUGH, DAVE see Kitty White

CHAIX, HENRI see BC 11/9/68

CHARLES, RAY
   7/13/63   Busted (with the Raelets-v) a
   7/13/63   In the Evening (When the Sun Goes Down) (with
                    the Raelets-v) a
                    Ol' Man Time (with the Raelets-v) a
   1964   Feudin' and Fightin' (with the Raelets-v) a
                    Ma (She's Making Eyes at Me) a
                    Smack Dab in the Middle (with the Raelets-v) a

CHASE, LINCOLN
   1953-1954   Johnny Klingaringding (with Spencer-Hagen Orch.)
                    a
                    You're Driving Me Crazy (with Spencer-Hagen
                    Orch.) a

CHATHAM, CHRISTINE
   4/6/44   Hurry Hurry (Mabel Smith [Big Maybelle]-v) c

CHEATHAM, DOC
   5/2/75   Blues in My Heart c

THE CHEER LEADERS see Jack Powers

CHESTER, BOB
   1941-1942   Blues in My Heart (Betty Bradley-v) c

CHILDS, REGGIE
   1939   Melancholy Lullaby (Marion Kaye-v) c

CHITTISON, HERMAN see Ethel Waters

THE CHOCOLATE DANDIES
   9/18/29   That's How I Feel Today a
   12/4/30   Goodbye Blues a, c
   12/31/30   Bugle Call Rag a
                    Dee Blues a, c
                    Got Another Sweetie Now (Jimmy Harrison-v) a
   10/10/33   Blue Interlude a, c
                    I Never Knew a
                    Krazy Kapers a, c
                    Once Upon a Time a, c
                    See also BC 8/23/46

CHRISTY, JUNE
   5/9/55   Lonely Woman (with Stan Kenton) c
   6/58   Rock Me to Sleep (accompanied by Bob Cooper) c
                    When Lights Are Low c
                    See also Stan Kenton

CHURCHILL, SAVANNAH

                    See chronological section of discography for vari-
                    ous arrangements and compositions recorded by
                    this vocalist with the Carter Orchestra during
                    1943-1946.

CLARKE, KENNY
   10/26/56   When Lights Are Low c

CLUMP, CLARENCE [pseudonym for Benny Carter]   see   BC 12/14/48

COBB, ARNETT
   2/27/59   Blues in My Heart   c
                       See also Milt Buckner

COLEMAN, BILL
   5/24/56   Blues in My Heart   c

COLIN, SID   see   R. A. F. Dance Orchestra

CONNOR, CHRIS
   4/9/62   Lonely Woman   c

COOK, J. LAWRENCE
   date unknown   Cow Cow Boogie   (piano roll)   c

COOPER, BOB   see   June Christy, Bud Shank

COTY, BILL   see   McKinney's Cotton Pickers

CRAYTON, PEE WEE
   ca. 1950   Blues in My Heart   c
   1953-1955   Hurry Hurry   c

CRISS, SONNY
   2/24/75   Blues in My Heart   c

CRISTOBAL, CHICO
   11/15/46   Cow Cow Boogie   c

CROTHERS, SCAT MAN
   ca. 1949   I'd Rather Be a Rooster   c

CUMMINGS, MILDRED   see   Little Miss Cornshucks

CURRY, IRMA
   ca. 1966   A Heart Must Learn to Cry   a
                       We Were in Love   c

DAHL, PAT
   1966   It's Alright with Me   a
                       Lonely Woman   a, c

DAHLANDER, NILS BERTIL [BERT DALE]
   1958   When Lights Are Low   c

DALE, BERT   see   Nils Bertil Dahlander

DAMONE, VIC
   1961   When Lights Are Low   c

DANIELS, BILLY
   11/56   Blue Prelude   a
                       Blue Skies   a
                       Comes Love   a
                       Hallelujah   a

                    How Am I to Know   a
                    It's De-Lovely   a
                    Just in Time   a
                    A Melody from the Sky   a
                    Time After Time   a
                    You Go to My Head   a
                    You Turned the Tables on Me   a
                    You're My Everything   a

DAVIS, BLIND JOHN
    ca. 1976   Cow Cow Boogie   c

DAVIS, EDDIE "LOCKJAW"
    ca. 1951   Blues in My Heart   c

DAVIS, LEM
    10/20/45   Blues in My Heart   c

DAVIS, MARTHA
    1949   I Ain't Gettin' Any Younger   c
    1957   A Hundred Years from Today   a
                        Red Red Robin   a
                        You Are Not My First Love   a
                        You'd Better Think it Over   a, c
                        See also Louis Jordan

DAVIS, MAXWELL   see   Rudy Render

DAVIS, MILES
    5/19/53   When Lights Are Low   c
    10/26/56

DAVIS, SAMMY, JR.   see   Soundtrack: <u>A Man Called Adam</u>

DECKER, BOB   see   BC 1/48

DeFRANCO, BUDDY
    10/15-17/61   When Lights Are Low   c

DELANE, NICK   see   Jimmy Zito

DELANEY, ERIC
    ca. 1968   When Lights Are Low   c

DEPPE, LOIS   see   Fletcher Henderson

DERWIN, HAL   see   Shep Fields

DOLPHY, ERIC
    8/30/61   When Lights Are Low   c
    9/6/61

DOMNERUS, ARNE
    3/4/55   Key Largo   c
    3/10/59   When Lights Are Low   c
    11/60   Melancholy Lullaby   c

DONAHUE, SAM
 1945   Paradise (see note in title listings) a
 1945?   Lonesome Nights c

DONOVAN, DAN see Henry Hall

DORN, PAT
 1965   Blue Train a, c
          Brazilian Twist a, c
          Gonna Build a Mountain a
          High Society Limbo a, c

DORSEY, JIMMY
 5/26/39   A Home in the Clouds (Helen O'Connell-v) c
 9/5/39   Melancholy Lullaby (Helen O'Connell-v) c

DORSEY, TOMMY
 7/25/38   Symphony in Riffs a, c
          6/22/40 (featuring Bunny Berigan)

THE DREAM DUSTERS
 1954   Spring Fever Blues (with Jimmie Maddin (v) and
          Orch.) a

DREW, KENNY see Jane Fielding

THE DRIFTERS
 ca. 1950   I'm the Caring Kind c

DURANTE, JIMMY
 ca. 1957   Swingin' with Rhythm and Blues (with Peter Law-
          ford-v) a

EBERLE, RAY see Glenn Miller

ECKSTINE, BILLY
 2/19/64   A Beautiful Friendship a
          People a
          Poor Fool a, c
          Wouldn't It Be Loverly a
 1968   I'll Be Here with You c

EDISON, HARRY "SWEETS"
 1964   Blues in My Heart c
          The Girl from Ipanema a
          I Don't Know What Kind of Blues I've Got a
          I'm Lost a
 ca. 1966   When Lights Are Low c

ELDRIDGE, ROY
 9/9/39   Lady Be Good a
 3/28/51   I Still Love Him So (as I'd Love Him So) c
          1/16/76
          See also BC 1/9/55

THE ELECTRECORD ORCHESTRA (ROUMANIAN)
 date unknown   Symphony in Riffs a, c

ELLINGTON, DUKE
    9/21/32   Jazz Cocktail a, c
    1947   Key Largo (Ellington Gang) c

ELLIOTT, LUCY
                            See chronological section of discography for vari-
                            ous arrangements and compositions recorded by
                            this vocalist with the Carter Orchestra during
                            1945-1946.

ELLIS, HERB see Charlie Byrd

ELRICK, GEORGE see Henry Hall

THE ENCHANTERS see BC 1/48

ERSTRAND, LARS see Bob Wilber

EVANS, DON
    1958   How Long Is a Moment a, c
                            It's So Frightnin' a, c

EWANS, KAI see BC 8/26/36, 8/29/36

FAYE, ALICE see Soundtrack: The Gang's All Here

FEATHERSTONHAUGH, BUDDY
    2/14/45   Blues in My Heart (with the Radio Rhythm Club
                            Sextet) c

FELDKAMP, ELMER see Bert Lown

FELTON, ROY
                            See chronological section of discography for vari-
                            ous arrangements and compositions recorded by
                            this vocalist with the Carter Orchestra during
                            1939-1941.

FERGUSON, MAYNARD
    1963   Rock Me to Sleep c

FIELDING, JANE
    2/56   Key Largo (with the Kenny Drew Quintet) c

FIELDS, SHEP
    5/22/39   A Home in the Clouds (Hal Derwin-v) c

FITZGERALD, ELLA
    11/3/43   Cow Cow Boogie (with the Ink Spots-v) c
    4/27/55   Between the Devil and the Deep Blue Sea a
                            Lover Come Back to Me a
                            Old Devil Moon a
                            That Old Black Magic a
    5/10/68   It's Up to You and Me a
    2/15-16/79   Ain't Misbehavin' (with Count Basie's Orch.) a
                            Don't Worry 'Bout Me (with Count Basie's Orch.) a
                            Honeysuckle Rose (with Count Basie's Orch.) a
                            I'm Getting Sentimental Over You (with Count
                            Basie's Orch.) a

Just A-Sittin' and A-Rockin' (with Count Basie's
Orch.) a
My Kind of Trouble Is You (with Count Basie's
Orch.) a, c
Organ Grinder's Swing (with Count Basie's Orch.)
a
Please Don't Talk About Me When I'm Gone (with
Count Basie's Orch.) a
Some Other Spring (with Count Basie's Orch.) a
Sweet Lorraine (with Count Basie's Orch.) a
Teach Me Tonight (with Count Basie's Orch.) a
NOTE: In addition, Carter arranged and played
on a series of medleys for Ella Fitzgerald's
Capitol LP 30 By Ella.   See 5/28, 5/29, and
6/3/68 in chronological section of discography.

FOLDS, CHUCK
2/12/74   When Lights Are Low   c

FORREST, HELEN   see   Artie Shaw

FOSLIEN, ORRIN   see   New McKinney's Cotton Pickers

FRANCIS, PANAMA   see   Milt Buckner

FREEMAN, ERNIE
date unknown   Poor Fool (Lawrence Stone-v)   c
                           See also Lawrence Stone

FRIEDMAN, BOB
11/71-3/72   All I Need Is You (Ernestine Anderson-v) a
                           Betty (Benny Carter Chorale-v) a
                           Bobby (Benny Carter Chorale-v) a
                           Bossa Nova Sonata (A Serenade to Genie) (Gene
                           Merlino-v) a
                           The Day Your Love Comes True (Ernestine
                           Anderson-v) a
                           How Do I Love Thee (Bob Grabeau-v) a
                           I Love You (Sue Raney-v, vocal group) a
                           Jane (Benny Carter Chorale-v) a
                           Jenny (Benny Carter Chorale-v) a
                           Little Bit O'Heaven (Bob Grabeau-v) a
                           Mary (Benny Carter Chorale-v) a
                           Pretty Girl (Bob Grabeau-v) a
                           Serenade to Genie (Bob Grabeau-v) a
                           Sleepy Baby (Benny Carter Chorale-v) a
                           Tender Loving Words (Benny Carter Chorale-v) a
                           Thank You, Mr. Moon (Ernestine Anderson-v) a
                           That's Love (Benny Carter Chorale-v) a
                           NOTE: Amateur songwriter Bob Friedman com-
                           missioned Carter to arrange and conduct a number
                           of his compositions for recording.   The record-
                           ings, made between November 1971 and March
                           1972 featured vocalists Carmen McRae and Joe
                           Williams among others.   Many top jazz players
                           also took part, such as Sweets Edison, Jimmy
                           Rowles, Flip Phillips, Barney Kessel and Jimmy
                           Jones.   The Williams and McRae tunes were re-
                           leased on LPs on Friedman's own label, Temponic,

and were widely available commercially. These performances are listed here under Carmen McRae and Joe Williams. The remainder of Carter's arrangements for Friedman appeared on a two-record Temponic limited issue, Twenty-Five Years, which Friedman dedicated to his wife on their anniversary. These items are listed above.

FULLER, CURTIS
   1959   When Lights Are Low c

GELLER, HARRY see Frankie Laine, Patti Page

GETZ, STAN
   8/19/64   Only Trust Your Heart (Astrud Gilberto-v) c

GILBERTO, ASTRUD see Stan Getz

GILLESPIE, DIZZY see BC 4/27/76

GONELLA, NAT
   9/26/41   Kansas City Moods c

GOODMAN, BENNY
   8/16/34   It Happens to the Best of Friends (Ann Graham-v) a
                       Lonesome Nights (as Take My Word) a, c
   9/11/34   I'm Getting Sentimental Over You (Tony Sacco-v) a
   1/15/35   Blue Moon (Helen Ward-v) a
                       Limehouse Blues a
   8/8/38   Blue Interlude (Martha Tilton-v) a, c
   2/9/39   A Home in the Clouds (Martha Tilton-v) c
   10/19/42   Cow Cow Boogie (Peggy Lee-v) c
                       See also Soundtrack: The Gang's All Here
                       NOTE: In addition to the recorded arrangements cited, Benny Goodman's files indicate the following scores were supplied by Carter: "Earful of Music" (signed score, dated 1934) and "Don't Let That Moon Get Away" (1938). Also, a 1934 arrangement of Carter's "Blues in My Heart" may have been by Carter. There are no known airchecks of these arrangements.

GRABEAU, BOB see Bob Friedman

GRACEN, THELMA see Freddie Slack

GRAHAM, ANN see Benny Goodman

GRAY, DICK see BC 5/21/44

GRAY, GLEN
   3/8/58   Symphony in Riffs (with Casa Loma Orch.) (Time-Life series The Swing Era) a, c
   8/14/59   Malibu (with Casa Loma Orch.) (Time-Life series The Swing Era) a, c
                       NOTE: These two recordings are recreations--

see notes in title listings.
See also Jonah Jones, Time-Life series

HACKETT, BOBBY
  ca. 1958   Blues in My Heart c
  1973   When Lights Are Low (with Vic Dickenson) c

HALL, AL
  1/24/46   Blues in My Heart c

HALL, HENRY
  4/4/36   I'm Putting All My Eggs in One Basket (Dan
                    Donovan-v, and the B. B. C. Dance Orch.) a
                    We Saw the Sea (Dan Donovan-v, and the B. B. C.
                    Dance Orch.) a
  5/2/36   What's the Name of That Song (Dan Donovan-v,
                    and the B. B. C. Dance Orch.) a
                    1936 (Dan Donovan-v, and the B. B. C. Dance
                    Orch.) a
  10/24/36   Bye Bye Baby (George Elrick-v, and the B. B. C.
                    Dance Orch.) a
  1/23/37   One, Two, Button Your Shoe (George Elrick-v,
                    and the B. B. C. Dance Orch.) a
                    NOTE: According to 1936 issues of the Melody
                    Maker, the following Carter arrangements were
                    broadcast over the B. B. C. by Henry Hall and the
                    B. B. C. Dance Orchestra. There are no known
                    airchecks.
  3/27/36   Blues in My Heart   a, c
                    I Got Rhythm a
                    Indiana a
                    Swingin' at the Maida Vale a, c
                    Way Down Yonder in New Orleans a
  5/7/36   Chickfeed   a, c
                    I Never Knew a
                    Nightfall a, c
                    The Melody Maker also lists the following Carter
                    arrangements as being aired around the same
                    time--ca. May 1936 (no known airchecks):
                    Hold Me Tight, I'm Falling a
                    I'm Tickled to Death I'm Me a
                    Let It Be Me a
                    Rise and Shine a
                    A Sunbonnet Blue a
                    When You're Smiling a
                    Finally, the Melody Maker reports that Carter
                    was commissioned to arrange the following tunes
                    for Henry Hall and the B. B. C. Dance Orchestra.
                    They may have been included in a broadcast:
                    Blue Interlude a, c
                    Dirty Hands, Dirty Face a
                    I Ain't Got Nobody a
                    The Man I Love a
                    Tiger Rag a
                    Transatlantic a, c

HALL, RENE see David Swift

HAMPTON, LIONEL
    7/21/38   Any Time at All a
                        I'm in the Mood for Swing a, c
                        Muskrat Ramble a
                        Shoe Shiner's Drag a
    9/11/39   Early Session Hop a
                        One Sweet Letter from You a
                        When Lights Are Low a, c
                        9/11/39 (take #2)
    ca. 1960   Lonesome Nights c
                        12/61

HARRIS, BIXIE see BC 1/5/46

HARRIS, WYNONIE see Lucky Millinder

HARRISON, JIMMY see The Chocolate Dandies, Fletcher Henderson

HAWKINS, COLEMAN
    4/28/37   Crazy Rhythm a
                        Honeysuckle Rose a
                        Out of Nowhere a

HEIDT, HORACE
    1955   Bugle Call Rag a
                        Riding to Glory on a Trumpet a
                        Trumpets Have Triplets a

HENDERSON, BOBBY
    3/69   A Home in the Clouds (two versions) c

HENDERSON, FLETCHER
    4/28/27   P. D. Q. Blues (see note in title listings) a
    12/12/28   Come on Baby a
                        Easy Money a
    ca. 4/29   Raisin' the Roof a
    5/16/29   Blazin' a
                        The Wang Wang Blues a
    10/3/30   Somebody Loves Me a
    12/2/30   Keep a Song in Your Soul a
    2/5/31   My Pretty Girl (Lois Deppe-v) a
                        Sweet and Hot (Jimmy Harrison-v) a
    10/16/31   Blues in My Heart (Les Reis-v) c
    9/11/34   Happy as the Day Is Long a
                        Limehouse Blues a
    3/2/37   Rhythm of the Tambourine a

HERBECK, RAY
    5/17/39   A Home in the Clouds (Betty Bronson, Kirby
                        Brooks-v) c

HERMAN, WOODY
    12/30/48   I Ain't Gettin' Any Younger (as I Ain't Gonna
                        Wait Too Long) c

HEYWOOD, EDDIE
    2/29/46   Pom Pom c

HILL, ALEX
   10/19/34   Let's Have a Jubilee   a

THE HIP STRING QUARTET   see   Milt Jackson

THE HIT PARADERS   see   Mark Warnow

HODGES, JOHNNY
   12/20/65   Someone to Watch Over Me   (with the Lawrence
                               Welk Orch.)   a

HOLIDAY, BILLIE
   10/15/40   Loveless Love   a
                               St. Louis Blues   a
                               See also Teddy Wilson

HOLLAND, CHARLES   see   BC 12/13/34

HOLMES, RICHARD "GROOVE"
   11/28/66   When Lights Are Low   c

HORNE, LENA   see   Soundtracks: Stormy Weather,   Thousands Cheer

HUGHES, SPIKE
   2/10/32   Blues in My Heart   (Joey Shields-v)   c

HUMES, HELEN
   5/9/50   Rock Me to Sleep   (accompanied by Marshall
                               Royal and His Orch.)   c

HUTTON, BETTY
   1947   Rumble, Rumble, Rumble   (with the Joe Lilley
                               Orch.)   a

HUTTON, MARION   see   Glenn Miller

HYMAN, DICK
   ca. 1956   Cow Cow Boogie   c

THE INK SPOTS   see   Ella Fitzgerald

ISHIHARA, YUJIRO
   8/30/74   Again   a
                               As Time Goes By   a
                               The Call of the Far Away Hills   a
                               Mona Lisa   a
                               The River of No Return   a
                               Ruby   a
                               September Song   a
                               Summertime in Venice   a
                               NOTE: 8/30/74 is the date of recording for the
                               instrumental backing for these tunes (done in Los
                               Angeles); the vocal tracks were added later by
                               Ishihara in Japan.

ITO, BENARD
   ca. 1970   Con Alma   a
                               Never Again   a

JACKSON, MILT
    5/68   A Walkin' Thing (with the Hip String Quartet) c
    4/76   My Kind of Trouble Is You c

JACKSON, QUENTIN see McKinney's Cotton Pickers

JAZZ AT THE PHILHARMONIC
    11/22/60   A Jazz Portrait of Brigitte Bardot c
                            Swedish Jam c

JAZZ GALA '79, CANNES, FRANCE
    1/22/79   Blues in My Heart (Joe Williams-v) c

THE JAZZ TODAY UNIT
    4/20/55   Symphony in Riffs (Kenny Baker-leader, featuring
                            Bertie King) c

JOHNSON, CHARLIE
    1/24/28   Charleston Is the Best Dance After All a
                            1/24/28 (take #2)
                            You Ain't the One (Monette Moore-v) a
                            1/24/28 (take #2)

JOHNSON, EDDIE
    June–July 1981   Blue Star c

JOHNSON, LAURIE
    early 1960's   Stick or Twist a, c

JOHNSON, PLAS
    1960   Blues in My Heart c

JOLLY, PETE
    1956   When Lights Are Low c

JONES, CLAUDE see Fletcher Henderson

JONES, DEAN
    ca. 1959   The Gypsy in My Soul a
                            Young and in Love a

JONES, JONAH
    9/61   After You've Gone a
                            Apollo Jumps a, c
                            Baubles, Bangles and Beads a
                            Boy Meets Horn a
                            Ciribiribin a
                            Echoes of Harlem a
                            Hot Lips a
                            I Can't Get Started a
                            Sugar Blues a
                            Tenderly a
                            Two O'Clock Jump a
                            West End Blues a
    1962   Blues in My Heart c

JONES, QUINCY see Peggy Lee

JORDAN, LOUIS
    12/8/47   Don't Burn the Candle at Both Ends (Martha
                            Davis-v) c
                            You're on the Right Track Baby (But You're
                            Goin' the Wrong Way) (Martha Davis-v) c

JOYCE, TEDDY
    1937   When Lights Are Low   c

JUGGERNAUT BAND   see   Frankie Capp

KPM MUSIC LIBRARY
    5/63   Be Cool - A   a, c
                            5/63 - B
                            5/63 - C
                            Blue Yonder - A   a, c
                            5/63 - B
                            Catfish Row   a, c
                            5/63 (link) #1
                            5/63 (link) #2
                            Discovery   a, c
                            Gotta Go Home   a, c
                            Heels Up   a, c
                            Imminent   a, c
                            Jazz Waltz - A   a, c
                            5/63 - B (thematic link)
                            5/63 - C (thematic transition)
                            Lonely Affair - A   a, c
                            5/63 - B
                            5/63 - C (thematic transition)
                            5/63 - D (thematic bridge)
                            Metropole   a, c
                            One Way Out   a, c
                            Show Break (ending) #1   a, c
                            5/63 (ending) #2
                            Vinho Verde   a, c
                            See also notes for this session (5/63) in chrono-
                            logical section of discography.

KASSEL, ART (recorded under pseudonym JOHNNY RIDGE)
    date unknown   Red Rose Waltz   a
                            The Ship That Never Sailed   a

KAWAGUCHI, GEORGE   see   Buddy Rich

KAYE, DANNY   see   Soundtrack: The Five Pennies

KAYE, MARION   see   Reggie Childs

KEENE, BOB   see   "Stringin' Along"

KEITH PROWSE MUSIC   see   KPM Music Library

KELLER, GRETA
    10/5/31   Blues in My Heart   c

KENNEDY, JOE
    1980   When Lights Are Low   c

KENTON, STAN
    12/6/47   Lonely Woman (June Christy-v) c
                            Nov. 25-Dec. 21 1947
                            9/21/59
                            See also June Christy

KESSEL, BARNEY see Charlie Byrd

KING, BERTIE
    4/6/55   Blues in My Heart c
                            Once Upon a Time c
    9/20/56   Blue Interlude c
                            Lazy Afternoon c
                            Skip It c
                            See also Jazz Today Unit

KIRK, ANDY see note under "Lonesome Nights"

KRAL, IRENE
    1963   Rock Me to Sleep (accompanied by Junior Mance
                            Trio) c

KRUEGER, JERRY
    4/25/39   Rain, Rain, Go Away a
                            Summertime a

KRUPA, GENE
    ca. 8/39   Melancholy Lullaby c
                            2/2/40
                          Symphony in Riffs a, c
                          9/20/39
                          11/5/39
    3/22/41   Rockin' Chair a
                          6/7/41
                          7/2/41
                          10/3/41
                          4/15/49 (possibly same arrangement)
                          4/22/49 (possibly same arrangement)
    1/23/42   Harlem on Parade (Anita O'Day-v) c
    11/13/42   Cow Cow Boogie (Anita O'Day-v) c

LAINE, FRANKIE
    ca. 1951   I Love You for That (with Patti Page-v, and
                          Harry Geller Orch.) a

LAMBERT, HENDRICKS, BAVAN
    12/20-21/63   Meetin' Time c

LANE, RUBY
    early 1950's   Baby, Won't You Please Come Home a
                          For Sale--One Broken Heart a

LARKINS, ELLIS
    11/74   Blues in My Heart c
                            7/21/77

LAWFORD, PETER see Jimmy Durante

LEE, JULIA
    11/11/47   King Size Papa c

1956-1957
Take It or Leave It   c

11/13/47   I Didn't Like It the First Time   c
4/49   Don't Come Too Soon   c
7/21/50   You're Gonna Miss It   c

LEE, PEGGY
ca. 7/47   Lonely Woman   c
1950   Rock Me to Sleep   c
early 1950's?   Melancholy Lullaby   c
1954   Love, You Didn't Do Right By Me   a
4/15-16/61   San Francisco Blues   (with Quincy Jones Orch.)   a
8/61   I Believe in You   a
7/62   I'm a Woman   a
                   See also Benny Goodman

LESTER, KETTY   see   Bruce Blalock

LEWIS, WILLIE
1/17/36   All of Me   a
                   I've Got a Feeling You're Fooling   a
                   Just a Mood   a, c
                   Rhythm Is Our Business   (Bobby Martin-v)   a
                   Star Dust   a
                   Stay Out of Love   a

LILLEY, JOE   see   Betty Hutton

LINCOLN, ABBEY
1956   I Didn't Say Yes (I Didn't Say No)   a
                   A Lonesome Cup of Coffee   a
11/5-6/56   The Masquerade Is Over   a
                   This Can't Be Love   a
                   Two Cigarettes in the Dark   a

LITTLE MISS CORNSHUCKS (pseudonym for MILDRED CUMMINGS)
1951   Papa Tree Top Blues   a
                   Rock Me to Sleep   a, c

LOMBARDO, CARMEN   see   Guy Lombardo

LOMBARDO, GUY
2/23/32   Blues in My Heart   (Carmen Lombardo-v)   c

LOVELLE, TONY
date unknown   Key Largo   c

LOWE, MUNDELL
1978   Souvenir   c

LOWN, BERT
9/16/31   Blues in My Heart   (Elmer Feldkamp-v)   c

LUNCEFORD, JIMMIE
12/23/40   O. K. For Baby   c
                   Nov. -Dec. 1940
                   1945?
                   See also note under Lonesome Nights (in title
                   listings).

LUNDBERG, VICTOR
    1968   On Censorship a, c
                              To the Destroyers a, c
                              NOTE: Carter composed and arranged background music for Lundberg's narrative vocal.

LUTER, CLAUDE see Sidney Bechet

M SQUAD (TV SHOW)
    3/59   (The) Juke Box a, c
                              A Lady Sings the Blues a
                              The Mugger a, c
                              Phantom Raiders a, c
                              The Search a, c

McCALL, MARY ANN
    2/1/50   The Sky Is Crying c

McGHEE, STICKS
    1/14/53   Blues in My Heart c

McKINLEY, RAY
    1955   Cow Cow Boogie c

McKINNEY'S COTTON PICKERS
    9/8/31   Do You Believe in Love at Sight (Quentin Jackson?-v) a
    11/4/30   Never Swat a Fly (Bill Coty-v) a

McRAE, CARMEN
    1968   I Haven't Got Anything Better to Do a
                              I'm Always Drunk in San Francisco a
    11/71-3/72   All That I Can Do Is Think of You a
                              All the Time a
                              Bobby a
                              The Happy Ones a
                              I'll Never Pass This Way Again a
                              Mr. Love a
                              Tender Loving Words a
                              When It's Time to Tell a
                              When Twilight Comes a

MacRAE, GORDON
    1950   Hongi Tongi Hoki Poki (with the Les Baxter Chorus and Paul Weston and His Orch.) c

McVEA, JACK
    8/45   O. K. For Baby c

MADDIN, JIMMIE
    1954   I Like a Shuffle Beat a
                              I Stole De Wedding Bell a, c
                              Play Ball a, c
                              See also The Dream Dusters

MALONE, ANNIE
    date unknown   Debbie's Debut a
                              Hell's Bells a

MANCE, JUNIOR see Irene Kral

MANN, HERBIE
   4/29/57   When Lights Are Low   c

MANTOVANI
   1962   Summer Night   c

MARTIN, BOBBY see Willie Lewis

MARTIN, DEAN
   6/20/58   Once Upon a Time (It Happened)   c

MASON, MARTHA
   1967   The Wine of Sweet Remembrance   c

MAY, BILLY see Time-Life series The Swing Era

MERLINO, GENE see Bob Friedman

MERRILL, HELEN
   1959   Blues in My Heart   c

MEZZROW, MEZZ
   11/6/33   Free Love   a, c
                      Love, You're Not the One for Me   a, c

MILES, EDDIE see Washboard Rhythm Kings

MILLER, GLENN
   9/11/39   Melancholy Lullaby (Ray Eberle-v)   c
   10/9/39   Bluebirds in the Moonlight (Marion Hutton-v)   a
   11/17/39
   11/25/39
   2/5/40   Symphony in Riffs   a, c
   3/4/40
   7/3/40   Blues in My Heart   c
   9/10/40
                      1943-1944 (with the Army Air Force Band)
   7/16/42   Rainbow Rhapsody   c
                      1959 (New Glenn Miller Orch.)

MILLER, MRS.
   9/29/70   I Said No   a
                      Ma (She's Making Eyes at Me)   a
                      She Had to Go and Lose It at the Astor   a
                      The Weekend of a Private Secretary   a

MILLINDER, LUCKY
   5/26/44   Hurry Hurry (Wynonie Harris-v)   c

MILLS BLUE RHYTHM BAND
   6/26/31   Heebie Jeebies (Chick Bullock-v)   a
   9/23/32   Jazz Cocktail   a, c
   10/4/34   Let's Have a Jubilee   a

THE MILLS BROTHERS see BC 10/23/40

MILTON, ROY
    1946   Blues in My Heart c

MISS RHAPSODY (pseudonym for Viola Wells)
    4/22/72   Blues in My Heart c

MOORE, JOHNNY
    1951   Blues in My Heart (Billy Valentine-v) c

MOORE, MONETTE see Charlie Johnson

MORGAN, DICK
    10/31/60   When Lights Are Low c

MORSE, ELLA MAE
    4/24/46   Your Conscience Tells You So (with Freddie
                      Slack) c
    ca. 1948   Cow Cow Boogie c
                      See also Freddie Slack

"MUCHO CALOR"
    10/57   Autumn Leaves (features Art Pepper) a

MULDAUR, GEOFF
    1/75   Livin' in the Sunlight (Lovin' in the Moonlight) a

MULDAUR, MARIA
    1974   It Ain't the Meat, It's the Motion a
                      12/22/74
                      Squeeze Me a
                      12/22/74
                      Sweetheart a
                      12/22/74
    12/22/74   Any Old Time a
                      Don't You Make Me High a
                      Gee, Baby, Ain't I Good to You a
                      It Don't Mean a Thing If It Ain't Got That Swing a
                      Lover Man a
                      Walkin' One and Only a
    9/75   Rockin' Chair (with Hoagy Carmichael-v) a
                      We Just Couldn't Say Goodbye a

MURPHY, MARK
    1962   Blues in My Heart c

MUSIC FROM M SQUAD see M SQUAD

MYLES, MEG
    date unknown   My Melancholy Baby a

NEUMAN, ULRICH see Alice Babs

NEW McKINNEY'S COTTON PICKERS
    3/31/71   Ol' Man River (arrangement dates from early
                      1930's) a
    9/20/75   Never Swat a Fly (Orrin Foslien, Jr.-v) (ar-
                      rangement originally recorded in 1930 by McKin-
                      ney's Cotton Pickers) a
                      6/26/80

NOTE: New McKinney's LP Bountiful B38003
lists Carter as the arranger of "China Boy"
(recorded 9/20/75) but Carter, upon hearing it,
finds no reason to believe it is his.

NEWBORN, PHINEAS
    4/1/64   A Walkin' Thing c

NEWMAN, ALFRED
    1955   The Girl Upstairs a
                        Blue Mountain (as To Ava) a
    1961   The Bad and the Beautiful a
                        Laura a
                        Pinky a

NOBLE, RAY
    2/12/32   Blues in My Heart (Al Bowlly-v) c

NORVO, RED
    10/14/47   Hollyridge Drive a, c

O'CONNELL, HELEN see Jimmy Dorsey

O'DAY, ANITA
    1947   I Ain't Gettin' Any Younger (with Ralph Burns
                        Orch.) a, c
                        Key Largo a, c
                        See also Gene Krupa

OLAY, RUTH
    ca. 1957   Slow But Sure c
    1958   Hurry Hurry c

OMER, JEAN
    ca. 12/40   The Blue Room a

PAGE, PATTI
    ca. 1951   Back in Your Own Backyard a
                        See also Frankie Laine

PARRY, HARRY
    6/19/46   O.K. For Baby c

PAYNE, JACK
    ca. 1932   Blues in My Heart c

PEPPER, ART
    10/24-25/60   How Can You Lose? c
                        See also "Mucho Calor"

PETERS, LOIS
    ca. 1958   Ask (with the Ravenscroft Singers and Orch.) a, c
                        How Deep Is the Ocean a
                        I'll Be Your Bride Again (with the Ravenscroft
                        Singers and Orch.) a

PETERSON, OSCAR
    7/58   When Lights Are Low c
                        1958

See also BC 9/52

PIERCE, NAT see Frankie Capp

POLK, LUCY ANN see Les Brown

POWELL, CHRIS
    4/6/50   Blues in My Heart c

POWERS, JACK
    ca. 1953   She Doesn't Laugh Like You (with the Cheer
                              Leaders) c

PRICE, SAMMY
    4/9/56   Blues in My Heart c

PRINCETON UNIVERSITY JAZZ ENSEMBLE see BC 4/8/77, 11/10/79

PROWSE, KEITH see KPM Music Library

R. A. F. DANCE ORCHESTRA (THE SQUADRONAIRES)
    7/27/43   Cow Cow Boogie (Sid Colin-v) c

THE RADIO RHYTHM CLUB SEXTET see Buddy Featherstonhaugh

THE RAELETS see Ray Charles

RALEIGH, DON
    late 1950's   Rainbow Rhapsody c

THE RAMBLERS (DUTCH) see BC 3/24/37

RANEY, SUE see Bob Friedman

RAVENSCROFT SINGERS AND ORCHESTRA see Lois Peters

RAWLS, LOU
    1965   Blues for the Weepers a
                              Charmaine a
                              Cold Cold Heart a
                              Du Bist Die Liebe a
                              Gee, Baby, Ain't I Good to You a
                              If I Had My Life to Live Over a
                              If It's the Last Thing I Do a
                              I'll See You in My Dreams a
                              Into Each Life Some Rain Must Fall a
                              It's Monday Every Day a
                              Margie a
                              Me and My Shadow a
                              My Buddy a
                              Nobody But Me a
                              Nothing Really Feels the Same a
                              Now and Then There's a Fool Such as I a
                              The Power of Love a
                              Three O'Clock in the Morning a
                              Two Tickets West a
                              What'll I Do a
                              Whispering Grass a

RAZAF, ANDY (recorded under pseudonym JOHNNY THOMPSON)
    1/17/28   Nobody Knows How Much I Love You   c

REIS, LES   see   Fletcher Henderson

RENDER, RUDY
    ca. 1951   Rock Me to Sleep   (with Maxwell Davis and His
                             Orch.)   c

RICH, BUDDY
    9/10/53   Let's Fall in Love   a
                             Me and My Jaguar   a, c
    1/18/65   Slides and Hides   (with Louis Bellson and the
                             George Kawaguchi Orch.)   a, c
                             See also BC 9/52

RICH, FREDDIE
    2/14/40   A House with a Little Red Barn   (Rosemary Cal-
                             vin-v)   a
                             How High the Moon   (Rosemary Calvin-v)   a
                             I'm Forever Blowing Bubbles   a
                             Till We Meet Again   a

RICHARDS, ANN
    1958   Blues in My Heart   c

RICHARDS, CHUCK
    12/19/34   Blue Interlude   c

RIDGE, JOHNNY (pseudonym)   see   Art Kassel

RIEDEL, GEORG
    9/5/55   When Lights Are Low   c

ROBERTS, HOWARD
    2/12-13/63   When Lights Are Low   c

ROBERTSON, DICK   see   Eubie Blake, King Carter

ROBINSON, BILL   see   Soundtrack: Stormy Weather

ROBINSON, JOE
    9/22/49   Don't Scream, Don't Shout   a
                             If I Can't Have You   a, c
                             Roll with the Boogie   a, c
                             Suspicious of My Woman   a, c

ROGERS, DICK (pseudonym)   see   Dick Robertson

ROSOLINO, FRANK   see   Conte Candoli

ROSS, CANDY
                           See chronological section of discography for vari-
                           ous arrangements and compositions recorded
                           featuring vocals by this musician with the Carter
                           Orchestra in 1946.

ROYAL, MARSHALL   see   Helen Humes

SACCO, TONY   see   Benny Goodman

ST. JOHN, DELL

See chronological section of discography for various arrangements and compositions recorded by this vocalist with the Carter Orchestra in 1939.

SANDERS, FELICIA
1959   My Kind of Trouble Is You   c

SANDERS, PHAROAH
1981   When Lights Are Low   c

SAVITT, JAN
1/24/40   Kansas City Moods   c
                              10/25/45

SCHROUDER, CHARLES   see   Helen Troy

SCOTT, BERYL   see   Bill Shepherd

SHANK, BUD
1/19/56   When Lights Are Low   (with Bob Cooper)   c

SHARON, RALPH   see   Tony Bennett

SHAW, ARTIE
4/28/37   Symphony in Riffs   a, c
                              7/8/38
2/15/38   Lonesome Nights (as Take My Word)   a, c
12/2/38   Blue Interlude   c
1949   Melancholy Lullaby   c
                              NOTE: The liner notes to RCA (F) FXM1-7336
                              (Artie Shaw and His Orch. v. 1, 1941-1945) state
                              that Carter was responsible for the arrangements
                              from Shaw's 6/24/61 session--"Confessin'," "Love
                              Me a Little Little," "Don't Take Your Love from
                              Me," and "Beyond the Blue Horizon." Shaw, however, has identified these arrangements as his
                              own (letter dated 5/31/77).

SHEARING, GEORGE
7/17/52   When Lights Are Low   c
8/57   Blues in My Heart   (Dakota Staton-v)   c
1963   Nightfall   c
                              See also Joe Williams

SHEPHERD, BILL
1959   When Lights Are Low   (with Beryl Scott Chorus)   c

SHIELDS, JOEY   see   Spike Hughes

SIMMONS, ART
4/15/58   Cow Cow Boogie   c

SIMMS, GINNY
1939   Melancholy Lullaby   c
12/17/40   I'm Out of Style   (with Eddie South and His Orch.)
                              c

Sighs and Tears (with Eddie South and His Orch.)
c

SIMPKINS, ARTHUR LEE
    date unknown   I Long for You a
                     I Resolve a

SIMS, LEE
    ca. 1931   Blues in My Heart c

SIMS, ZOOT
    8/14/79   Black Butterfly a
                     I Got It Bad a
                     I Let a Song Go Out of My Heart a
                     In a Mellotone a
                     It Don't Mean a Thing If It Ain't Got That Swing
                     a

SLACK, FREDDIE
    5/21/42   Cow Cow Boogie (Ella Mae Morse-v) c
                     1955 (Thelma Gracen-v)
    11/25/47   Boogie Minor a, c
                     Chopstick Boogie a
                     St. Louis Blues a
    12/16/47   Re-Bop Boogie (as Be-Bop Boogie) a, c
    1947   Two Left Hands (Charlotte Blackburn-v) c
    1955   Between 18th and 19th on Chestnut Street a
                     Rhumboogie a
                     See also Ella Mae Morse

SMITH, HALE see BC 12/3/73

SMITH, KEELY
    1964   Can't Buy Me Love a
                     A Hard Day's Night a
                     I Want to Hold Your Hand a
                     Please Please Me a

SMITH, MABEL (BIG MAYBELLE) see Christine Chatham

SONORA SWING BAND see BC 9/12/36

SOUTH, EDDIE see Ginny Simms

SPENCER-HAGEN ORCHESTRA see Lincoln Chase

SPIVAK, CHARLIE
    1/7/47   Devil's Holiday a, c
                     1/12/47
                     2/12/47

THE SQUADRONAIRES see R. A. F. Dance Orchestra

STAFFORD, JO
    1963   Oh! Look at Me Now a
                     The One I Love Belongs to Someone Else a
                     Whatcha Know Joe? a
                     Yes Indeed a

STARR, KAY
  11/26/47   Second Hand Love   a, c

STATON, DAKOTA
  1959   When Lights Are Low   c
  2/60   Be Anything   a
                        Body and Soul   a
                        Close Your Eyes   a
                        Congratulations to Someone   a
                        Dedicated to You   a
                        I Can't Get Started   a
                        My Wish   a
                        Old Folks   a
                        Solitude   a
                        The Very Thought of You   a
                        Whispering Grass   a
                        You're Mine Now   a
  6/60   Don't Explain   a
                        Don't Leave Me Now   a
                        Everybody's Somebody's Fool   a
                        First Things First   a
                        The Folks Who Live on the Hill   a
                        Hey Lawdy Mama   a
                        I Won't Worry   a
                        If I Love Again   a
                        I'll Close My Eyes   a
                        Indiana   a
                        Knock Me a Kiss   a
                        Let Them Talk   a
                        Make Me a Present of You   a
                        The Masquerade Is Over   a
                        Meet Me at No Special Place   a
                        On Green Dolphin Street   a
                        Pick Yourself Up   a
                        Rock Me to Sleep   a, c
                        'Round Midnight   a
                        So in Love   a
                        Trapped in the Web of Love   a
                        Weak for the Man   a
                        Will You Still Be Mine   a
                        You Call It Madness   a
                        See also George Shearing

STEVENS, INGER
  1968   Lasse Lasse Litten   a, c
                        The Loving Room   a, c

STEVENS, RAY
  1975   Cow Cow Boogie   c

STONE, LAWRENCE
  1950's   Without a Word of Goodbye   (with Ernie Free-
                        man's Orch.)   c
                        See also Ernie Freeman

"STRINGIN' ALONG"
  11/5/57   Once in a While   a
                        Polka Dots and Moonbeams   a

NOTE: Personnel includes Bob Keene (cl) and
session appears in Jepsen under his name.

SULLIVAN, JOE
   4/29/40   Pom Pom   c
   1944-1946   Blues in My Heart   c

SULLIVAN, MAXINE   see   BC   4/1/44, 1/8/46

SVENSKA HOTVINTETTEN
   1940   When Lights Are Low   c

SWIFT, DAVID
   1962   Cow Cow Boogie   (with Rene Hall's Orch.)   c

SYMS, SYLVIA
   1952   Lonely Woman   (with Barbara Carroll Trio)   c
                      1976

TATUM, ART
   12/28/53   Blues in My Heart   c
                      See also BC 6/25/54

TAYLOR, BILLY
   6/24/59   When Lights Are Low   c

TAYLOR, SAM
   1956-1957   Blues in My Heart   c

THOMPSON, JOHNNY (pseudonym)   see   Andy Razaf

THOMPSON, LUCKY
   4/22/47   Boulevard Bounce   a, c

THOMPSON, SIR CHARLES
   1/8/61   Cow Cow Boogie   c

THE THREE REASONS   see   Dick Todd

TILTON, MARTHA   see   Benny Goodman

TIME LIFE SERIES: THE SWING ERA
   8/3/70   Melancholy Lullaby   (Billy May-leader)   a, c
   11/30/70   Liza   (Billy May-leader)   a
   7/29/71   Happy as the Day Is Long   (Billy May-leader)   a
   8/2/71   Rockin' Chair   (Billy May-leader)   a
   2/17/72   I Surrender Dear   a
                      NOTE: These five recordings are recreations--
                      see notes in title listings.
                      See also Glen Gray

TJADER, CAL
   4/57   When Lights Are Low   c
                      9/77
   1960   Key Largo   c

TODD, DICK
   5/1/39   A Home in the Clouds   (with the Three Reasons-
                      v)   c

TORME, MEL
    8/2/54   It Don't Mean a Thing If It Ain't Got That Swing a
                              Tutti Frutti a
                              See also Soundtrack: A Man Called Adam

TROY, HELEN
    1954   You'll Never Get the Chance Again (with
                              Charles Schrouder-v, and Van Alexander's Orch.)
                              c

TURNER, JOE (pianist)
    5/29/76   Blues in My Heart c

UNIVERSITY OF BUFFALO JAZZ ENSEMBLE see BC 10/28/78

U. S. AIR FORCE JAZZ ENSEMBLE see The Airmen of Note

VALENTINE, BILLY see Johnny Moore

VAN BERGEN, FRANS
    1/2-4/61   When Lights Are Low c

VARSITY SEVEN
    1/15/40   Pom Pom c

VAUGHAN, SARAH
    4/8/56   Lonely Woman c
    1962   After You've Gone a
                              Falling in Love with Love a
                              A Garden in the Rain a
                              Great Day a
                              Honeysuckle Rose a
                              I Believe in You a
                              I Can't Give You Anything But Love a
                              I'm Gonna Live Til I Die a
                              The Lady's in Love with You a
                              Moonlight on the Ganges a
                              Nobody Else But Me a
                              The Trolley Song a
    1/63   Always on My Mind a
                              Friendless a, c
                              If I Had You a
                              I'll Never Be the Same a
                              Lonely Hours a
                              Look for Me, I'll Be Around a
                              The Man I Love a
                              So Long, My Love a
                              Solitude a
                              These Foolish Things a
                              What'll I Do a
                              You're Driving Me Crazy a
    ca. 1963   Key Largo c
                              When Lights Are Low c
    1965   The Pawnbroker a
    8/13/79   Day Dream a
                              In a Sentimental Mood a
                              Lush Life a
                              Solitude a

Sophisticated Lady   a
Tonight I Shall Sleep with a Smile on My Face   a
See also The Airmen of Note

VENTURA, CHARLIE
10/48   Lonely Woman   (Jackie Cain-v)   c

VENUTI, JOE
10/13/33   Everybody Shuffle   a, c

WALLER, FATS
1/23/43   Moppin' and Boppin'   c

WARD, HELEN   see Benny Goodman

WARING, FRED
8/23/45   My Twilight Reverie   c

WARNOW, MARK
2/2/42   Cocktails for Two   (Barry Wood-v)   a
2/9/42   The Music Goes 'Round and 'Round   (The Hit
                              Paraders-v)   a
                              These Foolish Things   (Barry Wood-v)   a

WARREN, EARLE
2/9/74   Blues in My Heart   c

WASHBOARD RHYTHM KINGS
9/23/31   Blues in My Heart   (Eddie Miles-v)   c

WATERS, ETHEL
1931-1934   Blues in My Heart   (with Herman Chittison Trio)
                              c

WAYNE, CHUCK
12/27/76   When Lights Are Low   c

WEBB, CHICK
3/30/31   Blues in My Heart   (Louis Bacon-v)   a, c
                              Heebie Jeebies   a
                              Soft and Sweet   a
5/3/38   Liza   a
8/13/38

WEBSTER, BEN
12/27/51   King's Riff   c
                              Randall's Island   c

WELCH, ELISABETH
1976   When Lights Are Low   c
                              See also BC mid 6/36, 6/20/36

WELCH, EMMA LOU   see   BC 1/48

WELK, LAWRENCE   see   Johnny Hodges

WELLS, VIOLA   see   Miss Rhapsody

WESTON, PAUL   see   Gordon MacRae

WHITE, KITTY
    7/8/49   It Pays to Advertise (accompanied by Dave
                                    Cavanaugh's Orch.) c
    ca. 1958   I Am Your Dream a
                                    The Old Man and the Sea a

WHITEMAN, PAUL

                                    The Whiteman Archive at Williams College has
                                    scores of three Carter compositions from the
                                    Whiteman book.   None were arranged by Carter
                                    and there are no known recordings.   The titles
                                    are: "Blue Interlude," "Blues in My Heart," and
                                    "Devil's Holiday. "

WICKMAN, PUTTE
    5/4/49   When Lights Are Low c

WIDESPREAD DEPRESSION ORCHESTRA
    1981   Night Hop a, c

WILBER, BOB
    5/30-31/79   I'm in the Mood for Swing (with the American
                                    All Stars featuring Lars Erstrand) c
                                    When Lights Are Low (with the American All
                                    Stars featuring Lars Erstrand) c

WILEY, LEE
    7/25/57   Blues in My Heart c

WILLIAMS, HARRY
    ca. 1961   Summer Night c

WILLIAMS, JOE
    3/1-2/71   Blues in My Heart (with George Shearing) c
    11/71-3/72   Always on Sunday a
                                    Care a
                                    God Bless You a
                                    Got That Feeling a
                                    I'm a Lucky Guy a
                                    Love Is a Feeling a
                                    Once Upon a Happy Time (The Big Band Days) a
                                    Right Here in My Heart a
                                    Satin Latin a
                                    When You're Young a
                                    See also Bob Friedman (note); Jazz Gala '79,
                                    Cannes, France

WILSON, GARLAND
    9/7/36   Just a Mood c

WILSON, JACKIE
    1/3-4/68   Chain Gang (with Count Basie's Orch.) a
                                    Even When You Cry (with Count Basie's Orch.) a
                                    For Your Precious Love (with Count Basie's
                                    Orch.) a
                                    Funky Broadway (with Count Basie's Orch.) a

I Never Loved a Woman (with Count Basie's Orch.) a
I Was Made to Love Her (with Count Basie's Orch.) a
In the Midnight Hour (with Count Basie's Orch.) a
My Girl (with Count Basie's Orch.) a
Ode to Billy Joe (with Count Basie's Orch.) a
Respect (with Count Basie's Orch.) a
Uptight (Everything's All Right) (with Count Basie's Orch.) a

WILSON, NANCY
    1968   Prisoner of My Eyes (I Can Never Let You Go) a

WILSON, STANLEY
    1960-1961   Champagne Waltz a
    5/63   Cherchez La Femme a, c
                      Dance with Me a, c
                      Domino (vocal group) a
                      If You Go a
                      Poor Little Rich Girl a
                      Roses of Picardy a
                      Show Me the Way to Go Home a
                      Under Paris Skies (vocal group) a
                      What Kind of Fool Am I a
    ca. 1963   A Kiss from You (as Lydia) c

WILSON, TEDDY
    10/31/38   Here It Is Tomorrow Again (Billie Holiday-v) a
    11/9/38   April in My Heart (Billie Holiday-v) a
                      I'll Never Fail You (Billie Holiday-v) a
                      Say It with a Kiss (Billie Holiday-v) a
                      They Say (Billie Holiday-v) a
                      11/9/38 (take #2)

WOOD, BARRY see Mark Warnow

WYATT, DON
    1968   All Tore Down a
                      Do I Need You a
                      I'll Never Leave You a
                      Point of No Return a, c

YOUNG, WEBSTER
    8/21/61   When Lights Are Low c

ZITO, JIMMY
    1947   Key Largo (Nick Delane-v) c

NOTE: Listed here are Carter arrangements and compositions which have been released on Soundtrack LPs. For a complete listing of his film work see Filmography.

THE BIG BROADCAST OF 1932   see   Cab Calloway

THE FIVE PENNIES
   Sept. -Oct. 1958   Bill Bailey, Won't You Please Come Home
                        (Louis Armstrong, Danny Kaye-v) a
                        Just the Blues a NOTE: Features Louis Armstrong, tp.

FLOWER DRUM SONG
                        Carter played in the orchestra and assisted in the orchestration of parts of this 1961 production. The soundtrack is on Decca DL79098 (later labelled MCA 2069).

THE GANG'S ALL HERE
   Mar. or Apr. 1943   No Love, No Nothing (Alice Faye-v, and the Benny Goodman Orch.) a

GUNS OF NAVARONE
   1961   Yassu a

THE HANGED MAN   see   Stan Getz

A MAN CALLED ADAM
   11/65   Ain't I a, c
                        All That Jazz (3 versions) (Mel Torme-v) a, c
                        Claudia (2 versions) a, c
                        Crack Up (Playboy Theme) a
                        Go Now a, c
                        Night Walk a, c
                        Soft Touch a, c
                        Whisper to One (Sammy Davis Jr. -v) c

STATE FAIR
   1962   That's for Me (Pat Boone-v) a

STORMY WEATHER
   Jan. -Feb. 1943   Ain't That Something (Bill Robinson-v) a
                        Good for Nothin' Joe (Lena Horne-v) a
                        I Can't Give You Anything But Love (Lena Horne, Bill Robinson-v) a

Stormy Weather   (Lena Horne-v)   a
Jan. -Feb. 1943   (vocal group)   (Carter arranged
last 29 measures)

THOUSANDS CHEER
    1943   Honeysuckle Rose   (Lena Horne-v)   a

VALLEY OF THE DOLLS
    1967   I'll Plant My Own Tree   a

CHRONOLOGICAL INDEX
OF COMPOSITIONS AND ARRANGEMENTS

a = Carter arrangement   c = Carter composition

1927
PDQ Blues a

1928
Charleston Is The Best Dance After
  All a
Come On Baby a
Easy Money a
Nobody Knows How Much I Love
  You c
You Ain't The One a

1929
Blazin' a
Raisin' The Roof a
The Wang Wang Blues a

1930
Bugle Call Rag a
Dee Blues c
Goodbye Blues ac
Got Another Sweetie Now a
Keep A Song In Your Soul a
Never Swat A Fly a
Somebody Loves Me a

1931
Blues In My Heart ac
Do You Believe In Love At Sight
  a
Heebie Jeebies a
My Pretty Girl a
Soft And Sweet a
Sweet And Hot a

1932
Hot Toddy ac
Jazz Cocktail ac
Sweet Rhythm a

1933
Blue Interlude ac
Blue Lou a
Devil's Holiday ac
Everybody Shuffle ac
Free Love ac
I Never Knew a

Krazy Kapers ac
Lonesome Nights ac
Love, You're Not The One For Me
  ac
Ol' Man River a
Once Upon A Time ac
Swing It a
Symphony In Riffs ac
Synthetic Love ac

1934
Dream Lullaby ac
Happy As The Day Is Long a
I'm Getting Sentimental Over You a
It Happens To The Best of Friends
  a
Let's Have A Jubilee a
Limehouse Blues a
Shoot The Works ac

1935
Blue Moon a
Nagasaki a

1936
Accent On Swing ac
All Of Me a
Big Ben Blues ac
Blue Interlude a [c: 1933]
Blues In My Heart a [c: 1931]
Bye Bye Baby a
Chickfeed ac
Gin And Jive ac
Gloaming a
Hold Me Tight, I'm Falling a
I Got Rhythm a
I Gotta Go ac
I Never Knew a
If Only I Could Read Your Mind ac
I'm Putting All My Eggs In One
  Basket a
I'm Tickled To Death I'm Me a
Indiana a
I've Got A Feeling You're Fooling a
I've Got Two Lips a
Just A Mood ac
Let It Be Me a

Nightfall   ac
Rhythm Is Our Business   a
Rise 'N Shine   a
Scandal In A Flat   ac
Some Of These Days   a
Star Dust   a
Stay Out Of Love   a
A Sunbonnet Blue   a
Swingin' At Maida Vale   ac
Swingin' The Blues   ac
These Foolish Things   a
Waltzing The Blues   c
Way Down Yonder In New Orleans
   a
We Saw The Sea   a
What's The Name Of That Song
   a
When Day Is Done   a
When Lights Are Low   ac
When You're Smiling   a
You Understand   ac

1937
Blues In My Heart   a [c: 1931]
Crazy Rhythm   a
Honeysuckle Rose   a
I Ain't Got Nobody   a
I'll Never Give In   a
I'm In The Mood For Swing   ac
Lazy Afternoon   ac
Mighty Like The Blues   a
My Buddy   a
One, Two, Button Your Shoe   a
Out Of Nowhere   a
Pardon Me, Pretty Baby   a
Rambling In C   c
Rhythm Of The Tambourine   a
Skip It   ac
Somebody Loves Me   a
Stars And You   c
There's A Small Hotel   a

1938
April in My Heart   a
Blue Light Blues   c
Farewell Blues   a
Here It Is Tomorrow Again   a
I'll Never Fail You   a
I'm Coming Virginia   a
I'm In The Mood For Swing   a
   [c: 1937]
Liza   a
Muskrat Ramble   a
Say It With A Kiss   a
Shoe Shiner's Drag   a
They Say   a

1939
Blue Evening   a

Blue Orchids   a
Bluebirds In The Moonlight   a
Early Session Hop   a
The Fable Of A Fool   ac
A Home In The Clouds   ac
Honeysuckle Rose   a
How Strange   a
I Cried For You   a
I'm Coming Virginia   a
I'm Forever Blowing Bubbles   a
Lady Be Good   a
Lilacs In The Rain   a
Love's Got Me Down Again   a
Melancholy Lullaby   ac
More Than You Know   a
My Heart Has Wings   a
One Sweet Letter From You   a
Patty Cake, Patty Cake, Baker
   Man   a
Rain, Rain, Go Away   a
Riff Romp   ac
Scandal In A Flat   a [c: 1936]
Shufflebug Shuffle   ac
Star Dust   a
Summertime   a
Tea For Two   a
Vagabond Dreams   a
What's New   a
When Lights Are Low   a [c: 1936]

1940
All Of Me   a
Among My Souvenirs   a
Blue Room   a
Boogie Woogie Sugar Blues   a
By The Watermelon Vine, Lindy
   Lou   a
Calling All Bars   a
Cocktails For Two   a
Fish Fry   ac
A House With A Little Red Barn   a
How High The Moon   a
I'm Out Of Style   c
I've Been In Love Before   a
Kansas City Moods   ac
The Last Kiss You Gave Me   a
The Lone Arranger   a
Loveless Love   a
Night Hop   ac
O. K. For Baby   ac
Pom Pom   ac
St. Louis Blues   a
Serenade To A Sarong   ac
Sighs And Tears   c
Sleep   a
Slow Freight   a
Takin' My Time   ac
Till We Meet Again   a
The Very Thought Of You   a

Who's Yehoodi a

1941
Babalu a
Back Bay Boogie ac
Cuddle Up, Huddle Up ac
Ev'ry Goodbye Ain't Gone ac
Ill Wind a
Lullaby To A Dream ac
Midnight a
My Favorite Blues ac
Rockin' Chair a
Sunday a
There I've Said It Again a
Tree Of Hope ac
What A Difference A Day Made a

1942
Cocktails For Two a
Cow Cow Boogie c
Harlem On Parade c
I Can't Get Started a
The Music Goes 'Round And
    'Round a
Ol' Man River a
Rainbow Rhapsody c
These Foolish Things a

1943
Ain't That Something? a
Good For Nothin' Joe a
Honeysuckle Rose a
Hurry Hurry c
I Can't Get Started a
I Can't Give You Anything But
    Love a
Love For Sale a
Moppin' And Boppin' c
No Love, No Nothin' a
Stormy Weather a

1944
I Can't Escape From You a
I Never Mention Your Name a
I Surrender Dear a
I'm Lost a
Star Dust a
Sweet Georgia Brown a
Two Again a

1945
All Alone a
Bunbelina ac
Cuttin' Time ac
Daddy Daddy a
June Comes Around a
Just You, Just Me a

Malibu ac
My Twilight Reverie a
Paradise a (arrangement probably
    dates back to early 30s but first
    recorded 1945)
Riffamarole c
Somebody Loves Me a

1946
Dream Castle ac
I Cover The Waterfront a
If I Can't Have You ac
I'm The Caring Kind ac
Jump Call ac
Looking For A Boy a
Night And Day a
Oofdah! ac
Out Of My Way a
Re-bop Boogie ac
Twelve O'Clock Jump ac
What'll It Be c
Where Or When a
Your Conscience Tells You So ac

1947
Boogie Minor ac
Boulevard Bounce ac
Chopstick Boogie a
Congoroo ac
Don't Burn The Candle At Both
    Ends c
Hollyridge Drive ac
I Ain't Gettin' Any Younger ac
I Didn't Like It The First Time c
I'm A Three Time Loser c
Key Largo ac
King Size Papa c
Lonely Woman c (composed 1937
    but first recorded 1947)
Re-bop Boogie a [c: 1946]
Rumble, Rumble, Rumble a
St. Louis Blues a
Second Hand Love ac
Take It Or Leave It c
Two Left Hands c
You're On The Right Track (But
    You're Goin' The Wrong Way) c

1948
Baby, You're Mine For Keeps a
Bop Bounce ac
I Don't Want It No More c
Let Us Drink A Toast Together a
An Old Love Story a
Reina a
You'll Never Break My Heart Again
    a

1949

Don't Come Too Soon c
Don't Scream, Don't Shout a
I Ain't Got Nobody a
I Lost You a
I'd Rather Be A Rooster c
If I Can't Have You a [c: 1946]
It Pays To Advertise c
Look Out For Tomorrow c
Roll With The Boogie ac
Stinkin' From Drinkin' c
Surf Board c
Suspicious Of My Woman ac

1950

Hongi Tongi Hoki Poki c
I'm Such A Fool To Be In Love
   With You c
Rock Me To Sleep c
The Sky Is Crying c
That Ain't It ac
You're Gonna Miss It c

1951

Back In Your Own Backyard a
I Love You For That a
I Still Love Him So c
King's Riff c
Papa Tree Top Blues a
Randall's Island c
Rock Me To Sleep a [c: 1950]

1952

Bewitched, Bothered And Be-
   wildered a
Blue Mountain a
Cocktails For Two a
Cruisin' ac
Georgia On My Mind a
Jam Blues c
Key Largo a [c: 1947]
Lullaby In Blue ac
Mama Lou ac
Rockin' Along ac
'Round Midnight a
Sunday Afternoon ac
Wanna Go Home a
Wish You Were Here a
You Belong To Me a

1953

All Alone And Lonesome ac
Beautiful Love a
Blue Star ac
Don't Lead Me On a
Flamingo a
I'll Be Around a
Johnny Klingaringding a

Let's Fall In Love a
Make Me A Present Of You a
Me And My Jaguar ac
She Doesn't Laugh Like You c
You're Driving Me Crazy a
You're Gone For A Long Long
   Time a

1954

Can't We Be Friends a
I Like A Shuffle Beat a
I Stole De Wedding Bell ac
I'm Sorry ac
It Don't Mean A Thing If It Ain't
   Got That Swing a
Love, You Didn't Do Right By Me
   a
Play Ball ac
Spring Fever Blues a
Symphony a
Tutti Frutti a
With A Song In My Heart a
You'll Never Get The Chance Again
   c

1955

Between 18th and 19th On Chestnut
   Street a
Between The Devil And The Deep
   Blue Sea a
Blue Mountain a
Bugle Call Rag a
Christmas In New Orleans a
Christmas Night In Harlem a
The Girl Upstairs a
Lover Come Back To Me a
Millions Of People ac
Moments To Remember a
My Kind Of Trouble Is You c
Old Devil Moon a
Only You a
Rhumboogie a
Riding To Glory On A Trumpet a
That Old Black Magic a
Trumpets Have Triplets a

1956

Blue Prelude a
Blue Skies a
Comes Love a
Hallelujah a
How Am I To Know a
I Didn't Say Yes (I Didn't Say No) a
It's De-Lovely a
Just In Time a
A Lonesome Cup Of Coffee a
The Masquerade Is Over a
A Melody From The Sky a

This Can't Be Love a
Time After Time a
Two Cigarettes In The Dark a
You Go To My Head a
You Turned The Tables On Me a
You're My Everything a

1957
Autumn Leaves a
Blue Lou a
But Now I Know a
How Can You Lose? ac
A Hundred Years From Today a
I'm Coming Virginia a
In The Dark a
Just Squeeze Me a
Lover Come Back To Me a
Old Fashioned Love a
Once In A While a
Peace a
Polka Dots And Moonbeams a
Red Red Ribbon a
'Round Midnight a
Song Of The Wanderer a
Sunset Eyes a
Swingin' With Rhythm And Blues a
A Walkin' Thing ac
You Are Not My First Love a
You'd Better Think It Over ac

1958
Ask ac
August Moon c
Bill Bailey, Won't You Please
  Come Home a
February Fiesta a
How Deep Is The Ocean a
How Long Is A Moment ac
I Am Your Dream a
I'll Be Your Bride Again a
I'll Remember April a
It's So Frightnin' ac
June In January a
June Is Bustin' Out All Over a
Just The Blues a
March Wind ac
The Old Man And The Sea a
Once Upon A Time (It Happened)
  c
Roses In December a
September Song a
Sleigh Ride In July a
Something For October ac
Swingin' In November ac

1959
Friendly Islands c
The Gypsy In My Soul a

The Juke Box ac
A Lady Sings The Blues a
The Mugger ac
Phantom Raiders ac
The Search ac
Young And In Love a

1960
Be Anything a
Blue Five Jive ac
Body And Soul a
Champagne Waltz a
Close Your Eyes a
Congratulations To Someone a
Dedicated To You a
Don't Explain a
Don't Leave Me Now a
Everybody's Somebody's Fool a
First Things First a
The Folks Who Live On The Hill a
Guiding Light c
Hey Lawdy Mama a
I Can't Get Started a
I Won't Worry a
If I Love Again a
I'll Close My Eyes a
Indiana a
Jackson County Jubilee ac
A Jazz Portrait Of Brigitte Bardot
  c
Katy Do ac
Knock Me A Kiss a
Let Them Talk a
Make Me A Present Of You a
The Masquerade Is Over a
Meet Me At No Special Place a
Meetin' Time ac
Miss Missouri ac
My Wish a
Old Folks a
On Green Dolphin Street a
Paseo Promenade ac
Pick Yourself Up a
Rock Me To Sleep a [c: 1950]
Rompin' At The Reno ac
'Round Midnight a
So In Love a
Solitude a
Sunset Glow ac
Swedish Jam c
Trapped In The Web Of Love a
The Very Thought Of You a
Vine Street Rumble ac
Weak For The Man a
Whispering Grass a
The Wiggle Walk ac
Will You Still Be Mine a
You Call It Madness a
You're Mine You a

1961

After You've Gone a
Amoroso ac
Apollo Jumps ac
The Bad And The Beautiful a
The Basie Twist ac
Baubles, Bangles And Beads a
Blue Star a [c: 1953]
Body And Soul a
Boy Meets Horn a
Cherry a
Ciribiribin a
Cottontail a
Crazy Rhythm a
Doozy ac
Easy Money ac
Echoes Of Harlem a
The Flower Drum Song (soundtrack)
   a
Goin' On ac
Honeysuckle Rose a
Hot Lips a
I Believe In You a
I Can't Get Started a
Laura a
The Legend ac
The Midnight Sun Will Never Set
   a
Pinky a
Row Row Row Row a
San Francisco Blues a
Sugar Blues a
Summer Night c
The Swizzle ac
Tenderly a
Tired a
Toot Toot Tootsie a
The Trot ac
Turnabout ac
Two O'Clock Jump a
West End Blues a
Who's Blue ac
Yassu a

1962

After You've Gone a
Amoroso a [c: 1961]
Blitzen a
Doozy a [c: 1961]
Falling In Love With Love a
A Foggy Day a
A Garden In The Rain a
Great Day a
Gumshoe ac
Honeysuckle Rose a
I Believe In You a
I Can't Give You Anything But
   Love a

I'm A Woman a
I'm Gonna Live Til I Die a
The Lady's In Love With You a
Lou's Blues ac
Lula c
The Moon Is Low a
Moonlight On The Ganges a
Nobody Else But Me a
That's For Me a
The Trolley Song a
Who's Who ac

1963

Always On My Mind a
Around The World In Eighty Days
   a
Bagatelle c
Be Cool ac
Black Knight a
Blue Yonder ac
Busted a
Catfish Row ac
Cherchez La Femme c
Cherokee a
Cuando Caliente El Sol a
Dance With Me a
Discovery ac
Domino a
Friendless ac
Gotta Go Home ac
The Gypsy a
Heels Up ac
If I Had You a
If You Go a
I'll Never Be The Same a
Imminent ac
In The Evening (When The Sun Goes
   Down) a
Jazz Waltz ac
A Kiss From You c
Lonely Affair ac
Lonely Hours a
Look For Me, I'll Be Around a
The Man I Love a
Metropole ac
Oh! Look At Me Now a
Ol' Man Time a
The One I Love Belongs To Some-
   one Else a
One Way Out ac
Poor Little Rich Girl a
Roses Of Picardy a
Show Break #1 ac
Show Break #2 ac
Show Me The Way To Go Home a
So Long, My Love a
Solitude a
These Foolish Things a

I Never Loved A Woman a
I Was Made To Love Her a
I'll Be Here With You c
I'll Never Leave You a
I'm Always Drunk In San Fran-
    cisco a
In The Midnight Hour a
It's Up To You And Me a
Lasse Lasse Litten ac
The Loving Room ac
My Girl a
Ode To Billy Joe a
On Censorship ac
Point Of No Return ac
Prisoner Of My Eyes (I Can
    Never Let You Go) a
Protect Me a
Respect a
To The Destroyers ac
Uptight (Everything Is All Right)
    a

1969
(none)

1970
Con Alma a
I Said No a
Ma (She's Making Eyes At Me)
    a
Never Again a
She Had To Go And Lose It At
    The Astor a
The Weekend Of A Private Secre-
    tary a

1971
All That I Can Do Is Think Of
    You a
All The Time a
Always On Sunday a
Bobby a
Care a
God Bless You a
Got That Feeling a
The Happy Ones a
Here's That Rainy Day a
A House Is Not A Home a
I Never Met A Stranger a
I'll Never Pass This Way Again
    a
I'm A Lucky Guy a
It's Impossible a
Love Is A Feeling a
Mama, A Rainbow a
Mister Love a
Once Upon A Happy Time (The
    Big Band Days) a

Right Here In My Heart a
Satin Latin a
Supper Time a
Tender Loving Words a
When It's Time To Tell a
When Twilight Comes a
When You're Young a

1972
Blues For Beginners ac
Doozy a [c: 1961]
Honeysuckle Rose a
I Can't Get Started a
The Juke Box a [c: 1959]
You Are ac

1973
Coalition ac
Cottontail a
Doozy a [c: 1961]
A Kiss From You a [c: 1963]
Souvenir ac
A Walkin' Thing a [c: 1957]
When Lights Are Low a [c: 1936]
You Are a [c: 1972]

1974
Again a
Any Old Time a
As Time Goes By a
The Call Of The Far Away Hills a
Don't You Make Me High a
Doozy a [c: 1961]
Gee, Ain't I Good To You a
It Ain't The Meat, It's The Motion
    a
It Don't Mean A Thing If It Ain't
    Got That Swing a
Lover Man a
Mona Lisa a
The River Of No Return a
Ruby a
September Song a
Squeeze Me a
Summertime In Venice a
Sweetheart a
Walkin' One And Only a

1975
Livin' In The Sunlight (Lovin' In
    The Moonlight) a
Rockin' Chair a
We Just Couldn't Say Goodbye a

1976
A Tea Vista c
Blues in D Flat c
The Courtship c

Green Wine   c
JJJJump   c
Johnny   c
Kansas City Line   c
Mama Don't Wear No Drawers   c
Stroll   c

1977
All My Love   a
Chinatown   a
Confessin'   a
Cottontail   a
God Bless The Child   a
Hobnobbin'   ac
In A Sentimental Mood   a
It Don't Mean A Thing If It Ain't
   Got That Swing   a
Jitterbug Waltz   a
Nuages   a
South Side Samba   ac
Souvenir   a [c: 1973]
Squatty Roo   a
Them There Eyes   a
Things Ain't What They Used To
   Be   a
When It's Sleepy Time Down
   South   a
When You're Smiling   a

1978
(none)

1979
Ain't Misbehavin'   a
Black Butterfly   a

Day Dream   a
Don't Worry 'Bout Me   a
Feasant Pheathers   c
Honeysuckle Rose   a
I Got It Bad   a
I Let A Song Go Out Of My Heart
   a
I'm Getting Sentimental Over You
   a
In A Mellotone   a
In A Sentimental Mood   a
It Don't Mean A Thing If It Ain't
   Got That Swing   a
Just A-Sittin' And A-Rockin'   a
Lush Life   a
My Kind Of Trouble Is You   a
   [c: 1955]
Organ Grinder's Swing   a
Please Don't Talk About Me When
   I'm Gone   a
Solitude   a
Some Other Spring   a
Sophisticated Lady   a
Sweet Lorraine   a
Teach Me Tonight   a
Tonight I Shall Sleep With A Smile
   On My Face   a

1980
(none)

1981
The Courtship   a [c: 1976]
I'm Beginning To See The Light   a
Mood Indigo   a

A BASIC SELECTION OF BENNY CARTER'S LPs

This list will help readers who want to obtain a basic selection of Carter's recordings. Most of these LPs are domestic labels or widely-distributed imports that are either still in print or only recently cut out. Essential items are marked with an asterisk.

In addition, at any given time there are usually available several bootleg LPs of Carter's recordings for the Armed Forces Radio Service by his mid-1940s orchestra. Most of them are imports carried by large record stores or by mail-order dealers.

*The Giants of Jazz: Benny Carter (Time-Life Records STL-J10, 3 records). Highlights of Carter's recording career from 1929 to 1977. Includes samples of Carter as multi-instrumentalist, arranger and composer with the Chocolate Dandies, Fletcher Henderson, McKinney's Cotton Pickers and his own orchestras among others. Available by mail from Time-Life.

*Benny Carter 1933 (Prestige 7643). First important recordings of the Carter orchestra and the 1933 Chocolate Dandies. Includes such seminal arrangements as "Symphony In Riffs" and "Lonesome Nights."

*Benny Carter (French RCA Black & White PM42406, Jazz Tribune series, no. 4, 2 records). A cross-section of recordings for Victor, 1928-1952. Includes Carter's first recording (with Charlie Johnson), Lionel Hampton all-star dates 1938-39, and a good representation of Carter's 1940-41 orchestra.

The Early Benny Carter (Everest Archive of Folk and Jazz FS225). British recordings, 1936-37.

Benny and the Hawk on the Loose in Europe (On the Loose, vols. 1-5). Recordings of Carter and Coleman Hawkins in Europe, together and separately. Includes many items never before on LP as well as previously unissued alternate takes. Limited edition import, not easily obtainable.

Benny Carter 1933/1939 (Tax m-8031). Includes 1933 Mezz Mezzrow date, 1934 Carter orchestra, 1936 British recordings with Elisabeth Welch, 1937 Dutch recordings with Hawkins and 1939 Carter orchestra. Swedish import.

Melancholy Benny (Tax m-8004). 1939-40 orchestra: studio recordings and Savoy Ballroom airchecks. Swedish import.

*Big Band Bounce (Capitol M11057, Capitol Jazz Classics series, vol. 11). 1943-45 West Coast recordings of Carter orchestra with Max Roach, J. J. Johnson and other younger musicians. (One side is Carter, the other Cootie Williams.)

*Jazz Giant (Contemporary S7028).   1957 small group and quartet in-
cluding Ben Webster.

*Swingin' the Twenties (Contemporary S7561).   Carter's only record-
ings with Earl Hines, 1958.

*Further Definitions (Impulse A12).   Carter leads and arranges for
sax quartet including Coleman Hawkins, Phil Woods and Charlie Rouse, 1961.

Additions to Further Definitions (Impulse A9116).   1966 date featuring
Carter's arrangements and compositions played by five-man reed section.

The King (Pablo 2310-768).   "Comeback" date in 1976 featuring Carter
with Milt Jackson, Tommy Flanagan and Joe Pass playing Carter originals.

Carter, Gillespie, Inc. (Pablo 2310-781).   1976 reunion with his former
trumpeter.

*Benny Carter 4 - Montreux '77 (Pablo Live 2308-204).   Live at 1977
Montreux Jazz Festival, with Ray Bryant; finest example of Carter's alto
in the 1970s as well as his first recordings on trumpet in fifteen years.

'Live and Well in Japan (Pablo Live 2308-216).   Ten-piece band recorded live in Tokyo, 1977; new Carter arrangements include tributes to
Louis Armstrong, Billie Holiday and Duke Ellington.

The Best of Benny Carter (Pablo 2310-853).   One side of material
from 'Live and Well in Japan album and one side from Benny Carter 4 -
Montreux '77 album.

Benny Carter Jazz All Star Orchestra, Live in Japan '79 (Paddle
Wheel GP3199).   Ten-piece band, loose jam-style arrangements leaving much
solo space, as well as a ballad medley.   Japanese import, hard to obtain.

Street of Dreams (LOB LDC1030).   Carter plays standards backed by
Japanese trio; recorded 1981.   Japanese import, hard to obtain.

FILMOGRAPHY

1. Theatrical Films by Major Studios

Carter's work on theatrical films made by the major Hollywood studios has been of two kinds. (a) On about a hundred films he plays on the soundtrack but has not written music. This category is omitted from this filmography. (b) We have traced thirty-three films, included in this filmography, in which he arranges, orchestrates, or composes music; in some of them he also plays or conducts on the soundtrack and appears on screen. The films are listed in chronological order by date of release, showing title, studio, music director, and Carter's specific contributions as indicated by the following abbreviations:

cmp:	composes
at:	arranges or orchestrates tunes or songs
ab:	arranges or orchestrates backgrounds
ps:	plays on soundtrack
cs:	conducts on soundtrack
scr:	appears on screen

Studio abbreviations: TCF--Twentieth Century-Fox; MGM--Metro-Goldwyn-Mayer.

1943	June 11	Jitterbugs. TCF. Alfred Newman (probably). at
	July 16	Stormy Weather. TCF. Alfred Newman. at ps
	August 2	Young Ideas. MGM. George Bassman. ab
	August 14	This Is the Army. Warner Brothers. Ray Heindorf. at ps
	September 17	Wintertime. TCF. Alfred Newman. at ps
	December 24	The Gang's All Here. TCF. Alfred Newman. at ps
1944	January	Thousands Cheer. MGM. Herbert Stothart. at ps cs scr
	July 29	The Canterville Ghost. MGM. George Bassman. ab
	December	Here Comes the Waves. Paramount. Robert E. Dolan. at
1949	April 22	Portrait of Jennie. Selznick. Dmitri Tiomkin. at ab
1950	March 3	Love Happy. United Artists. Ann Ronell. at cs
	September	My Blue Heaven. TCF. Alfred Newman. at ps cs
	September	Panic In the Streets. TCF. Alfred Newman. at ab cmp ps cs
	September 30	Edge of Doom. RKO Radio. Hugo Friedhofer. ab ps

393

September 30.	I'll Get By. TCF. Lionel Newman. at
October.	No Way Out. TCF. Alfred Newman. at

1951 November 9   An American in Paris.   MGM.   Johnny Green.   at
                    ps   cs   scr

1952 June   Clash by Night.   RKO Radio.   Roy Webb.   at   ps
                    cs   scr
     November   Night Without Sleep.   TCF.   Cyril Mockridge.   at
                    ps

1953 April   The Glass Wall.   Columbia.   Leith Stevens.   at   ps
                    cs
     July   The Snows of Kilimanjaro.   TCF.   Bernard Herr-
                    mann.   at   ps   scr   Note: release date is July 1953
                    but this film was reviewed in the New York Times,
                    September 19, 1952, p. 19.

1954 March   Red Garters.   Paramount.   Joseph L. Lilley.   at

1955 November   The View from Pompey's Head.   TCF.   Elmer
                    Bernstein.   at   ps   cs   scr

1957 September   The Sun Also Rises.   TCF.   Hugo Friedhofer.   at
                    ps

1959 August   The Five Pennies.   Paramount.   Leith Stevens.   at
                    ps
     December   The Gene Krupa Story.   Columbia.   Leith Stevens.
     (probably)   at   ps

1961 July   The Guns of Navarone.   Columbia.   Dmitri Tiomkin.
                    ab
     October   Town Without Pity.   United Artists.   Dmitri Tiom-
                    kin.   ab

1962 January   Flower Drum Song.   Universal.   Alfred Newman.
                    at   ps   Note: release date is January 1962 but this
                    film was reviewed in the New York Times, November
                    10, 1961, p. 40.

1966 July   A Man Called Adam.   Embassy.   Benny Carter is
                    music director: composer, arranger-orchestrator,
                    conductor on all music (does not play).

1967 December 14   Valley of the Dolls.   TCF.   John Williams.   at

1971 no release   Red Sky at Morning.   Universal.   Billy Goldenberg.
     date given   at   Reviewed in New York Times, May 13, 1971,
                    p. 53.

1972 April   Buck and the Preacher.   Columbia.   Benny Carter
                    is music director: composer, arranger-orchestrator,
                    conductor on virtually all music (does not play).

2.   Short Animated Films

Carter has written music for five short (four to ten minutes) animated films by John and Faith Hubley, as shown in The Hubley Studio list, "John Hubley: Faith Hubley," N. Y., n. d., ca. 1977.

Year of Release	Title
1957	Adventures of an Asterisk
1957	Harlem Wednesday
1966	Urbanissimo
1967	The Cruise
1975	People People People

In 1980 Carter composed for a short animated film, Opens Wednesday, by Barry Nelson Productions.

3.   Television

Carter has written at least ninety-five episodes ("segments") of twenty television serials or shows with an overall title for unrelated segments. There is no documentation to show all his television work, nor does he remember it all, but the following table certainly includes almost all. The list comes mainly from his statement of October 10, 1976 in connection with the composers' (CLGA) law suit against the major studios. The table shows the year, the overall name of the series, and the approximate number of segments Carter composed. All these shows were productions of the Universal studio, except for the last series, Banyon, which was by Warner Brothers.

Year of Contract or Airing	Overall Name of Series	Approximate No. of Segments
1958-1960	M Squad	35
1960	17 Battery Place	Pilot + 1
1961	The Investigators	Pilot
1963	Kraft Suspense Theater	1
1963-1966	Bob Hope Chrysler Theater	20
1964	Expose	Pilot
1964	Alfred Hitchcock	1
1964	General Electric Theater	4
1964	Project 120	1
1965	Jean Arthur	1
1965	Run for Your Life	1
1968	World Première	2
1968-1969	Ironside	8
1968-1970	Name of the Game	8
1969	It Takes a Thief	Pilot + 1
1969	The Outsider	1
1970	The Doctors	1
1970	Night Gallery	2
1970	The Bold Ones	2
1971	Banyon	1

Carter has also written for two feature telefilms: Man Hunter, 1968 (Universal), and Louis Armstrong, Chicago Style, 1976 (independent).

BIBLIOGRAPHY OF WORKS CITED

Adderley, Julian "Cannonball." "Paying Dues: The Education of a Combo Leader," In Williams, ed., q.v., pp. 258-263.

Albertson, Chris. Bessie. New York, Stein and Day, 1972.

Allen, Leonard. "The Battle of Tin Pan Alley." Harper's Magazine, October 1940, pp. 514-523.

Allen, Walter C. Hendersonia: The Music of Fletcher Henderson and His Musicians, A Bio-Discography. Highland Park, N.J., The Author, 1973.

Armstead-Johnson, Helen. "Blacks in Vaudeville: Broadway and Beyond." In Myron Matlaw, ed. American Popular Entertainment. Westport, Conn. and London, Greenwood, 1979, pp. 77-86.

Arvey, Verna. "Memo for Musicologists." In Robert B. Haas, ed., q.v., pp. 88-93.

The ASCAP Biographical Dictionary of Composers, Authors and Publishers. 3d ed. New York, ASCAP, 1966.

Atterbury, Grosvenor. "The Phipps Model Tenement Houses." Charities and the Commons (later, The Survey), October 1906, pp. 49-65.

Balliett, Whitney. "Profiles." New Yorker, February 14, 1977, pp. 43-52.

_____. Such Sweet Thunder. Indianapolis and New York, Bobbs-Merrill, 1966.

Barker, Danny. "Jelly Roll Morton in New York." Jazz Review, May 1959, pp. 12-14.

Barnouw, Erik. Tube of Plenty: The Evolution of American Television. New York, Oxford, 1975.

Bazelon, David. Knowing the Score: Notes on Film Music. New York, Van Nostrand Reinhold, 1975.

Bechet, Sidney. Treat It Gentle. New York, Hill and Wang, 1960.

Bérard, Madeleine. "Un Dîner avec Benny Carter." Hot-Revue (Lausanne). 1946 (month not indicated), vol. 1, no. 12, pp. 12-15.

Berg, Charles Merrell. An Investigation of the Motives for and Realization of Music to Accompany the American Silent Film, 1896-1927. New York, Arno, 1976.

397

Berger, Edward. "Benny Carter: A Discographical Approach." Journal of Jazz Studies 4, no. 1 (1976): 47-74, and 5, no. 1 (1978): 28-80.

Berger, Morroe. "Jazz Caravan." Aramco World Magazine, July-August 1977, pp. 1-2.

_____. "Jazz: Resistance to the Diffusion of a Culture-Pattern." Journal of Negro History 32 (October 1947): 461-494. Reprint, Charles Nanry, ed., q.v., pp. 11-43.

Berlin, Edward A. Ragtime: A Musical and Cultural History. Berkeley and Los Angeles, University of California Press, 1980.

Bernstein, Elmer. "What Ever Happened to Great Movie Music?" High Fidelity and Musical America, July 1972, pp. 55-58.

_____. "The Man with the Golden Arm." In Limbacher, ed., q.v., pp. 94-96.

The Billboard. Band Year Book. Suppl. September 26, 1942.

_____. Music Year Book. 5th annual ed. 1943.

_____. Music Year Book. 6th annual ed. 1944.

Blesh, Rudi. Shining Trumpets: A History of Jazz. New York, Knopf, 1946.

_____, and Harriet Janis. They All Played Ragtime. 4th ed. New York, Oak, 1971.

Bontemps, Arna, and Langston Hughes. Arna Bontemps-Langston Hughes Letters 1925-1967. Charles H. Nichols, ed. New York, Dodd, Mead, 1980.

Borneman, Ernest. A Critic Looks at Jazz. London, Jazz Music Books, 1946.

Bourne, Michael. "His Royal Majesty of Reeds: Benny Carter." Down Beat, February 24, 1977, pp. 20-21, 50.

Bowen, Louise De Koven. "Dance Halls." The Survey, June 3, 1911, pp. 383-387.

Boyer, Richard O. "Profiles: The Hot Bach--III." New Yorker, July 8, 1944, pp. 26-31.

Bradford, Perry. Born With the Blues: Perry Bradford's Own Story. New York, Oak, 1965.

Braithwaite, R. B. Theory of Games As a Tool for the Moral Philosopher. Cambridge, England, Cambridge University, 1955.

Brooks, Aubrey. "About Musicians." The Inter-State Tattler, September 13, 1929, p. 13.

Burley, Dan. "So He Laid His Bible Down." New York Amsterdam News, October 21, 1939, p. 20.

Burns, Jim. "Jazz and the Beats." Jazz Monthly (London), January 1971,
    pp. 17-22.

Burton, Jack. The Blue Book of Hollywood Musicals. Watkins Glen, New
    York, Century House, 1953.

_____. The Blue Book of Tin Pan Alley. New York, Century House,
    1951.

Butler, Jack, and Jean Poinsot. "Harlem en 1928." Bulletin du Hot Club
    de France, September 1960, pp. 5-7.

California Advisory Committee to the United States Commission on Civil
    Rights. Behind the Scenes: Equal Opportunity in the Motion Picture
    Industry. U. S. Commission on Civil Rights, Washington, D. C., 1978.

Calloway, Cab, and Bryant Rollins. Of Minnie the Moocher and Me. New
    York, Crowell, 1976.

Carpenter, Paul S. Music: An Art and a Business. Norman, Oklahoma,
    University of Oklahoma Press, 1950.

Carter, Benny. "Benny Carter Hits Out." Melody Maker, April 10, 1937,
    p. 2.

_____. "Benny Carter Sifts LA Union Issues." Down Beat, August 27,
    1952, p. 14.

_____. Interview, 1976. Jazz Oral History Project, Institute of Jazz
    Studies, Rutgers University, Newark, N. J.

_____. "My Nine Lives." Swing Music (London), May-June 1936, pp.
    55, 71.

_____. See Feather, The Pleasures of Jazz.

_____. See The Giants of Jazz.

Castle, Irene (as told to Bob and Wanda Duncan). Castles in the Air. New
    York, Doubleday, 1958.

_____. Irene and Vernon. Modern Dancing. New York, Harper, 1914.

Ceplair, Larry, and Steven Englund. The Inquisition in Hollywood: Politics
    in the Film Community 1930-1960. New York, Anchor/Doubleday, 1980.

Cesana, Otto. "Have Dance Orchestras Reached Their Peak?" Down Beat,
    March 1, 1942, p. 9.

Charters, Samuel B., and Leonard Kunstadt. Jazz: A History of the New
    York Scene. New York, Doubleday, 1962.

Cheatham, Adolphus "Doc." Autobiographical statement accompanying record
    album, Jezebel JZ-102-ST. New York, 1973.

Coleman, Bill. Interview, 1978. Jazz Oral History Project, Institute of
    Jazz Studies, Rutgers University, Newark, N. J.

Chilton, John. McKinney's Music: A Bio-Discography of McKinney's Cotton
     Pickers. London, Bloomsbury Book Shop, 1978.

_____. Billie's Blues: Billie Holiday's Story 1933-1959. New York,
     Stein and Day, 1975.

_____. Who's Who of Jazz. Rev. ed. Alexandria, Virginia, Time-Life
     Records, 1978.

Cogley, John. Report on Blacklisting. 2 vols. New York, Fund for the
     Republic, 1956. Vol. 1: Movies.

Cole, Bill. Miles Davis: A Musical Biography. New York, Morrow, 1974.

Collier, James Lincoln. The Making of Jazz: A Comprehensive History.
     Boston, Houghton Mifflin, 1978.

Collins, John. Interview, 1975. Jazz Oral History Project, Institute of
     Jazz Studies, Rutgers University, Newark, N.J.

Connor, D. Russell, and Warren W. Hicks. BG on the Record: A Bio-
     Discography of Benny Goodman. New Rochelle, New York, Arlington
     House, 1969.

Cook, Bruce. Dalton Trumbo. New York, Scribner, 1977.

Cook, Mercer. "Benny Carter Plays for Italian Students." New York Am-
     sterdam News, March 19, 1938, p. 19.

_____. "From 'Clorindy' to 'The Red Moon' and Beyond." Typescript of
     lecture at CUNY Graduate Center, New York, October 1978.

Cook, Will Marion. "Clorindy, the Origin of the Cakewalk." Theater Arts,
     September 1947, pp. 61-65. Reprint, Eileen Southern, ed., q. v., pp.
     217-223.

_____. Letter dated December 19, 1926, New York Times, December
     26, 1926, sec. 7, p. 8. Reprint, Cuney-Hare, q. v., pp. 135-136.

Cressey, Paul G. The Taxi-Dance Hall. Chicago, University of Chicago
     Press, 1932.

Cripps, Thomas. Slow Fade to Black: The Negro in American Film, 1900-
     1942. New York, Oxford, 1977.

Crosland, Margaret. Jean Cocteau. London, Peter Nevill, 1955.

Cuney-Hare, Maud. Negro Musicians and Their Music. Washington, D.C.,
     Associated Publishers, 1936.

Dance, Stanley. "Benny Carter Interviewed by Stanley Dance." Jazz, July
     1966, pp. 12-14.

_____. "Jazz at the White House." Saturday Review, November 15, 1969,
     pp. 73, 75, 101.

_____. The World of Count Basie. New York, Scribner, 1980.

_____. The World of Duke Ellington. New York, Scribner, 1970.

_____. The World of Earl Hines. New York, Scribner, 1977.

_____. The World of Swing. New York, Scribner, 1974.

Davis, Clive, with James Willnerth. Clive: Inside the Record Business. New York, William Morrow, 1975.

Davis, Fred. Yearning for Yesterday: A Sociology of Nostalgia. New York, Free Press, 1979.

Delaunay, Charles. "Biographie de Benny Carter." Jazz Hot, September-October 1935, p. 5.

_____. Django Reinhardt. Translated by Michael James. London, Cassell, 1961.

_____. Hot Discography. (1st ed. 1936.) Rev. ed. New York, Commodore Record Co., Inc., 1943.

de Lerma, Dominique-René, ed. Black Music in Our Culture. Kent, Ohio, Kent State University Press, 1970.

_____. "Will Marion Cook, Antonín Dvořák, and the Earlier Afro-American Musical Theater." Morgan State University Music Department, Baltimore, Maryland, 1979.

de Toledano, Ralph, ed. Frontiers of Jazz. New York, 1947. 2d ed. New York, Ungar, 1962.

Dexter, Dave, Jr. Jazz Cavalcade. New York, Criterion, 1946.

_____. Playback. New York, Billboard, 1976.

Dimmitt, Richard Bertrand. A Title Guide to the Talkies. 2 vols. New York, Scarecrow, 1965.

Dorr, Rheta Childe. What Eight Million Women Want. Boston, Small and Maynard, 1910. Reprint ed., New York, Kraus, 1971.

Driggs, Frank. "Don Redman, Jazz Composer-Arranger." In Williams, ed., q.v., pp. 91-104.

_____, Franklin S. [Frank] "Kansas City and the Southwest." In Hentoff and McCarthy, eds., q.v., pp. 189-230.

DuBois, W. E. Burghardt. "The Future of Wilberforce University." Journal of Negro Education 9(October 1940):553-570.

Durante, Jimmy, and Jack Kofoed. Night Clubs. New York, Knopf, 1931.

Dvořák, Antonin. "Music In America." Harper's, February 1895, pp. 429-434.

Edey, Maitland. "Dizzy Gillespie. An Interview." Paris Review, Fall 1965, pp. 137-146.

Eisen, Jonathan, ed. The Age of Rock. New York, Vintage Books, 1969.

Eldridge, Roy. "Little Jazz." Interview with Nat Hentoff, q. v.

Ellington, Edward Kennedy (Duke). Music Is My Mistress. New York, Doubleday, 1973.

Ellington, Mercer, with Stanley Dance. Duke Ellington in Person: An Intimate Memoir. Boston, Houghton Mifflin, 1978.

Emge, Charles. "Jazz' Most Underrated Musician? Benny Carter." Down Beat, May 18, 1951, pp. 2, 16, 18.

Ertegun, Nesuhi. "Benny Carter." The Record Changer, May 1948, pp. 5-6.

Esquire's Jazz Book. See Miller, Paul Eduard, ed.

Evans, Mark. Soundtrack: The Music of the Movies. New York, Hopkinson and Blake, 1975.

Ewen, David. A Journey to Greatness: The Life and Music of George Gershwin. New York, Holt, 1956.

_____. Panorama of Popular Music. Englewood Cliffs, N. J. , Prentice-Hall, 1957.

Falter, John, and Richard Gehman. "Greatest Jazz Band." Saturday Evening Post, Spring 1972, pp. 60-63, 153.

Fass, Paula S. The Damned and the Beautiful: American Youth in the 1920s. New York, Oxford, 1977.

Faulkner, Robert R. Hollywood Studio Musicians: Their Work and Careers in the Recording Industry. Chicago and New York, Aldine-Atherton, 1971.

Feather, Leonard. "Bennett L. Carter, Esquire." Melody Maker, October 31, 1936, p. 2.

_____. The Encyclopedia of Jazz in the Sixties. New York, Bonanza, 1966.

_____. "The Enduring Benny Carter." Down Beat, May 25, 1961, pp. 15-16.

_____. Inside Jazz. New York, Da Capo, 1977. (1st pub. as Inside Be-bop, New York, J. J. Robbins, 1949.)

_____. The New Edition of the Encyclopedia of Jazz. New York, Bonanza, 1962. (1st ed. , New York, 1955.)

_____. The Pleasures of Jazz. Introduction by Benny Carter. New York, Horizon, 1976.

Feather, Leonard, and Ira Gitler. The Encyclopedia of Jazz in the Seventies. New York, Horizon, 1976.

Federation of Social Agencies of Pittsburgh and Alleghany County, Bureau of Social Research. "Social Facts Concerning McDonald Borough." Pittsburgh, Pa., 1940.

Fitzgerald, F. Scott. "Echoes of the Jazz Age" (1931). The Crack-Up. New York, New Directions, 1945.

Fletcher, Tom. 100 Years of the Negro in Show Business: The Tom Fletcher Story. New York, London and Toronto, Burdge, 1954.

Flower, John. Moonlight Serenade: A Bio-Discography of the Glenn Miller Civilian Band. New Rochelle, N.Y., Arlington House, 1972.

Foote, Timothy. "Benny Carter." The Swing Era: One More Time. Philip W. Payne and Joan S. Reiter, eds. Time-Life Records, New York, 1972, pp. 28-38.

Foreman, Ronald Clifford, Jr. Jazz and Race Records, 1920-1932: Their Origins and Their Significance for the Record Industry and Society. Ph. D. Thesis, U. of Illinois, Urbana, 1968.

The Giants of Jazz: Benny Carter. Philip W. Payne, ed. Recordings by Carter, biography by Morroe Berger, music notes by Edward Berger. Time-Life Records, Alexandria, Va., 1980.

Gifford, Denis. The British Film Catalogue, 1895-1970. New York, Mc-Graw-Hill, 1973.

Gillespie, John Birks. "Conversation with John Birks 'Dizzy' Gillespie." By Josephine R. B. Wright. The Black Perspective in Music 4(Spring 1976):82-89.

_____. to BE, or not ... to BOP: Memoirs. New York, Doubleday, 1979.

Gitler, Ira. Jazz Masters of the Forties. New York, Macmillan, 1966.

Goddard, Chris. Jazz Away from Home. New York and London, Paddington, 1979.

Goffin, Robert. Aux Frontières du Jazz. 2d ed. Paris, Editions du Sagittaire, 1932.

_____. Horn of Plenty: The Story of Louis Armstrong. Translated by James F. Bezou. New York, Towne and Heath, 1947.

_____. Jazz: From the Congo to the Metropolitan. Translated by Walter Schaap and Leonard G. Feather. New York, Doubleday Doran, 1944.

Goldberg, Isaac. Tin Pan Alley: A Chronicle of the American Popular Music Racket. New York, John Day, 1930.

Goldblatt, Burt. Newport Jazz Festival: The Illustrated History. New York, Dial, 1977.

Goldman, Albert. Freakshow. New York, Atheneum, 1971.

Goldstein, Richard, ed. The Poetry of Rock. New York, Bantam, 1969.

Goodman, Benny, and Irving Kolodin. The Kingdom of Swing. New York, Stackpole Sons, 1939.

Granz, Norman. Just Jazz 2. Sinclair Traill and Gerald Lascelles, eds. London, Peter Davies, 1958, pp. 15-21.

Green, Johnny. "Johnny Green Tells Duties, Functions, and Details of Motion Picture Musical Director." Down Beat, August 22, 1956, pp. 13, 41.

Guback, Thomas H. The International Film Industry: Western Europe and America Since 1945. Bloomington and London, Indiana University Press, 1969.

Gutman, Herbert G. The Black Family in Slavery and Freedom, 1750-1925. New York, Pantheon, 1976.

Haas, Robert Bartlett, ed. William Grant Still and the Fusion of Cultures in American Music. Los Angeles, Black Sparrow, 1972.

Hall, Ben M. The Best Remaining Seats: The Story of the Golden Age of the Movie Palace. New York, Clarkson N. Potter, 1961.

Hammond, John, with Irving Townsend. John Hammond on Record. New York, Summit, 1977.

Handy, W. C., ed. Blues: An Anthology. New York, Boni, 1926. Introduction by Abbe Niles.

Harris, Rex. Jazz. Harmondsworth, England, Penguin, 1952.

Haskins, Jim. The Cotton Club. New York, Random House, 1977.

Henderson, Horace. Interview, 1975. Jazz Oral History Project, Institute of Jazz Studies, Rutgers University, Newark, N.J.

Henderson, Mae Gwendolyn. "Portrait of Wallace Thurman." In Arna Bontemps, ed. The Harlem Renaissance Remembered, chap. 8. New York, Dodd, Mead, 1972.

Hennessey, Thomas Joseph. From Jazz to Swing: Black Jazz Musicians and Their Music, 1917-1935. Ph.D. Thesis, Northwestern University, 1973.

Hentoff, Nat. "Dr. Jazz, and His Son, the Professor." New York Times Magazine, April 14, 1974, pp. 12-13, 28, 30, 32-35.

_____. "Little Jazz." Down Beat, September 19, 1956, pp. 13-14, 48.

Hentoff, Nat, and Albert J. McCarthy, eds. Jazz: New Perspectives on the History of Jazz. New York, Rinehart, 1959.

Heyward, Sammy. "Résumé of the New Amsterdam Musical Association." New York, 1974.

Hippenmeyer, Jean-Roland. Jazz sur Films (1917-1972). Yverdon, Editions de la Thièle, Switzerland, 1973.

Hobson, Wilder. "Fifty-second Street." In Ramsey and Smith, eds., q.v., chap. 11.

_____. "Introducing Duke Ellington." Fortune, August 1933, pp. 47 ff. Reprint, Ralph de Toledano, ed., q.v., pp. 137-147.

Hodeir, André. Toward Jazz. Translated by Noel Burch. New York, Grove, 1962.

_____. The Worlds of Jazz. Translated by Noel Burch. New York, Grove, 1972.

Hoefer, George. Liner notes to The Sound of Harlem, record album, C3L33, Columbia Jazz Archive Series, "Jazz Odyssey," Frank Driggs, producer. New York, 1964.

Holiday, Billie, with William Dufty. Lady Sings the Blues. New York, Lancer, 1965. (1st ed., New York, Doubleday, 1956.)

Horricks, Raymond, et al. These Jazzmen of Our Time. London, Gollancz, 1959.

Huggins, Nathan Irvin. Harlem Renaissance. New York, Oxford, 1971.

Hughes, Langston. The Big Sea: An Autobiography. New York, Knopf, 1940.

_____. Letters. See Arna Bontemps and Hughes.

_____. Something in Common and Other Stories. New York, Hill and Wang, 1963.

Hughes, Langston, and Milton Meltzer. Black Magic: A Pictorial History of the Negro in American Entertainment. Englewood Cliffs, N.J., Prentice-Hall, 1967.

Hughes, Patrick Cairns (Spike). Second Movement. London, Museum Press, 1951.

_____. "Sweet Sorrow." Swing Music (London), November-December 1935, pp. 250-252, 268, 270.

Hughes, Rupert. "A Eulogy of Rag-Time." Musical Record, April 1, 1899, pp. 157-159.

Hunt, David C. "Benny Carter: Controversial Jazz Giant." Jazz and Pop, May 1970, pp. 42-44.

International Cyclopedia of Music and Musicians. 9th ed. New York, Dodd, Mead, 1964.

International Motion Picture Almanac. Annual. New York, 1933--present.

Jablonski, Edward. Harold Arlen: Happy with the Blues. New York, Doubleday, 1961.

Jackson, Edgar. "Maestros of Jazz--No. 4. Benny Carter." "His Master's Voice" Record Review (London), December 1942, pp. 17-20.

"The Jazz Composers in Hollywood: A Symposium with Benny Carter, Quincy Jones, Henry Mancini, Lalo Schifrin, Pat Williams." Conducted by
Harvey Siders. Down Beat, March 2, 1972, pp. 12-15, 34.

Jepsen, Jörgen Grunnet. Jazz Records 1942--. 11 vols. Copenhagen,
Knudsen, 1963-1970.

Johnson, J. Rosamond. "Why They Call American Music Ragtime." The
Colored American Magazine 15(January 1909):636-639.

Johnson, James Weldon. Along This Way. New York, Viking, 1933.

_____. Black Manhattan. New York, Knopf, 1930.

Johnson, James Weldon, ed., and J. Rosamond Johnson and Lawrence
Brown, arrangers. The Book of American Negro Spirituals. New
York, Viking, 1925.

Johnson, James Weldon, ed., and J. Rosamond Johnson, arranger. The
Second Book of Negro Spirituals. New York, Viking, 1926.

Jones, Isham. "American Dance Music Is Not Jazz." The Etude 42 (August
1924):526.

Jones, LeRoi. Blues People: Negro Music In White America. New York,
William Morrow, 1963.

Jones, Max, and John Chilton. Louis: The Louis Armstrong Story 1900-
1971. Boston, Little, Brown, 1971.

Joplin, Scott. The Collected Works of Scott Joplin. Vera Brodsky Lawrence, ed. New York, New York Public Library, 1971.

Karshner, Roger. The Music Machine. Los Angeles, Nash, 1971.

Katkov, Norman. The Fabulous Fanny: The Story of Fannie Brice. New
York, Knopf, 1953.

Kellner, Bruce. Carl Van Vechten and the Irreverent Decades. Norman,
Oklahoma, University of Oklahoma Press, 1968.

Kennington, Donald. The Literature of Jazz: A Critical Guide. Chicago,
American Library Association, 1971.

Kimball, Robert, and William Bolcom. Reminiscing with Sissle and Blake.
New York, Viking, 1973.

Kinkle, Roger D. The Complete Encyclopedia of Popular Music and Jazz
1900-1950. 4 vols. New Rochelle, New York, Arlington House, 1974.

Kirkeby, Ed, with Duncan P. Schiedt and Sinclair Traill. Ain't Misbehavin':
The Story of Fats Waller. New York, Dodd, Mead, 1966.

Klamkin, Marian. Old Sheet Music: A Pictorial History. New York, Haw-
thorn, 1975.

Kolodin, Irving. "The Dance Band Business Today: A Study in Black and
White." Harper's Magazine, June 1941, pp. 72-83.

Kunstadt, Leonard. "The Story of Louis Metcalf." Record Research, October 1962, pp. 3-12.

Langeweg, Hans. "Benny Carter." Doctor Jazz (Utrecht, Holland), No. 93, September 1980, pp. 33-41.

Larkin, Dick. "Sir Bennett Arrives." Orchestra World, December 1943, p. 27.

Larkin, R. L. "Are Colored Bands Doomed as Big Money Makers?" Down Beat, December 1, 1940, pp. 2, 23.

Lees, Gene. Letter, Down Beat, December 29, 1966, pp. 8-9.

Leitch, Alexander. A Princeton Companion. Princeton, N. J., Princeton University Press, 1978.

Leiter, Robert D. The Musicians and Petrillo. New York, Octagon, 1974. (1st ed., New York, Bookman, 1953.)

Leonard, Neil. Jazz and the White Americans. Chicago, University of Chicago Press, 1962.

Levin, Floyd. "New Orleans--July 4, 1976." Fanfare (Southern California Hot Jazz Society), August 1976, pp. 3-6.

Lewis, Willie. "I Was Driven Out of Europe by Fascist Armies." Music and Rhythm, January 1942, pp. 18, 45.

Limbacher, James L., comp. and ed. Film Music: From Violins to Video. Metuchen, N. J., Scarecrow, 1974.

_____. Keeping Score: Film Music, 1972-1979. Metuchen, N. J., Scarecrow, 1981.

Locke, Alain. The Negro and His Music. Port Washington, N. Y., Kennikat, 1968. (1st ed., Washington, D. C., Associates in Negro Folk Education, 1936.)

_____., ed. The New Negro: An Interpretation. New York, Johnson Reprint Corp., 1968. (1st ed., New York, Boni, 1925.)

Lyons, Jimmy, with Ira Kamin. Dizzy, Duke, the Count and Me: The Story of the Monterey Jazz Festival. San Francisco, San Francisco Examiner, 1978.

Mannes, David. Music Is My Faith. New York, Norton, 1938.

Marbury, Elisabeth. My Crystal Ball: Reminiscences. New York, Boni and Liveright, 1923.

Marks, Edward B. They All Sang. New York, Viking, 1934.

McCarthy, Albert. Big Band Jazz. New York, G. P. Putnam's Sons, 1974.

_____. The Dance Band Era: The Dancing Decades From Ragtime to Swing 1910-1950. London, Spring Books, 1971.

McCarthy, Albert J., and Nat Hentoff. See Hentoff and McCarthy.

McCarty, Clifford. Film Composers in America: A Checklist of Their Work. New York, Da Capo, 1972. (1st ed., Glendale, California, distributed by J. Valentine, 1953.)

McDonald Diamond Jubilee, Inc. Souvenir Booklet: 75th Anniversary of the Founding of the Borough of McDonald, Pennsylvania, 1889-1964. McDonald, 1964.

McGinnis, Frederick A. A History and an Interpretation of Wilberforce University. Wilberforce, Ohio, 1941.

McKay, Claude. Home to Harlem. New York, Harper, 1928.

McLaughlin, Robert. Broadway and Hollywood: A History of Economic Interaction. New York, Arno, 1974.

McRae, Barry. "June Clark." Jazz Journal (London), May 1963, pp. 17-18.

Meeker, David. Jazz in the Movies: A Guide to Jazz Musicians 1917-1977. New Rochelle, N.Y., Arlington House, 1977. (1st ed., London, 1972.)

Mezzrow, Milton "Mezz." Really the Blues. New York, Random House, 1946.

Mialy, Louis Victor. "Benny Carter." Jazz Hot (Paris), February 1970, pp. 14-16.

Milhaud, Darius. Ma Vie Heureuse. Paris, Belfond, 1973.

Miller, Paul Eduard, ed. Esquire's Jazz Book. New York, Smith and Durrell, 1944.

_____. Esquire's 1945 Jazz Book. New York, Barnes, 1945.

_____. Esquire's 1946 Jazz Book. New York, Barnes, 1946.

Millinder, Lucky, as told to Dan Burley. "Negro Bands Are Not Doomed, Says Millinder." New York Amsterdam News, December 21, 1940, pp. 20-21.

Mills, Irving, with Charles Emge. "I Split With Duke When Music Began Sidetracking." Down Beat, November 5, 1952, p. 6.

Mooney, Hughson F. "Rock as an Historical Phenomenon." Popular Music and Culture 1(Spring 1972):129-143.

Morgenstern, Dan. Liner notes to record Bean and the Boys: Coleman Hawkins. Prestige 7824, New York, 1970.

_____. "Jazz on Film." Down Beat, 12th Yearbook, Music 67, suppl. to vol. 33, 1966, pp. 64-67, 69, 88-91.

Morgenstern, Dan, with Ole Brask. Jazz People. New York, Abrams, 1976.

Moss, Harry. "The Future of the Ballroom." 3 articles. Orchestra World, April 1933, p. 19; May 1933, p. 19; July 1933, p. 19.

Murray, B. J. "Dance Hall Versus Ballroom." Orchestra World, April 1931, p. 20.

M. W. "Benny 'King' Carter Confides." Musical News and Dance Band (London), May 1936, pp. 25-26.

Nanry, Charles. "Jazz and All That Sociology." In Nanry, ed., q. v., pp. 168-186.

Nanry, Charles. ed. American Music: From Storyville to Woodstock. New Brunswick, N. J., Transaction, 1972.

_____, with Edward Berger. The Jazz Text. New York, Van Nostrand, 1979.

Niles, Abbe. Introduction to Handy, q. v.

Noble, Peter. The Negro in Films. New York, Arno, 1970. (1st ed., London, Skelton, 1948.)

Osofsky, Gilbert. Harlem: The Making of a Ghetto, Negro New York, 1890-1930. 2d ed. New York, Harper 1971. (1st ed., New York, 1966.)

Ovington, Mary White. Half a Man: The Status of the Negro in New York. New York, Negro Universities Press, 1969. (1st ed., London, Longmans, Green, 1911.)

_____. The Walls Came Tumbling Down. New York, Schocken, 1970. (1st ed., New York, Harcourt, Brace, 1947.)

Owens, Thomas. Charlie Parker: Techniques of Improvisation. Ph. D. Thesis, University of California at Los Angeles, 1974.

Panassié, Hugues. Hot Jazz. The Guide to Swing Music. Translated by Lyle and Eleanor Dowling. New York, Witmark, 1936.

_____. Le Jazz Hot. Paris, R.-A. Corrêa, 1934.

Panassié, Hugues, and Madeleine Gautier. Guide to Jazz. Translated by Desmond Flower. Boston, Houghton Mifflin, 1956.

Paque, Glyn. "Bennet [sic] Carter." Jazz News (Basel), December 1940, pp. 7-8.

Pepper, Art and Laurie. Straight Life: The Story of Art Pepper. New York, Schirmer, 1979.

Perelman, S. J. Crazy Like a Fox. New York, Random House, 1944.

Pleasants, Henry. Serious Music--and All That Jazz! New York, Simon and Schuster, 1969.

Prendergast, Roy M. A Neglected Art: A Critical Study of Music in Films. New York, N. Y. U. Press, 1977.

Raksin, David. "What Ever Became of Movie Music?" Filmmusic Note-
book, Autumn 1944, p. 22.

Ramsey, Frederic, Jr., and Charles Edward Smith, eds. Jazzmen. New
York, Harcourt, Brace, 1939.

Randle, William, Jr. "Black Entertainers on Radio, 1920-1930." The
Black Perspective in Music 5(Spring 1977):67-74.

Rapee, Erno. Encyclopedia of Music for Pictures. New York, Arno, 1970.
(1st ed., New York, Belwin, 1925.)

Reis, Claire R. Composers, Conductors and Critics. New York, Oxford,
1955.

Reisner, Robert George. Bird: The Legend of Charlie Parker. New York,
Citadel, 1962.

Riley, Clayton. "We Thought It Was Magic." New York Times Magazine,
November 7, 1976, pp. 38 ff.

Roberts, John Storm. Black Music of Two Worlds. New York, William
Morrow, 1974.

Rogers, J. A. "Jazz at Home." In Locke, ed., q. v., pp. 216-224.

Rolontz, Bob. "Whatever Became of Jazz and Poetry?" Jazz Review,
February 1959, pp. 26-27.

Rosenkrantz, Timme. Dus Med Jazzen: Mine Jazzmemoirer. Copenhagen,
Erichsen, 1964.

Rosenthal, Harold, and John Warrack. Concise Oxford Dictionary of Opera.
London, Oxford, 1964.

Rowland, Mabel, ed. Bert Williams: Son of Laughter. New York, The
English Crafters, 1923.

Russell, Ross. Bird Lives! New York, Charterhouse, 1973.

Rust, Brian. The American Dance Band Discography 1917-1942. 2 vols.
New Rochelle, N.Y., Arlington House, 1975.

_____. The Dance Bands. New Rochelle, N.Y., Arlington House, 1974.
(1st ed., London, 1972.)

_____. Jazz Records 1897-1942. 2 vols. 4th ed. New Rochelle, Ar-
lington House, N.Y., 1978.

Rust, Brian, with Allen G. Debus. The Complete Entertainment Discography
from the Mid-1890s to 1942. New Rochelle, N.Y., Arlington House,
1973.

Rust, Frances. Dance in Society. London, Routledge and Kegan Paul, 1969.

Rye, Howard. "Visiting Firemen. 4: Benny Carter." Storyville, No. 93,
February-March 1981, pp. 84-87.

Sampson, Henry T. Blacks in Black and White: A Source Book on Black Films. Metuchen, N. J. , 1977.

Sanford, Herb. Tommy and Jimmy: The Dorsey Years. New Rochelle, N. Y. , Arlington House, 1972.

Sargeant, Winthrop. Jazz: Hot and Hybrid. New ed. New York, Dutton, 1946. (1st ed. , New York, 1938.)

Schary, Dore. Heyday: An Autobiography. Boston, Little, Brown, 1979.

Schiffman, Jack. Uptown: The Story of Harlem's Apollo Theater. New York, Cowles, 1971.

Schuller, Gunther. Early Jazz: Its Roots and Musical Development. New York, Oxford, 1968.

Schwartz, Charles. Gershwin: His Life and Times. Indianapolis, Bobbs-Merrill, 1973.

Shand, Gwendolyn Vaughan. "The Sociological Aspects of an Industrial Community. " M. A. Thesis, Carnegie Institute of Technology, Division of Social Work. Pittsburgh, 1923.

Shaw, Arnold. Honkers and Shouters: The Golden Years of Rhythm and Blues. New York, Macmillan, 1978.

_____. The Street That Never Slept: New York's Fabled 52d St. New York, Coward, McCann and Geoghegan, 1971.

Sheean, Vincent. Oscar Hammerstein I. New York, Simon and Schuster, 1956.

Shih, Hsio Wen. "Count Basie. " In Stewart, q. v. , pp. 195-206.

_____. "The Spread of Jazz and the Big Bands. " In Hentoff and McCarthy, eds. , q. v. , pp. 171-187.

Simon, George T. The Big Bands. Rev. ed. New York, Macmillan, 1971.

_____. "Carter Clan Clean. " Metronome, November 1940, p. 16.

_____. Glenn Miller and His Orchestra. New York, Crowell, 1974.

_____. Simon Says: The Sights and Sounds of the Swing Era, 1935-1955. New Rochelle, N. Y. , Arlington House, 1971.

Skvorecky, Josef. The Bass Saxophone. Translated by Kaca Polackova-Henley. New York, Knopf, 1979.

_____. The Cowards. Translated by Jeanne Nemcova. New York, Grove, 1970.

Smith, Charles Edward. "Jazz: Some Little Known Aspects. " The Symposium 1(October 1930):502-517.

_____. Liner notes to Swing Street, record album, Epic SN 6042, Frank Driggs, producer. New York, 1962.

Smith, Willie the Lion, with George Hoefer. Music on My Mind: The
    Memoirs of an American Pianist. New York, Doubleday, 1964.

The Sound of Harlem. See Hoefer.

Southern, Eileen, ed. "Black-Music Concerts in Carnegie Hall, 1912-1915."
    The Black Perspective in Music 6(Spring 1978):71-88.

_____. The Music of Black Americans. New York, Norton, 1971.

_____, ed. Readings in Black American Music. New York, Norton,
    1971.

Spaeth, Sigmund. A History of Popular Music in America. New York,
    Random House, 1948.

_____. They Still Sing of Love. New York, Horace Liveright, 1929.

Stearns, Marshall W. "Is Jazz Good Propaganda? The Dizzy Gillespie
    Tour." The Saturday Review, July 14, 1956, pp. 28-31.

_____. The Story of Jazz. New York, Oxford, 1956.

Stearns, Marshall W., and Jean Stearns. Jazz Dance: The Story of Amer-
    ican Vernacular Dance. New York, Macmillan, 1968.

Stefan, Paul. Anton Dvořák. Translated by Y. W. Vance. New York,
    Greystone, 1941.

Steiner, Max. "Scoring the Film." In We Make the Movies, ed. Nancy
    Naumburg, chap. 14. New York, Norton, 1937.

Stevens, Leith. "The Wild One." In Limbacher, ed., q. v., pp. 120-122.

Stewart, Rex, "The Benny Carter I Knew." Jazz Masters of the Thirties,
    pp. 168-180. New York, Macmillan, 1972. (Original publication:
    Down Beat, October 7, 1965, pp. 20-23.)

_____. "Rex Stewart Remembers Cuban Bennett." Down Beat, March
    10, 1966, p. 13.

Still, William Grant. "A Composer's Viewpoint." In de Lerma, ed., q. v.,
    chap. 8. Reprint, Haas, q. v., pp. 124-139.

_____. "How Do We Stand in Hollywood?" Opportunity: Journal of Negro
    Life, Spring 1945, pp. 74-77.

Stuart, Fredric. The Effects of Television on the Motion Picture and Radio
    Industries. New York, Arno, 1976.

Suber, Charles. "Jazz Education." In Feather and Gitler, q. v., pp. 366-
    381.

Sudhalter, Richard M., and Philip R. Evans. Bix: Man and Legend. New
    Rochelle, N. Y., Arlington, 1974.

Sutak, Ken. The Great Motion Picture Sound-Track Robbery: An Analysis
    of Copyright Protection. Hamden, Conn., Archon, 1976.

The Swing Era: One More Time. Philip W. Payne and Joan S. Reiter, eds. Time-Life Records. New York, 1972.

Sylvester, Robert. No Cover Charge: A Backward Look at the Night Clubs. New York, Dial, 1956.

Tendes, Antonio. "Figuras del Jazz." Ritmo y Melodia (Barcelona), no. 2, p. 3. (Date or volume not indicated. This was 2d issue of 1st year; in retrospect, November 1943.)

_____. "Galeria de Figuras del Jazz: Benny Carter, el Versatil." Jazz Magazine (Barcelona), June 1936, pp. 1-2.

Terrace, Vincent. The Complete Encyclopedia of Television Programs 1947-1976. 2 vols. South Brunswick, N.J. and New York, A. S. Barnes, 1976.

Terry, William E. "The Negro Music Journal: An Appraisal." The Black Perspective in Music 5(Fall 1977):146-160.

Thomas, Tony. Music for the Movies. South Brunswick, N.J. and New York, A. S. Barnes, 1973.

Thurman, Wallace. The Blacker the Berry ... A Novel of Negro Life. New York, Collier, 1970. (1st ed., New York, Macaulay, 1929.)

Tiomkin, Dmitri. "Composing for Films." In Limbacher, ed., q.v., pp. 55-61.

Tirro, Frank. Jazz: A History. New York, Norton, 1977.

Tynan, John. "Jazz in Hollywood Studios." Down Beat, March 1, 1962, pp. 14-15.

Ulanov, Barry. Duke Ellington. New York, Creative Age, 1946.

_____. "Thanks, Mr. Redman, for Modern Style." Metronome, June 1941, pp. 20-21, 25.

United States Copyright Office. Library of Congress. Catalogue of Copyright Entries. Part 3: Musical Compositions. Washington, D. C., annual.

United States Department of Labor. Children's Bureau. Publication No. 189. Public Dance Halls: Their Regulation and Place in the Recreation of Adolescents. By Ella Gardner. Washington, D. C., 1929.

United States Senate. Use of Mechanical Reproduction of Music. Hearings before a Subcommittee of the Committee on Interstate Commerce Pursuant to S. Res. 286, September 17, 18, and 21, 1942. Washington, D. C., 1943.

Valburn, Jerry. "Armed Forces Transcriptions as Source Materials." Studies in Jazz Discography I. Institute of Jazz Studies, Rutgers University. New Brunswick, N.J., 1971, pp. 47-52.

Walker, Leo. The Wonderful Era of the Great Dance Bands. New York, Doubleday, 1972.

Walker, Stanley. The Night Club Era. New York, Frederick A. Stokes, 1933.

Wall, Joseph Frazier. Andrew Carnegie. New York, Oxford, 1970.

Waters, Ethel, with Charles Samuels. His Eye Is On the Sparrow. New York, Doubleday, 1951.

Wells, Dicky, as told to Stanley Dance. The Night People: Reminiscences of a Jazzman. Boston, Crescendo, 1971.

Whiteman, Paul. "The All-America Swing Band." Collier's, September 10, 1938, pp. 9-12, 63-64.

_____. "So You Want to Lead a Band." Collier's, September 9, 1939, pp. 14, 51-52.

Williams, Martin. "Jazz at the Movies." Saturday Review, July 15, 1967, p. 49. Reprinted in Limbacher, ed., q.v., pp. 42-44.

_____, ed. Jazz Panorama. New York, Crowell-Collier, 1962.

Wilson, John S. "Cabaret and Jazz Are Active, But...." New York Times, August 29, 1976, sec. 2, p. 15.

Wilson, John S. The Collector's Jazz: Traditional and Swing. Philadelphia, Lippincott, 1958.

_____. "Jazz Makes a 'Comeback' With Broadest Range Yet." New York Times, January 24, 1974, p. 46.

_____. "Jazz: Serenading the Rock Fans." New York Times, August 28, 1977, sec. 2, p. 17.

_____. Jazz: The Transition Years. New York, Appleton-Century-Crofts, 1966.

_____. "Meet Professor Carter." Down Beat, April 2, 1970, pp. 19, 32.

Winkler, Max. A Penny from Heaven. New York, Appleton-Century-Crofts, 1951.

Witmark, Isidore, and Isaac Goldberg. From Ragtime to Swingtime: The Story of the House of Witmark. New York, Lee Furman, 1939.

Woll, Allen L. Songs from Hollywood Musical Comedies, 1927 to the Present: A Dictionary. New York and London, Garland, 1976.

Woodson, C. G. The Education of the Negro Prior to 1861. Washington, D.C., Associated Publishers, 1919.

Worthington, George E. "The Night Clubs of New York." The Survey 61(January 1, 1929):413-417.

Wright, Josephine R. B. See Dizzy Gillespie, "Conversations...."

Zissu, Leonard. "The Copyright Dilemma of the Screen Composer." Hollywood Quarterly 1(April 1946):317-320.

Zolotow, Maurice. "Harlem's Great White Father." Saturday Evening Post, September 27, 1941, pp. 37 ff.

Zwerin, Mike. "You're Not Going to Like This, But...." Down Beat, November 3, 1966, pp. 18-19.

DISCOGRAPHICAL ADDENDA

Changes to sessions already listed:

[94] Updated matrix and take information:

SLEEP: 1126-1 (complete); -2 (complete); -3 (breakdown); -4 (issued)

AMONG MY SOUVENIRS: 1127-1 (complete); -2 (complete); -3 (breakdown); -4 (issued)

FISH FRY: 1128-1 (breakdown); -2 (complete); -3 (breakdown); -4 (issued); -5 through -8 (breakdowns); -9 (complete); -10 (breakdown)

[371] Following titles issued in June 1982 on Storyville SLP4047, SUMMER SERENADE: INDIANA/LIKE SOMEONE IN LOVE (listed on LP as ALMOST LIKE BEING IN LOVE)/SUMMER SERENADE/ALL THAT JAZZ (vocal Richard Boone)/BLUE STAR/WHEN LIGHTS ARE LOW/TAKING A CHANCE ON LOVE

Additional Sessions:

Probably May 22, 1973   Holbaek Jazz Club, Denmark

Carter (as), Harry Edison, Arnvid Meyer (tp): John Darville (tb), Ben Webster, Jesper Thilo (ts), Niels Jorgen Steen (p), Hugo Rasmussen (b), Hans Nymand (d)

I CAN'T GET STARTED/SUNDAY/WHEN LIGHTS ARE LOW/KEESTER PARADE

July 19, 1973   Tokyo, Toranomon Hall

Carter (as), Gildo Mahones (p), Larry Gales (b), Duffy Jackson (d)

LULLABY OF BIRDLAND/ROBBINS NEST/I CAN'T GET STARTED/ UNDECIDED

July 22, 1975   Nice Festival

Carter (as), Joe Venuti (violin), George Barnes (g) Michael Moore (b)

SOMEBODY LOVES ME/DEEP PURPLE/UNDECIDED/SOMETIMES I'M HAPPY

July 25, 1975 Nice Festival

Carter (as), Illinois Jacquet (ts), Kenny Drew (p), Arvell Shaw (b), Bobby Rosengarden (d)

LADY BE GOOD

same date

Carter (as), Doc Cheatham (tp), Vic Dickenson (tb), Budd Johnson (ts), Kenny Drew (p), Arvell Shaw (b), Bobby Rosengarden (d)

JUST YOU, JUST ME/'DEED I DO

July 17-25, 1975 Nice Festival

Carter (as), Ruby Braff (tp), George Barnes (g) unknown b, d

WRAP YOUR TROUBLES IN DREAMS/I CAN'T GET STARTED/LOVER COME BACK TO ME

July 17-25, 1975 Nice Festival

Carter (as), Earl Hines (p) with several horns

CONFESSIN'

April 25, 1977 Fukuoka, Japan

same personnel as session no. 351

EASY MONEY/THEM THERE EYES/IN A SENTIMENTAL MOOD/NUAGES/ ARMSTRONG MEDLEY/CHINATOWN/THINGS AIN'T WHAT THEY USED TO BE/ ALL MY LOVE/GIRL TALK/THE COURTSHIP/JITTERBUG WALTZ/ SOUVENIR/COTTONTAIL

early July 1977 probably London, Pizza Express

Carter (as), Ralph Sutton (p), Jim Richardson (b), Tony Mann (d)

UNDECIDED/PERDIDO/IN A MELLOTONE

September 6, 1980 Osaka, Japan (Aurex Festival)

same personnel and similar titles to sessions no. 372 and 372A

May 21, 1982 Princeton University (Morroe Berger Memorial Concert)

Carter (as), Harry Edison (tp), Derek Smith (p), George Duvivier (b) Ronnie Bedford (d), Stanley Jordan (g--on last four titles)

EASY MONEY/AUTUMN LEAVES/THE COURTSHIP/LOVE FOR SALE (feat. D. Smith)/IN A MELLOTONE/AIN'T MISBEHAVIN' (feat. H. Edison)/ BASIC-ALLY THE BLUES (feat. G. Duvivier)/SOUTH SIDE SAMBA/UNDECIDED/ SOUVENIR/MISTY (S. Jordan solo)/PERDIDO/COTTONTAIL/BLUES

Arrangements: Julian Claes notes three Carter arrangements for the Ink Spots on Verve MGV2124, Favorites (released 1960).

Spelling correction: Phil Schaap has verified correct spelling of saxophonist Ben Whittett's last name to be Whitted.

Session no. 57 (8/18/37)

Newly released alternate takes (-2) of "Somebody Loves Me," "Pardon Me, Pretty Baby," and "My Buddy" on Panachord (Dutch) H2005.

Ella Fitzgerald/Count Basie Arrangements

Pablo Today D2312110 (A Perfect Match) recorded in Montreux, Switzerland 7/12/79 contains three Carter arrangements: "Please Don't Talk About Me When I'm Gone," Some Other Spring," and "Honeysuckle Rose." These are the same arrangements recorded in L.A. 2/15-16/79; "Honeysuckle Rose" from that session was issued on Pablo Today 2312-132 with other Carter arrangements from that date.

Sessions 277 and 278 (Impulse album Further Definitions) reissued on Jasmine JAS14.